CLASSICAL SCHOLARSHIP

Garland Reference Library
of the Humanities
(Vol. 928)

Classical Scholarship

A BIOGRAPHICAL ENCYCLOPEDIA

edited by

WARD W. BRIGGS AND

WILLIAM M. CALDER III

Garland Publishing, Inc.

NEW YORK & LONDON 1990

© 1990 Ward W. Briggs and William M. Calder III

LIBRARY OF CONGRESS CATALOGING-IN-PUBLICATION DATA

Classical scholarship : a biographical encyclopedia / edited by
Ward W. Briggs and William M. Calder III.
p. cm. — (Garland reference library of the humanities ; vol. 928)
Includes bibliographical references.
ISBN 0-8240-8448-9 (alk. paper)
1. Classicists—Biography—Dictionaries.   2. Classical philology—
Study and teaching—Biography—Dictionaries.   3. Civilization, Classical—
Study and teaching—Biography—Dictionaries
I. Briggs, Ward W.   II. Calder, William M.
(William Musgrave),1932–   .   III. Series.
PA83.C58   1990   880' .092'2—dc20   [B]   89-23294
CIP

Printed on acid-free, 250-year-life paper

MANUFACTURED IN THE UNITED STATES OF AMERICA

Hellmut Flashar

SEXAGENARIO

TABLE OF CONTENTS

PREFACE

Our task in this book was to choose fifty scholars through whose lives and work some idea of the history of classical scholarship in the modern period could be gained, in a way that the broader surveys of Sandys, Wilamowitz, and Pfeiffer could not.[1] The present volume is unlike these histories of classical scholarship in two respects: 1) We concentrate on the modern period, which we consider to extend from the matriculation at Göttingen of Friedrich August Wolf, *studiosus philologiae* in 1777, up to the death of Arnaldo Momigliano in 1986, some six generations. The lack of suitable materials available for the lives of earlier scholars was a factor in our decision, as well as the practical need to narrow the field. 2) We are primarily interested in giving full accounts of the lives of these scholars in order to show how the facts of their lives influenced the way they thought about the ancient world and thus how we think about the ancient world.

With the purpose and limits defined, we set about selecting the fifty scholars we had the space to treat. The fifty here in no way represent our view of the fifty greatest classicists of the era; some definitely are, a few definitely are not, and we leave it to the readers and reviewers to draw attention to those who have been omitted. Some scholars are missing here because the best people to write on them (see #3 below) were either unwilling or, the more common case, unavailable, to contribute. For the record, we state here that we should have liked to have included Jacob Bernays, August Böckh, Sir Arthur Evans, Moses Hadas, Richard Harder, Benjamin Jowett, Friedrich Leo, Paul Maas, B. G. Niebuhr, Mark Pattison, Louis Robert, Bruno Snell, Friedrich Gottlieb Welcker; *dis aliter visum*. Or for those who prefer Catullus to Virgil: *nummi desunt*.

In general there were three criteria for inclusion:

1. We wanted scholars who were innovative and exerted influence, bad as well as good. A good scholar who simply went on doing well what his teachers had

---

[1]John Edwin Sandys. *A History of Classical Scholarship*. 3 vols. (Cambridge, 1903–1908); reprinted 1964; Ulrich von Wilamowitz-Moellendorff, *History of Classical Scholarship*. English translation by Alan Harris (Baltimore, 1982); Rudolf Pfeiffer, *History of Classical Scholarship*. Vol. 1 (Oxford, 1968) and vol. 2 (Oxford, 1976).

done well did not merit inclusion, although we read his books and learn much from them; for example, Moriz Haupt, H. A. J. Munro, or A. S. Pease.

2. We sought people whose lives amounted to more than just bibliographies. This means that evidence must survive from which one may learn about them and that there was something about them that made them unusual. The tortured, mendacious Schliemann is one example; others are the homosexual Housman; the drunkard Porson; Jane Harrison, struggling against a man's world; the chauvinistic Germans Eduard Fraenkel and Werner Jaeger, whose careers were destroyed by their own people; or the survivors of defeated sides, Gildersleeve and Wilamowitz. Contrarily, so fine a scholar as Sir John Sandys was not included, for his books are useful but his life was dull.

3. We needed scholars for whom worthy biographers were available. We considered a biographer especially worthy if he were a citizen of his subject's country, if he were a known authority in some part of his subject's field, and if he knew something about the time in which his subject lived. In some cases (e.g., Beazley, Fraenkel, Frank, Highet, Page, Pasquali, and Schadewaldt), we were fortunate enough to secure biographers who had been students of their subjects and had gone on to excellence in the subject's field. Of these criteria, the third is the most important. We have avoided hacks. Our policy has been *laissez-faire* rather than Procrustean, so that the reader will find a considerable variety of approach and length in the articles here, and not the homogenized style and treatment of the ordinary biographical dictionary.

For those interested in the ideas, authors, and works that our subjects have treated, our index gives the browser access to views of these great figures on many of the questions and discoveries that have occupied classicists for the last two centuries.

Among our subjects, there is a preponderance of Germans, and the reason is not far to seek. The modern historical-philological study of classical antiquity, the modern conception of *Altertumswissenschaft*, is a German invention. Readers of this book will see how it began with C. G. Heyne and his student, F. A. Wolf. *Wortphilologie* reached its high point with Hermann in Greek and Lachmann in Latin. Karl Otfried Müller and F. G. Welcker (the teacher of Karl Marx), developing hints in Wolf, bequeathed to subsequent generations the conception of the *Totalitätsideal*, the conviction that one can only interpret the specific with knowledge of the whole. This meant the use of evidence provided by material objects, not just literary texts, and thanks to Otto Jahn and the work of men like Kekule and Adolf Furtwängler among others, and in spite of Schliemann and his protégé Wilhelm Dörpfeld, archaeology became a university subject in Prussia. Ernst Curtius, tutor of Friedrich III, arranged the first modern archaeological agreement with a foreign power. It resulted in the Germans excavating Olympia, publishing what they found, and building a museum there to house it. It has become the model for all subsequent such agreements. The influence of Nietzsche's teacher, Friedrich Ritschl, was regressive. Only briefly could he subvert the influence of his Bonn colleagues Welcker and Jahn by turning back to the antiquated *Wortphilologie*. His departure from Bonn and the influence of his follower, the problematical Usener, whose interests were far broader, repaired the damage.

Meanwhile the rising star of Mommsen, aided by the Prussian Academy and later the Göttingen Scientific Society (thanks to Paul de Lagarde, to the mathematician Felix Klein, and to Wilamowitz), created what Adolf Harnack called "the big business of scholarship," whose ability to acquire state funding created vast international projects like the *Inscriptiones Latinae*, the Church Fathers Commission, the *Thesaurus Linguae Latinae*, the corpus of sarcophagi, and others. The most productive period in the history of classical scholarship (1870–1914) coincided with the generation of Hermann Diels, Georg Kaibel, Friedrich Leo, Eduard Norden, Carl Robert, Wilamowitz, and their students, of whom Eduard Fraenkel, Felix Jacoby, Werner Jaeger, and Wolfgang Schadewaldt are represented in this volume.

With very few exceptions—Cobet in Holland, Grote in England, and Madvig in Denmark are the three obvious ones—the remaining scholars in this volume are either products of the German system or have been deeply influenced by it. Pasquali, a student underestimated by his greatest teacher, Wilamowitz, was the apostle of Prussia to the Italians. Of the English, only Jebb and Porson could not read German. Murray consciously sought to become the English Wilamowitz. Beazley, Dodds, Frazer, Harrison, Housman, and Page are unthinkable without their German predecessors. Throughout his unbroken sixty-year career of teaching and scholarship, Gildersleeve kept a bust of Ritschl on his desk as he pioneered German methods and educational systems in America. If Fraenkel is considered an Englishman (he is as English as Schliemann is American), he is the Englishman who fulfilled the dream of Mark Pattison and made the English dilettantism of Benjamin Jowett professional by Germanizing it.[2] Nilsson and Heiberg for most of their lives were encouraged or taught through books and letters by Wilamowitz.

The two most influential political figures in the history of American classical scholarship who were not themselves classicists are King George III of England and Adolf Hitler. The former, as the antagonist of the American Revolution, whose army could commit the atrocities of Valley Forge and Arcadia, followed a generation later by the War of 1812, created a climate of hostility to all things British at the time when the ascendency of German culture in this country was beginning. Even when Gildersleeve set off for Germany in 1850, with his head full of Goethe, he tells us that there were few anglophile youths in America.[3] One hundred and fifty years later, Hitler drove some thirty of the greatest classicists of his time to our shores.

American classical scholarship during its formative period (1853–1914) was entirely a product of the German. Gildersleeve, Oldfather, and Shorey, the three founders of scientific philology in the United States, all took German doctorates. The Russian immigrant Michael I. Rostovtzeff owed much of his international career to Wilamowitz, for it was on the advice of Wilamowitz that Georg Wissowa assigned him the article *Frumentum* in Pauly-Wissowa and thus the modern economic history of the

[2]See John Sparrow, *Mark Pattison and the Idea of a University* (Cambridge, 1967).

[3]For American classical scholarship as the product of the German see William M. Calder III, "Die Geschichte der klassischen Philologie in den Vereinigten Staaten," *Jahrbuch für Amerikastudien* 11 (1966) 213–240.

ancient world began. The Scottish immigrant Gilbert Highet translated the three-volume history of the Greek mind by Werner Jaeger, Wilamowitz's successor at Berlin, into English. A Scot, like Frazer and William Robertson Smith, he was early at home in German. Frank and Taylor were historians and so more influenced by the English tradition than those who worked with texts. The endowment of the Rhodes Scholarships and the sinking of the *Lusitania* ended the first period of German influence, ended the teaching of German in U.S. schools (it was replaced by Spanish, which is of minor importance to a classical scholar), and returned Americans to English dilettantism.

The second wave of German influence owed its momentum to the influx of victims of Hitler's anti-Semitism and comprised some thirty Jews, husbands of Jews, and Kurt von Fritz.[4] They were men like Elias J. Bickermann, Otto J. Brendel, Hermann Fränkel, Paul Friedländer, Otto Neugebauer, Alexander Turyn, and one woman, Margarete Bieber, a distinguished art historian, who was made assistant professor with tenure at Columbia. Werner Jaeger led them. They revived German scholarship; successfully transplanted ancient art history to the United States, where native classical archaeology had become a sterile discipline engaged in bloody wars about two- or three-bar sigma; and they once and for all opened classical posts in American universities to American Jews who had been barred from tenured United States posts in the discipline until the European Jews broke the anti-Semitic barrier. For example, Rostovtzeff only obtained his chair at the University of Wisconsin when proof was presented to the administration that he was neither a Jew nor a communist. No longer would we have to lose such men as James Loeb, the greatest benefactor of American classics, to Germany, whose universities attracted American Jews because they had neither required chapel nor a *numerus clausus*, usually a 7% limit on Jewish admissions.[5]

Milman Parry was different. He was the daring, independent, young American, educated in Paris, not Berlin, who had a brilliant idea that for fifty years has dominated historical Homeric criticism. Except for Elroy Bundy in Pindaric studies, no American has so affected international attention to a major classical author. And yet the cornerstone of his thesis that Homer was an oral bard remained Wolf's insistence that Homer was illiterate. And so from Parry back to Wolf, we end at the beginning again.

Most readers will come to this book to learn more about the lives of a few familiar figures; we sincerely hope the lives of others will attract them. Those who have more time are invited to use the list on pages xxiii–xxiv and read the lives chronologically, starting with Heyne, Wolf, and Porson and reading through to Page and Momigliano. It will make a continuous story. Perhaps the best way to proceed

---

[4] The fundamental study is Donald Fleming and Bernard Bailyn, *The Intellectual Migration: Europe and America 1930–1960* (Cambridge, 1969). See also Lewis A. Coser, *Refugee Scholars in America: Their Impact and their Experiences* (New Haven and London, 1984), especially 271–277 on classics.

[5] For the problem see Dan A. Oren, *Joining the Club: A History of Jews at Yale* (New Haven and London, 1985).

might be to take up volume three of Sandys' compendious *History of Classical Scholarship* or Wilamowitz's much shorter but greater history of classical scholarship, brief and authoritative and now available in English, and let the present accounts of men and ideas enlarge the figures that Sandys and Wilamowitz can only briefly describe.[6]

Abbreviations of journals (with the exception of *TAPA* and *AJP*) generally follow those of *L'Anée Philologique*.

For their fluent and accurate translations of some fifteen of these articles, we thank E. Christian Kopff (University of Colorado at Boulder) and Michael Armstrong (University of Illinois at Urbana/Champaign). We are also grateful to Professor Ernst Vogt, editor of *Gnomon*, for permission to print a translation of Karl Christ's obituary notice from that journal.[7] Finally, we express our gratitude to Tom Morton and the staff of the Humanities and Social Sciences Computing Laboratory at the University of South Carolina for their technical assistance in the preparation of this book.

Ward W. Briggs, Jr.
William M. Calder III

[6]In addition to Sandys and Wilamowitz (see note 1 above), see now *La Filologia Greca e Latina nel Secolo XX*. Atti del Congresso Internazionale Roma, Consiglio Nationale delle Ricerche, 17-21 Settembre 1984. Vol. 1, Edited by Scevola Mariotti (Pisa, 1989). The volume contains articles on the history of classical studies in such lands as Greece, Turkey, Australia, and New Zealand, United States, East Germany, Austria, Switzerland, etc. Volume II should be published soon.

[7]*Gnomon* 60 (1988) 571–575.

INTRODUCTION

Sir John Sandys was wrong to think that a collection of biographical details was "A History of Classical Scholarship." Politics, religion, ideas shape the individual. The spirit of the age does, what Tacitus called *Saeculum*, and after him Hegel called *Zeitgeist*. The history of a discipline becomes the interplay between its practitioners and the values of their time. The *Antigone* and *Oedipus Coloneus* of Jebb and Mendelssohn are Christian. Today Antigone is a female victim of a male establishment who would have made a far better ruler than the stubborn Kreon. That she will lay down her life for a friend is neither here nor there as far as Sophocles goes. Only because the play has become a document in the history of love do we see it in Christian terms. Pericles saw that Kreon was the hero and Antigone a troublemaker and rewarded Sophocles for a play he approved by making him a general.

In capitalist America Oedipus is a symbol for a Freudian transcendental truth applicable to all men. In Communist Berlin a public debate is held on whether Sophocles' play has anything to say to a socialist society.[1] Medea used to be a monster. Now she is a martyr defending her right to choose postnatal abortion. For our fin-de-siècle, Seneca the tragedian is an amoral nihilist who does not care anymore. Kris Kristofferson's "Freedom's just another word for nothing left to lose" is the message of his *Agamemnon*. For the Canadian classicist H. J. Rose he was a degenerate hypocrite. Friedrich Leo, his greatest editor, said he would sell all of Seneca's tragedies to buy Ovid's *Medea*. For men like the English historian of Latin literature J.W. Duff, Petronius was vile and depraved. Gilbert Highet, later abetted by Fellini, turned him into a moralist exposing vice in pursuit of virtue, and J. P. Sullivan urges us to admire Nero and his lascivious circle and discard Cato Uticensis as a conservative bore,[2] a view our founding fathers would not have approved.

Cebes's *Tablet*, a dialogue in Platonic style describing a picture on which Good and Bad Paideia (= Culture/Education) are represented, was a staple for Ameri-

---

[1] See Heiner Miller, *Sophokles Ödipus Tyrann nach Hölderlin* (Berlin and Weimar, 1969): 93ff.

[2] J.P. Sullivan, *Literature and Politics in the Age of Nero* (Ithaca and London, 1985) and the review by W.M. Calder III in CJ 81 (1985–1986) 263–265.

can undergraduates who read Greek a hundred years ago. Few professors of Greek today know that the tiresome work exists. Xenophon's *Education of Cyrus* has just been rescued from a similar obscurity not as the text it once was, one that improved the sons of the ruling class, but by the fashionable revelation that it contains a proto-novel. In at least one American university, Cicero and Caesar have been banished from the lower level curriculum because there are no women in their pages and have been replaced by Ovidian trifles that provide them. Contrarily, Wilamowitz in 1893 recommended Thucydides because no women stain his pages with the perfume of the boudoir. (In fact two do.) The texts remain the same, but fashion dictates the questions scholars ask them.

To phrase it differently, the history of classical scholarship is part of *Rezeption*, the way in which successive generations have received or reacted to the heritage of Greece and Rome. This is quite different from another German word which we are not permitted to use anymore: *Nachleben*, literally "afterlife." This word meant that there was one true meaning for, say, Sophocles' *Philoctetes*, namely what it meant to its first audience in 409 B.C. Later interpretations, like Edmund Wilson's,[3] are perversions against which students must be warned. Receptionists, however, are interested in tracing the sources for the thesis of *The Wound and the Bow* (one must pay a terrible price for a great gift) to nineteenth-century romantic notions (syphilis made Nietzsche great). They want to see why Edmund Wilson interpreted the play as he did and why he convinced so many people that he was right. His interpretation is not wrong. It is different and deserves consideration as a symptom of its age.

Because we have at most only "fragments of fragments" of the whole of literature produced by the ancient Greeks and Romans, the role of reception is surely more decisive in the field of classics than in the study of, e.g., nineteenth-century opera. We can know from letters and diaries what Wagner was trying to do and from other letters, diaries, and published reviews how his audience reacted to what he did. Only when one has worked in the nineteenth century does one see how futile are the attempts of generations of classicists to find what Sophocles or Thucydides "really thought" of Pericles or what Vergil, Horace, or Ovid "really thought" of Augustus. We need letters to a trusted friend. And these we have only for Cicero and Augustine, but Augustine is a Christian and does not count as a classical author. To phrase it differently, classical literature, because of its remoteness, is more vulnerable than modern to contemporary critical theories which replace authorial intent with structuralist and deconstructionist theory, just as it earlier was to New Criticism.

Wilamowitz, to explain this, took a metaphor from the *Odyssey*. He said in his Oxford lecture of 1908:[4]

---

[3] Edmund Wilson, *The Wound and the Bow* (London, 1952).

[4] Ulrich von Wilamowitz-Moellendorff, *Greek Historical Writing and Apollo: Two Lectures Delivered before the University of Oxford June 3 and 4, 1908*. Translated by Gilbert Murray (Oxford, 1908; reprinted Chicago, 1979): 25.

The tradition is dead; our task is to revivify life that has passed away. We know that ghosts cannot speak until they have drunk blood; and the spirits which we evoke demand the blood of our hearts. We give it to them gladly; but if they then abide our questions, something from us has entered into them; something alien, that must be cast out, cast out in the name of truth!

His ideal here mingles the opposing aims of the Prussian historians B. G. Niebuhr and Leopold von Ranke: Niebuhr declared that we must make the past alive again, while Ranke sought the past "as it really was."[5] Of course, one can edit papyri and inscriptions without the loss of much blood to the ghosts. When one starts emending literary texts more blood is required. How much of Bentley's Horace became Bentley? (To say nothing of Bentley's Miltonic forays.)[6] When one begins to interpret great literature, the tragedians, or Plato, the interpretation mirrors the critic as much as the text. A life of Alexander or Christ or Nietzsche is the best autobiography.

Paradoxically Wilamowitz wishes to expel precisely what causes his work to survive, its intense subjectivity, hence its urgency. Nietzsche taunted Mommsen for drawing modern parallels to ancient history. He believed they trivialized the subject. Wilamowitz after Welcker referred to Sappho's "girls' boarding school." The phrase was arresting and its aim pedagogical but it aroused the ire of the humanists. Similarly, the George Circle dismissed Wilamowitz's *Platon* as "Plato for serving maids." He saw Plato and Socrates as his own contemporaries. The opposite view was held by Werner Jaeger. Jaeger greeted the same book in a letter to Wilamowitz: "You have restored the man Plato to the world."[7] That is what Wilamowitz wanted to do.

We are actors who play the parts of the ancients we interpret. Wilamowitz took his metaphor from Diderot's *Paradoxe sur le comédien* and opposed it to the Nietzschean idea of the philologist as prophet. We must play the chosen role but never sacrifice our individuality. Nor must we be the virtuoso whose identity shines through the mask. Mommsen played Caesar; Gildersleeve played Pindar; Wilamowitz played Herakles, Hippolytus, and Plato; Gilbert Highet eagerly played Juvenal.

The decision to present the history of modern classical scholarship through the achievement of fifty of its most illustrious modern practitioners is owed to my teacher, Werner Jaeger. Werner Jaeger wrote: "For the noisy bustling activity of so-called scholarship with all the journals, encyclopedias, and mass-meetings has been little more than the long shadow cast by a few towering scholars."[8]

[5] See recently Ronald S. Stroud, " 'Wie es eigentlich gewesen' and Thucydides 2.48.3," *Hermes* 115 (1987) 379–382.

[6] One finds the best defense of Bentley's bizarre edition of *Paradise Lost* at R.C. Jebb, *Bentley* (London, 1889): 190: "It is a rule applicable to most of Bentley's corrections, that their merit varies inversely with the soundness of the text."

[7] See William M. Calder III, "The Correspondence of Ulrich von Wilamowitz-Moellendorff with Werner Jaeger," *HSCP* 82 (1978) 326.

[8] Werner Jaeger, *Five Essays*. Translated by Adele M. Fiske, R.S.C.J. (Montreal, 1966): 62.

Anyone familiar, as Jaeger was, with the secondary literature of his field knows this to be true. In *Paideia* he argued that great intellects like Plato mold *paideia* (that is, both "culture" and the process of transmitting it, "education") for succeeding generations. Smaller men, like Xenophon, are formed by it. The tradition of Classical scholarship is different because of men like F. A. Wolf, Karl Otfried Müller, Gottfried Hermann, Theodor Mommsen, Karl Lachmann, J. G. Frazer, Ulrich von Wilamowitz-Moellendorff, and even Heinrich Schliemann. To dismiss biography as irrelevant to intellectual history, of which the history of classical scholarship is a small part, is simply to deny facts. Welcker's defense of Sappho against the charge of tribadism has shaped Sapphic scholarship until this day by permanently putting the moral question first. Welcker, in defending Sappho's homosexuality, was defending his own. This gave his case its ferocity. George Grote's exaltation of Periclean democracy is the natural effect caused by his political liberalism and his friendship with Bentham and the Mills. No man could ever on the extant evidence put forth the thesis of Jane Harrison's *Themis*. She argued the direction of the universe by a benevolent female deity because she was a woman. Rohde's *Psyche* was the turning point in the modern rediscovery of Euripides. For the first time those qualities of Euripides which had been dismissed as vices by earlier generations were extolled as virtues. What caused Rohde to see them thus was his intimate friendship with Friedrich Nietzsche. His portrait of Euripides is a portrait of Nietzsche set in antiquity. The end of the American Civil War diverted Gildersleeve's attention from the tragedians and orators to Pindar, whose "experience of the losing side" echoed the despair of Southern defeat.

Similarly, Wilamowitz's famous characterization of Phaedra in *Hippolytus*, often wrongly attributed to the influence of Ibsen's *Hedda Gabler*, is a distorted portrait of his aunt. It has been known since antiquity that writers of fiction may base characters on extraordinary people whom they have met. Indeed, even classicists, Moriz Haupt, Benjamin Jowett, Mark Pattison, and Gilbert Highet, have all appeared metamorphosed in novels. Scholars do the same thing. My own views of Seneca as a poet of totalitarianism grew out of my years in eastern Europe. The young Wilamowitz's humiliation because he misinterpreted Pausanias on the way between Olympia and Arcadia caused him to despise Pausanias all his life. His hate infected his writings. His writings colored the German reception of Pausanias for 100 years. Or again Bacchylides has never recovered from the disappointment with which Wilamowitz first read him on 29 December 1897. He remains a poor man's Pindar. So long is the shadow of what Jaeger would call "a towering scholar."[9]

This leads to a further consideration. Classicists, at least American ones, may be the last people who believe in facts. Traditionally their business has been to make new facts out of facts. Housman said that a publication to be justified must contain

---

[9] See William M. Calder III, "The Riddle of Wilamowitz's *Phaidrabild*," GRBS 20 (1979) 219–236; Christian Habicht, *Pausanias' Guide to Ancient Greece* (Berkeley, Los Angeles, London, 1985): 165–175; Herwig Maehler, "Die Lieder des Bakchylides I. Die Siegeslieder," *Mnemosyne* Supplement 62 (Leiden, 1982) x.

something that is both new and true. Germans have long been less dogmatic. They speak of Droysen's Alexander or Wilcken's or Schachermeyr's; of Schadewaldt's Homer or Jaeger's Demosthenes. In a gripping book, Professor Alexander Demandt has recently traced the reception of a great historical event, the fall of Rome.[10] His book is not on why Rome fell but how the generations of men since its fall have reacted to the fall. Medieval Christians saw in it the judgment of God. The Renaissance and the Enlightenment lamented the end of paganism. Marxists see it as inevitable. The causes of Rome's fall are unimportant. What is important is how generations have interpreted the fall of Rome. Demandt has collected 210 reasons put forth for the fall of Rome, from the rise of Christianity to lead water pipes. Bolshevism or Capitalism is the villain. The Germans and Jews have been blamed. Others have indicted homosexuality or prostitution or impotence or celibacy. Find out what you do not like and say that it caused the fall of Rome. The evidence is there. Objective scholars devoted to the pursuit of truth will find what they have decided to seek. Arthur Darby Nock put it in a different way. He said: "The facts of history are what people believe."

William M. Calder III

---

[10] Alexander Demandt, *Der Fall Roms. Die Auflösung des römischen Reiches im Urteil der Nachwelt* (Munich, 1984).

LIST OF CONTRIBUTORS

ROBERT ACKERMAN (J.G. Frazer) is Chairman of Humanities at the University of the Arts, Philadelphia, PA. His biography of Frazer was published by Cambridge in 1987.

CHARLES ROWAN BEYE (Milman Parry) is Professor of Classics at Lehman College / Graduate Center City University of New York.

DIETRICH von BOTHMER (J.D. Beazley) is Chairman of the Department of Greek and Roman Art at the Metropolitan Museum of Art and Adjunct Professor at New York University. One of Beazley's last students, he revised his *The Development of Attic Black-figure* in 1986 and has lectured on Beazley in England and America.

JAN N. BREMMER (Hermann Usener) is Professor of Ancient History at the Rijksuniversiteit Utrecht.

WARD W. BRIGGS, JR. (Basil L. Gildersleeve) is Professor of Classics at the University of South Carolina and the editor of *B.L. Gildersleeve: An American Classicist* (1986) and *The Letters of Basil Lanneau Gildersleeve* (1987).

T. ROBERT S. BROUGHTON (Tenney Frank, Lily Ross Taylor) is Paddison Professor of Classics Emeritus at the University of North Carolina at Chapel Hill. A student of Frank, he was appointed to the faculty at Bryn Mawr one year after Lily Ross Taylor and was her colleague for a quarter of a century.

JOHN BUCKLER (William Abbott Oldfather) is Professor of Ancient History at the University of Illinois at Urbana-Champaign.

MARIA GABRIELLA CAGNETTA (Gaetano De Sanctis) is Instructor in Classical Philology at the Università di Perugia. She has written on fascism and its effect on classical scholars.

WILLIAM M. CALDER III (Werner Jaeger) is William Abbott Oldfather Professor of Classics at the University of Illinois. In addition to his extensive work on Wilamowitz and other classical scholars of Germany and America, he has written six articles of Jaeger, his professor at Harvard.

HUBERT CANCIK (Erwin Rohde) is Professor of Classical Philology at the University of Tübingen. He has recently published three articles on classical philology in the nineteenth century.

LUCIANO CANFORA (Giorgio Pasquali) is Professor of Classical Philology at the Università di Bari and editor of *Quaderni di Storia*. He wrote *Ideologie del classicismo* (1980).

MORTIMER H. CHAMBERS (Ernst Curtius, Felix Jacoby) is Professor of Ancient History at the University of California, Los Angeles. He is completing a biography of Felix Jacoby.

KARL CHRIST (Arnaldo Momigliano) is Professor of Ancient History Emeritus at the Philipps-Universität Marburg and a longtime friend of Arnaldo Momigliano.

ROGER D. DAWE (R. C. Jebb, D. L. Page, Richard Porson) is Lecturer in Classics at Trinity College, Cambridge and was a student of D. L. Page.

ALEXANDER DEMANDT (Theodor Mommsen) is Professor of Ancient History at the Free University of Berlin. He has written four articles on Mommsen and *Der Fall Roms. Die Auflösung des Römischen Reiches im Urteil der Nachwelt* (1984).

J. RUFUS FEARS (M. Rostovtzeff) is Professor and Chairman of the Department of Classical Studies at Boston University. He is an editor of the forthcoming series *The Classical Tradition and the Americas*.

HELLMUT FLASHAR (W. Schadewaldt) is Professor of Classical Philology at University of Munich and a director of the Thyssen Foundation. He wrote for *Gnomon* the obituary of Schadewaldt, who was his professor, and edited his *Festschrift*.

ROBERT L. FOWLER (Gilbert Murray, Ulrich von Wilamowitz-Moellendorff) is Associate Professor of Classics at the University of Waterloo. With W. M. Calder III he edited the letters of Wilamowitz to Eduard Schwartz and he has given the first account of the Gildersleeve *Nachlaß* at Johns Hopkins.

HERMANN FUNKE (F. A. Wolf) is Professor of Classical Philology at the University of Mannheim.

ANDREAS FURTWÄNGLER (Adolf Furtwängler) is Professor of Classical Archaeology at the University of Saarlandes. He is the grandson of Adolf Furtwängler.

CHRISTHARD HOFFMANN (Eduard Meyer) is Dozent in the Institute for Antisemitic Study at the Technical University of Berlin. He wrote his thesis and two articles on Meyer as well as *Juden und Judentum im Werk deutscher Althistoriker des 19. und 20. Jahrhunderts* (1988).

NICHOLAS HORSFALL (Eduard Fraenkel) taught at University College, London and now resides in Rome. He was a student of Fraenkel and compiled his bibliography.

L.P. JANSSEN (C.G. Cobet) is retired Dozent for Classical Philology at the University of Utrecht.

PAUL T. KEYSER (J.L. Heiberg) has a Ph.D. in Physics, is pursuing one in Classics, and has been guest professor at the Universities of Rostock and Illinois.

E. CHRISTIAN KOPFF (Paul Shorey) is Associate Professor of Classics at the University of Colorado. He has written a prizewinning essay on the reaction of American classicists, including Shorey, to German influence at the end of the nineteenth century.

BERNHARD KYTZLER (Eduard Norden) is Professor of Classical Philology at the Free University of Berlin. He edited Norden's *Kleine Schriften*.

JØRGEN MEJER (J.N. Madvig, M.P. Nilsson) is Dozent for Classical Philology at the University of Copenhagen.

CARL WERNER MÜLLER (Otto Jahn) is Professor of Classical Philology at the University of Saarbrücken.

P. G. NAIDITCH (A.E. Housman) is Publications Editor for the Department of Special Collections, University Research Library, University of California, Los Angeles. He has written numerous articles on Housman and is the author of *A.E. Housman at University College, London: The Election of 1892* (1988).

EDGAR PACK (Johannes Hasebroek) is Dozent for Ancient History at the University of Cologne. He has written biographical articles on Hasebroek at Cologne and his correspondence with Rostovtzeff.

ULRICH SCHINDEL (C.G. Heyne) is Professor of Classical Philology at the Georg-August Universität in Göttingen.

LIST OF CONTRIBUTORS

WOLFGANG SCHINDLER (Ernst Buschor) is Professor of Classical Philology at the Winckelmann Institut, Humboldt University.

BERNFRIED SCHLERATH (Franz Bopp) is Professor of Linguistics at the Free University of Berlin. He has recently written on Bopp in Germany.

RENATE SCHLESIER (Jane Ellen Harrison) is Dozent for the History of Religion at the Free University of Berlin.

ERNST GÜNTHER SCHMIDT (Gottfried Hermann) is Professor of Classical Philology at the Friedrich-Schiller Universität, Jena.

RÜDIGER SCHMIDT (Jacob Wackernagel) is Professor of Linguistics at the University of Saarlandes.

ECKART SCHÜTRUMPF (Hermann Diels) is Professor of Classics at the University of Colorado and Chairman of the Department.

THOMAS A. SUITS (Gilbert Highet) is Professor of Classics at the University of Connecticut and was a colleague of Highet at Columbia from 1958 to 1966.

DAVID A. TRAILL (Heinrich Schliemann) is Professor of Classics and head of the department at the University of California, Davis. He has published eleven articles on Schliemann and is working on a biography.

WOLFHART UNTE (Karl Lachmann, Karl Otfried Müller) is Director of the University Library at the Free University of Berlin.

JOHN VAIO (George Grote) is Associate Professor of Classics at the University of Illinois at Chicago.

ERNST VOGT (Friedrich Ritschl) is Professor of Classical Philology at the University of Munich and editor of *Gnomon*. He has published two articles on nineteenth-century philology.

DOUGLAS K. WOOD (F.M. Cornford) teaches at the Berkshire School in Sheffield, MA.

CHRONOLOGICAL ARRANGEMENT OF SUBJECTS

Christian Gottlob Heyne	25 September 1729–14 July 1812
F. A. Wolf	15 February 1759–8 August 1824
Richard Porson	25 December 1759–19 September 1808
Gottfried Hermann	28 November 1772–31 December 1848
Franz Bopp	14 September 1791–23 October 1867
Karl Lachmann	4 March 1793–13 March 1851
George Grote	17 November 1794–18 June 1871
Karl Otfried Müller	28 August 1797–1 August 1840
J. N. Madvig	7 August 1804–12 December 1886
Friedrich Ritschl	6 April 1806–8 November 1876
Otto Jahn	16 June 1813–9 September 1869
C. G. Cobet	28 November 1813–28 October 1889
Ernst Curtius	2 September 1814–11 July 1896
Theodor Mommsen	30 November 1817–1 November 1903
Heinrich Schliemann	6 January 1822–26 December 1890
Basil L. Gildersleeve	23 October 1831–9 January 1924
Hermann Usener	23 October 1834–21 October 1905
R. C. Jebb	27 August 1841–9 December 1905
Erwin Rohde	9 October 1845–11 January 1898
Hermann Diels	18 May 1848–4 June 1922
Ulrich von Wilamowitz-Moellendorff	22 December 1848–25 September 1931
Jane Ellen Harrison	9 September 1850–15 April 1928
Adolf Furtwängler	30 June 1853–11 October 1907
Jacob Wackernagel	11 December 1853–22 May 1938
J. G. Frazer	1 January 1854–7 May 1941
J. L. Heiberg	27 November 1854–4 January 1928
Eduard Meyer	25 January 1855–31 August 1930
Paul Shorey	3 August 1857–24 April 1934
A. E. Housman	26 March 1859–30 April 1936
Gilbert Murray	2 January 1866–20 May 1957

CHRONOLOGICAL ARRANGEMENT OF SUBJECTS

Eduard Norden	21 September 1868–13 July 1941
Gaetano De Sanctis	15 October 1870–9 April 1957
M. Rostovtzeff	10 November 1870–20 October 1952
F. M. Cornford	27 February 1874–3 January 1943
Martin P. Nilsson	12 July 1874–7 April 1967
Felix Jacoby	19 March 1876–10 November 1959
Tenney Frank	19 May 1876–3 April 1939
William Abbott Oldfather	23 October 1880–27 May 1945
Giorgio Pasquali	29 April 1885–9 July 1952
J. D. Beazley	13 September 1885–6 May 1970
Ernst Buschor	2 June 1886–11 December 1961
Lily Ross Taylor	12 August 1886–18 November 1969
Eduard Fraenkel	17 March 1888–5 February 1970
Werner Jaeger	30 July 1888–19 October 1961
Johannes Hasebroek	14 April 1893–17 February 1957
Wolfgang Schadewaldt	15 March 1900–10 March 1974
Milman Parry	20 June 1902–3 December 1935
Gilbert Highet	22 June 1906–20 January 1978
D. L. Page	11 May 1908–6 July 1978
Arnaldo Momigliano	5 September 1908–1 September 1987

J. D. Beazley

13 September 1885 – 6 May 1970

DIETRICH VON BOTHMER
The Metropolitan Museum of Art

John Davidson Beazley's entire adult life, from October 1903 until his death on 6 May 1970, was spent at Oxford. He attended first the King Edward VI school at Southampton, and, after his family went to live in Brussels, he entered Christ's Hospital in London on a scholarship in 1898. He was an excellent pupil, and his great promise was recognized at a very early age. At Christ's Hospital he was a "Classical Grecian," but he also won prizes in Religious Knowledge, French, and English Essay. In 1903 he went up to Balliol College on a classical scholarship, where Cyril Bailey and A. W. Pickard-Cambridge were his tutors. At Oxford he took a First in Classical Moderations and Literae Humaniores, winning just about every prize and scholarship the University had to offer: Ireland and Craven Scholar in 1904; Hartford Scholar in 1905; Derby Scholar in 1907; and the Gaisford Prize in Greek Prose in 1907.

Classical Archaeology at Oxford was not an independent discipline in those days, and a chair in this subject had not been established until 1885, the year Beazley was born. Percy Gardner, the second professor, had introduced in 1890 a paper on Greek sculpture in the first part of the Literae Humaniores program—Classical Moderations—and the Diploma in Classical Archaeology was introduced in 1907, the year Beazley took his B. A. As an undergraduate Beazley was one of Percy Gardner's many pupils, but graduate work leading to a D. Phil. in Classical Archaeology was not part of the Oxford curriculum until many decades later. Thus Beazley may be considered mostly self-taught in the field in which he was to establish his reputation and to win universal acclaim. He had been attracted to art at an early age, and visiting his parents in Brussels on school holidays gave him a taste of travel and exploration that stayed with him throughout his life. Within the realm of classical art his first and most abiding love was the linear beauty of Greek vase-painting. Vases were on view in all the great museums of Europe and America and had been published in one form or another for more than a century, but the middling quality of the reproductions, lithographs or engravings after drawings, or poor photographs, which usually masked the villainous restorations, was misleading and hardly encouraged stylistic studies. Paul Hartwig's *Die griechischen Meisterschalen* (Stuttgart 1893) and Adolf Furtwängler's *Griechische Vasenmalerei* (with drawings by Karl Reichhold, begun in 1904) set new standards and elevated the study of vase-painting to a level on which questions of style and attribution could be answered. It was in this area of scholarship that Beazley was to excel. In a series of early articles he blazed the trail: his success in recognizing three major Attic vase-painters of the red-figured technique—the Berlin Painter, the Kleophrades Painter, and the Pan Painter—encouraged him to set for himself the gigantic task of attributing *all* painted Attic vases of the sixth and the fifth centuries B.C. to their respective artists and to assemble the results of his findings in comprehensive listings that not only recognized individual hands but also grouped the artists stylistically and chronologically, distinguished the great talents from the lesser practitioners of the craft, separated imitators from originators, and the like.

His teaching career at Oxford began at the age of twenty-two in 1907 with his appointment as lecturer for Classical Moderations at Christ Church, a college that elected him "student" (i.e., Fellow) the following year. His official duties were those of a college tutor in Classics, but the University, taking note of his special talents and predilections, named him in 1920 University Lecturer in Greek Vases and five years later chose him as Percy Gardner's successor in the Chair of Classical Archaeology, a position he held for thirty-one years. His teaching at Oxford was interrupted by the Great War, in which he served first in the censorship office at Boulogne-sur-Mer and later in London at the Admiralty, but before its outbreak he went to St. Petersburg during Easter vacation in 1914 and to the United States in the summer of the same year. These visits, not at all common in those days, rounded out his knowledge of collections beyond his earlier itineraries that had taken him abroad to Belgium, France, Germany, Italy, and Greece. Travel was not only part of Beazley's training; he soon recognized it as the only way to learn of recent discoveries and museum acquisitions. To America he returned twice (1946 and 1949), and late in life he hoped to go again to Russia, but accepted instead an invitation to Australia. He also travelled to Poland, Denmark, Cyprus, Spain, Austria, Israel, the Netherlands, Switzerland, and on each visit to a private collection, museum, or excavation he took careful notes and made tracings (an art to which he was introduced by Karl Reichhold in 1908). The vast body of his archaeological *apparatus*, including thousands of mounted photographs, is now housed in the Beazley Archive at Oxford.

After his first visit to America, Beazley put together the attributions he had made in a book published by Harvard University Press entitled *Attic Red-figured Vases in American Museums* (1918). This book was well illustrated and, though ostensibly a book on Attic red-figured vases in America, Beazley used it as a springboard to publish lists of vases he had attributed to the painters he had isolated. By now their number had grown to over eighty. In his next book, printed in Germany and written in German (*Attische Vasenmaler des rotfigurigen Stils*) the number of distinct stylistic personalities had grown again, as it was to do until the end of his life. This German book became the model of a much-expanded English version, *Attic Red-figure Vase-painters* (1942), that appeared during the war seventeen years later, of which a second, enlarged edition came out in 1963, but in the years between the two wars Beazley did much else besides bringing his lists of Attic red-figure vase-painters up to date. Through his friendship with E. P. Warren, who resided in Lewes House, Beazley was entrusted with the publication of his engraved gems, and in the following year (1921) he published the Story-Maskelyne collection of ancient gems.

A journey to Poland in the spring of 1926 led to *Greek Vases in Poland* (1928), which in many ways represents a return to the format of *Attic Red-figured Vases in American Museums* published ten years earlier, in that Beazley wrote about and illustrated the more important of the vases he had seen in Castle Goluchow and Cracow. This time his justly famous tracings of vases were supplemented by photographs taken by his wife (whom he had married on 13 August 1919). The lists of attributions, though updated, were kept to footnotes. At the same time he included Attic black-figured vases on which he later read a paper for the British Academy in 1928, *Attic Black-figure: A Sketch*. Beginning in 1926 he also contributed chapters on Greek art to the *Cambridge Ancient History*, which, together with those authored by Ashmole, were printed as a book in 1932, *Greek Sculpture and Painting*. As to his preferred subject, Attic vases, he joined in the international undertaking *Corpus Vasorum Antiquorum* and published the Attic red-figured vases in the Ashmolean Museum at Oxford in 1927, followed four years later by a second fascicule, with H. G. G. Payne and E. R. Price as collaborators.

In 1931 the first part of *Attic Vase Painting in the Museum of Fine Arts, Boston* (by Lacey D. Caskey with Beazley's cooperation) set new standards in vase publications both for the accuracy of its drawings and the remarkably informative text (parts II and III, 1954 and 1963). Cooperation suited Beazley: when his friend Paul Jacobsthal launched an attractive series, *Bilder griechischer Vasen*, in 1930, Beazley contributed three monographs: on the Berlin Painter (1930), the Pan Painter (1931), and the Kleophrades Painter (1933), and he also collaborated with F. Magi in the publication of the Benedetto Guglielmi antiquities in the Vatican by describing and publishing the Greek and Etruscan painted vases (1939). The exposure to Etruscan painted pottery led in turn to a monograph on Etruscan vase-painting (1947).

The writings of Beazley are as clear and uncluttered as was his speech. Factual information is revealed with astonishing elucidations drawn from world literature and arts of other periods and countries. Totally human in his approach, he brings you as close to the artist and his works as is possible; with gentle humor he allows us to look at ancient art without the sham devotion of a religious cult. As generous in praise, where deserved, as he was uninhibited in his scorn for hackwork, his thumbnail sketches of artists and their style are as readable as they are entertaining, and his critical judgment based on intimate knowledge and constant observation remains as profound today as when it was first pronounced: he is one of the very few scholars that can and should be read in their total output by everybody laying claim to an interest in the subject.

In 1925 Beazley succeeded Percy Gardner in the Lincoln and Merton Chair of Art and Archaeology at Oxford, a position he held until 1956. His teaching duties were light, and the three terms at Oxford were only eight weeks each, leaving much time for what is today called "research," of which his hundred and fifteen articles (and an equal number of book reviews) bear eloquent witness. He also gave many lectures outside of Oxford—at the British Academy, in Newcastle, St. Albans, New York, Basel, Cambridge, Ferrara, Rome, and Melbourne, and most of his lectures were promptly published. The New York Gillender lectures of 1946 on Attic black-figure were expanded in 1949 when Beazley spent a semester as Sather Professor at the University of California and were printed in 1951 under the title *The Development of Attic Black-figure*, five years before his *Attic Black-figure Vase-painters*. The latter followed the format that Beazley had established for the painters of Attic red-figure: up-to-date lists of the painters and the vases attributed to them, arranged by chapters according to chronology and stylistic affinities, but otherwise devoid of full stylistic explanations. "I would rather not sum him up in a few sentences" is what Beazley said of the Berlin Painter at the conclusion of his Melbourne lecture (1964) when he was in his seventy-ninth year: what seemed so easy at the time of his first book, written when he was half a century younger, he now preferred to leave unexpressed.

The second English edition of his red-figure book had come out the year before, and the final task Beazley set for himself was to bring both his black-figure and his red-figure attributions up to date. Beginning in 1942 (the date of the first edition of *Attic Red-figure Vase-painters*) he had periodically typed up his manuscript additions, copies of which went to the Ashmolean Museum, the Athenian Agora, and the Metropolitan Museum of Art. Similar supplements were prepared by him after 1956 for *Attic Black-figure Vase-painters*, and when in 1963 (after the second edition of *Attic Red-figure Vase-painters* had come out) he realized that he could not count on enough time to bring out new separate editions for both the black-figure and the red-figure books, he decided to publish instead his accumulated additions to both works in one volume called (as were his manuscript supplements) *Paralipomena* (1971). This book was handed to the printer in 1968 but did not come out until a year after his death on 6 May 1970.

He had suffered a stroke in 1967 after the death of his wife, from which he did not recover, and while his thoughts were not affected, his growing aphasia, coupled with a deafness against which he had struggled valiantly for twenty years, increased his isolation. He died in Oxford in his eighty-fifth year.

Though Beazley exerted an enormous influence on archaeology, elevating almost single-handedly what had been treated as a minor manifestation of the Greek artistic genius to a well-documented level recognized by art historians, he was not a revolutionary genius. Far from upsetting established criteria of relative chronology and established identifications—both of style and subject matter—he poured his passion into a workable refinement of our understanding of a class of material remains that in sheer number outweighs any other category of ancient objects. An innate sense of artistic endeavor and a deep appreciation of differing degrees of quality prevented him from reducing his enormous knowledge to mere statistics. His sound knowledge of classical literature and his special familiarity with ancient Greek assured him of discovering the true meaning of many an obscure representation, be it mythological or taken from daily life. His forthright descriptive prose, based on accurate observations and an instinctive understanding of human relationships, will serve as a model for many generations to come.

Books and Monographs

Attic Red-figured Vases in American Museums. Cambridge, MA, 1918; reprinted Rome, 1967.

The Lewes House Collection of Ancient Gems. Oxford, 1920.

Catalogue of the Story-Maskelyne Collection of Ancient Gems. London, 1921.

Attische Vasenmaler des rotfigurigen Stils. Tübingen, 1925.

Corpus Vasorum Antiquorum. Great Britain. Fasc. 3, Oxford, Ashmolean Museum, Fasc. 1. Oxford, 1927.

Greek Vases in Poland. Oxford, 1928.

Attic Black-figure: A Sketch. PBA 14 (1928) 217–263. Published separately in London, 1929.

Suggestions for the New Exhibition of the Sculptures of the Parthenon. With D. S. Robertson and B. Ashmole. Privately printed September 1929.

Der Berliner Maler. Berlin, 1930; 2d ed., revised 1944 and 1947 and printed in the original English as *The Berlin Painter*, Mainz, 1974.

Der Pan-Maler. Berlin, 1931; 2d ed., revised 1944 and 1947 and printed in the original English as *The Pan-Painter*, Mainz, 1974.

Corpus Vasorum Antiquorum. Great Britain. Fasc. 9, Oxford, Ashmolean Museum, Fasc. 2. With H. G. G. Payne and E. R. Price. Oxford, 1931.

Attic Vase Painting in the Museum of Fine Arts. Part I. By L. D. Caskey with the cooperation of J. D. Beazley. Boston and London, 1931.

Greek Sculpture and Painting to the End of the Hellenistic Period. Sections I–III by J. D. Beazley; sections IV–IX by B. Ashmole. Cambridge, 1932; reprinted 1966.

Der Kleophrades-Maler. Berlin, 1933; revised 1944 and 1948; and printed in the original English as *The Kleophrades Painter*, Mainz, 1974.

Campana Fragments in Florence. London, 1933.

Attic White Lekythoi. Charlton Lecture 19. London, 1938.

La Raccolta Benedetti Guglielmi nel Museo Gregoriano Etrusco I. Rome, 1939; *Vasi dipinti greci ed etruschi* by J. D. Beazley: 1–100; *Buccheri e ceramic d'impasto* by F. Magi: 103–154.

Attic Red-figure Vase-painters. Oxford, 1942; 2d ed., 1963.

Potter and Painter in Ancient Athens. PBA 30 (1944) 87–125. Published separately in London, 1944.

Etruscan Vase-painting. Oxford, 1947.

Some Attic Vases in the Cyprus Museum. PBA 33 (1947) 195–242. Published separately in London, 1948.

The Development of Attic Black-figure. Sather Lectures Vol. 24. Berkeley, 1951; 2d ed. corrected, 1964; 3rd ed., 1986 revised by D. von Bothmer and Mary B. Moore. 1986.

Les vases attiques à figures rouges. Exploration archéologique de Délos, Fasc. 21. By C. Dugas with the collaboration of J. D. Beazley. Paris, 1952.

Attic Vase Painting in the Museum of Fine Arts, Boston. Part II. Boston, 1954.

Attic Black-figure Vase-painters. Oxford, 1956.

ΕΛΕΝΗΣ ΑΠΑΙΤΗΣΙΣ. PBA 43 (1957) 233–244. Published separately in London, 1957.

Attic Vase Painting in the Museum of Fine Arts, Boston. Part III. By L. D. Caskey with the cooperation of J. D. Beazley. Boston, 1963.

The Berlin Painter. Melbourne, 1964.

Paralipomena. Additions to Attic Black-figure Vase-painters and to Attic Red-figure Vase-painters; 2d ed., Oxford, 1971.

Sources

Bothmer, Dietrich von, et al. *Beazley and Oxford* (Oxford University Committee for Archaeology, Monograph Number 10, 1985). (Lectures delivered by Dietrich von Bothmer, Martin Robertson, Dale Trendall, and John Boardman in Wolfson College, Oxford, on 28 June 1985.)

Robertson, Martin. *Beazley and After. Münchener Jahrbuch der bildenden Kunst,* series III, vol. 27 (1976) 29–46.

Bibliography:

Ashmolean Museum, Department of Antiquities. *Select Exhibition of Sir John and Lady Beazley's Gifts to the Ashmolean Museum 1912–1966.* Oxford, 1967: 177–188.

Obituaries:

Ashmole, Bernard. PBA 56 (1970) 443–461.

Bothmer, Dietrich von. *Oxford Magazine* (12 June 1970) 299–302.

Cahn, Herbert A. *National-Zeitung* (Basel) (13 May 1970) 7.

Metzger, Henri. *Revue Archéologique* (1970) 297–299.

Robertson, Martin. *The Burlington Magazine* 112, no. 809 (August 1970) 541–542.

———. *Gnomon* 43 (1971) 429–432.

———. *Lincoln College Record* (1971–1972) 16–21.

Thompson, Homer A. *Year Book of The American Philosophical Society* (1972) 115–121.

Times (London) (7 May 1970) (unsigned).

Franz Bopp

14 September 1791 – 23 October 1867

BERNFRIED SCHLERATH
Freie Universität Berlin

Rarely in the history of science can the beginning of a discipline be ascribed to one single personage and the appearance of only one book signal the birth of that discipline, but such is the case with Comparative Indo-European Linguistics. In the year 1816 appeared Franz Bopp's book on the conjugational system of Sanskrit compared with that of Greek, Latin, Persian, and Germanic. The preface was dated 16 May 1816; every year thereafter Bopp celebrated the anniversary of that day, and on the fiftieth "birthday" of Indo-European studies, the Royal Prussian Academy created the Bopp Foundation.

There was, however, nothing in that monograph that was not known before. The importance of the book lies not in any single discovery but rather in the persistent and systematic grammatical comparison of the five languages in question without any consideration of philosophical problems or historical implications. The book's success derives from its thematic limitation and the systematic enlargement of its material. Using this method, Bopp advanced his field of study for the remainder of his lifetime and thus became the first comparative philologist and historical linguist. Because that domain is inexhaustible, he created not only a discipline but also a profession, which has not changed much in the course of history.

Bopp's character and personality corresponded exactly with his work. He was not a linguistic genius or a man of high-flown brilliance; he was famous for his rectitude, modesty, and his steady diligence. His special gifts were a sober instinct for tracing out grammatical correspondences and his remarkable powers of deduction.

Franz Bopp was born 14 September 1791 in Mayence, the sixth child of the bookkeeper in the division of horse fodder and carriages of the electoral administration (*kurfürstlicher Futter- und Wagenschreiber*) and his wife, Regina, née Linck. When Mayence became French in 1801, following the peace treaty of Luneville, the Bopp family followed the elector to Aschaffenburg in Bavaria. There Franz Bopp attended the gymnasium from 1801 to 1812 and later the university (which existed only from 1808 to 1814). His principal teacher was Karl Joseph Hieronymus Windischmann (1775–1838), physician-in-ordinary of the then elector in Mayence, historian and philosopher, freemason and later devout Catholic.

The decisive event in Bopp's life was the appearance in 1808 of Friedrich Schlegel's book on the language and wisdom of the Indians, *Über die Sprache und die Weisheit der Indier*. Schlegel had learned Sanskrit in Paris from Alexander Hamilton, a British naval officer who had acquired his knowledge of Sanskrit in India, and who stayed in Paris from 1802 to 1807 because political and military circumstances prevented his return to England. In his book Schlegel gave some information on specimens of Sanskrit literature along with a sketch of the most noticeable grammatical correspondences between Sanskrit and other languages, principally Greek and Latin. It was a *communis opinio* in the late eighteenth century that there was a genealogical relationship between these languages, but Schlegel was the first to compare not simply words but also grammatical structures. That was the decisive step forward. In his words, "The similarity lies not only in a great number of common roots, but includes also the innermost structure and the grammar. The correspondence is therefore not accidental but proves a common descent." And: "The decisive point that will make everything clear is the inner structure of the language; that is, the comparative grammar, which will bring us new information about the genealogy of the languages in much the same way as comparative anatomy threw light upon higher natural history."

Immediately after Schlegel's book came out in 1808 Bopp and Windischmann studied it thoroughly again and again. While Windischmann was more interested in the wisdom of the East, his student was fascinated by the language. One can suppose that even by that time in Aschaffenburg Bopp opposed Schlegel on one special point: Schlegel thought that Sanskrit had a *pure* inflection, namely reduplication and ablaut, the suffixes and endings showing the natural strength and ability of the root to create grammar without the help of other words or extraneous elements. In this point, according to Schlegel, Sanskrit differs from the other languages. Bopp, on the other hand, was brought up in the doctrine of the general linguistic notions of the eighteenth century, which taught that on grounds of general considerations, all languages of the world can have only *one* verb and that this verb is the one that means "to be," so that, e.g., English *loves* must by analyzed as *love-* "loving" plus ellipsis of the copula plus *-s,* "he." In the same way, *old hunter* has lost the copula, while *the hunter is old* has preserved it. That means that according to eighteenth century linguistics (following scholastic traditions), only the copula is able to connect the parts of speech in a sentence. It was Bopp's idea to apply that doctrine (which was based only on logical considerations) to the practical and historical analysis of languages. For him the analysis of *loves* given above is perfectly analogous to Latin *pot-es-t,* "mighty-is-he" (he can) and Latin *dic-s-it* (*dixit*) "saying-was-(*-s-* from Sanskrit *as-* "to be")-he" (he said) and *ama-b-at,* "loving-was (*-b-* from Sanskrit *bhû-* "to be")-he" (he loved). Bopp could therefore not follow Schlegel's opinion that morphemes, which he saw as formations sprouting out of the root, were a proof of the vitality and strength of the rootstock of the Sanskrit language. It must be added that Bopp had already developed his analysis of the Indo-European verb forms and his explanation of them as compounds with verbs meaning "to be" and/or pronouns, while he and his teacher Windischmann were reading Schlegel's book. In any case, the opposition against Schlegel gave Bopp the impetus to investigate the Indo-European verbal systems systematically, while Schlegel soon after lost interest in these problems.

But first Bopp had to learn Sanskrit, and as Napoleon's Continental System prevented his going to London, he assumed that he would study in Paris. Bopp moved to Paris in 1812, and with money provided by his father rented a small garret in Faubourg St. Germain and started immediately to work, only to discover, contrary to his expectations, that Sanskrit was not taught in Paris. With only the help of the imperfect grammars of H. Th. Colebrooke (1805) and William Carey (1806), and without a dictionary or an edition of a text, he taught himself so well that he deciphered a manuscript of the great Indian epic *Mahâbâratá*. He was encouraged only by Louis Langlois, the curator of oriental manuscripts of the National Library. Bopp started with some passages that were accessible through printed translations and gradually, in the course of time, progressed to the stage where he translated the entire huge work. Even today, with our good grammars, dictionaries, commentaries and translations, this would be a great performance. At this time Bopp studied Arabic and New Persian with the great Orientalist Silvestre de Sacy and taught himself Spanish, much as he had Sanskrit, finally reading Calderón and Lope de Vega.

Bopp stayed in Paris from 1812 to 1816, supported by his father for the first two years, then by a small scholarship granted by the king of Bavaria. On weekdays he would read from morning to evening in the National Library and then study at home for many hours at night and on weekends. He was interested in nothing else in the world except the study of languages. In his letters from Paris we do not find one word about Paris or its inhabitants, about manners and customs, about the food, about art treasures or edifices. Even the world-shaking political events, the repeated capture of Paris, and the fall of the Napoleonic empire are mentioned only briefly, emphasizing at the same time that these events cost him no time away from his studies. From 1814 to 1816 Bopp introduced August Wilhelm Schlegel, the elder brother of Friedrich, to Sanskrit. In 1819 Schlegel became the first professor of Sanskrit in Bonn.

The fruit of Bopp's studies in Paris was *Über das Conjugationssystem der Sanskritsprache*, mentioned above. Bopp's first aim in this book was the analysis of the verb forms and the etymological explanation of the elements he derived from his analysis. He tried to describe the formation of the verb forms in Sanskrit and the related languages. As he was interested in revealing the leading principles of Indo-European grammar, there was a strong typological element in his research. But he was not a historian in the proper sense; the historical element in his work was only an automatic consequence of the inclusion of a huge mass of linguistic material. Bopp's peculiar position as what Reinhard Sternemann calls a "non-historical historian" ("Bopp betreibt also gewissermassen einen 'unhistorischen Historismus'") who achieved results of the greatest importance for the history of the Indo-European languages (while he himself was rather a typologist and "etymologist of morphemes") becomes especially clear from his later books. In this respect Bopp's position is directly opposite to that of Jacob Grimm, who some time later worked in the field of Germanic languages as a mere and true historian. Historical phonology, in particular laws of sound—later the firm base of all research in language history—is not found in Bopp's work, nor is any systematic reconstruction.

When Bopp's royal scholarship ended in August 1816, he had to leave Paris and return to his parents in Aschaffenburg. In October he stayed in Munich applying for further financial support, but he first had to sit for an examination to prove that the king of Bavaria had not granted his aid in vain. Bopp was required to present a paper explaining the results and the methods of his research and he had to demonstrate in oral examination, with the help of a passage of a Gothic text of his own choosing, the relation between Gothic and Sanskrit. Before a wider public audience he had to translate the first two chapters of Herodotus into Latin. The procedure was finished in January 1817, but not until September of that year did the king decide to grant Bopp the extraordinary support of 1,000 guilders per annum for two years. Meanwhile, Bopp left Bavaria and stayed in Paris at his own expense, working in the library and reading Sanskrit texts twice a week with August Wilhelm Schlegel. It was at this time that he made the acquaintance of Hamilton, who was then visiting Paris. In October 1818 he went to London and there studied Sanskrit manuscripts in close contact with Colebrooke, G. C. Haughton, and C. Wilkins. In the summer of 1820 he went from London, via Paris, to Mommenheim, a village near Mayence, where his father had bought a small estate for Bopp's elder brother. In the same year the competent ministry in Munich tried to force the Philosophical Faculty of the University of Würzburg to inaugurate a chair for Bopp. But the faculty declared strictly that a chair for Sanskrit would be useless and furthermore that Bopp would not even be qualified for such a chair. Only one year later, the same faculty appointed Othmar Frank, a Sanskritist of limited knowledge, Professor of Oriental Languages.

In November 1820 Bopp went to Göttingen, where he enrolled in courses in Hebrew. In April 1821 the University of Göttingen bestowed upon him the honor of *doctor honoris causa* in appreciation of his work and discoveries in the Sanskrit language. In the same month Bopp visited Berlin for the first time and studied Sanskrit texts with Wilhelm von Humboldt nearly every day. Through Humboldt he came into contact with important personalities in the Ministry of Cultural Affairs: Minister Altenstein and the Privy Councillors (*Staatsräte*) Süvern and Nicolovius. On 9 September 1821 Bopp was appointed Extraordinary Professor of Oriental Literature and General Linguistics at the Friedrich-Wilhelms University (the document was granted on 14 September, his thirtieth birthday) and a short time later, full Professor. In 1822 he became a member of the Prussian Academy of Sciences. By 1820 a revised edition of his first book had appeared in English translation under the title *Analytic Comparison of the Sanskrit, Greek, Latin, and Teutonic Languages Showing the Original Grammatical Structure.*

In Berlin Bopp was now free from all worry about his daily existence and could, by hard labor day after day and year after year, and with his imperturbable determination, build up his immense life's work. In the early twenties he edited and translated some smaller Sanskrit texts: in 1827 his *Ausführliches Lehrgebäude der Sanskrita-Sprache* appeared, then the second edition in Latin (1833), a concise version (1834), a second German edition (1845), followed by a third (1863). A Sanskrit glossary came out in 1830, with a second edition in 1847. While the first edition was followed by a short etymological appendix, the second edition became a sort of etymological dictionary.

His main work, however, was the Comparative Indo-European Grammar. He started with five preliminary essays dealing with special problems, which appeared as *Akademieabhandlungen* (1824–1826, 1829, 1831). His *Vergleichende Grammatik des Sanskrit, Zend, Griechischen, Lateinischen, Litauischen, Gotischen und Deutschen* came out in six volumes (1833, 1835, 1837, 1842, 1849, 1852). The second edition appeared from 1856 to 1861 and in 1868, one year after Bopp's death, the third. Up to the end of the seventies, that work formed the firm and authoritative foundation of all Indo-European studies. Nevertheless, many questions about other languages remained, and Bopp treated them in special dissertations because it would have been too complicated to include them in the great grammar: he dealt with Celtic in a monograph of great importance (1839), and also produced monographs on Old Prussian (1853) and Albanian (1855).

His comparison of the Greek and Sanskrit accentual system was, even in the eyes of many contemporaries, unsuccessful. Unsuccessful also were his attempts to prove that the Malayan and Polynesian languages belong to the Indo-European language family (1840) and that Georgian was also an Indo-European language (1846). The reason for these failures lay in the lack of a reliable historical phonology. The concept of sound laws was developed only a short time after Bopp's death.

Happily and regularly progressing in his scholarly work, in a harmonious family circle and in close contact with Wilhelm von Humboldt, and surrounded by many students who admired him, he was witness to the rise and flourishing of "his" discipline. He was a modest and unpretentious man who knew no doubts or inner conflicts. He especially enjoyed living in Berlin, where he appreciated the free and easy form of social life and the high estimation and respect that the royal court and the administration showed towards the sciences, arts and humanities.

Bopp continued to lecture up to 1864 and died on 23 October 1867 after an attack of apoplexy.

Books

Über das Conjugationssystem der Sanskritsprache in Vergleichung mit jenem der griechischen, lateinischen, persischen und germanischen Sprache. Frankfurt-am-Main, 1816.

Ausführliches Lehrgebäude der Sanskrita-Sprache. Berlin, 1827; 2d ed. in Latin, 1833; concise version, 1834; 2d German ed., 1845; 3d ed., 1863.

Grammatica critica linguae sanscritae. Berlin, 1829; 2d ed., 1832.
Glossarium Sanscritum. Berlin, 1830; 2d ed., 1847.
Vergleichende Grammatik des Sanskrit, Zend, Griechischen, Lateinischen, Litthauischen, Gothischen und Deutschen. 6 vols. Berlin, 1833–1857; 2d ed., 1856–1861; 3d ed., 1868. English translation, *A Comparative Grammar of the Sanscrit, Zend, Greek, Latin, Lithuanian, Gothic, German, and Slavonic Languages*. Translated by E. B. Eastwick. London, 1845–54; French translation by Michel Bréal. Paris, 1866–74.
Kritische Grammatik der Sanskrita-Sprache in kürzer Fassung. Berlin, 1834; 2d ed., 1845; 3d ed., 1863; 4th ed., 1868.
Die celtischen Sprachen in ihren Verhältnisse zum Sanskrit, Zend, Griechischen, Lateinischen, Germanischen, Litthauischen und Slawischen. Berlin, 1839.
Über die Sprache der alten Preussen in ihren verwandtschaftlichen Beziehungen. Berlin, 1853.
Über das Albanesische in seinen verwandtschaftlichen Beziehungen. Berlin, 1855.

Sources

Benfey, T. *Geschichte der Sprachwissenschaft*. Munich, 1869: 370–379, 470–515.
Kuhn, Adalbert. "Franz Bopp." *Unsere Zeit*, IV Jahrg. 10 heft., 1868.
Lefmann, Solomon. *Franz Bopp, sein Leben und seine Wissenschaft*, 1. Hälfte. Berlin, 1891.
Leskien, August. "Franz Bopp." *Allgemeine Deutsche Biographie*. Bd. 3 (1876): 140–149.
Martineau, Russel. "Obituary of Franz Bopp." *Transactions of the Philological Society*, 1867.
Neumann, Günter. *Indogermanische Sprachwissenschaft 1816 und 1966*. Bd. 1. Franz Bopp. Innsbrucker Beiträge zur Kulturwissenschaft. Sonderheft 24. Innsbruck, 1967.
Schlerath, B. "Franz Bopp." *Berlinische Lebensbilder Geisteswissenschaftler*. Edited by M. Erbe. Berlin, 1989: 55–72
Sternemann, Reinhard. "Franz Bopps Beitrag zur Entwicklung der vergleichenden Sprachwissenschaft." *Zeitschrift für Germanistik*. Bd. 5. Heft 2 (1984).
———. *Franz Bopp und die vergleichende indoeuropäische Sprachwissenschaft*. Innsbrucker Beiträge zur Sprachwissenschaft 33. Innsbruck, 1984.
Windischmann, K. J. "Vorerinnerungen" in Bopp's *Conjugationssystem*.

Ernst Buschor

2 June 1886 – 11 December 1961

WOLFGANG SCHINDLER
Winckelmann Institut der
    Humboldt Universität

Ernst Buschor belongs to those pioneers of archaeology, who, after the First World War, deepened through interpretation the legacy of the collection and study of the artifacts that characterized archaeological research at the turn of the century. Buschor's method sought to connect the objects with the history and culture of their time, while also making them important for us on their own account. Such a goal may best be understood in the light of Werner Jaeger's Third Humanism. Buschor turned archaeology into an art history that tried to understand the objects by themselves.

Buschor was born on 2 June 1886 in Hürben near Krumbach (Bavaria) into a peasant family. After his school education he first studied law. By 1905 he had changed to classical archaeology at Munich under the influence of Adolf Furtwängler (1853–1907). Later he observed of himself when recalling his study under Furtwängler, that "he could only describe himself as thoroughly dependent on his teacher." Even before obtaining his doctorate in 1912, he wrote his book *Griechische Vasenmalerei* (1912). That was his first publication in which along with highly specialized research on the objects themselves, he already revealed his methodological approach that led to a more profound understanding of them in their historical context. His book immediately won for him a wide circle of admirers. He wrote his dissertation under Paul Wolters (1858–1936).

After his participation in the First World War, Buschor became in 1919, without habilitation, associate professor (= extraordinarius) for archaeology at Erlangen. One year later he became at age 34 full professor at Freiburg in Breisgau. From 1922 until 1929 he was Director of the German Archaeological Institute in Athens, which had reopened in 1921. During these years he reopened the excavations of the Sanctuary of Hera at Samos which had been discontinued in 1914. He contributed much to our understanding of the early architectural phases of this sanctuary, especially of the Rhoikos Temple, which preceded the Temple of Polykrates. In the same productive decade he also investigated the archaic poros pedimental sculpture from the Athenian acropolis, as well as completing the masterpiece of his teacher Furtwängler, *Griechische Vasenmalerei* (Vol. I, 1904; vol. II, 1905; vol. III, 1932).

In 1929 Buschor accepted the chair of classical archaeology at Munich, earlier held by his teachers, Furtwängler (1894–1907) and Wolters (1908–1929). He continued to direct the Samian excavations which he had begun in 1925. In the early thirties he presented to the scholarly world the quintessence of his method in a famous and brief article entitled "Begriff und Methode der Archäologie" ("The Idea and Method of Archaeology"). This was published in Iwan Müller's *Handbuch der Archäologie* first in 1939 and republished in 1969. He reveals clearly the concern and the limitations of his method as well as his interest in the ideology of the time. Because of his inclination toward the nationalistic movement of the Third Reich, he was at first deprived of his right to teach after World War II but soon again received the *venia legendi.*

After the war he devoted himself intensively to the translation and staging of Greek tragedies. He translated all extant Greek tragedies. At the same time he applied himself to a wider understanding of the development of Greek and Roman Art. Already in his book *Vom Sinn der griechische Standbilder* (1942) he had drawn a first sketch. Now he intensified these ideas in his publication, *Bildnisstufen* (1947) and widened them in his *Das Porträt* (1960).

Buschor was a member of the Bavarian and Berlin Academies of Science. In 1937 he received an honorary doctorate from the University of Athens. In 1959 he was elected to the Ordre pour le mérite, the last German archaeologist to receive this honor. He died in Munich on 11 December 1961. Among his students were L. Alscher, R. Hampe, N. Himmelmann, E. Homan-Wedeking, G. Kleiner, and D. Ohly.

Along with his teaching (he was a charismatic and brilliant lecturer), Buschor exerted influence far beyond archaeological and art historical circles through his publications which enjoyed wide circulation and were often translated. Beginning with the genre of painting, where throughout he was concerned with originals (*Griechische Vasemmalerei; Griechische Vasen*), he turned to the study of reliefs (poros pedimental sculpture; the Olympia pediments; Parthenon sculpture; friezes from the Maussolleion at Halicarnassus). He especially devoted his attention to freestanding sculpture (*Altsamische Standbilder, Plastik der Griechen, Das Hellenistische Bildnis*). Throughout all these studies he sought to discover an interdisciplinary *tertium comparationis*, that might provide the key to an understanding and interpretation that embraced the whole. His complex analytical method is brilliantly revealed in his publication, *Grab eines attischen Mädchens.*

What will remain of the published work of Buschor for posterity as a challenge and as an everlasting obligation (Verpflichtung) will be his devotion to the concrete and abstract aspects of the ancient works. In both aspects are implied their historical importance as well as their relevance to the modern beholder. The two remain in a dialectical tension one with the other. As long as they do, the message of ancient art, interpreted by the archaeologist, demands attention.

Buschor's activity is characterized by the break from historicism to phenomenological methodology. Interpretation in its deeper sense required the task of making the cultural legacy of antiquity relevant. Heidegger's conception of art demanded a great mediator capable of transmitting the greatness of his subject to his own time. Only this way from Heidegger's point of view, could art be truly experienced. In this sense Buschor tried to overcome history. That means to place the historical into a contemporary context that uses it but is not defeated by it. We see now that Buschor's work was able to accommodate the Third Humanism. Education in the sense of paideia was inseparable from this aspect of his teaching and writings.

From the point of view of hermeneutics Buschor reached a limitation where his method of stylistic analysis demanded entry into a wider cultural context, namely an historical totality. His biological metaphor for development with which he tried to comprehend wide periods of time at the very latest had to fail in regard to Roman art. With the rise of the iconological method (Aby Warburg; Erwin Panofsky) Buschor seemed dated. That does not mean that the quest for complex analysis and interpretation can be neglected.

Books

Griechische Vasenmalerei. Munich, 1912; 2d ed. 1914; English translation by G. C.
　　　Richards as *Greek Vase Painting*, London, 1921.
Die Skulpturen des Zeustempels zu Olympia. Marburg, 1924.
Größenverhältnisse attischer Porosgiebel . Berlin1924.
Die Tondächer der Akropolis. Berlin and Leipzig, Vol. 1 1929, vol. 2 1933.
Altsamische Standbilder I–V. Berlin, 1934–1960–1961.
Die Plastik der Griechen. Berlin, 1936; repr. Munich, 1958.
Grab eines attischen Mädchens. Munich, 1939; 2d ed. 1941; repr. 1959.
Begriff und Methode der Archäologie. In *Handbuch der Archäologie*, edited by W. Otto,
　　　Munich, vol. I 193;, repr. 1969.
Griechische Vasen. Munich, 1940.
Vom Sinn der griechischen Standbilder. Berlin, 1942.
Phidias der Mensch. Munich, 1948.
Das hellenistische Bildnis. Munich, 1949.
Maussollos und Alexander. Munich, 1950.
Das Porträt. Bildniswege und Bildnisstufen in fünf Jahrtausenden. Munich, 1960.

Sources

Benson, J. L. *On the Meaning of Greek Statues*. Amherst, 1980: ix–xxiii.
Diepolder, Hans. *Von griechischer Kunst: Ausgewählte Schriften*. Munich, 1963.
　　　2:5–12.
Homan-Wedeking, E. "Ernst Buschor," *Gnomon* 38 (1966) 221–224. (With portrait.)

Schefold, Karl. "Ernst Buschor 1886–1961." In *Archäologenbildnisse: Porträts und Kurzbiographien von Klassischen Archäologen deutscher Sprache*. Edited by R. Lullies and W. Schiering. Mainz, 1988:234–235.

Schiering, Wolfgang. *Allgemeine Grundlagen der Archäologie*. Edited by Ulrich Hausmann. Munich, 1969: 78–80.

Walter, Hans. "Ernst Buschor zum 75. Geburtstag," *Von griechischer Kunst: Ausgewählte Schriften*. Munich, 1963. 2:221–225.

Zanker, Paul. "Ernst Buschor, 1886–1961: Archäologe, Pädagoge, Weltdeuter," *Umbits* 5 (Munich, 1986) 16–17.

C. G. Cobet

28 November 1813 – 28 October 1889

L. F. JANSSEN
University of Utrecht

Charles Gabriel Cobet was born 28 November 1813 in Paris, the son of Johannes Cobet, a Dutch civil servant attached to the French Ministry of War from 1810 to 1815. His mother was a Frenchwoman, Marie Bertrand, a relative of Henri Count Bertrand, who, as *grand-maréchal du palais*, accompanied Napoleon to Elba and St. Helena. After returning to Holland, Cobet passed through the gymnasium at The Hague and was inscribed in the Faculty of Theology of Leiden University (1832). Being one of the few visitors of the university library, Cobet spent many days perusing Greek and Latin texts, and he became an intimate friend of the librarian Johan Jacob Geel, who guided his interests in a most beneficial way. Two years later Cobet switched over to classical philology and at about the same time (December 1835) he won the gold medal of the Faculty by writing a *Prosopographia Xenophontea*. This masterpiece resulted in his being welcomed gladly by the Leiden philologists Bake and Hofman Peerlkamp. In order to finish his studies a testimonial for hearing *historia iuris* by Thorbecke—in later years a famous Dutch statesman—was indispensible, but Cobet could not see the relevance of this subsidiary specialism and he was not inclined to meet this obligation; by this unusual behavior Cobet's independent and willful character made itself manifest at an early stage. The result was a deadlock, all the more serious because the Royal Institute wanted to patronize a new Simplicius edition and was prepared to send the young scholar to France and Italy in order to make the appropriate collations of manuscripts. Fortunately, Bake found an excellent way out by making Cobet defend an unauthorized but full-sized thesis (on 20 October 1840) that enabled Bake to confer the degree *doctor honoris causa* on Cobet some months later, on 17 March 1841.

At that time Cobet was already in Paris, where he had to discover for himself that the Aldina of the *Commentarii De caelo* was indeed a late Greek translation of the thirteenth-century Latin version by Willem van Moerbeke. He stayed abroad for five years exploring the libraries of Paris, Turin, Florence, Rome, Naples, Milan, and Venice, not only collating a total of some eighty-five Simplicius manuscripts, but also taking a keen interest in all other texts he came across, recording important *variae lectiones*, with a clear preference for Attic prose and Homeric scholia (on finding the codex Venetus B, Cobet immediately recognized its importance). As the government only paid for three years, Cobet accepted an invitation from Firmin Didot to provide a new edition of Diogenes Laertius, a task he finished with great reluctance, as he thought it absurd to add a Latin translation. However, the edition was published at last in 1850 without a foreword and it remained the leading one for more than a century. As the correspondence with his friend Geel was carefully preserved by the addressee, we are in the happy position of being able to follow Cobet week by week from November 1840 to July 1845 in his quest for manuscripts while he unremittingly ransacked French and Italian libraries and copied thousands of text variants; these letters, giving information and comments upon many difficult passages, betray both a youthful energy and enthusiasm, and a vehement, often improper criticism of librarians and other scholars.

After his return, Cobet in 1846 became Extraordinary Professor of Roman Antiquities at Leiden (succeeding W. L. Mahne, the insignificant panegyrist of Wyttenbach), but he soon rose to the chair of Hofman Peerlkamp, being entrusted with the teaching of Greek in accordance with an arrangement with Bake, who took charge of the Latin department. Cobet remained in function for more than thirty-five years, though in the end he suffered from apoplectic fits that impaired his memory; he died 28 October 1889.

Cobet was mainly concerned with textual criticism, and nearly all his publications, varying from his thesis *Observationes criticae in Platonis comici reliquias* (1840), through *Commentationes philologicae* (1853), *Variae* and *Novae Lectiones* (1854; 1859) to *Miscellanea* and *Collectanea critica* (1876; 1878), contain numerous emendations to and conjectures on the whole range of Greek prose literature (cf. the useful inventories in *Mnemosyne* n.s. 34 [1906] 430–448; 35 [1907] 440–449).

In his very instructive inaugural *Oratio de arte interpretandi grammatices et critices fundamentis innixa primario philologici officio* (1847), Cobet laid down the leading principles of his approach to Greek language and literature. These lines were further defined in his yearly *adhortationes* or *allocutiones* with which he began his lectures in order to encourage the students; some of these were published in 1852, 1853, 1854, 1856, and 1860. He honestly believed that the Greeks, and first and foremost the Athenians, were able, as long as they enjoyed freedom, to express in their Attic language a supreme rationality and lucidity in combination with a natural elegance and feeling for nuance. While learning the grammatical subtleties of pure Attic it should, however, be observed that each author had his own peculiar way of thinking and relating; students should be reminded that reading Greek meant listening to a human being with his own idiom and style. Consequently, *lexica abicere et sibi sufficere mature docendus est quicumque iustam certamque antiquae linguae scientiam quaerit*, as dictionaries usually mixed up forms and meanings from different authors and different periods. It was only during the classic period that Greek usage was consistent and precisely defined. With the arrival of Alexander the Great, Greece was deprived of its independence, Attic speech lost its natural purity and spontaneity, and it became ever more liable to degeneration and corruption. The post-Alexandrian authors, though still emulating the classical examples and writing an even more elegant Attic, were too much influenced by words and expressions borrowed from non-Attic dialects and from vulgar speech.

The normative power of Attic was mainly due to its grammatical perspicuity, the constancy in the meaning of words, and the clear structure of sentences; its grammar was ruled by the laws of analogy, and these guaranteed an ideal precision and adequacy of expression. A full knowledge of Greek might ultimately lead one to reach the highest grade of *humanitas*.

In these views Cobet proved himself to be a true representative of the early nineteenth-century trend of classicism. He had assimilated his mind so completely to Greek thinking that he confessed he usually read Latin by translating it into Greek. This mentality led him to a way of handling old manuscripts—always intent on making corrections in order to eliminate the grammatical faults and misinterpretations of medieval copyists—that was appreciated neither by many contemporary German colleagues nor by most of his modern Dutch successors. His hypercorrective attitude toward traditional readings made him neglect many peculiarities nowadays recognized as true and original Attic forms or phrases. So he would not accept the feminine dual forms τά, ταῖν, etc., and corrected them to τώ, τοῖν, etc., though these forms are doubtless good Attic (cf. G. L. Cooper III in *TAPhA* 103 (1972) 97–125, who showed that some feminine forms seem to have a hypocoristic connotation about them). Other typical Cobetian corrections were: 1) changing forms of the present (e.g., imperfect) into aorist, 2) changing imperfect to pluperfect, 3) inserting *optativi obliqui* instead of indicative forms, 4) preferring future infinitive or aorist infinitive + ἄν to aorist infinitive, 5) deleting *verba dicendi* in *oratio obliqua*.

In recent years Cobet's "critical philosophy" has been severely criticized by E. J. Kenney (*The Classical Text*, Berkeley and Los Angeles, 1974: 117–123), who rightly observes that Cobet did not avail himself of the innovative methods of *recensio* as espoused by his contemporaries Madvig and Lachmann, and in his *Observationes criticae et palaeographicae in Dionysii Halicarnassensis Antiquitates Romanas* (Leiden, 1877) ignored Ritschl's *stemma codicum*. Cobet stubbornly kept to the doctrine of restoring the text *sive ex antiquis membranis sive ex ingenio* sanctified by his illustrious predecessors Ruhnken and Scaliger. Nonetheless, it cannot be denied that Cobet gave an indisputable proof of his skill as a textual critic by collating and classifying the manuscripts of Simplicius' *Commentarii*; he indeed identified the Laurentianus 85.21 as the archetype of the *Commentarii de anima* and, as Sicking rightly noticed (1984), Cobet's method of differentiating between good and bad manuscripts does not actually depart from the rules laid down by M. L. West (*Textual Criticism and Editorial Technique*, Stuttgart, 1973: 37ff.) in the case of an open recension; in the same way, Cobet's harsh and damning qualification of medieval monks and scribes as mendacious falsifiers can easily be paralleled with comments made by modern authors in this field.

Unfortunately, Cobet's preliminary work on Simplicius' *Commentarii*—at first a complete edition was planned by the Royal Dutch Academy—only resulted in the publication of the *Commentarii de caelo* by S. Karsten in 1865. As Cobet himself did not have any philosophical inclinations and referred to such speculations as λῆροι λεπτότατοι, he concentrated all his acumen on the constitution and interpretation of Greek prose texts, especially the historical works of Herodotus, Thucydides, Xenophon, and the Attic orators like Demosthenes, Lysias, Antiphon, and Aeschines. He took a particular interest in Hellenistic scholarly literature (e.g. Athenaeus, Galen, Clement of Alexandria, Photius, Stobaeus, and Strabo), as it preserved countless quotations from lost drama or comedy. Having a quick and witty mind, Cobet found much pleasure in looking for comic fragments of Menander, and since many were stored by Athenaeus, he collated all the manuscripts in question on the basis of the Venetian archetype. Above all Cobet loved Homer—he thought him an Athenian!—and he did much to make his way of thinking better understood, e.g. by vindicating many ἀπρεπῆ in verses discredited by the bad taste of the Alexandrians. In drama, he contributed some good emendations to Sophocles and Euripides (i. e. *Helen*), though he frankly confessed that he did not feel at home in poetry, and the more so if he could not find an *animi sanitatem et* φρόνημα in it. Accordingly, he could not appreciate Callimachus because of his sophisticated erudition and artificial style, nor Theocritus, who confused old and new forms in an unpleasant way. When comparing the works of later prose writers with the rules set by the Atticistic grammarians, Cobet spent much time and energy in trying to distinguish faults caused by paleographic errors from those due to the grammatical carelessness of the prose writers themselves; while doing so he abominated the empty talk of Aelian and Longus, but he was very much pleased with Lucian's *veterum nitidam et tersam dictionem, cogitandi serenitatem, loquendi sanitatem*. Always looking for normative rules and clear expression he showed himself a real nineteenth-century Dutchman, who put *zeker weten en helder inzicht* ("definite knowledge and clear insight") above all.

This narrow-minded but consistent attitude made him an extraordinary mainstay to all those students who loved him intensely and spread his learning and ideas. After 1864 nearly all Dutch university chairs of classical philology were successively occupied by pupils of Cobet: in Utrecht, Van Herwerden, Van der Vliet, and J. C. Vollgraff; in Groningen, Halbertsma and Polak; in Amsterdam, Naber and Boissevain; in Leiden, Cornelissen, Van Leeuwen, Hartman, and Hesseling. Du Rieu and Scato de Vries made their mark as Leiden librarians. Many distinguished schoolmasters and *rectores gymnasii* had been trained in conformity with Cobetian standards, and even the later famous Sanskritists Kern and Caland owed their critical methods mainly to Cobet. This is all the more remarkable as Cobet had a dislike for comparative linguistics and severely criticized its lack of grammatical knowledge (λινγυιστικη!) and jeered at these συ/αγκριτισταί.

Neither the archaeological remains in Rome and Pompeii nor the works of art that Cobet saw in Florence and Naples left a strong impression on him; yet he was fully alive to new finds in papyrology and epigraphy and he took an active part in revising recently discovered texts or inscriptions. Thus, he prepared new editions of Hyperides' Ὑπὲρ Εὐξενίππου, Λόγος ἐπιτάφιος (1877) and of Philostratus' Περὶ γυμναστικῆς (1859), while his stay in Venice (1844) gave him the opportunity to study three Cretan inscriptions relating to Hierapytna (=*Inscr. Cret. III, 3,3*).

Greek and Roman antiquities had early aroused Cobet's interest, as he was put in charge of teaching this particular subject. Accordingly, several chronological problems and the analysis of sources in Plutarch's *Lives* I–XI (especially Pericles, Aristides, Themistocles, Alcibiades) were carefully studied as well as those in the writings of Duris of Samos and in Dionysius' *Roman Antiquities*, the latter being gathered in *Observationes in Dionysii Halicarnassensis Antiquitates Romanas* (1877). As to the Gracchi, Cobet tried, against Cicero, to justify their policy, while he did not shrink from caviling Mommsen.

This preferential treatment of historical authors, in combination with a resolute aiming at an improvement of Dutch educational practice, made Cobet prepare a clean Attic edition of Xenophon's *Anabasis* and *Hellenica* that became standard reading in the gymnasia for nearly a hundred years. Though at the outset destined only for school practice, these texts gradually achieved a prescriptive status. In the same way Cobet lent his genius to two other schoolbooks: 1) a revision of the Nepos edition originally prepared by his colleague W. G. Pluygers and 2) a strange phenomenon in Dutch pedagogic tradition—a collection of nearly 500 jokes (asteia) taken from Philogelos and remodelled into a fashionable Greek. Some people were a little shocked at this publication, but many teachers were glad to have their lessons spiced by these funny stories.

After all, Cobet was both a creative scholar and a brilliant speaker, who knew how to inspire his pupils with a lasting confidence in the superiority of classical literature and who was always ready to encourage and help them. Not a few foreign scholars acknowledged their debt to Cobet, "the greatest Greek scholar of this century," as W. G. Rutherford, the author of an exemplary Phrynichus edition, qualified him in the obituary in *CR* 3 (1889) 470–474. Yet the number of students attracted by Cobet from abroad was very limited; among these was the later Nestor of the Athenian faculty, Constantine Contos, who came to Leiden as a young man to improve his knowledge of Greek. Many scholars profited from the collations Cobet had made in Italy, and these were generously put at their disposal, like A. Emper (Dio Chrysostom), L. Kayser (Philostratus), W. Dindorf (Scholia Homerica), W. A. Hirschig (Erotici). In later years, Cobet's extreme negligence of German literature and his failing memory raised many sharp polemics and blunt insinuations by colleagues who, like Bernardakis and Th. Gomperz, thought they could prove the priority of other scholars in proposing conjectures. On glancing through the critical apparatus of some texts commented on by Cobet, it is not difficult to point to some emendations that can now justly be traced back to their originator, but at the same time it is curious to see other Cobetian corrections attributed to later distinguished scholars. Cobet would not worry about such questions; instead, he would probably have said: "nunc ad seriora transeamus," as he used to say when in university examinations it was his turn to test the knowledge of the candidate in Greek after philosophy or archaeology had been examined.

Books

Observationes criticae in Platonis comici reliquias. Amsterdam, 1840.
Commentationes philologicae. Amsterdam, 1853.
Variae Lectiones. Leiden, 1854.
Novae Lectiones. Leiden, 1859.
Miscellanea Critica. Leiden, 1876.
Observationes criticae et palaeographicae in Dionysii Halicarnassi Antiquitates Romanes. Leiden, 1877.
Collectanea critica. Leiden, 1878.

Sources

Fruin, R. and van der Mey, H. W. *Brieven van Cobet aan Geel.* Leiden, 1891.
Naber, S. A. *Vier tijdgenoten.* Haarlem, 1894: 159–357.
van Proosdij, B. A. *Two Thunderclouds Closing in Conflict.* Leiden, 1954.
Schouten, D. C. A. J. *Het Grieks aan de Nederlandse Universiteiten in de 19e eeuw.* Diss., Nijmegen, 1964: 124–211, 220–233.
Sicking, C. M. J. "Cobet." In *Een universiteit herleeft.* Leiden, 1984: 26–37.
Papers
At University Library, Leiden.

F. M. Cornford
27 February 1874 – 3 January 1943

DOUGLAS KELLOGG WOOD
Berkshire School

Francis Macdonald Cornford, Fellow of Trinity College and Laurence Professor of Ancient Philosophy in the University of Cambridge, was a revolutionary scholar who reinterpreted the origins of Western thought and a masterful translator of and commentator on the later dialogues of Plato. He was also a recognized authority on Greek science, an innovator in the methodology of the history of ideas, an historian and a poet, and an important student of human nature. In his work he achieved a rare combination of profound erudition and sympathetic imagination, which he expressed in an admirable English style that inspired students and colleagues, and enabled him to reach an audience far beyond Cambridge.

Cornford was born in Eastborne, Sussex, on 27 February 1874, a clergyman's son. During his youth he distinguished himself as a promising student of Latin and Greek and, upon graduating from St. Paul's School in London, he entered Trinity College, Cambridge, in 1894 on an Open Minor Scholarship to pursue a course of classical studies (Greek and Latin literature and ancient philosophy).

In his second year Cornford became the pupil of Henry Jackson, praelector in Ancient Philosophy at Trinity, who later became Regius Professor of Greek in the University, a member of the Order of Merit, and Vice-Master of his college. Cornford once compared Jackson to Dr. Johnson: "Both were masters of the peculiarly English wit that is near allied, not to madness, but to common sense; both were great talkers—Jackson the more congenial of the two, countering folly with a north-country bluntness that did not forget the claims of courtesy. He taught the young scholars of many academic generations to clear their minds of loose thinking and never to leave a stone unturned. Like Socrates, he was content to leave his mark upon the minds of his pupils." Jackson, Cornford continued, not only influenced him as well as three other Cambridge classicists he admired (Richard Archer-Hind, James Adam, and Robert Hicks) but also men outside "the academic world . . . who, if they met

Jackson only as unflagging host, perambulating those rooms in Nevile's Court with a syphon in one hand and a cigar-box in the other" would "count it an honour that they once received a friendly greeting from a great humanist and a great Englishman" (Cornford, *The Laws of Motion in Ancient Thought* 6–7).

Jackson, whose great interest was Plato's later theory of ideas (a subject he was never able to shape into a book) took Cornford under his wing and set him to reading ancient philosophy. Another important influence on Cornford at this time was that of Walter Headlam, Fellow of King's College, who was then working on his translations of Aeschylus. (He had previously translated fifty poems of Meleager and later would publish poems of Herodas.) Headlam was regarded by many in Cambridge and on the Continent—Wilamowitz praised his scholarship—as one of the most promising young classicists of his day. Rapport seems to have been established between Headlam and Cornford from the outset, and, until his premature death in 1908, Headlam called on his former pupil for assistance in interpreting difficult passages from Aeschylus.

After Cornford graduated from the University in the Jubilee Year of 1897 (he had taken Firsts in both parts of the Classical Tripos), he continued to live in Cambridge, where he supported himself with an Exhibition from Trinity and with the salary he received as editor of the *Cambridge Review*. It had seemed that he would have to become a schoolmaster, since he had been informed by his family that he would shortly have to be the sole support of his mother. Hence he momentarily ruled out the possibility of seeking a fellowship. Although he was offered a position in the sixth form at Clifton, he continued to mark time and in the end decided to gamble that he would be able to stand successfully for a fellowship before he might have to provide for his mother. Yet he almost lost his wager, for while he passed his Examination, Henry Jackson would not accept his thesis on the *Cratylus*. Cornford had evidently annoyed Jackson by disagreeing with his mentor's interpretation of the dialogue. In any event, he was determined to succeed on his last chance in 1899. Jackson, however, had warned him that there might not be any openings that year. Thus, at the age of twenty-five, he applied for the Professorship of Greek at University College, Cardiff. He was turned down by Cardiff, but he won his fellowship in Trinity on the basis of his dissertation, "Prolegomena to the *Nicomachean Ethics*."

The year before he became a teaching Fellow of Trinity Cornford met Jane Ellen Harrison, a Lecturer in classics in Newnham College. He had first heard her give one of her bravura performances at the Archaeological Museum: "I have a vision of her figure on the darkened stage of the lecture-room . . . which she made deserve to the full its name of theatre—a tall figure in black drapery, with touches of her favourite green, and a string of blue Egyptian beads, like a priestess' rosary." After hearing her public lecture on the *mystica vannus Iacchi*, Cornford "sent her a letter on some point that had struck me. She asked me to come talk it over, and so began the series of innumerable conversations over the black brew of Indian tea which we both found needful to revive the powers of thought after the idleness of the early afternoon" (Cornford, 1929). And so, too, began a period of scholarly collaboration that ended when Cornford joined the British army in 1914.

Shortly after meeting Cornford, Harrison introduced him to her Oxford friend, Gilbert Murray. This group of scholars, augmented on occasion by the participation of A. B. Cook, has been referred to as the Cambridge School or the Cambridge Ritualists. Either term, however, is a misnomer, since Murray was at Oxford (as Regius Professor of Greek from 1908). But the term "ritualist" was an appropriate description of their interest; they wished to discover the sources of Greek culture, and they thought that ritual was the bedrock from which all great symbolic forms emerge.

At the time Cornford and his group set out to revolutionize the study of Greek culture, classical scholarship was mainly confined to philology. Though Cornford and his collaborators appreciated the importance of strict linguistic study, they insisted that it should not dominate or circumscribe the scope of their investigations. The key, they thought, which would provide a more accurate and inclusive understanding of the intellectual achievements of ancient Greece, was not to be found in the study of syntax or textual criticism but in the relatively new disciplines of sociology and cultural anthropology. Borrowing concepts and methods of research from Emile Durkheim and from comparative mythologists such as James George Frazer, Cornford, Harrison, Murray, and Cook made a fresh examination of the *origins* of Greek historiography, philosophy, literature, and religion. The word "origins" is stressed because, until they applied the techniques and discoveries of contemporary social anthropology to classical studies, the vast majority of classicists ignored the beginnings and development of ancient Greek drama, religious practice, and philosophical speculation. By and large, most European students of antiquity in the late nineteenth and early twentieth centuries treated classical texts *in vacuo*, as if they were independent of time and change. Yet within twelve years (1903–1914)—twelve years in which Cornford and his intellectual compatriots published many of their most influential and controversial works—the case for the evolutionary approach to classical studies had been made quite convincing; it could be, and indeed was, attacked (mainly because the evolutionary thesis appeared to diminish the importance of invention and individual genius in the creation of works of art or systems of thought); but it could no longer be ignored. Henceforward classical scholars would have to take seriously the contention that Attic tragedy and comedy, Ionian cosmogony, and Olympian religion, had had their roots in earlier, more "primitive" stages of thought and action, namely, in archaic ritual—an idea that Cornford's article acquired from Robertson Smith—and mythology. Scholars could no longer accept with complacency the established view of the Greek "mind" as a static entity; rather, they now had to consider the possibility that it was a process demarcated by clearly definable stages analogous to the cultural strata unearthed by archaeologists. Just as archaeologists such as Schliemann (who had begun digging at Troy when Harrison was an undergraduate) and Arthur Evans (who "set sail for his new Atlantis and telegraphed news of the Minotaur from his own labyrinth") (J. E. Harrison, *Reminiscences of a Student's Life*: 83) had revealed a succession of different levels in the cultures of Troy and Crete, so Cornford, Harrison, Murray, and Cook thought they had dug up the past layers of the Greek mind and had revealed the historical series of mental and social events that led gradually but directly to the cultural triumphs of the fifth and fourth centuries.

The search for origins, however, did more than establish the evolutionary record by which the Greek mind emerged from ritual and myth. As Cornford notes in his first book, *Thucydides Mythistoricus* (1907): "Our view is that modern research into origins is not only recovering the temporal sequence of the several stages in the development of religious (and philosophic) representations, but is also, by that very fact, bringing to light the corresponding systems of association deposited, at those stages, in the racial tradition and memory of the Greeks—systems that lasted on in their minds like superimposed layers of alluvial stratification."

Discovery of these "corresponding systems of association" was invaluable, Cornford observed, in attempting to understand the history of ancient thought in general and the views of individual philosophers in particular. Philosophers do not think in a vacuum; they are influenced by their background and traditions perhaps even more than by their historical time and place. While acknowledging the significance of individual talent and authentic novelty in the history of ideas, Cornford persistently drew attention to the fundamental presuppositions, the commonly employed structures of thought and feeling, of metaphor and symbol that are taken for granted during a given epoch. For he believed that the process of discovering the presuppositions of a philosopher's work was as, if not more, important than perceiving the differences that divided him from his contemporary opponents: "In every age the common interpretation of the world of things is controlled by some scheme of unchallenged and unsuspected presupposition; and the mind of any individual however little he may think himself to be in sympathy with his contemporaries, is not an insulated compartment, but more like a pool in one continuous medium—the circumambient atmosphere of his place and time."

Thucydides Mythistoricus is devoted to elucidating the "systems of association," presupposition, or—to use a term Cornford later used—the "unwritten philosophy" in the *History of the Peloponnesian War*. Cornford argued in Part I that the policy of commercial expansion championed by the Piraeus party and annealed in the Megarian decrees—the so-called "Western Policy," which, for reasons of political expediency, was reluctantly supported by Pericles—led to the outbreak of the War. But—and this is the crucial point of Part I—Thucydides did not understand this fact, because he had no comprehension of the modern "science" of economics, since there was as yet no such thing. Nor did he possess, as Cornford argues in Part II, an understanding of historical causation in the modern sense, since his thought was still molded by traditional or mythopoeic forms. This led him to explain specific events of war in terms of nonhuman agencies (Tyche, for instance, in the case of the battle of Pylos) and to view the Peloponnesian War itself as the unfolding of tragic destiny (a model of historical explanation that he derived from Aeschylus). Hence Thucydides was not, as the majority of his recent students had claimed, a "modern of moderns" but rather a *myth*istoricus.

According to Cornford, historical events are frequently transformed in an author's mind by "traditional habits of thought." He called this process by which commonly inherited assumption transmutes fact into legend and legend into myth "infiguration." In Thucydides' case, tradition prevented him from perceiving the facts at Pylos. He was on the frontier of two ages, one still bound up in mythopoeic presupposition, the other—then just arising—seeking to establish a view of the world based on reason. He simply did not have the symbolic forms that might enable him to see things as they actually happened at Pylos or the Piraeus; he knew nothing of causation. Thus he relied on pre-Olympian or nonhuman agencies to explain reversals of fortune and borrowed the structure of Aeschylean tragedy to describe the crucial events of the war.

Reactions to Cornford's first book were mixed. The expected support was immediately at hand: Gilbert Murray praised it in a letter to his friend and gave it an excellent review in the *Albany*. Arthur Verrall, G. M. Trevelyan, Hugh Stewart, and G. E. Moore wrote letters of appreciation. He also received thoughtful and complimentary letters from Walter Leaf and Alfred Zimmern. But he was attacked by Phillimore, who thought he was misinterpreting Thucydides to suit his own devices. And he was as often praised as criticized in the newspapers. J. B. Bury, who presumably read *Thucydides Mythistoricus* when he was preparing his Lane Lectures (which he delivered at Harvard in the spring of 1908) agreed "that the style of Thucydides was influenced by the Attic drama . . . and it is one of the merits of Mr. Cornford's monograph to have illustrated this influence. But," he insisted, "the tragic phrases and reminiscences, and the occasional use of tragic irony, cannot be held to have more than a stylistic significance."

While some classicists, such as W. K. C. Guthrie, have recently praised *Thucydides Mythistoricus*, Bury's view has endured. There is another exception to this opinion, however, that is worth recording; in *The Idea of History* (1946) R. G. Collingwood points out that "legend, either in the form of theocratic history or in the form of myth, was" not "a thing foreign to the Greek mind. . . . F. M. Cornford in his *Thucydides Mythistoricus* . . . drew attention to the existence of such elements even in the hard-headed and scientific Thucydides. He was of course perfectly right."

The year following the appearance of *Thucydides Mythistoricus* Cornford published his immortal satire of academic politics, *Microcosmographia Academica*, with its portraits of the young-man-in-a-hurry, the Adullamites (scientists and engineers), Liberals and Conservatives, and its splendid description on acquiring influence: "Political influence may be acquired in exactly the same way as the gout; indeed, the two ends ought to be pursued concurrently. The method is to sit tight and drink port wine."

Cornford's venture into academic satire was consistent with his previous efforts at reform of the University and its Colleges. He had urged the Classical Society of Cambridge to reform the Classical Course in 1903; he had attacked compulsory chapel in 1904; and he had helped establish a summer course at Cambridge for the Working Men's College in 1901. He also questioned the role of religion in the University in 1911. It is important to note that Cornford's concern for University reform (he had supported University degrees for women as an undergraduate) reflects in part his desire to reform society as a whole. He opposed British imperialism, became a Fabian Socialist, assisted political refugees, and tried to save scholars from Nazi persecution. And he invariably defended democratic principles, especially the right of freedom of expression, a position that was sharply tested when he—at the time a Sergeant of Musketry—helped lead the effort to have pacifist Bertrand Russell's Lectureship in Trinity reinstated during World War I.

Four years after the appearance of *Microcosmographia Academica* Cornford published his second book, *From Religion to Philosophy*. The year of its publication, 1912, marked the greatest cooperation amongst the members of his scholarly circle. Harrison published *Themis* in the same year, a work that included chapters by both Cornford ("The Origin of the Olympic Games") and Murray ("Excursus on the Ritual Forms Preserved in Greek Tragedy"). And Murray himself, whose *Rise of the Greek Epic* had appeared during the same year as Cornford's *Thucydides Mythistoricus* (1907), also published a book in 1912, *Four Stages of Greek Religion*. In his new book Cornford continued to explore questions he had raised in *Thucydides*: the problems of deciphering the unconscious elements in ancient systems of thought, and the quest for origins. He had previously taken issue with contemporary scholars who imposed modern assumptions on Thucydides; now he criticized modern classicists (such as Deussen and Burnet) who mistakenly viewed the presocratics—to transpose a phrase of Jacob Burkhardt's—as the first-born sons of modern empiricism. The Ionian cosmogonists, for instance, appeared to them to be precursors of the natural philosophers of the seventeenth-century Age of Genius or, indeed, even the scientists of the Age of Darwin. The fallacy of misplaced empiricism ignores the importance of collective effort and tradition in the creation and transmission of ideas. To imagine "that Thales or Anaximander was like Adam on the day of his creation, with no tradition behind him, no inherited scheme of things, opening his innocent eyes on a world of pure sense impressions not as yet coordinated into any conceptual structure" is at the very least naïve, since the "philosophic Muse is not a motherless Athena: if the individual intellect is her father, her older and more august parent is Religion."

Philosophy, according to Cornford, has its roots in religion, or rather in a pretheological state of religion or myth, and the representations of religion develop from the social order of the primitive tribe. Borrowing from Durkheim, Cornford asserted that the collective consciousness of the primordial tribe generated the idea of the sympathetic continuum (of all life in nature), which itself became the first religious representation. The sympathetic continuum was eventually divided—the idea of division having been unconsciously inherited from antecedent totemic divisions of the primordial tribe—into two pools or channels of mana that resulted in the formation of two approaches to reality, one negative, the other positive. The former produced the collective religious representations of Moira, Nomos, and Physis, the emergence of the Olympian gods, and the advent of philosophy and the early development of scientific materialism. The latter led to the creation of mystery religions and the view of life as dynamic process. The negative channel spatialized reality—here Cornford, following Harrison, borrows from Bergson—while the positive stream of religious thought viewed life in terms of human time or becoming. The former ends by reducing life to particles in a machine, while the latter embraces life in the round of nature. Early philosophy comprises both channels in two historical traditions, first noted by Diogenes Laertius: the Ionian and the Pythagorean, the scientific and the mystical or, as Nietzsche would have it—and Cornford gives him credit for the intuition—the Apollonian and the Dionysian.

Like his first book, *From Religion to Philosophy* provoked controversy and received varied reviews. W. A. Heidel found some favorable things to say about his handling of the mystical tradition, but he was very critical of Cornford's assimilation of the complex history of Ionian philosophy to the simplified abstractions of Durkeheimian sociology. Contrary to Heidel, Gilbert Murray noted his agreement in *The Nation* (13 July 1912) with Cornford's analyses of the inherited mental background of the earliest Ionian philosophers. "For instance, Anaximander, in a famous sentence, says that all existing things of necessity must pass away into that from which they rose, because '*they pay to one another justice and retribution for their injustice according to the ordinance of time*.' That is not the free comment of a man of science, derived from the observation of nature. It is steeped in religious [and moral] preconceptions" that originate in the pretheological notion of Moira as "the portion of land, that by rights belongs to any division of the tribe. To transgress Moira is to trespass; to break Dike, or custom; to violate nomos, the tribal law or assignment." Since "the world of the gods is necessarily imagined on the model of the world of their worshippers, the rule of Moira over Zeus becomes plain." For, like the members of the totemic tribe, the gods have to follow the rules of apportionment. To exceed their proper portion would make both humans and gods culpable of *hybris* or force them, as Anaximander puts it, to pay recompense "for their injustice according to the ordinance of time."

While he accepted Cornford's view of the continuity between religion and philosophy, Murray could not entirely agree with his colleague's conclusions about the "origin of the conceptions of god, the soul and other religious ideas, and the derivation of the various forms of early Greek philosophy from divergent treatments of these fundamental totemic conceptions." Like Heidel, Murray also thought that Cornford neglected important "historical factors" in his account of the different philosophers because "he is sometimes obsessed by his own method."

Cornford's reviews were also varied in the press. Many reviewers had reservations about his thesis, and most still deemed Burnet's view that science began with Thales as essentially correct. While some complimented Cornford on the boldness of his interpretation, they had reservations or outright distaste for his use of French sociology.

From Religion to Philosophy has fared somewhat better in more recent evaluations. W. K. C. Guthrie, Cornford's most famous pupil and eventually his successor to the Laurence Chair of Ancient Philosophy, thought Cornford's theory "leaves one now with a certain feeling of inadequacy." Yet, he concluded, "it is fair to say that it represents a necessary stage on the way to that comprehensive understanding of the Greek mind which he afterwards achieved, rather than an example of the full understanding itself" (*Unwritten Philosophy*). D. S. Robertson, late Regius Professor of

Greek in Cambridge and also a pupil of Cornford's, expressed his admiration for the work at the time of Cornford's death: "Five years later came a far better book [than the *Thucydides*], his novel and stimulating *From Religion to Philosophy*, much influenced by Jane Harrison's *Themis*." Hugh Lloyd-Jones may have had the book in mind (as well as Cornford's later treatment of the subject, *Principium Sapientiae*) when he referred to Cornford's "important work on Plato and on presocratic philosophy and its prephilosophical background." Perhaps the greatest admirer of *From Religion to Philosophy* (as well as Cornford's other works on the presocratics) is the French scholar, Jean-Pierre Vernant, although Cornford also receives most favorable treatment by the philosopher of science Richard H. Schlagel, in his *From Myth to the Modern Mind: A Study of the Origins and Growth of Scientific Thought* (1985).

In his next book, *The Origin of Attic Comedy* (1914), Cornford put forward the hypothesis that the "*canonical plot formula*" of the Aristophanic play "*preserves the stereotyped action of a ritual or folk drama, older than literary Comedy, and of a pattern well known to us from other sources.*" He had been inspired to reexamine the structure of the Old Comedy by the works of Zielinski and Gilbert Murray. The latter's "Excursus on the Ritual Forms Preserved in Greek Tragedy" in Jane Harrison's *Themis* had especially inspired him to look for traditional forms in the plays of Aristophanes. He eventually concluded "that Comedy itself has sprung, not necessarily from the same ritual [as Tragedy], but from one closely allied to it and belonging to the same class."

Cornford thought scholars had overlooked the importance of the second part of the Aristophanic play. Although they had discussed the *Prologue*, *Parados*, and *Agon*, they had regarded the play as being virtually over after the *Parabasis*. Yet, Cornford argued, there is a "sequence of fixed incidents" in the second part of the play that is "no less canonical than the *Agon*": a "Sacrifice, Feast, [and] marriage *Komos*."

Following Aristotle, Cornford concluded that the fixed elements in the Old Comedy had originated in the Phallic ceremonies associated with the worship of Dionysus, an example of which can be found in Aristophanes' *Acharnians*. In his view we see in the *Agon* "the equivalent of the sacrifice which precedes the Phallic Song. The *Agon* is the beginning of the sacrifice in its primitive dramatic form—the conflict between the good and evil principles, Summer and Winter, Life and Death. The good spirit is slain, dismembered, cooked and eaten in the communal feast, and yet brought back to life. These acts survive in the standing features of the comic plot between the *Parabasis* and the *Exodos*. Finally comes the Marriage of the risen God, restored to life and youth to be the husband of the Mother Goddess. This marriage is the necessary consummation of the Phallic ritual, which, when it takes a dramatic form, simulates the union of Heaven and Earth for the renewal of all life in Spring."

His brilliant reconstruction of the origins of comedy was generally greeted with praise. He was criticized for exaggerating the significance of conjectural literary origins, for failing to substantiate fully the existence of the basic ritual drama, and for diminishing the significance of individual creativity, a charge he vigorously disputed: We can never know how creative "the wit of Aristophanes" was unless we can find out what Aristophanes "did not invent." Most of his reviews, however, stressed the importance of his analysis of the second part of the plays, complimented him for his ingenious and thorough examination of the extant comedies, and either accepted or were at least open to his suggestion that a ritual drama provided the traditional mold in which the Old Comedy was cast.

The thesis that drama originated in ritual, or that dramatists unconsciously used fixed forms inherited from fertility ceremonies, was vigorously challenged from the start by classicists such as William Ridgeway, Professor of Archaeology in Cambridge, who insisted that tragedy developed from the dramatic dances associated with the cult of heroes. Some reviewers of *The Origin of Attic Comedy* referred favorably to Ridgeway's theory when they criticized Cornford's chapter on comedy and tragedy. However, the scholar whose efforts to demolish the idea that drama (both tragedy and comedy) was associated with the rituals of Dionysus as Year Spirit (*Eniautus-Daimon*) or seasonal deity was A. W. Pickard-Cambridge, who maintained in his *Dithyramb Tragedy and Comedy* (Oxford, 1927) that the advocates of this theory proved neither the existence of a ritual from which drama emerged in classical Greece nor its use in the surviving plays. More recently, scholars such as Gerald Else have resumed Pickard-Cambridge's argument and have decried "the modern obsession with myth and ritual, or ritual origins of myth." The rejection of the ritualist interpretation of the origins of tragedy and comedy predominates at present (although it should be noted that T. B. L. Webster held to a modified variation of Murray's theory). As Cornford observed in his lecture on "The Unconscious Element in Literature and Philosophy" (1921), the theory that there are " 'fixed forms' of Attic Tragedy" and Comedy that "correspond to the moments in a ritual drama which survives all over Europe in the folk-play" reduces many scholars "for some cause I cannot fathom . . . to a state of frenzy." If it no longer provokes frenzy—and it may still—it is either largely dismissed or ignored.

Less than three months after the last reviews of *The Origin of Attic Comedy* appeared, Cornford joined the British Army as a (territorial) Instructor of Musketry. Whereas he was often embarrassingly quiet during supervision of his pupils, and while he was known for his uncanny ability to "dematerialize" or vanish without notice from a social gathering (he once told his children that he could have been "confidential butler to a wicked earl"), he thoroughly enjoyed the camaraderie of army life. He was rarely too far away from Cambridge to visit his growing family—he had married Frances Crofts Darwin, a granddaughter of the great naturalist, in 1909—and he often managed to keep a hand in college politics, even after he joined the Ministry of Munitions (where he rose to the rank of major).

After the war Cornford resumed his Lectureship in classics (he had been appointed Assistant Lecturer in 1902, Lecturer in 1904), and stood for the Regius Professorship of Greek in 1921. He lost to Alfred Chilton Pearson (a scholar in the Jebb tradition) but tried again in 1928, when he competed against his former pupil, D. S. Robertson, to whom he also lost. He consoled himself with the fact that he had previously been appointed Brereton-Laurence Reader in Classics (the first University post in ancient philosophy in Cambridge), and he continued to hope that the University would one day establish a chair in his subject, an aspiration that was fulfilled when he was appointed first Laurence Professor of Ancient Philosophy in 1931.

Two years after he first stood for the Regius Professorship Cornford started publishing again: articles on Pythagoreanism were followed by contributions to the *Cambridge Ancient History* on "Mystery-Religions and Presocratic Philosophy," and "The Athenian Philosophical Schools." In 1927, hearing that Philip Wicksteed, who was paralyzed and terminally ill, needed assistance in completing his translation and commentary on Aristotle's *Physics*, Cornford immediately offered his services. It took him longer than he had anticipated to revise Wicksteed's manuscript, and it was not until 1929 that the first volume of the *Physics* was published by the Loeb Classical Library; the second volume appeared in 1934. His generous labor may have diverted him from his own scholarship, but it influenced the form he chose for his great studies of Plato's later dialogues.

Beginning in 1935 with *Plato's Theory of Knowledge* (the *Theaetetus* and the *Sophist*) and followed by the *Timaeus* in 1937 and the *Parmenides* two years later, Cornford sought to elucidate the epistemology and cosmology of Plato by using a method (employed by Wicksteed in his analysis of the *Physics*) that was familiar to every lecturer on classical texts: translation with "running commentary." In his earlier books Cornford had examined the origins and background of early Greek speculation; now, in his Plato studies, he focused his attention on "the finished product." This allowed him "the opportunity for a more exact appreciation of the structure which the philosopher himself had built." Yet, although he was now dealing with the philosophy itself rather than the presuppositions it had inherited from the preclassical past, he still immersed himself in the study of the main currents of thought that formed the intellectual climate of Plato's age, and he made a serious effort to learn Greek mathematics—including the mathematics taught in the Academy—so that he could understand his subject in the round.

Cornford's accomplishment astounded many of his contemporaries. As Professor Guthrie has observed: "Those of us who knew Cornford at that time can only marvel at the completeness with which all this in itself indigestible material was assimilated and transmuted, so that the reader who is presented with the finished commentary can scarcely be aware of the amount of patient labour that has gone to its composition."

The books on the later dialogues were an immediate success and, even though they never achieved the popularity of Cornford's famous translation of the *Republic* (1941)—which was aimed "at conveying to the English reader as much as possible of the thought of the *Republic* in the most convenient and least misleading form"—they have been (and still are being) read by many academic generations.

After completing his Platonic studies, Cornford returned to the subject that had never ceased to fascinate him: the origins of Greek philosophical thought. Previously he had taken the view that one channel of Greek religion had ultimately evolved into science. Now, however, he revised his earlier opinion—which he still maintained in *Before and After Socrates* (1932)—and argued that both Pythagoreanism and Ionian "empiricism" had remained essentially religious (although pretheological). Indeed he demonstrated that Milesian cosmogony had ultimately derived from Near Eastern ritual, a thesis he first put forward in his lecture "A Ritual Basis of Hesiod's *Theogony*" (1941) and later examined at length in his posthumously published book, *Principium Sapientiae* (1952). By examining the sorts of questions the early philosophers had asked about the creation of the universe and by discovering "fossilized metaphors" of defunct mythologies in their philosophical fragments, Cornford was able to demonstrate that the Ionians were not only not conducting an empirical investigation of nature but were unconsciously framing their conclusions about the origins of the universe in the structure of prehistoric creation myths (ultimately derivable from the *Enuma Elish* and transmitted through the *Epic of Kumarbi*) that were based on cosmogonic ritual in the case of the Ionians and shamanism in the case of the "Italians." His last search for the origins of Western philosophy led Cornford to the conclusion that there were at least four distinct (yet dynamically interrelated) stages in the evolution of Western "thought": ritual, myth, religion ("quasi-rational"), and philosophy ("rational," although not "scientific"). He appears to have believed that through his study of the emergence of philosophy he had discovered a model of ideational change that might in fact be universal, applicable, in other words, not simply to the development of Greek thought but, at least in some important respects, to the intellectual evolution of the species as a whole.

Principium Sapientiae has not only influenced classicists but also historians and philosophers of science. Whether it has been criticized (by Vlastos, for instance, for failing to recognize the importance of the Ionians' formulation of the idea of an independent order of nature [*Gnomon* 27 (1955) 65ff.]) or praised by E. R. Dodds and W. K. C. Guthrie, it cannot be overlooked. It remains an outstanding treatment of the subject.

Cornford retired in 1939. Two years earlier he had received an honorary D. Litt. from Birmingham University for his outstanding scholarship in ancient philosophy. His last years also saw rewards outside academia: his wife, Frances Crofts Darwin, was restored to health after a long period of illness, some of his children married and, for a second time, he became a grandfather. According to his wife, he felt confident about his family's future when he died on 3 January 1943.

Books

Thucydides Mythistoricus. London, 1907.

From Religion to Philosophy. A Study in the Origins of Western Speculation. London, 1912; repr. New York, 1957.

The Origin of Attic Comedy. London, 1914; 2d impress., Cambridge, 1934. Edited with additional notes by Theodor H. Gaster. Gloucester, MA, 1968.

Greek Religious Thought from Homer to the Age of Alexander. New York and London, 1914; repr. New York, 1969.

The Laws of Motion in Ancient Thought. Cambridge, 1931 = *Selected Papers of F. M. Cornford.* Edited by Alan C. Bowen. New York and London, 1987: 367-409.

Before and After Socrates. Cambridge, 1932.

Aristotle: The Physics. With P. H. Wicksteed. 2 vols. Loeb Classical Library. Cambridge, MA, 1929–1934.

Plato's Theory of Knowledge. The Theaetetus and the Sophist of Plato. London, 1935.

Plato's Cosmology. The Timaeus of Plato. London, 1937.

Plato and Parmenides. Parmenides' Way to Truth and Plato's Parmenides. London, 1939.

The Republic of Plato. Oxford, London, and New York, 1941.

The Unwritten Philosophy and Other Essays. Edited by W. K. C. Guthrie. Cambridge, 1950.

Principium Sapientiae. The Origins of Greek Philosophical Thought. Cambridge, 1952.

Articles

"Plato and Orpheus." CR 17 (1903) 433–445.

"The Poems of George Meredith." *Supplement to the Working Men's College Journal* (1903) 103–118.

"Elpis and Eros." CR 21 (1907) 228–232.

"Note on Plato, *Phaedo* 105 A." CQ 3 (1909) 189–191 = *Selected Papers:* 239–241.

"Hermes, Pan, Logos." CQ 3 (1909) 281–284.

"Hermes-Nous and Pan-Logos." CR 26 (1911) 180–181.

"The Origin of the Olympic Games." In J. E. Harrison, *Themis. A Study in the Social Origins of Greek Religion.* Cambridge, 1912: 212–259.

"Psychology and Social Structure in the Republic of Plato." CQ 6 (1912) 246–265 = *Selected Papers:* 256–275.

"The So-called Kommos in Greek Tragedy." CR 27 (1913) 41–45.

"The *Aparchai* and the Eleusian Mysteries." In *Essays and Studies Presented to William Ridgeway.* Cambridge, 1913: 153–166 = *Selected Papers:* 21–34.

"The Unconscious Element in Literature and Philosophy." PCA 18 (1921) 104–119 = *Unwritten Philosophy:* 1–13.

"Mysticism and Science in the Pythagorean Tradition." CQ 16 (1922) 137–150; 17 (1923): 1–12 = *Selected Papers:* 99–112.

"The Idea of Immortality." CR 37 (1923) 132–133.

"Note on Aeschylus, *Eumenides* 945." CR 38 (1924) 113.

"Mystery Religions and Presocratic Philosophy." *Cambridge Ancient History.* Cambridge, 1926. 4:522–578, 650–653 (bibliography) = *Selected Papers:* 36–97.

"Psychology and the Drama." *New Adelphi* 1 (1927) 2–11, 136–144.

"The Athenian Philosophical Schools." *Cambridge Ancient History.* Cambridge, 1927. 6:302–351, 587–589 = *Selected Papers:* 312–589.

"Plato, *Theaetetus* 209 D." CR 44 (1930) 114.

"Anaxagoras' Theory of Matter." CQ 24 (1930) 14–30, 83–95 = *Selected Papers:* 144–173.

"The Division of the Soul." *Hibbert Journal* 28 (1930) 206–219 = *Selected Papers*: 242–255.

"The Harmony of the Spheres" (1930). In *Unwritten Philosophy*: 14–27.

"Note on [Plato,] *Eryxias* 393 B." CR 46 (1932) 156.

"Aristotle, *Physics* 250 A 9–19 and 266 A 12–24." CQ 26 (1932) 52–54.

"Mathematics and Dialectic in the *Republic* VI.–VII." *Mind* N.S. 41 (1932) 37–52, 173–190 = *Selected Papers*: 277–310.

"Parmenides' Two Ways." CQ 27 (1933) 97–111 = *Selected Papers*: 129–143.

"Innumerable Worlds in Presocratic Philosophy." CQ 28 (1934) 1–16 = *Selected Papers*: 175–190.

"A New Fragment of Parmenides." CR 49 (1935) 122–123 = *Selected Papers*: 126–127.

"Plato's Commonwealth." *Greece and Rome* 4 (1935) 92–108 = *Unwritten Philosophy*: 47–67.

"The Unwritten Philosophy" (1935). In *Unwritten Philosophy*: 28–46.

"The Invention of Space." In *Essays in Honour of Gilbert Murray*. Edited by J. A. K. Thomson. London, 1936: 215–235 = *Selected Papers*: 199–219.

"The Doctrine of Eros in Plato's *Symposium*" (1937). In *Unwritten Philosophy*: 68–80.

"Greek Natural Philosophy and Modern Science." In *Background to Modern Science*. Edited by Needham and W. Pagel. Cambridge, 1938: 1–22.

"The 'Polytheism' of Plato: An Apology." *Mind* n.s. 47 (1938) 321–330.

"Notes on the Oresteia." CR 53 (1939) 162–165.

"[Aristotle,] *De caelo* 288 A 2–9." CQ 33 (1939) 34–35.

"A Ritual Basis for Hesiod's *Theogony*." In *Unwritten Philosophy*: 95–116.

"Plato's *Euthyphro* or How to Read a Socratic Dialogue." Lecture read to the Peterhouse Society. *In Selected Papers*: 221–238.

"Was the Ionian Philosophy Scientific?" JHS 62 (1942) 1–7 = *Selected Papers*: 191–197.

"The Marxist View of Ancient Philosophy." *In Unwritten Philosophy*: 117–137.

Sources

Bowen, Alan C. "Introduction." *Selected Papers of F. M. Cornford*. New York and London, 1987.

Else, Gerald F. *The Origin and Form of Greek Tragedy*. Martin Classical Lectures 20. Cambridge, MA, 1965.

Guthrie, W. K. C. "Memoir" and "Appendix." *Unwritten Philosophy*: vii–xix, 138–139.

Hackforth, Reginald. "Francis Macdonald Cornford." *DNB 1951-1960*. Oxford, 1971: 177–79.

Harrison, Jane E. *Reminiscences of a Student's Life*. London, 1925: 83.

Heidel, W. A. Review of *From Religion to Philosophy*. JPhil 10 (1913) 103.

Lloyd-Jones, H. Introduction to *History of Classical Scholarship*, by U. von Wilamowitz-Moellendorff. London, 1982: xxiv.

Murray, Gilbert. "Francis Macdonald Cornford 1874–1943." *PBA* 29 (1944).

Robertson, D. S. "Obituary." *The Cambridge Review* (30 January 1943).

Letters

Cornford Papers Cambridge Spring House, Conduit Head Road, Cambridge, CB3 OEY, England.

Additional manuscripts in the British Library:

58401–58411 Frances Crofts Cornford: Correspondence with Francis Macdonald Cornford, 1908–1940.

58412 Frances Crofts Cornford: Correspondence with Christopher Cornford, 1924–1937. (Letters relating to Rupert John Cornford.)

58418 Francis Macdonald Cornford: Correspondence with Gilbert and Lady Murray, 1908–1954. (Letters from Rosalind Murray, 1905–1923.)

58420 Frances Crofts Darwin: Letters on her engagement, 1908; Francis Macdonald Cornford's death, 1943.

58427–58430 Francis Macdonald Cornford: Correspondence and Papers of 1885–1942, 4 vols.

Unpublished Lectures

In the Cornford Papers, Classical Faculty Library Mill Lane, Cambridge University, Cambridge, England, are nine boxes of lectures, lecture notes, and some letters on deposit, including lectures on the presocratics, Plato, and Aristotle.

Ernst Curtius

2 September 1814 – 11 July 1896

MORTIMER CHAMBERS
University of California, Los Angeles

Ernst Curtius represents, both in his life and in his work, the transition from the romantic infatuation with Greece and its aesthetic ideals to the solid professional study of antiquity, above all through archaeology. He willingly embraced the enthusiasm for Greek culture that arose during the nineteenth-century in Germany and as a scholar could still see Greek history in an idealizing light. Yet his approach to philology was stamped with the realism of his teacher and collaborator August Böckh, one of the greatest geniuses among Hellenists. To the scientific discipline of Böckh, who never visited Greece, Curtius could contribute in addition an intimate knowledge of the countryside, its monuments, and its artifacts. He established Germany's most prominent excavation, at Olympia, and set the pattern for the scientific recovery of the Hellenic world and its experience through exploration on the soil of Greece itself.

Curtius was born in Lübeck and always retained the Hanseatic unaspirated *s* in his speech. He studied first in Bonn, where he heard the philologist F. G. Welcker and the philosopher C. A. Brandis; in 1834 he moved to Göttingen, where he heard Karl Otfried Müller, who turned him toward the study of Greek geography, history, and culture. He then studied in Berlin under Böckh and F. W. Gerhard. In 1837 he accepted an invitation from Brandis, who was academic adviser to King Otto of the newly independent Greece, to accompany Brandis and his family to Greece as tutor to their children. He explored Greece widely in the company of the geographer Karl Ritter, translated Greek poetry into German, wrote emotional poems of his own celebrating the landscape, and fell in love with the country and people—but in a highly classicizing way. He deliberately turned his gaze from contemporary Greek politics and aspirations and showed the same lack of interest in political reality in his studies of Greek antiquity. His aim was, rather, to commune with the loftiest ideals of ancient civilization, even if this required overlooking moments when these ideals fell short of achievement.

In 1838 he first visited Olympia, which was to be the focus of his scientific work. He also visited Delphi and sent his parents an enthusiastic description of the site and its atmosphere (*Ein Lebensbild in Briefen*, 181–82):

I lived four days in Delphi, unforgettable days, when heaven favored us with sun again, though intermittently. You can forget the whole world in this pleasant nook in the mountains. The houses of Kastri lie exactly over the old temple of Pythian Apollo; the terrace of the temple, made of Pentelic marble, gleams at midday among the huts built over it. In the same way you can see between two poor hovels a part of the splendid curve of the theater and everywhere traces of temple-stones and inscribed blocks of marble. . . . When you reach the Castalian Spring you are actually in Delphi. There is a lovely open area around the source, immediately above are the mountains, reaching to heaven, then downward are the gentle slopes; they are watered by the sacred spring and thickly covered with the most beautiful olive trees, and in the middle there is a quiet monastery beneath the walls of the ancient gymnasium. You can climb up and reach another spring in a few minutes: this is the Cassiotis, from which the priestess drank her inspiration. This spring still has its old course through the middle of the temple area as the water trickles under the terrace of the temple. Even today it irrigates a bay tree, an honored descendant of the old grove of the priestess.

If you go farther toward the western end of the theater-like curve of the area of Delphi, you come to another street of graves and to a ledge from which you have a great view of the sea, down to the old harbor of Delphi, where once ships landed from all regions carrying horses for competition in the games as well as pack animals. . . . You cannot imagine the joy with which I looked for traces of the ancient remains here, since I got certain results beyond anything I might have expected and formed a clear picture of the sacred place.

And after I had spent the whole day with my architect in visiting and measuring, I enjoyed the evening in the gay company of the common people. Just then it was the marriage season and on the Sunday three marriages were in preparation. That always calls for a cycle of celebrations lasting two weeks. We went with the mayor to the bride's relatives. The music consisted of a muffled drum and a shrill shepherd's pipe. The men sit around on little benches that are crowded with food and wine. The main jollity is the toasts to one's health: first to the king, then to the bride and groom, then to the visitors, and so on. Each drinker usually gives a little speech to his drinking partners and then drains his glass to loud music as slowly as he can. The women stand around the bride and sing in the next room. . . .

With his former teacher, Müller, he visited Delphi in 1840 and, when Müller died on the trip from a heat-induced fever, had the sad duty of burying him in the living rock of the hill of Kolonos Hippios, overlooking the grove of Plato's Academy outside Athens—the home of Sophocles and the place where the outcast Oedipus at last found peace. This scene too he described to his parents (*Ibid.*, 232, 237):

> God in his grace has preserved me from all dangers and has kept me strong and well under the glowing rays of the July sun, which this time were frightful—but the miserable days I have lived through, and the horrible tragedy that has struck us here, must be the sad content of these lines. Our dear teacher and master has been the victim of his tireless enthusiasm: last Sunday, 2 August, we laid Karl Otfried Müller to rest on the hill of the Academy. . . . After the autopsy was performed on Sunday afternoon, which showed that the brain of the deceased was completely soft and decomposed, the burial was carried out towards evening. Students drew the coffin on a wagon, four deans of the university walked at its corners; all the ambassadors, the whole staff of the court, of the university, and of the schools, most of the Germans in Athens, and many Greeks all followed, a line seemingly without end. The high priest gave a speech in German, then the excellent Professor Ioannou spoke in Greek; military music accompanied the funeral procession. Schöll and I returned home from the grave of our dear teacher by clear, quiet moonlight, thinking mainly of the unfortunate widow with her five children, who were awaiting the happy return of the man in Ohlau. . . .

Curtius returned to Germany and obtained his doctorate in Halle (1841) and gained Habilitation in Berlin in 1843 with an edition of Delphic inscriptions that he had begun with Müller. He was invited in 1844 to become tutor to Prince Friedrich Wilhelm, the future Emperor Friedrich III, and established close relations with the royal house, which became enthralled with Greek culture and supported German research in Greece. From 1844 to 1856 he was professor of classical philology in Berlin. He now published his first major work, perhaps still his most important personal contribution to knowledge, the two-volume description of the Peloponnese, the fruit of his early explorations of Greece in the 1830s.

In 1856 he returned to Göttingen as professor of classical philology and archaeology, thus holding until 1868 the chair once occupied by his mentor and friend, Karl Otfried Müller. The crowning work of his years in Göttingen was his *Griechische Geschichte*, planned by the house of Weidmann as a companion to Mommsen's history of Rome. This became the most widely read Greek history written in German, reaching a sixth edition.

Curtius's aim was to present the most exalted possible view of Greek civilization. The work is written in ceremonious rhetorical style and found a ready public when Germans were constructing their adoring relationship toward classical Greece. The English historian Freeman thought that the best pages were the vivid descriptions of the Greek landscape, but he awarded the palm for political realism and insight to George Grote, whose history appeared at the same time.

For Curtius, history was mainly the result of decisions by great men, élite leaders, and he fearlessly discovered their noble motivations even when ancient sources failed him. Solon's aims (he thought) were shaped by long self-communion of the broadest philosophical sort. Cleisthenes was seen as a man of passionate ambition and a champion of the civil rights of the oppressed; part of his loyalty was to Solon's constitution, whose generosity to the lower orders he sought to expand. Pericles was to Curtius almost a philosopher-king. Yet Curtius was not a modern Livy: he knew his sources with the thoroughness of a great German scholar and a pupil of Welcker and Böckh, and the triumph of Greece over Persia is not naïvely portrayed as the victory of light over darkness.

The chronological limits of the history also tell their story. Only some fifteen years had passed since J. G. Droysen had written his history of Alexander and carried the survey down into the Hellenistic age, which in effect he discovered. He was under the powerful influence of Hegel and saw Greek history as fulfilling its assigned cycle and preparing the way for Christianity; for him, Alexander was the tool of history, and the whole story had a purpose that was validated by historical inevitability. Curtius had nothing to do with such modern theories. His third volume ends the narrative with the establishment of Philip II's domination over Greece. The resistance led by Demosthenes was for Curtius the final act of independent Hellenism. As his collaborator Mommsen, in the Weidmann series, ended his history of the Roman Republic before the death of his hero Julius Caesar, so Curtius evidently found no pleasure in letting Macedonian dynasts supplant Greek statesmen on the stage of history. His chief aim was an uplifting narrative, and Georg Busolt was right to admit that his own detailed, encyclopedic *Griechische Geschichte* should not be compared with that of Curtius in respect of enjoyable reading. Neither Busolt nor his more original rival, Julius Beloch, drove Curtius from the field among "general readers."

In 1868 Curtius returned to Berlin as Professor of Classical Archaeology. He had long recommended the undertaking of systematic excavations in Olympia but had not been able to move the German authorities to implement his plan. After the early successes of Schliemann at Troy, Curtius finally got his wish. In early 1874 he signed an agreement with the Greek government that allowed German scholars to excavate Olympia and provided that the finds should be permanently displayed in a museum, built by the Germans, at the site. This contract marked the beginning of systematic excavations by government-supported agencies in the Mediterranean (it will be remembered that Schliemann financed himself) and became the model for similar arrangements on behalf of the British, French, and other schools in Greece. This negotiation was an act of the highest academic statesmanship, and the following of the model by others has furthered the scientific study of the Greek world while avoiding the plundering of Greek antiquities.

Excavations at Olympia took place from fall 1875 to 1881; they were revived from 1936 to 1941 and have continued since 1952. The first results were edited by Curtius and Adler in five volumes; and here the scholarly work of Curtius moved into the scientific mode of the late nineteenth and twentieth centuries. He was also among those who brought into existence the German Archaeological Institute in Athens.

Curtius was especially noted for his addresses delivered on ceremonial occasions, especially in the presence of the royal family or for the emperor's birthday. Characteristic, for example, was his "Die Entwickelung des Preußischen Staats nach den Analogien der alten Geschichte" (1880), delivered on the anniversary of the accession of Friedrich II. He collected these orations in two volumes, to which a third, *Unter drei Kaisern*, was added. His many essays and papers were collected as *Gesammelte Abhandlungen*, and in his last years appeared his *Die Stadtgeschichte von Athen*.

Curtius' main scholarly monument was clearly his organization and editing of the excavations at Olympia, but, more than that, he inspired a generation of German scholars to become Hellenists. Others, such as his teacher Böckh, had indeed already devoted their lives to Greek studies, but Curtius contributed a love of the Greek landscape, long practical experience in Greece, and enthusiasm for his life work. He was from a deeply religious family, and all witnesses agree on his generous, affectionate personality. His *Griechische Geschichte*, though undeniably from another era so far as concerns historical accuracy and realism, is nonetheless a monument to that very era, to the earliest years of an independent Greece and to the time when the Hellenic message was rediscovered.

Books

De portubus Athenarum commentatio. Halle, 1842.

Anecdota Delphica. Berlin, 1843.

Peloponnesos. Eine historisch-geographische Beschreibung der Halbinsel. 2 vols. Gotha, 1851–1852.

Die Ionier vor der ionischen Wanderung. Berlin, 1855.

Griechische Geschichte. 3 vols. Berlin, 1857–1861; 6th ed., 1887–1889. English translation by A. D. Ward as *The History of Greece*. 5 vols. New York, 1867–1872; London, 1868–1873; revisions in later printings by W. A. Packard.

Beiträge zur Geschichte und Topographie Kleinasiens. With Regely, Adler, Hirschfeld, and Gelzer. *Abhandlungen der Königlich-preussische Akademie der Wissenschaften zu Berlin*, 1872: 1–96. Separately printed in Berlin, 1873.

Über Wappengebrauch und Wappenstil im griechischen Altertum. Abhandlungen der Königlich-preussische Akademie der Wissenschaften zu Berlin 1874: 1–96. Separately printed in Berlin, 1874.

Olympia. Die Ergebnisse der von dem Deutschen Reich veranstalteten Ausgrabungen. Edited with F. Adler, et al. 5 vols; 4 vols. of plates. Berlin, 1890–1897.

Karten von Attika. Edited with J. A. Kaupert. 8 parts. Berlin, 1881–1894.

August Böckh. Berlin, 1885.

Die Stadtgeschichte von Athen. Berlin, 1891.

Articles and Speeches (Collected)

Altertum und Gegenwart: Gesammelte Reden und Vorträge. Berlin, 1875; vol. 2 added, 1882; vol. 3, *Unter drei Kaisern,* 1893. Final ed., vol. 1, 5th ed., vol. 2, 3rd ed. Stuttgart, 1903.

Gesammelte Abhandlungen. 2 vols. Berlin, 1894.

Sources

Borbein, A. H. "Ernst Curtius." *Berlinische Lebensbilder Geisteswissenschaftler.* Edited by M. Erbe. Berlinische Lebensbilder 4. Berlin, 1989: 157–174.

Christ, K. *Von Gibbon zu Rostovtzeff.* Darmstadt, 1972; 2d ed., 1979: 68–83.

Curtius, F. *E. Curtius. Ein Lebensbild in Briefen.* Edited by Friedrich Curtius. Berlin, 1903; 2d ed., 1913.

Freeman, E. A. "Curtius' History of Greece." *Historical Essays.* Second series. London and New York, 1873: 148–160.

Gurlitt, L. "Erinnerung an Ernst Curtius." *JAW* 111 (1901) 113–144.

Kähler, H. *NDB* 3 (1957) 446–447. (With further references.)

Kern, O. *ADB* 47 (1903) 580–597.

Bibliography

Gurlitt, L. "Erinnerung an Ernst Curtius." *JAW* 111 (1901) 139–144.

Letters

Curtius, F. *E. Curtius. Ein Lebensbild in Briefen.* Edited by Friedrich Curtius. Berlin, 1903; 2d ed., 1913.

Gaetano De Sanctis

15 October 1870 – 9 April 1957

MARIELLA CAGNETTA
Università di Perugia

The renewal of research into ancient history in Italy is owed to Gaetano De Sanctis. With more coherence and rigor than such contemporaries as Pais and Bonfante, he successfully applied the German philological method to the study of scholarly problems larger and more complex than those that, up to his time, had been the subject of research by the dominant erudition, which tended to be antiquarian and archaeological in nature.

De Sanctis was born in Rome a few days after the capture of the city had made it part of the unified national state. The traumatic conclusion to the centuries-old temporal power of the popes was an event that had significant consequences in the years of his education. His early training took place in a climate marked by sharp tensions. On the one hand were sentiments of devotion to the papacy and hostility to the new national government, sentiments shared by his entire family. On the other hand was his adhesion to the new order of things, cultural in nature before it was political, which he developed as a young man. A climate of pride and hope reigned in Italy after the *risorgimento*, as well as the desire to give new life to a tradition of greatness that traced itself back to ancient Rome.

De Sanctis, a fervent Catholic, had made up his mind to guard the free development of his personality both from the reactionary conditioning of his family as well as from the attitudes of the dominant positivistic lay culture. While completing his studies at the University of Rome, in a rather advanced cultural environment, he found ways to reinforce his independence of judgment through contact with teachers of various orientations: among others, the Hellenist Piccolomini, the prehistorian Pigorini, the archaeologist Loewy, the epigrapher Halbherr, and above all the ancient historian Karl Julius Beloch, a German who had been living in Italy for many years. It was from Beloch, as well as from other scholars with whom he soon came in contact, particularly those who were in charge of the Deutsches Archäologisches Institut in

Rom, that De Sanctis derived a way of approaching classical antiquity that was far from rhetoric, not conditioned by nationalistic preconceptions, and placed on a rigorously scientific basis. Despite some differences, the relations of the rationalist Beloch and the Catholic De Sanctis were solid and deep. To the secure critical sense and realism derived from his teacher in the criticism of sources, the pupil joined interests of great range, which concentrated on the political and institutional aspects of ancient societies. At the center of his studies he placed the life of the state in its juridical and military articulations as well as its religious and cultural manifestations.

His first works show us De Sanctis as a precociously mature scholar capable of participating in the scholarly discussion of important topics. Significantly, his first work is dedicated to the *Athenaion Politeia* of Aristotle (1892), the text of which had recently arrived at London and was published in 1891. Such timeliness from one who was still a student demonstrated a lively attention to current questions, but also a singular sharpness. He argued that Aristotle's exposition was based on antiquarian sources of the fourth century, which should not be assumed to be superior to the information given us by the triad of great historians. It is still today a respectable view, while the thesis of Wilamowitz's monumental *Aristoteles und Athen*, which appeared in the next year, that there existed annalistic sources from the sixth and fifth centuries, is today obsolete.

This happy beginning happened to fall in years of important work for the study of the ancient world. Just then numerous wide-ranging and lasting works were appearing, such as those by Busolt (*Die griechischen Staats- und Rechtsaltertümer*, 1892), Meyer (*Forschungen zur alten Geschichte*, I, 1892; *Geschichte des Altertums*, II, 1893), Pöhlmann (*Geschichte des antiken Kommunismus und Socialismus*, 1893), Rohde (*Psyche*, 1894). There was also Beloch's *Griechische Geschichte*, a work very different from traditional introductory handbooks and innovative in its treatment of political and social problems. We should not forget that, even though Beloch was isolated from the world of Germany, he was nevertheless in fruitful correspondence with Meyer, whose teaching he mirrored and introduced to Italy.

De Sanctis's thesis (*tesi di laurea*) was devoted to the Athenian political history of the first half of the third century. It was subsequently published in Beloch's journal as "Contributi alla storia ateniese dalla guerra lamiaca alla guerra cremonidea" (1893). The young student showed himself capable of filling a void in the historiography of the Greek world on the basis of fragmentary witnesses, both epigraphic and literary in nature. (Cf. Ferguson, *Hellenistic Athens*, London, 1911: vii). His interests in the next period led him to a deeper knowledge of "Questioni politiche e riforme sociali" in the third century. He worked on a terrain all the more fertile because it was far from the usual beaten paths, with its tired treatment by Italian historical research.

The development of his scholarly personality tended to reinforce his deepest tendencies and sensibilities. He writes essays that confront problems in the religious beliefs of the Homeric poems ("La divinità omerica e la sua funzione sociale," 1896; "L'anima e l'oltretomba secondo Omero," 1897), where he is seen to have readily assimilated the lessons of Rohde. In other articles he demonstrated his vocation as epigrapher (in this field he would produce excellent results and give birth to a school of high quality). Other articles represent his first steps as student of the Roman world.

As an admirer of Eduard Meyer and to some degree a sharer of his vision of the centrality of the state, De Sanctis consecrated his first large work (*Atthis*, 1898) to the reconstruction of the process whereby the polis surpassed the limits of tribal structure and became a state. Wilamowitz's severe judgment, in refusing to write a review of the book, was communicated privately to the author: it would be impossible for him to write on it without saying "dass das hier gegebene Bild der Geschichte ein Spiel der Willkür ist" (letter of Wilamowitz to De Sanctis of 4 October 1898). The book received different and much more favorable opinions from many other reviewers. Théodore Reinach greeted the book's appearance with enthusiasm and noted the high level that scholarship in Italy had reached thanks to Italians such as Comparetti and Vitelli and "metics" such as Holm and Beloch. The time had passed in which one could say *a priori* of an Italian book on Greek antiquity: *italicum est, non legitur*. He praised the book's command of the facts and its mature critical sense, equidistant from credulity and extreme scepticism. This was no piling up of material but an organic rethinking of traditional facts and the hypotheses that had been formulated from them over the course of time. *Atthis* seemed worthy of the same interest that had greeted the great books of Wilamowitz and Busolt (*REG* [1898] 435–436).

In 1900 De Sanctis became *ordinarius* at Turin, where he taught Greek and Roman history in alternate years. He stayed there until 1929 and had as students, among others, Luigi Pareti, Aldo Ferrabino, Mario Attilio Levi, and, finally, the keenest and most versatile of all his students, Arnaldo Momigliano. The memories of his activity as a teacher indicate that the seminar was more congenial to him than lecturing. In seminars he shone in his ability to guide students by furnishing them with the necessary facts so that their intuition caught fire. It is significant that his commemoration of Mommsen at the Accademia delle Scienze di Torino began with a phrase of Otto Seeck's: "Teaching reveals a a man's nature. In no other area is there a clearer manifestation of the good and bad characteristics of one's scholarly personality than in his effect on his students."

In his first decade at Turin articles appeared that began from epigraphical and archaeological discoveries. The latter took account of the results of the Italian excavations at Crete, directed by Federico Halbherr. Several articles also dealt with papyrology. "Una nuova pagina di storia siciliana," 1905, deals with a new papyrus, variously attributed, that De Sanctis held to be by Philistus; "L'Attide di Androzione e un papiro di Oxyrhynchos" attributes to the Atthidographer the so-called "Oxyrhychus Histories." But it ought to be said that the work has an annalistic structure and adopts the Thucydidean framework.

Many of the articles of these years came together in 1909 in a "libro di battaglia" (as the author called it): *Per la scienza dell'antichità. Saggi e polemiche*. Besides articles on Homeric subjects, he reprinted a speech, *La guerra e la pace nell'antichità*, an opening lecture from 1904. The topic was a polemical treatment of a recent book by the Marxist historian Ciccotti (*La guerra e la pace nel mondo antico*, Turin, 1901). De

Sanctis echoed this title almost literally and developed his ideas further in an appendix, "Intorno al materialismo storico." De Sanctis claimed as the historian's role the "intuition of the reality of life" that hides behind documents, as well as the precise interpretation of those documents. De Sanctis attached himself explicitly to the teaching of Benedetto Croce and attacked the exponents of other historical currents: Bonfante for his sociological schematism, Pais for his prejudiced skepticism toward tradition, Ferrero for his dilettantism. De Sanctis's tone as a polemicist is energetic, on fire. "He felt pleasure in opposing, provoking, challenging," Momigliano remembered. He was himself later the victim of several polemical assaults by his teacher.

The 1909 book was intended to give a theoretical foundation to the great work he had started in 1907 and that would accompany De Sanctis through his life as *Lebenswerk:* the *Storia dei Romani.* The first two volumes of the history were intended to counter analogous reconstructions recently published in Italy, above all Pais's *Storia dei Romani.* They begin with the remoter periods and then give a lively reconstruction of the Regal era and the period of the early republic on the basis of a systematic reconsideration of all the epigraphical and archaeological material known up to that point, as well as the literary tradition. The clear narrative exposition was joined as far as possible to a critical analysis, which tripped up the development of the narrative every now and again. Here too, as in the *Atthis*, the basic theme of the work is the analysis of the city becoming a state.

The *Storia dei Romani* contains more transient aspects, as is only natural in a synthesis of such proportions, and even annoying elements. A certain phil-aryan racism was a constant factor in the man and in the scholar, a factor that often returns to the concept of "inferior races" and "sterile cultures" (Oriental, Semitic) from which Western civilization had to guard itself. ("Civiltà caduche e civiltà perenne" ["Transient cultures and lasting civilization"] is the title of an essay of 1943 on this topic.) These attitudes in historiography are in complete harmony with his position in 1911 in favor of Italian colonial expansion in Libya, in the name of the diffusion of a higher civilization, Catholic and Roman (not to mention an increased national power).

Once he had put himself on this dangerous slope, even though he was a lover of personal and political liberty, he could not then condemn Fascist aggression in Ethiopia in the thirties. Because of his hatred of England, the opponent of Italian pretenses in the Mediterranean, he will view Germany's cause in the Second World War with relative sympathy.

On the eve of the First World War he had publicly taken the position that Italy should remain neutral, the position of Benedetto Croce and the young philologist, Giorgio Pasquali. He did this both out of sympathy for the German world and its culture and because of his conservative political vision for which conflict, in the presence of strong social differences, represented a potential danger for the state system and constituted order. After Italy entered the war, like all conservative Catholics, he abstained from further manifestations in favor of neutrality.

In 1916–1917 De Sanctis published the two fascicles of volume III of *Storia dei Romani*, which was mainly devoted to political and military affairs. In the preface the author pointed out the similarity between the warlike background in which his work was written and the material it treated, but he dissuaded his reader from seeking easy and mechanical analogies between strategies and events that were apparently similar. (Many years later, in his late work *Pericle* of 1944, he found analogies of a political nature attractive, as he saw the end of Periclean Athens relived in the light of the tragedy that Italy was undergoing in those years.) The numerous appendices were rich in learning. Their outstanding aspect is a careful scrutiny of the sources for the history of the Punic Wars, but it is meaningful also for its treatment of "Dido in the Greco-Roman tradition," where, in the learned discussion on the sources of that character's legend, we find sensitive notes on the Virgilian version. In promising in the preface that the following volume would contain a general historical picture of Roman culture (such as he had to some degree given in volume III for Rome's enemy, Carthage), De Sanctis perhaps noticed the limits of an undertaking substantially closed to the new problems that had been placed before the attention of scholars, problems confronted by recent significant works on Roman history, such as Rostovtzeff on Roman colonies (1910), Warde Fowler on the religion of the Roman people (1911), and Gelzer in the prosopographical area. So, drawing his inspiration perhaps from Beloch's *Geschichte*, he will devote an entire large section of his *Storia* to the literature and religious life of Rome.

During the crisis that followed the First World War, when Italy was lacerated with serious political battles and social conflict, De Sanctis felt it necessary to participate directly in political life. He enrolled in the Partito Popolare, whose principles of devotion to the Church inspired an essentially conservative politics. In the years from 1919 to 1921 he was a candidate in political and administrative elections. His scholarly writing reflected these interests, although never in a fashion that was crudely "relevant." In 1920 he published an essay on "Dopoguera antico," in 1921 one on "Rivoluzione e reazione nell'età dei Gracchi." The latter closed with words that might seem prophetic of what was waiting for Italy in just a little while. With the death of Scipio Aemilianus, wrote De Sanctis, "there was no longer anything to stop the fierce strife between revolutionaries and reactionaries. Therefore the people who were the masters of the world hastened to pay for its own imperialism, by bowing its head under the yoke of military monarchy." It is in this spirit that we should understand the dedication/epigraph that opens volume four of the *Storia dei Romani*, which was already circulating before the March on Rome (Polverini, *ASNP* 3 [1973] 1056): *A quei pochissimi / che hanno parimente a sdegno / d'essere oppressi e di farsi opresssori.* ("To those very few who scorn equally the role of oppressed and oppressor.")

With this volume, devoted to the great conquests and their political consequences (which were negative according to his condemnation of imperialistic expansionism, a condemnation made in ethical language), the writing of the work was interrupted for about twenty years. When he took it up again, it had become something rather different. In the twenties, when De Sanctis had achieved full scholarly maturity and even international recognition of his worth (he received a degree *honoris causa* from Oxford in 1925), his research was directed toward the themes of the history of historiography. He would later collect the articles that came from this period devoted to Hecataeus, Herodotus, Thucydides, Xenophon, Sallust, and Livy in the volumes *Problemi di storia antica* (1932) and *Studi di storia della storiografia greca* (1951).

From 1923 De Sanctis's work became more and more devoted to cultural organization. In that year he assumed, together with the philologist and man of letters Augusto Rostagni, the editorship of Italy's oldest and most prestigious classical journal, *Rivista italiana di filologia e di istruzione classica*. He published there from time to time notes on Greek epigraphy (he was the head of the research group working on the inscriptions from Cyrenaica and Crete), "Cronache e commenti," and many book reviews. An especially important book review was devoted to Rostovtzeff's *Social and Economic History of the Roman Empire* in 1926. Rostovtzeff was a foreign scholar to whom De Sanctis was bound by ties of true friendship.

With the Fascist regime established in power, De Sanctis became involved, as did almost all Italian intellectuals of note, with the *Enciclopedia Italiana*, a cultural initiative of great prestige, supported by the government, which intended to make itself deserving of respect in the scholarly arena. This gigantic enterprise took a decade to reach its successful conclusion. De Sanctis was head of the Section for Classical Antiquity. He was given this position by Giovanni Gentile, the theoretical philosopher of fascism and scholarly director of the *Enciclopedia*, who nourished the greatest esteem for De Sanctis and served as his political patron on more than one occasion. In a climate of openness and tolerance notable for a totalitarian regime, De Sanctis worked for the success of the enterprise with a rhythm that was prodigious. He allowed the printing of no article without a careful reading and revision, often intervening, correcting, and improving. The articles on classical antiquity, entrusted to the greatest classicists, are admirable and can often still be useful today for their high level of information and scholarly originality. Among De Sanctis's collaborators I would record, for the philological side, Giorgio Pasquali, and then Momigliano (his student in ancient history from the last years at Turin), Fraccaro, Rostagni; from outside Italy, Maas and Rostovtzeff contributed articles.

Meanwhile, in 1929, De Sanctis moved to Rome as Professor of Greek History, filling the chair that had been Beloch's. His teaching in the capital was soon interrupted. In 1931 all university professors were asked to swear an oath of loyalty to the regime. De Sanctis refused and was removed from his chair, losing at the same time the use of the university buildings and libraries. He was among the few, some ten in all Italy, to give this example of intellectual honesty in opposing the dictatorship.

His old age was rendered harsh, besides the material problems attendant on his loss of work, from progressive blindness, even though voluntary readers were always present. It was in these difficult conditions that he began to work on another great work of synthesis, the *Storia dei Greci* (1939). Already in the early '30s he had returned to the history of the Greeks, the land of political liberty and free and critical thought. The volume *Problemi di storia antica*, published with timely solidarity by the anti-Fascist publishing house of Laterza soon after he lost his chair, began significantly with the 1930 essay "Essenza e carattere della storia greca," in which Ferrabino's *La dissoluzione della libertà nella Grecia antica* (1929) was implicitly discussed and criticized. It was under De Sanctis's guidance that the young Treves worked on *Demostene e la libertà dei Greci* (1933). The *Storia dei Greci* in the form in which it was published appeared without scholarly apparatus. It reflected scholarly positions that the author had matured much earlier and did not intend to open up again to discussion, e.g. the Doric invasion of Greece. It took no account of additions to knowledge that were being achieved in those years in the area of anthropology. It remains a work of great originality, where the prejudice in favor of national political unity coexists with a leading idea of great force and civil value, the idea of history as the ethical and political history of liberty. The influence of the liberal Croce on the Catholic De Sanctis could not be more evident. So in his less successful *Pericle* (1944) he repeated his thesis that the Duce of Athens had caused the collapse of Athens by an irresponsible pursuit of imperialist objectives, a formulation that had to appear to allude to the present.

The last part of his life was devoted to working on his great work, which was destined to remain unfinished, the *Storia dei Romani*. The second part of volume IV was already finished when, sharing a common fate with the Thucydides commentary of Gomme, the only copy was stolen. With a brave heart the old scholar devoted himself to reconstructing it. The first fascicle appeared in 1953, dedicated to religious, literary, and artistic aspects of the age of the conquests, while the second was published posthumously in 1957 and discussed the evolution of juridical institutions. The author did not live to reconstruct the treatment of economic and financial aspects. As in the *Storia dei Greci*, these last fascicles are not based on research and analysis but on a clear synthesis able to dominate an enormous field of knowledge.

With the fall of Fascism, he was restored to teaching and named Professor of Greek History for life. He became the president of the *Enciclopedia Italiana*.

Aside from his boundless productivity, the universal approbation accorded De Sanctis is based on his work as the head of a school. He showed respect to the human and scholarly personality of his students and was incapable in his relations with them of being conditioned by preconceptions, such as those concerning Indo-Europeans or the West, to which he was by no means immune. He had among his best students intellectuals of the most varied views: liberals and democrats like Momigliano and Treves, liberals and then Catholics like Ferrabino, Catholics like Accame, Fascists like Pareti and Levi. Mussolini himself intervened to brake the university careers of the numerous Jewish students of his school (Momigliano, Levi, Treves) in his preoccupation to guarantee an orthodox nationalistic imprint on the teaching of ancient history, and Roman history in particular. The school of epigraphy created by him (Guarducci, Moretti) has produced notable results. At the beginning of this century, in commemorating Mommsen, De Sanctis proudly proclaimed the rebirth of the study of ancient history in Italy. Everyone today acknowledges that that rebirth is due principally to him.

Translated by E. Christian Kopff

Books

ΑΤΘΙΣ. *Storia della Repubblica Ateniese dalle origini alla riforma di Clistene.* Rome, 1898; 3d ed. enlarged. Edited by S. Accame. Florence, 1975.

Storia dei Romani. La conquista del primato in Italia, vols. I–II. Turin, 1907; 3d ed. of vol. I. Edited by S. Accame. Florence, 1979.

Per la scienza dell'antichità, saggi e polemiche: I, Saggi omerici; II, Richerche di storia antica; III, A' miei critici. Turin, 1909.

Storia dei Romani. L'età delle guerre puniche, vol. III, 1–2. Turin, 1916–1917.

Storia dei Romani, vol. IV, *La fondazione dell' Impero: 1. Dalla battaglia di Naraggara alla battaglia di Pidna.* Turin, 1923.

Problemi di storia antica. Bari, 1932.

Storia dei Greci dalle origini alla fine del secolo V, vols. I–II. Florence, 1939; reprinted with bibliography by A. Momigliano, Florence, 1960.

Pericle. Milan and Messina, 1944.

Studi di storia della storiografia greca. Florence, 1951.

Storia dei Romani, vol. IV, *La fondazione dell'Impero: 2. Vita e pensiero nell'età delle grandi conquiste,* t. I–II. Florence, 1953–1957.

Ricerche sulla storiografia siceliota. Palermo, 1958.

Storia dei Romani, vol. IV, *La fondazione dell'Impero: 3. Dalla battaglia di Pidna alla caduta di Numanzia.* Florence, 1964.

La guerra sociale. Edited by L. Polverini. Florence, 1976.

Articles

"Studi sull' Ἀθηναίων πολιτεία attribuita ad Aristotele." *RFIC* 20 (1892) 147–163.

"Contributi alla storia ateniese dalla guerra lamiaca alla guerra cremonidea." *St. di storia antica* 2 (1893) 3–62.

"Questioni politiche e riforme sociali. Saggio su trent' anni di storia greca (258–228)." *Riv. intern. di scienze sociali* 4 (1894): I. "La guerra per la supremazia nell'Egeo.": 50–60; II. "Le riforme sociali di Agide IV.": 60–63; III. "La guerra demetriaca.": 229–238.

"Gli Scriptores Historiae Augustae." *Riv. di storia antica* 1 (1896) 90–119.

"L'anima e l'oltretomba secondo Omero." *Riv. di storia antica* 2 (1897) 38–52.

"Iscrizioni tessaliche." *MAAL* 8 (1898) 5–76.

"Una nuova pagina di storia siciliana." *RFIC* 33 (1905) 66–73.

"Nuovi studi e scoperte in Gortyna.": II, "Iscrizioni." *MAAL* 18 (1908) 297–348.

"Dopoguerra antico." *A&R* n.s. 1 (1920) 3–14, 73–89.

"Rivoluzione e reazione nell'età dei Gracchi." *A&R* n.s. 2 (1921) 209–237.

"La composizione della Storia di Erodoto." *RFIC* 54 (1926) 289–309.

Review of *The Social and Economic History of the Roman Empire,* by M. Rostovtzeff (Oxford, 1926). *RFIC* 54 (1926) 537–554.

"Postille tucididee.": I. "Il dialogo tra i Meli e gli Ateniesi."; II. "I trattati fra Sparta e la Persia."; III, "La oligarchia del 411." *RAL* 6th ser., 6 (1930) 299–341.

"La genesi delle Elleniche di Senofonte." *ASNP* 2d ser., 1 (1932) 15–35.

"Il 'logos' di Creso e il proemio della Storia erodotea." *RFIC* 64 (1936) 1–14.

"Essenza e carattere di un'antica democrazia." *Quaderni di Roma* 1 (1947) 43–58.

Sources

Autobiography

Ricordi della mia vita. Edited by S. Accame. Florence, 1970. (Published posthumously along with some pages of his diary and part of the correspondence concerning his refusal to take the oath of allegiance to the Fascist regime.)

Bibliography

Künzle, P. *Studi di storia della storiografia greca.* Florence, 1951: 173–194. (Writings up to 1949: to be integrated with the bibliography of *Scritti minori.* Cf. L. Polverini, "Gaetano De Sanctis recensore," 1047.)

Cf. *Scritti minori*, appendix to volume 5, for a list of the articles written by De Sanctis for the *Enciclopedia Italiana.*

Biographical

Accame, S. "Il pensiero storiografico di Gaetano De Sanctis." *Humanitas* 12 (1957) 431–446.

———. *Gaetano De Sanctis fra cultura e politica. Esperienze di militanti cattolici a Torino, 1919–1929.* Florence, 1975.

Bandelli, G. "Imperialismo, colonialismo e questione sociale in Gaetano De Sanctis (1887–1921)." *QS* 12 (1980) 83–126.

———. "Gaetano De Sanctis tra Methode e ideologia." *QS* 14 (1981) 231–251.

Cagnetta, M. *Antichisti e impero fascista.* Bari, 1979.

Ferrabino, A. "Gaetano De Sanctis." *Accademia dei Lincei: Problemi attuali di scienza e cultura* 43 (Rome, 1958) 15–33.

Gabba, E. "L'ultimo volume della Storia dei Romani di Gaetano De Sanctis." *RSI* 76 (1964) 1050–1075.

———. "Riconsiderando l'opera storica di Gaetano De Sanctis." *RFIC* 99 (1971) 5–25.

Mastromarco, G. "Il neutralismo di Pasquali e De Sanctis." *QS* 3 (1976) 115–137.

Momigliano, A. "In memoria di Gaetano De Sanctis (1870–1957)." *RSI* 69 (1957) 177–195 = *Secondo contributo alla storia degli studi classici.* Rome, 1960: 299–317.

———. "Gaetano De Sanctis (1870–1957)." *AAT* 104 (1969–1970) 69–77 =*Quinto contributo alla storia degli studi classici . . .* Rome, 1975: 179–185.

Pani, M. "Gaetano De Sanctis e l'imperialismo antico." In *Scritti sul mondo antico in memoria di Fulvio Grosso.* Edited by L. Gasperini. Rome, 1981: 475–492.

Polverini, L. "Gaetano De Sanctis recensore." *ASNP* 3d Ser., 3 (1973) 1047–1094.

———. "La 'Storia dei Romani' che non fu scritta." *StudRom* 30 (1982) 449–462.

Treves, P. "Nel centenario di Gaetano De Sanctis." *Il Veltro* 14 (1970) 217–255.

Papers

Scritti minori. Edited by A. Ferrabino and S. Accame. 6 vols. Edizioni di Storia e Letteratura. Rome, 1970–1983.

Hermann Diels

18 May 1848 – 4 June 1922

ECKART E. SCHÜTRUMPF
University of Colorado at Boulder

Hermann Alexander Diels, Ordinarius at the University of Berlin from 1886 to 1920, edited texts such as the *Fragmente der Vorsokratiker* that changed the course of study of early Greek philosophy, organized scholarly projects such as the *Commentaria in Aristotelem Graeca* and the *Corpus Medicorum Graecorum* that are still indispensable for modern scholarship, was a member of the Berlin Academy, and for twenty-five years was permanent secretary of its philosophical-historical section. He was also honored as a Knight of the Ordre pour le mérite, as well as a corresponding or honorary member of numerous academies in Europe and overseas.

He was born on 18 May 1848 in Biebrich (on the Rhine), the son of a railroad stationmaster. His father had intended that Hermann be a salesman, but the young Diels protested, finally getting his way, and was allowed to attend the Gymnasium in Wiesbaden (1858–1867). Nevertheless, his father still insisted that Hermann learn a trade, so Diels learned the profession of bookbinding. He bound many of the books in his own library, which bear witness to his skill (after his death Diels's library was acquired by the University of Louvain). Strong reinforcement to commit himself to classics came from his uncle Karl Rossel (1815–1872), who had a Ph.D. from the University of Göttingen (with a thesis, *De philosophia Socratis*, in 1837). Diels's schoolboy hobby of experimenting in chemistry and his interest in technical matters remained throughout his career and aided his work on ancient technology. His father, in addition to being a stationmaster, started several businesses (such as breeding silkworms) in order to finance his son's studies; all failed.

His first year of study of classical philology (spring 1867–1868) at the University of Berlin was on the whole disappointing. The only teachers Diels respected were J. G. Droysen (1808–1884) and, to a much lesser degree, Moriz Haupt (1808–1874). In 1867 Diels signed up for the seminar of August Böckh (born 1785), who became too ill to complete the course and died the same year (1867). Diels continued his studies (spring 1868) at the University of Bonn under Otto Jahn, as well as under Jahn's successor, Franz Bücheler (1837–1908), and in particular Hermann Usener. Fellow students were Ulrich von Wilamowitz-Moellendorff, Georg Kaibel (1849–1901), and Carl Robert (1850–1922). As a third-year student under Usener's guidance he started exploring the relationship of the collections of *Placita philosophorum* in Plutarch, Stobaeus, and Galen, a study from which Diels's *Doxographi* finally evolved. Diels mentions in his (unpublished and now lost) memoirs on his earlier years that the librarian Jacob Bernays (1824–1881), whose contributions to Aristotelian scholarship are still being discussed today, denied him access to some holdings of the library. For his work on the *Placita* Diels received the Faculty Prize in 1869. He graduated as Doctor of Philosophy with a thesis on *De Galeni historia philosopha* in 1870. For four months he traveled to Austria and Italy studying Greek manuscripts and searching for texts of *florilegia*. At the Archeological Institute in Rome he got to know a number of scholars, among them Rudolf Hirzel (1846–1917).

Financial constraints did not allow him to prepare for the "Habilitation" (therefore, he never was "Privatdozent") and forced him to teach at Gymnasia, first in Flensburg, then, from 1873 to 1877, at the *Gelehrtenschule* of the *Johanneum* in Hamburg (called by him the "Hamburg galley"). He worked regularly from 7 A.M. to 1 A.M. Moral support from Usener and Eduard Zeller (1814–1908) helped him persevere. Diels respected both men most highly and kept up a correspondence with each over many years.

During this time, Zeller had invited Diels to participate in projects to be undertaken by the Berlin Academy. When the Academy announced a prize in 1874 for the best study on Pseudo-Plutarch's *Placita*, Diels submitted the manuscript of the *Doxographi Graeci* and won the award in July 1877. The first part of the *Doxographi Graeci* (1879) contains a prolegomena, in which Diels attempted to demonstrate that the ancient texts dealing with the opinions of the philosophers go back to Theophrastus' *Physikai doxai*. He showed how excerpts were used by later authors for their excerpts and he attributed a crucial role to Aëtius (first or second century A.D.), whose Ξυναγωγὴ περὶ ἀρεσκόντων Diels regarded as one of the most important sources for the literature on the opinions of the philosophers. The volume contains an edition of the texts of the Doxographi and a large index. It has been said by Otto Regenbogen that Diels' *Doxographi Graeci* presents a new kind of scholarship in a new area applying a new method: Diels introduced the study of the tradition of Greek philosophy. By analyzing the relationships of dependencies between the different sources, he placed the research on the history of Greek philosophy on a new basis. Naturally, it was unavoidable that some of Diels's results would be rejected, in particular his reconstruction of Aëtius out of texts of Stobaeus and Plutarch, about whose validity there is serious doubt today.

In the fall of 1877 Diels moved to Berlin where he became a regular teacher at the Königstädtische Gymnasium. Soon afterward, upon the recommendation of Eduard Zeller, he was appointed editor of the edition of the *Commentaria in Aristotelem*

Graeca undertaken by the Berlin Academy. He succeeded Adolf Torstrik, who had been the editor of this project but under whom not a single volume was published. Diels organized the series as an international project, including scholars from England (Ingram Bywater; Frederic Kenyon), Denmark (J. L. Heiberg), Italy (Girolamo Vitelli), and Greece (Spyridon Lambros). Under Diels's direction it was completed in 1909, comprising 23 volumes plus 3 volumes *Supplementum Aristotelicum*.

It was Zeller who, supported by Mommsen, Hermann Bonitz, Adolf Kirchhoff, and Johannes Vahlen, recommended that Diels be elected an ordinary member of the Berlin Academy. When Diels became a member of the Academy in August 1881, he was still employed as a teacher at the Königstädtische Gymnasium, a post he did not leave until fall 1882. Contemporaries say that the decade he served as a schoolmaster shaped his personality, even his way of teaching at the university and the style of his many public addresses and speeches.

In 1882 he received his first appointment at the University of Berlin as Extraordinarius for Classical Philology in the Philosophical Faculty. In the following years he received and turned down calls to the chairs of classics at the Universities of Gießen (1883), Greifswald (1885), and Heidelberg (1886). In 1886 he was promoted to Ordinarius in Berlin. He taught there until his retirement in 1920. As colleagues he had Wilamowitz (from 1897) and Eduard Norden (from 1906). All of them dedicated works to one another: Wilamowitz dedicated his *Platon* (1919) to Diels; Diels his edition of Lucretius (1923) to Wilamowitz; Norden dedicated his *Die germanische Urgeschichte in Tacitus' Germania* (1920) to Diels, proving the high respect these scholars had for each other despite all their differences in personality and style (Diels disapproved of the injurious harshness with which Wilamowitz dealt with colleagues).

In order to concentrate on scholarship, Diels turned down the offers from Mommsen to become editor of *Hermes* and of the *Deutsche Literaturzeitung*, but in 1888 he cofounded the *Archiv für Geschichte der Philosophie*, in whose first volume he published a research report on the presocratics, something he continued in 1889 and 1891.

Diels's edition of books I–IV of Simplicius' commentary to Aristotle's *Physics* (CAG IX [Berlin 1882]) was the first volume of the whole series of *Commentaria in Aristotelem Graeca* to appear. His edition of the other four books of Simplicius' commentary followed in 1895, and he contributed to this series as well the *Anonymi Londinensis ex Aristotelis Iatricis Menoniis et aliis medicis eclogae* (*Suppl. Aristotelicum* vol. III, 1893). While working on Simplicius he had already conceived the idea of collecting the fragments of the presocratic philosophers. In the preface to his edition of the first four books of Simplicius' *Commentary on the Physics* (1882) he announced a plan to edit the presocratic philosophers that would be fulfilled more than twenty years later.

In his first position, as Extraordinarius at the University of Berlin, Diels succeeded F. W. A. Mullach (1807–1882), whose boring teaching he had detested even as a student. Mullach had edited a collection of fragments of Greek philosophers, which comprised the fragments of presocratics in volumes I (1860) and II (1867). This collection did not satisfy even the most modest standards of scholarship, and the articles published by Diels since 1880 (many of which are reprinted in the *Kleine Schriften*) prove that presocratic philosophy already occupied his mind at that time. Editions by Diels of Parmenides (1897), Heraclitus (1901), and, in the same year, the poetic fragments of Greek philosophers were harbingers of his edition of *Die Fragmente der Vorsokratiker* (1903). The principles of his approach to both the transmitted texts of presocratic philosophy and the tradition of textual criticism had already displayed his virtuosity (for example, in transposing the order of lines in the transmitted text). These principles appear already in the preface to his *Parmenides*, where he claims more modest intentions, namely, not to bring the Eleatic philosopher up to the heights of modernity and not to give him in bold conjectures a beauty or elegance he simply never had. The errors of previous editors in dealing with the transmitted text, he explains, arose from a lack of understanding "for the poetic individuality and the ability of the Eleatic philosopher."

The edition of the "Vorsokratiker" opened a new area in the study of the history of early Greek philosophy. The differences between the editions of Mullach and Diels are evident: Mullach's text could never have created the strong revival of the study of presocratic philosophy that took place after Diels's edition. In his presentation of the material of presocratic philosophy Diels followed principles he had adopted in his edition of Parmenides: Rather than treating the philosophical schools as a whole, Diels wanted to focus on the individuals, the few big names and the innumerable less important ones who, with their industry, explain the almost incomprehensible development of philosophy in the sixth and, particularly, fifth centuries B.C. Diels aimed at presenting the complete material of the verbally transmitted fragments—in each new edition he added new material—because he regarded his selections as a tutorial for the student. It was with students in mind that he had written this book, for he planned that it would serve as the textbook for lectures on early Greek philosophy. Thus Diels did not cite all texts in which verbally transmitted fragments are quoted.

Diels introduced a new way of presenting the material by dividing it into three sections. For each author in section A, Diels gave the ancient biographical and doxographic evidence, the latter according to the disposition adopted by Theophrastus in his *Physikai doxai*; in section B, he printed only the verbally transmitted citations of the presocratic philosopher in question, marking off material of dubious value; in section C, he added imitations, for example, the myth in Plato's *Protagoras* (320 c ff.) presented there by the interlocutor of that dialogue, Protagoras. To the texts listed in section B, Diels added his own translation. He resisted the temptation of ordering the fragments according to some theory about their original connection (his method is particularly evident in his dealing with Heraclitus when compared with that of earlier editors like F. Lasalle). Instead, he printed them in the order in which the ancient excerpts contain them; when ordering the authors of ancient excerpts he simply followed the alphabet. His intention was to provide a collection of fragments as complete as possible in a way that allowed a comprehension of the conditions of transmission of the fragments, because he regarded such an understanding as necessary for an assessment of these texts. Diels wanted to avoid the subjective view of the editor obstructing or influencing the study of these documents of the presocratic philosophers; only the order in which he placed the philosophers betrays his view on the development of presocratic philosophy. In the first edition Diels did not include a critical apparatus to the fragments, because he was not satisfied with the quality of the editions of the authors he referred to. It appears that the work on the presocratics was probably the scholarly achievement that meant most for Diels. Wilamowitz called it a work "indispensable for each philologist and for each philosopher, a work incomparable in its kind."

Just two years after the first edition a new one was necessary. Volume I was published in 1906, vol. II in 1907. Diels's disciple, Walther Kranz (1884–1960), added a detailed index (1910). The third edition appeared in 1912, and for a fourth edition, published after his death in 1922, Diels had written a new preface and valuable supplements. Kranz was in charge of the revision of the fifth edition (1934–1937), which was again and again reprinted with additional changes.

In 1895 Mommsen resigned as secretary of the philosophical-historical section of the Berlin Academy and Diels was elected to become his successor. He took the post for financial reasons and was active in this capacity until 1920, and the influence of his work went far beyond the limits of Berlin. He was committed to furthering international cooperation und understanding among European universities. The same commitment to the course of international cooperation he showed as Rector of the Berlin University in 1905–06, when, in his speech on the anniversary of the founding of the University, he addressed the international duties of universities. He was critical of attempts to introduce the artificial creation of Esperanto as a world language. At the same time, he rejected attempts to reinstate Latin as the language of international scholarship; English, French, and German should be treated equally within the international academic community. The teaching of French and English should be strengthened at German Gymnasia and universities, an academic exchange program should further international understanding. Diels compares favorably with less open attitudes at German universities during the decade preceding the First World War. During that time Diels received honors from the most prestigious national and international institutions, too many to be mentioned here. To name but a few: He became Corresponding Fellow of the British Academy in 1904; the American Academy of Arts and Sciences in the section Philology and Archaeology made him a foreign honorary member in 1907; the American Philosophical Society made him a member in 1909; in the same year the University of Cambridge awarded him an honorary doctorate; in 1913 he was awarded membership in the Ordre Pour le Mérite. After 1914 he deplored the breakdown of international relations among scholars, and turned, very much from a patriotic position, against the anti-German attitude maintained chiefly by French scholars. Immediately after the end of the war he worked to re-establish scholarly contacts and, a few weeks before his death at the age of 74, he undertook an extended lecturing tour through the Scandinavian countries, hoping to lead their scholarship out of national isolation.

The plan of an edition of a *Corpus Medicorum Graecorum* was formed at the first general assembly of the Association of Academies in Paris 1901, initiated by J. L. Heiberg. Following the proposal by Diels, the Berlin Academy decided to edit the texts of Greek medical writers in partnership with the Academies of Leipzig and Copenhagen. Diels was certainly the driving force behind the project. The basis for this work, the catalogue of the manuscripts of ancient medical writers, was already published in 1905 and 1906. Diels himself was prepared for this area of scholarship through his work on Galen as part of the *Doxographi Graeci* and his edition of the Anonymus Londinensis in the *Supplementum Aristotelicum* vol. III (1893). Numerous articles and reviews on Greek medicine written since 1899 prove Diels's focus on this area. His contribution to the *Corpus Medicorum Graecorum* was his edition *Galeni In Hippocratis Prorrheticum I* (1915).

Diels was active as well in founding the *Thesaurus Linguae Latinae*, a project initiated by four German Academies (Berlin, Göttingen, Leipzig, Munich) and that of Vienna. His study "Elementum" (1899) was written in this context as his model of a lexicological study.

His work in the history of religion, begun in 1886 with "Antike Heilwunder," started in earnest with the *Sibyllinische Blätter* (1890), in which he dealt with the Sibylline oracles for the year 125 B.C. For his argument he referred to cults and rituals outside of the Greek and Roman world. A number of articles and lectures belong to the same area. He studied religious aspects, in the words of Walter Burkert, "from the standpoint of an enlightened-liberal point of view."

Halfway between ancient medicine and religion are his studies (published in the *Abhandlungen* of the Berlin Academy 1907 and 1908) on παλμομαντική, a form of divination based on the convulsions of the sick. Here, again, he proved to be the talented organizer; he went beyond the boundaries of Greek antiquity by enlisting his colleagues' support to compile a corpus of Arabic, Hebrew, Slavic, and Indian literature on throbbing.

Diels took part as well in the edition of the papyri that had been acquired by the Berlin Museum. Together with Wilhelm Schubart (1873–1960) he published the commentary of Didymus to the Philippic speeches of Demosthenes and an anonymous commentary to Plato's *Theaetetus* (1904).

From his schoolboy days he had an interest in chemistry and studied all kinds of technical matters. In Berlin he included this in his scholarly work. To his *Parmenides* (1897) he added an appendix on Greek doors and locks (117–51). In 1913 he published in the *Abhandlungen* of the Berlin Academy a study on the discovery of alcohol in antiquity. When invited to give a series of lectures at the University in Salzburg in September 1912, he chose as subject matter ancient technology. These lectures formed the core of his book *Antike Technik*. In *Sechs Vorträge* (1914), apart from his scholarly purpose of explaining aspects of ancient technology, he wanted to show that, in its approach to technical progress, antiquity came closer to the modern age than the Middle Ages did. He saw the hostility of modern natural scientists to antiquity that characterized the nineteenth century and was still influential in the beginning of the twentieth as based partly on their ignorance of antiquity and partly on the narrowness of the classicists themselves. Diels expressed (in the preface) the strongest criticism of the humanists who, caught in nebulous idealism, did not know enough about the real world of antiquity and therefore misunderstood its connection with the reality of modern times. Diels was particularly interested in the mutual relationship of ancient technology and science. He not only used literary sources but drew on archaeological material as well. In this area, again, he went beyond antiquity, when he pursued, for instance, the development of ancient siege machines into the cannons of modern times (111ff.). This booklet on ancient technology proved so successful that already in 1919, in spite of the difficult time after the First World War, a second edition was published to which Diels added an additional chapter. A third edition appeared after his death in 1924. Together with Erwin Schramm, Diels published an edition with German translation of Hero's *Belopoiika* and Philo's *Belopoiika* (*Transactions of the Berlin Academy*, 1918).

In 1920, after twenty-five years, Diels resigned as secretary of the philosophical-historical section of the Academy. In the same year he retired as professor and on 4 June 1922 he died of heart failure.

Diels's last works were an edition and a translation of Lucretius, which both appeared after his death. The edition was dedicated to Wilamowitz. It stands out for two reasons: It provided the fullest critical apparatus published to that date, and it recorded in the most complete way the quotations from and references to Lucretius' work. As an editor Diels restored archaic forms in the transmitted text. He tried to emulate the style of the original through various poetical devices, at the same time keeping a freshness that did not smell of translation. Albert Einstein wrote the introduction, praising the clarity of Diels' version. However, Diels's textual decisions have not regularly been accepted by later editors. His metrical translation of Lucretius' poem was not altogether completed at his death; his pupil Johannes Mewaldt (1880–1964) had to revise it.

The lasting achievement of Hermann Diels is his edition of *Die Fragmente der Vorsokratiker*, which made the scattered material of presocratic philosophy available and put the study of this important area on a firm basis.

Books

Doxographi Graeci collegit recensuit Prolegomenis Indicibusque instruxit. Berlin, 1879.
Simplicii in Physicorum Libros quattuor priores, Commentaria in Aristotelem Graeca. Vol. IX. Berlin, 1882.
Sibyllinische Blätter. Berlin, 1890.
Anonymi Londinensis ex Aristotelis Iatricis Menoniis et aliis medicis eclogae, Supplementum Aristotelicum. Vol. III, part I. Berlin, 1893; reprinted 1961.
Simplicii in Physicorum Libros quattuor posteriores, Commentaria in Aristotelem Graeca. Vol. X. Berlin, 1895.
Parmenides' Lehrgedicht. Griechisch und Deutsch. Mit einem Anhang über griechische Türen und Schlösser. Berlin, 1897.

Elementum. Eine Vorarbeit zum Griechischen und Lateinischen Thesaurus. Leipzig, 1899.

Poetarum philosophorum fragmenta. Berlin, 1901.

Herakleitos von Ephesos. Griechisch und Deutsch. Berlin, 1901; 2d ed., 1909.

Die Fragmente der Vorsokratiker. Griechisch und Deutsch. Berlin, 1903; 2d ed., revised and enlarged. Vol. I, Berlin 1906; Vol. II, 1907, 2nd half, *Wortindex,* compiled by W. Kranz. Foreword and supplement by H. Diels, 1910; 3rd ed., 1912; 4th ed., 1922; 5th ed., 1934–1937. English translation of the fifth edition by Kathleen Freeman as *Ancilla to the Pre-Socratic Philosophers.* Oxford, 1948. See also K. Freeman, *The Presocratic Philosophers: A Companion to Diels' Fragmente der Vorsokratiker.* Oxford, 1946.

Didymos' Kommentar zu Demosthenes (Papyrus 9780) nebst Wörterbuch zu Demosthenes' Aristocratea (Papyrus 5008). Compiled by Diels and W. Schubart. In *Berliner Klassikertexte* 1. Berlin, 1904.

Didymi de Demosthene Commenta cum Anonymi in Aristocrateam lexico post editionem Berolinensem. Edited by Diels and W. Schubart. Leipzig, 1904.

Anonymer Kommentar zu Platons Theaetet (Papyrus 9782) nebst drei Bruchstücken philosophischen Inhalts (Papyrus N. 8; Papyrus 9766; 9569). Under the supervision of J. L. Heiberg. Compiled by Diels and W. Schubart. In *Berliner Klassikertexte* 2. Berlin, 1905.

Colloquium über antikes Schriftwesen (1908): Vorlesungen über Herodot (1907–08). Introduction by J. Dummer and W. Rösler. Epilogue H. Hommel. Leipzig, London, and New York, 1984.

Theophrasti Characteres. Oxford, 1909; reprinted 1920; 1944; 1952; 1961; 1964.

Antike Technik. Sechs Vorträge. Leipzig and Berlin, 1914; enlarged 2d ed., 1919; 3rd ed., 1924.

Galeni In Hippocratis Prorrheticum I. In *Corpus Medicorum Graecorum,* V.9, 2. Leipzig, 1915: 1–178.

T. Lucretii Cari de rerum natura libri sex. Berlin, 1923.

Lukrez von der Natur. Edited by Hermann Diels. Foreword by J. Mewaldt. Preface by Albert Einstein. Berlin, 1924.

Articles (Collected)

Hermann Diels. Kleine Schriften zur Geschichte der antiken Philosophie. Edited by W. Burkert. Hildesheim, 1969.

Sources

Bibliographies

Kleine Schriften: xiv–xxvi.

See Kern, below: 136–146.

Biographical

von Arnim, H. "Nachruf H. Diels." *Almanach Österreichische Akademie der Wissenschaften* 73 (1923) 206–211.

Bickel, E. "Hermann Diels." *Nassauische Lebensbilder* 5 (1955) 253–259.

Dümmer, Jürgen. "Hermann Diels' 'Colloquium über antikes Schriftwesen.' "
    Philologus 121 (1977) 150–156.

Jaeger, W. "Hermann Diels. Zum goldenen Doktorjubiläum am 22. Dezember 1920."
    Internationale Wochenschrift 15 (1921) 133–146.

Kern, O. *Hermann Diels und Carl Robert. Ein biographischer Versuch.* Jahresbericht
    über die Fortschritte der klassischen Altertumswissenschaft. Suppl. 215,
    1927.

Rösler, Wolfgang. "Hermann Diels als Kartograph." *RhM* 115 (1972) 92–93.

de Strycker, Emile. "Der Nachlass von Hermann Diels." *Philologus* 121 (1977)
    137–145.

von Wilamowitz-Moellendorff, U. "Gedächtnisrede auf Hermann Diels."
    Sitzungsberichte der preussischen Akademie der Wissenschaften zu Berlin. Berlin,
    1922: cv–cviii.

Letters

Hermann Diels und Ulrich von Wilamowitz-Moellendorff: Briefwechsel 1869 bis 1921.
    Edited by W. M. Calder III and D. Ehlers. Berlin, 1991.

Hermann Diels und Hermann Usener: Briefwechsel. Edited by D. Ehlers. Berlin, 1990.

Hermann Diels und Eduard Zeller: Briefwechsel. Edited by D. Ehlers. Berlin, 1990.

Eduard Fraenkel

17 March 1888 – 5 February 1970

NICHOLAS HORSFALL

Eduard Fraenkel was one of the most distinguished of Wilamowitz's pupils, equally eminent in Greek and Latin, in Germany and in England, equally influential in England and in Italy.

Eduard David Mortier Fraenkel (born in Berlin, seven days into Frederick III's brief reign) was a first cousin (paternal) of the philologist Ernst Fraenkel; his father was a first cousin (maternal) of Ludwig Traube, and Eduard's sister married Hermann Fränkel. Fraenkel's father was a wine merchant; his mother, Edith, to whom he was deeply devoted, nursed him through osteomyelitis and its consequences; her brother, the publisher Hugo Heimann, helped found Fraenkel's remarkable library. Fraenkel wrote meticulously with a withered right hand, enjoyed a remarkably robust constitution, a superb memory, and tireless energy, and applied these to a severe routine. His classical education began at the Askanisches Gymnasium, under, notably, Otto Gruppe. But it was above all Wilamowitz who fascinated the schoolboy and law student. On Fraenkel's return from Italy in 1907, he turned decisively to classical philology and studied under Eduard Meyer, Diels, and Norden (for whom he shared Wilamowitz's strange disdain). Most of 1909–1912 he spent at Göttingen: Wackernagel and Leo exercised a lasting influence, and the preface to his edition of Leo's papers is tender and masterly. There Fraenkel met his great friends Jachmann, Pasquali, and Von der Mühll. Though he returned briefly to Berlin in 1910–1911 (where his influences were Vahlen and Schulze; the latter's studies of "Wort- und Sittengeschichte" remained an inspiring element in Fraenkel's teaching for the next sixty years); from Göttingen he graduated in 1912 with a thesis *De media et nova comoedia quaestiones selectae*, and the next year he joined the *Thesaurus Linguae Latinae*, which he always maintained was a crucial influence. In 1917 he returned to the University of Berlin as Privatdozent and soon married (see below). Thereafter, his German career moved swiftly upwards: 1920, Extraordinarius, Berlin; 1923, Ordinarius, Kiel; 1928, Göttingen; 1931, Freiburg. He was Norden's likely successor at Berlin until the Aryan Law of 1933. *Plautinisches im Plautus* (1922; beautifully translated and expanded in the Italian version of 1960) is "one of the most exciting works of classical scholarship," as Wilamowitz recognized. In the twenties, Fraenkel concentrated also on Roman law (and remained a great admirer of the *Digest*, for content and for Latinity), on Lucan, and on "Iktus und Akzent" ("il mio disgraziato libro," he said; "a disaster" comments a necrologist).

He left Germany in 1934. Fortunately, the Chair of Latin at Oxford fell vacant in the next year, and he towered over the field. Housman, cordially respectful of Fraenkel's *Gnomon* review of his Lucan, lent strong support. His early years at Oxford were uncomfortable; refugees did encounter xenophobia and anti-Semitism; professors there are not especially important, and college tutors jibbed at his rough language and new ways. The autobiographies of Dodds and Bowra are suggestively unrevealing; his great friend and helper, though, was Sir John Beazley. And there arrived a remarkable flood of fellow exiles helped and gathered by Gilbert Murray, Hugh Last, and Sir David Ross. They did not form a unified and loving whole, but with Fraenkel, Pfeiffer, Jacoby, Jacobsthal, Klibansky, Maas, Labowsky, Brink, Wellesz, Walzer, and Weinstock all gathered, it became easier to understand what Germany had to offer, and the grand scale of the *Agamemnon* commentary established Fraenkel's unchallengeable professional eminence. The crushing review of the Harvard Servius was undertaken as a diversion before ordering the final draft of the *Agamemnon*. Forty years have not treated that commentary kindly, but it remains a monument of scholarly technique, of mastery of detail, of huge and varied erudition. Fraenkel's seminars (see below) on the play transformed Oxford teaching methods and standards.

At Corpus, he became a "good college man"; colleagues also learned to respect his ferocities and his genius, while he came to admire the traditional English grounding in Latin and Greek (and regularly went to talk in the older schools). But *Horace* (1957), admired at the time, has not weathered well; see D. Armstrong, *Arion* 3 (1964) 116–28 for a feline but largely just summary of its defects. Fine observations and rich annotation coexist with unfruitful critical approaches and (twenty years after *Roman Revolution*) a naïve view of the Augustan principate. In the same period there appeared also a great flood of substantial articles and reviews on central Latin topics (usually poetic). Retirement changed nothing; exceptionally, he retained his college rooms and his two yearly seminars (the often entertaining introduction to Greek meter—he did have a notable musical ear and a splendid reading voice—and the more demanding study of a text) continued. His Roman publisher friend, Don Giuseppe De Luca, brought out his reissue of two of Schulze's monographs, selections of Leo's papers and of Fraenkel's own, a collection of essays on and elucidations of Aristophanes, and *Leseproben aus Reden Ciceros und Catos* (1968), on the rhythms of the individual *cola* of Latin oratory. He received six honorary degrees (including Oxford's); his eightieth birthday was celebrated throughout Europe, and age barely touched his memory, his energy, and his urge to teach.

Fraenkel was by birth a Jew (*fidem profiteor Mosaicam*, in his doctoral *vita*), which did not impede his career under Weimar; his master Leo's Lutheranism he could not accept and finally did not need to. Momigliano's interpretation of Fraenkel as an essentially Jewish teacher is deeply perverse and unconvincing. Fraenkel did visit Israel, wrote (once) for a Jewish journal, visited Jewish excavations on holiday, yet loved Bach's cantatas and Anglican Oxford and, as a European, spoke of "we who are Christians . . . ." Both his determination to transmit what he had learned and the manner of his death are as much Roman as Jewish. His wife, Ruth ("the best thing about Fraenkel," said Wilamowitz), was of Lutheran extraction; they met in Schulze's seminars (Fraenkel viewed with proprietary interest the numerous matches made in his own) and married in 1918. There were five children. Ruth set his work loyally before hers (she was Ph.D. Berlin 1917), though she continued to publish sporadically, to translate from the German, to type, to index, and to discuss everything with him. She gave gentle, wise, and unfailing support. Fraenkel had no intention or desire to survive her. We revere his suicide, for love. They are buried in St. Cross Cemetery, Oxford.

Of Fraenkel's books, I have deliberately said very little. Though he still lives powerfully in the *Elementi* and in the *Kleine Beiträge*, his greatest and most lasting contribution to scholarship was through his teaching—"For us, the last representative in flesh and blood of the great *Altertumswissenschaft* of nineteenth-century Germany"; at the same time "Lehrer aus Passion." He showed his British and Italian students what that tradition meant, how and why they should revere it, and how they could seek, by *aemulatio* and *imitatio*, to become part of it themselves. R. G. M. Nisbet noted rightly that Fraenkel "fertilized the minds even of those who reacted against him." Perplexingly, he adds that he "failed to found a school." Rather, spurning mass-produced imitators, he preferred to exercise widespread, indirect, but decisive influence on generations of English and Italian classicists.

The Oxford inaugural is dated 13 Feb. 1935; Housman died on 30 April 1936, a strikingly isolated figure. Fraenkel introduced new levels of perceptivity and professionalism. My copy of Nisbet-Hubbard on Horace *Carm.* 1 is dated five weeks after his death. The best of Berlin *Wissenschaft* came to flower triumphantly transplanted on English soil. When Fraenkel reached Oxford, graduate research was not esteemed; even when he retired from the chair, that form of apprenticeship was still taking root. The seminar, not individual supervision, was his instrument; that included some younger dons (there had been more, but he had found their presence inhibited the young), graduate students, undergraduates, and some varied *extranei*. Few of the noted *Fraenkeliani* were formally his graduate students. In his last fifteen years there come to mind Reeve, Pecere, Taplin, Rizzo, Macleod, Cassio, Passalacqua, Anna Morpurgo, König, Keudel, Livrea, Muecke, Wallace-Hadrill, Hine; to go a little further back, Wilson, Lloyd-Jones, G. W. Williams, Delz, Fedeli, Nisbet, Knauer, Canfora, Cavallo, Dell' Era, Questa, Tandoi, Hubbard, L. E. Rossi.

Williams quoted a description of the Oxford seminar as "a circle of rabbits addressed by a stoat." Very true, especially on a bad day. Unlike Pasquali (the distinction is Timpanaro's), Fraenkel knew in advance the answer he wanted to emerge from discussion. Debate was directed, and at Oxford, disagreement was far less tolerated than—to judge from the printed record—was the case in Italy. Fraenkel stood like a shepherd beyond a fence: his (Oxford) flock was not lured, wooed, coaxed to choose the right gate; most of us, fearful and bemused, rushed blindly, trusting to luck, instinct, or guesswork. But strangely, years later, facing fences of our own choice, we found we knew how to choose our gates. He harassed us until he got us thinking roughly as he had been trained to think himself. The seminars could be grim, bullying affairs; equally, his approval could warm you for twenty years. Those he held at Florence, Urbino, and Pisa in the '50s were recognizably close kin to those of Oxford; at Rome and Bari, a decade later, he was still awe-inspiring, but also notably relaxed and tolerant. Even at Oxford, *non omnia possumus omnes* sometimes elegantly let off the uninformed. He did enjoy, warmly, but most decorously, female beauty; that counted, in the seminars. He likewise loved great music, and a remarkable range of composers are mentioned in his footnotes. Most appropriately, a late and particularly treasured Oxford pupil is now an internationally renowned soprano!

Between Italy and England there is a crucial distinction: "Eduard è sempre agitato quando è a Oxford, qui in Italia è felice" (Ruth, to Italo Mariotti). He certainly found great happiness in Italy, from a first trip in the winter of 1906–1907. He was there briefly in 1936 with a group of younger Oxford colleagues: "when I act as a guide in Rome, I like to be with someone who is *completely* ignorant." For the '50s, Timpanaro, and for the '60s, Rossi have given us memorable pictures. The review of G. Pasquali's *Storia dello spirito tedesco nelle memorie d'un contemporaneo* helps explain (*Gnomon* 26 [1954] 337–41 = *Kleine Beiträge* 2:601–7): the portrait of Pasquali radiates loving envy of his dear friend's exuberant unconventionality and informality. The photographs of the Rome seminar's outings show Fraenkel truly beatific. He loved the country and all its beauties, the language and literature (both Dante and Pinocchio!), the food, drink, art, and, notably, the cigars. He knew his students would be less well prepared: "io non sono carnivoro," he assured them; "I get angry with colleagues, not with students."

Peter Levi refers to Fraenkel's constant maxim that "learning was easy and all too common in Oxford, but what we needed was judgment." Though Fraenkel's publications moved in wide orbits, admirably charted by Timpanaro, and his interests, as footnotes often reveal, were vaster still, his teaching concentrated on a small canon, particularly, in the later years, of the dramatists. There is a compact unity in his approach and method from the first to the last; he was delighted to see *Elementi* reissued after forty years.

But what did we learn? Part of the answer is to be found in the books and articles, part in the published seminars, part in the obituaries; the heart of the matter is still "oral tradition."

How to say "I love you" in idiomatic Italian (on Terence *Eun.* 655, I suspect); how to look at the whole scene, not just at the line or word; how to distinguish, on the other hand, the word or idiom as anomalous and therefore as especially significant in its context; how to suspect elegant emendations and admire ruthless deletions (he came rather to rue his Jachmann-inspired hatchet work on Petronius, in Müller's first edition); how to recognize in individual words the echo of a custom, or a ritual, or an outlook, distant from, but adding greatly to, its context; how to maintain an informed general interest in the history of classical scholarship, and how not to drown in bibliographical or editorial trivia; how to be right without having a parallel to back you up; how to proceed and where to turn when Kühner-Gerth disagrees with Schwyzer and all editors of Sophocles are at odds; how to respect your predecessors while maintaining your independence; how to think clearly and simply; how to cite the one truly relevant parallel; how to give due weight to the staging and visual impact of an ancient play; how to listen intelligently to a passage from an ancient author, and to learn from its rhythms and cadences; how to be alert for patterns in sound, language, meter and thought; how to learn from what you see, not just from what you read; how to distrust the artificial and cleave to the simple; how to avoid the prolix, the pedantic, the quibbling, the opaque; how to despise wanton erudition and superfluous parallels, elder-worship and standard handbooks; how to love Greek and Latin and how to love working on them; how to find fulfillment, and excitement, through *Sitzfleisch*. Those who actually enjoyed the seminars will of course have learned far more than this. A strong fellow-feeling binds those who took his seminars, though they are characterized by no unity of thought.

Fraenkel's impact is perhaps uniquely complex: in Italy he did a very great deal to reinforce what Pasquali had transplanted from Göttingen; in Oxford he dominated for thirty-five years and still dominates Greek and Latin studies. His sense of the profession's seriousness and high standards, and his real belief in the excellence of the authors taught coincided better than might have been anticipated with old English views of the desirability of refined linguistic training and the real moral and spiritual value of the best classical authors: Thomas Arnold and Wilamowitz unite as the intellectual grandparents of, notably, Colin Macleod, Fraenkel's most admired pupil.

Books

De media et nova comoedia quaestiones selectae. Diss., Göttingen, 1912.
Plautinisches im Plautus. Phil. Unters. 28. Berlin, 1922. Italian translation by F.
        Munari, with numerous additions, as Elementi Plautini in Plauto. Florence,
        1960.
Iktus und Akzent im lateinischen Sprechvers. Berlin, 1928.
Aeschylus. Agamemnon. Edited with a commentary. 3 vols. Oxford, 1950.
Horace. Oxford, 1957. German translation by G. and E. Bayer. Darmstadt, 1963. 2d
        ed. (revised), 1970–1971; 3d ed., 1971; 4th ed., 1974.
Beobachtungen zu Aristophanes. Rome, 1962.
Kleine Beiträge zur klassischen Philologie. 2 vols. Rome, 1964.
Leseproben aus Reden Ciceros und Catos. Rome, 1968.

Articles

"Zur Geschichte des Wortes *Fides*." *RhM* 71 (1916) 187–99 = *Kleine Beiträge* 2:15–26.

"Das Geschlecht von *Dies*." *Glotta* 8 (1917) 24–68 = *Kleine Beiträge* 2:27–72.

Review of *Lucan*, ed. A. E. Housman. *Gnomon* 2 (1926) 497–532 = *Kleine Beiträge* 2:267–308.

"Kolon und Satz," *NGG, Phil.-hist.Kl.* 1932: 197–213 = *Kleine Beiträge* 1:73–92.

Review of *Servianorum in vergilii carmina commentariorum editionis Harvardianae*, Vol. 2, ed. E. K. Rand, et al. *JRS* 38 (1948) 131–43 and 39 (1949) 145–54 = *Kleine Beiträge* 2:368–90.

"Der Einzug des Chors im Prometheus." *ANSP* 2.23 (1954) 269–84 = *Kleine Beiträge* 1:389–406.

"Ein Motiv aus Euripides in einer Szene der neuen Komödie." *Studi in Onore di Ugo Enrico Paoli.* Florence, 1955: 293–304 = *Kleine Beiträge* 1:487–502.

"Die sieben Redepaarenim Thebanerdrama des Aeschylus." *ABAW, phil.-hist. Kl.* Heft 3. Munich, 1957 = *Kleine Beiträge* 1:273–328.

Introduction to F. Leo, *Ausgewählte Kleine Schriften.* Edited by Fraenkel. Rome, 1960.

Review of *Catullus, A Commentary*, ed. C. J. Fordyce. *Gnomon* 34 (1962) 253–63.

Review of *The Authenticity of the Rhesus of Euripides*, by W. Ritchie. *Gnomon* 37 (1965) 228–41.

Note that the *Kleine Beiträge* was the result of notably rigorous selection and rejection: much not there printed is therefore implicitly disavowed.

Sources

Bibliography

Horsfall, N. M. "Eduard Fraenkel. Bibliography." *JRS* 66 (1976) 200–5.

Addenda to Wilamowitz, *Glaube der Hellenen* 2. Berlin, 1932: 549–52.

Lloyd-Jones, H. "Preliminary Notes on Menander's *Dyskolos*." *CR* 9 (1959) 183–92.

Macleod, Colin. "Wilamowitz." *QS* 5 (1977) 101–18. (A fragmentary Italian lecture on Wilamowitz.)

Letters

Calder, W. M., III. "Seventeen Letters of Ulrich von Wilamowitz-Moellendorff to Eduard Fraenkel." *HSCP* 81 (1977) 275–97 = Calder, W. M., III, *U. von Wilamowitz-Moellendorff, Selected Correspondence 1869–1931.* Naples, 1983: 93–116 (with 306–7).

Prete, S. *Pagine amare di storia della filologia classica.* Sassoferrato, 1987. (Fraenkel's correspondence with G. Jachmann.)

Obituaries

A list of obituaries is given by H. Lloyd-Jones, 634, n. 1 and by L. E. Rossi, xxxi. Momigliano's obituary is reprinted in *Quinto Contributo*, 1026–9.

Mariotti, I. "Eduard Fraenkel, concittadino di Plauto." *A&R* 30 (1985) 170–8.

Lloyd-Jones, H. *Gnomon* 43 (1971) 634–40.

Macleod C. W. *Collected Essays.* Oxford, 1983: 347–8.

Rizzo, S. *Rassegna di Cultura e vita scolastica.* 24, 4–5 (1970) 13.

Timpanaro, S. "Ricordo di Eduard Fraenkel." *A&R* 15 (1970) 89–103.

Williams, G. *PBA* 56 (1972) 415–42.

Papers

Fraenkel had a remarkable private library: the Ashmolean Museum, Library, Oxford from 1972 has held all pamphlets and offprints, all books heavily annotated, and those others which did not duplicate its already existing holdings and the (almost complete) collection I assembled of F.'s own *opuscula.* His papers, including some unpublished work, are held by Corpus Christi College, Oxford, and a handlist may be obtained on application to the Librarian.

Seminars

Horsfall, N. M. *Due seminari Romani di Eduard Fraenkel: Aiace e Filottete di Sophocle.* Rome, 1977.

L. E. Rossi's preface contains a remarkable portrait of the Rome seminars (vii–xxx), *Belfagor* 38 (1983) 433–51 (Ajax) overlaps. Cyclostyled versions at least of the Bari seminars on Ar. *Birds,* Plaut. *Pseud.* (1965) and Soph. *Aj.* and Cat., (1966) exist. It is a pity that the project of publication outlined at *Belfagor* 27 (1972) 634, n. 1 was not carried out.

For their help, I am grateful to Otto Skutsch, Scevola Mariotti, Frances Muecke, Frank and Colin Hardie, Albio Cesare Cassio and Silvia Rizzo, Tonino Pecere and Chico Rossi.

Tenney Frank

19 May 1876 – 3 April 1939

T. ROBERT S. BROUGHTON
University of North Carolina

Tenney Frank, Professor of Latin at the Johns Hopkins University, was recognized at home and abroad as the foremost American historian of ancient Rome of his time. He was also a brilliant and inspiring teacher, a humanist of wide interests with an active and original mind, a patient and vigorous investigator who made important contributions in several disciplines, whose qualities of character and personality made him a wise counselor and a good friend.

His origins and background were common to many midwestern Americans. He was born on a farm near Clay Center, Kansas, of pioneer Swedish-American stock, his father an immigrant from Sweden and his mother the daughter of one. The un-Swedish name Frank was said to have been assigned to an ancestor, a military recruit, at a Francophile moment in the time of Bernadotte. His early years were spent in the discipline of farm life and with a strict religious upbringing. The reading allowed on Sundays was restricted to the Bible and the Lives of the Saints, in Swedish, which was the language of the household. These years did much to give him his characteristic habits of independent observation and persistent endeavor and his practical idealism. Bad seasons led to the loss of the farm in 1890. His father worked in the stockyards in Kansas City, Missouri, as he did himself during school vacations, both there and, later, in Chicago. He was proud of his Scandinavian origin, his rural upbringing, and his experiences with manual labor and different kinds of employment. In later life he held that such experiences were a great aid to ancient historians, and that they had given him a better understanding of the Italian countryside and the agricultural basis of Roman social and economic life. He never lost his love of the land and his sympathy with the people on it. He kept up a lively interest in birds and flowers all his life, was proud of the ferns in his garden, and used to place on a par with his scholarly achievements his success in inducing arbutus to grow.

In secondary school in Kansas City a teacher of German birth and education named von Minckwitz gave him confidence in himself and aroused his interest in classical studies. He majored in classics at the University of Kansas, with the unusual addition of special study in geology, won his A.B. in 1898 with highest distinction and election to Phi Beta Kappa, and his A.M. the following year. Professor A. T. Walker there had interested him in grammar and syntax, subjects then at the height of their vogue. So he applied for a fellowship at the University of Chicago, attracted by the reputation of William Gardner Hale. He quickly became one of Hale's preferred pupils while studying also with other distinguished scholars in the classical faculty at that time: Paul Shorey, G. L. Hendrickson, F. F. Abbott, Edward Capps, and C. D. Buck. He held an appointment as Instructor in Latin from 1901 to 1904, and received his Ph.D. in 1903 with a dissertation entitled *Attraction of Mood in Early Latin*.

Appointed as Associate in Latin at Bryn Mawr College in 1904, he quickly won recognition for his stimulating teaching and his activity as a scholar and was promoted to Associate Professor in 1909 and to Professor in 1913. His first studies were in the field of his dissertation, but it was at Bryn Mawr that he developed the breadth of interest in all aspects of ancient Roman life and achievement that were the mark of his career as a whole. One of the first fruits of his new direction, his book *Roman Imperialism*, and several major articles gave him an international reputation. When, after fifteen years at Bryn Mawr, he accepted an appointment to Johns Hopkins University as Professor of Latin, his colleague, Professor Arthur Wheeler, wrote that no American classical scholar of his years was his equal in the range and quality of his work. During the immensely productive years that followed he received other invitations, notably one from Harvard University, but declined them and remained at Johns Hopkins.

Frank's unflagging energy, the "Energie der Forschung" that Hermann Dessau praised in a letter to him, appears in the volume of his published works. The list in the *American Journal of Philology* (60 [1939] 280–287) includes fifteen books or monographs, several of considerable size, over 150 articles in periodicals, and many reviews besides. No less impressive is the wide range of disciplines with which he was familiar and in which he made contributions: grammar and linguistics, textual criticism, metrics, literary criticism and interpretations, social and political history, economics, law, epigraphy, and archaeology. A guiding principle was the view that true scholarship on ancient Rome, as in general, aims above all at the fullest possible acquaintance with every aspect of its life. A second was the view, evident in his treatment of literature and history, that these disciplines go hand in hand and illuminate each other.

As noted above, his early articles reflected his philological training, as, for example, "Latin vs. Germanic Modal Conceptions" (*AJPh* 28 [1907] 273–286) and his Scandinavian background, as in "The Use of the Optative in the *Edda*" (*AJPh* 27 [1906] 1–32) and "Classical Scholarship in Medieval Iceland" (*AJPh* 30 [1909] 139–152). But from 1909 on, several articles reveal his growing interest in historical problems. Such were "Commercialism and Roman Territorial expansion" (*CJ* 5

[1910] 99–110), "A Chapter in the Story of Roman Imperialism" (*CPh* 4 [1909] 118–138), "The Import of the Fetial Institution" (*CPh* 7 [1912] 335–342), and "Mercantilism and Rome's Foreign Policy' (*AHR* 18 [1913] 235–252). That interest increased still further during a sabbatical year (1910–11) that he spent in study at Göttingen and Berlin, where he attended the lectures of Eduard Meyer and other historians and reacted against their point of view. The book on which he was working, *Roman Imperialism*, appeared in 1914 and won him immediate recognition for his independent interpretations and his clear and cogent style. It aroused a lively debate, which continues still, on the nature of Roman expansion: how far should it be considered defensive, action taken against injury and aggression of others in wars that were just under the fetial rules, or how far due to acquisitiveness and individual desire for glory, while the fetial rules were ignored or became nothing but ceremonies? In later life Frank was willing to grant that Roman desire for conquest did increase in the second century before the period of Pompey and Caesar, but he continued to believe that the fetial tradition did not lose all of its moral influence.

Among the many articles and notes of the next years, "Race Mixture in the Roman Empire" (*AHR* 21 [1916] 689–708) aroused special attention. It was a detailed analysis of the epitaphs, mainly those of the city of Rome as listed in *Corpus Inscriptionum Latinorum* VI, which showed clearly the great extent to which the older free Roman stock had been replaced by the stock of foreigners and their progeny, largely easterners of slave origin, and raised questions about the social and political results. Some articles, like "*Caelianum illud*, Cic. *Ad Att.* X, 15, 2" (*CPh* 14 [1919] 287–289), were incidental to his reading, but a goodly number show him already at work on the materials for his books of the 1920s. Such were his skeptical "The Economic Interpretation of Roman History" (*CW* 11 [1917] 66–71), "Some Economic Data from *CIL*, Volume XV" (*CPh* 13 [1918] 155–168), and "Agriculture in Early Latium" (*Am. Econ. Rev.* 9 [1919] 267–276), or "Notes on the Servian Wall" (*AJA* 22 [1918] 175–188), the first fruit of study at the American Academy in Rome as Annual Professor in 1917 to 1918. Such studies as "Horace on Contemporary Poetry" (*CJ* 13 [1918] 550–564), "Cicero and the Poetae Novi" (*AJPh* 40 [1919] 396–415), and "Vergil's Apprenticeship I, II and III" in (*CPh* 15 [1920] 23–38, 103–119, 230–244) look to his later books on Vergil and on Catullus and Horace. But his immediate achievement was *An Economic History of Rome to the End of the Republic*, published in 1920, a pioneer work in a field neglected by the ancient authors, in which he brought together the scattered bits, often difficult to find, of literary, historical, inscriptional, and archaeological evidence, with analysis and conclusions in chronological order. It received a warm welcome both in America and abroad, and was published in Italian translation in 1924.

Meanwhile, in another field, E. K. Rand's essay on "Young Vergil's Poetry" (*HSPh* 30 [1919] 103–185) had greatly encouraged acceptance of the poems in the *Appendix Vergiliana* as composed by Vergil himself in his youth. Some are attributed to him by Quintilian, Martial, and the Donatus Life. The poems of the *Appendix* are not in the great early manuscripts but appear in ninth-century ones. Frank believed firmly in Vergilian authorship of almost all of these and made them in large part the basis of his *Vergil, A Biography*, a bold and original work, attractive in both content and style. The dispute about authorship of the *Appendix* continues, but even the more skeptical recent discussions grant some of the *Catalepton* to Vergil himself and are inclined to admit that these poems were composed near his time and with good information. (See the summary by J. Richmond, *ANRW* II, 31, 2 [1981] 1112–1154.) Frank's book therefore still preserves much of its value, in the words of one critic, "for the many suggestive lines of thought by which Frank endeavors to coordinate Vergilian poetry with contemporary history and politics."

The same aim and the same approach characterize his *Catullus and Horace, Two Poets in their Environment*. Their works and the social and political history of their times are used together to illuminate each other. The intent is not of course to explain the genius of either poet but rather to show the context of their lives, the forms that were natural to them, and the nature of their experiences. Literary criticism of both authors has advanced greatly since Frank's time, but he was successful in his purpose—and besides, one rarely meets such passages as the vivid evocation of life in the Sirmio and Verona of Catullus' youth or in the setting of Horace's Sabine farm.

Frank's studies in this field culminated in his Sather Lectures, published in 1930, with the significant title *Life and Literature in the Roman Republic*. He first describes the social forces, especially the contacts with Greek literature and culture and the changes in Rome itself, during the formative period of Latin literature, in order to show how Roman writers, although they made generous use of their Greek predecessors, reacted independently. "The really personal literature of the Republic," he wrote, "is neither conformist nor monotonous, neither Greek nor classical in spirit" but "frankly experimental" and "always proves to reflect some phase of Roman life." A review of the long development from early tragedy and epic, through Greek comedy at Rome, Terence and his successors, to Accius and the *togatae*, Roman historiography and the rise of Roman oratory, and notable comments on Cicero, Lucretius, and Livy, reveal the Roman adaptations to their own conditions and their increasing assertion of their own independence. Perhaps one may paraphrase in translation R. Helm's judgment (*BPhW* 51 [1931] 845), who notes the stimulating content of the book, the new points of view on every subject, whether in prose or poetry, and the unusual gift for presentation that arouses interest even in questions that appear dull, and adds, "He has certainly been successful in his aim: to visualize a few of the early Roman writers in their response to the desires and demands of their environment."

The History of Rome, which appeared in 1923, was planned as a general textbook suitable for college classes and was widely in use for a long time. In it he chose to emphasize a theme close to his own background and of greater interest to American readers, one that he had also stated in his *Roman Imperialism*: "The older peoples of Europe are more interested than we in the imperialistic problems of Rome. We are naturally more concerned with Rome's earlier attempts at developing an effective government while trying to preserve democratic institutions. Whereas modern European nations have experienced a devolution, as it were, from late Roman autocracy, our state, like the Roman Republic, plunged at once into experimenting with more or less accepted theories of popular sovereignty." Discoveries and discussions have modified his statement in some degree, but the importance of popular assemblies and popular elections remained clear throughout the Republic. His interest in this theme may explain why he seems to show less interest in the later part of the Principate. Even so, a reviewer of his time welcomed the *History* as "the best college textbook of Roman History in our language" (W. W. Hyde in CW 17 [1923–24] 44–47).

Appointments to the American School of Classical Studies in Rome as Annual Professor in 1917–18 and Professor in Charge in 1922–23 and 1924–25 had given him the opportunity to become familiar with the structure and topography of the buildings of ancient Rome. Using his early training in geology, he concentrated his attention on identifying the tufas that were the regular building materials under the Republic and in investigating the quarries from which these tufas had been brought. The dates at which these quarries became available in the course of the early expansion of Roman territory in Italy provided important additional evidence for the history of the buildings. The resulting book, *Roman Buildings of the Republic*, remains an important work of reference. He gave his collection of matching fragments from the buildings and from the quarries to the American Academy as a permanent aid to study.

By 1927, exhaustion of the first edition of *An Economic History of Rome* made a second edition necessary. The appearance in the meantime (1926) of Rostovtzeff's great *Social and Economic History of the Roman Empire* had made a full scale addition of chapters on the Empire, as originally planned, no longer necessary, but he decided to include in the new edition several new chapters, not in rivalry, but to bring out some differences in interpretation and point of view. Such chapters are "The First Decades of the Empire," "The Provinces in Hadrian's Day," and "Beginnings of Serfdom." The volume has remained in demand, in most subjects still a good base for further work, but the chapter "Roman Coinage" is now completely out of date since the discovery that the first issue of the silver denarius must be dated about 211 B.C., and not in 269 as Frank had thought (See M. H. Crawford, *Roman Republican* Coinage [London 1974] 1: 28–35).

The year 1932 saw the appearance of two valuable works. One was the Annual Lecture on a Master Mind, delivered on the Henriette Hertz Trust before the British Academy. Frank's subject was Cicero, whom he presented more as a pervasive influence than as a master mind, and to whose apparently inconsistent career he gave some unity by showing that in fact Cicero had tried to hold a moderate centrist position and opposed extremists both to the right and the left as occasion arose. The other is volume II of the Martin Classical Lectures at Oberlin College, entitled *Aspects of Social Behavior in Ancient Rome*. The first of the five lectures points out the apparent equality of women in social position and property rights in the actual working of the patriarchal system at Rome, the second discusses the effect of the steady infusion of other peoples on Roman religious rituals, especially those bringing in oriental cults, the third is on the influence of agrarian economics and agrarian mentality on politics and conduct, the fourth on the attitude of different forms of government at different periods toward public charities, and the last presents interpretations of passages in the Twelve Tables to show how, even then, early law of the Republic was responding to social and business needs. Incidentally, he held that *coemptio* marriage never meant purchase of the bride.

Although articles and notes continued to appear and he was editor of the *American Journal of Philology* from 1936 to 1939, a major part of his effort and time from 1932 on was occupied with the planning and preparation of *An Economic Survey of Ancient Rome*, probably his most impressive and most enduring scholarly achievement. When representatives of the Rockefeller Foundation approached him for a recommendation of some large cooperative scholarly enterprise that would advance the study and understanding of the ancient world, he welcomed the opportunity, as he had felt that, in comparison with other countries, there had been a lack of such enterprises in American scholarship. He proposed in the *Survey* the making of an Empire-wide collection of the vast amount of ancient social and economic evidence, literary, inscriptional, and papyrological, with attention also to archaeology, for the various Roman periods up to the fourth century A.D. An important aim was to present together the widely scattered and incidental texts, so neglected by ancient sources, and, with the needs of economists and other nonclassicists in mind, to provide English translations of the significant ones, using standard translations whenever they were available in order to avoid possible bias. Comments and interpretation would present only assured results, not fill gaps in the evidence with conjectures.

For himself he undertook the preparation of the first volume on *Rome and Italy of the Republic*, published in 1933, and a final volume on *Rome and Italy of the Empire*, well advanced but not yet completed at the time of his death. As editor, he arranged for the group of collaborators, named below in the bibliography, and supervised the publication of the three intervening volumes on the eastern and the western provinces. It soon became apparent that no single pattern of presentation was possible as the sources varied and different areas and different periods required different approaches. The obvious value and convenience of such a collection and presentation ensured a hearty welcome for all the volumes, whatever difference of opinion there might be about details. It is a pity that Frank was not able to include the Danubian and the Balkan provinces. At his death most of volume V had been written and was ready for publication with editing, according to his instructions, by his student, Mrs. Loane. But instead of the three final chapters he had planned, "The Economics of Septimius Serverus," "The Third Century," and "Diocletian," it was possible only to sketch his conclusions by putting together materials from lectures he had given in Oxford and London, and Diocletian could be represented only by an up-to-date text and translation of his *Edict on Maximum Prices*, on which Dr. Elsa Graser, another student of his, was working. On the whole series of volumes, those he wrote and those he edited, one may quote from the review by M. Cary (*CPh* 36 [1941] 72): "For all the vast ground which it covers, the Survey is a handy and eusynoptic encyclopedia. Though it lacks a capstone it is a proud monument to a great scholar and a great leader."

The breadth and originality of his scholarship gave stimulus and inspiration to his teaching, while the example of his patient investigation and unflagging energy aided students to keep searching "for the last refractory fact" and to fit it into its place. Work with him became a cooperative search for truth and the satisfaction of mutual interests. He studied the needs of his students and gave them tasks that would open windows for future endeavors, and the supply of suggestive ideas never ran low. His understanding of human motives, his keen perceptions and wise judgments made him a good counselor and a generous friend. His intellectual and moral integrity was unwavering, and he asked nothing of others he did not ask of himself. He was not distant or austere. A quiet and dry humor pervaded his lectures and played in his conversations. In seminar or out of it, students soon learned to recognize the quizzical expression that preceded a question that would catch them out or the overconfident twinkle that preceded a salutary bit of teasing. His modest and unassuming manner often surprised those who knew from his works the boldness and originality of his mind.

In 1907 he married Grace Edith Mayer of Chicago, who later became well-known as an accomplished scholar in Romance philology and medieval drama. She was a constant partner in all his interests and avocations, and no small support as his health declined in his final years.

Many honors, not without responsibility, came to him. While Professor at the American Academy in Rome he was appointed the American Delegate to the Union Académique Internationale. He was President of the American Philological Association in 1929 and gave the Horace White Lecture at Bryn Mawr College that same year. His Sather Lectures at the University of California in 1930, the Martin Lectures at Oberlin College, and the Lecture on a Master Mind to the British Academy in 1932 have been mentioned above. He was elected a member of the Swedish Royal Society of Letters in Lund, a member of the American Philosophical Society (1927), Fellow of the American Academy of Arts and Sciences (1935), Corresponding Fellow of the British Academy (1934), and received the degree of L.H.D. from Union College. The final honor was his appointment to the prestigious Eastman Professorship at Oxford University for 1938–39, the first American classicist to be so honored. He lectured there for the first two terms with great success but died suddenly on 3 April before the beginning of the third term. He is buried in Wolvercot Cemetery with many of the famous names of Oxford on the gravestones about him.

Books (Authored)

Attraction of Mood in Early Latin. Diss., University of Chicago, 1904.
Roman Imperialism. New York, 1914.
An Economic History of Rome to the End of the Republic. Baltimore, 1920.
Vergil, A Biography. New York, 1922.
A History of Rome. New York, 1923.

Roman Buildings of the Republic. An Attempt to Date Them from their Materials. Papers and Monographs of the American Academy in Rome, 3 (1924).

An Economic History of Rome. Baltimore. 2d ed. (revised), 1927.

Catullus and Horace. Two Poets in their Environment. New York, 1928.

Life and Literature in the Roman Republic. Sather Classical Lectures 7. Berkeley, 1930.

Aspects of Social Behavior in Ancient Rome. The Martin Classical Lectures 2, Oberlin College. Cambridge, MA, 1932.

An Economic Survey of Ancient Rome. Vol. I: *Rome and Italy of the Republic.* Baltimore, 1920.

An Economic Survey of Ancient Rome. Vol. V: *Rome and Italy of the Empire.* Baltimore, 1933.

Books (Edited)

American Journal of Philology (1936–1939).

An Economic Survey of Ancient Rome. Vol. II: *Roman Egypt to the Time of Diocletian,* by A. C. Johnson. Baltimore, 1936.

An Economic Survey of Ancient Rome. Vol. III: *Roman Britain,* by R. G. Collingwood; *Roman Spain,* by J. J. Van Nostrand; *Roman Sicily,* by V. M. Scramuzza; *La Gaule Romaine,* by A. Grenier. Baltimore, 1937.

An Economic Survey of Ancient Rome. Vol. IV: *Roman Africa,* by R. M. Haywood; *Roman Syria,* by F. M. Heichelheim; *Roman Greece,* by J. A. O. Larsen; *Roman Asia Minor,* by T. R. S. Broughton. Baltimore, 1938.

Books (Translated)

Cornelius van Bynkershoek. *Quaestiones iuris publici libri duo.* The Classics of International Law, no. 14, vol. II. Oxford and London, 1930.

Articles (Selected)

"Race Mixture in the Roman Empire." *AHR* 21 (1916) 689–708.

"The Economic Life of an Ancient City." *CP* 13 (1918) 225–240.

"Epicurean Determinism in the Aeneid." *AJPh* 41 (1920) 115–126.

"The Inscriptions of the Imperial Domains in Africa." *AJPh* 47 (1926) 55–73.

"Roman Historiography before Caesar." *AHR* 32 (1927) 232–240.

"'Dominium in Solo Provinciali' and 'Ager Publicus'." *JRS* 17 (1927) 141–161.

"Notes on Roman Commerce." *JRS* 27 (1937) 72–79.

"Pyrrhus" (Chapter 20); "Rome and Carthage: The First Punic War" (Chapter 21); "Rome after the Conquest of Sicily" (Chapter 25). In *The Cambridge Ancient History.* Vol. VII. Cambridge, 1928.

"Italy" (Chapter 11) and "Rome" (Chapter 12). In *The Cambridge Ancient History.* Volume VIII. Cambridge, 1930.

"Italy: 'Archaeology.' " "Rome: 'The Ancient City.' " and "Rome: 'Ancient History.' " In *Encyclopaedia Britannica.* 14th Edition. Chicago, 1929.

"Introduction." and Chapter III: "The Roman World." In the *Encyclopaedia of the Social Sciences*. Edited by E. R. A. Seligman. New York, 1930 1:42–60.

Sources

Bibliography

[Clift, Evelyn Holst.] Bibliography appended to DeWitt's obituary, *AJPh* 60 (1939) 280–87. (Prepared as a tribute by Evelyn Holst Clift.)

Biographical

Albright, W.F. "Tenney Frank (1876–1939)." *Year Book of the American Philosophical Society* (1939) 444–446.

Anon. Obituary. "Professor Tenney Frank. The Study of Roman Antiquity." *London Times*, 4 April 1939. Note another by C. R. in the same journal on 6 April 1939.

Broughton, T. Robert S. "Tenney Frank–Humanist, Historian, Originator." *Johns Hopkins Alumni Magazine* 27 (1939) 107–110.

DeWitt, Norman W. "Tenney Frank." *AJP* 60 (1939) 273–280.

Pease, Arthur Stanley. "Tenney Frank (1876–1839)." *Proceedings of the American Academy of Arts and Sciences* 74 (1940–42) 123–125.

Who's Who in America. 20th Edition. 1938–39.

Details remembered from conversations with both Professor and Mrs. Frank.

J. G. Frazer
1 January 1854 – 7 May 1941

ROBERT ACKERMAN
University of the Arts

Sir James George Frazer, OM, FRS, FBA, Fellow of Trinity College, Cambridge, was a prolific scholar whose deep and broad classical learning underlay his epochal explorations into the comparative evolutionary history of religion. His most important work was folkloristic and anthropological, as those terms were understood before the First World War, but he also produced a larger quantity of first-class classical work than do many scholars who never stray from the beaten paths of classical antiquity. Although his writings met a mixed reception from the start among scholars, they arguably had a greater impact on the thinking of the educated lay reader in the English-speaking world in the first third of this century than those of any other British scholar. During that time they caused thoughtful people to understand the origins, development, and meaning of human mental and spiritual evolution in a new way, and even now, half a century after his death, some range him with Darwin, Marx, and Freud as a prime architect of the modern consciousness. The statement by T. S. Eliot in the notes to his landmark modernist poem *The Waste Land* (1922) that the work could be understood fully only by a reader conversant with *The Golden Bough* is only the best-known acknowledgment of that influence.

James Frazer was born in preindustrial Glasgow, on 1 January 1854, the eldest son of a pious (Free Church of Scotland), middle-class family. His father, self-educated, was activist by temperament and rose to become a leader among the businessmen of Glasgow and the pharmacists of Scotland. James, by contrast, was shy, retiring, and bookish from the start. His academic career began brilliantly in 1874, when he swept most of the classical honors in taking his first degree at the University of Glasgow. There (Frazer says) the Latinist G. G. Ramsay played a critical part in shaping his understanding of the classical world. It was also at Glasgow that his religious faith seems to have slipped painlessly away.

It is worth noting that the standard expected of the students at Glasgow was not as high as it was in an English university, but the curriculum was much broader. In a technical sense Frazer was not as well prepared as his English contemporaries who were products of classical preparatory schools; on the other hand, Glasgow introduced him to subjects like psychology and philosophy that undergraduates in England never encountered. This early exposure may have predisposed him to taking the wide views that characterize all his mature work.

At this time Scottish graduates interested in pursuing an academic career regularly took a second B.A., usually in England; accordingly, Frazer entered Trinity College, Cambridge, in 1874. This was to be his spiritual home, as student and fellow, for the rest of his long life. There, as he continued to read widely, the great influence was his teacher Henry Jackson, Praelector in ancient philosophy. After coming second in the classical Tripos of 1878, he won a college fellowship in 1879 with a Jacksonian dissertation on *The Growth of Plato's Ideal Theory*. (This fellowship, having been renewed in 1885, 1890, and 1895, became tenable for life. Except for one year, 1907–1908, when Frazer left Cambridge to take up a chair in social anthropology at Liverpool but then returned, homesick for Cambridge, the fellowship was his only academic position. In later years—especially after he married a French widow with two teen-aged children in 1896—he depended for much of his income on book royalties. He did no teaching and had no students, which explains to some extent why his later eclipse was so total.)

At Trinity he also absorbed great doses of evolutionary social thought in the work of Herbert Spencer, then at the height of his influence, and the rationalist anticlericalism of the French Orientalist Ernest Renan. By the 1880s, then, Frazer had much broader interests than the typical Cambridge classical graduate of the time, who tended to be content in a rather antlike way to add his tiny contribution to the mountain of textual commentary. Frazer revised a school text of Sallust's *Catilina* and *Jugurtha* and had already begun a translation of and commentary upon Pausanias when, in 1884, he met and fell under the spell of the brilliant Scottish Semiticist and historian of religion, William Robertson Smith (1846–1894). It was Smith who gave Frazer his first intimations of anthropology and "primitive" religion.

Smith had publicized the results of German Biblical criticism in the volumes of the ninth edition of the *Encyclopaedia Britannica*, of which he was the editor. For his pains he became the defendant in the last important heresy trial in Britain. Although exonerated, he was too notorious for provincial Scotland and as a result emigrated to Cambridge. Smith quickly enlisted the young but already erudite Frazer, possessor of a clear and graceful style, as a contributor to the encyclopedia. At that time volumes were published as they were completed, and for this reason everything through the letter O had already appeared. Thus it was that he first had Frazer write a few small classical articles on subjects beginning with *P*, and when all went well entrusted to him the major articles on "Taboo" and "Totemism." The younger man never looked back. The new field of anthropology, although at the time not a university subject and thus without professional prospects, must have appeared to him more inviting than classics, where all must have seemed set in stone.

His eyes having been opened by anthropology, Frazer suspended work on Pausanias and turned to an ambitious and speculative general work on the nature and origins of religion: *The Golden Bough* (1890). From the point of view of intellectual history, the book may be seen as a late contribution to the long-term movement to topple the Greeks and Romans from the privileged positions in the European historical imagination that they had occupied since the Renaissance. Frazer, demythologizing, asserted that the Greeks and Romans were at the same (not very advanced) stage of mental evolution as contemporary European peasants and so-called primitive peoples. (The discovery—or the invention—of the "folk" and folklore was one of the great enterprises of European romanticism, and masses of data about "savages" had flowed into the European capitals throughout the nineteenth century as a result of imperialism and colonialism. In terms of its main sources, then, *The Golden Bough* could not have been written much earlier than it was.) For this reason, the best way to understand the spiritual life of classical antiquity, Frazer argued, was through the lens of the religious behavior of peasants and savages and the mentality such behavior bespoke. The book was generally well received, the reviewers praising especially Frazer's deftness in guiding the reader through veritable Saharas of dry facts.

The Golden Bough's novelty lay in the way it juxtaposed materials from the classical and "savage" worlds, using the latter to illuminate the former. Its hidden agenda lay in what was *not* discussed: although the reader learns much about Attis, Adonis, Dionysus, and the other gods of the eastern Mediterranean, there is not a word about the most well-known of that pantheon, Jesus. Only the slowest reader, however, could not notice this striking omission, and only the same kind of reader could fail to make the connection between the heathen gods that Frazer argues are the products of mental confusion and the Son of God. Thus, by seeming to follow the comparative method and the ethnographic data wherever they led him, Frazer made many of his points by indirection while avoiding religious polemic, for which he had no taste. For all its masses of exotic facts, *The Golden Bough* is an attempt to employ the prestige of an objective "scientific" methodology to hammer the last nail into the coffin of Christianity in post-Darwinian Britain. His book was well received not merely because of its accomplished style but because there existed in 1890 an educated audience that was deeply interested in any work that promised to shed light on the question of whether religion remained viable as a guide to life.

As soon as *The Golden Bough* appeared, Frazer returned to Pausanias. (It is not wholly fanciful to see Frazer as a modern Pausanias: both share in a marked degree the qualities of digressiveness, curiosity, and a special interest in the religion, mythology, and customs of the past.) He traveled to Greece in 1890 and again in 1895, visiting the archaeological sites then being excavated in order to gather the most up-to-date information. As he labored, the commentary grew in a way that alarmed his publisher and foreshadowed the relentless ballooning of his later work. In 1898, some fourteen years after Frazer had begun, Macmillan finally brought out the six quarto volumes of

Pausanias's Description of Greece, which magisterially assembled and weighed all the evidence on the myriad of large and small archaeological, historical, and topographical questions that studded that author's problematic guidebook. Many believe it to be Frazer's most completely successful work.

Significantly, the only aspect of Pausanias that is scanted is the text—essentially that of Schubart, as emended by various hands—which Frazer chose not to edit. Instead, to his translation he merely appended a long list of textual variants and emendations. For Frazer, though an excellent scholar, the text was never of interest in itself, and although subsequently he twice returned to pure classical scholarship (Apollodorus' *The Library* and Ovid's *Fasti*), those works were chosen only because they lent themselves to the application of folklore and anthropology.

With Pausanias at last out of the way, Frazer returned to *The Golden Bough*, eager to revise it in the light of new information concerning the religious and social institutions of the Australian aborigines. These peoples, then regarded as the most primitive in the world, were thought to afford a glimpse into "the childhood of the race." It was the Australian evidence that impelled him in the second edition to the thesis with which he is most closely identified: that magic, religion, and science characterize the three successive stages in the evolution of the mind. Although *The Golden Bough*'s ostensible *raison d'être* is an explanation of a strange ritual combat that took place in the grove of Diana at Nemi, as the work relentlessly grew (from two volumes in 1890 to three in 1900 to twelve in 1911–1915), it became increasingly clear that Nemi existed merely as a peg from which Frazer might hang his immense excursus into the world's folklore and mythology, and that in fact he was stalking bigger game: nothing less than an analysis of the evolution of the human mind. Indeed, in the concluding pages of the third edition, Frazer finally acknowledged his true subject to be epistemology.

The years 1900–1914 Frazer dedicated to anthropology. He was especially preoccupied with the evolution of the institution of the sacred kingship in ancient and primitive cultures and the vexed question of the origins and meaning of totemism. On the first of these his most important work was *Lectures on the History of the Kingship* (1905), which emerged from an energizing series of discussions with A. B. Cook (1868–1952). Their collaboration marked the first time since 1894, the year of Robertson Smith's death, that Frazer had worked in a significant way with anyone.

During these same years Frazer also proceeded to distance himself from "ritualism"—the idea that ritual preceded (and therefore was more important than) myth in ancient religion, a position associated with Robertson Smith that he had seemed to endorse in the first edition of *The Golden Bough*. As he did so, ritualism was being enthusiastically embraced by a group of Frazer's classical colleagues who came to be known as the Cambridge Ritualists: Jane Ellen Harrison, F. M. Cornford, A. B. Cook, and Gilbert Murray (despite his being an Oxford man). They drew heavily upon Frazer's work but augmented it where in their view it was weakest, in sociology and psychology. Frazer saw all social change as the result of individual thought and effort. He implicitly assumed in the best British utilitarian tradition that the ancient/

primitive community was to be understood as an atomistic assemblage of competing selves; in psychology he likewise assumed rationalistic utilitarian motives, at least among those in the tribe who were least benighted mentally (the "primitive savants"). The Ritualists, on the other hand, combining the collectivist sociology of Emile Durkheim with the vitalism of Henri Bergson and the "animatism" of the English anthropologist R. R. Marett, came to understand primitive religious institutions as originating in collective manifestations and not as the products of individual ratiocination.

By 1914, in the conclusion of the third edition of *The Golden Bough*, Frazer had moved so far from ritualism as to endorse euhemerism as the best explanation of ancient religion. Needless to say, he became increasingly uncomfortable with the Ritualists, especially because they levied upon his work so freely. He made his views known unequivocally in 1921, when, in the introduction to his Loeb edition of Apollodorus' *The Library*, he went out of his way to disavow the Ritualists. This gradual but unmistakable evolution of his position on the origins, meaning, and relationship of myth to ritual fatally undermines any formulation that associates Frazer directly and closely with ritualism.

The publication of the great third edition of *The Golden Bough* brought Frazer recognition: a knighthood in 1914, fellowship in the Royal Society in 1920, membership in the select Order of Merit in 1925. The immense success of the one-volume abridgment he prepared in 1922 finally gave him the financial security he had long sought. It may be an indication of his deepest allegiances that as soon as he was relieved of money worries he immediately returned to the classics. Long a friend of James Loeb, he had been involved in the Loeb Library from its inception before the war; indeed, Loeb had asked him to be its first general editor. But Frazer, loath to leave his friend George Macmillan, was unwilling to assume the responsibility of directing the Loeb series. As noted above, however, he did edit two titles in it—*The Library* and *Fasti*—because they represented opportunities for anthropological and folkloristic commentary. Indeed, the *Fasti* was Pausanias all over again, with the copiousness of the commentary such that the narrow confines of the Loeb format could contain only a small part of it; Macmillan published the entire edition in five quarto volumes.

There is an important difference in tone and subtext between the Pausanias and Frazer's Loeb classical work of the 1920s. In the 1890s Pausanias had been a distinctly embattled author because twenty years earlier Wilamowitz concluded that the Greek traveler's account was an unreliable farrago of plagiarism and invention and accordingly he and his students carried on a lengthy anti-Pausanian polemic. Therefore, no one working on Pausanias at the time could remain neutral. As a result of his lengthy immersion in Pausanias, Frazer, normally the least combative of men, found himself engaged in a protracted battle that he found distasteful but in which he acquitted himself handily. (He had the great advantage of being right, for the archaeological evidence supported Pausanias nearly every time.) As a result he conceived a lifelong animus against Wilamowitz. By comparison the Apollodorus and the Ovid, although, like the Pausanias, still useful today, were anything but controversial, and as a result perhaps lack the decisiveness and emotional energy that sometimes result from intellectual tension.

The *Fasti*, completed when Frazer was seventy-five, was his last great achievement. He had suffered from eye trouble for many years, and suddenly in 1931 he went blind. When he learned that his sight would never return, Frazer gamely kept working for another decade with the help of readers and amanuenses, and even published an embryonic attempt at a fourth edition of *The Golden Bough*, entitled *Aftermath*, in 1936.

When he died from the degenerative effects of old age at the age of eighty-seven in 1941, his passing was not greatly mourned. In the 1920s Bronislaw Malinowski and A. R. Radcliffe-Brown had revolutionized anthropology by changing its focus from the comparative study of the evolution of institutions to the study of social structures in individual societies and by insisting on the importance of fieldwork as a *sine qua non* for any general formulations. By the 1930s Frazer had thus come to be seen as the incarnation of how *not* to do anthropology, and the decline in his reputation was precipitous and long-lasting. Only since the 1960s has Frazer's importance (to all but classics) come to be understood as essentially cultural in his contributions to the fund of significant images and metaphors of our time. Indeed, at moments he achieved truly prophetic stature as he plumbed the irrational side of the human psyche, albeit with some distaste, in cataloguing the "errors" that underlay religion. He outlived the era of Western intellectual, social, and political confidence that made his work on religion possible—his important contributions in that field were complete by 1914—and unhappily survived to see the recrudescence of that dark side in the Second World War.

Books

Totemism. Edinburgh, 1887.

The Golden Bough. 2 vols. London, 1890; new eds. 1900 [3 vols.], 1911–1915 [12 vols.]. Abridged edition. London, 1922.

Passages of the Bible. London, 1895.

Pausanias's Description of Greece. 6 vols. London, 1898.

Lectures on the Early History of the Kingship. London, 1905.

Psyche's Task. London, 1909.

Totemism and Exogamy. 4 vols. London, 1910.

The Belief in Immortality. London, 1913.

Folk-Lore in the Old Testament. 3 vols. London, 1918. Abridged edition. London, 1923.

Sir Roger De Coverley. London, 1920.

Apollodorus. The Library. 2 vols. Loeb Classical Library. London and Cambridge, MA, 1921.

The Gorgon's Head. London, 1927.

Publii Ovidii Nasonis Fastorum Libri Sex. 5 vols. London, 1929; text and translation
reprinted with abridged notes in one volume, Loeb Classical Library.
London and Cambridge, MA, 1931.

Garnered Sheaves. London, 1931.

Sources

Ackerman, Robert. *J. G. Frazer: His Life and Work.* Cambridge, 1987.

———. "Frazer on Myth and Ritual." *J. History of Ideas* 36 (Jan.–March 1975)
115–134.

———. "Sir J. G. Frazer and A. E. Housman: A Relationship in Letters." *GRBS* 15
(Autumn 1974) 339–364.

———. "J. G. Frazer Revisited." *American Scholar* 47 (Spring 1978) 232–236.

——— and W. M. Calder III. "The Correspondence of Ulrich von Wilamowitz-
Moellendorff with Sir James George Frazer." *PCPhS.* 204, n. s. 24 (1978)
31–40.

Besterman, Theodore. *A Bibliography of Sir James George Frazer, O. M.* London,
1934.

Douglas, Mary. "Judgments on James Frazer." *Daedalus* 107 (Fall 1978) 151–164.

Downie, R. A. *James George Frazer: Portrait of a Scholar.* London, 1940.

———. *Frazer and the Golden Bough.* London, 1970.

Gaster, T. H. *The New Golden Bough.* New York, 1959.

———. *Myth, Legend, and Custom in the Old Testament.* New York, 1969.

Hyman, Stanley Edgar. *The Tangled Bank.* New York, 1962.

Jarvie, I. C. *The Revolution in Anthropology.* London, 1964.

———. "Academic Fashions and Grandfather Killing—In Defense of Frazer."
Encounter 26 (April 1966) 53–55.

Jones, R. A. "Robertson Smith and James Frazer on Religion: Two Traditions in
British Social Anthropology." In *Functionalism Historicized.* Edited by G. W.
Stocking, Jr. Madison, WI, 1984: 31–58.

Leach, Edmund R. "Golden Bough or Gilded Twig?" *Daedalus* 90 (1961) 371–399.

MacCormack, Sabine. "Magic and the Human Mind: A Reconsideration of Frazer's
Golden Bough," *Arethusa* 17 (Fall 1984) 151–176.

Vickery, John. *The Literary Impact of the Golden Bough.* Princeton, 1973.

Papers

The two largest collections of Frazer materials (mainly letters) are those in the
Wren Library, Trinity College, Cambridge, and in the Macmillan Company
publishing archive in the British Library. The British Library also holds a
few of Frazer's notebooks. The important exchange between Frazer and his
friend Sir Edmund Gosse is to be found in the Brotherton Collection,
University of Leeds. The biography by Ackerman contains a complete list of
the locations of the papers.

Adolf Furtwängler

30 June 1853 – 11 October 1907

ANDREAS E. FURTWÄNGLER
Universität des Saarlandes

When the archaeologist Adolf Furtwängler died at the age of fifty-four in the Evangelismos Hospital in Athens, the loss was felt far beyond the boundaries of his own discipline. The famous French classical scholar Salomon Reinach declared that Furtwängler's character had possessed "la marque du génie" (Reinach: 309). Even Franz Studniczka, whose relations with Furtwängler had been distant and who had criticized his work, honored the deceased in these words: "Despite all his weaknesses, he was the greatest archaeologist of our . . . time" (Studniczka: 8).

Adolf Furtwängler himself had by no means felt predestined to a career in *Altertumswissenschaft*. On the contrary, he was at first undecided and remained so even during his first years at the university. Born in 1853 in Freiburg, he came into close contact with classical antiquity even as a child. His father, Wilhelm Furtwängler, a classical philologist and director of a Gymnasium in Freiburg, had devoted himself chiefly to Greek mythology and religion, and had also worked in archeology. The open and tolerant approach to religion that is evident in the last works (*Die Siegesgesänge des Pindaros* [Freiburg, 1859]; *Die Idee des Todes bei den Griechen* [Freiburg, 1857, 1860]) of this "unworldly humanist" (Schuchardt [1956]: 2) is indicative of the atmosphere in which the son grew up. Adolf Furtwängler's father and his deeply loved mother allowed him the greatest possible freedom for growth; for the development of his outstanding gifts as well as his impatient, angular, energetic, and unconventional character they provided the best possible environment.

By the fall of 1870 Adolf Furtwängler was already studying classical philology in his home town, Freiburg im Breisgau. On his father's advice he transferred to Leipzig in 1872 to work under Friedrich Ritschl and Georg Curtius, the true founder of comparative linguistics. As teachers, however, they roused no enthusiasm in him. "I simply felt that I could never work up any interest in such things . . . , but nevertheless

I continued to study philology" (Vita: 6). Furtwängler, however, was active in the "Free Student Union" and even considered a political career in the "German Progressive Party," the party that was working for democracy and parliamentary representation in Prussia and later, under the leadership of Eugen Richter, was to stand in opposition to Bismarck. "For at that time I still had no taste for actual scholarship" (Vita: 5–6). Even J. A. Overbeck, the leader of the school within archaeology that concentrated on art and mythology, just managed to awaken in Furtwängler some interest in the study of religion.

It was neither his teachers nor any scientific school that opened the way to a scholarly career for Adolf Furtwängler, but rather the Leipzig museum of plaster casts, which he often visited with his long-time friend Georg Loeschke and which filled him with enthusiam. "I felt how utterly I lacked any notion of a detailed understanding of forms, but I was resolved to acquire it" (Vita: 7). The necessary consequence of this decision was his transfer in 1873 to the University of Munich, where the important scholar Heinrich von Brunn, the founder of the art-historical school of German archaeology, was teaching. Here Furtwängler felt at home. He and Brunn both looked on archaeology as the study of the history of ancient art; this is undoubtedly one of the reasons that Furtwängler admired his teacher. Now at last Furtwängler's passionate temperament and his creative impulses (Brunn on Furtwängler: "He is all fire"—Curtius [1935]: 673) came to the fore—characteristics that undoubtedly helped to produce the flood of publications that was interrupted only by his death.

From the beginning Furtwängler's publications were noteworthy for their careful organization and extensive knowledge of the monuments. He had already laid the cornerstone for the latter in 1872–1873. "I set to work with a will on Stephani's Comptes-rendus [de la Commision Impériale Archéologique], which Papa took in. [I also went through] the whole of the Archäologische Zeitung as well" (Vita: 12). In Munich he was often to be found at the Staatsbibliothek, where he collected material for his enormous personal collection of data on monuments and discoveries, one of the largest such collections known to the archaeological world at that time. Adolf Furtwängler's method of working was rigorously economical; he made use of the most modern means that the age could afford him, especially photography, which had then recently come into fashion. Without a decidedly sharp visual memory, on the other hand, he could not have completed his dissertation (1874) in so short a time. This work, though traditional in its approach, already goes beyond the principles of his teacher. To be sure, the extensive material is treated, for the most part, iconographically, but the cautious stylistic classification upon which his total concept is based must be regarded as entirely novel.

In April 1875 Furtwängler was obliged to serve as substitute for his father, who had died in March of that year, at the Bertholdsgymnasium in Freiburg, where he taught Greek and Latin. "All [the other teachers] look on me as an arrogant man who is aiming at something higher," he noted regretfully (Vita: 20). The aspect of his character that was often interpreted as arrogance by those who knew him no better, was merely a cloak for his sensitive vulnerability; in the future this characteristic would often make life difficult for him. On the other hand, he now had an excellent opportunity to study "Pliny on the visual arts and his sources." A thorough and detailed study allowed him to distinguish Pliny's primary sources (Cornelius Nepos, Pasiteles, and Varro), the secondary sources (Mucianus), and Pliny's own additions. The study *Plinius und seine Quellen für die bildenden Künste* did not appear until 1877, whereas *Der Dornauszieher und der Knabe mit der Gans*, a work on scenes from everyday life in Greek sculpture that had been begun later but was supported by his study of Pliny, was published in 1876. Here he deals in depth with formal problems without, however, going beyond a traditional approach. His results are no longer convincing today, yet the style of these early works is as "easy and unconstrained as all that he later did" (Curtius [1935]: 673). Obviously this was understood in Berlin, for on the strength of his monograph on Pliny he was awarded stipendia from the Deutsches Archäologisches Institut that permitted him to travel in Italy and Greece for three successive years.

Furtwängler spent the years 1876–1878 in Italy and 1878–1879 in Greece. The numerous monuments of ancient art that lay yet unstudied in the museums, the almost infinite masses of generally ignored objects, the still unanalyzed material that lay scattered in countless private collections, were a challenge to Adolf Furtwängler's energetic classifying intellect. But it was not only the antiquities that inspired the twenty-five-year-old scholar. From now on all his love was focussed on Greece, "its landscape, which he declared to be the most beautiful in the world, its people, above all the Greek peasant, and its primitive lifestyle" (Curtius [1935]: 674). And it is not surprising that beneath this sun he succeeded in producing his first important pioneering works. In two beautifully illustrated works, *Mykenische Tongefäße* (1879) and the monograph *Mykenische Vasen* (completed in 1883 but not published until 1886), Furtwängler and his friend Loeschke first gave the world scholarly descriptions of the vases from Schliemann's excavations in Mycenae, as well as further sherd material from other excavations in Greece. The publications were unanimously hailed, and, though they are now superseded, they laid the foundations for our understanding of Mycenaean styles of decoration—foundations on which the great works of Furumark were later based.

Of greater importance for us today is his work on the Olympian bronzes, which he began in the same year, 1878. Ernst Curtius, director of the excavations at Olympia, had succeeded in recruiting Furtwängler as the stipendiary for his 1878 campaign. Furtwängler observed the stratigraphy of the site with painstaking accuracy, describing in detail the sequence of the strata, thereby securing important evidence for understanding the relative chronology of the site; this then became the basis for the study of an enormous mass of material. As early as 1879 he published a preliminary report: "Die Bronzefunde aus Olympia und deren kunstgeschichtliche Stellung," in which he confidently described and classified the formal characteristics of early Greek art and introduced a consistent use of the terms "geometric," "Mycenaean," and "oriental/orientalizing," which today are so indispensable as to seem self-evident. Adolf Furtwängler's study of early Greek art finally culminated in the fourth volume (1890) of the Olympia publications, a catalogue with commentary of the Olympian bronzes which is also a summary history of the art of early Greek antiquity. This volume is without doubt one of the most outstanding achievements of positivistic archaeological research, and it is consulted no less frequently today than in the past.

After his return from Greece in 1880, Furtwängler habilitated under Kekulé von Stradonitz and then taught as a *Privatdozent* in Bonn. One year later he advanced to the position of assistant director in the Berlin museums. At first he served in the Sculpture Department under A. Conze, but since Conze could not endure his all-too-direct, critical, and forthright manner, Curtius, who felt great sympathy with Furtwängler, had him transferred to the Antiquarium in 1882. During his fourteen years in Berlin, a period in which he played a large part in the rise of the Berlin museums (cf. Furtwängler's acquisition reports in AZ [1883–1885] and AA [1886–1895]), his productivity was nothing short of Herculean. For although many people would shrink from such a prospect, he delighted in working on and carrying forward as many tasks as possible, simultaneously and side by side (*in extenso*, see Zazoff: 206–212). Apart from numerous smaller works, Furtwängler's extensive catalogues of the Berlin collections are of particular importance. In his *Beschreibung der Vasensammlung im Antiquarium* (1885) he discusses over four thousand objects, describing them with painstaking accuracy and fitting them into a pioneering historical classification—that is, for the first time they are classified chronologically as well as by type-specific criteria. He dealt in similar fashion with the Antiquarium's collection of engraved stones, gems, and cameos, nearly twelve thousand in all; his catalogue (1896) was a sort of preliminary study for his epoch-making multi-volume work *Die Antiken Gemmen*.

Though these catalogues won unanimous acceptance and are esteemed even today as examples of catalogue work of the highest quality, the critical response to his *Meisterwerke der Griechischen Plastik* (1893–1895)—actually a polemic—was mixed. Among Furtwängler's colleagues a virtual polarization resulted between supporters and opponents of the book. Moreover, the criticism that the work received was motivated, in many cases, not only by scholarly disagreement. For along with Furtwängler's increasing mastery of an overwhelming mass of material came a certain inability to empathize with the more limited spectrum of his colleagues' professional knowledge, and thus his criticism could "appear hard and hurtful when he was merely going forward untroubled and regardless, clear in his own mind of the right way" (Bissing: 4). Clear indications of this harsher manner can already be detected in the catalogue of the Sabouroff collection (1884–1887), in which, for each of the different classes of monuments, disquisitions on art history alternate with discussions on the history of religion. Here Furtwängler, in accordance with his positivistically colored understanding of religious development, provides in his detailed introduction a history of the evolution of the Greeks' belief in the immortality of the soul. Derived though it is from animistic views, the introduction is still well worth reading today.

Though Furtwängler wrote his *Meisterwerke* in a partisan style that could not fail to "make the fur fly," the violence with which many scholars, such as Kekulé von Stradonitz, reacted to the book is surprising (cf. GGA [1895] 625–643). Furtwängler proceeded from the assumption that a great many Roman statues were copied directly from Greek originals or could at least be traced back to original Greek models; through precise formal analysis these originals could be assigned to Greek artists and artistic schools that are mentioned in the literary tradition. In any case, the assurance with which Furtwängler grasped the essential characteristics of the formal language of fifth- and fourth-century art is remarkable. And though it later became clear that many of his hypotheses were untenable and that, lacking the proper distance from classicism, he failed to understand the language of Roman classicizing sculpture, still his *Meisterwerke* influenced succeeding generations of classical archaeologists as did no other work on classical sculpture. It is also characteristic of Furtwängler that his truer insight allowed him to correct many false views—hence the liveliness of the discussion that the book provoked. Moreover, it was he who, in his paper "Ueber Statuenkopieen im Alterthum" (1896), introduced the necessary critical study of ancient copies. And how consistently he was right in these discussions is shown by the latest attempt to invalidate Furtwängler's reconstruction in the *Meisterwerke* of the "Athena Lemnia" (AJA 87 [1983]: 335–346). A close examination of the newly advanced arguments (*Jahrbuch der Staatl. Kunstsamml. Dresden* [1984]: 7–22; AJA 91 [1987]: 81–84) confirms the correctness of Furtwängler's reconstruction.

Today "Meisterforschung" (assignment of Greek originals or Roman copies to artists or artistic schools that are mentioned in the literary tradition), as it was practiced by Furtwängler, is generally viewed with great suspicion. Nevertheless, Furtwängler's *Meisterwerke* remains one of his most stimulating works.

Furtwängler could no more get over the attacks on his *Meisterwerke* than he could accept the fact that not he but Kekulé was appointed Director of the sculpture collection in 1889. He felt slighted and was deeply wounded, and not merely out of pride or blind ambition. Even in his youth he had admitted that "one of my fundamental failings is my constant readiness to believe that another is hostile to me or despises me" (*Vita:* 12).

In 1894 Furtwängler moved to Munich as successor to Brunn at the university; at the same time he was also appointed director of the Glyptothek and conservator of the vase collection and the plaster cast museum. Now began the twelve happiest and most independent years of his life. Devoted to his family, he derived great joy in particular from the musical talent of his son Wilhelm Furtwängler, the future conductor, to whose performances he listened with reverence. The memoirs of his daughter Märit, who later married the philosopher Max Scheeler, give a lively picture of these years.

His own research left him no time for careful classroom preparation, "but nevertheless the influence that radiated from him was overwhelming, because he always spoke from the abundance of his own experiences and his own work, with its continually new perceptions and discoveries, and because his enthusiasm was genuine" (Curtius [1935]: 684). He treated his pupils as his peers and presupposed that their knowledge was on a level with his own—an extreme incitement to learning. Several of his students later became distinguished archaeologists: Walther Riezler (diss. 1902), Ludwig Curtius, and the Balt Oskar Waldhauer (diss. 1903). Rudolf Hackl (diss. 1906), Georg Lippold, Eduard Schmidt (diss. 1907), and the Hungarian Antal Hekler published studies and dissertations in *Münchner Archäologische Studien* (1909), a Festschrift dedicated to Furtwängler's memory. Even Ernst Buschor, who began to attend Furtwängler's lectures in 1905, was so fascinated by his teacher that, as he later confessed, he felt utterly dependent on him.

Outstanding among the torrent of works that Furtwängler produced in his Munich years are the *Intermezzi* (1896), in which (*inter alia*) he establishes that portions of a sacrificial relief in the Louvre and portions of a relief in the Glyptothek depicting Poseidon and the marine Thiasos belong together, both coming originally from the altar of Domitius Ahenobarbus, and his *Neuere Fälschungen von Antiken* (1899), in which he gives proof of the sharpness of his eye. But the undisputed masterpiece of this period is *Die Antiken Gemmen* (1900). This is undoubtedly the most mature and, together with *Olympia IV*, the most important of his works; in many respects it is still valuable today. Furtwängler's partiality for ancient gems and engraved stones is due in part to the fact that this class of monuments, to a greater degree than any other, permits an overview of the totality of ancient art, from the ancient Orient to late antiquity, and can be described with art-historical methods of stylistic analysis. The first two volumes, which reproduce and discuss thousands of catalogue numbers, are rigorously organized by criteria of content, form, and chronology; the accompanying third volume is the actual synthesis, the brilliantly written historical survey of the art of stone-engraving in antiquity. At its publication the work was enthusiastically received, and it is still esteemed today as the "phenomenal achievement of its marvellously productive century" (Zazoff: 223).

As his last major task Furtwängler had selected Thorwaldsen's classicistic restorations of the Aeginetan pedimental sculptures in the Glyptothek; Furtwängler felt that Thorwaldsen's restorations had disfigured the statues, and he aimed to restore the pediments in accordance with their original plan. New evidence was required for such a large general project, and Furtwängler decided to excavate in Aegina. By 1906 his results, together with those of H. Thiersch and E. Fiechter, were published in *Aegina. Das Heiligtum der Aphaia*, a hastily prepared but exemplary work in which Furtwängler used old drawings by Cockerell and Haller as well as newly discovered fragments as evidence for the reconstruction of the pediment groups. Because of his early death, the plan to free the sculptures in the Glyptothek from classicistic additions and to achieve an accurate reconstruction of the pediments came to nothing. Not until much later did D. Ohly (*Die Aegineten I* [Munich, 1976]) succeed in removing the classicistic additions and producing an authentic restoration. Aside from a few minor differences, his reconstruction simply confirms the correctness of that sketched out in Furtwängler's drawings of 1906.

Despite Furtwängler's extensive knowledge of Roman art—as evidenced, for example, by his reconstruction of the Adamklissi *tropaion* (*Abhandlungen der Bayerischen Akademie der Wissenschaften* XII, vol. 3 [1903]: 455–516, *contra* O. Benndorf, *ÖJh* I [1898]: 122–137)—he never managed to feel close to it. Imbued with the liberalistic tendencies of the nineteenth century, he felt too intimately bound to "Hellenism."

The confidence with which the modern classical archaeologist deals today with Greek antiquities is due in no small measure to the fundamental researches of Adolf Furtwängler, who—in the words of L. Curtius—did for classical archaeology what Theodor Mommsen did for Roman history and Ulrich von Wilamowitz-Moellendorff did for ancient Greek literature.

Translated by Michael Armstrong

Books

Eros in der Vasenmalerei. Diss., Munich, 1874.

Der Dornauszieher und der Knabe mit der Gans. Entwurf einer Geschichte der Genrebildnerei bei den Griechen. Berlin, 1876.

Plinius und seine Quellen für die bildenden Künste. IX. Supplementband der Jahrbücher für Classische Philologie. Leipzig, 1877.

Der Satyr aus Pergamon. 40. Programm zum Winckelmannsfeste der Archäologischen Gesellschaft zu Berlin. Berlin, 1880.

Mykenische Tongefäße. With G. Loeschke. Berlin, 1879.

Königliche Museen zu Berlin. Beschreibung der Vasensammlungen im Antiquarium. Vols. 1 and 2. Berlin, 1885.

Mykenische Vasen. Vorhellenische Tongefäße aus dem Gebiet des Mittelmeeres. Berlin, 1886.

Die Sammlung Sabouroff. Kunstdenkmäler aus Griechenland. Vols. 1 and 2. Berlin, 1883–1887.

Olympia, die Ergebnisse der vom Deutschen Reich veranstalteten Ausgrabung. Band IV: Die Bronzen und die übrigen kleinen Funde von Olympia. Edited by E. Curtius and F. Adler. Berlin, 1890.

Meisterwerke der griechischen Plastik. Leipzig and Berlin, 1893. English translation: *Masterpieces of Greek Sculpture*. London, 1895; Chicago, 1964.

Intermezzi. Kunstgeschichtliche Studien. Berlin and Leipzig, 1896.

Königliche Museen zu Berlin. Beschreibung der geschnittenen Steine im Antiquarium. Berlin, 1896.

A Guide to the Glyptothek of King Ludwig I at Munich. Munich, 1896.

Denkmäler griechischer und römischer Skulptur. With H. L. Urlichs. Munich, 1898; revised 1904 and 1911. Japanese ed. Tokyo, 1986.

Sammlung Somzée. Antike Kunstdenkmäler. Munich, 1897.

Neuere Fälschungen von Antiken. Berlin, 1899.

Griechische Vasenmalerei. Auswahl hervorragender Vasenbilder. With K. Reichhold. Munich, 1900 et seq. (The work was continued after Furtwängler's death.)

Die antiken Gemmen. Geschichte der Steinschneidekunst im Klassischen Altertum.
Leipzig, 1900.

Ein Hundert Tafeln nach den Bildwerken der Glyptothek zu München. Munich, 1903.

Die Aegineten der Glyptothek König Ludwigs I. nach den Resultaten der neuen Bayerischen Ausgrabung. Munich, 1906.

Aegina. Das Heiligtum der Aphaia. With E. R. Fiechter and H. Thiersch. Munich, 1906.

Articles

Fifty of the most important articles are collected in *Kleine Schriften von Adolf Furtwängler.* Edited by J. Sieveking and L. Curtius. 2 vols. Munich, 1912–1913.

"Die Bronzefunde aus Olympia und deren kunstgeschichtliche Stellung." *APAW* (1879): 3–106 = *Kleine Schriften:* 339–426.

"Athene." "Atlas." "Atreus." "Chariten." "Dioskuren." "Elektra." "Eros." "Gorgones, Gorgo." "Gryps." "Herakles." *Ausführliches Lexicon der griechischen und römischen Mythologie I, 1–2.* Edited by W. H. Roscher. Berlin, 1884–1890.

"Eine altgriechische Porosstatue in München." *MDAI 21* (1896) 1–10.

"Ueber Statuenkopieen im Alterthum. Erster Theil." *ABAW 20* (1896) 527–588.

"Der 'Apollo Stroganoff'." *MDAI 25* (1900) 280–285.

"Ancient sculptures at Chatsworth House." *JHS 9* (1901) 209–228.

"Aphrodite Diadumene und Anadyomene." *Monatsberichte über Kunstwissenschaft und Kunsthandel.* 1 (4) (1901) 177–181.

"Über ein griechisches Giebelrelief." *ABAW 22* (1902) 99–105.

"Zu früheren Abhandlungen. I. Zu den marathonischen Weihgeschenken der Athener in Delphi. II. Zu den Tempeln der Akropolis. III. Zum Tropaion von Adamklissi." *SBAW* (1904) 365–417.

"Die Klassische Archäologie und ihre Stellung zu den nächstbenachbarten Wissenschaften." *Deutsche Revue* (January 1905) Sep. 1–14.

"Über griechische Kunst." *Deutsche Rundschau 31* (7) (1905) 44–59.

"Zu Pythagoras und Kalamis." *ABAW* (1907) 157–169.

"Die neue Niobidenstatue aus Rom." *SBAW* (1907) 207–225.

"Zur Einführung in die griechische Kunst. I." *Deutsche Rundschau 34* (5) (1908) 235–260; II. 34 (6) (1908) 357–379.

Sources

von Bissing, F. W. In *Münchner Neueste Nachrichten* (14 October 1907) 3–4.

Bulle, H. In *Allgemeine Zeitung* No. 188–189 (23–24 October 1907) Appendix.

Buschor, E. In *Geist und Gestalt, Biographische Beiträge zur Geschichte der Bayerischen Akademie der Wissenschaften I.* Munich, 1959: 276–278.

Church, J. E., Jr. "Adolf Furtwängler: Artist, Archaeologist, Professor." *University of Nevada Studies* 1 (2) (October, 1908) 61–67.

Curtius, L. *Badische Biographien VI.* Heidelberg, 1935: 672–685.

————. *Deutsche und Antike Welt*. Stuttgart, 1958: 111–115; 128–142; 174–177; 208–211; 334.

Döhl, H. *Heinrich Schliemann, Mythos und Ärgernis*. Munich and Lucerne, 1981: 46–47.

Greifenhagen, A. "Der Archäologe Adolf Furtwängler an den Berliner Museen (1880–1894)." *Jahrbuch der Stiftung Preußischer Kulturbesitz 1964–65* (1966) 136–39.

Hauser, F. *Süddeutsche Monatshefte* (1908) 461.

Helbig, W. *Neue Deutsche Biographie 5* (1961) 738–740.

Lullies, R. "Adolf Furtwängler." In *Archäologenbildnisse*. Edited by R. Lullies and W. Schiering. Mainz, 1988: 110–111.

————. "Der Archäologe Adolf Furtwängler im Kreise von Schülern und Wiener Kollegen, Wien 1905." *Opus Nobile, Festschrift U. Jantzen* (1969) 99–105.

Protzmann, H. "Antiquarische Nachlese zu den Statuen der sogenannten Lemnia in Dresden." *Jahrbuch der Staatlichen Kunstsammlungen Dresden* (1984) 7–22.

Reinach, S. [Obituary]. *Chronique des Arts. GBA Suppl.* (1907) 309.

Riezler, W. "Nekrolog auf Adolf Furtwängler." *Müncher Jahrbuch der bildenden Kunst* 2 (1905) [1907] vii–xi.

————. "Adolf Furtwängler zum Gedächtnis." *Süddeutsche Zeitung* 245 (12–13 October 1957).

Schuchhardt, W. H. *Adolf Furtwängler*. Freiburger Universitätsreden N.F. 22. Freiburg, 1956.

Sieveking, J. *Biographisches Jahrbuch für die Altertumswissenschaft* (145) 32 (1909) 119–131.

————. *Biographisches Jahrbuch und Deutscher Nekrolog* 12 (1907) [1909] 188–191.

Studniczka, F. *Neue Jahrbücher für das Klassische Altertum* 21 (1) (1908) 3–8.

Wegner, M. *Altertumskunde*. Freiburg, 1951: 273–277.

Weickert, C. AA (1954) 304–311.

Wolters, P. "Adolf Furtwängler. Gedächtnisrede gehalten in der Festsitzung der Kgl. Bayer. Akad. der Wiss. am 20 November 1909." *Süddeutsche Monatshefte* (1910) 90–105.

Zazoff, P. and H. *Gemmensammler und Gemmenforscher. Von einer noblen Passion zur Wissenschaft* (1983) 203–231.

Letters

Adolf Furtwängler, Briefe aus dem Bonner Privatdozentenjahr 1879/1880 und der Zeit der Tätigkeit an den Berliner Museen 1880–1894. Edited by A. Greifenhagen. Stuttgart, 1965.

Heres, G. "Zwei Briefe A. Furtwänglers." *FBSM* 14 (1972) 194–98.

Papers

Furtwängler, Adolf. *Vita 1872–1875*. (With unpublished autobiographical notes from 1878–79.)

————. *Tagebuch 1884–1886* [unpublished].

M. Furtwängler-Scheeler. *Erinnerungen* [unpublished manuscript 1966].

Letters to Furtwängler in the Archive, German Archaeological Institute, Berlin.

Basil L. Gildersleeve

23 October 1831 – 9 January 1924

WARD W. BRIGGS, JR.
University of South Carolina

A career as long and distinguished as that of Basil Lanneau Gildersleeve divides almost naturally into two quite distinct parts: the first, comprising two decades at the University of Virginia, is marked by dedication to teaching southern undergraduates, advancing southern causes, and maintaining his regional isolation; the second career, more than twice the length of the first, is marked by training professional classicists from across the nation, advancing American classical scholarship on the world stage, and enlarging his reputation in Britain and Europe. Always an advocate of his region's sectionalism, he was also a scourge of his nation's provincialism. His devotion to the South created a loyalty so intense that he eagerly fought on the Confederate side in the Civil War, but the concomitant isolation determined the nature of his career: "It prepared me for slow and scant recognition, which might have been slow and scant in any case, and it taught me to seek my solace in my work and to do that work without regard to the praise of man." In later life he spoke of his fear of having lost the great game, but if he could not see the general revival of his literary tastes nor the economic resurrection of his native region, he could well claim that the classical scholarship of his nation, after (and to an extent as a result of) his sixty years in the profession, was a significant factor in the world of learning. He was above all our most literary classicist at the same time that he was our most scrupulous and masterful grammarian, and he appeals to us today at least as much in the noble humanity of his style as in the humbling regality of his learning. At the time of his death, he could claim such pervasive influence in his own land as few scholars can: his edition of Pindar's Olympian and Pythian Odes was recognized as a standard commentary on these poems of the most vexatious classical poet; his *Latin Grammar* was still in print and widely used; the journal he founded, *The American Journal of Philology*, continued to hold the first rank among international classics journals and attracted the best contributors from this country and Europe. It is the more remarkable that each of these statements remains true today, some sixty-five years after his death.

He was the first classicist inducted into the American Academy of Arts and Letters, and his life's work was rewarded with honorary degrees from Harvard, Yale, Princeton, Oxford, and Cambridge. His motto all his life was "Grow, not climb" and he was proud of the fact that "all my honors came to me unsought," for his goal was to enlarge the world of classical philology, to improve it where possible, to correct it when necessary, without regard to whether his personal stamp were affixed or not, or whether his personal star rose any higher in the heavens.

If asked to select his own monument, Gildersleeve would likely have placed above these achievements the more than three score students whose dissertations he directed and the countless others whose lives he touched. His students were among our finest classicists: H. W. Smyth, Kirby Flower Smith, F. G. Allinson, C. W. E. Miller, A. T. Murray, H. L. Ebeling, H. R. Fairclough, Gordon J. Laing, John Adams Scott, G. L. Hendrickson, J. E. Harry, G. M. Bolling, L. L. Forman, and Gonzalez Lodge. Among the non-classicists touched by his teaching were John Dewey, Walter Hines Page, the publisher and diplomat, and the economist Richard T. Ely. The full range of work these men and others he taught accomplished can be seen in his *Festschrift, Studies in Honor of Basil L. Gildersleeve*, to which forty-four former pupils contributed. Through his students and, in turn, their students, the great work of his life lives on.

Paul Shorey applied to Gildersleeve Oliver Wendell Holmes' sly remark about the man who had chosen his ancestors well. His grandfather, Finch Gildersleeve (1750–1812), served with Washington at Valley Forge and, for his services to his native New York state, was given 1,200 acres of bounty lands. Finch's second son, Benjamin (1791–1875), Basil Gildersleeve's father, sold his interest in the family farm to pay his tuition at Middlebury College and Princeton Theological Seminary, intending to be a teacher. Since he had received some schooling at the Hopewell Seminary in Georgia, he sought his calling in the south and after two years' teaching in a classical school, he founded in 1819, the year before his ordination, the first of the several religious newspapers that he would edit. Following the death of his first wife, he gave up editing and became an itinerant preacher in Georgia and South Carolina, where he met and married his second wife, who died on their first anniversary in 1825. In 1827 he founded the *Charleston Observer*, which he edited in that city until 1845, when he moved his third wife and his five children to Richmond and merged his newspaper with another to form the *Watchman and Observer* and finally the *Central Presbyterian* (1856–1860). His father set the young Basil an example of the strong pull of religion, the willingness to fight for one's beliefs, the love of journalism, and his overriding sense of the duty of work, but the "doughty controversialist" wearied his son: "I was soon sated with controversy and have never had a relish for debates of any kind. If, however, one has to fight, it is well to hit hard." Fortunately, Gildersleeve needed to hit hard only rarely in his career and preferred the épée of wit to the claymore of diatribe.

Gildersleeve's maternal grandfather was Bazile Lanneau (1746–1833) of Bal-isle, Acadia, Canada. At the age of eleven Bazile had been deported to America with his family and many other Acadians. His entire family was lost to smallpox as they awaited permission to land at Charleston, and the boy was forced to make his way more or less alone at that tender age, refusing the support of Henry Laurens (1724–1792), a prominent Charlestonian and signer of the Declaration of Independence. By 1781 Bazile had acquired enough capital to open a small store, and by 1830 he owned eleven slaves. He was a notable patriot during the Revolution and afterwards served three terms in the South Carolina Legislature. His daughter, Emma Louisa (1805–1859), was, according to Gildersleeve, "a loving woman of quick sensibilities, who had a heart full of true religion and a head free from theology, true or false."

When Gildersleeve was born, America was still largely a frontier, and a frontiersman named Andrew Jackson was in the White House. The proudest bastion of civilization in the south was Charleston, South Carolina, Gildersleeve's birthplace. Pride in his natal city was a concomitant part of his innate sectionalism: "I was a Charlestonian first, Carolinian next, and then a southerner—on my mother's side a southerner beyond dispute." In his essay of 1891, "Formative Influences" (from which come most of the unattributed quotations that follow), he says of his Charleston period, "all that came after lay implicit in that first period." Gildersleeve grew up in a storybook city full of exotics, patricians, slaves, politicians, poets, and the other stimulations of a cosmopolitan port. By the age of thirteen he had yet to leave the city, and, like his future mentor and friend Friedrich Ritschl, he had been entirely educated by his father. "My lessons were heard at odd hours, often when my father was tired from work; and hard was the work that would tire that heroic soul. . . . I could read when I was between three and four years of age, and I signalized the completion of my fifth year by reading the Bible from cover to cover." The precocious boy read Virgil, Horace, and other Latin authors "before the time when boys of to-day [1891] have fairly mastered the rudiments," and at the age of twelve he made a translation of Plato's *Crito* and of Anacreon. This early introduction to Greek gave him a double advantage in his subsequent career, for he not only had a headstart on others in the field, but he was able the more easily to learn other languages as well. Thus the depth of knowledge and breadth of reading evident in the "Brief Mention" essays was acquired early. He picked up French, German, and Spanish as a boy, and his father encouraged him to read Milton, though he condemned the "immoral" Shakespeare, as he did any novel by any author.

In 1844 Gildersleeve entered the College of Charleston, where he remained one year. His natural bent was for literature, and he quickly discovered that "composition in prose did not give me half the pleasure that versification did," but he soon after realized that, though he had what he called "the poetic temperament," he was nevertheless "unblest with poetic power." He continued to court the Muse all his life, though she seems to have graced him but periodically. The first entries in his bibliography are two poems for a children's newspaper in Charleston; the last is a sonnet to South Carolina written in his ninety-second year.

The family moved to Richmond after Gildersleeve's year at the College of Charleston, and "my Presbyterian father sent me to a Presbyterian college, although I pleaded for the University [of Virginia]." It was Jefferson College (now Washington and Jefferson College) in Canonsburg, Pennsylvania, where Gildersleeve was bored by the classwork and appalled at the unseriousness of the students. After a year at Jefferson, he begged to go to Yale, where a beloved uncle had gone and where his father had once intended to go, but instead he was sent to his father's alma mater, Princeton, entering at the age of fifteen and in 1849, at the age of seventeen, graduating fourth in a class of seventy-nine.

Even at Princeton, the instruction was "hit-or-miss" and an insufficient challenge: "I gave a couple of hours to my classes each day, and then ho! for the wide field of literature—English, French, German, Italian, Spanish." One day while hunting with his Greek professor, his rifle accidentally discharged in his face. Sitting beneath a tree while a doctor was summoned, and "with the affected stoicism of a boy, I sent up to my room for a copy of the Everlasting Yea, if the worst came to the worst. I did not know the pretty anecdote of Solon, who wished to know the last sweet thing of Sappho's before he died." One permanent result of the incident was a scar that he covered with a magisterial beard all his life.

It was at this time that Gildersleeve began his "Teutonomania" ("There was no such thing as Anglomania then"), and particularly his devotion to Goethe. He read Goethe as a student at Princeton and in Germany, and, for a time following the death of his mother in 1859, Goethe supplanted Gildersleeve's deep-set religious convictions: "Goethe's aphorisms were my daily food. I committed my favorite passages to memory. I repeated them over and over to myself in my long solitary rambles, and Goethe was my mainstay at a time when my faith had suffered an eclipse." His heart knit briefly with a comrade in the war who quoted Goethe and was later killed. Goethe remained a source of comfort and inspiration (and allusion) for Gildersleeve throughout his career.

His sixty-five-year teaching career began at the private academy of Socrates Maupin in Richmond, where Gildersleeve taught for a year, saving the money for his pilgrimage to Germany and beginning a long, semi-autobiographical novel. To polish and quicken his own knowledge before passing it on to his students, he made himself compose in Latin and Greek, and here were planted the seeds of his later teaching method and his successful Latin series: "The necessity of close observation, the necessity of formulating rules, first for my own guidance, then for the guidance of my pupils, made me in time a fair grammarian, and has given me my only claim to have contributed something to the science of my chosen province" (SBM: 614). As long as Gildersleeve taught, he taught one course in composition per year and recommended composition as an excellent way to learn a language (Allinson, 134).

At last Gildersleeve set off for Germany, determined to complete his novel and experience his *Wanderjahre*, while incidentally enhancing his classical education. He arrived in Bremen by tobacco boat in 1850 "an imaginative, impulsive, *prime-sautier* boy, proud, shy, self-conscious," and on the day of his matriculation at Berlin for the winter semester 1850–1851 his life was altered by meeting August Böckh, whose "teaching made a passionate classicist out of an amateurish student of literature." "It was a great thing for an American boy to see scholars in the flesh," he later wrote (BM: 141), and in a Lucianesque essay entitled "Professorial Types" (1893) he limned his German teachers for us as an American boy saw them, with much amusement, but with much more admiration. Gildersleeve promptly abandoned his novel and, for the moment, his other literary ambitions under the influence of Böckh's dictum that "Grammar is the highest problem of science." He also studied with Johannes Franz (1804–1851), "the first real teacher of Greek I ever had," and Friedrich August Maercker (1804–1889). With only five Americans at Berlin that semester, including William Dwight Whitney (1827–1894), Gildersleeve felt isolated and awed by the great capital, and out of a "desire to migrate from university to university to preserve a freedom from bias," he moved to the friendlier Göttingen for the Easter Term 1851. There he roomed with three old friends from Charleston and the Bostonian George Martin Lane (1823–1897), who would become professor of Latin at Harvard, and whose son, Gardiner Martin Lane (1859–1914), would marry Gildersleeve's only daughter. He took courses from Karl Friedrich Hermann (1804–1855), the Platonist Heinrich Ritter (1791–1869), and Friedrich Wilhelm Schneidewin (1810–1856), "one of my favorite teachers."

He moved to Bonn for the spring semester of 1852 and the winter semester 1852–1853, where he studied with Ritschl, who welcomed him into his home and became a correspondent, Joseph von Aschbach (1801–1882), F. G. Welcker (1784–1868), Franz Ritter (1803–1875), and the young Jacob Bernays (1807–1881), who "led me into the study that resulted in my doctoral dissertation." Among his fellow-students were Johannes Vahlen (1830–1911) and the man with whom he would form a sixty-year friendship, Emil Hübner (1834–1901).

Gildersleeve returned to Göttingen to defend his dissertation, De Porphyrii studiis capitum Homericis trias, and to swear his oath on the Ides of March, 1853. After a brief European tour, he sailed for home with a paucity of prospects and a multiplicity of impressions of his German friends and teachers.

For three years he pursued his ambition "to be a poet or failing that to be a man of letters" by writing free-lance articles, re-working his novel, and resuming his relations with the Charleston literati, particularly those in the circle of the novelist and man of letters William Gilmore Simms (1806–1870). Though offered a job at Princeton, he considered it "so far inferior to what I, a conceited youngster, deemed my due as a Ph.D. with high honours from a German university, that the negotiations were broken off with some show of anger on both sides." Instead, through his old friend John R. Thompson (1823–1873), the editor of The Southern Literary Messenger, he met Edgar Allan Poe and heard him read "The Raven" in Richmond. He wrote some lengthy review articles, "tasted the salt bread of tutorship in a private family" near Charleston for one winter, and helped his father with the Watchman and Observer. "School room and printing office have been parts of my life from the beginning until now." The critic and the professor both intend to instruct and persuade, and the connection seems not only clear, but, for an understanding of Gildersleeve's career, crucial, as this period of essentially literary activity fostered aspects of Gildersleeve's career that made him unique: not only his literary sensitivity and critical ability, but also the rare and precious gift of a fine literary style.

"Fortunately for my reputation an opening in the University of Virginia closed my career as a novelist," Gildersleeve wrote to Whitney in 1858. At Virginia, Greek and Latin had both been under the purview of Gessner Harrison (1807–1862), who had been a recent medical graduate when Thomas Jefferson appointed him in 1828 to succeed the University's original classicist and Harrison's mentor, the Englishman George Long (1800–1876). Wearied after thirty years of teaching all the Greek and Latin, the most populated discipline, Harrison demanded that his chair be split and that he be given the Latin courses. In May of 1856 the professorship was divided into a chair of Latin, assumed by Harrison, and a chair of Greek and Hebrew, to which the Board, after surmounting the only objection raised against Gildersleeve's candidacy, that of his "non-Virginian name," elected the twenty-four-year-old, who wrote, "My only regret was that I was in port so early."

"Let us imagine," Gildersleeve wrote in 1879, "a young man fresh from the best German schools. . . . Our young friend begins his novitiate either as a tutor in one of our large universities, or as a professor in some half-endowed college. The transition is one of the most painful that can be imagined. . . . He comes from the best in quality and the richest in resource to our average. In the meagerly furnished library he misses his favorite books, or rather books which by frequent citation he seems to know; . . . He has no one who will suffer him to talk about the themes of his personal research . . . His duties are eminently distasteful." Though he loved the university and treasured his years there, he began his career with an acute sense of the distance that lay between this university, begun only thirty years before at the edge of Indian country, and the venerable lecture-halls of Berlin, Göttingen, and Bonn, in the center of European intellectual life. As a consequence both of his youth and his isolation, he wrote almost nothing for publication in these years; "I planned several books, but finished none, and never wrote a line for the press, or appeared before the general public in any way, from the date of my election until 1863—seven long years." In his presidential address to the American Philological Association in 1878 he defended his dedication to teaching at the expense of publication: "It were not only foolish but criminal to measure a professor's efficiency simply by his written work. There is often a sublime self-denial in the resolute concentration of a teacher on the business of the class-room; and the noiseless scholarship that leavens generation after generation of pupils is of more value than folios of pretentious erudition. It was with profound insight that the Greeks called higher study by the same name as personal intercourse. To the Greek, university students were οἱ συνόντες [disciples] and he who has made faithful use of this power of personal influence shall have his reward, even if he has nothing to show in black and white" (E&S: 95–96).

But Gildersleeve's superior learning and bearing did not make his early career in Charlottesville easy. In 1856 a student wrote home to his father "Prof. Gildersleeve, our new Prof. of Greek does not succeed very well. He is young and there is room for improvement. Though a man of ability he cannot impart his knowledge well to his class" (H.C. Allen to John Allen, University of Virginia Archives # 9780). He was even rebuked by the faculty for rudeness to a student and was reputed to have been uncivil to some local ladies.

Moreover, he had fallen into immediate conflict with his colleague Harrison. Gildersleeve's up-to-date scientific training clashed explicitly with Harrison's atavistic English humanism, and among alumni and others connected with the University there was considerable resentment of Gildersleeve's intellectual domination of this beloved figure even after Harrison had retired in ill health in 1859, just three years after Gildersleeve's arrival: When Gildersleeve resigned to go to Johns Hopkins in 1876, an editorial in a Richmond newspaper crowed, "Now we shall have the Greek of the Greeks, not the Greek of Gildersleeve."

The years before the war were devoted to class work and the reading of primary texts, largely without benefit of commentaries and reference works, rare to find in the antebellum South. But as he kept one eye on the students of Virginia, he kept another on the scholars of Germany, maintaining his correspondence with his student-friend Emil Hübner and managing to return to Europe in 1860, just before the start of the Civil War, to visit his old teacher Ritschl, whom he recalled in a loving memoir of 1884.

Gildersleeve's love of his native region allowed him no hesitation in enlisting for the Confederate cause in April of 1861. He saw himself in the tradition of Lachmann, who "dropped his Propertius to take up arms for his country," and of Reisig, "who annotated his Aristophanes in camp, and everybody knows the story of Courier, the soldier Hellenist" ("Southerner in the Peloponnesian War" 338). Gildersleeve's three brothers enrolled as well, and his father, aged 70, enlisted in the Richmond Home Guard. All five survived, though Benjamin (1834–1921) was a prisoner of war for nearly a year. Basil claimed to have earned "the right to teach Southern youths for nine months . . . by sharing the fortunes of their fathers and brothers at the front for three." His war service, which he called "desultory," included stints as aide-de-camp to General Fitzhugh Lee in 1861, as a private in the First Virginia Cavalry in 1863, and finally as an aide on the staff of General John B. Gordon during General Jubal T. Early's campaign in the Shenandoah Valley in the Summer of 1864. It was while carrying orders during a skirmish at Weyer's Cave near Staunton, Virginia, on 25 September 1864 that his thigh was shattered by a Spencer bullet. "I lost my pocket Homer, I lost my pistol, I lost one of my horses, and finally I came very near to losing my life by a wound which kept me five months on my back."

He was treated at the field and brought to "Hillandale," the estate of Raleigh Colston, a wealthy wheat farmer of Albemarle County, Virginia, near Charlottesville, who had given his large home over as a convalescent hospital for Confederate soldiers and who had enlisted his three beautiful daughters as nurses. The wound and the limp that Gildersleeve retained as a result for the rest of his life added to the romantic picture of this Southern Paladin: to one, he fought "like some veteran of Fabius who had striven to do his part towards driving the Carthaginian invader from his native soil" (P. A. Bruce), while to another he "had shown that he could emulate the courage of the heroes of Hellas as successfully as he could expound the intricacies of their beautiful language" (R. H. McKim).

He later wrote a friend, "The close of the war left me poorer by four years—I had nothing much else to lose—and a broken leg. Of course while I was wounded I had nothing better to do than become sentimental. When I began to convalesce I fell in love and in 1866 I was married." Gildersleeve left "Hillandale" "after five months of racking pain," telling Colston he would return one day to marry one of his daughters, and on 18 September 1866, he duly married Elizabeth Fisher Colston (1846–1930). The marriage produced a son, Raleigh Colston (1869–1944), and a daughter, Emma Louise (1872–1954).

From 1861, when Harrison's replacement, Lewis Minor Coleman, had been killed in the field at Fredericksburg, Virginia (indeed, the only two faculty members even touched by gunfire in the war were the two classicists), Gildersleeve taught a full complement of Latin as well as Greek courses. He had begun at some point, either before or during the war, to collect examples for a complete syntax of all departments of Greek (the fruits of which survive in a notebook dated 1874 in the Johns Hopkins *Nachlaß*), for he had long desired to express fully his strong disagreements with the most commonly used grammar, R. Kühner's *Ausführliche Grammatik der griechischen Sprache* (Gildersleeve used Curtius instead). In addition, W. W. Goodwin, his colleague at Berlin and his chief rival for supremacy as the greatest American hellenist of the day, had before the war published his *Syntax of the Moods and Tenses of the Greek Verb* (1859), which was widely praised. In light of the need to provide for his new wife, his experience teaching Latin during the War, and the greater need for Latin texts than for Greek, he converted his outline from Greek to Latin and produced in 1867 his *Latin Grammar*. Following the original publication, by Richardson & Co., the man for whom Gildersleeve was carrying orders when he was wounded, General John B. Gordon, began (with Horace Greeley and August Belmont of New York) the University Publishing Co., dedicated to producing a series of textbooks for Southern students written by Southern teachers. Gildersleeve happily obeyed his old commander's new orders and produced an entire Latin Series, with an exercise book (1871), primer, and a reader (both 1875).

Though the *Latin Grammar* began from a translation of the German of Lattmann, Gildersleeve made it unique by the clarity and logic of its structure, by the brevity and acuity of his definitions, rules and the like, and by the wit and approximation to the original Latin style of the translations, all prepared with his decade of experience in teaching Southern undergraduates. Few who have used the grammar fail to have their favorite passages, such as his observation that there are as many subjunctives as there are frames of mind, and as many frames of mind as there are minds to frame. The grammar remains an indispensable source and is still in print today.

Gildersleeve's grammar won its author renown in the South, but only there. He was awarded an honorary degree by William and Mary in 1869 and gratefully wrote the president of that institution that he regarded the award "only as a tribute to endeavour, not to attainment . . . so noiseless and even and unobtrusive has been the discharge of my duties." In another letter he quoted the words of Ovid's *Tristia*, 3.4.25: *Bene qui latuit bene vixit.*

The spring of 1875 brought two momentous changes in Gildersleeve's life. The first was the visit to Charlottesville of Daniel Coit Gilman (1831–1908), the designated president of the projected Johns Hopkins University in Baltimore, Maryland. He was searching American colleges and universities for faculty and his eye fell upon Gildersleeve. His first choice for a classicist was Goodwin of Harvard, who, like Lane, whom Gilman also tried to attract, was so encumbered with undergraduate teaching that he was not free to do research. Goodwin declined and suggested Gildersleeve, as did Lane and Whitney. Gilman and Gildersleeve met formally in Washington to discuss the position, and a few days later Gildersleeve became the first faculty appointment to the new university.

The second event was the death of his father in Tazewell, Virginia, at the age of eighty-four. Of this he wrote to Hübner, "So long as the father lives, the son is not in the front and the whole aspect of life is strangely altered when the headship is changed." Gildersleeve was about to alter his life significantly.

The enormity of these two events almost obscured a third, the publication of his school-text of Persius, "a vacation study," he wrote to a friend, "undertaken simply for the purpose of replenishing a lank purse." The first-century A.D. satirist appealed to Gildersleeve because of his moralism, his bookishness, his obscurity, and, of course, his humor. Persius' association with Attic Comedy and his literary kinship with Lucian appealed as well. The first of Gildersleeve's commentaries sets the pattern for its two successors: a learned but sprightly homiletic introduction chiefly emphasizing the biographical and the prosodical, which he considered some of his best writing, with notes and commentary that on the one hand constantly looks at the relationship of the poem in question to the collection as a whole, and on the other hand treats obscure matters of grammar with brevity and clarity. The volume remains serviceable to any student of satire.

Gildersleeve and The Johns Hopkins University were in many ways an ideal match. The university was the first in this country to be founded explicitly on the German model, with graduate study in the academic professions a priority, along with the publication of journals and the creation of a university press to serve not simply the faculty but academics throughout the world. Such a concept required staff who were not only products but partisans of the German system. A second agreeable aspect was the provision in Johns Hopkins' will that set aside free scholarships for students from Maryland, Virginia, and North Carolina. President Gilman eagerly desired an eminent southerner for this new university in a Civil War border state, and Gildersleeve obviously found the sympathies both of the administration and the city congenial.

At last he could upgrade his level of work. In 1875–1876, Gildersleeve taught three levels of Greek—four hours per week of senior Greek and three hours each for juniors and intermediates—with the constant composition of lectures and grading of exercises and examinations, in addition to a private reading course that accompanied each class. He also was in charge of the post-graduate studies and was obliged to teach Hebrew upon demand. A student called it "Socrates trundling a baby carriage." Though he was a professor of Greek, his Latin series, which he called "decided failures" and his edition of Persius were his only book-length publications.

The man whom Gildersleeve credits with relieving him of the burdens of this position, the man for whom he accomplished his greatest legacies, his *Pindar* and the *American Journal of Philology*, the man who kept him from further squandering his talents and education, who would take up the role of guiding his career virtually from the moment his father died, and the man he referred to as "the head of the house," was Daniel Coit Gilman. Indeed, as is clear from their correspondence, Gildersleeve loved Gilman second only to his family, and expressed his devotion by seeking advice and sharing confidences, advertising The Johns Hopkins and interviewing students, and searching out faculty, not only for the Latin chair, but also for the chairs of English and German. Gildersleeve later reflected that his sense of "happiness and usefulness," if not his entire career, was due to Gilman, and Gilman's resignation in 1901 was a deep blow. Gildersleeve said of his chief: "Wherever he appeared there came light and hope and confidence. His wide vision was matched by the discernment of spirits which is the secret of power, his marvellous resourcefulness by his wonderful sense of order."

At his last commencement in Charlottesville, the students gave a resounding call for their Grecian, and Gildersleeve responded with a touching farewell, whose last words were: "To the University I shall give my allegiance, her fame is mine, and her lofty standard of morals, her unswerving adherence to truth and purity, and all high and noble learning shall be my standard forever."

With this farewell he exchanged Charlottesville's rural ease for Baltimore's urban activity, the "absolute independence" of his Virginia position for the synergistic effort to found Gilman's idea of a university, which Gildersleeve said "was the same as a Presbyterian's idea of heaven, namely, 'a place where meetings ne'er break up and congregations have no end.'"

With the translation to Johns Hopkins and his second career launched, his perspective changed: the sense of duty to preserve the values of his region became a duty to advance the contributions of his nation, which he performed as adamantly in the pages of *AJP* as he had performed the former in the pages of the *Examiner* and numerous southern journals. He was now himself on a national stage and charged with the responsibility of putting American classics on an international stage. His shorter publications had been in regional or state journals, he had visited Europe more often than New York, and he had not even joined the American Philological Association (founded in 1870), though encouraged by its secretary, his old Berlin colleage W. D. Whitney.

His first tasks were to set a curriculum, stock the library, and populate his seminary. His first class comprised Ernest Gottlieb Sihler (1853–1942), who received the first Ph.D. in Greek given by Hopkins and went on to a long career at New York University (1892–1923); Alexander Duncan Savage (1848–1935), a student of Gildersleeve's at Virginia who had helped check references in the *Latin Reader*, who went on to various posts in libraries and museums; John Henry Wheeler (1850–1887), who took a Ph.D. from Bonn in 1879 and went on to positions at Bowdoin and the University of Virginia before his premature death; and Walter Hines Page (1855–1918), from rural North Carolina, who stayed only two years before embarking on a career in journalism during which he was editor of the *Forum* (1891–1895; to which Gildersleeve contributed "Formative Influences"), the *Atlantic* (1895–1899; to which Gildersleeve contributed three articles), and the *World's Work* (1900–1913). He also founded the publishing firm of Doubleday, Page (1899) and later was appointed Ambassador to the Court of St. James (1913–1918). With this sterling group assembled, Gildersleeve was sent by Gilman on the first day of classes into a bare classroom with but one instruction: "Radiate."

From the outset, Gilman wanted each department to publish a journal, and Gildersleeve began at once not only the establishment of the *American Journal of Philology* but also the establishment of his scholarly credentials in the presence of the nation's best scholars and in print by gathering some fruits from his reading and note-taking of the past two decades. To do so, he presented a paper on εἰ with the future indicative and ἐάν with the subjunctive in the tragic poets at a session of the APA meeting (at which Goodwin was to preside) in New York on 18 July 1876. He then agreed to host the 1877 meeting in Baltimore and at that meeting was elected president for 1877–1878. For that occasion he needed another scholarly paper and so enlisted the help of his Fellows in counting the frequency of the articular infinitive in the Greek orators, upon which he based his address at the 1878 convention in Saratoga, New York.

In the midst of all this he had to finish his edition of the *Apologies* of Justin Martyr, begun in Charlottesville for the Douglass Series of Christian Greek and Latin Writers at the request of F. A. March of Lafayette College. It was the last outgrowth of his strict, perhaps fundamentalist, religious upbringing and shows the last traces of the cast of mind evident in the essays of the 1860s in which he scored the paganism of Julian, Marcus Aurelius, and Apollonius of Tyana. But the translation to John Hopkins meant an enlargement of his views and a mellowing of his fervor. Consequently, his notes are chiefly historical and grammatical, with theological matters "touched as lightly as possible." Clearly Gildersleeve's wide reading in the fathers of the Christian church yielded numerous syntactic examples of the various usages. His structural analysis of argument, employed also in his Persius and Pindar, is here again, as Gildersleeve makes plain that the grammar illuminates the argument, and analysis of both reveals the author's meaning. It is a valuable commentary today and presages much of his later grammatical work. Gildersleeve made only three hundred dollars for being, as he put it, "chained for two years to Justin Martyr by my friend Professor

March," and as he and his wife were planning how to spend it, the bank in which they had deposited the money failed.

With the program established, *Justin Martyr* published, and the APA hosted and led, the journal could at last be got underway. The prospectus announced that the journal would have three main parts: it would contain articles on all branches of philology, not just classical; it would contain reports on articles in foreign journals, since many were not held in American libraries; and it would contain reviews by American specialists. However, just as the establishment of Johns Hopkins was looked upon with suspicion by the universities who thought their faculties would be plundered to staff the new enterprise, so the prospectus for the *AJP* was greeted with scorn in those quarters where it was felt that the journal would draw contributors away from *Transactions of the American Philological Association*, our only classics serial. It would be twenty-five years before another American classics journal would be founded.

But Gildersleeve braved the doubters and with incredible energy pressed on to drum up contributions from the leading men of America not only in classics but in all fields of philology. "It certainly betokens great supineness on the part of our scholars that a country which boasts a Journal of Speculative Philosophy should not have even a solitary periodical devoted to a science which counts its professed votaries by hundreds, if not by thousands, and that our professors and teachers should be satisfied with consigning an occasional paper to the slow current of a volume of transactions or exposing a stray lucubration to struggle for notice amidst the miscellaneous matter of a review or the odds and ends of an educational magazine" (*E&S*: 98). It must have seemed the fulfillment of his boyhood dream to be a journalist and/or editor, as when he worked for his father's editorial offices in 1845–1846. "If I had not been a philologian, I should have been a journalist and I can understand the fascination of the life. One can hardly be both—as I know by sad experience." But he came as close as he could, not only contributing popular reviews and articles on classical subjects to the *Nation*, but, beginning in volume 5 (1884) his quarterly column "Brief Mention," which he maintained for 37 years, until 1921.

The prospectus was mailed in May 1879 and by October he had 217 charter subscribers. The first issue of *AJP* appeared 1 January 1880. Pride of place in the first number was given to the Eliot Professor of Greek Literature at Harvard, Goodwin (who never contributed again), with Gildersleeve's own "Encroachments of μή on οὐ in Later Greek" following after, "wrung from me by the necessity of making a beginning with the Journal, most of my friends having left me in the lurch" (*AJP* 3 [1882] 195 n. 1).

The necessity of acquiring foreign contributions was made plain to him from the first, and so, when Gilman sent him to Europe in the summer of 1880 to find a Latinist and other faculty, he used the opportunity to advertise his journal. He met J. P. Mahaffy in Dublin, the editor John Tulloch, the Sanskritist Julius Eggeling and the mathematician P. G. Tait at St. Andrews, the classicist and vice-chancellor of Manchester, Joseph Gouge Greenwood, Jebb, Ingram Bywater (see *AJP* 38 [1917] 392–410), Robinson Ellis, and Lewis Campbell at Oxford, the Plautine scholar

Wilhelm Studemund and the professor of English literature Bernhard ten Brink at Strassburg, and the historian Hermann Eduard von Holst at Freiburg. He spent nearly a month in London with access to prominent clubs and their members. He was received at Bonn, Leipzig, Berlin, Dresden, and Munich, where he secured a European distributor for *AJP* and renewed old acquaintances. He received promises of contributions from Jebb, Campbell, J. B. Mayor, Henry Nettleship, and Ellis, though Mayor never contributed, but with the exception of the very best men, he could find no one suitable for an American classroom, for he sought the particular combination of qualities that made a man first of all a great teacher, secondarily a great scholar: industry, intelligence, sensitivity, and attractiveness. He finally realized that the learned of Europe were not the best suited to training our young men and that the American character may after all be best for combining the needs of science and teaching in one personality: "An audacious, inventive, ready-witted people, Americans often comprehend the audacious, inventive, ready-witted Greek *à demi-mot*, while the German professor phrases, and the English 'don' rubs his eyes, and the French *savant* appreciates the wrong half. No nation is quicker than ours to take in the point of a situation, and there is no reason discernible why Americans should not excel in the solution of the most subtle problems of antique manners and politics" (*E&S*: 105).

His friend Hübner in 1881: "My own life has not been a success from the philological point of view but I think I can do something towards helping the new generation to better things." He actively involved his students in his work and contributed numerous reports from the seminary to the *Johns Hopkins University Circulars*. He continued to prise contributions out of his friends and to make the journal a vehicle for his own work: In the years 1880–1885 he contributed five major articles on syntactical matters, twenty-one reviews, four notes, and a long reminiscence of Friedrich Ritschl. In this same period, he also published the articles "Athena Parthenos" in *Harper's*, "Grammar and Aesthetics" in the *Princeton Review*, six entries for Liddell and Scott's Greek Dictionary, and thirteen reviews for the *Nation*. Having written three commentaries in ten years and at the height of his powers at age fifty-four, he would not publish another book until he was nearly seventy.

His edition of Pindar's *Olympian and Pythian Odes*, "another nail in the coffin," as he called it, was published in 1885. Like his other two commentaries, it provided a lengthy (100 pages) biographical, literary, grammatical and prosodical introduction with notes stressing the grammatical. Its goal was usefulness for the student, not primarily enlightenment for the specialist. Nevertheless, this quite practical book made it clear to readers everywhere that Gildersleeve was, as an English reviewer said, "a true master of Greek grammar and syntax." Gildersleeve felt that "the fruitful study of Pindar lies through synthesis, not through analysis," and in this he pays homage to his great mentor, August Böckh, a pioneer in treating these poems as parts of an organic whole. Gildersleeve considered his central task "the endeavor to follow the evolution of the poet's thought and the correspondence between form and content" (JHU Circulars no. 287 [July 1916] 35). Gildersleeve's comments on Pindar's subject matter, style, and art ("His song does not fly on and on like a bird of passage. Its flight is the flight of an eagle, to which it has often been likened, circling the heavens, it is true, stirring the ether, but there is a point on which the eye is bent, a mark, as he says, at which the arrow is aimed" [xxv]), on approaches to understanding the poet ("The fact is, a man who has read himself into Pindar is a poor judge of the relative difficulty of the odes unless he has made actual trial in the class-room, and the experience of most lovers of Pindar has of necessity been limited, as Pindar has seldom been read in our colleges." [lxiii]), his metre, dialect, and, of course, syntax. "It is intended for beginners . . . , " he wrote Hübner, "I have had no time to work at it except at night when I was tired out or in the hot early summers and I am afraid that the book betrays my fatigue as well as other things." Occasionally, late at night, Gildersleeve may have "read himself into Pindar" too much, as when the Confederate veteran writes "The man whose love for his country knows no local root, is a man whose love for his country is a poor abstraction; and it is no discredit to Pindar that he went honestly with his state in the struggle. . . . A little experience of the losing side might aid historical vision" (xii). Some lapses of style rankled one English critic, particularly Gildersleeve's description of Pindar's "earliest poem [*Pythian* 10], which is an arrangement in God and blood" (*Saturday Review* 60 [22 August 1885] 261) and surely moderns will not be charmed by his characterization of Corinna, as showing "the sweet inconsistency of her sex." Nor will Gildersleeve's advocacy of the metrical schemes of J. H. H. Schmidt, which rely perhaps too heavily upon musical analogy and which were most notably vitiated by another former Schmidtean, John Williams White, be of service to scholars of today.

Upon publication, the book was scarcely noticed in America, while English and German reviewers were "decidedly frigid." The first to warm to the book were the Italians L. Cerrato and G. Fraccaroli, and then the British Pindarists, R. Y. Tyrrell, his student J. B. Bury, and particularly C. A. M. Fennell, also an editor of Pindar, who supported "the method of seeking the organism of the Odes in their strophic structures" (*Ibid.*). Subsequent editions by Wilhelm von Christ and Otto Schroeder as well as the Loeb translation by Sir John Sandys, declare the influence of Gildersleeve's commentary. The Europeans, however, led by A. B. Drachmann and Wilamowitz, objected to some of Gildersleeve's "overstrained historical interpretations and fanciful attempts to establish a mechanical unity in the several Odes," and reverted to studying the various odes individually. Even twenty-five years later, he still felt trepidation awaiting Wilamowitz's response to his article on the Seventh *Nemean*.

As the book was a commercial failure, the publisher did not commission a companion volume on the *Nemeans* and *Isthmians*, yet the volume remains useful for scholars and indispensable for students (and in print) over a century after its initial publication.

The exhausting work on Pindar was the watershed event of his second career. From now on, his scholarly energies would be almost exclusively directed to the *AJP*, as he realized that the life of scholarship enjoyed by his German teachers and colleagues, who enjoyed state support for their grand projects and who had considerable freedom from teaching, would never be available to him. For a time he still managed to publish his syntactical studies on the final sentence in Greek (1883–1884), the consecutive sentence (1886), the articular infinitive (1887), and participles (1888), all of which point toward the *Syntax* that C. W. E. Miller was taking agonizingly long to check and correct for the press. As he saw the failure of his plans for editions of Aristophanes' *Frogs* and Plato's *Symposium*, and as a projected series of commentaries edited by himself and Benjamin Ide Wheeler of Cornell fell through, he managed only to revise and reprint his Latin textbook series with the help of his pupil Gonzalez Lodge. The great burst of original work that followed the appointment to Hopkins had drained him, and his production began to decline as his reputation grew. Having been President of the APA, he was offered the directorship of the American School for Classical Studies at Athens, was given honorary degrees by the University of the South (Sewanee) (1884), Harvard on its 250th anniversary (1886), Yale on its 200th (1901), Cambridge, and Oxford (both 1905). His family continued to flourish. His daughter Emma married Gardiner Martin Lane, the son of his old Göttingen classmate, the Harvard Latinist George Martin Lane, and his son Raleigh became a prominent architect, whose most notable designs were for two buildings at Princeton University.

His lifelong sense of duty compelled him to serve the nation's needs as he saw them without regard to achieving the kind of personal glory that accrued to his counterparts in Germany and England, Wilamowitz and Jebb. Instead he devoted the remainder of his life to three areas: 1) his teaching; 2) his editing of *AJP*; 3) his public role as, in Paul Shorey's words, "the ideal type of cultured and scholarly American" (Shorey: 142).

Like Housman, Gildersleeve saw himself first and foremost as a teacher. Contrary to the notion that teaching is ephemeral, Gildersleeve found it eternal: "Much of our science passes away: the theory of to-day pushes away the theory of yesterday, to be thrust away in turn by the theory of to-morrow. One by one books, like men, drop into the night, and shade is lost in shadow. What is not lost, what lives forever, is the spirit of love to learning and love to the learner, which, once kindled, passes from teacher to learner, onward to the end of time" ("Friedrich Ritschl": 355). Scholarship and publication was for him the natural outgrowth of teaching, as he learned when he prepared for classes at Maupin's Academy in 1849. His eight o'clock (A.M.) lectures at the University of Virginia on historical Greek grammar were the source of much later publication: "Many of the formulae reached during twenty years of teaching were deposited in the notes of my edition of *Justin Martyr* (1877), and much that I have written since is little more than a justification of rules and principles established or verified in the course of my class-work."

He taught only the authors of Attic Greek: Thucydides, Plato, Aristophanes, Sophocles, and the orators, particularly Lysias and Demosthenes. He did not teach Homer because we know so little of his period that we cannot reconstruct his culture as fully as we can that of the fifth century; he did not teach authors who survive in fragments. He was interested in Euripides but never taught and rarely mentioned Aeschylus. In all of his courses, the emphasis was on understanding the author's style. As one of his students put it, "He seemed to care little for what Plato said, but he was immensely impressed by the way he said it" (Scott, xxiii). He also seemed to care little for secondary bibliography or for explaining the rapid fire of allusions that characterized his discourse.

A strict teacher, barely forgiving of errors, he believed that the devil inhabited dry places and so habitually followed discourse on arid technical matters with a characteristic joke. As previously mentioned, he was an advocate of composition, particularly the simultaneous translation into Greek of church sermons as an anodyne to boredom. In his sixty years of teaching he was never late to class, never missed a class, and only once cancelled his seminar at Johns Hopkins (the day after the Rotunda at the University of Virginia burned), setting his students an example of discipline and devotion that many carried as an ideal for the rest of their lives. His vast knowledge of literature enlarged not only their appreciation of Greek grammar, but also the world of European and American literature. His student Francis Allinson wrote, "I have always felt, in my own modest attempts at scholarly work, that Gildersleeve was there, looking over my shoulder and ready to castigate any intellectual laziness or slovenly inaccuracy" (Allinson: 133–134). In *Hellas and Hesperia*, his 1909 lectures at the University of Virginia to inaugurate the Barbour-Page Foundation Lectures, Gildersleeve touches on the central feature that made him so effective a teacher: "A man who simply raves about the glory that was Greece and the grandeur that was Rome is one for whom the real lover of antiquity has little respect. A man who exhausts his English vocabulary in extolling a Greek orator and mistranslates the passage that he selects for especial comment is worse than the infidel who does not believe in Greek. . . . Specialization may readily degenerate into what is the worst characteristic of our guild, specialization in the interest of personal vanity, . . . No truth stands alone, and the most effective work is done by those who see all in the one as well as one in the all . . . The scholar of this type has life in himself, and has it so abundantly that he can communicate it to others. The principle may be mysterious, it may be undefinable, but it is no less patent for all that" (*Hellas and Hesperia*: 46).

Gildersleeve had at first imagined that he would edit *AJP* for only ten years, after which another man would take over. When no successor appeared in 1890, however, he resigned himself to the "ball and chain," as he called it, that would be his for the next thirty years. At length, "after decades of ploughing in grammatical furrows and stubbing the waste lands adjacent thereunto, I found myself hankering after the key of fields in which I disported myself in the early years of my long life of endeavour" (*SBM*: 396). He had found a way to continue his scholarship while at the same time exercising his journalistic impulse to express his views on the relation of ancient and modern literature, on the state of the profession, and on the value of American work in a form that was, among classicists, uniquely his own.

When the *AJP* was young, an excess of books and a paucity of space and reviewers led Gildersleeve to create a section of the journal initially called "Lanx

Satura," later changed to "Brief Mention." In these pages, he, and occasionally others, wrote brief reviews of notable books, but it gradually became the editor's own vehicle for essays on personal reminiscences, literary analogies, or historical precedents that would elevate the column to new heights, while the impulse for the essay, "the bit of cork with which I try to float my trimestrial net" (AJP 28 [1907] 217), was often lost in the tide of learned allusions and graceful digressions. Some little criticism was directed at the essays for being on the one hand too recondite and on the other for being simply a rehash of his classroom notes. But most recognized that, from his "seat on the backdoorsill of the journal," Gildersleeve produced little Alexandrian jewels of learning and wit which were often the items in the journal that readers would turn to first. There is scarcely a reader today who can dip into Miller's collection, *Selections from the Brief Mention of Basil Lanneau Gildersleeve* (=SBM) without profit and pleasure.

With the founding of the English *Classical Review* in 1890, many of his British contributors defected, but by this time the field was sufficiently built up in this country (largely through Gildersleeve's efforts) that native work of excellent quality could sustain the journal into the twentieth century. In 1905 the founding of *Classical Philology* and *Classical Journal* gave him some pause, but he suppressed his anxiety: "It is a droll thing that an antique secessionist like myself should be called to support the national standard of an American journal," he wrote to a friend.

His role on the larger public stage is his third sphere of activity in this period. He contributed a magisterial introduction to H. Cary's translation of Herodotus (1899), which he considered "one of the best things I ever wrote," and he wrote the entries on classical authors for *Johnson's Universal Cyclopedia* (1893–1897). He continued to be the public embodiment of proper philological endeavor, which he defined in addresses such as "The Spiritual Rights of Minute Research" (1895) and "Oscillations and Nutations of Philological Studies" (1901).

Increasingly an international figure, he also became known as an apologist for the Old South of his young manhood. Horace E. Scudder, the editor of the *Atlantic*, commissioned from him the essay by which he is perhaps most widely known outside his field, "The Creed of the Old South," which first appeared in the *Atlantic* in January, 1892. Gildersleeve had written Scudder that "even the most charitable of my Northern friends find it difficult to understand how a Southerner could have gone into the conflict with a clean conscience." He set out to show that many Southerners were men of true honor, whose theory of government "had become what is called a faith and where there is faith there is conscience." Gildersleeve had stridently and passionately defended the Southern cause (while attacking Southern problems) in his editorials in the Richmond *Examiner* while the war was being fought, and he was happy to gather up his views again after the passage of a quarter century.

"Begun as mere literature and finished under the pressure of strong emotion," the essay begins by recounting his war experiences. He recalls the proud mien of a captured Yankee officer, who was clearly a gentleman of the sort many Southern officers prided themselves upon being. A young Southern captain, a lover of Goethe, with whom Gildersleeve rides to the front is suddenly killed. From these vivid memories and others, Gildersleeve resurrects the sense of duty and local patriotism that brought intelligent Southerners into the conflict, particularly his dearest friend David Ramsay (1830–1863), even though he "was . . . utterly at variance with the prevalent Southern view of the quarrel and died upholding a right which was not a right to him except so far as the mandate of the State made it a right." "To us, submission meant slavery, as it did to Pericles and the Athenians. . . . where does submission begin? . . . That is a matter which must be decided by the sovereign; and on the theory that the States are sovereign, each State must be the judge." He once put forth the view that the whole war was fought on a point of grammar: The North says "The United States is . . ." and the South says "The United States are . . ." Because southern politicians had a tradition of debating before the masses on courthouse greens, all southerners were keenly aware of the issues and went to battle with clear understanding. In the end, it is a question of the local patriotism Gildersleeve learned as a boy in Charleston: "Take away this local patriotism and you take out all the color that is left in American life." Slavery itself, the great question of the war, was probably doomed in any case, but it was part of the southern way of life, rightly or wrongly, and it had to be defended. The cause was "civil liberty, not human slavery," but with the war over, "we have learned to work resolutely for the furtherance of all that is good in the wider life that has been opened to us by the issue of the war, without complaining, without repining."

The essay was immediately popular, called by the *Nation* "A poetical view of the Southern cause in the Civil War." William Archer in *America To-Day* (London, 1900: 121) called it, "an essay—one might almost say an elegy, so chivalrous in spirit and so fine in literary form that it moved me well nigh to tears," and it was taken as a serious historical document by J. F. Rhodes in his *History of the United States* (New York, 1904: 5:350).

Five years later, his former student Walter Hines Page was editing the same magazine and, recalling Gildersleeve's love of historical parallels, commissioned "A Southerner in the Peloponnesian War," a cunning collection of coincidences between the Peloponnesian and American Civil War. The war was a good time to study classical literature generally, since few new books got through the Yankee blockade and few books were reprinted in the Confederate states. With training in Greek and Latin so widespread in the South, it was not uncommon to find soldiers re-reading the ancients in the field, and it is Gildersleeve's thesis that knowledge of the elder conflict enlarges our understanding of the recent one; while conversely the firsthand experience of war does much for one's understanding of Thucydides.

Beginning in 1891, at age 60, following another suggestion of Page, Gildersleeve began to sum things up in a series of autobiographical articles, beginning with "Formative Influences" and continuing with "Professorial Types" and "A Novice of 1850." With these articles he lay before the public his view of himself, fulfilling the legend of scholar, soldier, patriot, and teacher.

Finally, in 1900, came the long-awaited first part of the *Syntax*. The framework, which he had devised forty years earlier, then adapted for his Latin grammar, had been re-adapted for Greek as early as 1882. Gildersleeve turned back to the project in 1885, following completion of his *Pindar*. In 1891 Johns Hopkins assigned him his former student Charles William Emil Miller (1863–1934) as his special assistant for the express purpose of doing "the detail work" of the *Syntax*. But Miller took such exquisite pains with the checking and was slowly given so many additional duties involving *AJP* and classroom instruction, that Gildersleeve finally had to realize that he would never see his complete syntax in print.

The 190 pages of the first part are devoted to the syntax of the simple sentence as found in Attic Greek, with examples arranged in reverse chronological order, from Demosthenes back to Homer and by genre, beginning with the orators, "the standard of conventional Greek, we have worked backward through philosophy [chiefly Plato; Aristotle is left out] and history to tragic, lyric, and epic poetry, comedy being the bridge which spans the syntax of the Agora and the syntax of Parnassus" (iv). The book is notable for the clarity and ease of use of its arrangement and for the copiousness of its examples, though an English reviewer remarked that the formulas must be so familiar to Gildersleeve that some of the more elliptical explanations may be clear only to their author. He cites the sentence "the pluperfect is sometimes used to denote rapid relative completion," asking the meaning of "relative" (CR 16 [1902] 178). But the majority of the explanations are marvels of lucidity, e.g., on the use of cases in exclamations: "the nominative *characterizes*, the vocative *addresses*, the accusative implies an *object of emotion*, and the genitive the *source or sphere of emotion*" (*Syntax*, 3). Within its somewhat limited scope, the number of matters treated and the number of quotations surpassed both the revised Kühner that he had despised at Virginia, and even his erstwhile American rival Goodwin's *Moods and Tenses of the Greek Verb*.

The preface makes plain that the project arose from the wishes of his students to put down in final form the precepts he had taught for so long. Consequently the book was a synthesis of his syntactical writing in *AJP*, his commentaries, and his classroom lectures, with many new examples. The *Syntax*, published in the same period as the grammatical work of Goodwin and of Goodwin and Gildersleeve's student Herbert Weir Smyth (1857–1937), realized the long dream, once thought impossible, of American preeminence in the field of Greek grammar. The volume was also Gildersleeve's greatest personal scholarly triumph. He was finally widely reviewed in his beloved Germany, though his style and puckish wit led one S. Witkowski to call him the "naughty boy of Greek syntax" while Hans Meltzer, in the same journal, called him the "Marc Twain der griechischen Syntax" (BJ 159 [1912] 13, 310).

Nevertheless, the strain of Miller's slowness obliged him to put much of the work he intended for the *Syntax* into reviews or in such articles as "Problems in Greek Syntax" (1902), "Temporal Sentences of Limit in Greek" (1903), and "Notes on the Evolution of Oratio Obliqua" (1906).

Finally the Second Part, on the simple sentence expanded, appeared in 1911. The strain of the relationship shows in the limited breadth of the book, though among its features is a treatment of the article, chiefly done by Miller. But the frustration of working with his assistant meant that the project could not go forward, and in 1912 Gildersleeve wrote a friend, "[Miller's] deliberation and meticulousness are the real cause of the abrupt termination of our joint work on the Syntax." Thus we shall never have Gildersleeve's treatment of oblique cases, prepositions, infinitives and participles, the subjects planned for the third part, much less his treatment of compound and complex sentences. A nearly obsessive proofreader and hater of errors, his life's work was stalled by one even more scrupulous than he; one who had often longed in print for the exactitude of the German masters of his youth now found in extreme old age an exactitude in his assistant that prevented the realization of his dreams of raising American accomplishment in his field even higher.

Gildersleeve's physical bearing, at six feet tall and 200 pounds, had always reinforced his overwhelming learning. Two accounts by former students give similar testimony. Wrote the first: "Inseparable, in fact, from his invincible scholarship was his imposing physical personality. His tall and well proportioned figure was the normal support for his Olympian head with the dominating eyes, humorous or devastating as the occasion demanded" (Allinson, 281). In a similar vein Miller wrote, "he was not only distinguished looking but handsome. . . . His face was usually animated with a genial smile, but, at times, there was a stern, forbidding look that might strike terror into the heart of even the boldest student. He was heavily bearded, and in his sterner moods recalled to members of the philological guild the figure of the Olympian Zeus" (SBM: xxix).

But after sixty years of uninterrupted teaching, it was the body that betrayed Gildersleeve with cruel afflictions, confining, but not hampering the mind that remained as sharp as ever: the brilliant talker was kept from conversation by the failure of his ears and the voracious reader was kept from his books by the cataracts that dimmed his eyes. Although Gilman had urged him never to resign, he retired from his chair as Francis White Professor of Greek in his eighty-fourth year, continuing to edit AJP through volume 40 (1919) and to write "Brief Mention" until 1920. As night fell figuratively and literally, he turned again to the composition of sonnets for his friends. The deaths of friends and colleagues, and particularly of Gilman in 1908 and of his son-in-law Gardiner Lane, in 1914, depressed him, as did the intimation of his own mortality in the form of a massive heart attack on 29 February 1916. The illness of his wife and his own infirmity prevented him accepting Wheeler's offer of a Sather Lectureship in Berkeley, but he was increasingly adored by students and non-students old and young and became the subject of newspaper articles in Baltimore and New York as he approached and achieved his ninetieth year.

On 9 January 1924, Gildersleeve died in Baltimore at the age of 92 of a bronchial infection and was buried in Charlottesville in the University Cemetery on 14 January. The gravestone at Plot 58 gives his chosen epitaph, from a fragment of Aeschylus (265 Nauck): διαπεφρούρεται βίος, which he translated "Life's bivouac is o'er."

It was a career rich in rewards and, unlike that of nearly any scholar of his magnitude, was remarkably free from enemies. Such complaints as he voiced about his career stemmed from the lateness with which he, a southerner, was recognized by his northern colleagues, and the lateness with which he, an American, was noticed by his European colleagues. A man with all the clear-cut prejudices of his age, region, and station, Gildersleeve nevertheless felt himself a victim of the prejudice of others. But he also allowed that he suffered with foreign readers because of what he called his "kaleidoscopic" style, which made him as devilish for Europeans to read as he is delightful for readers of English. His style of thought is noted for the density of its reference and quotation and for the dazzling leaps he makes from topic to topic. His prose style is noted for his mellifluous compound sentences with extended balanced cola, bold Americanisms, and particularly "Biblical phraseology . . . because I can cling to the altar of the Authorized Version and feel myself fairly safe" (SBM: 41). Hans Goelzer, reviewing *Problems in Greek Syntax* and referring to a remark of Sainte-Beuve's, wrote "Il y a aussi 'un poète mort jeune' à qui le grammarien survit" (*REG* 16 [1903] 287) and A. Martin in *RPh* 29 (1905) 167 wrote of him, "Ce grammarien est cependant toujours un peu poète."

Gildersleeve enjoyed referring to himself and his fellow grammarians as γωνιοβόμβυκες, or "corner-hummers," but he was "imbued with the conviction that the study of syntax is of the utmost importance for the appreciation of literary form" (*Syntax*, iv), for "it is the literary man in me that seeks the aid of the grammarian at every turn. . . . To follow the r-sound is as thrilling to the lover of languages as a voyage in the track of Odysseus from the throat of the Cyclops to the lips of Penelope" ("Spiritual Rights"). Though it was his pleasure to compare himself to Greek figures of the second rank, the grammarian Diotimus, Lucian's *Hireling Professor*, and "the lame Spartan schoolmaster Tyrtaeus," comparisons with Nestor and Zeus were common both before his death and since. Shorey compared him to his advantage with the greatest Hellenists of England and Germany, Jebb and Wilamowitz, and noted that birth and experience had given him the four "elements" necessary for greatness in our field: "the solid earth of German erudition, the murmur of the oceanic waters of our English inheritance, the nimble and eager air of French esprit, and the elemental American fire clasping all strongly in its warm embrace" (Shorey, 143).

Gildersleeve himself should have the last word, and one that characterizes his wit, charm, and *selbstironie*. It is a sonnet that he wrote for a friend in 1915:

B. L. G.

His nature was remotely kin to Puck;
His efforts to be witty some called frantic;
Had he been gifted with the spirit mantic,
He would have sunk into the common rut.

Pierian roses he essayed to pluck;
He fluttered round Parnassus' peaks gigantic.
He wrote some papers for the old Atlantic,
But with his literary venture had no luck.

He was the author of a Latin grammar
By many schoolboys vehemently cursed,
Whose imprecations stopped not at doggone it.
His muse was feeble, but he would not damn her;
He loved her to the last as at the first
And died while getting up a parlous sonnet.

Books

De Porphyrii studiis Homericis capitum trias. Diss., Göttingen, 1853.
Latin Grammar. New York, 1867; rev. ed. New York, 1872; rev. and enlarged by
    Gildersleeve and Gonzalez Lodge, New York, 1894.
A Latin Exercise-Book. New York, 1871; rev. ed. 1873.
The Satires of A. Persius Flaccus. New York, 1875; reprinted, New York, 1979.
A Latin Reader. New York, 1875.
A Latin Primer. New York, 1875; rev. ed. by Gildersleeve and Chapman Maupin,
    New York, 1882.
Pindar. The Olympian and Pythian Odes. New York, 1885; reprinted 1890.
Latin Grammar, School Edition. With G. Lodge. New York, 1898.
Latin Composition. With G. Lodge. New York, 1899; 2d ed., 1904.
Key to Latin Composition. With G. Lodge. New York, 1899; 2d ed., 1904.
Syntax of Classical Greek, Part I. With C. W. E. Miller. New York, 1900; reprinted
    Groningen, 1980.
Hellas and Hesperia, or The Vitality of Greek Studies in America. New York, 1909.
Syntax of Classical Greek Second Part. With C. W. E. Miller. New York, 1911.
The Creed of the Old South. Baltimore, 1915.

Articles (Collected)

Essays and Studies. Baltimore, 1890; New York, 1924; New York, 1968.
Selections from the Brief Mention of Basil Lanneau Gildersleeve. Edited by C. W. E.
    Miller. Baltimore and London, 1930.

Articles (Classical)

"The Legend of Venus." *Southern Review* (Baltimore) 1 (1) (April 1867) 352–382 =
    E&S 161–205.
"Xanthippe and Socrates." *Southern Review* (Baltimore) 2 (3) (July 1867) 172–200 =
    E&S 209–248.
"The Emperor Julian." *Southern Review* 3 (5) (January 1868) 179–209 = *E&S*
    355–398.
"Apollonius of Tyana." *Southern Review* 4 (7) (July 1868) 94–125 = *E&S* 251–296.
"Lucian." *Southern Review* 6 (12) (October 1869) 389–426 = *E&S* 299–351 and
    Library of Southern Literature 4:1799–1804.

"A Word or Two on Comparative Syntax." *Educational Journal of Virginia* 1 (4) (February 1870) 97–101.

"The Grammarian's Tools." *University Monthly* 2 (2) (February 1872) 36–38; 2 (3) (March 1872) 56–58; 2 (5) (May, 1872) 103–105. Part 3 reprinted in *Educational Journal of Virginia* 3 (9) (July 1872) 333–337.

"On the Steps of the Bema: Studies in the Attic Orators." *Southern Magazine* (= *New Eclectic Magazine*) 12–13 (n.s. 5–6) (April, May, June, July, August, September 1873) 395–404, 559–569, 664–671, 4–22, 129–137, 272–283.

"On εἰ with the Future Indicative and ἐάν with the Subjunctive in the Tragic Poets." *TAPA* 7 (1876) 5–23.

"Contributions to the History of the Articular Infinitive." *TAPA* 9 (1878) 5–19.

"Encroachments of μή on οὐ in Later Greek." *AJP* 1 (1880) 45–57.

"On ΠΡΙΝ in the Attic Orators." *AJP* 2 (1881) 465–483.

"Notes from the Greek Seminary: I. The Articular Infinitive in Xenophon and Plato; II. οὐ μή." *AJP* 3 (1882) 193–202; 202–205.

"Athena Parthenos." *Harper's New Monthly Magazine* 64 (April 1882) 666–674.

"Studies in Pindaric Syntax: I. The Conditional Sentence in Pindar; II. On AN and KEN in Pindar; III. Aorist and Imperfect."*AJP* 3 (1882) 434–445; 446–455; 4 (1883) 158–165.

"ΕΣΤΕ, ΙΝΑ, ΟΠΩΣ, ΟΥ, ΜΗ, ΠΡΙΝ." *Liddell and Scott's Greek Lexicon*, 7th ed. Oxford, 1882.

"Note on the Seventh Edition of Liddell and Scott's Greek Lexicon." *AJP* 3 (1882) 515–516.

"Weiske on the Articular Infinitive." *AJP* 4 (1883) 241–242.

"Symmetry in Pindar." *JHU Circulars* no. 25 (August 1883) 138–140.

"On the Final Sentence in Greek." *AJP* 4 (1883) 416–444; 5 (1884) 53–73.

"Friedrich Ritschl." *AJP* 5 (1884) 339–355.

"The Consecutive Sentence in Greek." *AJP* 7 (1886) 161–175.

"The Articular Infinitive Again." *AJP* 8 (1887) 329–337.

"On the Stylistic Effect of the Greek Participle." *AJP* 9 (1888) 137–157.

"On the Article with Proper Names." *AJP* 11 (1890) 483–487.

"The Construction of ΤΥΓΧΑΝΩ." *AJP* 12 (1891) 76–79.

"On εἰ with the Future Indicative, or Statistics and Statistics." *JHU Circulars* no. 99 (June 1892) 102–104. Repr. "Brief Mention," *AJP* 13 (1892) 123–125.

"Aristophanes," "Euripides," "Hesiod," et al.." *Johnson's Universal Cyclopaedia* 8 vols. New York 1893–1897.

"My Sixty Days in Greece: I. The Olympic Games, Old and New; II. A Spartan School; III. My Traveling Companions." *Atlantic Monthly* 79 (February, March, May 1897) 199–212, 301–312, 630–641.

"Introduction." In Henry Cary, *The Histories of Herodotus*. New York 1899: iii–xviii.

"Problems in Greek Syntax." *AJP* 23 (1902) 1–27, 121–141, 241–260; reprinted Baltimore 1903.

"Temporal Sentences of Limit in Greek." *AJP* 24 (1903) 388–407.

"Notes on the Evolution of Oratio Obliqua." *AJP* 27 (1906) 200–208.

"A Syntactician among the Psychologists." *AJP* 31 (1910) 74–79.
"The Seventh Nemean Revisited." *AJP* 31 (1910) 125–153.
"Usque recuret MH." *AJP* 33 (1912) 447–449.
"Paulus Silentarius." *AJP* 38 (1917) 42–72.

Articles (Reviews)

"B. Delbrück, *Die Grundlagen der griechischen Syntax.*" *AJP* 2 (1881) 83–100.
"Friedrich Mezger, *Pindars Siegslieder.*" *AJP* 2 (1881) 497–501.
"Josef Sturm, *Geschichte Entwickelung der Constructionen mit prin.*" *AJP* 4 (1883)
     89–92.
"Bruno Keil, *Analecta Isocratea.*" *AJP* 6 (1885) 107–109.
"Theodor Mommsen, *Römische Geschichte*, Fünfter Band." *AJP* 6 (1885) 483–486.
"W.G. Hale, *The Sequence of Tenses in Latin.*" *AJP* 8 (1887) 228–231.
"F.W. Schmidt, *Kritische Studien zu den griechischen Dramatikern.*" *AJP* 10 (1889)
     87–91.
"C. Ritter, *Untersuchungen über Platon.*" *AJP* 10 (1889) 470–480.
"Peter Schmitt, *Ueber den Ursprung des Substantivsatzes mit Relativpartikeln im
     Griechischen.*" *AJP* 14 (1893) 372–376.
"Hermann Usener, *Götternamen.*" *AJP* 17 (1896) 356–366.
"Hermann Usener, *Die Sintfluthdsagen.*" *AJP* 20 (1899) 210–215.
"Stahl's *Syntax of the Greek Verb.*" *AJP* 29 (1908) 257–279, 389–409; 30 (1909)
     1–21. Published in booklet form as *Notes on Stahl's Syntax of the Greek Verb.*
     Baltimore, 1909.

Articles (Southern)

"The Proposed Epitaph for the Monument to Stonewall Jackson." *New Eclectic
     Magazine* 7 (November 1870) 527–530.
"The Creed of the Old South." *Atlantic Monthly* 69 (January 1892) 75–87; reprinted
     in *The Creed of the Old South* (Baltimore, 1915; New York, 1979) 7–52; C.
     D. Morley, *Modern Essays Second Series* (New York, 1951), 103–121; *Library
     of Southern Literature* 4:1804–1824.
"A Southerner in the Peloponnesian War." *Atlantic Monthly* 80 (September 1897)
     330–342; reprinted in *The Creed of the Old South* (Baltimore, 1915) 55–103.

Sources

Autobiographical

"Formative Influences." *The Forum* 10 (February 1891) 607–617.
"The College in the Forties." *Princeton Alumni Weekly* 16 (16) (26 January 1916)
     375–379.
"A Novice of 1850." *JH Alumni Magazine* 1 (November 1912) 3–9.
"Professorial Types." *The Hopkinsian* 1 (1893) 11–18.

"Modest Critique of 'A Sketch after Landseer'." *Southern Literary Messenger* 20 (February 1854) 118–120.

"The Hazards of Reviewing." *Nation* 101 (8 July 1915) 49–51.

"Retrospect." *AJP* 25 (1904) 486–490.

"An Unspoken Farewell." Privately printed, 1915.

"Announcement." *AJP* 40 (1919) 451.

Bibliography

Selections from the Brief Mention of Basil Lanneau Gildersleeve. Edited by C. W. E. Miller. Baltimore and London, 1930: xxx–liii.

Biographical

Allinson, F. G. "Gildersleeve as a Teacher." *Johns Hopkins Alumni Magazine* 13 (2) (January 1925) 132–136.

Ames, J. S. "Professor Gildersleeve and the University." *Johns Hopkins Alumni Magazine* 13 (2) (January 1925) 129–132.

Basil Lanneau Gildersleeve: An American Classicist. Edited by Ward W. Briggs, Jr. and Herbert W. Benario. *American Journal of Philology Monographs* 1. Baltimore and London, 1986. Contains "Basil Lanneau Gildersleeve: The Charleston Background" by Deborah Reeves Hopkins (1–8); "Basil Lanneau Gildersleeve at the University of Virginia" by Ward W. Briggs, Jr. (9–20); "The Foundation of Johns Hopkins and the First Faculty" by Herbert W. Benario (21–26); "Gildersleeve on the Study of the Classics" by Stephen Newmyer (27–35); "Gildersleeve the Syntactician" by John Vaio (36–41); "Gildersleeve, *The Journal*, and Philology in America" by George A. Kennedy (42–49); "Gildersleeve and the Study of Attic Tragedy" by Seth L. Schein (50–55); "Gildersleeve in American Literature: The Kaleidoscopic Style" by E. Christian Kopff (56–61); and "The Gildersleeve Archive" by Robert L. Fowler (62–105).

Garant, Geraldine. "Basil Gildersleeve, the American Scholar." Thesis, Vanderbilt, 1942.

Griffin, E. H. "Professor Gildersleeve as Friend and Colleague." *Johns Hopkins Alumni Magazine* 13 (2) (January 1925) 126–29.

Miller, C. W. E. "Gildersleeve the Scholar." *TAPA* 56 (1925) xix–xxii, xxviii–xxxii.

———. "Biographical Sketch" in *Selections from the Brief Mention of Basil Lanneau Gildersleeve.* Edited by C. W. E. Miller. Baltimore and London, 1930: xxiii–xxx.

Scott, John Adams. "Gildersleeve the Teacher." *TAPA* 56 (1925) xxii–xxviii.

Shorey, Paul. "Gildersleeve the American Scholar and Gentleman." *Johns Hopkins Alumni Magazine* 13 (2) (January 1925) 136–148.

Thornton, W. M. "Basil Lanneau Gildersleeve at the University of Virginia." *Johns Hopkins Alumni Magazine* 13 (2) (January 1925) 122–126.

Festschrift

Studies in Honor of Basil L. Gildersleeve. Baltimore, 1902.

Indices

"Indiculus Syntacticus." *AJP* 36 (1915) 481–87. (An index of Gildersleeve's writings on Greek syntax in *AJP*.)

"Index Scoliodromicus." With Lawrence H. Baker. *AJP* 42 (1921) 370–82. (An index of Gildersleeve's non-syntactical work in *AJP*.)

Letters

The Letters of Basil Lanneau Gildersleeve. Edited by Ward W. Briggs, Jr. Baltimore, 1987.

Papers

The two major collections of Gildersleeve's papers are held at Special Collections, Milton S. Eisenhower Library, Johns Hopkins Library and in the Manuscripts Department, Edward O. Alderman Library, the University of Virginia. For a comprehensive description of the former, see Robert L. Fowler, "The Gildersleeve Archive," *Basil Lanneau Gildersleeve: An American Classicist*. Edited by Ward W. Briggs, Jr. and Herbert W. Benario. *American Journal of Philology Monographs* 1. Baltimore and London, 1986: 62–105.

George Grote

17 November 1794 – 18 June 1871

JOHN VAIO
University of Illinois at Chicago

In 1952 Arnaldo Momigliano informed the learned world that Greek history had been invented by the British. It is no surprise then that one of the most illustrious names in this field is that of an Englishman, George Grote, whose *History of Greece* fundamentally shaped the perception of ancient Greek culture and history among English-speaking scholars and readers in the Victorian age and had a major impact on the Continent as well, especially in Germany, where "all . . . studies on Greek history of the last fifty years of the nineteenth century are either for or against Grote" (Momigliano, 65).

Yet this great historian began his professional life not as a scholar but as an employee in his father's bank. Taken from school at the age of fifteen and a half, the man who helped found a new university was himself deprived of a university education by a practically minded father anxious for his son to enter the family business. In later years Grote deplored "that mistaken impatience with which parents . . . abridge those years requisite for their son's complete education, and hurry him into professional life a half-educated man" (H. Grote, 10n). In Grote's case, how was the half made whole? And of what did it consist?

Grote's formal education was traditional for a boy of his class. In 1800, at age five and a half, he was sent to a grammar school to prepare for Charterhouse, one of the great English public schools, which he attended from 1804 to 1810. Other notable Carthusians were the rival historian of Greece Connop Thirlwall (later Bishop of St. David's), the lexicographer H. G. Liddell, and the novelist Thackeray. The latter two attended the school in the 1820s, but Thirlwall, who entered in 1809, met Grote there and became a lifelong friend.

This was the extent of Grote's schooling, but we should add that his mother had taught him at home to read and write "and had even grounded him in the rudiments of Latin; she having a strong desire to see her son excel in learning" (*Ibid.*,

6). This information supplied by Grote's wife and biographer suggests that the impulse and interest that carried the future historian far beyond the narrow confines of a British public-school education had their basis in this early maternal influence.

After leaving school the young banker devoted much of his spare time to a rigorous course of self-education despite the demands of his profession. He continued and broadened his study of Greek and Latin authors—Charterhouse had, after all, given him a thorough grounding in the classical languages. And he embarked on a study of philosophy, political economy, and above all German, the key to the most important classical scholarship of the time. Grote initially learned the language in order to read literature and philosophy: by 1819 he was deep into Kant. Still, it was not all work and study with no play: he played cricket regularly and began the cello, which he learned well enough to play Handel.

From 1810 to 1818 the stimulus for all this study came from himself and from his close friendship with several young men who shared his intellectual interests. But about 1818 a major change occurred. Grote became acquainted with the great economist David Ricardo, who in turn introduced him to James Mill, the father of John Stuart Mill and Grote's chief intellectual mentor for almost twenty years. About this time Grote also met Jeremy Bentham, and the circle was complete.

Three of the greatest intellects in Europe became Grote's "professors" in politics, philosophy, and economics (the "Modern Greats" of twentieth-century Oxford). It was beyond anything a young Englishman might expect at either of his own great universities and could hardly be matched even on the Continent. The effect on Grote was decisive: in politics he became an ultrademocrat, in religion, an unbeliever, and in philosophy, a Utilitarian. Of particular importance was the influence of James Mill, historian and philosopher, to whom Grote owed "an amount of intellectual stimulus and guidance such as he [could] never forget" (*Minor Works*, 284).

Who or what inspired a London banker to write the finest Greek history of his age? There are rival claimants, chiefly James Mill and Harriet Lewin, the woman Grote married in 1820. And what of Grote himself? Two unpublished essays on Greece and Macedon in the fourth century B.C. date from 1815, three years before the meeting with Mill and five years before marriage. The beginnings of the *History* may be traced back to the historian himself and perhaps also to the encouragement he received from his closest friend of this period, George Warde Norman. Next came induction into the circle of Utilitarian philosophers under the aegis of James Mill, where the idea for the *History* took concrete form. Certainly Grote's historical method is essentially that of the elder Mill in his *History of British India*, and it was Mill who inspired the passionate dedication to democratic principles that underlies Grote's concept of Greek political history. But one can hardly deny the support and influence of the strong-minded wife, who ever aided and abetted her husband's scholarly efforts by deed (e.g., correcting proofs, drawing maps) as well as word. Modern research, however, has conspired to rob her of the title she claimed for herself, that of sole muse and inspiration.

Mrs. Grote was a woman of remarkable vigor and independent character, who later made her mark in the literary, musical, and social life of London. And it is both curious and noteworthy that the storms and intrigues that clouded Grote's budding romance with this formidable lady in 1815 are emblematic of his position within the tradition of English scholarship. The scope and force of Grote's intellect were acknowledged by all but his most inveterate detractors: he was a great historian, but not a "great Greek Scholar." His rival in love, however, who schemed and lied to separate Grote from his beloved and win her for himself, was precisely that: one Peter Elmsley, a notable master of the niceties of Attic verse and diction. In the end neither philological subtlety nor the strong opposition of Grote's family prevailed: our historian wed his Harriet.

By 1822 Grote was hard at work on the *History*, progressing steadily until early 1831. (By 1829 he had reached the end of the Sicilian Expedition—413 B.C.) But the political frenzy leading inexorably to the passage of the Reform Bill in 1832 caught him up, put an almost decade-long hiatus to the *History*, and landed him in Parliament, where he served until 1841. Work on the *History* was not resumed until 1842, when it was substantially rewritten. But preliminary and primary research had been done in the 1820s, when Grote was under the intense and steady influence of James Mill. Though it did not appear until 1846–1856, one may agree with Grote's modern biographer in calling his *History* "the most distinguished example of Benthamite historiography" (Clarke, 106).

During the 1820s, in addition to the early draft of the *History* and his work at the bank–he had become a full partner in 1816—Grote wrote several papers and edited a book, all of which shed important light on his concept of history. In 1821 he published a pamphlet on parliamentary reform, followed ten years later by a more elaborate work on the same subject. The ancient historian also wrote on contemporary politics, and the conceptual basis for applying current models to ancient forms of government is evident.

The historian of religion also learned his craft at this time. In 1820 Grote produced an essay on magic, which James Mill called "a very learned, and what is more, a truly philosophical discourse on the subject of Magic" (Bain, *James Mill*, 193ff.). "Magic" in this case meant the realm of the supernatural. The paper was recommended for publication in the *Encyclopedia Britannica* but never appeared. In addition, Bentham handed over to Grote "four volumes of illegible notes" on religion, out of which Grote, with immense labor, produced *An Analysis of the Influence of Natural Religion on the Temporal Happiness of Mankind* (published in 1822 under the pseudonym Philip Beauchamp). More directly historical is a review of Clinton's *Fasti Hellenici* published in the Benthamite *Westminster Review* for April 1826. This gave Grote the opportunity to launch a full-scale attack on the antidemocratic bias of the current standard Greek history by William Mitford. It was, in effect, Grote's political-historical battle cry and the rationale for his own *History*.

As if this were not enough, to round out his activities in this period Grote turned his hand to founding a new university free from the religious shackles and elitism of Oxford and Cambridge. From 1825 to 1830 he served on the council and several key committees of what later became University College. According to the *Dictionary of National Biography* (8:729) he was one of "the pioneers of a movement that . . . had the effect of transforming the whole higher education of the country." In 1830 Grote resigned from the council over a disputed professorial appointment but returned in 1849, becoming Treasurer in 1860 and President in 1868.

The University of London (established in 1836) also was the scene of Grote's educational activities. In 1850 he became a member of the academic senate and from 1862 to the end of his life he held the post of Vice-Chancellor. This academic *cursus* brought special honor and distinction to a politician and man of business who held no regular university degree. (Honorary doctorates were awarded in 1853 from Oxford and 1861 from Cambridge.)

Grote's parliamentary career (1833–41) was on the whole not a success. A political thinker of considerable intelligence and a good speaker, the future scholar lacked the personal talents necessary for success in the public arena. As the famous wit Sydney Smith put it, he was "an honest and able man who would have been an important politician if the world had been a chess board" (Clarke, 65). Nevertheless, the practical experience of parliamentary debate and maneuver for over eight years gave Grote a profound understanding of political reality that few historians can claim. Certainly his passionate advocacy of Athenian democracy is as much the pleading of a committed party man—Grote was a "Philosophical Radical" on the extreme left of the Whig party—as it is the reasoned argument of the historical interpreter.

Grote's *History* began to appear in 1846 with the publication of the first and second volumes and ended ten years later with the completion of the twelfth volume. From an exhaustive survey and analysis of myth and legend it proceeded with painstaking detail, bold innovation, and scrupulous argument to the death of Alexander the Great. A kind of preview had appeared in the *Westminster Review* of 1843 (=*Minor Works*, 75–134) presenting at considerable length Grote's extreme skepticism on the historical value of ancient Greek legend: for Grote, true history begins only with the first Olympiad in 776 B.C. Such skepticism is not without serious modern adherents: for example, Sir Moses Finley in *Aspects of Antiquity* (London, 1968, 24ff, esp. 29). And it is all too easy to forget that the first excavation of "Troy" by the Englishman Frank Calvert took place some ten years after the *History* was completed.

Noteworthy also is Grote's pioneering reevaluation of Thucydides as an historical source. It was chiefly from Grote that we learned to distinguish the careful reporting of facts from the sometimes flawed judgment on political integrity and military competence (especially true in the case of the notorious Athenian demagogue, Cleon). Even today Grote merits being read as an important historical commentary on the greatest of Greek historians.

". . . Grote's history set new standards and gave new impulse to the writing of Greek history. Under Grote's archonship a new era started" (Momigliano, 65). But Grote was also a trained philosopher and a notable historian of Greek philosophy.

Indeed, intellectual history forms a vital part of the *History*, nowhere more so than in the famous defense and vindication of the Sophists. This was Grote's major contribution to the history of Greek thought and redirected the course of all subsequent research on the subject. ". . . Theodor Gomperz took pride in acknowledging how much his *Greek Thinkers* owed to Grote, whom he knew personally. I suspect that Gomperz was in fact Grote's greatest pupil" (*Ibid.*, 66).

Grote had originally intended to include a study of Plato and Aristotle in his account of the fourth century, but the impracticality of this scheme convinced him that separate treatment was necessary. By 1858 he was hard at work on Plato and in 1865 published three volumes entitled *Plato and the Other Companions of Sokrates*. This monumental achievement would lead W. K. C. Guthrie, the author of the standard modern history of Greek philosophy, to place Grote in the ranks of Zeller and Wilamowitz as one of the "few indestructibles" of Platonic scholarship (*A History of Greek Philosophy*, 4:xv). As John Stuart Mill put it, it was "quite wonderful for one man to have written the best history and the best philosophical history of Greece" (*Amberley Papers*, 1: 372).

Of particular importance for contemporary scholarship was the sober and thorough account of the Platonic canon. Here Grote cogently defended the authenticity of certain dialogues now universally accepted as genuine but which at that time had been seriously called into question. In addition, Grote decisively rejected the theory of Schleiermacher, the leading German Platonist of the early nineteenth century, who held that Plato wrote his dialogues according to a preconceived scheme and in an intentional sequence. For Grote there was no grand plan behind the dialogues: they were independent works whose date and order remained in general unknown and unknowable. Again, Grote proved that none of the dialogues had been written before the death of Socrates, though many Platonists of that time thought otherwise. Finally, as regards the general interpretation of Plato's philosophy Grote's most important contribution was to emphasize the skeptical side of Plato's method as opposed to the dogmatic: "[Plato's] purpose is to provoke the spirit of enquiry—to stimulate responsive efforts of the mind by a painful shock of exposed ignorance—and to open before it a multiplicity of new roads with various points of view" (Grote, *Plato*, 3d ed., 2:15).

"No sooner had the Plato been completed, and the printing begun (viz. in Sept. 1864), than the author 'set the loom' afresh for his Aristotle. Scarcely permitting himself breath, as it were, he applied his spare hours to the preparation of what he used to call 'my Trilogy' " (H. Grote, 277). Grote had retired from banking in 1843 in order to devote himself fully to scholarship. But by the 1860s much of his time was taken up by administrative work for University College, the University of London, and the British Museum—he had been made a Trustee in 1859. Indeed, a disputed appointment to the chair of philosophy at the College embroiled Grote in "bitter and noisy controversy" that cost him six months work on *Aristotle*. It was, in fact, the many demands on his time in addition to his research that prompted Grote to decline a peerage offered him in 1869.

Nor did Grote's personal life provide the peace and tranquility needed for work on the great Peripatetic. By 1864 he had, according to the confidante of his embittered wife, "conceived a passion" for the sculptress, Susan Durant, and "had made an old fool of himself" (*Amberley Papers*, 1:477). This affair with a woman at least 25 years younger than himself lasted until the end of 1868 and caused a serious estrangement from his wife, whose health broke down under the strain. Half a decade of storm and stress must have taken its toll on poor *Aristotle* as well.

In any case, the work was left unfinished at Grote's death in 1871 and was published posthumously in the following year. The fragment begins with an account of Aristotle's life that won much praise from contemporaries and includes careful discussion of the Aristotelian canon. For the most part, the extant study is devoted to an analysis of the logical treatises, a subject of limited interest for the general reader: thus *Aristotle* had less impact than *Plato*. Papers on the *Ethics* and *Politics* were later published in *Fragments on Ethical Subjects* (1876) and included in the second edition of *Aristotle* (1880).

Grote died on 18 June 1871 and was buried in Westminster Abbey with much pomp and ceremony on June 24th. Among the pallbearers were John Stuart Mill, the illustrious son of Grote's great mentor, and Benjamin Jowett, the Master of Balliol and Grote's chief Platonic rival. As was fitting, the major ancient historian of Victorian England was laid to rest near the grave of Edward Gibbon, his most famous eighteenth-century predecessor.

Books

A History of Greece. London. Vols. 1–2, 1846; new eds. 1849, 1851, 1854, 1859.
Vols. 3–4, 1847; new eds. 1849, 1851, 1859. Vols. 5–6, 1848; new eds. 1854, 1859. Vols 7–8, 1850; new eds. 1851, 1860. Vols 9–10, 1852; new ed. 1857. Vol. 11, 1853; new eds. 1856, 1861. Vol. 12, 1856; new ed. 1857. New editions of the whole work were published in 1862 (8 vols.), 1869 (12 vols.), 1872 (10 vols.), 1884 (12 vols.), 1888 (10 vols.) and 1907 (12 vols., Everyman Library); French translation by A.-L. de Sadous, 1864–67; German translation by N. N. W. Meissner, 1850–55; Italian translation by O. Colonna 1855–57 (incomplete).

Plato and the Other Companions of Sokrates. 3 vols. London, 1865; new eds. 1867 (3 vols), 1875 (3 vols.), 1885 (4 vols.), 1888 (4 vols.; repr. New York, 1973); index vol., 1870.

Aristotle. Edited by A. Bain and G. C. Robertson. 2 vols. London, 1872; 2nd ed., 1880 (1 vol.).

The Minor Works of George Grote. Edited by A. Bain. London, 1873.

Fragments on Ethical Subjects. Edited by A. Bain. London, 1876.

Articles

Review of *Fasti Hellenici*, by H. F. Clinton. *Westminster Review* 5 (April 1826)
269–331; summarized in *Minor Works*: [12]–[18]).

Essentials of Parliamentary Reform. Pamphlet, 1831 = *Minor Works*: 1–55.

"Grecian Legends and Early History." Review of *Griechische Heroen Geschichte* by B.
G. Niebuhr. *Westminster Review* 39 (May 1843) 285–328 = *Minor Works*:
73–134.

Sources

Bibliography

For a complete bibliography see Clarke, 189–191.

Biographical

Bain, A. "The Intellectual Character and Writings of George Grote." In *Minor
Works*: [1]–[170].

———. *James Mill: A Biography*. London, 1882; reprinted New York, 1967.

Clarke, M. L. *George Grote: A Biography*. London, 1962.

Dow, E. F. "George Grote, Historian of Greece." *CJ* 51 (1956) 211–219.

Dow, S. "Grote's History of Greece: A Bibliographical Note." *Ibid*. 220.

Lady Eastlake (Elizabeth Rigby). *Mrs. Grote: A Sketch*. London, 1880.

Freeman, E. A. *Historical Essays, Second series*, 3d ed. London, 1889: 109–178.

Gomperz, T. *Essays und Erinnerungen*. Stuttgart and Leipzig, 1905: 184–195.

Grote, H. *The Personal Life of George Grote*. London, 1873.

Guest, I. *Fanny Essler*. London, 1970.

Lehrs, K. *Populäre Aufsätze aus dem Alterthum*, 2d ed. Leipzig, 1875: 447–478.

Mill, J. S. *Autobiography*. Edited by R. Hawson. New York, 1924; reprinted 1969.

Momigliano, A. D. "George Grote and the Study of Greek History." *Studies in
Historiography*. London and New York, 1966: 56–74 = *Contributo alla storia
degli studi classici*. Rome, 1955; repr. 1979: 213–231. (Originally an Inaugural
Lecture delivered at University College, London, in 1952.)

Robertson, G. C. "Grote, George." *DNB* 8:727–736.

Ross, J. *Three Generations of English Women*. London, 1893.

Thirlwall, J. C. Jr. *Connop Thirlwall*. London, 1936.

Tollemache, Mr. and Mrs. L. A. *Safe Studies*. London, 1891: 131ff., 211ff.

Turner, F. M. *The Greek Heritage in Victorian Britain*. New Haven and London,
1981.

Letters

The Amberley Papers. Edited by B. Russell and P. Russell. 2 vols. London, 1937.

Gomperz, H. *Theodor Gomperz, Briefe und Aufzeichnungen*. Vol. 1. Vienna, 1936.

——— and Kahn, R. A. *Theodor Gomperz, Briefe und Aufzeichnungen*. Vol. 2.
Vienna, 1974.

Letters Literary and Theological of Connop Thirlwall. Edited by J. J. Stewart Perowne
and L. Stokes. London, 1881.

Letters of J. A. Symonds. Edited by H. M. Schueller and R. L. Peters. Vol. 1. Detroit, 1967.

Niebuhr, B. G. *Briefe 1816–1830.* Edited by E. Vischer. Vol. 3. Bern and Munich, 1983.

Papers

Posthumous Papers . . . of the Late George Grote. Edited by H. Grote. Privately printed, 1874.

Lewin Letters. Edited by T. H. Lewin. Privately printed, 1909.

Jane Ellen Harrison

9 September 1850 – 15 April 1928

RENATE SCHLESIER
Freie Universität Berlin

Jane Ellen Harrison remains even today one of the most influential and controversial of the classical scholars working at the turn of the twentieth century. She was the earliest and the most consistent of those who integrated archaeology and anthropology, sociology and psychology into the study of the history of Greek religion. Her vivid, immediate, mystically emotional attitude toward the traditions of archaic religion had an inspiring effect on the younger generation of scholars, especially on her comrades in arms in the Cambridge Ritualists, Gilbert Murray and Francis Cornford. Her innovative heterodoxy and her enthusiastic idiosyncrasy in dealing with textual and pictorial evidence discredited her work with the majority of her conventional colleagues. Nevertheless, what Gilbert Murray wrote in 1955 is still true: "Few people would accept the whole of J. E. H.'s conclusions, but nobody can write on Greek religion without being influenced by her work" (Stewart, xi).

Jane Ellen Harrison was born in 1850 in Yorkshire; she grew up there and in Wales. Thanks to the business connections of her father, a timber merchant, she conceived in early childhood an enthusiastic interest in Russia, which, finally, in the last fifteen years of her life, was to determine her interests almost exclusively. The death of her mother four weeks after her own birth was decisive for the dramatic course of her life and work: idealization of religious matriarchy was united with rebellion, in theory and practice, against patriarchal rule, marriage, and family. To the end of her life her strong passions and her capacity for enthusiasm toward human beings, animals, and the subjects of her studies remained undiminished. She, for whose sake her mother had to die, identified herself not only with the she-bear, but above all with the ker, the *daimon* of death. In numerous friendships with congenial men—friendships that often lasted for years and were characterized by intellectual excitement and sublimated eroticism—she again and again experienced disappointments in love.

She was predisposed to these experiences by her father's remarriage five years after her birth. Her extremely mystical and puritanical stepmother (who had previously been her governess), a Welsh Evangelical "of the fervent semi-revivalist type" (*Reminiscences*: 19), subjected her to a strict religious upbringing that included training in playing the organ, memorization of entire sermons, and the fundamentals of Latin, Greek, Hebrew, and German. When her stepmother objected to her close attachment at age seventeen to a young curate, she was sent away in 1868 to Cheltenham Ladies' College, a strictly evangelical boarding school for daughters of the upper middle class; the school offered an ambitious program of education that went far beyond training in housekeeping and also sought to inculcate the silence and self-control appropriate to a convent. In 1869–70 Harrison broke with her principal, Dorothea Beale, whom she revered, when she read David Friedrich Strauß's *Leben Jesu* and began to advocate an historical and mythological interpretation of the Bible. After taking honors in Women's Matriculation at the University of London in 1870, she returned to her family as governess to her younger siblings and, gradually and increasingly breaking free from her Christian upbringing, became an agnostic.

In 1874 she passed the Higher Local Examination for Cambridge University, and her excellent marks won her a scholarship at Newnham College, Cambridge. The college had been founded in 1871 by the philosopher and former Fellow of Trinity, Henry Sidgwick, as Cambridge's second women's college after Girton. Harrison quickly became the dominant figure among the residents and came into conflict with the principal, Ann Clough, who, like Harrison's stepmother and the director of Cheltenham, was a Welsh evangelical conservative and watched over the modesty and decency of her charges. Although the students were permitted to perform the *Medea* in 1876 Clough vetoed the performance of Euripides' *Electra* that was planned for 1877. Playing the title role in the Oxford University Dramatic Society's production of the *Alcestis*, Harrison was a great success. Among her closest student friends was Ellen Crofts, who later became the wife of Charles Darwin's son Francis, his father's secretary and biographer.

Her teachers in Greek and Latin were the Trinity College Lecturers in Classics Samuel Henry Butcher (from 1874) and Arthur Woollgar Verrall (from 1877), who later became the husband of Margaret de G. Merrifield, her lifelong closest friend from the Newnham days. Henry Butcher was already engaged but was also paying court to Harrison; in 1876, however, he went to Oxford to marry the other woman. The fact that most Cambridge Fellows showed mistrust and resistance toward the newly founded women's colleges was one of the bitterest experiences of Harrison's academic life. Female students received certificates only and were excluded from taking degrees in Cambridge until 1947 (in Oxford until 1920). Newnham quickly became a focal point for distinguished visitors. During Harrison's student days, she met liberal politicians such as William Ewart Gladstone, the Russian writer and social critic Ivan Turgenev, and George Eliot, whom she especially esteemed. In 1878 a lecture on Olympia by Sidney Colvin, then director of the Fitzwilliam Museum, stimulated her interest in classical archaeology. After receiving only a Second Class in the Classical Tripos in 1879 and teaching Latin without enthusiasm for a term at Notting Hill High School and at Oxford High School, she went to London in 1880 to study ancient Greek art and archaeology. Not she, but her rather more conventional friend Margaret de G. Merrifield, was chosen as Classical Lecturer at Newnham.

During the last two decades of Queen Victoria's reign, which Harrison spent in London beginning with her thirtieth year, she was one of a circle of artists and writers (Edward Burne-Jones and Walter Pater were also members) who devoted themselves to an "aesthetic" enthusiasm for Greek classicism in the footsteps of Shelley and Keats; she appeared in "Homeric theatricals" and tableaux in elegant salons and encouraged Isadora Duncan in her first attempts to introduce ancient Greek elements into the dance. By becoming a member of two clubs, teaching at the Girl's Public High School, and sharing rooms with a teacher of nursing, she came into contact with the movement for women's rights. Throughout her life, however, her attitude toward the suffragettes was skeptical. Harrison's teacher in archaeology, Charles Newton, keeper of Greek and Roman antiquities at the British Museum, who had visited Olympia with Colvin in 1875, gave her the opportunity to deliver lectures in the galleries of the sculpture and vase collections, and arranged for her to publish in the *Journal of Hellenic Studies*.

In her first book, *Myths of the Odyssey in Art and Literature* (1882), one can already detect something of the unconventional spirit, receptive to new intellectual currents, which unmistakably predominates in her later publications. Here Edward Burnett Tylor's *Primitive Culture* (1871), which was soon to exert a decisive influence on the anthropological studies of Andrew Lang, William Robertson Smith, and James George Frazer, was already used as a basis for drawing analogies between the myths of "primitive" peoples and those of the Greeks. The use of vase-paintings as evidence for rituals and festivals, which was to figure largely in Harrison's major works, here makes its first appearance. Harrison's claim to offer the English reader something new is fulfilled in the treatment of works of visual art as myth—"commentaries" that stand on an equal footing with the literary evidence; for Homer and the vase-painters "drew their inspiration from one common source, local and national tradition" (*Ibid.*, ix). This was precisely the epoch-making insight of Karl Otfried Müller (1797–1840), to whose authority Harrison from this point on appeals. His works and the writings of other, chiefly German, archaeologists had been brought to her notice by Wilhelm Klein, her exact contemporary, who had been staying in London in 1880 and would later be Professor Ordinarius of Classical Archaeology in Prague. In 1881, on the first of her many research journeys, which she financed in part by means of an inheritance left her by her mother, she examined collections of antiquities abroad and made the acquaintance of Ernst Curtius and Carl Robert in Berlin, Heinrich Brunn in Munich, Wolfgang Helbig in Rome, and, most important, the young architect Wilhelm Dörpfeld, who had been Curtius's collaborator at Olympia since 1877 and after 1882 directed Schliemann's campaigns of excavation in Troy and Tiryns.

In her lectures at the British Museum, Harrison at first inspired herself and her fashionably blasé audience—chiefly wealthy London society ladies ("British

Lionesses")—with an enthusiasm for a classicizing aestheticism that declared the Elgin Marbles to be the supreme artistic and educational ideal. In her second book, *Introductory Studies in Greek Art* (1885), which was intended for a more general, educated public and stands out among her other works by its conventionality, she celebrated the ideality, harmony, and humanity of classical Greek art in contrast to the art of the ancient Orient, which she condemned as magical, monstrous, and inhuman. In 1886 she met Dugald Sutherland MacColl, a man nine years her junior and artistically talented, who later became keeper of the Tate Gallery. His stern criticism of her sermonizing style of lecturing precipitated an intellectual crisis, which she experienced as a sort of conversion. Under the influence of MacColl, who gave lectures on folklore and spread the gospel of Impressionism, she began to think of her taste for art in the Olympian and transfigured style as a "sin." She rejected his proposal of marriage but nonetheless maintained close relations with him until his marriage in 1897. Together they attended Dörpfeld's lectures in Athens in 1888 and took part in the first of his legendary sightseeing tours. In her autobiography she writes, "It was worth many hardships to see forty German professors try to mount forty recalcitrant mules" (*Reminiscences*, 65). In the course of an adventurous journey of several months through Greece to Constantinople, alone with MacColl, she gave the abbot of a monastery, who was quite taken with her, a photograph of herself in a ballroom gown and was delighted when he placed it beside the icon of the Theotokos.

After her return from the trip she published in 1890 *Mythology and Monuments of Ancient Athens*, a decisive step toward the establishment of the ritualistic school. In a detailed commentary on sections of Pausanias' *Attica* (translated by Margaret de G. Verrall), she consistently developed the method of archaeological "mythography" that she had sketched out in her first book. Like Pausanias, and in the spirit of Schliemann and Dörpfeld, she treated figures of myth as historical persons, and she amalgamated the ancient aetiological method of interpretation with a theory of myth explanation that went back to Friedrich Max Müller, the Oxford scholar of comparative religion and linguistics: "In the large majority of cases *ritual practice misunderstood* explains the elaboration of myth" (*Ibid.*, iii). During her London years between 1880 and 1898, her three much-discussed books, her numerous articles and reviews, and the interest roused by her lectures (which were delivered even at prestigious boys' schools like Eton) won her a reputation as a scholar of the first rank and personal recognition from respected scholars in Britain and abroad. She was elected to the Council of the Classical Association, received honorary doctorates from the universities of Aberdeen and Durham, and in 1896 became a corresponding member of the Deutsches Archäologisches Institut in Berlin. Yet despite abundant testimonials from scholars throughout Europe, she twice (1888 and 1896) failed to secure appointment to the Yates Professorship in Archaeology at University College, London.

At the age of forty-eight she was awarded one of the first Newnham Research Fellowships, and in 1898 she returned to her college as Resident Lecturer in Classical Archaeology; even after the expiration of her fellowship in 1903 she was to remain on the staff of the college until 1922. The sixteen years preceding the outbreak of the First World War were the high point of Harrison's career and of her scholarly productivity. This period also brought perhaps the most intense, and yet the most painful, personal experiences of her life. In Cambridge (under Edward VII the center of innovations in the sciences in England) she took an active role in intellectual activities that extended far beyond the field of classics, together with her teachers and friends from student days and above all with the circle of Henry Sidgwick, the Verralls, and the family of Ellen and Francis Darwin. She studied Sanskrit and the history of Indian religion with Robert Alexander Neil (born 1852), a Fellow of Pembroke, who as a classical scholar and Orientalist had been giving lectures in women's colleges since the late 1870s, and she discussed with him the preliminary stages of new works. They had planned to be married when he unexpectedly died in 1901.

Jane Harrison's most fruitful and, from the point of view of the history of scholarship, her most significant ties were the friendships that she formed, shortly after her return to Cambridge, with the newly elected Fellow of Trinity and later Classical Lecturer, Francis Macdonald Cornford (1874–1943) and with Gilbert Murray (1866–1957), who in 1889 had succeeded Richard Jebb as Professor of Greek at Glasgow. In 1899 Murray withdrew into the country for reasons of ill health; in 1905 he returned to Oxford and became Regius Professor of Greek there in 1908. Harrison had enthusiastically hailed his first book, *A History of Ancient Greek Literature* (1897), and in 1900 the Verralls introduced her to him and his wife. Despite differences in outlook—Harrison, the mystical agnostic, sympathized with the Tories, whereas Murray, a teetotaller and vegetarian, who believed that the immortality of the soul could be scientifically demonstrated, was a politically active Liberal—he remained until her death, as her eight hundred letters to him testify, the most reliable source of order in the chaos of her life and the most sympathetic critic of her scholarly work.

No less stimulating, but full of emotional drama, was the course of her relationship with Francis Cornford, twenty-four years her junior, who had sought a conversation with her after one of her public lectures. With him she took many trips—to the east coast of England, to France, and most importantly to Crete and the Greek mainland; with him she studied ancient oriental languages and entered enthusiastically into academic and religious heresy. His name for her was "Queen of Sheba"; she called him "Solomon." His marriage in 1909 to her student Frances, the daughter of Ellen and Francis Darwin, the friends of her own student days, was probably the deepest emotional wound she ever received.

In the period of her first acquaintance with Cornford and Murray, two long essays of hers appeared in the *Journal of Hellenic Studies*: "Delphika" (1899) and "Pandora's Box" (1900). In these articles the central themes of her epoch-making book *Prolegomena to the Study of Greek Religion* (1903) are already clearly visible. 1) Her dualistic theory, which has points of reference in Aeschylus, Isocrates, Plato, and Plutarch and appropriates Bachofen's evolutionistic concept of matriarchy, contended that a "division of labor" existed between the Greek deities; this finds expression in two contrasting forms of ritual: the formula *do ut abeas* corresponds (she maintains) to the cult of the older matriarchal Chthonic deities, whereas the formula *do ut des* corresponds to that of the younger patriarchal Olympians. 2) Influenced by Robertson Smith's totemism theory, she held that in the evolution of the Greek gods and ghosts theriomorphism was a primitive stage that preceded anthropomorphism; this is most clearly visible in their worship in serpent form. 3) She interpreted the Olympic pantheon, almost canonical since Homer, as a mythological and theological construct that was meant to expel the preliterate archaic worship of the maternal earth-divinities and amorphous demons, though these still retained their importance as "survivals" (in E. B. Taylor's sense) in local cult festivals in the classical age.

Literary sources that pointed to Crete and, above all, the excavations begun there in 1900 by Arthur John Evans were construed by Harrison as suggestive confirmations of these postulates. In 1901, accompanied by her student Jessie Graham Crum (later Mrs. Hugh F. Stewart), she traveled to Italy and Greece; in Athens she met the Swedish historian of religion Sam Wide, who would later become an active proponent of her theory of the metamorphosis of the chthonic gods into sky gods, and she took part in Dörpfeld's tours of the Peloponnese and the islands. On Crete, Evans showed her his first discoveries. A clay seal was in her eyes a revelation of the Mountain-Mother, escorted by lions and worshipped ecstatically by a youth. This was one of the basic motifs of her book in progress: the ritual connection between mother-goddess and son that had preceded the worship of the patriarchal usurpers.

Religious ecstasy had been a preoccupation of Harrison's since her earliest studies of vase-painting. Erwin Rohde's book *Psyche: Seelencult und Unsterblichkeitsglaube der Griechen*, the two volumes of which (1890 and 1894) she had immediately and enthusiastically reviewed in the *Classical Review*, had brought the uniqueness of the worship of Dionysus and the question of asceticism in the Orphic mysteries to the center of her own researches. Her fascination with Dionysian ecstasy, further stimulated by Rohde's former friend and predecessor Nietzsche, was intensified during the writing of the *Prolegomena* by conversations and correspondence with Murray about his simultaneous studies of Euripides and, especially, about his translation of the *Bacchae*. She confided to him, "The whole centre of gravity of the book has shifted. It began as a treatise on Keres with a supplementary notice of Dionysus. It is ending as a screed on Dionysus with an introductory talk about Keres" (Stewart, 25). Her exchange of ideas with Murray also left its mark on the thesis, developed in the book's final chapters, that Orphism was a mystical spiritualization and transcendence of the ecstatic religion of Dionysus. In 1902 they studied together in the British Museum and in Naples the gold tablets that had recently been discovered in graves in southern Italy and in Crete; inscriptions on these tablets speak of the dead being deified, which Murray and Harrison interpreted as evidence of an Orphic eschatology. Murray, whom Harrison recognized as her main authority in philological matters, added to the *Prolegomena* a "Critical Appendix on the Orphic Tablets."

In 1928, in the first of the Jane Ellen Harrison Memorial Lectures that Newnham College had instituted, Murray praised the *Prolegomena* as a "work of genius" (Murray, 11). Here for the first time the study of ancient Greek religion found its focus in the rituals. These, the "things done," are the "some neglected aspects" (*Ibid.*, vii) to which Harrison, supported by the concreteness of her examples from the visual arts, wished to draw the attention that had hitherto been preoccupied with things thought and written, the myths. The work is brilliantly written; it is learned, though often imprecise in details; it still retains its fresh and revolutionary effectiveness; and, despite objections and reservations on the part of the scholarly guild, it was an immediate success in Britain and abroad. Only one year after its appearance, five of the examination questions in the Classical Tripos, part II, referred to the *Prolegomena*, as Harrison remarked with pride (Stewart, 54).

But she was beginning to have serious problems with her health, and because of nervousness and shortness of breath, perhaps due to a malfunction of the thyroid gland, she was obliged to undergo medical treatment and to renounce temporarily the cigarette smoking and whisky drinking that she loved. She wrote sarcastically to the Murrays, "If giving up drink is like the wrench from a lover . . . , giving up smoking is like parting from the best friend" (Stewart, 101).

Her predilection for these two delightful poisons, like her fashionable outfits, was among the eccentricities with which she had been provoking dons and bluestockings since her student days. Her lectures, rhetorically polished and furnished with a background of sound and lighting effects, were famous for extravagance and drama. Even her use of lantern slides as visual aids, a practice that dated back to her London period, was an original innovation; far more so were the drums and bull-roarers on which friends, concealed in the background, were obliged to perform in order to bring home to the audience at her Newnham lecture on Orphism the religious awe in the fragment of Aeschylus' *Edonoi*. The great value she ascribed to the most authentic possible presentation of ancient cult appears in her attempt, the failure of which she deeply regretted, to find in the Louvre adequate *xoana* (primitive wooden images of the gods) to serve as models for Aphrodite and Artemis for the Lyric Theatre's 1904 production of the *Hippolytus*, the first staging of one of Gilbert Murray's Euripides translations. To enable her to exhibit the *liknon* (winnowing basket), during a lecture on the Eleusinian mysteries, as the cradle of the Holy Child at the moment of its revelation, Francis Darwin obtained an antique winnowing fan from some French peasants; covered at first, it was unveiled at the fitting moment.

Her detailed study of the *liknon*—"Mystica Vannus Iacchi"—appeared in the *Journal for Hellenic Studies* in 1903 and 1904. In this *paralipomenon* to the *Prolegomena*, the new directions that Harrison's work was taking were already apparent. Referring to Frazer's *Golden Bough* yet in partial disagreement with it, she intended to focus on the social significance of vegetation cults.

But for the present she was consolidating what she had already achieved. After publishing in 1905 the booklet *The Religion of Ancient Greece*—a schematic but still instructive summary of the postulates and problems sketched out in the *Prolegomena*—she traveled with Cornford to Greece and Crete. In 1906 she published *Primitive Athens as Described by Thucydides*, a tribute to Dörpfeld, which was related to the Pausanias commentary in Harrison's third book. Here she attempted to support Dörpfeld's interpretations of his excavations in the Athenian agora with her expertise in the history of religion and to defend them against Frazer's 1898 Pausanias commentary.

Harrison continually encouraged her friends and coworkers Cornford and Murray in their studies on the origins of Greek religion, literature, and historiography, and her encouragement bore its first fruits in 1907. In that year appeared both Cornford's first book, the still debated *Thucydides Mythistoricus*, which brought to light the religious undercurrents in the history of the Peloponnesian War, and Murray's *The Rise of the Greek Epic*, his Harvard lectures of 1907, which presented Homer as having transcended barbaric institutions and cults. Both authors emphasized their debt to Harrison, who was the undisputed center of the triad that came to be known as the Cambridge School and/or the Ritualists, which left its mark on several generations of scholars and still influences the study of ancient Greek religion.

Affiliated loosely with the group was Arthur Bernard Cook, who began his researches on Zeus in 1900, while their friend Verrall remained skeptical toward their ritualistic credo. But they were met with especially embittered resistance by their colleagues William Ridgeway in Cambridge and Lewis Richard Farnell in Oxford. These two Hellenists, archaeologists, and historians of religion, who were Harrison's slightly younger contemporaries, shared with the Ritualists an anthropological orientation, but they particularly opposed the universalistic concept of a pretheistic "year-spirit," the *eniautos-daimon*, a concept that Harrison had been pondering since 1904. The name is derived from a Hymn to Zeus Kouros and the Curetes, an inscription dated to the second or third century A. D. that R. C. Bosanquet had discovered at Palaikastro in Crete and published, jointly with Murray and Harrison, in 1908–09. The name of the goddess mentioned at the end of the hymn was chosen by Harrison as the title of her next book, which she had previously intended to call "Epilegomena" and that she would later describe as her "central work" (*Reminiscences*, 73): *Themis: A Study of the Social Origins of Greek Religion* (1912). In this year the collaboration of Harrison, Cornford, and Murray culminated in the simultaneous publication of Cornford's *From Religion to Philosophy*, Murray's *Four Stages of Greek Religion*, and Harrison's *Themis*. Cornford contributed to Harrison's book a chapter, "The Origin of the Olympic Games" and to Murray's, "Excursus on the Ritual Forms Preserved in Greek Tragedy."

Modifying her previous theory, Harrison no longer defined ritual as the "thing done"—for that, she said, is never religious—but as the "thing *re*-done or *pre*-done," i. e., as a commemorative or anticipatory form of representation. "The element of action re-done, imitated, the element of *mimesis*, is, I think, essential. In all religion, as in all art, there is this element of make-believe. Not the attempt to deceive, but a desire to *re*-live, to *re*-present" (*Themis*, 43). The ritual *par excellence* was the *dromenon*; according to Harrison this was a primeval new-year's cult play, ancestral within the tribe; in Greece it was performed in the spring and had originally lacked a deity; it was connected with male puberty rites and served the purpose of initiation into matriarchal mysteries. The young men in this rite would identify themselves with the dying and resurrected *megistos kouros*, the holy *eniautos-daimon*. Building on Harrison's thesis that "the myth is the plot of the *dromenon*" (*Themis*, 331) and his own researches on Pindar, Cornford interpreted the Olympic victor as the incarnation of the year-spirit, whose death and rebirth Murray likewise found embodied in the structure and the characters of tragedy. In Harrison's view, the goddess who presided over the religious system that derives from the seasonal festivals was Themis, the personification of the life-preserving ties of social cohesion, to whom even the Olympians had to submit and who preceded all religion: "Behind Gaia the Mother, and above even Zeus the Father, stands always the figure of Themis" (*Themis*, 2d ed., xxii).

In the years after the *Prolegomena*, Harrison had come to regard the Olympians as not merely nonprimitive, but even as nonreligious, figures, while Dionysus and Orpheus crystallized in her thoughts as being essentially religious. She understood their myths to be descriptions of bloody rites that had actually been practiced, and Harrison, sometimes called "Bloody Jane," felt repelled by their barbaric cruelty and obscenity. For, essentially, despite her enthusiasm for serpent-cults and archaic mysteries, she remained loyal all her life to the Puritanism of her Christian upbringing, the rationalism of the theory of evolution, and the classical ideal of Greece. In the introduction to *Themis* she formulates an *apologia*: "I . . . still confess, that I have little natural love for what an Elizabethan calls 'ye Beastly Devices of ye Heathen.' Savages, save for their reverent, totemistic attitude towards animals, weary and disgust me, though perforce I spend long hours in reading of their tedious doings. My good moments are when, through the study of things primitive, I come to the better understanding of some song of a Greek poet or some saying of a Greek philosopher" (*Themis*, 2d ed., xxv).

She found welcome support for her attempts to accept and justify these fundamentally religious "errors and licences" (*Themis*, 2d ed., xi) in Emile Durkheim and his school, whose studies on the sociology of religion had begun to appear in the 1890s and in the philosophical and psychological works that Henri Bergson began to publish in 1907. Disregarding the differences between them, Harrison amalgamated Durkheim's interpretation of religion as the primeval representation of collective thought and emotion with Bergson's sublime conception of *durée*: the persistence of social and organic life she found unconsciously expressed in Dionysus, god of the mysteries, but consciously reflected in the Olympians. Against this background, and with the help of extensive data from comparative cultural anthropology, she gave special emphasis to the theory of religion to such concepts as *mana*, magic, *tabu*, and totemism. Here she drew on Frazer's postulate of the sacral king as the original medicine-man, Evans's interpretation of Minoan tree- and pillar-cults, and Arnold van Gennep's *Rites de passage* of 1909. Appealing to the neutral deity Themis, Harrison damns both chthonic phallic worship and the Olympian individualism that is realized in the institution of marriage. This monumental work is the ultimate expression of the religious experiences she had suffered through and the emotional scars that she bore.

In 1912 Jane Harrison journeyed to Greece for the last time. In Athens she met Samuel Butler, who tried without success to win her over to his theory that the *Odyssey* was written by a woman, and she traveled across the sea to the coast of Athos. To her, Mt. Athos was a shrine of the Mountain-Mother, and the monks, who forbade women to set foot on the promontory, were the descendants of the Curetes. On board ship her *Themis*, which had just appeared, and Murray's book on Homer were being studied by Arthur Pickard-Cambridge, whose theory of the origin and development of tragedy, which was aimed directly at Harrison and Murray, was to become canonical.

Harrison's new book provoked a far more massive protest than the *Prolegomena* had, and the "sound scholars" replied to it with valid criticisms. Her health, which had long been fragile, was further weakened by operations, and in the fall of 1912 she traveled to Switzerland to undergo electrotherapy. There she was vouchsafed in a dream the easing of her hatred for Frances Darwin, who three years earlier had become Mrs. F. M. Cornford; at the same time she experienced a spiritual rebirth, comparable to mystic communion with a being which, however, did not in Harrison's view deserve the name of "God." Writing to Murray of this experience, she asked, "Do you think a blasphemous Ker could be converted?" (Stewart, 113).

Her last journey to Italy took her in 1913 to Venice, where Titian and Tintoretto left her indifferent. In the same year she published *Ancient Art and Ritual*; the book, not so unwieldy as *Themis*, was an attempt to explain the transformation of ritual (*dromenon*) into art (*drama*). Despite all the emotional setbacks of her life she remained physically vigorous and intellectually youthful. Even in 1913 she made reference to the Turkey Trot and Ragtime in an article "for fear of being out of touch with the young," as she acknowledged to Murray (Stewart, 182). She maintained close relations with friends a generation younger than herself—writers, painters, actors, London's "latest-fashion people" in the Bloomsbury circle of Virginia Stephen (after 1912 Mrs. Leonard Woolf); among them were Roger Fry, whom she had known since the days of her boys' school lectures, the Post-Impressionist Clive Bell, her Newnham colleague Pernel Strachey, and the latter's brother Lytton.

The outbreak of the First World War was for Jane Harrison a painful turning point in her scholarly interests and in her relations to her friends of the Ritualist group. In 1915 she published a collection, entitled *Alpha and Omega*, of lectures and pamphlets composed between 1907 and 1913, which contained autobiographical elements. The views therein expressed seemed to her now "like faded photographs" (*Alpha and Omega*, vi), and she added to the volume a stirring appeal for pacifism, composed after the beginning of the war. She, who shortly before had glorified collective emotional ties as forces making *per definitionem* for unity and the preservation of life, now reacted with shock and bewilderment to the masses' aggressive enthusiasm for war and to the anti-German political and military activities of her colleagues and friends, Murray and Cornford among them. Seeing her theoretical principles refuted in practice and forfeiting the maieutic conversations that she sorely needed with the men who had hitherto been closest to her, she felt paralyzed; her energy for work was diminished and her tendency to depression deepened, and she began to look about for new tasks. The fulfillment of her obligation to review new publications on Greek religion and mythology for Cyril Bailey's *The Year's Work in Classical Studies* in 1915 and 1917 was, she felt, like a visit to a grave.

During the winter of 1914–15, she went to Paris for treatment by a heart specialist; there she came into contact with the École des Langues Orientales and began to learn Russian. In 1916 she gave English lessons to foreign refugees in Cambridge, and in the "Union for Democratic Control" she supported Bertrand Russell, who had been dismissed from his lectureship at Trinity because of his pacifism. Meanwhile, her study of the language and culture of Russia had became the center of her interests, and in this study she found consolation and renewed energy. She hailed the March revolution in Russia in 1917 as the only good thing the war had brought about. In 1919 she studied Russian at the École Orientale in Paris together with her student and friend Hope Mirrlees, who had come to Cambridge in 1909 and was to be her companion to the end of her life in 1928. In 1919 she also published *Aspects, Aorists, and the Classical Tripos*, in which she underscored the similarities between Russian and Greek. At her first encounter with the language of the land of bears of her childhood dreams, she had confessed to Murray, "Nothing has made me so happy as the 'aspects' of Russian verbs since I first had sight of the Greek particles" (Stewart, 156).

From 1919 until her final departure from Cambridge in 1922 she taught Russian at Newnham; after a trip to Spain in 1920 she also taught Spanish. In 1920 she gave a lecture on the similarities between Cretan and Spanish bullfighting, and she outraged Cambridge society, in which Communism was not yet à la mode, by her acquaintance with a "real live Bolshevik bear" (Stewart, 175). In 1921 she witnessed male-chauvinist demonstrations and a vandalistic attack on Newnham by rioting students after the proposal to admit women to degrees (a proposal that had been accepted at Oxford and was supported at Cambridge by many dons) failed once more. Not only her opponents, such as Ridgeway, but also such close scholarly colleagues as A. B. Cook, had voted against the measure.

The last work she wrote while still at Cambridge was the *Epilegomena to the Study of Greek Religion* (1921), a résumé of her two great books. Here she drew on Durkheim's *Les formes élémentaires de la vie religieuse* of 1912, the second volume of Cook's *Zeus* (1921), and the third edition of Frazer's *The Golden Bough*, as well as her reading in the latest psychological and philosophical literature—C. G. Jung's *Psychologie des Unbewußten*, Vladimir S. Soloviov's *Justification of the Good*, and, not least, Sigmund Freud's *Totem und Tabu* (1912–13), the sexual theory of which, however, she did not accept. The *Epilegomena* begins with a dualistic division of primitive ritual into rites of expulsion, directed against evil, on the one hand, and rites of impulsion, operating in favor of good (i.e., fertility and nourishment), on the other. After an attempt at biological justification of both primitive and Olympian theology, she ended the book with a panegyric on asceticism, which she felt was necessary in the modern world. Gilbert Murray, who had long sought to bring Harrison to such a view, assured her that this was "the best thing you have ever written about religion" (Stewart, 182).

In 1922, the year of the third and last edition of the *Prolegomena*, Harrison gave up her residence at Newnham College, and most of academic Cambridge bade her farewell with expressions of gratitude and respect. She burned all letters and manuscripts, dispersed her library, and settled in France with Hope Mirrlees "to see things more freely and more widely" (*Reminiscences*, 90). From 1922 to 1925 she lived in the American University Women's Club in Paris and took an active part in the cultural life of the French capital, in which the Russian avant-garde was also active. In 1923 and 1924 Paul Desjardins, Professor at the Collège de Sèvres, invited her to the "Décades"—"Entretiens" on literature, religion, and politics—that he conducted at the Abbaye de Pontigny; there she met the *crème* of the Nouvelle Revue Française and its internationalist comrades in arms. Desjardins's guests too welcomed and honored her; among them were André Gide, André Maurois, Jean Schlumberger, and Heinrich Mann, as well as Harrison's final passion, the Russian Prince David Mirsky. Jean Jaurès, the Socialist politician who had been murdered at the beginning of the First World War, had been one of the first French intellectuals to applaud Harrison's *Themis*, and in 1925 it was placed on the syllabus of the Paris École des Hautes Études.

In her *Reminiscences of a Student's Life*, which was published by the Woolfs' Hogarth Press in 1925, Jane Harrison praised the passions that stirred her even in old age. "Life does not cease when you are old, it only suffers a rich change. . . . You even go on falling in love, and for the same foolish reasons—the tone of a voice, the glint of a strangely set eye—only you fall so gently; and in old age you may even show a man that you like to be with him without his wanting to marry you or thinking you want to marry him" (*Reminiscences*, 89–90). During the last four years of her life she affirmed anew her old love for the pure beauty of the poetic imagination in the classical literature of all ages, signifying the conquest of anxiety as the quintessence of all transcendent religion, in her last two brief books, *Mythology: Our Debt to Greece and Rome* (1924) and *Myths of Greece and Rome* (1927). In two works of Russian religion and folklore that she edited and translated together with Hope Mirrlees, *The Life of the Archpriest Avvakum* and *The Book of the Bear* (1926), she celebrated the Russian soul as a model to be emulated.

Before she finally settled in London in 1926, she traveled through the south of France and visited Cambridge once more, where she became interested once again in her old favorite subject, Orphism—now from the diffusionist and Orientalist point of view—a subject that she had studied long before, with Cornford and Murray. In her last publication, the preface to the second, almost unaltered edition of *Themis*, she noted that her "dangerous" book had turned many young scholars into freethinkers and that her old "heresies" were now generally accepted: "that gods and religious ideas generally reflect the social activities of the worshipper; that the food supply is of primary importance for religion; that the *daimon* precedes the full-blown god; that the Great Mother is prior to the masculine divinities" (*Themis*, 2d ed., ix). She herself, she said, could not take part in the further development of these theories, for "between the two editions lies the great war which shattered much of academic tradition, scattered my fellow-workers all over Europe to be killed or drilled, and drove me, for I am no Archimedes, to fly from Greece and seek sanctuary in other languages and civilisations—Russian, Oriental, and, finally, Scandinavian—bringing with them no bitter tang of remembrance" (*Ibid.*).

In the spring of 1928, Jane Harrison died of leukemia in London at 11 Mecklenburgh Street.

Jane Ellen Harrison was one of England's first women scholars, and in her fields of study she attained outstanding rank, comparable to that of Beatrice Potter Webb. She was an energetic woman and a fascinating personality whose enthusiasm was contagious. Her shining eyes and expressive hands were famous; her appearance reminded contemporaries of a sybil and also of a sailor. Her rebellion against educational, religious, social, and political institutions made her a lifelong outsider, despite all the recognition and the friendships that her knowledge, her powers of persuasion, and her personal charm won for her. That she was not broken by her deep-seated ambivalence toward religion and sexuality is probably due to her inexhaustible vitality; with its help she managed time and again, in the face of numerous disappointments, to respond enthusiastically to all that was new and vivid.

Thanks to her life's work, one cannot imagine *Altertumswissenschaft* ignoring the supreme importance of anthropology and vase-painting for the study of the history of religion. This is shown most clearly by the Vernant school in Paris, who are working to understand the Greek "*imaginaire*" from the comparative and social-psychological viewpoint. Harrison made a permanent contribution to overcoming the concept of classicism that was derived from poetry and sculpture. That the analysis of ritual is inseparable from that of myth, that older traditions remain potent in both, and that both may contain contradictory material from different periods—insights that Harrison was the first to follow up consistently—now belongs to the scholarly *communis opinio*. Despite the rationalistic dogmatism with which she clung to the idea of historical evolution, her tendency to identify with or respond uncritically to her sources and her teachers, and her pleas for mysticism and asceticism, she decisively influenced both the pioneer in the study of Greek irrationality who followed in her footsteps, E. R. Dodds, Murray's successor at Oxford, as well as Walter Burkert, whose methodology stresses biological and prehistoric dimensions of ritual. Nevertheless, many Hellenists and archaeologists even today look upon her as a sort of *femme fatale* of classics, and her work, to a large extent, lies under the ban of a *damnatio memoriae*. Some of the theories of Harrison's chief work—e.g., the notions of the year-spirit or of Themis as a fundamental all-embracing deity, have long since proven to be untenable, and the heresies that won acceptance in her lifetime are controversial once more, since the modern study of religion has grown skeptical toward theories of step-by-step development and no longer accept the possibility of definite reconstruction of origins. Doubtless, many of the allied questions to which Harrison first directed the attention of classical scholars continue to be hotly debated: the relationship between matrilinear and patrilinear societies and the religious conceptions bound up with each, the assumption of an early phase of ritual without divinities followed by actual worship of the gods, the specific role of the female and the Chthonic deities in contrast to that of the male and the Olympian deities, or, not least, the significance of initiation rites and the misogynistic tendencies in ancient religion and literature, as well as the question of the function of psychoanalysis and social history in interpreting ancient texts and works of art. Likewise, the study of mystery cults, of Orphism, and of tragedy can derive profit from Harrison's preliminary investigations, provided such study frees itself from her prejudices and does not establish new *idées fixes* in their place. Jane Harrison's intuitive skill at discovering fruitful methods and posing irritating questions, as well as her courage in following them up, remain unique to this day in the field of classics.

Translated by Michael Armstrong

Books

Myths of the Odyssey in Art and Literature. London, 1882.

Introductory Studies in Greek Art. London, 1885; 2d ed., 1892; 3d ed., 1894; 4th ed., 1897; 5th ed., 1902.

Mythology & Monuments of Ancient Athens. Being a translation of a portion of the "Attica" of Pausanias by Margaret de G. Verrall. With an introductory essay and archaeological commentary by Jane E. Harrison. London and New York, 1890.

Prolegomena to the Study of Greek Religion. Cambridge, 1903; 2d ed., 1908; 3d ed., 1922; reprinted New York, 1955; 1962; 1975; 1980.

The Religion of Ancient Greece. London, 1905; reprinted 1913, 1921.

Primitive Athens as Described by Thucydides. Cambridge, 1906.

Themis: A Study of the Social Origins of Greek Religion. With an excursus on the ritual forms preserved in Greek tragedy by Gilbert Murray and a chapter on the origin of the Olympic games by F. M. Cornford. Cambridge, 1912; 2d ed. revised with preface and supplementary notes, 1927; reprinted with a preface by John C. Wilson, New York, 1962; 2d printing 1966.

Ancient Art and Ritual. London, 1913; reprinted 1918; London, 1927, 1935, 1948; Oxford,1951.

Alpha and Omega. London, 1915.

Aspects, Aorists, and the Classical Tripos. Cambridge, 1919.

Epilegomena to the Study of Greek Religion. Cambridge, 1921; reprinted in *Themis.* Edited by John C. Wilson: xvii–lvi.

Mythology: Our Debt to Greece and Rome. Boston, MA, 1924; reprinted New York, 1963.

Reminiscences of a Student's Life. London, 1925; reprinted in *Arion* 4 (1965) 312–346.

The Book of the Bear. London, 1926. (Twenty-one tales newly translated from the Russian by Jane Ellen Harrison and Hope Mirrlees, with a preface and epilogue.)

Myths of Greece and Rome. London, 1927; reprinted 1928, 1933.

Articles (Selected)

"Erwin Rohde. *Psyche. Seelencult und Unsterblichkeitsglaube der Griechen. Erste Hälfte.*" Review. CR 4 (1890) 376–377.

"Erwin Rohde. *Psyche. Seelencult und Unsterblichkeitsglaube der Griechen. Zweite Hälfte.*" Review. CR 8 (1894) 165–166.

"Delphika.—(A) The Erinyes. (B) The Omphalos." *JHS* 19 (1899) 205–251.

"Pandora's Box." *JHS* 20 (1900) 99–114.

"Mystica Vannus Iacchi." *JHS* 23 (1903) 292–324; 24 (1904) 241–254.

"Greek Religion and Mythology." *The Year's Work in Classical Studies*, ed. Cyril Bailey (London, 1915): 71–80; (London, 1917): 79–101.

Sources

Bibliography

A complete bibliography of works by and about the Cambridge Ritualists (including Jane Harrison) by Shelley Arlen is forthcoming.

Biographies

Cornford, F. M. "Jane Ellen Harrison." *DNB 1922–1930:* 408–09.

Stewart, Jessie. *Jane Ellen Harrison. A Portrait from Letters.* London, 1959.

Peacock, Sandra J. *Jane Ellen Harrison. The Mask and the Self.* New Haven and London, 1988.

Biographical

Ackerman, Robert. "Some Letters of the Cambridge Ritualists." *GRBS* 12 (1971) 113–136.

———. "Jane Ellen Harrison: The Early Work." *GRBS* 13 (1972) 209–230.

McGinty, Park. "Jane Ellen Harrison and the Study of Dionysos." In *Interpretation and Dionysos. Method in the Study of a God.* Religion and Reason 16. The Hague, Paris, and New York, 1978: 71–103, 207–222. (Reviewed by Robert Ackerman, *Gnomon* 52 [1980] 673–75.)

Murray, Gilbert. *Jane Ellen Harrison.* An Address. Delivered at Newnham College, Cambridge, 27 October 1928. Cambridge, 1928 = *Themis.* Ed. John C. Wilson, 559–577.

Letters

Jane Ellen Harrison Papers, Newnham College Archive, Cambridge.

Johannes Hasebroek
14 April 1893 – 17 February 1957

EDGAR PACK
Universität zu Köln

Immer fremder werden wir den Erben,
schon die Enkel kennen uns nicht mehr.
Dieses nochmal nach dem Tode sterben
fällt uns Armen fast nochmal so schwer.
Immer noch in unsern morschen Tüchern
geistern wir umher und schwören stumm
auf die Wahrheit in den alten Büchern.
Keiner kehrt sich um . . .

Notwithstanding the somewhat gothic imagery, there is much relevance in these verses (from "The Dead," by Peter Gan [Richard Moering, 1894–1974], the German *émigré* poet who was Hasebroek's classmate) to the unhappy life of Johannes Hasebroek, one of this century's most distinguished German historians of ancient Greek social and economic history. For some scholars, personal misfortune and political circumstances deny them the satisfaction of publishing the results of a lifetime's scientific work and of forming a school around themselves. It is most difficult even now, only three decades after his premature death, to reconstruct a full idea of the man who produced the two books on economy and society in ancient Greece. They not only made a great impression on the contemporary public and established his international renown among his peers as a reputable and—since he was still relatively young—a promising scholar but also produced a highly commendable, if not obligatory, source that must be taken into consideration by all those who, even today, are interested in Greek society from the archaic through the early classical periods and in the nature of ancient economy. It is a fine tribute to the enduring impact of his closely documented research that even those who would now profoundly reformulate the secular debate on the "primitivism" or "modernism" of economy and society on different terms, still feel it necessary to demonstrate carefully what Hasebroek would have been the last to deny, i.e., that his position, based on a solid study of one or two epochs of Greek history, cannot any longer be an unquestioned universal clue to a general characterization of the economies of the Mediterranean during that one and a half millennia that usually forms the chronological framework of ancient Greek and Roman history. If so, the more important scientific theses, though naturally more or less appropriately restated by subsequent research, remain forcefully present in the still-current debates that began in the early sixties. The following sketch is intended to furnish those biographical data that might be useful for assessing more correctly Hasebroek's scientific achievement and, incidentally, to disprove, at least in part, the melancholic end of the verses cited above as an epigraph.

Johannes (or John, as he was christened originally, following an onomastic variant typical of northern Germany) Hasebroek was born in Hamburg on 14 April 1893, the son of a distinguished physician of wide interests who profoundly influenced the intellectual formation of his promising offspring. Not without self-irony, he once remarked to a younger university colleague that he was "a scion of an old Hamburg patrician family," and though this is hardly correct in the narrow sense, it shows quite clearly the social pretensions and the moral atmosphere of an upper-middle-class family in the second great city of the Germany of the post-Bismarck era. "Old" the family was indeed, since its Dutch and Flemish origins can be traced back to the late fifteenth century, as young Hasebroek established by a personal, quasiprofessional genealogical research that occupied him repeatedly at various times in his life and was written down in his last years in a lengthy manuscript now, unfortunately, lost. A great-uncle, who served as a minister to a Dutch denomination, and a great-aunt distinguished themselves as romantic poets who, though perhaps in a marginal way, contributed to the formation of the modern Dutch national conscience, while another member of the family emigrated from Leyden to the United States, where he died a citizen of Missouri in 1866. The son of this man was Hasebroek's father, who came to Germany with his mother after his father's early death and, after studying medicine, settled at Hamburg, ran a doctor's office, and published the results of personal experiments in fields as different as cardiology, anatomy, entomology (!), and the psychology of visual perception. In the deep moral crisis pervading Republican Germany after its defeat in World War I, he even felt compelled to participate in the debate over a moral refounding of the upset equilibrium of German society and politics by publishing (with the aid of his son) a full-length essay on the necessity of believing in (a somewhat deistic) God. Unsurprisingly for a German citizen of rather recent stock in those times, he seems to have shared strongly the patriotic feelings of the age, making his young son read the heavy volumes of Treitschke's German history and giving his consent to his son's wish to change (in 1914!) his English-sounding name to the more Germanic Johannes. Nevertheless, the Anglophone world remained a self-evident reference point, and when Hasebroek's younger sister married a

Danish diplomat from the family of the poet Pontoppidan, it seemed natural that conversation between the families should be in English.

Scions of Hamburg families of this type traditionally got their schooling at the Johanneum, a *Gelehrtenschule* once directed by such eminent men as the Thucydides scholar Johannes Classen (1805–1891) and the school of famous students of antiquity such as Erwin Rohde, Jacob Bernays, J. Geffcken, C. F. Lehmann-Haupt and, first and foremost, Eduard Meyer. There young Hasebroek studied, though it seems that he did not entirely approve or enjoy the encyclopedic way of teaching then canonical at this sort of school. In one of the few surviving autobiographical texts, he reluctantly recalls a feeling of being overfed with too much knowledge of a disconnected nature and of having no time for developing his more personal interests. If not misled by hindsight, we may discover here an early manifestation of Hasebroek's personal style of working, i.e., digging up deeply and effectively a field of research of his own choice, thus reaching good and valuable results, but sometimes risking to cling to his own individual, if not (in a few respects) idiosyncratic, insights, irrespective of a more balanced view that could perhaps have been gained by taking note more fully of the conceptual framework proposed by his coresearchers. It is true, however, that this subjective inclination enabled him to state his views very effectively, leaving no doubt where he stood and marking dissenting opinions most clearly.

So it remains uncertain how much prep school may have influenced his intellectual formation, and the same tendency to independence of work and autonomy of judgment seems to have prevailed in his years as a university student. Under the influence of Eduard Meyer's *Geschichte des Altertums*, a work he had read as a pupil, he chose to supplement his central subjects (history, especially ancient, and classical philology) by a full course of archeology and at least the rudiments of some ancient Near Eastern languages, especially Egyptian, which he studied under Hermann Ranke, who had recently come back from the United States, where he had been a coworker of the Nippur excavations of the University of Pennsylvania. This extensive attempt to master different, though connected, fields shows quite clearly that young Hasebroek had made up his mind to strive for the erudite life of a German professor, and had been brought into contact with some of the best teachers of Heidelberg University, the archaeologists F. von Duhn and Rudolf Pagenstecher, the philologists Fritz Schoell and Franz Boll, the art historian Carl Neumann, and the historian Hermann Oncken. His real teacher, however, was the ancient historian Alfred von Domaszewski (1856–1927), a somewhat scurrilous pupil of Mommsen's, who had done *inter alia* some very good research on Latin epigraphy and Roman military history, and who was best known at that time for an idiosyncratic two-volume history of the Roman emperors written for a wider public and making some doubtful concessions to what its author deemed the gusto of the times. It was he who proposed to Hasebroek a study on the emperor Septimius Severus as the passport to a university career and, when this proved too long to be done in the then usual four-year course, accepted a preparatory research on two pertinent *vitae* from the notoriously unreliable *Scriptores Historiae Augustae* as Hasebroek's doctoral dissertation in June 1916. Though not called to arms, Hasebroek's further career was influenced infelicitously by the difficulties of a nation at war and the straits of the post-war years. So it was only five years after the doctoral examination that he could present his full study on Severus as a thesis in partial fulfilment of the requirements for the Habilitation at Hamburg University in 1921. Meanwhile, he had done war service as a compulsory stopgap teacher at a Berlin Gymnasium, had collaborated with Hermann Dessau in preparing a volume of the *Corpus Inscriptionum Latinarum* on a part-time basis, and had tried to complete his knowledge of the ancient world by frequenting some courses at Berlin University, an institution that was not unknown to him, since he had interrupted his Heidelberg years for two (as it seems, not wholly successful) semesters at Berlin. As far as we can know, during the Berlin years Hasebroek received those scientific influences and had those new experiences that led him to the subjects that made him famous. If Assyriology under Friedrich Delitzsch was an experience he did not pursue in later life, it must have been the papyrological seminar of Ulrich Wilcken (publishing soon afterwards his well-known paper, "Alexander and the Hellenistic economy," in 1921) and the lectures of the economist Werner Sombart that guided him to his new field of research.

The doctoral dissertation and the *Habilitationsschrift* admittedly showed a young man mastering in a respectable way the whole set of tools necessary for a solid interpretation of literary, epigraphic, and numismatic evidence and, moreover, though being firmly rooted in Domaszewski's teaching, are a good testimony to his independence of thought, kindly conceded by the liberal temper of his fatherly teacher. The usefulness and the solidity of his book on Septimius Severus, acknowledged even fifty years later by the author of the latest full study of that emperor (A. Birley, *Septimius Severus: The African Emperor* [1971] xi; 2f.; 5; 5n; for Hasebroek's dissertation, see *Ibid.*, 11f.), earned him the deserved liberty of teaching at the new university of his hometown, where he had returned for economic reasons after temporarily holding an assistantship under Friedrich Preisigke at the Papyrological Institute of Heidelberg University; but it cannot be overlooked that, measured against the vigorous new approach of the later books on Greek history, both his doctoral dissertation and *Habilitationsschrift*, do indeed smack a bit not only of the virtues, but also of the limitations, of what is nowadays disdainfully called "career literature."

This was noted also by the faculty referee, the Greek historian Erich Ziebarth, but it should not be presumed that it might have influenced the fact that Hasebroek had to wait more than four years before winning his first associate professorship (*Extraordinariat*) at Zürich University in late 1925. Economic difficulties of German universities and, as their corollary, deoccupation were a widespread fact of life among university graduates in these years. Hasebroek, though sometimes suffering from bad health, took all pains to make the best of his, on the whole, unsatisfying situation: He used his four years as an unpaid lecturer (i.e. receiving only a small honorary fee that did not amount to a living wage) to establish a well-arranged sequence of systematic lectures, covering the whole range of Greek and Roman history. They enjoyed even more success when he moved to his later professorships and alternated this cycle with lectures on more specific topics and seminars dealing with problems related to his own research or discussing new findings of extraordinary importance. It was this type of teaching that he maintained all his professional life and that gained him a grateful audience of impressive size even among the new (and still small) universities where he spent most of his teaching life.

As early as 1920 he had published a long paper on Greek banking and bankers, exploring successfully an important aspect of his new interests and showing unmistakably the directions that he intended to take in the following decade (for a fair recent evaluation of this first paper see R. Bogaert, *Banques et banquiers dans les cités grecques* [Leiden, 1968] 19). In fact, a second essay on the organizational characteristics of Greek trade was subjoined before long. Though dedicated mainly to a very close mustering of Attic orators and inscriptions of the fifth and fourth centuries B.C. and though he steered clear of generalities, he circumspectly tried to connect his specialist research to the more general problem of the nature of ancient economy. This had provoked a violent controversy some twenty-five years before, involving such eminent scholars as Karl Bücher and L. M. Hartmann on one side and R. von Pöhlmann, K. J. Beloch, and Eduard Meyer on the other. Hasebroek, who, on a more general level, was an admirer of Meyer's historical achievement and in his student years had temporarily thought of making himself a pupil of this leading Berlin professor, now carefully avoided reopening the controversy as such but made it perfectly clear that, in his view, the proud position of the modernizers, then sometimes called the Meyer-Beloch orthodoxy, could not stand any longer and that Bücher, though exaggerating and propounding an untenably schematic theory of stages of economic development, had discerned the "primitive" character of ancient economy, and especially that of archaic Greece, in an essentially correct way. Sharpening and refining this general view with relation to Greek history from the "Dark Ages" to the fourth century B.C. was to become his main occupation for the next ten years, the decade of his greatest activity and achievement. While these two preparatory articles kept strictly to the documents and avoided making more theoretical involvements explicit, his lecture on the idea of imperialism in antiquity, given to Swiss schoolteachers in 1926, revealed for the first time the strong impact of Max Weber's historico-sociological typifications and conceptualizations, made more generally accessible by the publication of Weber's collected papers soon after his death in 1920. It has been observed, rightly, that Hasebroek was the first (and for a long time the only) ancient historian in Germany to try to put to a fuller use (though surely in a version of reduced complexity) the Weberian approach. On the contrary, it has been deplored by some recent critics that Hasebroek tended to narrow too much the theoretical dimension and consequences of what had been at stake in the debate of a generation before and of what should have been a consequence of a really full appreciation of what Weber offered. Perhaps it should be noted, in fairness, that Hasebroek began his respective research as a rather "lonely hunter" who did the best he could reasonably do. He stressed the necessity of laying solid philological foundations for that field that looked most appropriate for proving his case and avoided what was then considered the kind of excessively high-brow theorizing that might have compromised the acceptability of the whole of his intentions, at least to some colleagues. Though it is not quite clear to what extent Hasebroek believed "primitivism" (as opposed to "modernism"; he seems to have been the first to use exactly this opposition in that context) to be characteristic of the whole span of time called antiquity (probably not so), it is beyond doubt that Weber's approach, which, at that time, could be a guarantee of originality and novelty in ancient history, served him well in at least two respects. In 1927, when his great book on trade and politics (*Staat und Handel im alten Griechenland*) was known to be imminent, it procured him his first full professorship at Cologne University, recently refounded from an earlier trade school and, in harmony with some trends of the Weimar years, strongly emphasizing the new "social sciences" (his unsuccessful rivals were Joseph Vogt and Helmut Berve, later to become the leaders of the two most influential schools in German ancient history). More important still, this approach was the main factor leading to the impressive revival and, in a sense, to the first real debate of his more important theses in the broadened intellectual context after World War II and also, sadly, after his death. *Staat und Handel* provoked a rather intense, though not always wholly amiable, debate, mostly in the form of lengthy reviews in which some of the rising generation took part quite forcefully, noting the originality of the views expressed and the solidity of their philological basis but criticizing a sometimes polemical unilaterality and minor deficiencies. Regrettably, we don't hear anything of how the older protagonists of the earlier controversy reacted, especially K. J. Beloch and Eduard Meyer, but 81-year-old Karl Bücher, though not participating in public discussions any longer, is said to have shown signs of pleased approval. One of the finest tributes to the importance of the book undoubtedly was the proposal, made by still unidentified British scholars immediately after its publication, to arrange for an English edition, a rather rare event in those days for a scholarly book whose technical details evidently had little appeal to a general public with little Greek. Ever since its publication in 1933, it has secured his ideas a wide notoriety, especially in the Anglophone world, where, to the testimony of some distinguished scholars, the book was recommended as obligatory reading for students specializing in Greek history in more than one university even in the fifties, that is, before its revival in the context of the Finleyan debate initiated in 1962 on the occasion of the Second Congress of Economic History at Aix-en-Provence.

Meanwhile, Hasebroek had rounded out his systematic approach with another book expounding his theories in a more historical perspective, remedying in this way some of the shortcomings of his previous study and emphasizing the usefulness of his Weberian concepts for a structuring of Greek economy and society from Homeric times to the end of the Persian Wars. Though obviously less innovative in those aspects already expounded in the previous book, it still contributed forcefully to establishing his renown as one of the very few serious German students of ancient economic history. The intensity of elaborating this second book; the friendly conversation with some of his colleagues, among whom should be noted the liberal historian Johannes Ziekursch—a firm opposer to the Bismarck myth—and the sociologist Paul

Honigsheim, one of the younger members of the famous Weber circle at Heidelberg; successfully teaching to a growing audience; discussing problems (human and professional) with his first pupils, supervising their doctoral dissertations and entertaining them at home once a semester; some motor touring in the beloved Mediterranean landscape of southern France, Italy, and Greece (driving his own car and and thus stressing, too, his distance from the then-still-dominating professorial type of the "Geheimrat"); and the incisive participation in current debates through some extended, carefully pondered reviews (e.g. of Berve's *Griechische Geschichte I*, of Hans Schaefer's *Staatsform und Politik* and of Rostovtzeff's *History of the Ancient World*)—all this made him feel that the first *quinquennium Coloniense* was the happiest period and, in a sense, the acme of his personal and scholarly life.

But all this was soon to come to a rather sad end. Human problems—the trauma of a divorce from his first wife, a red-haired beauty too fond of life to share the tranquil existence of this scholar—and serious pulmonary disease, which prevented him for several years from fulfilling his teaching duties, not only brought him to the verge of depression, but hindered him from throwing himself energetically into the study of a new project or from resuming older working plans, such as a full-scale study on slavery in Greco-Roman Egypt, begun in his Berlin years and never brought to an end. A temporary plan of procuring a new edition of the epigraphical monuments of Roman Cologne had to be rejected for lack of funds. This sort of (partly enforced) inactivity seems to have contributed to some degree to weakening, in the end, his professional position in his own faculty. Some of his friends had left Cologne as victims of the Nazi reorganization that struck the university in the first months of the new régime. Others preferred silence. Indeed, for those who neither actively opposed nor actively supported the new governance, there was not much left to stimulate grand-scale original research that was by no means certain to reach an interested public. Illness did the rest, necessitating several serious operations and prolonged stays in Alpine health resorts. Paradoxically, it was the friendly *ambiance* of a Swiss sanitorium that provided the context for that shameful political denunciation that led to his ultimate removal (in late 1937) from his university post. Some friends in the faculty, hoping to avoid a political scandal and cooperating with some more moderate collaborators of the Berlin Education Department, saw to it that the removal was made for "reasons of bad health" and not for "political reasons," which would have involved loss of all means of support.

At age forty-five, having lost his wife, his post, and most of his friends, Hasebroek was a very lonely man. If ever he had seriously thought of emigrating (there are some hints of such plans in 1933, though not wholly conclusive), the best opportunity now seemed to have passed by unused. After some years of wandering about, he tried to settle down at Heidelberg and to resume work on a private basis. In 1936, when he believed that disease would cease within a short time, he had made up his mind to write a social and economic history of early Rome (up to the end of the Struggle of the Orders). He began to work through those ancient authors he could easily take to his health resort, but of course he lacked the support of a large library and the helpful discussions of specialized scholars. Again his chief idea was to find in Weberian concepts the guidelines for a rethinking of early Roman history, which was still dominated by Mommsen's public-law approach. The manuscript of this book, nearly completed in 1942, has survived, though it lacks one chapter at the end. Intended as a Roman counterpart to his book on Greek history of 1931, it cannot be said to have come up to Hasebroek's previous standards in every respect. He somewhat mechanically tried to discover the same structural principles in early Rome that he had found in archaic Greece, construing some of his sources' information in a quasi-mathematical spirit so as to fit onto the grid of his concepts, ignoring or underrating occasionally the different situation in Rome. So, the outcome of his long endeavor was a not wholly conclusive mixture of constitutional and social history, revealing that Hasebroek's main ideas had evolved little in the past decade. Still more than the Greek studies it showed the difficulties Hasebroek felt in keeping in touch with the new developments, especially in the field of archaeological research, so fundamental for a new assessment of early Rome. In part this is surely a consequence of his fatal isolation (first imposed from the outside and then continued as a personal choice in consequence of his self-image as an "outsider" and a "failure") that prevented continuous conversation with colleagues and pupils, usually a most efficient antidote to reasoning in isolation. As it seems, the only partner to whom he revealed his plans in these years and whom he asked for scholarly opinions was his Zürich succcessor Ernst Meyer (1900–1975), who in 1948 published his most successful monograph, *Römischer Staat und Staatsgedanke*, which treated some of Hasebroek's problems in a more balanced way and in a broader context.

The scarcity of the paper supply precluded any thought of publication in the war years and in the early fifties, when Hasebroek made the last effort to find an editor for his unfortunate manuscript. After the war, he seems never to have tried again seriously to update his materials and to rewrite those parts that most needed a new discussion in the light of new findings. One of the few scholars who met him after the war, Wolfgang Liebeschuetz, the son of his famous classmate Hans and himself a distinguished student of antiquity, recalls the vivid impression of a friendly though somewhat depressive man looking older than he really was and largely living in a world of ideas and *connaissances* now lost: "The creative spark had been knocked out of him." When the Cologne faculty invited him to resume his chair in 1946, he characteristically felt unable to do so. The never-quite-vanquished consequences of his pulmonary disease prevented him from pursuing prolonged oral teaching duties, and, moreover, he probably then already felt a stranger to many of the new scholarly developments of the preceding decade.

He passed his last years as a private scholar in a small village near Lübeck, reading his old books (and much *belles lettres*), discussing problems of democracy and of religion with the village physician and the parson, speaking on friendly terms to the neighbors' children in the garden, looking up documents on the history of his family and meditating, now and then, on the problems of his social history of early Rome. Fits of discontent and a sense of "failure," however, never again permitted his brooding mind to resume his former fancy in cello playing, a joyful pastime of his Berlin years, which he occasionally exercised in a chamber quartet that included such celebrities as Ulrich Wilcken and Albert Einstein. A second marriage to a sensible and helpful woman unfortunately came too late to restore him to serious work. Of what he might have written, he never published anything after 1937. His life as a scholar had ended long before he died in early 1957. There were no colleagues at his burial, and nobody thought of writing an obituary worthy of this scholar.

It is not known whether Hasebroek ever knew of that fundamental article by which Edouard Will (*Annales: Economies, Sociétés, Civilisations* 9 [1954] 7–19) resumed the old debate in a most influential way, setting the standard for all further discussions and paying a very honorable tribute to the achievements of his German predecessor. He did not live to see the renewed interest given to his approach in the new climate of the sixties; in Germany, for example, the critical sympathy of parts of the Christian Meier school, where it may be considered a hereditary reference point deriving from the work of their *archegetes* Hans Schaefer; in the English-speaking countries and then all over the world through H. L. Pearson, Karl Polanyi, and most conspicuously through the work of M. I. Finley; in France through Edouard Will and his followers; and last but not least in Italy, with its strong interests in the history of historiography, where a full collection of Hasebroek's more important works was brought out only five years ago. Few of all these distinguished scholars will now subscribe to Hasebroek's theses *telles quelles*, but there are still fewer who believe that modern students could do their work ignorant of his insights. So it is not only for *pietas* that we should recall this man and the difficult circumstances against which he struggled to achieve a work of scholarship that, though small and forced to remain unfinished, proved intellectually coherent and vigorously innovative.

Books

Die Fälschungen der Vita Nigri und Vita Albini in den Scriptores Historiae Augustae. Diss., Heidelberg, 1916.

Untersuchungen zur Geschichte des Kaisers Septimius Severus. Habilitation thesis, Hamburg, 1921. Heidelberg, 1921.

Staat und Handel im alten Griechenland. Untersuchungen zur antiken Wirtschaftsgeschichte. Tübingen, 1928; reprinted Hildesheim, 1966. English translation by L. M. Fraser and D. C. MacGregor as Trade and Politics in Ancient Greece. London, 1933; reprinted New York, 1965.

Griechische Wirtschafts- und Gesellschaftsgeschichte bis zur Perserzeit. Tübingen, 1931; reprinted Hildesheim, 1966.

Articles and Monographs

"Griechisches Bankwesen." Hermes 55 (1920) 113–173

Das Signalement in den Papyrusurkunden. Papyrusinstitut Heidelberg, Schrift 3. Berlin and Leipzig, 1921.

"Die Betriebsformen des griechischen Handels im IV. Jahrhundert." *Hermes* 58 (1923) 393–425.

Der imperialistische Gedanke im Altertum. Stuttgart, 1926.

Sources

Golczewski, F. *Kölner Universitätslehrer und der Nationalsozialismus.* Studien zur Geschichte der Universität Köln 8. Cologne and Vienna, 1988: 112 with note 24 (not wholly satisfactory), 283, 453.

Heimbüchel, B. "Die neue Universität. Selbstverständnis–Idee und Verwirklichung." In *Kölner Universitätsgeschichte.* Bd. II. Cologne and Vienna, 1988: 101ff. (Important for the general background of Cologne University; for Hasebroek see p. 506f., with some factual errors.)

Kürschners Deutscher Gelehrtenkalender. 1921ff.

Losemann, V. *Nationalsozialismus und Antike. Studien zur Entwicklung des Fachs Alte Geschichte 1933–1945.* Hamburg, 1977: esp. 41 and 201 f.

Marcone, A. "Una poco conosciuta recensione di M. Rostovtzeff." *Athenaeum* 65 (1987) 541–542.

Näf, Beat. *Von Perikles zu Hitler? Die athenische Demokratie und die deutsche Althistorie bis 1945.* Bern, 1986: esp. 176 f., but see index 327.

Pack, E. "Johannes Hasebroek und die Anfänge der Alten Geschichte in Köln. Eine biographische Skizze." *Geschichte in Köln* 21 (June 1987): 5–42. (With full bibliography of Hasebroek's writings and the doctoral dissertations written under his guidance.)

———. "Una lettera di Johannes Hasebroek a M. I. Rostovtzeff." *Athenaeum* 65 (1987) 542–547.

Weiss, A. "Johannes Hasebroek." *Rupertenblätter* (Heidelberg). No. 18 (May 1957).

Papers

Personal files in the University Archives of Cologne, Hamburg, Heidelberg, and Zürich; private letters; personal information from various contemporaries.

J. L. Heiberg

27 November 1854 – 4 January 1928

PAUL T. KEYSER
University of Colorado and
Wilhelm-Pieck-Universität Rostock

Johan Ludvig Heiberg, confused by the ignorant with his more famous playwright-critic namesake, obscured by the better-known studies of his teachers Madvig and Ussing, his friend and fellow student A. B. Drachmann and his colleagues Carl Hude, Hans Henning Ræder and (in the next generation) Frederick Poulsen, probably deserves to be remembered as the greatest of the Danish scholars of the golden age of classical studies. (Madvig, who overtops him, belongs properly to the previous generation.) Dyed in science rather than fatally tainted with literature, Heiberg chose to study the Greek mathematicians and doctors—a field neglected (to our detriment) by modern scientists and classicists alike. This choice and the fact that well over half his articles and books were in Danish have vitiated his fame.

Born to Læge Emil Theodor Heiberg, an Aalborg physician from whom he drew an interest in pharmaceutics, and Johanne Henrietta Jacoba Schmidt, from whom he gained an enthusiasm for the philosopher Kierkegaard, whom he later edited, and named after the most popular playwright of his parents' teen years (and occasionally called "J. L. II"), Heiberg was awakened to the charms of Greek and mathematics in the Aalborg Katedralkskole. At age seventeen, he went to the Kopenhagen University, where his teachers were Siesbye, Ussing, and, most importantly, Madvig. From Ussing he learned archaeology and art history, on which he often wrote (but only in Danish and on postclassical times). He was Madvig's last and perhaps best student, to whom he remained always loyal (he was asked to write the necrology in *Bursian's Jahresbericht*) and saw himself first as a philologist (as is clear from his editions of Archimedes, Apollonius, Euclid, and so forth). Important for Heiberg's development in graduate school was the Greek study-circle gathered by the archaeologist Christian Jørgensen. In 1875 he began his reading of Archimedes and four years later (1879) he took his doctorate with a dissertation, *Quaestiones Archimedeae*, on the man who held his interest for the rest of his life. He traveled to Italy for the first time in the same year (to examine manuscripts of Archimedes), a land to which he was to return more often than to his beloved Greece. At this time he also married Cathrine Asmussen, two years his junior (7 Oct. 1856–29 Aug. 1929), by whom he had a daughter, Cathrine.

His postgraduate career began in Kopenhagen private schools, though he had supported himself since 1876 as an instructor and continued to take part in instruction at his old school till his death. From 1884 (the year after his mother's death) till 1895 he was *Bestyrer* (Director) of the *Borgerdydskole* in Østerbro (founded 1787). In 1896 he was called back to the University, where he was a professor for a mathematically "perfect" twenty-eight years (retiring at seventy). He was a member of the Danish Academy of Sciences (Danske Videnskabernes Selskab) from 1883 and its editor (Redaktør) from 1902 to 1913. In 1915–1916 he was Rector of the University.

The works for which he is best known are his editions of the Greek mathematicians and scientists, for which he had been well prepared by his schooling, by Madvig, and by his contacts in graduate school with the mathematicians H. G. Zeuthen and Ludwig Oppermann. As he began his work on Euclid, he wrote in *Philologus* 44 (1884) 322:

> And the philologist also has here (that is, in the field of the history of Greek and Roman mathematics) a task to perform which he ought not to shirk. He must establish and clean the text with the utmost certainty and so correctly lay the foundation-stones for the historian of mathematics. And he need not feel himself to be the mathematician's handworker, for he is pursuing thereby his own scholarly goals and much appears to him in a different light and of another meaning than to the mathematician. The latter understands and evaluates Greek and Roman mathematics as steps in the progress of science; philology is concerned with its place in the intellectual history of antiquity.

And great was the work to be done: of editions then available, only Friedrich Hultsch's Pappos (1876–9) was any good; for Apollonius one had to depend on Edmund Halley's 1710 edition, for others on even earlier or worse editions. It was his lot to recover more Greek texts of importance than any other philologist of his era (? *Analemma*, Euclid *Optics*, Archimedes *Floating*—known only in late versions or translations, and Archimedes *Method*—not known at all). All of these editions are today *the* standard texts of the authors: his work is unsurpassed.

The first of these editions was his Archimedes in three volumes (1880–1881), later superseded by the second edition (1900–1915), which incorporated the newly discovered *Method*. Here he shows himself a Madvigian in his zeal to examine *every* manuscript (which he did) and to establish the exact history of the text from antiquity through the manuscripts he used. Moreover, unlike some editors who give only a "translation" of the MS figures (i.e., only redrawn figures), Heiberg was wise (and Madvigian) enough to give the MS figures themselves. Next came Euclid's *Elements*, including scholia and Theon's recension, in five volumes (1883–1888), and later the

Optics (1895; completed in 1890); much later the Euclidean fragments appeared, with other Euclideana by Heinrich Menge. In the interval Heiberg had completed his edition of Apollonius (of those books, the first four extant in Greek) with fragments and Eutocius' commentary (1890–1893). Hermann Diels convinced Heiberg to undertake the editing of Simplicius' *De Caelo*, which appeared in the *Commentaria in Aristotelem Graeca* in 1894.

All this before he was called back to Copenhagen. Already in 1895 Heiberg had turned to Ptolemy (the palimpsest of *Analemma*; from his university chair he produced editions of the *Syntaxis* ("Al-magest") and the *Opera Astronomica Minora* (1898; 1903; 1907); for the first time he did not provide a Latin translation. When Wilhelm Schmidt died leaving the Heron edition an *opus imperfectum*, Heiberg saw his duty and completed the last two (of five) volumes (1912, 1914). During this time he also found and restored to the world Archimedes' *Ephodos* (1907ff.) and brought out only his second edition of a Greek text, *Archimedes* (1910–1915). The last ten years of his university professorship, perhaps originally distracted by his Rektorat, were marked by a lower productivity—the works are mainly Danish or popular save the edition of the historian of mathematics P. Tannery's works (1912–1927). The survey of Greek science which he wrote at this time (1912) is probably his most widely read book, and the English translation is still used in history of science courses.

Late in life he turned back to his mathematicians (e.g., Theodosius, 1927) and to medicine and alchemy. In fact, the first impulse for the *Corpus Medicorum Graecorum* came from Heiberg, according to Diels, and in any case volume 1, part 1 appears over Heiberg's name (1927). He had long ago written on Hippocrates (1904) and then in 1921 and 1924 (also in the *Corpus Medicorum Graecorum*) had appeared Heiberg's edition of Paul of Aegineta (who may be called the last scientist of antiquity). In alchemy he contributed to the important *Catalogue des manuscrits Alchimiques Grecs* (1924, 1927).

He was not, however, only a historian of science and editor of Greek scientists; he also wrote (though always in Danish) on art history and made numerous trips to Italy for the purpose. He contributed occasional notes (derived from his wide reading of Greek literature) on various texts, especially Aristophanes and Herodotus, two of his favorites. He edited, with H. O. Lange and his friend and *commilitone* A. B. Drachmann, the works of the philosopher Søren Kierkegaard in fourteen volumes (1901–1906), with a second edition (cp. Archimedes), which he did not live to see completed (1920–1936). Hansen lists over 140 items of contributions to Danish scholarship by Heiberg (exceeded only by the archaeologist and art historian Friedrich Poulsen, with nearly 175). Heiberg thus outstrips in sheer numbers his teachers Madvig (ca. 125) and Ussing (ca. 85) as well as his colleagues Carl Hude (ca. 100), who wrote on Thucydides and Herodotus, Hans Henning Ræder (ca. 125), who wrote on Plato, and A. B. Drachmann (ca. 60). His virtue was to work on Greek mathematics and medicine where textual criticism was needed more than ideas (not his strong suit, according to Høeg). The virtue of the better-known Danes was to work on authors every schoolboy pretends to have read—and who has chosen the better life?

His love for things Greek went to the edge of monomania, according to a colleague at his seventieth birthday party, yet he could say that the Roman aqueducts were a better measure of the true greatness of Rome than all of Roman literature. He saw it as his duty to transmit the cultural values of the Greek intelligentsia and to present the cultural inheritance of Greece. This he did, primarily in Danish, in a long series of short, readable monographs beginning in 1891 (for example *Eros, en culturhistorisk Skitse* [1894]), many of which were collected in *Fra Hellas og Italien* (1929). His own views were rationalistic (he rejected as un-Greek all mysticism), and he stated:

> That we can create an existence worthy of a man on the foundation that Socrates has laid, he himself has shown by his life and death. He has once and for all pointed the way for all those who wish to lead their life without supernatural assistance.

(I cite the text of Junge who claims these are his "eigenen worte"; Hoeg quotes a similar passage but has made a number of verbal changes [wir uns . . . schaffen können aufgebaut werden kann, Dasein Leben, Sterben durch seinen Tod, Führen leben, for examples] which seem unlikely to be his. Hoeg says nothing about "eigenen worte." Heiberg would not approve.)

He was an embittered, even fanatical, anti-Christian (some of his monographs are directed against Christianity). For him rhetoric was a "Pestilenz," aesthetics were distant, and he was not open to the more refined art (despite his studies of postclassical art!). In the wide expanse of Greek literature he sought a field where naught but iron endurance and cool fact entered: thus his interest in Greek mathematics and medicine for their observation of reality and mistrust of speculative philosophy. I would add that only where we can control the results of Greek thought with our own knowledge (mathematics and physical science) can we understand the *processes* of Greek thought. He loved Greek symmetry and self-control and the dry humor of Aristophanes.

His personal life was complicated by a decades-long and never consummated Platonic love affair with the wife of his friend Drachmann, who allowed it (as recollected by Drachmann's younger son; see Calder and Meyer). He and Drachmann were close friends of Wilamowitz. Heiberg was completely unaffected and free of all vanity—he spoke German, Italian, and even French with the same Danish accent. He rarely raised his soft and muffled voice, even in his Rektoratrede. He was a passionate smoker, he rejected the telephone, and he preferred kerosene lamps to electric. In spite of his quirks, all who were familiar with him felt strongly that he was a powerful and pure personality. He gave to the world scientific texts of the Greek scientists (and of Kierkegaard), which then as now are standard; he advanced *Altertumswissenschaft* in the land that gave us the designations Stone, Bronze, and Iron Age by his writing and his work at the University (influenced by Wilamowitz) and he was a scientific humanist in the best sense.

Books

Quaestiones Archimedeae. Inest de arenae numero libellus. Diss., Copenhagen, 1879.

Archimedis Opera omnia cum commentariis Eutocii. 3 vols. Leipzig, 1880–1881; 2d ed., 1910–1915.

Literargeschichtliche Studien über Euklid. Leipzig, 1882.

Euclidis Opera Omnia. Vols. 1–5, 7, 8.2. Leipzig, 1883–8, 1895, 1916.

Apollonii Pergaei quae Graece exstant cum commentariis antiquis. 2 vols. Leipzig, 1891–3.

Aphorismer om Hippokrates. Copenhagen, 1892 = *Studier fra Sprog og Oldtidsforskning* 7.

Codex Leidensis 399, 1. Euclidis Elementa ex interpretatione Al-Hadschaschadschii cum commentariis Al-Narizii. With R. O. Besthorn. 3 vols. Copenhagen, 1893–1911.

Simplicii in Aristotelis de caelo commentaria. Berlin, 1894 = *Commentaria in Aristotelem Graeca* 7.

Eros, en culturhistorisk Skitse. Copenhagen, 1894 = *Studier fra Sprog og Oldtidsforskning* 19.

Attiske gravmaeler. Copenhagen, 1895.

Sereni Antinoensis Opuscula. Leipzig, 1896.

Beiträge zur Geschichte Georg Vallas und seiner Bibliothek = *Centralblatt für Bibliothekwesen.* Beiheft 6.16 (1896).

Claudii Ptolemaei Opera quae exstant omnia. 1: *Syntaxis mathematica.* Leipzig, 1898, 1903; 2: *Opera Astronomica Minora.* Leipzig, 1907.

Søren Kierkegaards samlede Værker. With A. B. Drachmann and H. O. Lange. 14 vols. Copenhagen, 1901–1906; 2d ed. [15 vols.], 1920–1936.

Anonymer Kommentar zu Platons Theaetet nebst frei Bruchstüchen philosophischen Inhalts. Edited by H. Diels and W. Schubart in cooperation with Heiberg. Berlin, 1905 = *Berliner Klassikertexte* 2.

Italien, Spredte Studier og Rejseskritser. Copenhagen, 1904. In part as 2d ed. = *Fra Helas og Italien.* Copenhagen, 1929.

Eine neue Schrift des Archimedes. With H. G. Zeuthen. Leipzig, 1907. Cf. T. L. Heath. *The Method of Archimedes Recently Discovered by Heiberg. A Supplement to the Work of Archimedes 1897.* Cambridge, 1912; reprinted New York, 1953.

Græske Læsestykker. With A. B. Drachmann. Copenhagen, 1912; 2d ed. with Hans Ræder and Drachmann, 1927.

Pauli Aeginetae libri tertii interpretatio Latina antiqua. Leipzig, 1912.

Naturwissenschaften und Mathematik im klassischen Altertum. Leipzig, 1912; reprinted 1920 = *Aus Natur und Geisteswelt* 370. English translation by D. C. Macgregor as *Mathematical and Physical Sciences in Classical Antiquity.* Oxford, 1922.

Den helliage Porphyrios, Bishop af Gaza. Et Tidsbillede Fra Hendnsabets sidste Dage. Copenhagen, 1912; reprinted 1922 = *Religionshistoriske smaa-shriffer.* Series 1, vol. 9. 1912.

Heronis Alexandrini Opera 4: Heronis definitiones cum variis collectionibus. Heronis quae Feruntur geometrica. Leipzig, 1912, 5: *Heronis quae Feruntur stereometrica et de mensuris.* Leipzig, 1914. .

Paul Tannery: Mémoires scientifiques. With H. G. Zeuther. 8 vols. Toulouse and Paris, 1912–1927.

Paulus Aegineta. 2 vols. Leipzig and Berlin, 1921 = *Corpus Medicorum Graecorum* vol. 9, fasc. 1–2.

Glossae medicinales. Copenhagen, 1924 = *Corpus Medicorum Graecorum* vol. 9, fasc. 1. (1924).

Catalogue des manuscrits Alchimiques Grecs. With J. Bides, F. Cumont and O. Lagercoante. 3 vols. Brussels, 1924, 1927, 1924.

Geschichte der Mathematik und Naturwissenschaten in Altertum. Munich, 1925 = *Handbuch der Altertumswissenschaft* vol. 5, fasc. 1, pt. 2.

Et Christent Verdensbillede. Copenhagen, 1926 = *Studier fra Sprog og Oldtidsforskning* 138. (On Cosmos Indicopleistas.)

Hippocratis Opera. 1.1 Leipzig and Berlin, 1927 = *Corpus Medicorum Graecorum* vol. 1, fasc. 1.

Mathematici Graeci Minores. Copenhagen, 1927 = *Dansk Videnskabernes Selskab. Historisk-Filologiske Meddelelser* 13.3 (1927).

Theodosius Tripolites Sphaerica. Berlin, 1927 = *Abh. Geswiss. Gött., Phil.-Hist. Klasse. N. s.* 19,3 (1927).

Fra Hellas og Stalien. Udvalgte Afhandlinger. Edited by A. B. Drachmann, Casten Hoeg and E. Spang-Hanssen. 2 vols. Copenhagen, 1929.

Anonymi logica et quadrivium, cum scholiis antiquis. Copenhagen, 1929 = *Dansk Videnskabernes Selskab. Historisk-Filologiske Meddelelser* 15.1.

Articles (Collected)

J. L. Heibergs Samlede Skrifter. 22 vols. (Vols. 1–11: Prose Writings; Vols. 12–22 Poetic Writings). Copenhagen, 1833–1862.

Articles (Selected)

"Einige von Archimedes vorausgesetate elementare Sätze." *Zeitschrift fur Mathetatik und Physik, Hist.-Lit Abt.* 24 (1879) 177–182.

"Die Kentnisse des Archimedes über die Kegelschnitte." *ZMP* 25 (1880) 41–67.

"Philologische Studien zu griechischen Mathematikern. I. Ueber Eutokios. II. Ueber die Restitution der Zwei Bücher des Archimedes περὶ σφαίρας καὶ κυλίνδρου." *Neue Jahrbücher für classische Philologie.* Suppl. 11 (1880) 355–99.

"Die Archimedes handschrift Georg Valls." *Philologus* 42 (1883) 421–37.

"Archimedis περὶ ὀχουμένων Graece restituit." *Mélanges Graux* (Paris, 1884) 689–709.

"Die Arabische Tradition der Elemente Euclids." ZMP 29 (1884) 1–22.

"Ein Palimpsest der Elemente Euklids." *Philologus* 44 (1885) 353–66.

"Johan Nicolai Madvig, geb. den 7. August 1804, gest. den 12. December 1886." *Biog* 9 (1886) 202–221.

"Om Scholiene til Euklids Elementer. Avec un résumé en Français." *Dansk Videnskabernes Selskab, Skrifter. Historisk og Philosofiske Afdeeling.* Series 6, vol. 2.3 (1888) 227–304.

"Neue Studien zu Archimedes." ZMP 34, Suppl. = *Abh. Gesch. d. math. Wiss.* 5 (1890) 1–84.

"Beiträge zur Geschichte der Mathematik in Mittelalter." ZMP 35 (1890) 41–58, 81–100.

"Ptolemäus de Analemmate." ZMP 40, Suppl. = *Abh. Gesch. d. math. Wiss.* 7 (1895) 1–30.

"Die Überlieferung der griechischen Mathematik." *Vorhandlungen der 43. Versammlung deutscher Philologen ond Schulmanner in Köln 1895.* Leipzig, 1895: 27–34.

"Græshe Vaser." With drawings by Joakin Skorgaard. *Kunstblakt* (1898) 337–53.

"De locis nonnullis Ranarum Fabula Aristophanis adnotatiunculae." *Nordisk Tidsskrift for Filologi.* Series 3, vol. 7 (1898–1899) 60–67.

"Bidrag til Belysning af Herodots relrgeuse Standpunkt." *Festskrift til J. L. Ussing.* Copenhagen, 1900: 91–109 = *Fra Hellas og Italien* 1:341–56.

"Quelques papyrus traitant de mathématiques." *Oversigt over det kgl. Danske Videnskabernes Selskabs Forhandlinger* (1900) 147–71.

"Anatolius sur les dix premiers nombres." *Annuaire International d'Histoire, Congrès de Paris 1900, 5e section* (Paris 1901): 27–57.

"Paralipomena zu Euklid." *Hermes* 38 (1903) 46–74, 161–201, 321–56.

"Antik Polemik mod Kristendommen." *Det ny Aarhundert* 1.2 (1903–1904) 84–102.

"Mathematisches zu Aristoteles." *Abh. Gesch. math. Wiss.* 18 (1904) 1–49.

"Die handchriftliche Grundlage der Schrift ΠΕΡΙ ΑΕΡΩΝ ΥΔΑΤΩΝ ΤΟΠΩΝ." *Hermes* 39 (1904) 133–45.

"Mathematik, Mechanik und Astronomie." *Die Altertumswissenschaft im letzten viertel-jahrhundert. Eine Übersicht über ihre Entwicklung in der Zeit von 1875–1900, in Verein mit meheren Fachgenossen.* Edited by Wilhelm Kroll. Leipzig, 1905: 129–43.

"Græsh Kultur." *Verdenskulturen.* No. 2. Edited by Aage Fris. Copenhagen, 1905–1906: 127–300.

"Et par Punkter af den byzantinske Kunsts Historie." *Tidsskrift for Filologi.* Series 3, vol. 16 (1907–1908) 1–20.

"Bemærkninger til Aristophanes' 'Fuglene.'" *Nordisk Tidsskritt for Filologi.* Series 3, vol. 16 (1907–1908) 1–20.

"Eine neue Archimedeshandschrift." *Hermes* 42 (1907) 235–303.

"Einige griechischen Aufgaben der unbestimmten Analytik." With H. G. Zeuthen. *Bibliotheca Mathematica.* Series 3, vol. 8 (1908) 118–34.

"Exakte Wissenschaften und Medizin." *Einleitung in die Altertumswissenschaft.* Edited by A. Gercke and E. Norden. Vol. 2, Leipzig and Berlin, 1910: 391–432; 2d ed., 1912: 385–425; 3rd ed., 1922: 315–57.

"Eine mittelalterliche Übersetzung der Syntaxis des Plolemaios." *Hermes* 45 (1910) 57–66 and "Noch einmal die mittelalterliche Ptolemaios-übersetz ung," *Hermes* 46 (1911) 207–16.

"Exegetische Bemerkungen." *Hermes* 46 (1911) 458–63. (Ad. Paus. 5.10.4, 11.6, Plutarch *Solon.*)

"De codicibus Pauli Aeginetae observationes." *REG* 32 (1919) 268–77.

"Bemærkinger om Josephus." *Historisk Tidsskrift.* Series 9, vol. 2 (1921) 281–306.

"Les sciences grecques et leur transmission." *Scientia* 31 (1922) 1–10, 97–104.

"Geisteskrankheiten im klassischen Altertum." *Allg. Zeitschr. f. Psychologie* 88 (1927); reprinted as *Geisteskrankheiten im klassischen Altertum.* Berlin, 1927.

Sources

Adler, Ada. "Heiberg, Johan Ludvig." *Dansk Biografisk Leksikon* 9 (1936) 560–7.

Arnim, H. "Johan Ludvig Heiberg. Ein Nachouf." *Almanach der Akademic der Wissenschaften im Wien* 78 (1928) 264–73.

Hansen, Peter Allen. *Bibliography of Danish Contrbutions to Classical Scholarship from the Sixteenth Century to 1970.* Danish Humanist Texts and Studies 1. Copenhagen, 1977.

Harrassowitz, O. *Bibliothek J. L. Heiberg und andere Bestände.* 2 vols. Leipzig, 1929 = Bücher-Katalog: 423–424.

Hoeg, Carsten. "Johan Ludvig Heiberg. Geboren 27. November 1854, gestorben 4. Januar 1928." *Jahresbericht über die Fortschritte der klassischen Altertums wissenschaft.* 233.4 (1931) 38–77.

Junge, Gustav, "Johann [sic] Ludvig [sic] Heiberg." *Jahresbericht der Deutschen Mathematiker-Vereinigung.* 38 (1929) 17–23.

Mejer, Jørgen. "Wilamowitz and Scandinavia: Friendship and Scholarship." *Wilamowitz nach 50 Jahren.* Edited by W. M. Calder III, et. al. Darmstadt, 1985: 513–37.

J. C. Poggendorff's Biographisch-Literarisches Handwörterbuch. 3 (Leipzig, 1898) 604; 4 (Leipzig, 1903) 605; 5 (Leipzig, 1926) 512–3; 6 (Leipzig, 1937) 1063.
   Bibliography
Spang-Hanssen, E., *Filologen J. L. Heiberg.* 2d ed., Copenhagen, 1969.

Gottfried Hermann

28 November 1772 – 31 December 1848

ERNST GÜNTHER SCHMIDT
Friedrich-Schiller-Universität Jena

Johann Gottfried Jacob Hermann was, with Richard Bentley (1662–1742) and Richard Porson (1759–1808), one of the triad of the greatest textual critics of history, and with Friedrich August Wolf (1759–1824) and August Böckh (1795–1867) he was one of the trinity of the greatest German classical philologists of the first half of the nineteenth century. He did not achieve the spectacular, albeit transient, success of Wolf's work on Homer nor the far-reaching and abiding influence of Böckh's studies of Greek inscriptions and institutions; yet, as the recognized leader of the linguistic and text-critical school of classical philology, as one of the greatest scholars of Greek and Latin of all time, and as a brilliant academic teacher and the educator of a whole generation of outstanding philologists, he acquired a fame that was, for a time, virtually legendary and that continues to reverberate to this day.

Hermann's accomplishment is all the more astounding in that it was achieved in a narrow, even provincial, environment. Born and buried in Leipzig, he hardly ever left his home town. The events of his life show but few travels outside the city: one semester as a student at Jena (1793–1794), two journeys to Switzerland (1815, 1825), brief excursions within central Germany (Thüringen, the Harz, Dresden, and vicinity), several visits to the spa at Karlsbad (Karlovy Vary), and attendance at philological congresses in Gotha (1840), Dresden (1844), and Jena (1846). So far as is known, he never saw Berlin, then beginning its rise as a center of scholarship, even though after 1841 he could easily have made the journey by rail. It is not without embarrassment that one sees Hermann, the celebrated editor, referring to his personal inspection of *codices* in such third-class manuscript libraries as Leipzig and Zwickau; he failed to make use of the great manuscript collections in southern Germany, France, and Italy, even when his scholarly rivals, such as Elmsley, began to do so. He never visited the classical lands.

That these circumstances did not more grievously diminish his influence is due to the fact that within the limits that were set for him—or which he set for himself—he aimed at and achieved a perfection hitherto unknown in his discipline. His successes, however, were not handed to him. Son of a senior member of the Leipzig court of sheriffs and of a mother who, though born in Halle, was of French extraction (a heritage that Hermann all his life tended rather to disavow than to cherish, though it doubtless influenced him), his family was respected but devoid of any loftier intellectual ambitions. His father intended that his son should study the law, and after the appropriate studies young Hermann devoted his first publication, in 1793, to a subject in jurisprudence—the basis of criminal law. But from the first he was far more seriously interested in classical philology than the law, though he never attended a preparatory school and his frail early years were followed by a period of overflowing youthful energy during which he was disinclined to study. But then he found men who gave him discipline and guided him to the classical authors. The first of these mentors was his private tutor, Karl David Ilgen (1763–1834), who later, on Hermann's recommendation, became rector of the famous boys' boarding school Schulpforte. Matriculating next at the University of Leipzig in 1786, he encountered Friedrich Wolfgang Reiz (1733–1790), the Professor of Philology, who pointed him toward the pioneering accomplishments of the English philologists and recommended to him as his life's work an edition of Plautus. (Hermann's student Friedrich Ritschl later produced this edition.) Hermann revered Reiz all his life and as late as 1844 publicly celebrated his memory at the philological congress in Dresden.

Becoming acquainted by chance with the philosophy of Kant, Hermann went briefly to Jena to attend the lectures of the Kantian Karl Reinhold (1758–1823). Clearly, however, he was more deeply influenced there by the philologist Christian Gottfried Schütz (1747–1832), an Aeschylean scholar, who eagerly recommended this tragedian to him. And although Hermann finally gave up his plans for an edition of Plautus, he was fascinated with the project of an edition of Aeschylus and worked on it all his life, though he failed to complete it. Only after his death was it published by his son-in-law, Moriz Haupt.

Though Hermann was not unaffected by external influences, his early mastery of philology cannot be explained by his training. It derived rather from a strong inner talent that, in addition, ripened quickly. Even in his first discussions of ancient meter (1796 and 1799) and in his early editions of Aeschylus (1799), Aristophanes (1799), and Plautus (1800), his command of his major field of endeavor—the explication of ancient, particularly Greek, poetry—was that of a master, and recognition came with appropriate rapidity. He became *magister artium liberalium* in 1793 and habilitated in 1794 with the thesis *De generibus poeseos*; in 1797 he was appointed Extraordinarius; in 1803 Ordinarius of Eloquence (*eloquentiae*); and in 1809 Professor of Poetry (*poeseos*) as well. This old and prestigious double professorship gave him a more respected position at the University of Leipzig than a professorship of philology would have done.

In his own eyes, the focus of his pedagogical influence was the "Greek Society" (*Societas Graeca*), which he founded in 1797. Here he came together with his best students for scholarly discussion—in Latin, of course. But his public lectures—he delivered his philological lectures in Latin, while those of more general interest were in German—exerted a consistently strong influence for many years.

Hermann declined calls from other universities: one from Kiel in 1803, after prolonged negotiations, and another from the newly founded University of Berlin in 1811. (August Böckh, who was still quite young, was appointed in his stead.) Hermann had not foreseen that Berlin would rise meteorically to become the intellectual center of Germany, and when it happened, he probably viewed that rise with some suspicion. He was twice Rector of the University of Leipzig, which in 1840 honored him in princely style on the occasion of the fiftieth anniversary of his master's degree. He reached the zenith of his public activity as president of the Philological Congress at Dresden in 1844. He married Wilhelmine Schwägerichen, the daughter of a Leipzig merchant, in 1803, and he was the father of six children. Grieving over the collapse of the German Reich in 1806, he gave his sons the names of medieval German emperors—Otto, Konrad, Rudolph.

In the course of his life Hermann received numerous honors. He was, for example, Knight of the Saxon Civil Service Order, a member of the Peace Class of the Prussian Order of Merit, the Greek Order of the Redeemer, and the Russian Order of Stanislaus. On the other hand, he declined appointment as *geheimer Rath* (Privy Councillor), which had been projected in honor of the fiftieth anniversary of his professorship. He was a member of academies or scientific societies in Berlin, Munich, Nancy, Oslo, St. Petersburg, and Rome, as well as being one of the eight associated members of the Académie des Inscriptions et de Belles Lettres of the Institut de France in Paris. In Leipzig in 1846 he was among the founding members of the Royal Society of Sciences (today the Saxon Academy of Sciences) and was its first secretary. In the same city shortly before his death he became member of the old and highly respected Prince Jablonowski Society of Sciences, which appeared before the public chiefly in setting subjects for prize essays.

One ought not to omit the fact that, as was customary for scholars in the Germany of this period, Hermann was assigned by the Saxon government to take part in the censorship of books. He received almost daily the proofs of novels and the like, the perusal of which he generally left to his wife. When the government proposed in 1836 to set up a separate Board of Censorship, Hermann strenuously opposed it, fearing that censorship would tighten its grip. This strong protest of 1836 was his only political activity of note. During the French Revolution his attitude toward contemporary events was less enthusiastic than that of the mass of young people, and later his political stance was half-liberal and half-conservative. He was sympathetic toward the revolution of 1848, which brought troubles to Leipzig among other places, without being shaken in his monarchical principles. His death at the threshold of the revolutionary years 1848 and 1849 spared him the disappointment of seeing his younger and highly talented colleagues Moriz Haupt (also his son-in-law), Otto Jahn, and Theodor

Mommsen, who were enmeshed in the events of the revolution, dismissed from their posts in 1850. He had felt entitled to hope that their connection with the University of Leipzig would long guarantee to his university a leading position in the disciplines of philology and *Altertumswissenschaft*.

All observers agree in their descriptions of Hermann's temperament and outward appearance. He was short of stature but slender and well-built; his mental and physical health was sound; harmonious by nature, he was personally unassuming but resolute and energetic. His city knew him not only as a scholar but also as a passionate horseman. In studies on the Greek terms to describe the gaits of the horse (*Op.* 1:63–80) and on horse-racing at Olympia (1839), in an excursus on equitation in his 1799 work on metrics, and in a posthumously published description of a ride to Karlsbad, he made good literary use of this hobby.

Hermann's scholarly conceptions were rooted in the theoretical heritage of the European Enlightenment; little affected by the contemporary spirit of Romanticism, he developed this heritage further, moving in the direction of the Positivism of the nineteenth century. True, he modified the Enlightenment's system of categories by making language, rather than reason, the central concept in his view of humanity, but he interpreted language as the reflection of reason and thus looked upon man, in the final analysis, as an *animal rationnel*, just as the Enlightenment had. From the category of the understanding he derived his characteristic application of the idea (conceived in *a priori* fashion) of law, by which he sought to transcend—or rather, by a unity of empirical and rational methodology, to replace—the more empirically grounded philological rules of the English scholars. He stressed that the details of texts under philological analysis must be understood as manifestations of general principles as well as in their own unique individuality. Impressed by Kant's critical philosophy, he took into serious consideration the category of the beautiful and thus emphasized, among other aspects, the aesthetic side of the phenomena under investigation, as had Kant in the *Critique of Judgment*. Hermann's insistence on high scientific standards made him skeptical toward hypotheses and speculations, for, as he formulated it, there was after all an art and science of not-knowing: *est etiam aliqua nesciendi ars et scientia* (*De Musis fluvialibus*, 1819).

Devoting himself to the ideal of the strictest possible methodology, Hermann worked out *a priori* three bases on which to ground the investigation and interpretation of texts: a general science of literature, sketched out at least in outline, a more broadly developed grammar, and—the fundamental philological discipline that he dealt with in most detail—metrics.

A science of literature requires a theoretical conception of literature, and Hermann produced his by deriving it from a system of the arts that was, in turn, based upon 1) the fundamental human ability to receive external impressions, 2) the capacity for conceptual thinking, and 3) (like a good Kantian) the perception of space and time (*Handbuch der Metrik*, 1799). From these elements he deduced dichotomies of poetry and rhetoric (*Handbuch der Metrik*), prose and poetry (*De differentia prosae et poeticae orationis*, 1803), as well as several individual poetic genres (*De poeseos gener-*

ibus, 1794). He worked on similar lines in his study of Aristotle's *Poetics* (edition with commentary, 1802) and, in a later study, on the tasks of the interpreter (*De officio interpretis*, 1834). Prose, he thought, is objective in its point of view, whereas poetry is subjective; the former aims at truth, the latter at beauty. The three intellectual functions of thought, feeling, and desire correspond to descriptive, epideictic, and practical prose. The inner structure of poetry can also be grasped by a deductive process that takes into account both content and form and leads to positing sixteen different poetic genres altogether, including lyric and epic, song, fable, and drama. The competent judge of literature must be familiar with the typical characteristics of each genre.

The grammar of the ancient languages, Hermann found, was a mass of rules too numerous and confused in themselves to be readily systematized and further complicated by the addition of countless inescapable exceptions. Even in his early work *De emendanda ratione Graecae grammaticae* (1801), he attempted to reduce the plethora of phenomena to comprehensible fundamental principles. Investigating the question of the pronunciation of the sounds symbolized by the Greek letters, he passed beyond accidence and into the realm of syntax, where his most fruitful discussions dealt with the phenomena that had been least clearly understood, e.g., enclisis, conjugation, cases, and moods.

But before he could perfect his own system, he was called away by a publisher's proposal for a new edition of the work of the French Jesuit François Vigier (1591–1647) on the chief characteristics of the Greek language (*De praecipuis Graecae linguae idiotismis*), a work that in Hermann's day was still much in use. Hermann added his own insights to the work of Vigerus (1802) in the form of appendices and thus passed up the chance to produce his own independent treatment of the subject. Moreover, he exaggerated the systematic character of a few of the phenomena that he discussed, for instance, he traced ellipse and pleonasm, *confusio notionum* (e.g., the use of a genitive where an adjective is expected), zeugma, attraction, anacoluthon, and substitution of moods back to the philosophical categories of quantity, quality, relation, and modality. Posterity is therefore not mistaken in judging that Philip Karl Buttmann (1764–1829), who reasoned more cautiously, was the true founder of the science of Greek grammar, and not Hermann. Yet Hermann's achievements in this field, among them his great study in four books on the particle ἄν (1831), must not be underestimated. Moreover, he also laid the foundations for a better understanding of Greek dialects (*De Graecae linguae dialectis*, 1807) and of the individual styles of ancient poets; here his examples were Pindar (1809) and Homer (1812–1813). Neither he nor Buttmann, however, felt any sympathy for the novel insights being put forward by the newly founded science of comparative historical linguistics.

What Hermann failed to accomplish in his grammatical studies he achieved in metrics: construction of a system, worked out in the smallest details, that embraced Greek and Roman literature equally. His chief work here, in terms of abundance of rules and examples, is the *Elementa doctrinae metricae* (1816). But his other three works on meter—*De metris poetarum Graecorum et Latinorum libri III* (1796), *Handbuch der Metrik* (1799, the most important of Hermann's few publications in German), and *Epitome doctrinae metricae* (1818), though they are built on basically similar principles, nevertheless have each an independent value. Like all his predecessors, Hermann took Hephaestion as his starting point; modern authorities like Heath and Brunk, in his view, had if anything lagged behind the ancient critic. Bentley had been the first to develop the requisite sensitivity to the rhythms of the ancients. He, to be sure, like a poet, had merely stated what he felt and had left it to others to develop this "feeling." But "no one did so, because no one felt as Bentley did" (*Handbuch der Metrik*: iv). Even Porson, Hermann maintained, valuable as his remarks were, had not really gone beyond Bentley. Hermann felt that he himself had the talent and the duty to take the decisive step by adopting a characteristically double approach to ancient metrics. On the one hand, he sought to understand the structure of the ancients' verses from feeling alone, from his sensitivity to the individual phenomena; on the other hand, however, he sought to comprehend the strict regularity and conformity to law that contained and transcended the particular details. Once again it was Kant who supplied him with a law, this time by means of his concept of causality. Before analyzing individual meters, Hermann declared, one must understand the "general law" of rhythm, and this was "the temporal form of causality, which is determined by the effect of alternation." According to this rule, the arsis necessarily draws the thesis after itself and so forms metrical series that are divided into units by caesurae. The first book of the *Elementa*, for example, is devoted to these general postulates; the second and third books then analyze simple, mixed, and compound meters. Generally speaking, Hermann's observations are excellent, and the rules he formulates—the most famous is the so-called "Hermann's Bridge" in the hexameter—are valid. Deriving everything from "causality" does seem arbitrary, as was noted by such contemporary critics as Geppert (see Bio-Bibliography). But by his principle we must look not to individual "meters," and certainly not to "feet," but to "series"—that is, larger metrical systems—as both the starting point and the goal of metrical analysis. Thus he paved the way for the modern understanding of meter—a way on which, e.g., Wilamowitz then traveled farther. Hermann was justly proud of having been the first to formulate the rules that govern the structure of ancient strophes (*Handbuch*, 415–448). And without doubt it is due to Hermann's work that even the most complicated ancient metrical forms—the verses and strophes of Pindar, of the Attic tragedians, and of the Roman comic poets—are intelligible today.

However highly Hermann valued genre theory, grammar, and metrics, in his eyes they were merely tools to be used in the philologist's real work: the editing and interpretation of texts. At the center of this major subdivision of his scholarly efforts were the works of the Attic tragedians. Hermann began his edition of Aeschylus as early as 1799 (*Eumenides*); the complete edition appeared posthumously in 1852. Completing and gradually superseding the edition of Sophocles begun by K. G. A. Erfurdt (1780–1813), he edited all the tragedies, beginning with the *Ajax* (1817) and ending with the *Oedipus Coloneus* (1825). He edited eleven plays by Euripides between 1800 (*Hecuba*) and 1840 (*Phoenissae*); he worked intensively on five more plays and on the recently discovered fragment of the *Phaethon*, while to four plays (*Hippolytus*, *Heracleidae*, *Electra*, *Orestes*) he devoted but a few remarks in passing. His splendid edition of the poems that have been transmitted under the name of Orpheus (*Orphica*, 1805) put an end to speculation on their supposed great antiquity, and his discussion of the place of these poems in the history of the Greek hexameter as it evolved from Homer to Nonnus was epoch-making. His other editions include the Homeric Hymns (1806), Aristophanes' *Nubes* (1797 and 1830), and, in the last years of this life, various Hellenistic poets, such as Moschus and Bion (posthumous, 1849). He published texts of prose writers in connection with his studies on grammar, metrics, and the evolution of genres: Aristotle's *Poetics* (1802), the *Lexicon* of Photius (1808), and the metrical work of pseudo-Draco (1812). Furthermore, he subjected Hesiod to more detailed text-critical analysis (1844), and, over the years, he repeatedly returned to textual studies of Pindar, to whom he had first been led by Christian Gottlob Heyne. His services to Roman poetry are great in his studies of Plautus (editions of the *Trinummus*, 1800, and of the *Bacchides*, 1845) and Terence (illustrating his difference of opinion with Bentley, 1819); but he was less fortunate in the case of Horace, particularly in his treatment of *Carm*. 1.1 (1842). His genius for divination was brilliantly confirmed when Friedrich Ritschl in 1837 found support in the Milan palimpsest of Plautus for many of the readings that Hermann had "predicted."

The quality of Hermann's conjectures varies in individual cases, but their excellence when taken together is undisputed. The Oxford Classical Texts of the tragedians, for example, (*Aeschylus*, ed. Murray; *Sophocles*, ed. Pearson; *Euripides*, ed. Murray) cite nearly 900 of Hermann's readings, counting both those accepted into the text and those cited in the apparatus (Aeschylus, 236 times; Sophocles, 204 times; Euripides, 456 times)—more citations than are granted to any other critic (see article on Richard Porson, pp. 378–380 of this volume). Hermann's results in textual criticism were achieved without the fundamental manuscript studies that Elmsley, for example, undertook, and quite apart from the method of systematic *recensio* by which Lachmann revolutionized textual studies. Wilamowitz called attention to one important characteristic of Hermann as a textual critic (*Geschichte der Philologie*: 49): while Elmsley applied the principle of analogy like a master, Hermann was able to grasp the completely individual character of a given textual passage. Today we can say that much of what Elmsley or Lachmann achieved would, in the present state of textual criticism, be accomplished by a computer. But Hermann's style of approaching a text transcends the capacities of mechanical data processing and herein lies its exemplary value for philology—if not for the philology of this generation or the next, then for the generation after that.

Hermann believed that interpreting a literary work consisted of more than merely constituting the text; he also insisted on extended treatment of questions of form, content, and characterization. So much is clear from what has been said above. But even Hermann's own students regretted that Hermann did not carry out his full program of interpretation for at least one text. Here Karl Otfried Müller anticipated him with his edition, with rich commentary, of the *Eumenides*. Unfortunately Hermann was not prepared to recognize the younger man's achievement and became entangled with Müller in one of those polemical affairs that characterized nearly the whole of his scholarly career.

The positive side (relatively speaking) of these polemical contests is that they led Hermann to areas of work that he otherwise might not have approached. This is true of the earliest of his quarrels, that with his contemporary Georg Friedrich Creuzer (1771–1858) who, unlike Hermann, was open to the influence of Romanticism and (rashly enough) traced mythology back to a primeval revelation couched in symbols. Hermann, on the other hand, in his own discussions of the question (e.g., *De mythologia Graecorum antiquissima*, 1817; *Briefe über Homer und Hesiod*, 1818; *Über das Wesen . . . der Mythologie*, 1819), clung firmly to the older principles of nature-mythology, which held that the gods and the figures of mythology were to be viewed as relatively simple personifications of the realms of nature and natural phenomena. His writings on this subject enjoy today no higher a reputation than those of Creuzer, but they deserve to be judged differently from the latter's works. Certainly we are taken aback when Hermann identifies Io with the Nile and her father, Inachos, with the Nile's source (*De historiae Graecae primordiis*, 1818). On the other hand, in his studies of Apollo, Artemis, and Athena (1837) he refrained from reckless etymologizing and derived these divinities from pre-Greek religion; in this regard, he was on the right track.

Stubborn antagonism arose between Hermann and F. G. Welcker (1784–1868). Among other subjects, they quarreled about the structure of the larger tragic forms. From his study of the single preserved specimen of a trilogy—Aeschylus' *Oresteia*—Hermann deduced that the first play of a trilogy exhibited a strict form, the second loosened the form of the first, and the third, bringing in spectacular stage effects, displayed the most colorful and variable structure of the three (*De compositione tetralogiarum*, 1819). Hermann successfully applied this rule to the fragments of the concluding play in the Danaid trilogy; his view of the putative court scene and the entrance of Aphrodite is precisely that of modern philologists. Yet when Welcker tried to do the same thing for the *Promethea*, Hermann accused him of fantasizing and quite failed to see the heuristic value of Welcker's hypothesis. Welcker replied in the same vein, and the polemics from both sides multiplied.

Hermann and Welcker also disagreed about the treatment of Greek verse inscriptions. This point led to a third scholarly quarrel, which was particularly instructive and far–reaching. Here Hermann threw all his authority onto the scale and yet did not come off the victor. His opponent was Böckh, and Hermann's chief point of attack was Böckh's collection of Greek inscriptions—a work whose usefulness was obvious from the first, as Hermann should have realized. But his fundamental principle was the prime importance of mastery of the languages, even in the "study of things," in which it was only superficially apparent that other considerations—for example, the breadth of the scholar's knowledge of the material—could be decisive. This principle, he felt, was under attack.

Hermann has often been praised for carrying on his scholarly feuds in a truly "chivalrous" manner, for confining himself to remarks on the subject at hand and refraining from personalities, for being always ready for reconciliation (as indeed he was in the case of Böckh), and for having, on the whole, "meant no harm" (as in the quarrel with Welcker). But the "chivalrous" Hermann also declared in 1838, in an unpublished letter (in the Universitätsbibliothek in Leipzig) to his student Funkhänel, with reference to Welcker's criticism of his study *De Aeschyli Aetneis* (1837), "This man [Welcker] is *a priori* my opponent, just as I know *a priori* that when he writes anything, I will not be able to agree with him." Hermann is here clearly entangled in prejudice—an aspect of his personality that cannot be excluded from a complete portrayal of the man.

But in an evaluation of Hermann as a polemicist, the question of his scholarly point of view is more important than the individual style of his polemicizing. Unquestionably he attributed such importance to his quarrel with Böckh primarily because it concerned the category of language, which for him was central. While Böckh saw in language one area of research among others, Hermann claimed first place for it and accordingly claimed first place for philology among the other subjects within *Altertumswissenschaft* that were then taking shape—ancient history, archaeology, epigraphy, history of law, etc. Certainly the dichotomy that here arose has been oversimplified by those who have maintained that since Hermann and Böckh classical philology has been virtually divided into two camps: the philology of words and texts and the philology of "things." But it must be confessed that the two men who here vied with each other represented two types of philologists—types that at least tended in the directions indicated above. Likewise it must be admitted that, though the barriers between the two may have been torn down, the two are not fully reconciled to this day. If we grant that Hermann's sphere included not only the narrow subjects of grammar and textual criticism but also the somewhat broader subjects of linguistic, formal, and aesthetic textual analysis, then we will agree that it is certainly to be encountered at the present time.

And it would be incorrect to conclude from Hermann's polemics that his principles obliged him to close his eyes to everything new in his discipline. The enthusiastic recognition that he granted to Niebuhr, for example, tells us otherwise. He embraced without hesitation and without reserve the revolutionary ideas of Friedrich August Wolf and Karl Lachmann in Homeric criticism; indeed, he himself took a hand in Homeric research in the spirit of Wolf by calling attention to the different linguistic and stylistic levels in the text of Homer.

Two further aspects of Hermann's influence deserve mention: his relation to the intellectual leaders of contemporary Germany and to the English philologists.

Mutual esteem united Goethe and Hermann. In 1800 Goethe visited him in Leipzig, and in 1820 they met again at Karlsbad. "Goethius"—as the name appears in Hermann's Latin writings—profited from Hermann's studies in metrics, had a share in the publication of the fragment of Euripides' *Phaethon*, (Hermann dedicated his 1831 edition of Euripides' *Iphigenia in Taurus* to the aged Goethe), and in one of his geological treatises adopted Hermann's maxim about the art of not-knowing. Hermann translated a section of Schiller's *Wallenstein* into Greek verses of great formal perfection. He was Wilhelm von Humboldt's adviser for the latter's translation of Aeschylus' *Agamemnon* (on this subject cf. the letters published by Leitzmann). Hermann ranked Humboldt far above other German translators of Greek texts, such as the meritorious and popular Johann Heinrich Voß. It was Hermann, incidentally, to whom Humboldt is said to have made the famous remark in conversation on the battleground of Leipzig in 1813, "Empires fall, but a good verse endures forever" (Leitzmann: 236).

As chance would have it, no less a figure than Goethe is also our witness for Hermann's early successes in England. At the aforementioned meeting in Leipzig in 1800, Hermann's most important publisher, Fleischer, was present, and he made the remark, which Goethe immediately noted in his diary, that Hermann's *Metrik* was "selling well" in England (Goethe, *Tagebücher* 1800). Hermann always emphasized the decisive importance of what he had learned from the English philologists. With a few of them, too, he quarreled—Elmsley, for example, whom he reproached for holding too closely to the rules he had formulated. Yet these differences of opinion never got out of hand as did those with his German colleagues. Hermann published in the *Classical Journal*, whose editors publicly congratulated themselves on having secured the collaboration of the famous scholar, and he corresponded with such English philologists as Gaisford (a letter to Gaisford is preserved in the Gennadeion, according to W. M. Calder III). In Leipzig he received visitors from England. In 1825 he was gratified when the respected English philologist Samuel Parr (1747–1825) left him, the "greatest of critics," a gold ring in his will.

Naturally Hermann's influence was even more potent in Germany than in England. No other German philologist in the first half of the nineteenth century led so splendid a troop of outstanding students as did Hermann. Only the most famous of them can be mentioned here (in order of seniority and with their dates and the places in which they chiefly worked): Christian August Lobeck (1781–1860; Königsberg), Friedrich Wilhelm Thiersch (1784–1860; Munich), Ferdinand Gotthelf Hand (1786–1851; Jena), Franz Passow (1786–1833; Weimar, Breslau), August Meineke (1790–1870, Berlin), Carl Christian Reisig (1792–1829; Halle), Adolf Trendelenburg (1802–72; Berlin), Leonhard Spengel (1803–80; Munich), Karl Friedrich Hermann (1804–55; Göttingen), Johannes Classen (1806–91; Lübeck, Frankfurt, Hamburg), his son–in–law Moriz Haupt (1808–74; Leipzig, Berlin), Hermann Sauppe (1809–93; Göttingen), Theodor Bergk (1812–81; Halle, Bonn), Hermann Bonitz (1814–88; Vienna, Berlin), and Hermann Koechly (1815–76; Heidelberg; Hermann's biographer). Karl Lachmann and Friedrich Ritschl also briefly attended Hermann's lectures. Thus there was nearly no important German university without a student of Hermann's active in teaching and research. Hermann's ability both to inspire his students and to induce them to work with the greatest methodological exactitude was incomparable.

Hermann was thus entitled to feel that he had plowed and sowed for the future, and yet his view of the future was gloomy. "Today everything is so out of joint that we are already fairly in the midst of barbarism." Only later would "a better time some day come, when philology too will be resurrected" (unpublished letter to Funkhänel, 1 February 1847, now in the Universitätsbibliothek in Leipzig—written one year before the birth of Wilamowitz!).

In the judgment of many, Hermann was the acclaimed leader of philology in his time; two hundred years after he began his work, his glory has lost not a little of its luster. Hermann brought to perfection older methods of philology without also becoming the champion of entirely new methods. The nineteenth century in philology was not the century of Hermann. But that century's philology cannot be imagined apart from Hermann's influence.

Translated by Michael Armstrong

Books (University programs included)

(*Op.* = *Opuscula*; see below)

De fundamento iuris puniendi. Leipzig, 1793 = *Op.* 1:1–19.

De poeseos generibus. Leipzig, 1794 = *Op.* 1:20–43.

De metris poetarum Graecorum et Latinorum libri III. Leipzig, 1796.

Observationes criticae in quosdam locos Aeschyli et Euripidis. Leipzig, 1798.

Handbuch der Metrik. Leipzig, 1799.

De emendenda ratione Graecae grammaticae, I. Accedunt Herodiani aliorumque libelli nunc primum editi. Leipzig, 1801.

Aristotelis de arte poetica liber, cum commentariis [and Latin translation]. Leipzig, 1802.

Francisci Vigeri de praecipuis Graecae dictionis idiotismis liber . . . . Edited with notes by Hermann. Leipzig, 1802; 4th ed., 1834.

De differentia prosae et poeticae orationis disputatio, I. II. Leipzig, 1803 = *Op.* 1:81–123.

Observationes de Graecae linguae dialectis. Leipzig, 1807 = *Miscellanea maximam partem critica.* Edited by F. T. Friedemann and J. D. G. Seebode, Wittenberg, London, Paris, Strasbourg, 1823: 2.2:278ff. = *Op.* 1:129–47.

De dialecto Pindari observationes. Leipzig, 1809; repr. in *Pindari carmina,* ed. C. G. Heyne, Leipzig, 1817:3.1:250–75 = *Op.* 1:245–68.

De praeceptis quibusdam Atticistarum. Leipzig, 1810 = *Miscellanea critica* 2.2:278–92 = *Op.* 1:269–89.

De usu antistrophicorum in Graecorum tragoediis. Leipzig, 1810.

De argumentis pro antiquitate Orphei Argonauticorum maxime a Koenigsmanno allatis. Leipzig, 1811 = *Op.* 2:1–17.

De Aeschyli Glaucis. Leipzig, 1812 = *Op.* 2:59–75.

De legibus quibusdam subtilioribus sermonis Homerici, I. II. Leipzig, 1812–13 = *Miscellanea critica,* 2.3:511–41 = *Op.* 2:18–58.

De Aeschyli Persis. Leipzig, 1814 = *Op*. 2:87–104.

De versibus spuriis apud Aeschylum. Leipzig, 1814 = *Op*. 2:76–86.

De metrorum quorundam mensura rhythmica. Leipzig, 1815; repr. in *Pindari carmina*, ed. C. G. Heyne, Leipzig,1817, 3.1:230–49 = *Op*. 2:105–23.

Elementa doctrinae metricae. Leipzig, 1816.

De choro Eumenidum Aeschyli, I. II. Leipzig, 1816 = *Op*. 2:124–66.

De mythologia Graecorum antiquissima. Leipzig, 1817 = *Op*. 2:167–94.

Dissertationes Pindaricae. In *Pindari carmina*, ed. C. G. Heyne, Leipzig, 1817: 3.1:179–410.

Über die bestrittene Cäsur im Trimeter der griechischen Komödie . . .Beilage zum 1. Heft der Analekten. Berlin, 1817.

Epitome doctrinae metricae. Leipzig, 1818; 4th ed., 1869.

De historiae Graecae primordiis. Leipzig, 1818 = *Op*. 2:195–216.

Briefe über Homer und Hesiodus, vorzüglich über die Theogonie. With Friedrich Creuzer. Heidelberg, 1818.

De compositione tetralogiarum tragicarum. Leipzig, 1819 = *Op*. 2:306–18.

De Musis fluvialibus Epicharmi et Eumeli. Leipzig, 1819 = *Op*. 2:288–305.

De Ricardo Bentleio eiusque editione Terentii. Leipzig, 1819 = *Op*. 2:236–87.

Über das Wesen und die Behandlung der Mythologie. Ein Brief an Herrn Hofrath Creuzer. Leipzig, 1819.

De Aeschyli Danaidibus. Leipzig, 1820 = *Op*. 2:319–36.

Euripidis fragmenta duo Phaethontis e codice Claromontano edita. Leipzig, 1821 = *Miscellanea critica*, Hildesheim, 1822: 1.1:1–17 = *Op*. 3:3–21.

Euripidis Medea. Edited by P. Elmsley with the notes of Hermann. Leipzig, 1822; notes reprinted in *Op*. 3:143–261.

De Sogenis Aeginaetae victoris quinquertii. Leipzig, 1822 = *Op*. 3:22–36.

De Aeschyli Niobe. Leipzig, 1823 = *Op*. 3:37–58.

Emendationes ad editionem Euripidis Alcestae . . . J. H. Monkii. Leipzig, 1824.

De emendationibus per transpositionem verborum. Leipzig, 1824 = *Miscellanea critica*, 2.4:717–27 = *Op*. 3:98–112.

De epitritis Doriis. Leipzig, 1824 = *Op*. 3:83–97.

De Aeschyli Philocteta. Leipzig, 1825 = *Op*. 3:113–29.

De Aeschyli Heliadibus. Leipzig, 1826 = *Op*. 3:130–42.

Über Herrn Professor Böckh's Behandlung der griechischen Inschriften. Leipzig, 1826.

Opuscula, vols. I–VII. Leipzig, 1827–39; vol. VIII, ed. Theodor Fritzsche. Leipzig, 1877.

De Aeschyli Prometheo soluto. Leipzig, 1828 = *Op*. 4:253–83.

De Archimedis problemate bovino. Leipzig, 1828 = *Op*. 4:228–38.

Emendationes Coluthi. Leipzig, 1828 = *Op*. 4:205–27.

De hyperbole. Leipzig, 1829 = *Op*. 4:284–302.

Incredibilium liber I. Leipzig, 1830 = *Op*. 4:341–72.

De particula ἄν libri IV. Leipzig, 1831 = *Op*. 4:1–204.

De Aeschyli Lycurgia. Leipzig, 1831 = *Op*. 5:3–30.

De interpolationibus Homeri. Leipzig, 1832 = *Op.* 5:52–77.

De Pauli epistolae ad Galatas tribus primis capitibus. Leipzig, 1832 = *Op.* 5:118–35.

De Aeschyli Myrmidonibus, Nereidibus, Phrygibus. Leipzig, 1833 = *Op.* 5:136–63.

De epigrammatis quibusdam Graecis. Leipzig, 1833 = *Op.* 5:164–81.

De fragmentis poetarum in scholiis Vaticanis ad Euripidis Troades et Rhesum. Leipzig, 1833 = *Op.* 5:182–206.

De certaminibus Graecorum [usually cited in this form; published without title]. Leipzig, 1834.

De officio interpretis. Leipzig, 1834 = *Op.* 7:97–128.

De quinque iudicibus poetarum. Leipzig, 1834 = *Op.* 7:88–96.

De veterum Graecorum pictura parietum coniecturae. Leipzig, 1834 = *Op.* 5:207–29.

Emendationes Pindaricae. Leipzig, 1834 = *Op.* 7:129–54.

De Aeschyli trilogiis Thebanis. Leipzig, 1835 = *Op.* 7:190–210.

De duabus inscriptionibus Graecis. Leipzig, 1835 = *Op.* 7:174–89.

Defensio dissertationis de ὑπερβολῇ. Leipzig, 1835 = *Op.* 7:65–87.

Ad Pindari Pyth. VII–XII. Leipzig, 1835 = *Op.* 7:155–73.

De tragoedia comoediaque lyrica. Leipzig, 1836 = *Op.* 7:211–40.

De Atlante. Leipzig, 1836 = *Op.* 7:241–59.

De Aeschyli Aetneis. Leipzig, 1837 = *Op.* 7:315–30.

De Apolline et Diana, I. II. Leipzig, 1837 = *Op.* 7:285–314.

De Graeca Minerva. Leipzig, 1837 = *Op.* 7:260–84.

De Aeschyli Psychostasia. Leipzig, 1838 = *Op.* 7:343–61.

De Aeschyli tragoediis fata Aiacis et Teucri complexis. Leipzig, 1838 = *Op.* 7:362–87.

De hippodromo Olympiaco. Leipzig, 1839 = *Op.* 7:388–404.

De iteratis apud Homerum. Leipzig, 1840 = *Op.* 8:11–23. German translation by J. Latacz as "Über die Wiederholungen bei Homer." *Homer. Tradition und Neuerung.* Wege der Forschung 463. Edited by J. Latacz. Darmstadt, 1979: 47–59.

Non videri Aeschylum Ἰλίου πέρσιν scripsisse. Leipzig, 1841 = *Op.* 8:129–44.

Retractiones adnotatorum ad Sophoclis Philoctetam. Leipzig, 1841 = *Op.* 8:185–202.

De Horatii primo carmine. Leipzig, 1842 = *Op.* 8:395–400.

De L. Attii libris Didascalicon. Leipzig, 1842 = *Op.* 8:390–94.

De choro Vesparum Aristophanis. Leipzig, 1843 = *Op.* 8:249–67.

De Dionysii et Mesomedis hymnis. Leipzig, 1843 = *Op.* 8:343–51.

De Hesiodi Theogoniae forma antiquissima. Leipzig, 1844 = *Op.* 8:47–67.

De Io. Nic. Madvigii interpretatione quarumdam verbi Latini formarum. Leipzig, 1844 = *Op.* 8:415–32.

De Pindari ad solem deficientem versibus. Leipzig, 1845 = *Op.* 8:75–89.

Pindari Nemeorum carmen sextum. Leipzig, 1845 = *Op.* 8:68–74.

De Prometheo Aeschyleo. Leipzig, 1846 = *Op.* 8:144–57.

De re scenica in Aeschyli Orestea. Leipzig, 1846 = *Op.* 8:158–72.

De loco Callimachei hymni in Delum et quibusdam epigrammatis. Leipzig, 1847 = *Op.* 8:360–70.

De quibusdam locis Euripidis Troadum. Leipzig, 1847 = Op. 8:203–17.
De interpolationibus Euripideae Iphigeniae in Aulide, I. II. Leipzig, 1847–48 = Op.
    8:218–41.
Emendationes quinque carminum Olympiorum Pindari. Leipzig, 1848 = Op. 8:110–28.
De arte poesis Graecorum bucolicae (includes *Bionis et Moschi carmina*). Leipzig, 1849
    = Op. 8:329–42.

Editions

Aeschyli Eumenides. Leipzig, 1799.
Aristophanis Nubes. Leipzig, 1799.
Euripidis Hecuba. Leipzig, 1800; Ed. G. Lange based on Hermann's edition. Halle,
    1806; 2d ed., 1828.
Plauti Trinummus. Leipzig, 1800.
Orphica. Leipzig, 1805.
Homeri hymni et epigrammata. Leipzig, 1806.
Photii Lexicon (combined with *Iohannis Zonarae Lexicon*, ed. T. A. H. Tittmann).
    Leipzig, 1808.
Euripidis Hercules furens. Leipzig, 1810.
Euripidis Supplices. Leipzig, 1811.
Draconis Stratonicensis Liber de metris poetices. Io. Tzetzae Exegesis in Homeri Iliadem.
    Leipzig, 1812.
Sophoclis Aiax. Leipzig, 1817; 4th ed., 1851.
Sophoclis Electra. Leipzig, 1819; 3d ed., 1864.
Sophoclis Trachiniae. Leipzig, 1822; 3d ed., 1851.
Euripidis Bacchae. Leipzig, 1823.
Sophoclis Antigona. Leipzig, 1823 (second edition of Erfurdt's text); 3d ed., 1830.
Sophoclis Oedipus Rex. Leipzig, 1823 (second edition of Erfurdt's text).
Sophoclis Philoctetes. Leipzig, 1824; 2d ed., 1839.
Sophoclis Oedipus Coloneus. Leipzig, 1825; 2d ed., 1841.
Euripidis Ion. Leipzig, 1827.
Hermesianactis elegi. Leipzig, 1828 = Op. 4:239–52.
Aristophanis Nubes. Leipzig, 1830.
Euripidis Tragoediae. Vol. I [*Hecuba, Iph. Aul., Iph. Taur.*]; Vol. II [*Hel., Andr., Cycl.,*
    Phoen]. Leipzig, 1831–40.
Plauti Bacchides. Leipzig, 1845.
Aeschyli Tragoediae. Vols. 1–2. Edited by M. Haupt. Leipzig, 1852; 2d ed., Berlin,
    1859.

Articles

   Only a few can be cited here, especially some of Hermann's reviews, which
were extremely famous in his day. More titles are to be found in the *Opuscula* (see
above).

"Commentatio de verbis, quibus Graeci incessum equorum indicant, ad Xenophontem de re equestri cap. VII." *Op.* 1:63–80.

"De ellipsi et pleonasmo in Graeca lingua." *Op.* 1:148–244.

"Censura in novam editionem Stephaniani Thesauri Gr. Londiniensem." *Classical Journal* 18, no. 35 (September 1818) 169–92 = *Op.* 2:217–51.

[Review of P. Elmsley's *Euripidis Medea.*] *Classical Journal* 19, no. 38 (June 1819) 267–89; 21, no. 42 (June 1820) 338–57; 22, no. 44 (December 1820) 402–28; reprinted as *Euripidis Medea,* edited by P. Elmsley, with annotations by G. Hermann, Leipzig, 1822: 325–407 = *Op.* 3:143–261.

"De Rheso tragoedia." *Op.* 3:262–310.

"Recension von Herrn Dissens Pindar." *Neue Jahrbücher für Philologie und Pädogogik* 1 (1831) 44–91 = *Op.* 6.1:1–69.

"Recension von Herrn Göttlings Hesiodus." [*Wiener*] *Jahrbücher der Literatur* 59 (1832) 192–248; 60 (1832) 1–49 = *Op.* 6.1:142–287.

"Über die Behandlung der griechischen Dichter bei den Engländern, nebst Bemerkungen über Homer und die Fragmente der Sappho." [*Wiener*] *Jahrbücher der Literatur* 54 (1832) 217–70 = *Op.* 6.1:70–141.

"Recension von Herrn [Otfried] Müllers Eumeniden des Aeschylus." [*Wiener*] *Jahrbücher der Literatur* 64 (1833) 203–44; 65 (1834) 96–155 = *Op.* 6.2:3–215.

"Über die Horazische Ode an Censorinus." *Berichte über die Verhandlungen der Königlich Sächsischen Gesellschaft der Wissenschaften zu Leipzig* 1 (1847) 274ff. = *Op.* 8:401–14.

"Über Friedrich Wolfgang Reiz." *Op.* 8:453–63.

In addition, some of Hermann's official speeches and poems, e.g., on the anniversary of Martin Luther's Reformation, the Russian Czar Alexander I, and the Saxon King Friedrich August I, are printed in the *Opuscula.*

Sources

Bibliography

"Gottfried Hermann." *Bibliographie zur Geschichte der Stadt Leipzig, Sonderband II: Karl-Marx-Universität Leipzig. Bibliographie zur Universitätsgeschichte 1409–1959.* Leipzig, 1961: 239.

Hartung, H. *Catalogus Bibliothecae Godofredi Hermanni.* Leipzig, 1854.

Biographical

Ameis, K. F. *Gottfried Hermann's pädagogischer Einfluß. Ein Beitrag zur Characteristik des altclassischen Humanisten.* Jena, 1850.

Bursian, C. *Geschichte der classischen Philologie in Deutschland.* Munich and Leipzig, 1883; reprinted New York and London, 1965: 2:666–87.

Fraenkel, E. "The Latin Studies of Hermann and Wilamowitz." *JRS* 38 (1948) 28–34.

Freese, C. *De Hermanni metrica ratione.* Halle, 1829.

Geppert, C. E. *Über das Verhältnis der Hermannschen Theorie der Metrik zur Überlieferung.* Berlin, 1835.

Jahn, O. "Gottfried Hermann. Gedächtnisrede." Leipzig, 1849; reprinted in *Otto Jahn. Biographische Aufsätze.* Leipzig, 1866: 89–132.

"Johann Gottfried Jakob Hermann." *Neuer Nekrolog der Deutschen* 26 (1848) 803–11.

Koechly, H. *Gottfried Hermann.* Heidelberg, 1874. (The richest source of information.)

Lehmann, C. "Die Auseinandersetzung zwischen Wort- und Sachphilologie in der deutschen klassischen Altertumswissenschaft des 19. Jahrhunderts." Diss., Humboldt-Universität Berlin, 1964.

Mette, H. J. "Gottfried Johann Jakob Hermann." *NDB* 8 (1969) 657–58. Berlin, 1969.

Pfeiffer, R. A *History of Classical Scholarship from 1300 to 1850.* Oxford, 1976: 178–9 = *Die klassische Philologie von Petrarca bis Mommsen.* Translated by Marlene and Erwin Arnold. Munich, 1982: 219–20.

Platner, E. "Reminiscences of the Late Gottfried Hermann." *Classical Museum* 7 (1849) 470–78.

Pruner, P. *Goethes Beziehungen zu Gottfried Hermann.* Schulprogramm. Frankfurt-am-Main, 1913.

Sandys, J. E. A *History of Classical Scholarship.* Cambridge, 1908; reprinted New York, 1958: 3:88–95.

Vogt, E. "Der Methodenstreit zwischen Hermann und Böckh und seine Bedeutung für die Geschichte der Philologie." In *Philologie und Hermeneutik im 19. Jahrhundert.* Edited by H. Flashar, K. Gründer, and A. Horstmann. Göttingen, 1979: 103–21.

Wilamowitz-Moellendorff, U. von. *Euripides: Herakles, I.* Berlin, 1889; 4th ed., Berlin, 1959: 235–9. = *Einleitung in die griechische Tragödie.* Berlin, 1907: 235–9.

———. *Geschichte der Philologie.* Leipzig, 1959: 51–2 = *History of Classical Scholarship.* Translated by Alan Harris. London, 1982: 109–10.

Letters

Hermann, G. *Carmina latina Carolo Einerto inscripta.* Dresden, 1852.

———. "*Reise nach Karlsbad*" [Greek verses]. *Berlin, 1863.*

Leitzmann, A. "Wilhelm von Humboldts Briefe an Gottfried Hermann." *Festschrift Walter Judeich.* Weimar, 1929: 224–70.

Volkmann, A. B. *Gottfried Hermanns lateinische Briefe an seinen Freund Volkmann.* Heidelberg, 1882.

A *Nachlaß* of Hermann does not exist; several unpublished letters are preserved in the libraries of Leipzig, Dresden, Berlin, and other German and European cities.

C. G. Heyne

25 September 1729 – 14 July 1812

ULRICH SCHINDEL
University of Göttingen

Among German philologists it was Heyne who laid the foundations for the development of a modern study of antiquity. Heyne was born in Chemnitz (today Karl-Marx-Stadt in Saxony in the German Democratic Republic), since his father, a linen weaver, had been driven out of Silesia for religious reasons. Since the weaver's trade in Saxony in those preindustrial times was chiefly a cottage industry, Heyne's family lived in extreme poverty; only with the help of godfathers and relations could he scrape together the money to pay for a relatively limited education at the town Latin School in Chemnitz. In 1748 he went to the University of Leipzig, where, to the extent his complete lack of funds permitted, he attended Johann August Ernesti's philology lectures and those by Johann August Bach on law and ancient history. Bach awarded him the Master's degree in 1752, but his poverty condemned him to autodidacticism, and he carried on the greater part of his studies independently.

In 1753 he received a subordinate post as copyist in the library of the Saxon Minister of State, Count Brühl, in Dresden. There he first became acquainted with the evidence of ancient art as a complement to the literary tradition and there, in addition, he met Johann Joachim Winckelmann, who was also working in Brühl's library. In this period he published his first editions—Tibullus and Epictetus—which established his fame as a philologist, and also his translation of the romance of Chariton. Driven out of Dresden by the disturbances of the Seven Years' War between Prussia and Austria (1756–1763), he eked out an existence by producing ephemeral translations for the booksellers and working as a private tutor ("Hofmeister") in well-to-do families.

In 1763 he was freed from this misery by a call, engineered by the Leyden philologist David Ruhnken, to the "Enlightenment" University of Göttingen, which had been founded only twenty-five years earlier but had already taken a leading place (with Halle) among German universities. As successor to Johann Matthias Gesner,

Heyne became Professor of Poetry and Eloquence as well as director of the Seminarium Philologicum (founded by Gesner in 1737), librarian of the University Library with its lavish holdings, and member of the Academy of Sciences.

Upon taking up his duties, Heyne busily immersed himself in literary and editorial work. From 1763 on there appeared an unbroken series of so-called programs and prolusions, which he, as Professor Eloquentiae et Poeseos, was obliged to produce for solemn academic occasions (one hundred thirty-five in all, by 1809); from 1770 to 1813 he prepared the Academy's forty-seven proceedings and until 1811, twenty eulogies. In addition to this he produced an unending sequence of reviews for the *Göttingische Gelehrte Anzeigen*, of which he became editor in 1770; by 1812 he had published several thousand reviews. Beside this mass of *opuscula* are his chief works: a *History of the World from the Creation to the Present Time* (translated from the English, 1765–72) and editions with commentary of Virgil (1767–75), Pindar (1773), and Homer (1802–03), as well as his edition of the Bibliotheca of Apollodorus (1782).

Comparable to this indefatigable scholarly productivity were his important achievements in scholarly administration. Heyne became Secretary of the Academy in 1770 and immediately put through a successful reorganization; the Academy, which had remained torpid since Haller's departure, was spurred on to renewed scholarly productivity. As librarian he achieved extraordinary results by organizing an acquisition program on an international scale. As a result, the holdings increased during his tenure of office from 60,000 to 200,000 volumes. But his greatest accomplishment as librarian was in setting up an alphabetical author catalogue (1776–1789), which became the model for many European libraries and is still used. He also left his mark on secondary education: His plans for school reform in the Electorate of Hannover, as well as the systematic philological and pedagogical training of future Gymnasium teachers in his Seminarium Philologicum, decisively influenced education at the Gymnasium level in northern Germany. His intimate and confidential relationship over the years with successive University administrators gave him a lasting influence on the appointments and the organizational development of the University, so that he became, as it were, the director behind the scenes. Thus it was not chance, but rather Heyne's authority and his acquaintance with Napoleon, which dated back to 1803, that thwarted the new French officials of the Kingdom of Westphalia in their plans to close the University of Göttingen.

In spite of numerous invitations—among them an offer from Copenhagen to reorganize the University there and the entire educational system of Denmark (1789)—he did not leave Göttingen. After 1755 he lived with his large family in an imposing house on the Leine canal; the house still exists (Papendiek, No. 16). In 1809 he retired from his professorship, but he retained his other posts until his death. At the end of his life he was a member of thirty learned societies in Germany and abroad: Berlin, Copenhagen, London, Moscow, Munich, St. Petersburg, Stockholm, and Utrecht, among others.

Heyne's importance in the history of scholarship lies in his having replaced an antiquarian polyhistorism, as it had hitherto been practiced, with a conception of the study of antiquity that aimed at a universal reconstruction of the literary, historical, and cultural life of the ancient world and also brought the knowledge thereby gained into relation with the present. This was visible even in the style of his academic teaching. His interpretative lectures dealt primarily with the poets (Homer, Hesiod, Pindar, Aeschylus, Sophocles, Euripides, Apollonius Rhodius, Callimachus; Lucretius, Virgil, Horace, Propertius, Statius), and here he was always concerned not only with the elucidation of the sense of the words and the pertinent factual background of the poem but also with the immediate perception and appreciation of its aesthetic beauty. "Nun kömmt der Tichter" ("now comes the poet") was his constant remark when he felt that he had sufficiently clarified the verbal meaning and the factual data and set himself to fathoming the venustates of the text and their causae. But his far-famed archaeological lectures, too, which were delivered in the midst of a collection of plaster casts collected to illustrate his remarks and which attracted such listeners as the Humboldt brothers and the Schlegel brothers, were chiefly concerned with "formation of taste," "perception of the beautiful," or quite generally "refinement and illumination of the understanding." These lectures were intended particularly for future travelers to Greece or Rome, so as to prepare them for authentic acquaintance with the works of ancient visual art. And the Seminarium Philologicum, finally, aimed in a similar fashion at a lively immersion in ancient literature; the members "exercise themselves and are guided in interpretation, Latin composition, speaking, and debate and must themselves, one after another, construe an ancient author grammatically and critically, and finally each must compose and defend a well-written Latin essay on a subject pertinent to this kind of scholarship." This school produced philologists like Friedrich August Wolf and Karl Lachmann and poets like Ludwig Hölty and Johann Heinrich Voß.

The same striving for universality and relevance to the present is visible in Heyne's *opera* and *opuscula*. The strength of his editions of the poets lies in his firmly grounded aesthetic judgement. Again and again the poets' expressions are paraphrased in sober prose that brings into relief the poetic turn of phrase. "The constant emphasis on the transformation of factual content into poetry is the salt that everywhere permeates this mass of commentary" (Friedrich). And among his manifold opuscula on literature, history, constitutional law, mythology, archaeology, and numismatics, each with its concise survey of the subject matter and the present state of knowledge, there is scarcely one that fails to employ reflections on the present to gain new perspectives on the study of the past.

Heyne's influence on modern classical philology lies in his having broadened philology's outlook in all directions. Not only history and its subdisciplines, such as epigraphy, constitutional and legal history, mythology, and the archaeology of art, but also numismatics and Etruscology are fields that in Heyne's scholarly practice first take shape as integral parts of a universal study of antiquity.

Heyne put his new principles into effect chiefly in the day-to-day practice of research and teaching rather than by embodying them in a systematic theoretical concept. As a result, his achievement, from the point of view of the history of philology, was thrown into the shade by Friedrich August Wolf's and August Böckh's works on methodology. But Heyne's influence was not limited to professional scholarship. By teaching his students to see the ancient world in perspective, by focusing on the existential connection between antiquity and the present, he brought the "humaniora," which had previously been the scholarly preoccupation of a minority, into the general consciousness of his age. He was thus able to set free the impulses that two generations later led to the intellectual movement of neo-humanism that dominated the German-speaking countries.

Translated by Michael Armstrong

Books

Charitons Liebesgeschichte des Chäreas und der Callirrhoe. Translated from the Greek. Leipzig, 1753.

Albii Tibulli quae exstant carmina. Leipzig, 1755; 3d ed., 1798; 4th ed. revised and enlarged by C. F. Wunderlich with supplement by L. Dissen, Leipzig, 1817–19; reprinted Hildesheim, 1975.

Epicteti enchiridion. Dresden and Leipzig, 1756; Warsaw and Dresden, 1776.

Allgemeine Weltgeschichte von der Schöpfung bis auf die gegenwärtige Zeit . . . ausgefertigt von Wilhelm Guthrie und Johann Gray. Translated from the English, vols. 1–4, 6–7, Leipzig, 1765–72.

P. Virgilii Maronis opera. Vols. 1–4. Leipzig, 1767–75; 3d ed., London, 1793; Leipzig, 1803; vols. 1–6, 3d ed., Leipzig, 1797–1800; vols. 1–5, 4th ed. revised by G. P. E. Wagner. Leipzig and London, 1830–41; reprinted Hildesheim, 1968.

Pindari Carmina. Göttingen, 1773. Vols. 1–3. Göttingen, 1798; 2d ed., Leipzig, 1817.

Apollodori Atheniensis bibliotheca. Text: Göttingen, 1782. Commentary: vols. 1–3. Göttingen, 1783; Text: 2d ed. in 2 vols. Göttingen, 1803; reprinted Hildesheim, 1972.

Homeri carmina. Vols. 1–9. Leipzig and London, 1802–22.

Articles

"Einleitung in das Studium der Antike." Göttingen und Gotha, 1772.

"Lobschrift auf Winckelmann." Kassel, 1778.

"Sammlung antiquarischer Aufsätze." Theil 1–2. Leipzig, 1778–79.

"Opuscula Academica." Vols. 1–6. Göttingen, 1785–1812.

Further articles in:

Deutsche Schriften von der königlichen Societät der Wissenschaften zu Göttingen. Vol. I. Göttingen, 1771.

Novi Commentarii Soc. Reg. scient. Götting. Vols. 1–8. Göttingen, 1770–78.

Commentationes Soc. Reg. scient. Gotting. recentiores. Vols. 1–11. Göttingen, 1808–13.

Reviews in:
Göttingische Anzeigen von Gelehrten Sachen. Göttingen, 1763–1812.

Sources

Berthold, H. "Bewunderung und Kritik. Zur Bedeutung der Mittlerstellung Christian Gottlob Heynes." In *Schriften der Winckelmann-Gesellschaft*, Bd. 7, Stendal, 1988: 161–170.

Bursian, K. *ADB* 12:375–378.

———. *Geschichte der classischen Philologie in Deutschland.* Munich and Leipzig, 1883: 476–496.

Carlyle, Thomas. "The Life of Heyne." *Miscellaneous and Critical Essays.* London, 1839: 1:351–89.

Döhl, H. "Die Archäologie-Vorlesungen Chr. G. Heynes. Anmerkungen zu ihrem Verständnis und zu ihrer Bedeutung." In *Winckelmanns Wirkung* (see below): 123–147.

Friedrich, W. H. "Heyne als Philologe." In *Der Vormann der Georgia-Augusta.* Edited by N. Kamp et al. (see below) 15–31.

Der Vormann der Georgia-Augusta. Christian Gottlob Heyne zum 250. Geburtstag. Sechs Akademische Reden. Edited by N. Kamp et al. Göttinger Universitätsreden 67. Göttingen, 1980.

Hirsch, E. and Karl, I. "Christian Gottlob Heyne zwischen Philanthropismus und Neuhumanismus." In *Winckelmanns Wirkung*: 113–122.

Irmscher, J. "Christian Gottlob Heyne—Altertumsforscher, Wissenschaftsorganisator, Winckelmann-Verehrer." In *Winckelmanns Wirkung*: 113–122.

Klingner, F. "Christian Gottlob Heyne" (1937). In *Studien zur Griechischen und Römischen Literatur.* Stuttgart and Zürich, 1964: 701–718.

Leo, F. "Heyne." *Historische Festschrift der königlichen Gesellschaft der Wissenschaften zu Göttingen.* Berlin, 1901: 155–234.

Menze, C. *Wilhelm von Humboldt und Christian Gottlob Heyne.* Ratingen, 1966.

Mettler, W. *Der junge Friedrich Schlegel und die griechische Literatur. Ein Beitrag zum Problem der Historie.* Zürcher Beiträge zur deutschen Literatur- und Geistesgeschichte 11. Zürich, 1955.

N. "Life of Heyne." *Classical Journal* 19, 37 (March 1819) 136–168; 20, 39 (September, 1819) 17–42.

Muhlack, U. "Philologie zwischen Humanismus und Neuhumanismus." In *Wissenschaft im Zeitalter der Aufklärung.* Edited by R. Vierhaus. Göttingen, 1985: 93–119.

Sandys, J. E. *A History of Classical Scholarship.* 3 vols. Cambridge, 1903–1908. 3:36–44.

Sauppe, H. "J. M. Gesner und C. G. Heyne." In *Göttinger Professoren.* Gotha, 1872: 78–98.

Schindel, U. *NDB* 9 (1972) 93–95.

————. "In memoriam C. G. Heyne." *Göttingische Gelehrte Anzeigen* 232 (1980) 1–5.

————. "Heyne als Schulreformer." *Gymnasium* 88 (1981) 193–208.

————. "Von der 'Poesie und Beredsamkeit' zur Philologia classica: Die Entwicklung der lateinischen und griechischen Philologie in Göttingen im 18. Jahrhundert." To be published in *Anfänge der Philologie in Göttingen im 18. Jahrhundert*. Edited by R. Lauer. Göttingen, 1989.

————. "Heyne und die Historiographie." To be published in *Festschrift für C. J. Classen*. Wiesbaden, 1989.

Winckelmanns Wirkung auf seine Zeit. Lessing, Herder, Heyne. Edited by J. Irmscher. Schriften der Winckelmann-Gesellschaft, Bd. 7, Stendal, 1988.

Bibliographies

Work-lists in:

A. H. L. Heeren. *Christian Gottlob Heyne. Biographisch dargestellt.* Göttingen, 1813: 489–522.

Christian Gottlob Heyne (1729–1812). Ausstellung anläßlich seines 250. Geburtstags, Staats- und Universitätsbibliothek Göttingen. Ausstellungskatalog von B. Bendach. Göttingen, 1979: 81–108.

Biography

A. H. L. Heeren. *Christian Gottlob Heyne. Biographisch dargestellt.* Göttingen, 1813. With autobiographical sections pages 5–28, 48–68.

Letters (*not yet collected*)

Heyne's letters to:

G. Forster, in *Georg Forsters Werke*. Edited by the Akademie der Wissenschaften der DDR. Vol. 18. Berlin, 1982.

G. E. Lessing, in *Lessings Werke*. Edited by Karl Lachmann and F. Muncker. Vols. 19–21. Berlin, 1904–07.

S. Th. Sömmerring, in R. Wagner. *S. Th. Sömmerrings Leben und Verkehr mit seinen Zeitgenossen. 1. Abt. Briefe berühmter Zeitgenossen an Sömmerring.* In S. T. Sömmerring. *Vom Baue des menschlichen Körpers.* Edited by W. T. Bischoff and others. Leipzig, 1844; reprinted Stuttgart and New York, 1986.

J. J. Winckelmann, in *Briefe*. Edited by W. Rehm und H. Diepolder. 4 vols. Berlin, 1952–1957.

F. A. Wolf, in: S. Reiter. *F. A. Wolf: Ein Leben in Briefen.* 3 vols. Stuttgart, 1935.

See also:

J. Joachim. "Aus Heynes Brief an J. A. Carus." In *Aufsätze F. Milkau gewidmet.* Leipzig, 1921.

A. Leitzmann. "Aus Heynes Briefen an seine Tochter Therese und seine Schwiegersöhne Forster und Huber." In *Archiv für das Studium der Neueren Sprachen und Literaturen* 121 (1908) 1–23.

A. C. Lucht. *Heyne an K. F. Heinrich. Bisher ungedruckte Briefe aus dem Nachlaß des letzteren.* Rendsburg, 1867. Schulprogramm, Rendsburg, 1867.

G. Meyer. "Heynes Briefwechsel mit J. von Müller über Ilfeld." In *Jahresberichte über die Klosterschule zu Ilfeld*. Göttingen, 1910.

H. Ruppert. "Aus Heynes Briefen." In *Aus dem 18. Jahrhundert, Th. Apel und H. Seeliger zum 8. 6. 1922 zugeeignet*. Leipzig, 1922.

Papers

134 volumes of manuscripts in the Handschriftenabteilung of the Staats- und Universitätsbibliothek Göttingen.

Gilbert Highet

22 June 1906 – 20 January 1978

THOMAS A. SUITS
University of Connecticut

"For many years he was the most famous classical teacher in the world. The most highly respected in his own profession: no. A dry specialist like A. E. Housman, a diamond-hard and many-faceted genius like Wilamowitz-Moellendorff, although less widely known to the public, stood higher in the regard of their colleagues. But for many years everyone in the English-speaking world who heard any mention of Greek poetry at once thought of [him]. . . . He became famous for a number of convergent reasons: because he was a superb teacher; because he translated Greek dramas into modern verse . . . because he wrote fluently and gracefully on many themes, not all of them classical; because he talked well and often on the B.B.C. . . . ." So wrote Gilbert Highet of Gilbert Murray (*The Immortal Profession*, 145–146), and much the same, *mutatis mutandis*, might be said of Highet himself, who clearly saw in Murray's career a model for his own. A scholar of no inconsiderable stature, a teacher of unsurpassed skill, he was best known for his exposition of the classics to the wider public. Here his gift for communication both oral and written, combined with the astonishing range of his intellectual interests, changed for untold thousands the image of classics from that of a narrow, dusty discipline to one of an exciting study with broad relevance to modern literature and life.

Gilbert Arthur Highet was born in Glasgow, that "hideous nineteenth-century industrial city." His allusions to the early years were few and bleak: relief from the "glutinous gloom of a Scottish Sabbath" came from the world of books—the beginning of Highet's lifelong passion for reading. His young mind was especially susceptible to the charms of poetry, and he later credited his early exposure to Macaulay's *Lays of Ancient Rome* with not only contributing toward his choice of classics as a profession but also preparing him emotionally for the eventual decision to be a citizen of a republic rather than a monarchy. As a pupil at the Hillhead High

School he received excellent preparation for his future studies, beginning at age eleven to learn French and Latin. Here he also had an early taste of the tutorial system when a schoolmaster, James Buchanan, noticing his promise, generously taught him Greek during lunch hours.

He went on to study classics at Glasgow University, where J. S. Phillimore was one of his teachers. He had mixed feelings about Phillimore. He found him "suave" and his translations "graceful," but he was also put off by his unimaginative, plodding approach to the ancient authors and by his indulging in pointless scholarly polemics while at the same time neglecting meaningful questions that would have addressed the real interests and needs of the students. The negative lesson would be an important one for Highet's future career. As contributor to, and later editor of, the *Glasgow University Magazine*, he gave a sample of the wide range of critical and creative writing that would mark his later work. (This was the period, as he mockingly recalled, when he was "an aesthete, trying to be one of the avant-garde.") Not least in importance of the events of the Glasgow University years was the meeting and winning of his future wife, the charming and talented Helen MacInnes, whose literary interests would complement and stimulate his own.

After the Glasgow M.A. with highest honors in Greek and Latin (1929), he went up to Balliol College, Oxford, as a Snell Exhibitioner. He loved Oxford, despite its creeping urban blight, and regarded his involvement in the tutorial system there in both the learning and teaching roles as one of the best experiences of his life. His tutor at Balliol was Cyril Bailey, but Gilbert Murray and C. M. Bowra were also molding forces. As he had at Glasgow, Highet contributed a broad range of pieces to university literary magazines, including poetry, fiction, and reviews. He even dabbled in theater, a not altogether surprising interest for one who would become a master showman in the classroom.

In 1932 he earned the Oxford B.A. with a double first, won appointment as Fellow of St. John's College, and on 22 September married Helen MacInnes. The remaining five years at Oxford were busy with teaching and more ambitious writing projects. In collaboration with his wife, who taught him German, he translated Kiefer's *Kulturgeschichte Roms* as *Sexual Life in Ancient Rome* and Gustav Mayer's life of Engels—choices that show that at this stage of his life, at least, he was scarcely a prim conservative. During this period he also produced two textbooks, which he later omitted from his bibliography as "little juvenilia," but which illustrate his lifelong concern for effective pedagogy. *An Outline of Homer* was addressed to the pupil with simple Attic Greek and contains twenty-odd annotated passages from the *Iliad* and *Odyssey* selected to represent the whole spectrum of Homeric poetry and arranged under the heads "Character," "Imagination" (viz., heaven, hell, Calypso's island), and "Life." *Beginning Latin* was for even younger pupils and stopped short of the subjunctive, but it incorporated substantial amounts of Roman history in its exercises. At the same time Highet was composing lively versions for the *Oxford Book of Greek Verse in Translation* and launching a study of the poet Juvenal that would occupy him off and on for twenty years.

In 1937 he came to Columbia University on a one-year appointment as Visiting Associate in Greek and Latin at the invitation of President Nicholas Murray Butler. The recommendation had come from Bowra, whom Butler had attempted to recruit without success. Within the year Highet was invited to stay permanently and was named Professor of Greek and Latin in a department recently decimated by death and retirements. Not only did his vigorous approach to teaching help his own department to survive at a difficult time for the classics, but his talents were also admirably suited to Columbia's Humanities program, where he joined such luminaries as Moses Hadas, Mark Van Doren, and Lionel Trilling.

In 1941 Highet went on leave for war service and joined British Security Coordination headquarters in New York, the hub for all branches of British intelligence. Commissioned in the British Army in 1943, he left as a lieutenant colonel in 1946 after having served with the British military government in Germany, where he was involved in helping to recover booty taken by the Nazis from occupied countries. The events of the war and the revelations of the warcrimes trials—some of which he attended—affected him profoundly, and very few of his subsequent books are without at least some allusion to Nazi barbarity or the evils of totalitarianism. (See, for example, the bibliographical note on concentration camps in *Juvenal the Satirist*, 289.) Even during the difficult wartime conditions Highet continued his translation of Werner Jaeger's *Paideia*, the first volume of which had been completed before the war. The second and third volumes were translated directly from the German manuscript. In his preface to the former, Jaeger acknowledges Highet's contribution in checking and discussing with him every disputable passage and in the whole process giving up several years of his own working life.

With release from the military came the crucial decision to return to academe rather than to accept one of several more lucrative offers. So began a decade and a half of remarkable activity and productivity, in the course of which he published eleven books, lectured to packed classes at Columbia, wrote reviews for the popular press, gave weekly syndicated radio talks, and—in short—came as close as perhaps any American classicist will to being a household name. He could even be caricatured as the central figure in a murder mystery, Professor Campbell Craig, suave popularizer of the classics: see R. H. R. Smithies, *An Academic Question* (New York 1965).

The Classical Tradition (1949), Highet's first original scholarly book, was described by him as "an outline of the chief ways in which Greek and Latin influence has moulded the literatures of western Europe and America." Twenty-four chapters rich in detail survey the classical legacy from the Dark Ages through the first half of the twentieth century. It was a bold enterprise of the sort that few men would attempt even at the end of a career and that nowadays would more likely be parceled out to a committee; yet Highet undertook it single-handedly in his early forties and, by and large, did it well. Virtually all the author's hallmarks are already present: crispness of style, clarity of organization, control of a vast range of material, confidence in his own critical judgment, and belief in the moral value of literature. Some would see his style as "writing down," his outline as oversimplified, his judgments as too uncompromising; but in most of his scholarly books Highet was also addressing the student and educated layman. Coverage is inevitably uneven: *The Classical Tradition* is strong on English and French literature, surprisingly thin on the Latin Middle Ages. E. R. Curtius, in a largely negative review, complained of a bias against German culture (*Gnomon* 23 [1951] 121–125). Generally, however, the work was well received (see the balanced reviews by J. A. K. Thomson, *CR* 1 [1951] 42–45, and J. Hutton, *AJPh* 73 [1952] 79–87), and it remains a valuable handbook, a passport between classical and modern literatures.

The Art of Teaching (1950) enjoyed phenomenal commercial success, going through fourteen English printings and being translated into sixteen languages, from Arabic to Urdu. In it a master teacher shared not only practical suggestions drawn from his experience but also his sense of the awesome responsibility that went with the calling. For Highet felt his primary obligation was to teach, and he applied himself to the task with the utmost conscientiousness. His classroom performances were legendary. Attired in elegant pin stripes or jaunty tweeds, he would make his entrance, a smile on his face and a gleam in his eye, and proceed to keep the attention of every student riveted for the duration of the precisely timed lecture. He would punctuate his characteristic rapid, clipped delivery with an occasional roar or laugh and sometimes resort to gesticulation, mimicry, song, or even the use of props. Yet behind the theatricality lay scrupulous preparation and careful organization designed to make the student understand and remember each important point.

The 1950s were momentous years for Highet. He became Anthon Professor of Latin in 1950 and a United States citizen by naturalization in 1951. Glasgow and Oxford awarded him the D.Litt. in 1951 and 1956 respectively, and he was elected a Fellow of the Royal Society of Literature in 1959. Chief literary critic for *Harper's Magazine* from 1952 to 1954, he resigned to become a judge for the Book-of-the-Month Club, a position he would hold until his death. In 1958 he was appointed chairman of the editorial advisory board of the new periodical, *Horizon*, to which he became a frequent contributor. His weekly radio talks, "People, Places, and Books," begun in 1952 on WQXR in New York, proved enormously successful, and by the time they were discontinued in 1959 they were carried by more than 300 stations in North America as well as by the B.B.C. At once erudite and entertaining, they covered topics as diverse as *haiku* and Housman, Bruegel and Bach. (Highet himself was an accomplished amateur pianist and was given to drawing analogies between literary and musical styles.) Some of the talks were made accessible on audio cassettes, and many of them were subsequently revised and published in five books of essays. Meanwhile, Helen MacInnes had established herself as a best-selling author of novels featuring international intrigue, and husband and wife were soon dubbed "the Lunts of literature."

The decade also saw the appearance of two of Highet's books on classical subjects. He had long found Juvenal particularly congenial: as he remarked in another context but with personal insight, "Scots have never been averse from indulging in strong and even somber moralizing." Twenty years of study had already resulted in a series of articles and now bore full fruit in *Juvenal the Satirist* (1954), the first major modern study of Juvenal as a poet. It consists of three parts: a reconstruction of the life of Juvenal from scraps of external and internal evidence (based on his 1937 article); a series of lively explications of the individual satires, which are given an extra dimension by copious modern parallels; and a survey of the survival and influence of Juvenal's work from the late empire to modern times. The reception was mixed. While the *Fortleben* section was almost universally applauded, the biographical approach was just as widely decried: the reconstructed life is highly hypothetical, and using it to interpret the poems is hazardous, if not circular; indeed, most would consider it irrelevant. This approach permeates and to a certain extent flaws the entire central section. (See the reviews of E. J. Kenney, CR 5 [1955] 278–281 and R. G. M. Nisbet, JRS 45 [1955] 234–235.) An indication, however, of the book's staying power may be seen in the fact that W. S. Anderson, who had expressed a harsh judgment at CP 50 (1955) 146–148, later revised his estimate in favor of a more balanced view: while not retreating from his criticism of the biographical approach, he acknowledges the book's overall strengths (PACA 6 [1963] 45–49). Prominent among these are the notes and bibliography, which fill more than 100 pages and reflect Highet's firm control of previous scholarship and interpretational problems; they have provided and will continue to provide a starting point for studies of the individual satires.

Poets in a Landscape (1957) is in many ways the most personal of Highet's classical books. Based on a visit to Italy and furnished with his own photographs and original verse translations, it represents in effect a pilgrimage in search of places associated with seven Roman poets (Catullus, Vergil, Propertius, Horace, Tibullus, Ovid, and Juvenal); there are chapters on each of the seven, plus a concluding one on Rome itself. Highet's propensity for taking the poems at face value, as though their authors were writing autobiography in verse, is here especially evident. (See the strictures of B. Otis at AJPh 79 [1958] 438–439.) But the book was scarcely intended as a significant contribution to scholarship. Charming by its often conscious fancifulness, it strikes a responsive chord in anyone who has ever visited a classical site on a similar quest, and it was fittingly honored by the Italian government with its Premio ENIT (Ente Nazionale Italiano per il Turismo).

In 1960 Highet delivered four Trask Lectures at Princeton, the end product of which was *The Anatomy of Satire* (1962). In it he examines the nature of satire, considering it under the three heads—not mutually exclusive—of monologue, parody, and narrative. Although ancient examples are naturally included, he also discusses representatives as diverse as Mort Sahl, the "Dreadnought" hoax, Hogarth's "Gin Lane," and ironic chapters in Gibbon. The book is thus not a work of classical scholarship nor even a systematic analysis of satire as a literary form. In its extraordinary range it is reminiscent of *The Classical Tradition*; but, while its scope is greater, it does not differ greatly in kind from some of the general essays derived from his radio talks. The fair assessment by W. Krenkel in *Gnomon* 35 (1963) 355–359 is more appropriate, given the author's intentions, than the wickedly amusing attack by E. C.

Witke in CP 58 (1963) 260–264. In 1963, Highet received the American Philological Association's Award of Merit for *The Anatomy of Satire*. It was certainly less deserving of that honor than *The Classical Tradition* or *Juvenal the Satirist*, but the likelihood is that the committee, while nominally recognizing his most recent book, was in reality paying homage to his lifetime achievement.

The surge in graduate classics enrollments in the 1960s caused Highet to devote an increased portion of his time to directing doctoral dissertations. Over the course of his career he sponsored more than two dozen dissertations on Greek and Latin subjects, and nearly three-quarters of these were completed during the last ten years before his retirement. He took this aspect of his teaching responsibility as seriously as he did all others and gave generously of his time in providing meticulous criticism and guidance. It was characteristic of his flair and style that he would mark a successful defense by inviting the candidate to oysters and champagne. A number of his doctoral students became productive teacher-scholars, and one, Howard Jacobson, himself won the Award of Merit of the American Philological Association.

Vergil was one of Highet's favorite authors, and his graduate course on the *Aeneid* was a fixture of the Columbia curriculum. This long interest culminated in his last book on a classical subject, *The Speeches in Vergil's Aeneid* (1972), completed shortly before his retirement. Whereas all of his other books had been designed to be accessible to the general reader, this work was clearly for the specialist and made no concessions to those without Greek and Latin. The author observes that nearly half the epic is devoted to direct speech but that the speeches as such have been largely neglected or imperfectly treated; he modestly hopes to fill the "small gap." What is offered is a multifold analysis of the speeches, with attention to such aspects as the degree of formal rhetoric represented (Highet finds relatively little and thinks that Vergil distrusted oratory), the various types of informal speeches, and the distribution of speeches among the several characters. In seven careful appendixes occupying more than fifty pages, the speeches are catalogued and cross-catalogued by sequence, type, grouping, speaker, etc. Taken together, text and appendixes constitute a mine of statistics, but the book, far from being dry, is rich with perceptive obiter dicta, particularly in the chapter "The Speeches and Their Models," where excellent use is made of G. N. Knauer's fundamental work *Die Aeneis und Homer* (Göttingen, 1964). The book was generally well received, cf. E. J. Kenney at *JRS* 64 (1974) 276–277. It will certainly continue to be consulted for its valuable appendixes if nothing else.

His retirement on 30 June 1972 was hastened in part by his disillusionment with Columbia and New York City. He was appalled by the student riots of 1968 and spoke of the revolutionaries with undisguised contempt. The sound of amplified oratory and rhythmic crowd shouts were chillingly reminiscent of a Nazi rally to a man who, while on his honeymoon in Bavaria, had heard Hitler speak at one. Butler Library was not burned, but Columbia was never the same for him. Nor was the increasingly dangerous New York, which at one time had ranked in his affections with Oxford and Paris. Although he and his wife retained their Park Avenue apartment, in 1970 they transferred their official residence to their summer home in East Hampton,

Long Island. Freed from seminars and dissertations, he returned after a twenty-year hiatus to publishing scholarly articles in classical journals. A dozen appeared in four years, including a series of pieces on Dio Chrysostom and a parting defense of his biographical approach (*Hermes* 102 [1974] 321–337). In 1976 he brought out his last book, *The Immortal Profession*, which, fittingly, dealt with teaching. Published a quarter-century after *The Art of Teaching* and dedicated to his students of forty years, it is at once a touching retrospective and a resounding reaffirmation of his tenets, now with particular application to the life of the teacher-scholar and the training of college teachers.

On 20 January 1978, Gilbert Highet died of cancer at the age of seventy-one. His personality and career have been variously judged. The brisk, hearty manner struck some as distant and lacking in real warmth, if not arrogant, and many even of his immediate colleagues were too awed by the overwhelming force of his person to become close. Yet beneath the sophisticated, man-of-the-world exterior some would see a certain diffidence. He remained in many ways a product of his Scottish Calvinist upbringing, a rigid moralist with faith in such old-fashioned virtues as hard work. He believed in the effectiveness of literature as a force on men's lives and in the particular value of Greek and Latin authors as embodying permanent moral and intellectual standards. He dedicated his extraordinary mental energy to studying this literature and—in the fullest sense—to teaching it. Although certain members of his profession applied the label "popularizer" to him as though it were a badge of shame, he wore it equably, confident in the rightness of his creed that the classical scholar's "first duty is to know the truth, and his second is to make it known" (*Classical Tradition*, 500).

Books

Kiefer, O. *Sexual Life in Ancient Rome.* Translated with Helen Highet. London, 1934.
An Outline of Homer. London, 1935.
Mayer, G. *Friedrich Engels: A Biography.* Translated with Helen Highet. New York, 1936.
Beginning Latin. Oxford, 1938.
Jaeger, W. *Paideia: The Ideals of Greek Culture.* Translated. Vol. 1. Oxford, 1939; 2d ed. New York, 1945. Vols. 2–3, New York, 1943–44.
The Classical Tradition. New York, 1949.
The Art of Teaching. New York, 1950.
People, Places, and Books. New York, 1953.
Juvenal the Satirist. New York, 1954.
Man's Unconquerable Mind. New York, 1954.
The Migration of Ideas. New York, 1954. (Also published with the preceding as *The Mind of Man.* London and New York, 1954.)
A Clerk of Oxenford. New York, 1954.
Poets in a Landscape. New York, 1957.

Talents and Geniuses. New York, 1957.
The Powers of Poetry. New York, 1960.
The Anatomy of Satire. Princeton, 1962.
Explorations. New York, 1971.
The Speeches in Vergil's Aeneid. Princeton, 1972.
The Immortal Profession. New York, 1976.

Articles (Collected)

Ball, R. J. *The Classical Papers of Gilbert Highet.* New York, 1983.

Articles (Selected)

"The Life of Juvenal." *TAPA* 68 (1937) 480–506.
"Petronius the Moralist." *TAPA* 72 (1941) 176–194.
"Rostagni's *La letturatura di Roma repubblicana ed Augustea.*" Review. *AJPh* 63
        (1942) 92–104.
"The Philosophy of Juvenal." *TAPA* 80 (1949) 254–270.
"Juvenal's Bookcase." *AJP* 72 (1951) 369–394.
"Sound-Effects in Juvenal's Poetry." *SPh* 48 (1951) 697–706.
"Libertino Patre Natus." *AJP* 94 (1973) 268–281.
"Consonant Clashes in Latin Poetry." *CP* 69 (1974) 178–185.
"Lexical Notes on Dio Chrysotom." *GRBS* 15 (1974) 247–253.
"Speech and Narrative in the *Aeneid.*" *HSCP* 78 (1974) 189–229.
"Masks and Faces in Satire." *Hermes* 102 (1974) 321–337.
"Lexical and Critical Notes on Dio Chrysostom." *GRBS* 17 (1976) 153–156.
"Mutilations in the Text of Dio Chrysostom." In R. J. Ball, *The Classical Papers of
        Gilbert Highet.* New York, 1983: 74–99.
For a complete bibliography, see Ball: 349–378, where almost 1,000 items are listed.

Sources

Ball, R. J. *The Classical Papers of Gilbert Highet.* New York 1983: 1–11. (Many
        personal details.)
Bovie, P. "Highet and the Classical Tradition." *Arion* 6 (1967) 98–115. (Some-
        what hostile.)
Calder, W. M., III. "Gilbert Highet, Anthon Professor of Latin, Emeritus." *CW* 66
        (1972–73) 385–387.
———. "Gilbert Highet." *Gnomon* 50 (1978) 430–432.
Campbell, B. "Gilbert Highet, Scholar and Poet, Dies of Cancer at the Age of 71."
        The New York Times (21 January 1978) 24.
Crosby, M. "Gilbert Highet: A Remembrance." *College Board Review* 108 (Summer
        1978) 28–30.

Farber, M. A. "Columbia's Highet is Retiring Today." *The New York Times* (30 June 1972) 12.

Anon. "Professor Gilbert Highet: Teacher and Popularizer of the Classics." *Times* (London) (26 January 1978) 16.

[For additional items, see Ball, 13–14.]

Papers

"Gilbert Highet" file, Columbiana Collection, Rare Book and Manuscript Library, Columbia University.

Others

Autobiographical details scattered throughout Highet's books of essays on general subjects.

Personal reminiscences.

A. E. Housman

26 March 1859 – 30 April 1936

P. G. NAIDITCH
University of California, Los Angeles

A.E. Housman is commonly regarded as one of the greatest classical scholars in the history of Great Britain. His rigorous intelligence and precision of thought; his genius for textual criticism; his wide, detailed, and systematic knowledge of the classical languages and literatures; and his elegant command of the English tongue go far to explain the reputation he has long possessed; but almost as significant as these, though perhaps less obvious than these, was a deadly seriousness of purpose that made him a proponent for the highest of standards in his chosen studies. Yet Housman's place in history is not limited to classical scholarship. In addition, he enjoys considerable standing as a poet. Many readers consider his verse amongst the most moving and melodious of modern English poetry; and his chief works, *A Shropshire Lad* (1896) and *Last Poems* (1922), have remained continuously in print since their publication. But Housman himself was more interested in his standing as a scholar than in his rank as a poet.

Alfred Edward Housman was the eldest of the seven children of Edward Housman (1831–1894), a Worcestershire solicitor, and his first wife, Sarah Jane Williams (1828–1871). Theirs was a talented family. Clemence (1861–1955) became a noted artist, novelist, and suffragette; Katharine Elizabeth (1862–1945) composed a history of King Edward VI Grammar School, Bath, where her husband, Edward Symons, was headmaster; Laurence (1865–1959) was variously an illustrator, novelist, playwright, and supporter of pacificism and women's rights. Others of the children became, respectively, a physician, a munitions expert, and a soldier, the last killed in combat during the Boer War.

Housman was born in a house called either The Little Valley or The Valley House, Fockbury, in the parish of Catshill, Worcestershire. Soon afterwards, the family moved to the neighboring town of Bromsgrove. The new home, Perry Hall, was a large manor, formerly the property of an elderly relation. But the size and extent of the house did not accurately reflect the financial standing of the family: the Housmans were thus far not so much prosperous as fortunate.

About the year 1870 Sarah Jane developed cancer and on 26 March 1871, her eldest son's twelfth birthday, she died. Housman had been sent away a few days before, and his mother's demise contributed greatly to his dark view of existence. But he was not the only member of the family badly affected by this sad event. His father did not support the death of his wife well, though two years afterward he married a cousin, Lucy Housman (1827–1907), who had introduced him to Sarah Jane. He endeavored, without conspicuous success, to continue his profession and, eventually, took to drink. Edward Housman died, nearly insolvent, in 1894.

A. E. Housman's academic career began propitiously. He won a scholarship in 1870 to King Edward VI Grammar School, Bromsgrove. He was studious and, when he respected an instructor, worked well. Under Herbert Millington, who became headmaster in 1873, his studies advanced until, in 1877, he stood at the head of the school. In this last year, Housman was ranked as one of the first twelve students in the annual Oxford and Cambridge Schools Examinations; and he won, in open competition, a classical scholarship to St. John's College, Oxford.

Housman's career at Oxford was, except for its conclusion, unremarkable. He worked at his studies; he contributed to undergraduate periodicals; and he stood, without making serious efforts to succeed, for the Newdigate Prize and the Ireland Scholarship. Despite his taking first class honors in Classical Moderations in 1879, the Fellows of St. John's were probably disappointed in him. For his part, Housman should have realized that the College to which he belonged was not one of the chief academic institutions at Oxford. Its tutors were not generally either the most learned or the most efficient in the University; and Housman, who had a history of neglecting work when he disliked or despised an instructor, was not inspired to put forward his best efforts.

In 1880 Housman and the other two scholars of his year, A. W. Pollard (1859–1944), afterwards Keeper of Printed Books in the British Museum, and Moses J. Jackson (1858–1923), took rooms outside the College. Probably, Pollard and Housman had come to be on friendly terms from the first. They each had won a classical scholarship; they involved themselves in the production of the undergraduate periodical *Ye Rounde Table*; and they visited each other's homes during the vacations. Jackson, on the other hand, had won the Holmes Science scholarship; he had little respect for, and indeed was openly contemptuous of, the humanities; and his outside interests centered not on literature but on athletics. In later years, however, Housman identified Jackson as his greatest friend, and said he had had more influence on him than anyone else. Not improbably, at Oxford, this influence was principally intellectual.

Like his College, the University of Oxford was not an institution for which Housman had great respect. The master of the most prestigious college was the Regius Professor of Greek, Benjamin Jowett of Balliol; and Jowett despised technical scholarship. Having heard Jowett lecture once, Housman never returned to hear him again. Henry Nettleship, the Professor of Latin from 1878 to 1893, though a man of considerable erudition and no mean intelligence, did not share Housman's high opinion of textual criticism; and the learned and industrious Robinson Ellis (1834–1913) was foolish and absurd and eccentric. Ingram Bywater and Herbert Richards, for both of whom Housman latterly had a measure of esteem, do not seem then to have come his way.

In 1881 Jackson received first-class honors in the natural science examinations, and Pollard received a first class in Literae Humaniores. Housman was failed. The explanation for his poor performance in Greats has long been a subject of discussion and debate. As early as 1881 Pollard was interviewed by the College authorities in the hope of determining why Housman had performed so badly. The reason may have been nothing more than Housman's disinterest in the subjects of the examinations and a false faith in his ability to deal satisfactorily with the philosophical questions. But writers have conjectured other causes, ranging from religious troubles to a misplaced romantic interest in Jackson; and it does not now seem possible to determine why Housman turned in such inadequate answers. But the examiners probably failed him because they felt he was treating them with contempt. They allowed him neither a fourth-class honors degree nor credit towards the pass examinations. This failure almost ended Housman's professional career before it had properly begun. Very few have proved able to surmount so disastrous a beginning in the classics, and no classical scholar has done so in as spectacular a fashion as Housman.

Housman returned to Bromsgrove. In 1881 and 1882, he worked as a sixth form master for Millington at his school and readied himself for the examinations for the pass degree at Oxford and the Civil Service in London. He was successful in these tests and, at the end of November 1882, accepted a position in the Patent Office in London, where his friend M. J. Jackson was employed as a special indexing clerk. Probably, Housman began his career as secretary to the head of the Patent Office. By 1883 or 1884, however, he was transferred to the Trade Marks Division, and worked as a higher division clerk until his resignation.

At this time, Housman dwelt in London with the brothers Moses and Adalbert Jackson, who were both students at University College, London. In 1883, Moses received a doctorate in science from the University of London; in the following year, Adalbert was awarded a bachelor's degree, and moved away to work as a schoolmaster. Apparently in 1885, after a serious altercation, whose causes are uncertain, Housman and Moses Jackson took rooms in different parts of London. Housman lodged at Byron Cottage, 17 North Road, Highgate, where he stayed until 1907, when he moved to 1 Yarborough Villas, Pinner.

Jackson had been greatly annoyed and disgusted by a major reorganization of the Patent Office, and in 1887 resigned to accept the position of Principal of Sind College, Karachi. He remained there, except for long and numerous holidays, until his retirement in 1910. His attempts to obtain a chair or headmastership in London during the late 1890s were unsuccessful and, on retirement, he moved to British Columbia. The break with Housman had been eventually healed, and in 1900 Housman was asked to stand as godfather to Jackson's fourth son.

It was in the 1880s that Housman began seriously to study the classics. At Oxford, he was considered highly intelligent, but his tutors did not view him as a prodigy, and on one occasion he was publicly told that he was not a genius. Even in those days, it is apparent that it was Housman's plan to become a professional classical scholar. As early as 1879 he began work on an edition of Propertius and, whilst still technically an undergraduate, he published an article in a Cambridge philological journal. Not improbably, it was with this article that he introduced himself to H. A. J. Munro (1819–1885), the one British scholar of the day whose labors he greatly admired. But if Housman entertained any hopes for aid from Munro in retrieving the position his failure had cost him, they were unfulfilled. Munro's reply was polite and friendly but apparently offered no help.

Housman's first article, "Horatiana," published in the *Journal of Philology* for 1882, reveals a young man of respectable though no exceptional learning, and of considerable intellectual ability and knowledge of Latin and the errors of scribes. The paper seems to have attracted little comment at the time. His second classical publication, a note on Ovid's *Ibis*, was even less ambitious, and appeared in the same periodical in 1883.

After his workday as a clerk in the Patent Office, Housman pursued his private classical studies at the British Museum. In 1885, he tried to interest the Oxford University Press and Macmillan in an elaborate edition of Propertius. The former declined the proposal on the advice of Robinson Ellis, who sent Housman a letter explaining his reasons for thinking the work unsatisfactory; Macmillan refused, without discussion, almost immediately. At length, in October 1886, Housman completed a long article, his third paper, "Emendationes Propertianae," and submitted it to the *Journal of Philology*. It was accepted and appeared in 1887. It is with this paper that Housman's career may be said to have properly begun.

Housman divided "Emendationes Propertianae" into two parts. After a brief preface, he listed about two hundred and fifty of his conjectures, without supporting argument, in the text of Propertius. This was followed by a detailed examination of the first elegy: a discussion with the subordinate purpose of showing that textual critics do not propose alterations without reasons. Housman displayed brilliance in argument and evidence of wide and careful reading in the Latin classics.

This article attracted the attention of R. Y. Tyrrell, the Regius Professor of Greek at Trinity College, Dublin, who, "struck by the brilliancy of some emendations of his published in one of the learned journals . . . introduced [himself to Housman] by letter." Likely enough, it was also at this time that Housman came to be on friendly terms with J. P. Postgate (1853–1926), then Professor of Comparative Philology at University College, London, who in 1891 entrusted him with the task of editing Ovid's *Ibis* for the *Corpus Poetarum Latinorum* (published 1894; corrected edition, 1905). Postgate also was greatly impressed by Housman's labors on Propertius and, in his own edition of 1894, accepted over sixty of his conjectures, transpositions, and changes in punctuation; and no name appears more often in his apparatus criticus than Housman's.

During the next few years, Housman continued to write on problems in classical texts. By the beginning of 1892, he had published over two hundred pages of notes, articles and reviews. These were principally concerned with the textual criticism of important ancient authors and were about equally divided between Greek and Roman writers: notably, Aeschylus, Sophocles, Euripides, Horace, and Ovid. In addition, he had contributed English verse translations of three passages in the tragedians to his friend Pollard's *Odes from the Greek Dramatists*: versions admired, among others, by Walter Headlam. In 1889, Housman was elected, with Postgate proposing him, to the Cambridge Philological Society.

Early in 1892 the chair of Greek and Latin at University College, London, became vacant, and the Council of the College resolved to engage two classical professors. The advertisement, when it appeared, attracted nineteen applicants, including R. S. Conway, A. B. Cook, J. Wight Duff, and G. F. Hill. Housman's testimonials, both in the number and eminence of his sponsors and in the force of their several asseverations, marked him as the strongest and most interesting of the candidates; and, taken as a whole, he was far the best supported applicant in the contest. He was able to submit favorable, even exceptionally laudatory, letters from the Professors of Latin at Oxford, Cambridge and Dublin and the Professors of Greek at Dublin and St. Andrews. He did not, however, include letters from the Regius Professors of Greek at Oxford and Cambridge and it is highly unlikely that he sought their support. Jowett he despised; and he probably realized that R. C. Jebb had as little liking for his philosophy of scholarship as he had for Jebb's.

As was permitted by the advertisement, Housman offered himself for either the Latin or the Greek chair, with a preference for the former. The election committee, of which Postgate was a member, recommended his appointment to the Professorship of Latin. The Chair of Greek was conferred on Wyse and, after his resignation in 1894, on Arthur Platt (1860–1925), a whimsical, delightful, and very erudite man, who became one of Housman's closer friends.

At University College, London, Housman fulfilled all of the duties that were set him both consistently and well. Since he was now Professor of Latin, and since he felt he was unable to attain to excellence in both Latin and Greek, Housman restricted his professional investigations in the main to problems in Latin textual criticism. But his idea of excellence was high, and his occasional contributions to the correction of new papyri texts, especially Bacchylides, remain notable. As a teacher Housman was efficient, though deliberately dry; and practically all of the students who left accounts concur in picturing an excellent instructor. None of his students at University College, London, however, attained eminence in classical studies and, whilst two or three became professional classical scholars, and Mortimer Wheeler an archaeologist, Housman later remarked in effect that he "seldom had pupils who possessed a native aptitude for classical studies or intended to pursue them far." As an administrator, Housman took, as was required of him, an active though not a dominant role in meetings: he served as Dean of his faculty (1894–1896) and as a member of the University College Council (1899–1902). Additionally, he involved himself, again as was expected of him, in the social activities of the College: notably in the Debating Society, especially in his first years, and in the Literary and Arts Societies. To the Literary Society he periodically delivered much-applauded lectures on various English poets. For the Union Society, he twice delivered the annual Foundation Oration. As an orator, be it in formal or informal settings, all accounts portray Housman as superb: witty, amusing, interesting, and delightful.

During his years at University College Housman began the work that was to become his most renowned contribution to classical studies. His labors on Propertius had been mostly abandoned after an unpleasant and regrettable controversy with Postgate in 1895, a conflict that took its origin in Housman's earlier work. Some time before, Housman had written a book on *The Manuscripts of Propertius*, and Postgate had sponsored it to the Cambridge University Press. The Press declined it in 1891, but the work was accepted by the *Journal of Philology* as three long articles (1892–1893). The series was brilliantly and charmingly argued. "Controversy," Housman remarked, "is inseparable from the discussion of our subject, and the ensuing pages will of necessity contain a certain amount of polemical matter; but my purpose is not in the main controversial. My purpose is to establish my own theory: to demolish the theories of others is only a necessary incident in the process." Realizing that true readings could not in themselves prove that a manuscript preserved a genuine element from antiquity, he used an intriguing methodology for evaluating manuscript lections: he gave emphasis to readings which stood "half way between the true reading and the corruption" in the lost common parent of the surviving codices.

Postgate believed, with reason, that Housman's *stemma codicum* was defective. It was indeed a fault in Housman's methodology that he often was willing to rely on others' reports of manuscripts; and the false datings and false reports on occasion seriously damaged the logical premises on which he built his arguments. His critic, in discussing another manuscript of Propertius, identified this defect as well as additional problems. Housman's rebuttal failed in its purpose; and Postgate's reply, bitter and harsh and deadly, silenced him. For nearly two years Housman published almost nothing in the journals. In 1897, however, he turned himself to Ovid's *Heroides* and, about the same time, to Manilius' *Astronomica*. In 1898 and 1900, he published his first papers on Manilius: dry lists of conjectures in the opening and final books of the poem. These papers led to his first book.

Housman's first published classical book, M. *Manilii astronomicon liber primus*, was published when its editor was forty-four years of age. It appeared in 1903 in an edition of four hundred copies, and it was published at Housman's expense. The volume was dedicated neither to teacher nor family member but to his friend M. J. Jackson, *harum litterarum contemptor*. This astrological poem remained at the center of Housman's studies for the rest of his life. In 1912 he published an edition, with commentary, of the second book; in 1916, of the third; in 1920, of the fourth; and, in 1930, of the fifth and final book. In 1932, he brought out an *editio minor*.

Housman's Manilius marked a considerable advance in Latin studies. He was not of course the first in Great Britain to work on the poem. In England, interest in Manilius had languished after Bentley's edition of 1739. But at length, during the last part of the nineteenth century, attention was again directed to the *Astronomica* chiefly by Robinson Ellis and J. P. Postgate, and it was their labors, not Bentley's, that first brought Manilius to Housman's critical notice. Ellis in particular had made available a partial collation of a new, important manuscript, though he failed to make good use of it himself; and it may be supposed that it was this publication that first led Housman seriously to consider Manilius as a subject on which to work.

Following a lengthy, polemical preface, Housman listed his conjectures in books II, III, and IV. Then, he provided a corrected text of the first book with a commentary written in Latin. The work was distinguished by the editor's erudition, the large number of intelligent and even brilliant alterations he proposed—a recent editor has accepted over two hundred of his conjectures—and by his disagreeable comments on other classical scholars, both dead and living: the slashing style, as one reviewer styled it, which all know and few applaud. The reception of the volume was mixed. Postgate welcomed Housman's volume as "the most substantial contribution to the criticism and elucidation of Manilius since the time of Bentley"; many others, especially in Germany, were less enthusiastic. Friedrich Vollmer, in particular, complained that Housman had no "inkling" of *Überlieferungsgeschichte*; and several, both on the Continent and in England, commented adversely on the savage, carping, disagreeable tone that pervaded the editor's preface and commentary.

Housman's seemingly ceaseless criticisms, especially of conservative critics, has led to the belief that his own philosophy was radical. He himself had no such delusion. In a private letter, he wrote: "Radicalism in textual criticism is just as bad as conservatism; but it is not now rampant, and conservatism is. Radicalism was rampant thirty or forty years ago, and it was then rebuked by Madvig and Haupt: now it is conservatism that wants rebuking."

But it was less his general remarks than his comments on distinguished or well-known scholars of the day that gave considerable offense. "I imagine that Mr Buecheler, when he first perused Mr Sudhaus' edition of the Aetna, must have felt something like Sin when she gave birth to Death"; "But suppose that we could blunt our grammatical perceptions to the hebetude of Mr Ehwald's . . ."; "Mr Vollmer's notion of the dative case is a case which he can translate by für." This polemical manner effectively disguised the fact that Housman was, in a special sense, a singularly courteous writer.

This courtesy consisted in the care with which Housman presented his case in favor of or against manuscript readings and the conjectures of other scholars. Readers were not required to have faith in his omniscience: they were given opportunity to see how he reached conclusions. It was a courtesy only accidentally given to the world at large, for Housman had little respect for mankind in general. His words, "the reader whose good opinion I desire and have done my utmost to secure is the next Bentley or Scaliger who may chance to occupy himself with Manilius," were not designed to win applause, and Housman clearly wished to annoy and alienate certain of his readers. There is no doubt that he fulfilled his desire. But there exists in his attitude a pride of purpose and loftiness of ambition that deserve admiration. He asked no quarter and, so far as his contemporaries could see, he gave none; he evaluated the writings of others by that same intelligent, learned standard by which he wished his own compositions to be judged. By standards such as his, few works deserved strong commendation and, accordingly, few received it from him.

In 1905 appeared Housman's second classical book: an edition of Juvenal. The satirist was not, until the close of the nineteenth century, a writer that especially interested Housman. But the discovery, in a manuscript at Oxford, of some thirty lines otherwise unknown in the tradition intrigued him, and he began to write on the problems the new text presented. As a result, Postgate asked Housman to review the Oxford Classical Text of Juvenal by S. G. Owen for the *Classical Review*. Following Housman's critique, Owen resigned his rights to preparing the text for Postgate's *Corpus*. The critic was invited to supply it in his stead, and his text, composed in about a twelvemonth, was issued both in the *Corpus* and, with a preface and revised apparatus, as a separate volume. As usual, for the separate book, Housman paid for the publication.

Juvenal's popularity has long been considerable. From the invention of printing to the beginning of the twentieth century, over nine hundred texts, translations, and reprints of the satires had appeared. The rate of correction of the work was not, however, commensurate with the interest the work attracted: "the fact is," wrote Housman, "that Juvenal has never been taken in hand by a critic of the first order. If, instead of Pithoeus and Rigaltius and Ruperti and Jahn, it were Scaliger and Gronouius and Bentley and Lachmann that had been here before us, not much would now remain unexplained or uncorrected except the inexplicable and the incorrigible."

The separately issued text of Housman's Juvenal, again of only four hundred copies, carries on the title page the words "editorum in usum edidit A. E. Housman." The preface was equally trenchant, with references to "the sloth and distaste for thinking which are the common inheritance of humanity" and "that habit of treading in ruts and trooping in companies which men share with sheep."

Housman's text of Juvenal is intelligently constituted. Although the apparatus criticus is superior in design and in detail to anything which had gone before, it nonetheless was inadequate. It wants emphasis, however, that Housman did not pretend that his was a polished edition. He wrote: "This work . . . is not meant for a model; it is an enterprise undertaken in haste and in humane concern for the relief of a people sitting in darkness." But he had an additional purpose. He designed not merely to provide a good text with a competently constructed apparatus criticus, he wished also to reform editorial technique in the classics. Therefore, Housman addressed himself to beginners "who are not critics yet, but are neither too dull to learn nor too self-satisfied to wish to learn." The brilliance, the sanity, the modesty with which he expressed himself—"The superstitious have full faith in their superstitions, but those who follow reason are well aware that reason is no infallible guide"—go far to mitigate the cruel satire with which he attacked fools; and Housman's improvements to the text, especially in punctuation, are not despised by more recent editors.

At the close of 1910 the Latin Chair in Cambridge, subsequently called the Kennedy Professorship, became vacant on the death of John E. B. Mayor. Housman was persuaded to stand and, though J. P. Postgate, J. S. Reid, T. R. Glover and others were candidates for the position, he was appointed to the Chair. His appointment was not inevitable, though he was recognized by some as the foremost Latinist in Great Britain. Amongst his champions were the Regius Professor Greek at Cambridge, Henry Jackson, and W. T. Lendrum, who actively worked on his behalf. Of the other electors, only Robinson Ellis, who had not forgiven Housman the discourteous treatment he had received from him in a review of Catullus, seems to have been mildly against his appointment. Jackson had long wished to see him Professor of Latin at Cambridge or Oxford; Lendrum believed him the greatest Latinist since Madvig. Shortly after Housman was offered the chair, he was elected to a fellowship at Trinity College. In Cambridge, his modest rooms were, except for the last few months of his life, in Whewell Court.

Housman took little part in academic politics at Cambridge, albeit he was President of the Cambridge Philological Society in 1912 and 1913. Only once, more than twenty years later, did he involve himself in a question concerning the classics in a nontechnical publication. In 1934, when a chauvinistic British writer in the *Sunday Times* complained about the election of the German Eduard Fraenkel to the Corpus Professorship of Latin in the University of Oxford, Housman was asked to intervene. His letter effectively silenced the opposition to the appointment. But this intervention was unique, though now and again he might write to the newspapers on some other matter. Ordinarily, Housman wrote papers and edited texts, served on the necessary boards, and delivered his lectures in Cambridge.

Housman's lectures in Cambridge were attended not only by students but by professional scholars. They seem rarely to have attracted large audiences. The lecturer limited himself almost entirely to problems in textual criticism; the substance of his discourse was precise and spare and polemical remarks were not numerous. But twice he delivered a special course on "The Application of Thought to Textual Criticism." In this series, he declined to give a systematic exposition of textual criticism and preferred to avoid as much as possible general propositions. He believed that it was very difficult for people, himself included, to generalize successfully. Instead, he gave particular examples of the way in which scholars had failed to approach their topics honestly or intelligently. The topics in the course ranged from the use of inscriptions for studying Saturnian meters to W. M. Lindsay's discussion of textual criticism; from H. W. Garrod's glib and foolish remarks on textual studies to Sir Richard Claverhouse Jebb's comments on a passage in Euripides' *Medea*.

The rest of Housman's lectures at Cambridge concerned Catullus, Horace, Juvenal, Lucretius, Martial, Ovid, Persius, Plautus and, over ten years, one book after another of Lucan. His labors on the *Bellum Civile* culminated in an edition that, declined by Macmillan, was issued by Blackwell in 1926. It was an edition that, like his Juvenal, depended not on an examination of new manuscripts but on an intelligent reading and assessment of others' collations and a carefully cultivated knowledge of how silver age poets expressed themselves. In addition, the editor's mastery of ancient astrology permitted him to deal with the writer's inaccurate references to that peculiar art: "that intricate fraud" as Housman styled it elsewhere "by which Asia revenged herself on Europe for the conquests of Alexander."

Housman's edition of Lucan in 1926 at last won him the respect and regard of continental scholars, notably Fraenkel, whose elaborate essay in *Gnomon* was the signal to others to take him seriously as the first scholar of Great Britain. Wilamowitz, Löfstedt, and Pasquali all soon declared themselves to be admirers of Housman's labors, and placed him at the head of classical studies in Britain. Much of the opposition Housman had encountered earlier now died down. Even old enemies began to seek excuses to praise Housman's work. In particular, the publication of the fifth and final book of Manilius in 1930 occasioned enthusiastic congratulations from many who were in no position to judge the quality of the work. Housman's reaction to this praise was restrained. He noted it and privately remarked that people did not like or understand his work any better than they had before, but as he now had a name in the world, they therefore thought it safer to treat him with respect. Like Nietzsche, he seems never to have read a word without seeing an attitude.

Having no high respect for the ability of his fellow man to assess quality —"You would be welcome to praise me if you did not praise one another"— Housman refused most of the honors that were offered to him. The chief exception was, thirty years after his academic disgrace in Literae Humaniores, an Honorary Fellowship at St. John's College, Oxford, in 1911. He declined at least eight honorary doctorates, election to the British Academy, and, in 1929, the Order of Merit, always with great courtesy and, when offered by those he liked, with considerable charm. "I must begin with grateful acknowledgment to you and my other friends," he wrote, "because I could not read your letter without feelings which had some pure pleasure in them; but this was swallowed up in surprise, and surprise itself was engulfed in horror. Not if the stipend were £150,000 instead of £150 would I be Public Orator." But friendship would oblige him to undertake even uncongenial tasks. Most notably, he composed addresses for Sir James G. Frazer and Henry Jackson and a biographical memoir for Arthur Platt, and he wrote addresses to King George V both for his College and for his University. Finally, he agreed to deliver the Leslie Stephen Lecture for 1933: a work much commended at the time, even by T. S. Eliot, though Housman himself took no pleasure or satisfaction in it.

Housman's refusal to accept unmerited or ignorant praise was mirrored by his reluctance to award commendation to others. His consciousness of high standards, and of the limits of his own expertise outside certain areas, made him at once a difficult critic to please when he was competent to judge, and a critic slow to commend when his learning or understanding seemed to him imperfect. And his anger and annoyance with "that vague and conventional laudation which is distributed at large, like the rain of heaven, by reviewers who do not know the truth and consequently cannot tell it" led him to adjust the scales of justice by preferring severity to kindness.

Harsh, seemingly merciless, criticism rarely wins friends, and few recognize a reluctance to give praise as an endearing trait. Nor does the student, who consciously designs to raise standards, usually win admiration from a population that had rather be left to pursue its work at its own low level; and the hatred and animosity that Housman still excites is due, in part, to wounded vanity and a desire to avenge savaged friends or respected predecessors. For his own part, Housman had especially great admiration for Richard Bentley (1662–1742), and reacted to casual attacks on Bentley as others have reacted to Housman's own careful invective against their friends.

The last few years of Housman's life were, as his health declined, physically painful. "The doctor does not want me to take walks of much more than a mile, and I myself am often inclined not to do much more than twice that amount. I still go up my 44 stairs two at a time, but that is in hopes of dropping dead at the top." He continued however, almost to the last, to deliver the lectures he had agreed to give. At length, he was compelled to abandon his rooms for a set on the ground floor of the Great Court. On 25 April 1936, he returned to the Evelyn Nursing Home, Cambridge, and died there of advanced heart disease in the evening of 30 April 1936. He was cremated, and his ashes buried in Ludford, a town he had commemorated in *A Shropshire Lad.*

In person, Housman was of medium height (5'9"), of slight physique, with a severe and forbidding countenance. He enjoyed long walks and ecclesiastical architecture, was very knowledgeable about plants and an excellent judge of wine and food. His holidays were, after his translation to Cambridge, usually restricted to France. Earlier in life, he often visited Italy, especially Venice, and, once, Istanbul. From 1920 he regularly flew to Paris for his gastronomical and architectural tours. His standing as a gourmet is reflected by the creation, by the chef of La Tour d'Argent, of the dish Barbue Housman. So far, indeed, as Housman willingly took part generally in society, it was as host or guest of university dining clubs, notably the Family, to which he had been elected. Philosophically, he described himself as a Cyrenaic or an egoistical hedonist, though twice, at the start of the first World War and during a financial crisis, he sent substantial sums of money to the government. Observation and experience and a certain sense of justice made Housman an atheist and, except in textual criticism, a conservative.

Controversy has long surrounded Housman and his labors. During his lifetime, there were numerous complaints about the severe and brutal tone of his criticisms; after his death, eminent classicists complained that his influence in these studies had been regrettable. He had, by making the discipline seem too difficult or dangerous, frightened students away from Latin studies; he had, by his example, encouraged a harsh, indeed cruel, tone of polemics in the compositions of those whom he influenced. Housman himself, who valued talent and competence and honesty and brains, was not noticeably moved by the first group and should not have been overly troubled by the second. Although many classical scholars desire to interest students in the cultures of ancient Greece and Rome and to encourage research in the humanities, Housman did not share these ambitions. He regarded it as no part of his business to popularize the classics or even to attract students to the field. A superb lecturer, he purposefully refrained from making his courses generally interesting; "the leading classic of his generation," his uncompromising invective caused some scholars to abandon classical studies as a profession. He never designed to found a school and despised the impulse that led to such foundations, for he judged, on the basis of observation, that schools impeded the quest for truth. Accordingly, though at Cambridge for almost a quarter of a century, he directed only one graduate student (W. H. Semple).

Housman's friend and biographer A. S. F. Gow has characterized him as "a man at war," and it is a fair description. "There is no rivalry" wrote Housman "between the studies of Arts and Laws and Science but the rivalry of fellow soldiers in striving which can most victoriously achieve the common end of all, to set back the frontiers of darkness." But the ranks of Housman's fellow soldiers only included those who shared his hatred for incompetence and dishonesty and impudence and sloth, and those whose abilities permitted them to advance learning.

Books

M. Manilii astronomicon liber I [II, III, IV, V]. London, 1903, 1912, 1916, 1920, 1930; corrected impression, vol. V, Cambridge, 1937; *editio minor,* Cambridge, 1932.

D. Iunii Iuuenalis saturae. London, 1905; revised ed., Cambridge, 1931.

M. Annaei Lucani belli ciuilis libri decem. Oxford, 1926; corr. impr., 1927.

Articles (Collected)

The Classical Papers of A. E. Housman (= Cl.Pap.). Edited by J. Diggle and F. R. D. Goodyear. Cambridge, 1972.

Articles (Selected)

"Emendationes Propertianae." *JPh* 16 (1887) 1–35 = Cl.Pap. 29–54.

"The Manuscripts of Propertius." *JPh* 21 (1892–93) 101–97, 22 (1893) 84–128 = Cl.Pap. 232–304, 314–47.

"Greek Nouns in Latin Poetry from Lucretius to Juvenal." *JPh* 31 (1910) 236–66 = Cl.Pap. 817–839.

"ΑΙΟΣ and ΕΙΟΣ in Latin Poetry." *JPh* 33 (1913) 54–75 = Cl.Pap. 887–902.

"The Application of Thought to Textual Criticism." *PCA* 18 (1922) 67–84 = *Selected Prose.* Edited by J. Carter. Cambridge, 1962: 131–50 = Cl.Pap. 1058–1069 = *Collected Poems and Selected Prose.* Edited by C. Ricks. London, 1988: 325–39.

"Prosody and Method." I, II, CQ 21 (1927) 1–12; CQ 22 (1928) 1–10 = Cl.Pap. 1114–26, 1136–46.

"Praefanda." *Hermes* 66 (1931) 402–12 = Cl.Pap. 1175–84.

Sources

Chambers, R. W. *Man's Unconquerable Mind.* London, 1939: 365–386. (Memoir of Housman's life at University College, London.)

Gow, A. S. F. *A. E. Housman: A Sketch*, corr. impr. Cambridge, 1936. (Biographical memoir; the best introduction to Housman's life; see Naiditch, *A. E. Housman at University College, London*, 26f.)

Graves, Richard Perceval. *A. E. Housman: The Scholar–Poet*. Corr. impr. Oxford, 1981. (Unreliable biography; see *CJ* 77 [1982] 361–64; 81 [1986] 365.)

Haber, T. Burns. *A. E. Housman*. New York, 1967. (Biography, with considerable material on Housman's verse; knowledgeable but uncritical and inaccurate.)

Hawkins, Maude M. *A. E. Housman: Man behind a Mask*. Chicago, 1958. (Foolish and preternaturally inaccurate biography; see W. White, *American Book Collector* 9 [February 1959] 23f.)

Housman, Laurence. *A. E. H.* London, 1937. (Memoir.)

Naiditch, P. G. *A. E. Housman at University College, London: the Election of 1892*. Leiden, 1988.

Page, Norman. *A. E. Housman: A Critical Biography*. New York, 1983; partly corrected impression, 1985. (Intelligent but indolent biography; see *CJ* 81 [1986] 362–365.)

Richards, Grant. *Housman 1897–1936*, Corr. impr. London, 1942. (Memoir accompanied by essays of varying value.)

Symons, Katharine E., et al. *Alfred Edward Housman: Recollections*. New York, 1937. (Memoirs and essays.)

Watson, George L. *A. E. Housman: A Divided Life*. London, 1957. (Intelligent, but badly biassed biography; see J. Sparrow, *Independent Essays*, London, 1963: 134–145.)

Withers, Percy. *A Buried Life*. London, 1940. (Memoir.)

Bibliographies

Ehrsam, T. G. *A Bibliography of Alfred Edward Housman*. Boston, 1941.

Carter, J. and Sparrow, J. *A. E. Housman: A Bibliography*. Revised by William White. Godalming, 1982 (see *CJ* 79 [1984] 269–272).

Letters

The Letters of A. E. Housman. Edited by H. Maas. London, 1971.

Other

Hundreds of works, including several books, have been dedicated to Housman's poetry and poetical theory. Cf. Ehrsam, Carter and Sparrow, the *Housman Society Journal* (Bromsgrove), and the *A. E. Housman Journal* (Tokyo).

Housman's Cambridge lecture notes survive (University Library, Cambridge, Add. Mss. 6874–6902). His library was dispersed, though large portions of the classical sections are preserved at St. John's College, Oxford; Trinity College, Cambridge; University Library, Cambridge; and Waseda University, Tokyo. Other libraries, possessed of large Housman collections, include the British Library, London; Bryn Mawr College, Pennsylvania; the Library of Congress, Washington, D. C.; the Lilly Library, Indiana University, Bloomington; the Pierpont Morgan Library, New York; University College, London; and the University of Illinois, Urbana-Champaign.

Felix Jacoby

19 March 1876 – 10 November 1959

MORTIMER CHAMBERS
University of California, Los Angeles

Felix Jacoby achieved during his long working lifetime a colossal feat that will not be superseded for centuries, if ever: a collection of the fragments (that is, quotations in other writers) of the incomplete or lost Greek historians. In its current format this collection, *Die Fragmente der Griechischen Historiker* (Jacoby requested the abbreviation *FGrHist*), comprises seventeen volumes; yet it remains a torso for, since Jacoby's final volumes on the historians of the non-Greek states (1958), no further installment has appeared. Beyond this immense work, he wrote dozens of articles for Pauly-Wissowa, among which the masterpiece is that on Herodotus: it is of book length and furnishes the most detailed analysis and survey of the vast canvas on which the first historian painted. Jacoby also edited a work of Hesiod and wrote many long articles on Greek literature and on Latin poetry. In the opinion of Robert Dundas, his colleague at Christ Church, Oxford, he was "the most learned man in Europe."

Jacoby was of a Jewish family but was baptized as a Protestant at age eleven. He attended the Pädagogium zum Kloster unserer lieben Frauen in his native city, Magdeburg, and studied first at the Universities of Freiburg im Breisgau and Munich, also serving one year in the Bavarian field artillery. His move to Berlin in 1906 brought about the decisive influence on his studies: here he wrote his dissertation, *Apollodors Chronik*, under Hermann Diels and dedicated the work (published 1902) to him; but in the preface he thanks his "zweiten Lehrer," Wilamowitz, for much useful criticism.

In 1901 Jacoby married Margarete von der Leyen (1875–1956), who had a good classical education in a Gymnasium and attended lectures on classical philology in Berlin. She was to help him indispensably in his work on *FGrHist*. Jacoby now began work on his *habilitationsschrift*, the second book normally required from a scholar who wants to teach in a German university. At this time there was a position vacant in Breslau for a Privatdozent, a young scholar who lectured for minimal pay.

Accordingly, on 7 May 1903, Wilamowitz wrote to Eduard Norden, then professor of classics in Breslau,

> Within the next few days Dr. Jacobi [sic], the author of the collection of the fragments of Apollodorus, will present himself to you in the hope that he may be able to achieve Habilitation in Breslau. . . . He had already made fairly good progress in his studies here when I arrived [1897]: I first had a stronger personal influence over him when he submitted his dissertation, which I then accepted for my series, the [Philologische] Untersuchungen. I may well have turned him from purely historical studies more toward philology . . . [University of Göttingen Library]

Jacoby thus went to Breslau in 1903 and gained his Habilitation there in the autumn of that year with an edition (published in 1904 and dedicated to Wilamowitz) of the Marmor Parium, an inscription preserving a chronicle of events in Greece compiled on Paros in 263 B.C. He reedited this text in FGrHist (239). His inaugural lecture in Breslau, after his Habilitation, was on Eratosthenes, the great scholar of the third century B.C., nicknamed "Beta" in antiquity because he ranked (at least) second in many fields of study; Jacoby edited his chronological writings as FGrHist 241.

Jacoby was already making a reputation through his articles for Pauly-Wissowa, published from 1905 onward (the first longer one was on Euhemerus of Messene); in 1906 he was called to Kiel (as a Latinist) as Professor Extraordinarius and became Ordinarius on 23 January 1907. He remained in Kiel (declining a call to Hamburg in 1927) until his retirement in 1934. He had about a dozen Ph.D. pupils, all in classical philology. One of his few female pupils was Rose Zahn (Die erste Periklesrede [in Thucydides] [Borna-Leipzig, 1934]), whose narrative he often entertainingly interrupts with notes signed "Jac." He lived in Kitzeberg, across the harbor from Kiel, and had to take a ferry into town to reach the university. When the weather was bad or he had urgent work to do he would telephone his assistant (a pupil, Marie Wünsch) and announce that "das Schifflein fährt heute nicht"; this "little boat" was commemorated in the title of the Festschrift presented to him in 1956, Navicula Chiloniensis.

On 6 August 1908 Jacoby spoke at an international congress of historical studies in the Philharmonie, Berlin, about his plan for a new collection of the fragments of the Greek historians. In the next year he published a long paper surveying the development of Greek historiography and outlining his program. The final form of the immense FGrHist differed in details from the scheme he presented here (123), but the principle remained the same. Jacoby cut through to the proper method, namely to edit the historians according to the development of historiography and the type or form of a given historian's work. Thus the large groupings are genealogy and mythography, histories limited in time, and histories limited by states (historians of several states, historians of a single state—above all, the historians of Athens or Atthidographers—, and ethnographers of non-Greek states). Only through this method are the lines of development apparent.

Along the path to the first volume, Jacoby published the most important of his articles for Pauly-Wissowa: on Hecataeus, Hellanicus, and Herodotus (1912–1913). During the Great War, he was called to active service, as he wrote to Johannes Kirchner (22 November 1915), in a note of thanks for the gift of a fascicule of *Inscriptiones Graecae* II, 2d ed. [Staatsbibliothek Preussischer Kulturbesitz, Berlin, Sammlung Darmstadt 1878, 2f., once wrongly assigned to Georg Busolt]:

> Dear Professor, I ought to have thanked you a long time ago for your nice gift. But instead of having more free time because of the small number of students, I have sunk myself so deep in my historians that I have found time for nothing else. But now I am taking the Attic inscriptions as reading matter with me to Hamburg, where I am going to get some practice in on my rusty skills in riding, in connection with my being called up for service. With cordial thanks and sincere greetings I remain your sincerely grateful
>
> FJacoby.

In the war Jacoby was a private; he became ill and was discharged on grounds of health. After the war, in 1923, the first volume of *FGrHist* (nos. 1–63) appeared, containing the major figures Hecataeus (1) and Hellanicus (4). The texts, divided into T(estimonia) (the references in other writers to the separate historians) and F(ragmente), after the manner of Jacoby's master, Diels, in his edition of the fragments of the presocratic philosophers, all have a brief critical apparatus. Jacoby also began the practice, which he continued through all the volumes, of printing in parallel columns fragments that occur in similar form in more than one source; this exposes immediately the variations within the citation of fragments and makes clear the dependence of later writers on the historians under study. The second huge Teil (historians of certain periods) appeared in 1926–1930.

But now the progress of the mighty work collided with the politics of the Nazi epoch. Any study of Jacoby must, with sympathy and caution, use whatever sources are available to recover his activities during the period. All who knew Jacoby testify to his conservative politics and life style. The late Gerhard Müller, a student of Jacoby in Kiel and later professor in Münster and Giessen, informed me that Jacoby shared for a time the optimism of many Germans over the proclaimed policies of the Nazi party, which he saw as reviving discipline and stability. He even advised his students to enter the party in order to bring into it reasonable and honest young men; were he not of a Jewish family, he said, he would enter it himself. He maintained this misguided optimism into 1933 and perhaps even 1934. But then neither his being a baptized Protestant nor his sympathy for the professed ideals of the Nazis could save his position. He taught until summer semester 1934, when he was forced by anti-Semitic regulations to take leave; seeing that his future at Kiel was hopeless, he accepted the inevitable and applied for retirement. He then moved to Finkenkrug, a northwestern suburb of Berlin (now in East Germany).

Jacoby continued work on the *Fragmente*, but his Jewish origins blocked further publication in Germany. He was later forbidden to use libraries in Berlin, and there is little doubt that he would have been imprisoned in due course, perhaps killed (although some Jews married to non-Jewish women were spared). This persecution, and a violent invasion of Jacoby's house by five Nazis thugs during the "Kristallnacht" (9–10 November 1938), induced in him a willingness to leave Germany. On 3 December 1938 the Dean (then A. T. P. Williams) and Governing Body of Christ Church, Oxford, wrote to him, with delightful British understatement, that they "wish to enable you to continue your important work on the fragments of the Greek historians as soon as possible here in Oxford where conditions seem to be particularly favourable for carrying on such an undertaking" (letter from The Governing Body of Christ Church, Oxford). One of the agents behind this invitation was Eduard Fraenkel, himself a baptized Jew, who had already taken refuge in Oxford and held the chair of Latin. At first Jacoby was refused permission to leave, but through the discreet intervention of Werner Otto von Hentig (1886–1984), an official in the Foreign Office who assisted other Jews in emigrating, he was allowed to move. He and his wife reached Oxford in April 1939 and were naturalized in 1948.

Their financial situation was difficult: a grant of £180 was arranged, and for months they lived in two furnished rooms in Crick Road. Later they found a home at 6 St. Margaret's Road. There he and his wife sat at two desks facing each other and worked on the *Fragmente*. Jacoby held no official position at Christ Church and was seldom seen outside his college or his home. Oxford scholars remember him as short, upright, and bristling in a military way, extremely German in manner.

In 1940 the firm of Brill published the first installment of volume III of *FGrHist* and continued through the last volume so far published. In these years appeared the massive crowning stone of the whole structure, as Jacoby reached the Athenian local historians. In 1949 he published his only large synthetic book, *Atthis*, an introduction to his commentary on the Atthidographers. This part of the commentary appeared in English as a huge two-volume Supplement to *FGrHist* III b ("What a book!"—A.W. Gomme). Jacoby later found it possible to return to Germany, owing largely to the unblocking of his salary. On 25 February 1956, just before his leaving, Oxford created him D. Litt. *honoris causa*. Soon after returning to Germany, Frau Jacoby died (21 March 1956), two days after Jacoby's eightieth birthday. Jacoby now lived with his son in Archivstrasse in West Berlin until his death.

FGrHist is Jacoby's monument; no other name in the field of Greek historiography can be mentioned beside his. Yet his interests in philology, attested above all by his work on Latin elegists, are in danger of being overlooked in the shadow of the *Fragmente*. He is said to have asked, "Why do these people in Oxford think I'm a historian?" Wilamowitz brought him nearer to philology, and in a letter to the sons of his pupil and friend Julius Stenzel he wrote, "I live more and more with two departed ones in perpetual spiritual connection—with Wilamowitz and with your father" (shown to me by Joachim Stenzel).

Books

Apollodors Chronik. Eine Sammlung der Fragmente. Berlin, 1902 = *Philologische Untersuchungen* 16; reprinted New York, 1973.

Das Marmor Parium herausgegeben und erklärt. Berlin, 1904.

Die Fragmente der Griechischen Historiker. Teil I–Teil III C. Berlin and Leiden, 1923–1958.

Hesiodi Carmina. Pars I. Theogonia. Berlin, 1930. (No more published.)

Atthis. The Local Chronicles of Ancient Athens. Oxford, 1949; reprinted New York, 1973.

Articles (Collected)

Griechische Historiker. Stuttgart, 1956; from Pauly-Wissowa, *Realencyclopädie* = GH.

Abhandlungen zur griechischen Geschichtschreibung. Edited by H. Bloch. Leiden, 1956 = AGG.

Kleine philologische Schriften. Edited by H. J. Mette. 2 vols. Deutsche Akademie der Wissenschaften zu Berlin, Schriften der Sektion für Altertumswissenschaft 21. Berlin, 1961 = KPS.

Articles (Selected)

"Die attische Königsliste I." *Klio* 2 (1902) 406–439. (No more published.)

"Über das Marmor Parium." *RhM* NF 58 (1904) 63–107.

"Zur Entstehung der römischen Elegie." *RhM* NF 60 (1905) 38–105, 320 = *KPS* 2.65–121.

"Über die Entwicklung der griechischen Historiographie und den Plan einer neuen Sammlung der griechischen Historikerfragmente." *Klio* 9 (1909) 80–123 = AGG 16–64.

"Tibulls erste Elegie. Ein Beitrag zum verständnis der Tibullischen Kunst." *RhM* NF 64 (1909) 601–632; 65 (1910) 22–87 = *KPS* 2.122–206.

Review of *The Ancient Greek Historians*, by J. B. Bury. *BPW* 29 (1909) 419–429 = AGG 65–72.

"Zu Hippokrates περὶ ἀέρων ὑδάτων τόπων." *Hermes* 46 (1911) 518–567.

"Hekataios von Milet." *RE* VII.2 (1912) 2667–2750 = GH 186–227.

"Hellanikos von Lesbos." *RE* VIII.1 (1912) 104–153 = GH 262–287.

"Herodotos von Halikarnassos." *RE* Suppl. II (1913) 205–520 = GH 7–164.

"Drei Gedichte des Properz." *RhM* NF 69 (1914) 393–413, 427–463 = *KPS* 2:216–265.

"Studien zu den älteren griechischen Elegikern. (I. Zu Tyrtaios. II. Zu Mimnermos)." *Hermes* 53 (1918) 1–44, 262–307 = *KPS* 1:268–344.

"Das Prooemium des Lucretius." *Hermes* 56 (1921) 1–65 = *KPS* 2:8–64.

"Griechische Geschichtschreibung." *Die Antike* 2 (1926) 1–29 = AGG 73–99.

"Thukydides und die Vorgeschichte des peloponnesischen Krieges." *NGG* 1929, 1–34 = AGG 207–238.

"Theognis." *SBBerl* 1931, 90–180 = *KPS* 2:345–455.

"Homerisches II. Die Einschaltung des Schiffkatalogs in die Ilias." *SBBerl* (1932) 572–617 = *KPS* 1:54–106.

"Homerisches I. Der Bios und die Person." *Hermes* 68 (1933) 1–50 = *KPS* 1:1–53.

"Die geistige Physiognomie der Odyssee." *Die Antike* 9 (1933) 159–194 = *KPS* 1:107–138.

"Der homerische Apollonhymnos." *SBBerl* 1933, 682–751 = *KPS* 1:139–218.

"Charon von Lampsakos." *SIFC* n.s. 15 (1938, publ. 1939) 207–242 = AGG 178–206.

"Die Überlieferung von Ps. Plutarchs Parallela Minora und die Schwindelautoren." *Mnemosyne* ser. 4, 8 (1940) 73–144 = AGG 359–422.

"Some Athenian Epigrams from the Persian Wars." *Hesperia* 14 (1945) 157–211 = *KPS* 1:456–520.

"*Patrios Nomos*: State Burial in Athens and the Public Ceremony in the Kerameikos." *JHS* 64 (1944, publ. 1946) 37–66 = AGG 260–315.

"The First Athenian Prose Writer." *Mnemosyne* ser. 4, 13 (1947) 13–64 = AGG 100–143.

"Diagoras ὁ Ἄθεος." *Abhandlungen Berlin Akademie*, Klasse für Sprachen, Literatur und Kunst, 1959, no. 3: 1–48.

Sources

Bibliography

"Verzeichnis der Schriften Felix Jacobys 1900–1956." Abhandlungen zur griechischen Geschichtschreibung. Edited by H. Bloch. Leiden, 1956: 1–15.

Biographical

Andrewes, A. *The London Times*, 20 November 1959, 16.

Mensching, E. "Texte zur Berliner Philologie-Geschichte. VI: Felix Jacoby (1876–1959) und Berliner Institutionen 1934–1939." In his *Nugae zur Philologie-Geschichte* II. Berlin, 1989: 17–59. (On Jacoby's retirement and emigration.)

Schindel, U. "Felix Jacoby." *NDB* 10 (1974) 252–253.

Theiler, W. "Felix Jacoby." *Gnomon* 32 (1960) 387–391.

International Biographical Dictionary of Central European Emigrés 1933–1945. Vol. 2, part 1: The Arts, Sciences, and Literature. Edited by H. A. Strauss and W. Röder. Munich, New York, London, Paris, 1983: 560.

Letters

No collection has been published, but letters are housed in Universitäts-bibliothek, Kiel; Universitätsbibliothek, Göttingen; Bodleian Library, Oxford; Corpus Christi College, Oxford; Bayerische Staatsbibliothek, Munich.

Werner Jaeger

30 July 1888 – 19 October 1961

WILLIAM M. CALDER III
University of Illinois
  at Urbana-Champaign

Werner Jaeger held the chairs of Friedrich Nietzsche, Ulrich von Wilamowitz-Moellendorff, and Paul Shorey. A University Professorship, above all departments and requiring small teaching and no administrative obligations, was created for him at Harvard University. He enjoyed the finest education available in the history of classical studies. He founded two journals and what Eduard Spranger first called "The Third Humanism." He published widely in the fields of Greek education and philosophy and the Greek church fathers. He stressed Christianity as the continuation of Hellenism rather than its destroyer. His students included men of the rank of Richard Harder, Viktor Pöschl, and Wolfgang Schadewaldt. Today what was acclaimed as his most famous work is read only by dilettantes too naïve to perceive its defects. The Third Humanism has become a passing fashion, an aberration of the dying Weimar Republic, of as little abiding influence as its rival, the George Circle. His name is rarely cited in footnotes of the learned. Modern students of his own subject no longer recognize his name. Who was this man? What did he do? Why is he forgotten? Is there a permanent achievement?

Werner Wilhelm Jaeger was born 30 July 1888 to Karl August Jaeger and Helene, née Birschel, in the small town of Lobberich in the lower Rheinland near the Dutch border. He lived the first twenty-one years of his life there. We know almost nothing of this crucial formative period and he is our only source. He was an only child. His father, like his grandfathers, held a managerial post in a local textile factory. Jaeger's background was small-town and petit-bourgeois. It was also Protestant, not pious, but the Protestantism of the Enlightenment. This made his family distinctive, for Lobberich was overwhelmingly Catholic. The Protestant boy attended the Catholic Thomas à Kempis Gymnasium (today the Werner Jaeger Gymnasium), but was forbidden to play with Catholic boys. He watched the Bishop of Münster visit his diocese, followed by the faithful peasantry on foot and horseback. Every house displayed the red-and-white church flag. One was a Catholic first, a Prussian second. The pattern of life and thought remained late medieval and ecclesiastical. The powerful Christian impact of the Lobberich years eroded but was never obliterated.

Precocious and intelligent, with no close friends among his contemporaries, young Jaeger was always in the company of doting adults, the darling of parents and grandparents, and without a rival, either at home or at school. As a result, when he had grown to manhood, he found he could never abide a rival. He early learned to get his way by wheedling, for a child has no other way. The legacy was that throughout his life he lacked a strong moral sense and easily resorted to flattery. This led to accommodation with National Socialism and a loose way with women. In addition, his teaching never really agreed with the man.

"The start of my own work was History," he wrote. Growing up where Belgium, Germany and Holland meet, hearing low German, Dutch, Flemish, and French early gave him an idea of Europe. Round about him were the walls, castles, and churches of the Middle Ages and the roads and excavated forts of Rome. He enjoyed the inestimable advantage of beginning Latin at age nine and Greek at age thirteen. Latin never seemed a foreign language to him and he spoke and wrote easily what he called the "lingua angelorum." He first learned Greek the better to understand Rome and saw Greece through the eyes of Cicero and Horace. He had nothing like the intellectual conversion that Wilamowitz experienced at Schulpforte. The teaching must have been uninspired and by rote. He told me once that the Rector ordered his pupils to memorize the names of Horace's friends. When the boy Jaeger asked why, the Rector snapped, "When you are as old as I am, you will know why." Jaeger continued, "I am older than he was and I still do not know why." Such stupid mechanical drill must have provided an impulse in later years for his missionary zeal in restoring life to the classics.

Poor teaching caused him to read widely on his own. When he wrote a paper on the foolish theme, "What would have happened if Alexander had marched West?," he astounded his teachers by citing the Alexander historians in Greek. At age sixteen he read privately Wilamowitz's *Griechisches Lesebuch* and his edition with introduction and commentary of Euripides' *Herakles*. "I became from far away a student of Wilamowitz. . . . A new world opened up for me." The stupendous erudition, the mastery of Greek, and the colorful depiction of Greek life stood in starkest contrast to the pale *epigoni* of the great period of German idealism and the philology of the first half of the nineteenth century. He learned the universality of his field by reading August Böckh's *Enzyklopädie und Methodenlehre der philologischen Wissenschaften*. In summer-semester 1907 Jaeger, age eighteen, matriculated at the University of Marburg. He could later write of his school years: "I always sought to perceive the intellectual in its connection with the reality of Greek life and Greek history. There the original, existential motive for my life operated." He had learned two difficult ancient languages well, had read far beyond the normal schoolboy's need in them, and already was a convinced historist.

Jaeger was only one semester at Marburg. It was long enough. A conversion took place there. He described it himself over fifty years later: "In my first semester at the University of Marburg, I came into close contact with philosophy which there, in the neo-Kantian school of Cohen and Natorp and under the influence of the logical insights gained from it, had turned to the study of Plato. Plato, interpreted in the neo-Kantian sense, was the very center of the intellectual life of the university—no small matter for a young man who was looking for a guide and who cherished the idea of an antiquity that was alive. This influence turned me definitively toward Greek philosophy" (*Essays*, 29). Here for the first time men of intelligence were taking an ancient author, Plato, seriously, as a guide for living, rather than a collection of syntactical peculiarities. Jaeger saw suddenly, after the arid apprenticeship of school, that his adored Greeks possessed "obvious philosophical relevance." Ironically the Marburg semester, although philosophical in its effect, intensified his philological proclivities, because the interpretation of Plato that he was given conflicted "with my historical-philological sense." This provocative misunderstanding of Plato made him an historian of ideas or, as he expressed it, turned him to *Geistesgeschichte*, not remote and antiquarian but vital and of central importance. "Quae philosophia fuit, philologia facta est." Seneca's epigram describes Jaeger at Marburg.

In the Prussia of 1907 the center of philological research was certainly not Marburg and was no longer Bonn. Usener had died in 1905. Buecheler had retired in 1906. Berlin, since the appointment of Ulrich von Wilamowitz-Moellendorff in 1897 by Friedrich Althoff, had become the center of philological science in Europe. Four Berlin scholars molded Jaeger's approach to Greek literature and thought. The aged Johannes Vahlen, who still lectured in Latin, continued the narrow word philology he had learned from Friedrich Ritschl in Bonn over fifty years before. Jaeger heard his lectures and benefited from the severe discipline of his seminar for two semesters. Vahlen taught him to beware brilliant conjectures and to study the linguistic usage of an author with microscopic attention. Often a conjecture is unnecessary if only the difficult passage is correctly understood. Vahlen braked the young student's impetuosity; and Jaeger to his credit remembered what he owed Vahlen's method, while Wilamowitz contrarily was often impatient with him. Jaeger was able to share in a continuing seminar concerned with readings in Aristotle held by the lively octogenarian, Adolf Lasson, "the last Hegelian," who had heard Böckh and Lachmann and had known the learned schoolmaster, August Meineke, personally. Already Jaeger was alert to tradition. Lasson taught with fiery passion and wit. He continued the exegetical method of Trendelenburg and Bonitz. On Friday evenings he met advanced students (Jaeger was by far the youngest) in his house. There they read together select problematical Aristotelian texts. Lasson read to understand the thought, as opposed to Vahlen, who wished to understand only the word. Jaeger sought to combine the best of both.

But the two great figures remained the *dioskouroi*, Hermann Diels and Ulrich von Wilamowitz-Moellendorff. The content of Jaeger's later work recalls often Diels's interests: Aristotelian philology and chronology, presocratic thought, and Greek medicine. His dissertation, later expanded into the book that made his reputation, was directed by Diels and colored by Vahlen's method. But it was Diels *per libros non vir* that influenced him. The *Doxographi Graeci* and *Die Fragmente der Vorsokratiker*, volume I of which had appeared shortly before Jaeger's arrival in Berlin, provided a scientific foundation, along with his monographs on Parmenides and Heraclitus, for the transmission, authenticity, and therefore interpretation of preserved fragments of the presocratic philosophers. The edition in twenty-eight volumes of the *Commentaria in Aristotelem*, edited by Diels and younger colleagues, provided invaluable early material for the elucidation as well as variant renderings necessary for any scientific reconstruction of Aristotle's texts. Jaeger owned the set and continually cited it in publications and lectures. Of the man he reports that he did not attend his lectures Über die Ethik des Aristoteles and that Diels lacked any inner affinity (*innere Wahlverwandschaft*) for Plato. Jaeger would become something like an enlightened Christian Platonist and often called *Paideia* "a road to Plato." Diels's lack of interest in Plato was a defect. There is a further reason. "Papa Diels," with his long snowy beard, was a productive, thoroughly honest, hardworking scholar to whom we can only be grateful. As a man he was uninteresting; as a lecturer, dull. In later life Jaeger spoke as often of Wilamowitz as he was silent about Diels. The Berlin letters (after 1897) of Diels to Wilamowitz are loyal, correct, thoroughly to the point and eminently forgettable. The modest son of a railroad employee never had the personality of the confident Junker from east of the Elbe. Wilamowitz was field marshal, actor, prima donna. Jaeger wanted to be all three. And Wilamowitz was a Platonist: "*Fidem profiteor platonicam.*"

Jaeger had read Wilamowitz at school. At Marburg he encountered his oldest student, who was also the son-in-law of Vahlen, Ernst Maaß, who suggested that he read Belger's life of Moriz Haupt. At Berlin in the winter-semester of 1907–1908 he met the man whom he would call "master" and to whom after his death he would offer *Heroenkult*. Wilamowitz lectured with brilliance on expansive topics. In that semester: the history of Greek literature in the Attic period; next semester: exegesis of his Greek reader, a title that belies the importance of his theme; in the following semesters: the cultural history of antiquity since Nero, introduction to philology, the epic poetry of the Greeks and the Romans, Hellenistic poetry. Seminars held concurrently with the lectures were devoted to the great authors or subjects: Thucydides, Sophocles, Horace, Plato, Aristotle, *Athenaion Politeia*, Menander. Years later Jaeger described the lecturer to Americans: "He was an actor, a brilliant *conferencier*, a spectacular figure, enthusiastic, with a high tinny voice that snapped when touched by pathos."

Schadewaldt detects three abiding characteristics that Jaeger's work owed Wilamowitz: 1) expert acquaintance with texts and manuscripts that early turned him into a brilliant textual critic, emendator, and editor; 2) the conviction that *Geistesgeschichte* must be built on concrete examples; 3) the conviction that *Philosophiegeschichte* cannot be pursued in isolation but as part of what Jaeger's student, Harald Patzer, called Wilamowitz's *Totalitätsideal*, itself a legacy from Friedrich Gottlieb Welcker and

Otto Jahn. I should add three others to these: 1) the preference for great writers and little patience with the second-rate, whom he gratefully left to others; 2) the conviction, itself Platonic, that the teacher is more important than the research scholar; 3) the unshakeable conviction that what he was doing was not a luxury but of supreme urgency. Jaeger became more than a student. A friendship began. He soon attended regularly the Wednesday evening at-homes at Eichenallee 12, where Wilamowitz met informally with gifted students. The preserved correspondence between the two (1911–1928) chronicles the rise and fall of the friendship.

The twenty-two-year-old's dissertation, *Studien zur Entstehungsgeshichte der Metaphysik des Aristoteles*, appeared in 1912. This was expanded in 1923 to *Aristoteles: Grundlegung einer Geschichte seiner Entwicklung*. The impact was immediate and dominated the interpretation and historical criticism of Aristotle for half a century. In the last quarter of the nineteenth century the Scottish Hellenist Lewis Campbell discovered that Plato's increasing avoidance of hiatus in his prose, an avoidance owed to Isocrates, provided a convincing criterion for establishing the relative chronology of his dialogues. Jaeger, after reconstructing Aristotle's earliest work, the lost *Protreptikos*, noticed its strong Platonic coloring in form and content. He went on to argue that the missing criterion for the relative chronology of Aristotle's esoteric works is his progressive distancing from his master, Plato. Necessary for this insight was his stress on the origin of the Aristotelian corpus as lecture notes (the Hegelian parallel may have given him the idea) and the need to explicate them in terms of genre as well as content. After a stay in Italy devoted to manuscripts, in 1914 he submitted his Habilitation on the church father, Nemesius of Emesa, and his indebtedness to Poseidonius. As the book concerned authors out of the classical mainstream, it never enjoyed the influence of the dissertation.

Before leaving the crucial formative years, I should note what Jaeger did not study. I know no testimony that he ever attended lectures on archaeology or on ancient history (Eduard Meyer!). Archaeologists dealt with objects and not with ideas, which are nobler. History, as Aristotle tells us in the *Poetics*, deals with the particular; poetry (one might add philosophy) with the universal. Historians were bound to use their sources for lesser ends than the philologist. Part of this aversion to *Realien* is the fact that Jaeger spent his *Wanderjahre* in libraries rather than museums and, unlike Wilamowitz, never visited Greece until old age and then largely to receive an honorary degree from the University of Athens. His idea of Greece could only be damaged by the reality. He told me on his return to Cambridge that, while driving him to Delphi, his chauffeur offered by a small detour to show him the crossroads where Oedipus slew Laius. " 'No!' I said to him. 'Drive on!' " This is symptomatic of the vagueness and excessive abstraction that historians find in *Paideia*. Arnaldo Momigliano wrote of the book: "But this historiography, with its scant grip on reality, bears the mark of an epoch of political dissolution. . . . That this historiography could degenerate into Nazism was a danger, which was confirmed by some of Jaeger's pupils who had remained in Germany."

Jaeger was never *assistent* and only briefly *dozent*. Between dissertation and habilitation he presumably survived on stipendia and maternal support. In the epochal year 1914, he habilitated (inaugural lecture at Berlin 14 June 1914), married Theodora Dammholz (28 March 1914), and at the age of twenty-six accepted the chair of Friedrich Nietzsche at Basel. He never fought for his country, so his influential discussion of Homeric military heroism in *Paideia* I is all secondhand. He was only a year at Basel and had neither influence nor doctoral students. His inaugural oration, *Philologie und Historie*, is programmatic and, seen in retrospect, anticipates the Third Humanism. He accepted an *Ordinariat* at Kiel in 1915, where Wilamowitz had advised his appointment. There he became a colleague of Eduard Fraenkel and Felix Jacoby and there he found his first and loyal disciple, Richard Harder. The shattering experience of World War I, the trauma of being on the defeated side, and the attendant collapse of everything, convinced him of the rare value of continuity and tradition. He was an eyewitness of the November Revolution at Kiel (3 November 1918). His letter to Wilamowitz of 24 July 1917 already reveals his awakening. It is a document of fundamental biographical importance. Jaeger writes: "From week to week this war tears more deeply apart the foundations upon which until now my life was built and accordingly, because I am a young man, the more existentially and painfully I must endure and struggle with these problems, the less aware I am of anything at all about me that is solid and so I lapse all the more into silence. Doubt about everything that had become second nature to me from childhood has sometimes so brutally overmastered the initial momentum of my rather shy attempts at flight that even my philological work suffers."

Schadewaldt wrote of his teacher: "Intellectual continuities were for him what really constituted history and also what turned its changes into rational changes. For most men the fact that something persists and stays is scarcely worth notice. One takes it for granted and it requires no explanation. For Werner Jaeger the fact that in the passage of time there was any continuity at all was a marvel. The alertness to tradition had been there since boyhood. The November Revolution transformed a tendency into an obsession."

Jaeger always saw Christianity as a culmination of the Hellenic tradition rather than a rejection of it. He could never understand Tatian. On the wall of Jaeger's Harvard office hung two icons, a portrait of the aged Wilamowitz and another of one whom as a young philologist I did not recognize. It was the church historian Adolf Harnack. Jaeger saw the two great men united in himself. He was never Harnack's student at Berlin nor did Harnack turn Jaeger to Gregory. Wilamowitz vigorously maintained, in the *Kirchenväterkommission* against Harnack—who preferred theologians—that a trained classical philologist was more competent to edit a Greek church father. Hence Schwartz's Eusebius and Jaeger's Gregory of Nysssa. In a letter accompanying the first copy to Wilamowitz, dated 8 March 1921, he writes: "You are entitled to the first: you summoned me to the task when after my doctoral examination I stood for the first time without any idea of what to do and you added an important dimension to my philological education. You loyally advised me during composition and proof reading; and you placed your vast philological experience at my service. That way you often preserved me from error or set me in new directions." Four days later Jaeger was offered the Berlin chair. He could do things on time. Ironically, the endless project that in his lifetime seemed to classicists so remote, even unnecessary, may well prove his most enduring contribution. Early Christian texts, like Byzantine ones, had lagged far behind their classical counterparts in accuracy and scientific reporting of manuscript evidence. Believers usually make poor editors and often knowledge of a pagan source can determine the true reading, knowledge that a theologian usually lacks. Jaeger later discovered that the preparation of a minor work of Gregory appealed to American doctoral students, who wanted something concrete with a clear beginning and end—a text, not ideas. E. K. Rand, his Harvard colleague, dealt with Servius, not always happily, in the same way. The Kiel years had prepared the teacher and orator, provided the psychic impetus for *Paideia*, and initiated the Gregory. But Jaeger was too great for Kiel.

Wilamowitz was forced by new and unwelcome legislation to retire from his Berlin chair in 1921. This was a blessing for posterity, because it freed him for research and the last period of great creativity. By exceptionally good luck, Jaeger, who was fourth on the list, secured the post. Eduard Schwartz (*aet.* 63) and Hans von Arnim (*aet.* 62) were named by the faculty *honoris causa* and expectedly passed over by the Ministry because of their age. The Minister of Higher Education, the Orientalist Carl Becker, could not have approved their politics. Franz Boll (*aet.* 54) was asked but unexpectedly declined to stay at Heidelberg. That left Jaeger, who accepted immediately, For years, as proven by his letters, he had shamelessly flattered Wilamowitz. Here was the reward. He was entirely apolitical and, unlike Wilamowitz, had no difficulty in accommodating the Weimar liberal, Becker. The Jaegers lived at Kaiser Wilhelm Straße 11 in Steglitz. In spring 1927 his later Harvard colleague, J. H. Finley, visited him. He reports:

> In the Berlin years he and the tall, beautiful first Mrs. Jaeger . . . with their two sons and a daughter inhabited a square, high-ceilinged, mansard-roofed, tree-surrounded house in the suburb Steglitz. Its resemblence to certain houses on older back-streets of Cambridge suggests that German tastes accompanied German academic standards to Mr. Eliot's Harvard. I was kindly included in a Sunday-afternoon party for students which nobly stretched from tea to well past dinner. The others all wore frock coats; I thought myself lucky in a fairly new blue serge suit.

There was a garden where roses grew. Wilamowitz visited them in 1926 and transmitted to his wife "a description of your castle . . . which impressed me enormously." There is a hint of irony. Jaeger's wife was rich.

Except for *Paideia* I in 1934, the fifteen Berlin years yielded no great publication. The reason was that Jaeger put first things first. A thirty-three-year-old from provincial Kiel had succeeded the greatest Greek scholar of modern times, in the most prestigious chair of the subject in the world. For the first ten years of Jaeger's professorship, Wilamowitz was very much there. He taught a full schedule. He regularly visited the department that he had founded in the University's west wing, which he had built. He directed dissertations. He served tirelessly in the Academy and the German Archaeological Institute. Although deprived of his vote upon retirement, Wilamowitz regularly attended faculty meetings. Jaeger told me that members, as in the Roman Senate, were asked their opinion in order of seniority. Wilamowitz would rise, say *No* emphatically, and no one dared oppose him as he watched the vote. Jaeger either could become dispensable or he must prove his independence even if the cost was that Wilamowitz would think him disloyal. Of course he chose the latter and paid the expected price. Rather than compete vainly with Wilamowitz in research, he emphasized what age had made unwelcome or difficult for the septuagenarian. Jaeger excelled in three areas: charismatic teaching; work within the profession among colleagues and schoolmasters; popularization of his subject on a national scale. As part of this effort he founded for his students a monograph series, *Neue philologische Untersuchungen*, where they could publish dissertations written under him. For the guild he founded a journal devoted to scholarly reviews of high quality. He appointed his Kiel student, Richard Harder, managing editor of *Gnomon*. For pastoral work among the educated laity he founded *Die Antike*. Only *Gnomon* survived World War II. *Antike und Abendland* (*mutatis mutandis*) continues *Die Antike* in Western Germany; *Das Altertum* continues in the German Democratic Republic.

Just the fact that he was so young made him less remote to students. He was an older brother, not a grandfather. There was room for change. Since 1918 there had been impatience with the traditional unquestioning reverence for all things Hellenic. The brutality of the war and the devastation of defeat had destroyed illusions. The unspoken assumption of historicism that the innate excellence of antiquity justified the attention lavished by a nation's most brilliant men no longer went unchallenged. Paul Friedländer states the dilemma in a moving letter of 4 July 1921 to his teacher Wilamowitz:

> The war has changed me a great deal; and I could not, like other men, start in again in 1919 where I had broken off in 1914. For me now things must have far higher demands. Also I should not like to say anything any more that is not finished and of importance. I do not want to write any more notes and articles simply because chance has cast something in my path. I do not want to "share in the debate": that is, to make an observation as C because A and B have made observations . . . and as to editing texts: I do not have the strength, my life is simply too short, to edit what is peripheral simply for the sake of editing it. . . . So you see, here are all sorts of inhibitions. But I find it good that these inhibitions are there.

Because of his naïveté and self-assurance Jaeger lacked the self-doubt of the Berlin Jew and war veteran, Friedländer. A return to Hellenism had revitalized Europe twice before, in the Renaissance and the age of Goethe. Why not a Third Humanism with Jaeger as Erasmus and Berlin as Weimar? His energy, his organizational skill, his ability to delegate work to others (students called him "our unmoved mover"), and his flair for showmanship worked wonders. There were endless speeches, meetings of schoolmasters and colleagues, scholarly conferences led by Jaeger with speeches by the faithful. The most famous he held at Naumburg Whitsuntide 1930, a colloquium on the spacious theme of "Antiquity and the Problem of the Classical." There were eight addresses by men like Johannes Stroux, Wolfgang Schadewaldt, Paul Friedländer, Eduard Fraenkel, Bernhard Schweitzer, and Matthias Gelzer. Teubner hastened to publish the addresses in a handsome volume. Wilamowitz thundered from Berlin: "Whenever I read *Die Antike*, a millwheel goes round and round in my head; but the wheel does not grind any meal; for me it does not. . . . I have an idea what classical Physics are, and classical music also exists. But other than these? English literature is rich enough. Does one find the classic there? Is Shakespeare classic? . . . I have never been able to make a start with the word classic which for me is a horror; and so I do not expect that others do."

The movement was well-meant. Jaeger wanted to preserve an endangered civilizing tradition that he believed irreplaceable. The catchword was *paideia*, the Greek word that Cicero translated as *humanitas* (*puerilitas* was not possible) and that meant both culture and its transmission, that is, education. The word provided the title of what Jaeger often called his "three-volume history of the Greek mind." Eduard Spranger early gave the movement its name in his address "The Position of the Humanities Today and the School," delivered at the Fifty-third Congress of German Philologists held at Jena on 27 September 1921. He said, "But a difference between our Humanism, which one might call the Third and that Second, lies in the breadth of our quest and the understanding which we moderns are able to bring to it." The friendly voice of a former believer, Wolfgang Schadewaldt, summarizes what Jaeger tried to do: "Jaeger's new humanistic approach is characterized by the fact that he set the Greek world of human values as a system of rationally working formative power into the history of Europe. It was, to state the matter epigrammatically, an historicizing of human values or as well a humanizing of our European history."

But there was something sham about it all. The time had passed when the values of Periclean Athens could be a formative educational force in Germany. In 1935, in a famous review of *Paideia* I, the Hamburg classical scholar, Bruno Snell, with wit and learning wrote the epitaph of a Third Humanism just fourteen years old. He showed how Jaeger was forced to interpret evidence (Homer is the obvious case) unhistorically in order to sustain his thesis that *paideia* provides the cornerstone on which to build an intellectual history of Greece. The educational function of poetry is a discovery of the Sophists, foreign to Homer. Snell corrects specific misinterpretations and then prophetically warns of the dangers of Jaegerian humanism. These he sees particularly in what Jaeger considered the superiority of his Third Humanism to the Second Humanism of Goethe and Humboldt; namely, its politicization. Greek political institutions cannot be exemplary in 1935 in the way that a Greek drama was circa 1800 for Goethe, a statue for Schadow, a building for Klenze. Jaeger misses the difference. Greek tolerance of slavery alone is decisive. Indeed, says Snell, Jaeger's

Greek politics easily boil down to heroism and Platonic authoritarianism. The vagueness of Jaeger's humanism allows it to become the servant of any kind of politics. That means it is always in danger of becoming a literary game (*Literatentum*). It was the *Dienstbarkeit* of Jaeger's politics, the readiness to serve any master, the preference for accommodation over reform, that made them unacceptable to Bruno Snell. At the risk of making his Greeks trivial, Snell prefers the revival of Wilamowitzian historicism to Jaeger's humanistic evangelism. We scholars can do no more than describe what was Greek truthfully and without presuppositions.

In 1980 Johannes Irmscher stated clearly the dangers only implied by Snell in 1935. "Many used to speak of the Third Humanism as the correlative in educational policy to the Third Reich's theoretical vision of the state." Obviously Jaeger did not devise nor Spranger name the movement for that purpose. On the other hand, Jaeger undeniably sought, albeit unsuccessfully, accommodation with National Socialism. Of the some seventy classical scholars who fled Nazi Germany, the Minister of Education in the Hitler government thanked Jaeger *alone* for his German work and granted him official permission to accept the Chicago post. A secret directive of the Hitler government in 1941 forbade critical mention of Jaeger in the German press. The same directive forbade posthumous mention of the seventy-fifth birthday of Eduard Norden, Jaeger's Jewish teacher and colleague. Jaeger never resigned from the Berlin Academy, which had expelled Norden and many others, and continued to publish in Nazi Germany as late as 1944 (*Paideia* II), after he had become a citizen of a country at war against Hitler! The document most often cited by scholars to prove Jaeger's early attempt to reconcile his Third Humanism with the Third Reich is "Die Erziehung des politischen Menschen und die Antike" ("Antiquity and the Education of the Political Man") (*Volk im Werden* 3 [Leipzig, 1933] 43–49). Jaeger argues that the classical curriculum in the schools could be presented in a manner supportive of the new system. He draws attention to the ideal of the Spartan citizen in Tyrtaeus, the prophetic strength of Solon's political poetry, the presentation of work as heroism by the peasant poet Hesiod ("Arbeit ist keine Schande; Nichtarbeiten ist Schande"—so much for welfare programs), and the Homeric "heroism of the defender of his fatherland" (Hector, presumably, rather than Achilles). The "fateful struggle" of tragedy would strike a welcome note and we climax with Thucydides' Pericles as a *Führergestalt*. History has granted to the classicists of Germany an urgent task: "The particular task which History today has set before the German people is the forming of the political human being. We ought not of course to demand from the schools and scholarship what has not earlier grown organically within the reality of national life. But at the moment when a new type of political man is taking shape, we shall obviously have need of antiquity, as a formative force."

Jaeger nowhere perverts his sources. He simply picks, chooses, and ignores to make a welcome point. But if one recalls Jaeger's immense prestige at the time, publication of such an article at such a time in such a place must have weakened considerably the hand of any decent schoolmaster who sought in the classics approval of the democracy just lost. Hitler had become Reichskanzler on 30 January 1933.

Jaeger's essay appeared a month later. The Association of German Classicists met in July. In 1933 the only high government official who dealt with classics in education was Bernhard Rust, a former student of the subject, later Reichsminister für Wissenschaft, Erziehung, und Volksbildung. At the urging of Rust, Jaeger, along with the chairman of the association, Kroymann, presented to the teachers of classics in Germany the program that the new government expected of them—that is, Jaeger, with all the prestige of his Berlin chair, agreed to act as mouthpiece to his profession for the new regime.

After a divorce from his first wife, whom he placed in a mental institution, Jaeger married his Jewish student, Ruth Heinitz, on 29 December 1931. A child followed. In 1934 Jaeger was Sather Professor at the University of California, Berkeley. His lectures were published in 1938 as *Demosthenes: The Origin and Growth of His Policy*. German and British scholarship of the time regularly extolled Alexander the Great at the expense of Demosthenes, an unscrupulous lawyer and *laudator temporis acti* obstinately refusing to acknowledge the reality of history and urging his fellow Athenians to a suicidal struggle against the inevitable. Jaeger rejected this view. He argued that the moral tragedy of the man Demosthenes was of greater interest than the political events of the time. By stressing a passage in the third *Philippic*, he sought to show that Demosthenes felt obliged to urge his fellow citizens to preserve the outmoded city-state against Macedonian expansion, although he feared the cause had already been lost. He did this because he was convinced that it was the only right course of action. To what degree was Jaeger's *Demosthenesbild* a self-portrait of his own predicament? One must defend humanism even if the cause had already been lost. Events moved rapidly. In 1936 Jaeger resigned the chair of Wilamowitz and accepted exile in Chicago, a city of gangsters and cattlemen, rather than divorce his wife and abandon his child. He immediately wrote an English article: "Greeks and Jews: The First Greek Records of Jewish Religion and Civilisation" (1936). What could not appear in *Volk im Werden* was eagerly accepted by the *Journal of Religion*. Jaeger was not an anti-Semite.

Ernst Bickel, the Bonn *ordinarius*, in 1943 called Jaeger in his Harvard period "the swan among geese." The swan left the Chicago geese, who had provided him and his family asylum, as soon as he could. In 1956 their bitterness still was undisguised. In 1939 he wisely declined the Laurence Professorship of Ancient Philosophy at Cambridge University (letter of F. M. Cornford to W. Jaeger 23 April 1939) and accepted the University Professorship at Harvard. He quickly learned that there were two great differences between Cambridge, Massachusetts, and Berlin, and expectedly accommodated. From the start he was denied any political influence of the sort he had wielded from his Berlin throne. E. K. Rand informed him on arrival that Americans expected Americans to run their departments. At a time when posts were few and those few allotted on the old-boy system, only women and priests, whose futures were secure, dared write dissertations with him. He could not place them. In over twenty years he had no student, in the sense of one whose dissertation he directed, who compared with his great German ones. Within the profession he went from leader to outsider. The second difference Jaeger himself noted in his introduction to the *Scripta Minora*: "Without the continuing prestige of the ancient idea of Man in human culture, classical scholarship is just a waste of time. Anyone who does not see this ought to come to America and let himself learn from the way classical studies have developed there."

The history of Hellenism in America has yet to be written. In his epoch-making book, *Classica Americana: The Greek and Roman Heritage in the United States* (Detroit, 1984), Meyer Reinhold has meticulously documented the formative influence of the classical heritage in the colonial, revolutionary, and early republican periods. The populism, materialism, and attendant anti-intellectualism that accompanied the expanding frontier and the industrial revolution in nineteenth-century America relegated classics to a handful of underpaid professors of Greek, men not distinguished by a capacity to influence the great issues of their time. The middle twentieth century saw a revival of Greek influence on American literature and thought, not always directly but through three German thinkers, Freud, Marx, and Nietzsche. But in general Greek influence has remained in the architecture of banks, railroad stations, and plantation homes.

The classics Jaeger found at the Harvard of the thirties were a game of grammar and translation played by boys from good families who had graduated from pale American imitations of the great English public schools. No one dreamt of "believing" anything he read in an ancient author in the way Winckelmann, Wilhelm von Humboldt, Niebuhr, Wilamowitz, or Jaeger himself had. American classical scholarship derives historically from the German during its Ritschlian phase (that is, after K. O. Müller and before Wilamowitz), with its preference for the objective and technical (which too easily means the trivial and uninteresting), for what needs doing before what matters. Jaeger had no chance of influencing American thought the way he had briefly influenced German thought. Jaeger's last accommodation was resignation. Like Wilamowitz after 1921, he left the arena and wrote books: *Paideia*, three volumes in English translation (1939–1944); *The Theology of the Early Greek Philosophers* (1947); the Oxford critical edition of Aristotle's *Metaphysics* (1957); *Scripta Minora*, two volumes (1960); *Early Christianity and Greek Paideia* (1961). There was also volume after volume of the Gregory. Even so, much remained unwritten. He often called the footnotes of *Paideia* "the graveyard of projected monographs."

American students were colossally naïve. Recently a woman revealed in a national journal how, during written examinations, a friendly old man would give her and her friend chocolate cookies. This is what she remembered. He was a kindly eccentric, a man of stupendous learning and quaint ideas, harmless and liked from afar. He was sought after for doctoral examinations because he never expected American students to know anything and asked simple questions, often answering them himself. Again and again he lamented, "I have no school."

Americans did not think in terms of schools, of messiahs, apostles, and disciples. The reason was simple. The subject was not that important to them. American professors are dilettantes, Jaeger used to say, classicists from 9:00 to 5:00.

You must live your *paideia*! A *vox clamantis in desertis*—for them it was just a job, not a way of life.

Hildegard von Wilamowitz-Moellendorff, in her memoirs of her father, recalls how, on his deathbed in September 1931, he delivered his final verdict on his student and successor, Werner Jaeger: "At that time Frau Jaeger came to my mother. He could not wait until my mother returned. When she brought the report of the divorce from Professor Jaeger, my father said: 'Up to now I have again and again defended him against all others. I see now; he is a bastard.' "

Dorothea Freifrau Hiller von Gaertringen said to me, "On his deathbed my father cursed Werner Jaeger." Not one member of the family attended Jaeger's memorial address to the Academy.

Wilamowitz condemned the man. Few could dispute him. He lacked moral conviction and inner courage, the assurance that he was right. This was in part the plight of his generation. The crisis of self-doubt that we saw in Friedländer necessarily brought an end to certainty. Why can't we sunder the work from the man? Wrong scholarship is forgotten. Right scholarship is absorbed—and then forgotten. Only in their conjectures do philologists win immortality. Jaeger's Oxford *Metaphysica* remains the standard text. Gregory has eclipsed all previous texts and provided a corpus of the genuine works and a paradigm for editions of other early Christian authors. Any history of Aristotelian scholarship in the twentieth century must evaluate Jaeger's contribution to the history of the corpus and the biography of the man. A brilliant idea, eloquently argued, led to a deeper historical understanding of the texts. Jaeger was an historian and philologist, never a philosopher.

What happened to the center of Jaeger's work during the Berlin years, "The Third Humanism"? It could not survive Bruno Snell and National Socialism. In one part of Jaeger's Germany, Marxism-Leninism replaced it; in the other part a revival of the historicism of Jaeger's teachers. In 1959 Jaeger denied ever having himself used the term, although in fact he had begun *Paideia I* with it. In America he won two influential apostles. His young Harvard colleague, John Huston Finley, Jr., learned from Jaeger that classics had something to say that mattered to young Harvard men of the forties and fifties. In a total break with his philological colleagues, most of them grammarians, paleographers, and exegetes, he delivered dazzling lectures on Greek literature in English translation to hundreds of undergraduates in the largest lecture hall of the university. He presented Homer as a text that could change our lives and won two generations of friends of classics in high places.

The other notable convert exerted a national, not a parochial, influence. Gilbert Highet, a naturalized Scot of boundless energy, translated all three volumes of *Paideia* into elegant English. That done, he began a popularization of the classics on a scale of which Jaeger never dreamed, introducing large lecture courses of classics in translation, writing endless articles and reviews for the popular press, lecturing tirelessly to schoolteachers and educated laity, and so on. But there was a striking difference from Jaeger. His message was not at all political; it was bellelettristic. Highet transformed into Anglo-Saxon terms Jaeger's profound conviction that classics had something to say to the modern world and he embodied this conviction in a comprehensive work that parallels but also productively contrasts with *Paideia, The Classical Tradition* (New York, 1949). Inspired by the failed Third Humanism, Highet returned to the apolitical Second Humanism with the result that while in 1936 several thousand American students read Homer in Greek annually, in 1986 several million read the poet annually in English, and the several thousand continue to read him in Greek. The beginnings of this vast popular movement owe much to Finley and Highet, who themselves had been ultimately inspired by Jaeger.

Within the profession, by his example and by his English books, which regularly cited German scholars, Jaeger did much to revive the German tradition that had dominated American philology from 1853 to 1914. This revival, in which Jaeger was aided by over thirty other refugees from Hitler's Germany, sought to rescue American scholarship from English dilettantism and return it to German scientific professionalism. The success of the von Humboldt stipendia and the emigration of outstanding German philologists to American universities are in part a result of Jaeger's revival of what Gildersleeve called our "Teutonomania." This transplantation of the Berlin humanistic tradition to the New World may not impossibly be Jaeger's most enduring achievement.

Books

Emendationum Aristotelearum Specimen. Diss., Berlin, 1911 = *Scripta Minora* 1:1–38.
Studien zur Entstehungsgeschichte der Metaphysik des Aristoteles. Berlin, 1912.
Aristotelis de animalium motione et de animalium incessu, Pseudo-Aristotelis de spiritu libellus. Leipzig, 1913.
Nemesios von Emesa. Quellenforschung zum Neuplatonismus und seinen Anfängen bei Poseidonius. Berlin, 1914.
Gregorii Nysseni Opera I: Contra Eunomium libri Pars Prior Liber I et II (Vulgo I et XIIb). Berlin, 1921.
Gregorii Nysseni Opera II: Contra Eunomium libri Pars Altera Liber III (Vulgo III–XII); Refutatio Confessionis Eunomii (Vulgo II). Berlin, 1921; 2d ed., 1960.
Aristoteles: Grundlegung einer Geschichte seiner Entwicklung. Berlin, 1923.
Das Problem des Klassischen und die Antike. Edited by Jaeger. Leipzig and Berlin, 1931; reprinted Darmstadt, 1961.
Paideia: Die Formung des griechischen Menschen I. Leipzig and Berlin, 1934; 2d ed., 1936.
Aristotle: Fundamentals of the History of His Development. Translated by Richard Robinson. Oxford, 1934; 2d ed., 1948.
Humanistische Reden und Vorträge. Leipzig and Berlin, 1937; 2d ed., 1960.
Demosthenes: The Origin and Growth of His Policy. Translated by Edward S. Robinson. Berkeley, 1938.
Diokles von Karystos: Die griechische Medizin und die Schule des Aristoteles. Berlin, 1938; 2d ed., 1963.

Paideia: The Ideals of Greek Culture. Vol. I. Translated by Gilbert Highet. New York and Oxford, 1939; 2d ed., 1945.

Paideia: The Ideals of Greek Culture. Vol. II: *In Search of the Divine Centre.* Translated by Gilbert Highet. New York and Oxford, 1943.

Paideia: The Ideals of Greek Culture. Vol. III: *The Conflict of Cultural Ideals in the Age of Plato.* Translated by Gilbert Highet. New York and Oxford, 1944.

The Theology of the Early Greek Philosophers. Translated by Edward S. Robinson. Oxford, 1947; 2d ed., 1948; 3d ed., 1960.

Gregorii Nysseni Opera VIII.1: Opera Ascetica De instituto Christiano, De professione Christiana, De perfectione. Edited by Jaeger with Johannes P. Cavarnos and Virginia Woods Callahan. Leiden, 1952.

Two Rediscovered Works of Ancient Christian Literature: Gregory of Nyssa and Macarius. Leiden, 1954.

Aristotelis Metaphysica. Edited by Jaeger. Oxford, 1957.

Scripta Minora I–II. Rome, 1960.

Early Christianity and Greek Paideia. Cambridge, 1961.

Articles (Collected)

Jaeger's more popular smaller publications are available in *Humanistische Reden und Vorträge,* 2d ed. (1960); his more scientific ones in *Scripta Minora,* 2 vols. (1960). Not included is: "Die Erziehung des politischen Menschen und die Antike." *Volk im Werden* 1 (1933) 43–48.

Sources

Calder, William M., III. "The Correspondence of Ulrich von Wilamowitz- Moellendorff with Werner Jaeger." HSCPh 82 (1978) 303–347 = Ulrich von Wilamowitz-Moellendorff, *Selected Correspondence 1869–1831.* Edited by William M. Calder III. *Antiqua* 23. Naples, 1983: 167–211.

———. "The Credo of a New Generation: Paul Friedländer to Ulrich von Wilamowitz-Moellendorff." *Antike und Abendland* 26 (1980) 90–102 = *Selected Correspondence:* 127–139.

———. "Werner W. Jaeger." *DAB, Supp. 7, 1961–1965,* ed. John A. Garraty (New York, 1981): 387–389 = *idem. Studies in the Modern History of Classical Scholarship. Antiqua* 27. Naples, 1984: 55–57.

———. "Werner Jaeger and Richard Harder: An *Erklärung.*" *Quaderni di storia* 17 (1983) 99–121 = *Studies in the Modern History of Classical Scholarship:* 59–81.

———. "Werner Jaeger." *Berlinische Lebensbilder Geisteswissenschaftler.* Edited by M. Erbe. Berlin, 1989: 343–363.

Calder, William M., III and Hoffmann, Christhard. "Ulrich von Wilamowitz-Moellendorff on the Basel Greek Chair." MH 43 (1986) 258–263.

Hörner, Hadwig. "Über Genese und derzeitigen Stand der grossen Edition der Werke Gregors von Nyssa." *Écriture et culture philosophique dans la Pensée de*

Grégoire de Nysse. Actes du colloque de Chevetogne (22–26 Septembre 1969), ed. M. Harl. Leiden 1971: 18–50.

Hölscher, Uvo. "Angestrengtes Griechentum: Die dritte Wiederkehr des Klassischen / Zu Werner Jaegers 100. Geburtstag." *Frankfurter Allgemeine Zeitung* 30 July 1988. (Feuilleton.)

Irmscher, Johannes. "Die klassische Altertumswissenschaft in der faschistischen Wissenschaftspolitik." *Altertumswissenschaften und ideologischer Klassenkampf.* Edited by Horst Gericke, *Martin-Luther-Universität Halle-Wittenberg: Wissenschaftliche Beiträge 35* (1980). Halle, 1980: 75–97.

Jaeger, Werner. *Five Essays.* Translated by Adele M. Fiske, R.S.C.J., with a Bibliography of Werner Jaeger prepared by Herbert Bloch. Montreal, 1966.

———. "Zur Einführung." *Scripta Minora* I. Rome, 1960: ix–xxviii.

Momigliano, Arnaldo. *Studies in Historiography.* London, 1966: 252–253.

Park, Clara Claiborne. "At Home in History: Werner Jaeger's *Paideia.*" *The American Scholar* (Summer 1983) 378–385.

Schadewaldt, Wolfgang. "Gedenkrede auf Werner Jaeger 30. Juli 1888–19. Oktober 1961, Gehalten an der Freien Universität Berlin am 12. Juli 1962." *Hellas und Hesperien: Gesammelte Schriften zur Antike und zur Neueren Literatur in zwei Bänden*, vol. II. Edited by Klaus Bartels, Reinhard Thurow, and Ernst Zinn. Zürich and Stuttgart, 1970: 707–722.

Snell, Bruno. "Rez. Werner Jaeger: *Paideia.* Die Formung des griechischen Menschen, Bd. I (35)." *Gesammelte Schriften.* Göttingen, 1966: 32–54.

Solmsen, Friedrich. "Werner Jaeger." *NDB* 10 (Berlin, 1974) 280–281.

Staehelin, Martin. " '. . . bei den Meinigen, nicht immer unter Wildfremden': Hugo von Hofmannsthal in Briefen an Werner Jaeger." *Catalepton: Festschrift für Bernhard Wyss zum 80. Geburtstag.* Edited by Christoph Schäublin. Basel, 1985: 203–212.

Wilamowitz-Moellendorff, Hildegard von. "Erinnerungen an meinen Vater." In Ulrich von Wilamowitz-Moellendorff. *In wieweit befriedigen die Schlüsse der erhaltenen griechischen Trauerspiele? Ein ästhetischer Versuch.* Edited with introduction and notes by William M. Calder III. Leiden, 1974: 159–163.

Papers

The Jaeger papers are available at the Houghton Library, Harvard University, Cambridge, Massachusetts. Jaeger's professional library is part of the library of the Center for Hellenic Studies, Washington, D.C. A number of the books contain annotations.

Otto Jahn

16 June 1813 – 9 September 1869

CARL WERNER MÜLLER
Universität Saarbrücken

Otto Jahn was probably the most versatile of nineteenth-century German scholars of *Altertumswissenschaft*. As a philologist he produced many exemplary editions of ancient authors, several of them with commentary. As an archaeologist he placed the study of Greek vase-painting on a new scientific basis, and in the realm of iconography he put an end to the symbolist fantasies of Creuzer and Panofka. As a musicologist he wrote a model biography of Mozart, the first to be erected on a documentary foundation. Finally, he contributed to the study of German literature two collections of Goethe's letters and a series of biographical essays and studies on the history of scholarship.

Jahn was born on 16 June 1813, in Kiel. His father, Jacob Jahn, was a respected and successful attorney; his maternal grandfather, Adolf Trendelenburg, was Professor of Jurisprudence at the University of Kiel. The house of Jahn's parents was a center of the city's musical life, and Jahn's musical training went far beyond the dilettantism that was usual in the education of a young bourgeois. The decision not to make music his profession was finally made only during his student days at Berlin. It was with the intention of offsetting the musical ambitions of the boy of seventeen with the strict discipline of exacting philological instruction that his father sent him in 1830 to the famous Gymnasium at Schulpforte, where A. G. Lange (1778–1831), Christian Friedrich Neue (1798–post 1861), and K. A. Koberstein (1797–1870) were his teachers in Greek, Latin, and German. Lange welcomed the boy into his home and, though Jahn stayed at Schulpforte for only a year, his hospitable teacher remained a father figure to him forever (*Briefe*, 117).

In 1831 Jahn returned to his home town of Kiel and began to study philology at the university there. The director of the philological seminar—to which he was at once admitted—was Gregor Wilhelm Nitzsch (1790–1861); Jahn praises him for combining a strict work ethic with an easy intercourse with his students (*Biographische Aufsätze*, 148–149). Johannes Classen (1805–1891), who later produced a commentary on Thucydides, was then a *Privatdozent* in Kiel; he directed Jahn's attention to the Roman satirists, who were to occupy him for the rest of his life and would form the subject of the greater part of his philological work. In the autumn of 1832 Jahn went to Leipzig, where he was even more impressed by Gottfried Hermann's personality than by his scholarly method. A year later he transferred to Berlin. Here he attended the lectures of August Böckh but was more attracted to Karl Lachmann, whom he regarded as his real teacher in philology (*Briefe*, 115). It was in Berlin that Jahn first encountered the study of archaeology. Julius Ambrosch (1804–1856) introduced him to the study of vases (then still in its infancy), and the lectures of Eduard Gerhard (1795–1867) on the antiquities of the Berlin museums brought him into close contact with one of the founding fathers of archaeology as a scholarly discipline in Germany. Returning to Kiel in 1835, he took his doctorate there in 1836 with a dissertation on the myth of Palamedes. This dissertation reveals an extensive knowledge of the ancient sources without, however, displaying the interconnection of literary and archaeological data that characterized Jahn's later works.

With a travel stipend from the Danish government (Schleswig–Holstein was then under Danish rule), Jahn traveled to Paris in the autumn of 1837, busied himself chiefly with studying the manuscripts of Juvenal and Persius, and formed connections with French archaeological scholars. He entered into close friendships with Désiré Raoul-Rochette (1790–1854) and Jean Joseph de Witte (1808–1889). In October 1838 he came to Rome; here his teacher was Emil Braun (1809–1856), a student of Karl Otfried Müller and at that time First Secretary of the Archaeological Institute. He introduced Jahn to the antiquities of Rome, assigned him the publication of this or that newly discovered monument (e.g., the tombstone of the baker Eurysaces near the Porta Maggiore), and brought home to the student of Hermann and Lachmann the importance of Friedrich Gottlieb Welcker. Finally, he directed him to the field of Latin inscriptions. Jahn acquired, with the financial support of the Berlin Academy, the epigraphic *Nachlass* of Olaus Kellermann (1805–1837), with the obligation to publish it. After travels to southern Italy and Sicily, Jahn came to Florence, where he met Karl Otfried Müller, who was on his way to Greece. Jahn returned to Kiel in the summer of 1839.

At the beginning of the winter semester he took up the teaching duties to which his doctorate from Kiel entitled him. One of his first students was Theodor Mommsen (only a few years younger than his teacher), who supplemented his law studies by attending Jahn's lectures on Juvenal and Persius and his archaeological classes. What the encounter with Jahn meant to the young Mommsen is revealed in his memoir written after his friend's death: Jahn "opened for me the doors of scholarship and of society" (*Briefwechsel*, 360). The correspondence between the two (1842–1868) is among the most impressive exchanges between scholars that the nineteenth century can show.

In 1842 Jahn was called to Greifswald as Professor Extraordinarius of Philology and Archaeology. In 1843 appeared his commentary on Persius—probably his most important achievement in philology. All later interpretation of Persius is based on this work (Knoche, *Römische Satire*, 86), and the fact that it was reprinted in 1962 shows that it is not yet entirely superseded. In 1845 came the edition of Censorinus, *De die natali*, a recension that for the first time placed the text on a solid foundation. After declining a call to the Imperial Academy of Sciences in St. Petersburg (Leningrad), Jahn was appointed Professor Ordinarius in 1845. While at Kiel he had already followed the model of the philological seminar to institute the first archaeology classes in Germany. He also introduced such classes at Greifswald, and the practice of annual celebration of Winckelmann's birthday at German universities, as was already the custom at the Roman Institute, goes back to him. The Berlin Academy's long-projected plan for a *Corpus Inscriptionum Latinarum* entered a new phase in 1845, when Savigny, then the Prussian Minister of Justice, asked Jahn to prepare a memorandum on means to complete the project. The Academy had previously planned to prepare a mere reprint of inscriptions from already available collections and publications, but Jahn's scheme involved collecting the texts—including the large number of previously unpublished inscriptions—by personal inspection of the originals, which presupposed a sojourn of many years in Italy. Mommsen in particular was to join Jahn as editor. Jahn opposed a topographical classification of inscriptions (the scheme that Mommsen ultimately followed) and advocated a classification by subject (Harnack, *Geschichte des königlich preussischen Akademie der Wissenschaft zu Berlin* II, 505 ff.). Because of the intrigues of August Böckh—"Böckh and his *Böcklein*" (goats), as Mommsen called the opponents—the plan could not at first be carried out. But Jahn gave himself credit for having kept matters open until Mommsen could "enter upon the task which a favorable destiny had reserved for him" (*Gerhard*, 84).

In 1847 Jahn was called to a professorship in Archaeology at the University of Leipzig, where, along with Gottfried Hermann and Moriz Haupt, he also lectured on philological subjects. During Jahn's Leipzig period he produced commentaries on Cicero's *Brutus* (1849) and *Orator* (1851), as well as editions of Persius (1851), Florus' epitome of Livy (1852), and Julius Obsequens (1853). Most important, however, was the great edition of Juvenal with the *scholia vetera* (1851); the treatment of the textual transmission offered by this edition forms the essential basis of Juvenal criticism to this day (Knoche, *Römische Satire*, 96–97). The projected commentary on Juvenal was never written.

In an address before the Leipzig *Gesellschaft der Wissenschaften* during the Leibnitz anniversary celebrations in 1848, Jahn presented his ideas on the nature and most important tasks of archaeology. He opposed Gerhard's conception of archaeology as "monumental philology" and gave it an independent role as a science of art—a role that it could only fulfill, however, in close partnership with the other historical *Altertumswissenschaften*, especially philology (cf. *Briefe*, 93, 164, 175).

Jahn worked successfully to have Mommsen called to Leipzig in 1849. For both men this was, according to their own testimony, the happiest period of their academic lives. They belonged to a sociable circle of friends—professors (Haupt), men of letters (Gustav Freitag), and publishers (Härtel, Hirzel, Reimer, Weigand)—whose political home was the *Deutscher Verein*, which occupied the bourgeois liberal middle in the Frankfurt Parliament. Jahn and Mommsen both took an active part in the political movements of 1848, first in their home province of Schleswig-Holstein and later in Leipzig. Here in 1849 the two friends, together with Haupt, joined in the agitation in Saxony for adoption of the imperial constitution drawn up by the Frankfurt Parliament. For this they were prosecuted, after the victory of reaction, for high treason. Jahn appealed the case and was acquitted, as were Mommsen and Haupt after repeated appeals, but nonetheless all three were dismissed from their professorships in 1850. Although the University soon tried to lure Jahn back, he rejected all compromise because of his feelings of solidarity with his two friends. It was all the more painful to him that he suffered longer and more grievously than they from the dismissal: Mommsen was called to Zürich in 1852 and Haupt to Berlin in 1853.

During the Leipzig period Jahn (favored by the *genius loci*) was occupied with a number of important musicological projects. The founding of the Bachgesellschaft, which aimed to produce a historical-critical edition of the works of J. S. Bach, was due largely to Jahn's initiative. Here, for the first time, the philological principles that had long been followed in critical editions of ancient texts were applied to the editing of music, and this methodology thereafter became the model for complete editions of the works of other great composers. When Wagner's *Tannhäuser* was performed in Leipzig in 1853, followed by *Lohengrin* in 1854, Jahn discussed these music-dramas—dubbed "music of the future" in the propaganda of Wagner's proponents—in critical reviews (*Gesammelte Aufsätze über Musik*, 64ff., 112ff.). Jahn's criticism of Wagner later affected the course of philology, since Friedrich Nietzsche, in *The Birth of Tragedy*, used it as an excuse for an ugly polemic against Jahn. The possibility that Nietzsche hoped thereby to gratify not only Wagner but also his own teacher, Friedrich Ritschl, does not excuse what he did. It was Nietzsche's outburst against Jahn—or so said Wilamowitz in his later years (*Erinnerungen*, 129)—that provoked his own pamphlet against Nietzsche: *Zukunftsphilologie!* ("Philology of the Future!").

Now that Jahn had been reluctantly released from university duties, he was able to travel extensively, and in 1852–53 he journeyed to Vienna, Salzburg, Berlin, and Frankfurt to collect and examine the *Nachlaß* of Mozart and Beethoven and to prepare his great book on Mozart. Originally planned as an introduction for a biography of Beethoven, the Mozart book grew into an independent work as the material multiplied. But before he could put this mass of material into shape, Jahn received from Munich a commission to catalogue the vase collection of Ludwig I, and this task occupied him in the years 1853–54. The introductory volume of the catalogue is an exhaustive discussion of the study of vases in its various aspects—history and subdivisions of the study, topography, evolution of styles, and iconography. A healthy skepticism in interpretation frees the paintings from all supposed connection with the mystery religions; interpretation is limited to factual description of content. Jahn's *Einleitung* long performed the function of a handbook on the study of vases.

Without Welcker's knowledge, Ritschl had been carrying on negotiations with the Ministry in Berlin, and at the end of 1854 Jahn was called to Bonn; he took up his teaching duties in the summer of 1855. Jahn had always affirmed that, with a call to Bonn as Welcker's presumptive successor, one of his fondest dreams would be realized (*Briefe*, 91, 92). However, it happened under circumstances that were anything but gratifying and that hampered his work at Bonn from the outset. Jahn came to Bonn under the assumption that he had been called at Welcker's desire or at least with his consent. Now he discovered that Welcker, who had been temporarily absent from Bonn, had been taken completely by surprise by the course of events and felt deeply insulted, believing that the creation of a new professorship of philology and archaeology was directed personally at him. Welcker's sense of propriety forbade him to inflict on Jahn the anger and mortification that he felt. Jahn, for his part, did all he could to let the grand old man see his veneration and his friendly feelings. It was Ritschl who had to bear the unpleasantness. Welcker broke off all ties with his longtime colleague and friend, by whom he felt he had been hoodwinked, while Jahn was intent on preserving his independence from Ritschl and took pains not to appear a member of his party. This conspicuous reserve—which was heightened by the difference in temperament between the two men—could not fail to annoy Ritschl, and he took it to be ingratitude. Within a few months they were estranged (*Briefe*, 95–96; *Briefwechsel*, 196); the ultimate results were mistrust and aversion. Yet their relations remained correct (*Briefe*, 197; *Briefwechsel*, 246); in particular Jahn, whatever his personal feelings toward his colleague, always acknowledged that the respect enjoyed by the Bonn Philological Seminar was chiefly due to Ritschl's teaching (*Briefe*, 174). Moreover, in their manner of conducting a seminar and in their methodological principles the two were clearly in agreement when it came to defending the formal orientation of essentially grammatical and text-critical training against instruction that concentrated on content, which the historians especially were demanding. Jahn's teaching enjoyed considerable popularity among the students (*Briefe*, 166, 174). "Jahn possessed a great personal magnetism for young people. . . . As a solitary man he felt, more than others, the need to maintain friendly and social relations with the students, to whom the treasures of his library, as well as his house, stood open in all generosity"—so judges a witness who is above suspicion (Otto Ribbeck, *F. W. Ritschl* 2:342). In 1857 the philosophical faculty elected Jahn their Dean, and in 1858 he was Rector of the University. Both these offices testify to the position of respect that Jahn had won among his colleagues within a short time.

In his first years at Bonn, Jahn completed his monumental biography of Mozart (1859) and produced a series of useful editions of texts, which had grown directly out of the needs of academic instruction: the elegant little volume, seeming to beckon to the reader, which contains Apuleius' tale of Amor and Psyche (1856); Pausanias' description of the Acropolis (1860); and the *Electra* of Sophocles (1861), including a collection of testimonia on the poet's life and work that was superseded only by Radt's collection of the fragments of Sophocles (*Tragicorum Graecorum Fragmenta* IV [Göttingen, 1977]).

Although Ritschl and Jahn also gave lectures and reading classes in Greek literature, the greater share of their philological work was in the field of Latin. Jahn's efforts to recruit a respected Hellenist (he had in mind his friend Hermann Sauppe [1809–1893] in Göttingen) are thus understandable (*Briefe*, 177–178). Jahn's fear that Ritschl would reject the suggestion— and no doubt also his fear of his colleague's tactical skill, to which he did not feel equal ("a past master of university intrigue"—Mommsen to Henzen, *Briefwechsel*, 331n4)—induced Jahn to negotiate with the Berlin government for Sauppe's appointment without consulting Ritschl (*Briefwechsel*, 333). His action bears certain similarities to Ritschl's behavior toward Welcker at the time of Jahn's own appointment. In the spring of 1865, Jahn seemed finally to have reached his goal. Having received a preliminary inquiry from Vienna, Jahn informed Berlin that he would remain at Bonn if Sauppe were appointed, whereupon the Ministry accepted this condition and offered the post to Sauppe. But Sauppe, who had already agreed to accept the post if it were offered, now declined it. Only now did the Bonn faculty—and Ritschl, who was then Dean—learn of the affair, since the Ministry had not previously consulted them, and "the storm" (Mommsen) burst over Jahn's head.

It was to become the most famous quarrel between philologists in the history of modern scholarship, and the exchange between Nietzsche and Wilamowitz furnished the concluding satyr play. The report of Sauppe's refusal called forth from Jahn's opponents indignation and gleeful malice, while his friends felt embarrassment and bewilderment. For, aside from the disgrace, even those well-disposed toward Jahn had to admit that his behavior and the means he had employed were a breach of courtesy between colleagues. But the campaign of slander that was immediately launched by some of Ritschl's supporters with the aim of defaming Jahn's moral character evened the balance of blame. While the faculty, with few exceptions, understandably took the part of their Dean, the majority of the students, "among them nearly the whole of the Seminar" were partisans of Jahn (Erwin Rohde to his parents, 27 June 1865). Nietzsche too sided with Jahn (Colli-Montinari, eds., *Briefe* No. 467); during his year as a student at Bonn, he had attached himself to Jahn (*Ibid.*, no. 463, 464), and his departure from Bonn had nothing to do with the quarrel between Jahn and Ritschl (*Ibid.*, no. 466).

The tactlessness of the Ministry, which published the sharp rebuke it issued to Ritschl for his official conduct as Dean in the affair, had meanwhile transformed a local Bonn University quarrel into a political scandal of widespread interest; it led to an attack on Bismarck's government by the liberals in the Prussian *Landtag*. Jahn found it all depressing. In spite of his personal integrity and his honorable intentions in trying to have an additional professorship of Greek created (*Briefe*, 218), his position was, for the moment, precarious. And the situation was paradoxical: in Parliament the liberals (Jahn's party) took up the cause of the archconservative Ritschl, while the liberal Jahn seemed to have joined forces with the "Junker Ministry." When Ritschl submitted his resignation from the Prussian civil service and left Bonn the next semester to accept the Saxon government's call to Leipzig, it was not, as a pamphlet by one of Ritschl's students prophesied, "the end of the Bonn school of philology"; but Jahn was sensible of the magnitude of the loss the University had sustained, and he suffered from the expectation that he would be held responsible for it (*Briefwechsel*, 304). Ritschl, on the other hand, could present himself to the public as the victim of the ingratitude of the state and of his colleague, and of a Holstein nepotism as well: the Bonn University curator Beseler was Jahn's cousin, and Olshausen, the responsible officer in the Ministry, was his childhood friend. In contrast to Ritschl's more robust nature, which allowed him to declare himself the moral victor with an easy conscience, Jahn, perpetually tormented by scruples and self-doubts, felt compelled again and again to resort to self-justifications, to which no one would listen. It was a conflict in which there were only defeats and no victories.

"He is incredibly unhappy," said so unsentimental a character as Mommsen—on another occasion—of Jahn (*Briefwechsel* 359). He was a man who needed friendship and was to a high degree capable of friendship; but the strokes of fate, human disappointments, and his own mistakes had transformed him into a lonely man who had given up on himself (*Briefe*, 222–225; *Briefwechsel*, 360). Jahn's guilelessness, his eagerness to admire, and his expressions of gratitude were often exploited, even by his friends; Haupt's contemptuous remarks about him require the interpretation of a psychologist. His few years of teaching in Bonn after Ritschl's departure were overshadowed by the onset of lung disease. But to the last he fought against his own physical decline, producing work after work—among them the edition of pseudo-Longinus Περὶ Ὕψους, which, in Vahlen's re-edition, has not yet been superseded, and above all the completely rewritten second edition of the Mozart biography, now in two volumes instead of four. In 1867 he declined a call to Berlin as Eduard Gerhard's successor and the offer of a one-year journey to Italy for study and recuperation, because he was well aware of his condition and wanted to use the short time remaining to him to complete the projects he had planned. On 9 September 1879, Jahn died in Göttingen in the home of the parents of Eduard Schwartz, whose mother was Jahn's niece. The library he left behind, one of the greatest private scholarly libraries of the nineteenth century, comprised more than 30,000 volumes. The *ex libris* with the motto *Inter folia fructus* was a gift from Ludwig Richter, given in gratitude for an essay Jahn had written about him (*Biographische Aufsätze*, 221ff.).

Agreement seems to exist among musicologists that Jahn's biography of Mozart is the most important work on music history written in the nineteenth century. The dedication of the *Köchel-Verzeichnis* to Jahn is a monumental evidence of this evaluation. Applying historical and philological methods to the examination of written sources for the purpose of portraying the life and work of a great composer was a pioneering achievement that served as the model for other biographies of composers; in the case of Mozart, Jahn's *Life* was superseded only in the 1920s—in a revision of Jahn's text (Abert, ed. [5th ed.], 1919; 1921).

A just appraisal of Jahn's influence on *Altertumswissenschaft* is much more difficult to formulate. This is partly because of the extreme diversity of his works, thematically as well as bibliographically; unhappily, no collection of his *Kleine Schriften* has ever been published. But the difficulty also lies in the nature of his researches. Jahn's scholarly interests lay in the concrete particular, not in the general. Speculation and systematization were not for him. He was concerned to portray descriptively the multiplicity of phenomena, with each in its historical context. In philology this meant, above all, producing a text as authentic as possible by examination of the textual transmission and interpreting the text by means of commentary. In archaeology it meant exact description, as well as collection, of the monuments (the idea of a corpus of sarcophagi goes back to Jahn). In the history of scholarship it meant biographic portrayal of its great figures. In mythology the concern was no longer with hypotheses on the original meaning of a given myth but rather with the exact understanding of its concrete portrayal in individual texts and monuments. The purposeful union of archaeology and philology was, for Jahn, entirely at the service of interpretation as the true goal of both disciplines. But it also provided access to the daily life of antiquity as a new subject of historical research, and this benefited literary and iconographic interpretation equally with the history of religion ("Über den Aberglauben des bösen Blickes") and the portrayal of commerce and handicrafts in the visual arts.

Jahn's oldest student was Mommsen; his youngest was Wilamowitz. These two were also his most important students, and both went far beyond their teacher. He directed the former to the study of Latin inscriptions; his influence on the latter was greater than is generally supposed. It is seen in the concept of a reconciliation between philology as a linguistic study (Hermann, Lachmann) and as a historical study (Böckh, K. O. Müller, Welcker), and in the preference given to single-work interpretation connected with a commitment to putting the individual phenomenon into its historical context; but it also appears in the new appreciation of Hellenistic poetry (Wilamowitz, *Geschichte der Philologie*, 68) as well as in the art of the essay on subjects in the history of scholarship. Though Wilamowitz liked to invoke the name of Welcker, he was a student of Jahn. As for archaeology, Jahn helped to establish it as a university discipline. At the same time, his insistence that the archaeologist be also a student of philology remained valid into the period after the Second World War. His archaeology students included his nephew Adolf Michaelis (1835–1910), Eugen Petersen (1836–1919), Otto Benndorf (1838–1907), Karl Dilthey (1839–1907), Wolfgang Helbig (1839–1915), and Carl Robert (1850–1922). Helbig's *Wandgemälde der vom Vesuv verschütteten Städte Campaniens* (1868) is unthinkable without Jahn, and Robert's *Hermeneutik der Archäologie* (1919) still betrays Jahn's influence. Almost all of these scholars also wrote philological works. By taking into account the phenomena of daily life in antiquity, including popular beliefs and superstitions, and by reappraising Hellenistic poetry, Jahn founded the philological tradition of the "Bonn School," the influence of which ranges from Hermann Usener and Adolf Brinkmann (1863–1923) to Hans Herter (1899–1984).

Translated by Michael Armstrong

Books (Classical Philology)

Palamedes. Kiel dissertation. Hamburg, 1836.

Specimen epigraphicum in memoriam Olai Kellermanni. Kiel, 1841.

Auli Persii Flacci satirarum liber cum scholiis antiquis. With commentary. Leipzig, 1843; reprinted Hildesheim, 1967.

Censorini de die natali liber. Berlin, 1845; reprinted Hildesheim, 1965.

Ciceros Brutus de claris oratoribus. Leipzig, 1849; 2d ed., Berlin, 1856; 3d ed., 1865; 4th ed., 1877 revised by A. Eberhard; 5th ed., 1908 revised by W. Kroll; 7th ed., 1964 revised by B. Kytzler.

D. Iunii Iuvenalis saturarum libri V, ex recensione et cum commentariis Ottonis Iahnii, vol. I: *D. Iunii Iuvenalis saturarum libri V cum scholiis veteribus.* Berlin, 1851. (Vol. II [commentary] was never published.)

Auli Persii Flacci satirarum liber. Leipzig, 1851 (*Editio minor* without commentary.)

Ciceros Orator. Appendix: *De optumo genere oratorum.* Leipzig, 1851; 2nd ed., Berlin, 1859; 3d ed. 1869; new ed. 1913 by W. Kroll, reprinted 1964. French translation of the introduction in F. Gache and J. S. Piquet, *Cicéron et ses ennemis littéraires.* Paris, 1886.

Iuli Flori epitomae de Tito Livio bellorum omnium annorum DCC libri II. Leipzig, 1852.

Periochae de T. Livio et Iulius Obsequens. Leipzig, 1853.

Apuleii Psyche et Cupido. Leipzig, 1856; 2d ed., 1873 revised by A. Michaelis; 3d ed., 1883; 4th ed., 1895; 5th ed., 1905.

Pausaniae descriptio arcis Athenarum. Bonn 1860; 2d ed., 1880 revised by A. Michaelis; 3d ed., 1901.

Sophoclis Electra. Bonn, 1861; 2d ed., 1872 revised by A. Michaelis; 3d ed., 1882.

Platonis Symposium. Bonn, 1864; 2d ed., 1875 revised by H. Usener.

Διονυσίου ἢ Λογγίνου περὶ ὕψους. Bonn, 1867; 2d ed., Leipzig, 1887 revised by J. Vahlen; 3d ed., 1905; 4th ed., 1910; 5th ed., Stuttgart, 1967 revised by H.-D. Blume.

A. Persii Flacci, D. Iunii Iuvenalis, Sulpiciae saturae. Berlin, 1868; 2d ed., 1886 with the scholia vetera, edited by F. Bücheler; 3d ed., 1893; 4th ed., 1910 revised by F. Leo; 5th ed., 1932.

Aus der Altertumswissenschaft. Populäre Aufsätze. Bonn, 1868.

Books (Archaeology)

Vasenbilder. Hamburg, 1839.

Die Gemälde des Polygnotos in der Lesche zu Delphi. Kiel, 1841.

Telephos und Troilos. Ein Brief an Herrn Professor F. G. Welcker in Bonn. Kiel, 1841.

Pentheus und die Mainaden. Kiel, 1841.

Paris und Oinone. Greifswald, 1844.

Archäologische Aufsätze. Greifswald, 1845.

Die hellenische Kunst. Greifswald, 1846. Revised version in *Aus der Alterthumswissenschaft* [see above]: 115–182.

Peitho. Greifswald, 1846.

Archäologische Beiträge. Berlin, 1847.

Prométhée. Paris, 1848.

Ficoronische Cista. Leipzig, 1852.

Beschreibung der Vasensammlung König Ludwigs in der Pinakothek zu München. Munich, 1854. Introduction (vol. 1) published separately, Leipzig, 1854.

Kurze Beschreibung der Vasensammlung Sr. Maj. König Ludwigs in der Pinakothek zu München. Munich, 1854; 2d ed., 1871; 3d ed., 1875; 4th ed., 1887.

Telephos und Troilos und kein Ende. Ein Brief an Herrn Professor F. G. Welcker zum 16 October 1859. Leipzig, 1859.

Der Tod der Sophonisba auf einem Wandgemälde. Leipzig, 1859.

Die Lauersforter Phalerae. Bonn, 1860.

Römische Alterthümer aus Vindonissa. Mitteilungen der Antiquarischen Gesellschaft in Zürich. Vol. 14.4. Zürich, 1862.

Über bemalte Vasen mit Goldschmuck. Leipzig, 1865.

De antiquissimis Minervae simulacris Atticis. Bonn, 1866.

Die Entführung der Europa auf antiken Kunstwerken. Denkschriften der philosophisch-historischen Classe der Kaiserlichen Akademie der Wissenschaften XIX. Vienna, 1870.

Griechische Bilderchroniken. Aus dem Nachlass des Verfassers herausgegeben und beendigt von Adolf Michaelis. Bonn, 1873.

Books (Musicology)

Leonore, Oper von Beethoven. Vollständiger Klavier-Auszug der zweiten Bearbeitung mit den Abweichungen der ersten. Leipzig, 1851.

W. A. Mozart. Leipzig, 1856–59 [4 vols.]; 2d ed., 1867 [2 vols.]; 3d ed., 1889–91 revised by H. Deiters; 4th ed., 1905–07; 5th ed., 1919–21 revised by H. Abert; 6th ed., 1924; 7th ed., 1955–56. *Life of Mozart* by Otto Jahn. Translated by Pauline D. Townsend. With a preface by George Grove. 3 vols. London, 1882; 2d ed., 1891; reprinted New York, 1970.

Gesammelte Aufsätze über Musik. Leipzig, 1866; 2d ed. 1867.

Books (history of German Literature; Biography)

Goethes Briefe an Leipziger Freunde. Leipzig, 1849.

Ludwig Uhland. Bonn, 1863.

Biographische Aufsätze. Leipzig, 1866. (Winckelmann; G. Hermann; L. Ross; Th. W. Danzel; L. Richter; Goethe.)

Goethes Briefe an Christian Gottlob von Voigt. Leipzig, 1868.

Eduard Gerhard. Ein Lebensabriss. Berlin, 1868.

Goethe und Leipzig. Leipzig ; 2d ed., 1909; 3d ed., 1910; 4th ed., Berlin, 1914 = *Biographische Aufsätze: 286–372.*

Articles

"Bassirilievi e le iscrizioni del monumento di Marco Vergilio Eurisace." *Annali dell' Instituto di Correspondenza Archaeologica* 10 (1838) 231–248.

"Über das Wesen und die wichtigsten Aufgaben der archäologischen Studien." *Berichte über die Verhandlungen der Königlich Sächsischen Gesellschaft der Wissenschaften zu Leipzig.* Philol.-hist. Cl. (1848) 209–226.

"Über die Kunsturtheile des Plinius." *Ibid.* (1850) 105–142.

"Über den Aberglauben des bösen Blicks bei den Alten." *Ibid.* (1855) 28–110.

"Die Wandgemälde des Columbariums in der Villa Pamfili." *Abh. kgl. bayer. Akad. Wiss., Philos.-philol. Cl.* (1857) 231–284.

"Priapos." *Jbb. d. Vereins v. Alterthumsfreunden i. Rheinlande* 17 (1859) 45–62.

"Über Darstellungen griechischer Dichter auf Vasenbildern." *Abh. Kgl. Sächs. Ges. Wiss., Philol.-hist. Cl.* (1861) 697–760.

"Darstellungen antiker Reliefs, welche sich auf Handwerk und Handelsverkehr beziehen." *Ber. Verh. Kgl. Sächs. Wiss. Leipzig., Philol.-hist. Cl.* (1861) 291–374.

"Einige antike Gruppen, welche Orestes und Elektra darstellen." *Ibid.* (1861) 100–132.

"Über Darstellungen des Handwerks und Handelsverkehrs auf Vasenbildern." *Ibid.* (1867) 75–119.

"Über Darstellungen des Handwerks und Handelsverkehrs auf antiken Wandgemälden." *Abh. Kgl. Sächs. Ges. Wiss. Leipzig,* Philol.-hist. Cl. (1868) 236–318.

"Die Cista Mystica." *Hermes* 3 (1869) 317–334.

Sources

Bursian, C. *Geschichte der classischen Philologie in Deutschland.* Munich and Leipzig, 1883, 2:1070–1080.

Calder, W. M. III. "Why Did Wilamowitz Leave Bonn? The New Evidence." *RhM* 130 (1987) 366–384.

Gruber, G. "Die Mozart-Forschung im 19. Jahrhundert." *Mozart-Jahrbuch* (1980–1983) 10–17.

Halm, K. "Otto Jahn." *Sb. kgl. bayer. Akad. Wiss. (I. Cl.)* (1870) 393–402.

Henseler, T. A. "Das musikalische Bonn im 19. Jahrhundert." *Bonner Geschichtsblätter* 13 (Bonn, 1959) 259–265.

Hübinger, P. E. "Heinrich von Sybel und der Bonner Philologenkrieg." *Historisches Jahrbuch* 83 (1964) 162–216.

King, A. H. "Jahn and the Future of Mozart Biography." In *Mozart in Retrospect.* London, 1955; 3d ed., Oxford, 1970: 66–77.

Langlotz, E. "Otto Jahn." In *Bonner Gelehrte. Beiträge zur Geschichte der Wissenschaften in Bonn. Philosophie und Altertumswissenschaft. 150 Jahre Rheinische Friedrich-Wilhelms-Universität zu Bonn 1818–1968.* Bonn, 1968: 221–226.

Luck, G. "Otto Jahn." *Ibid.* 144–164.

Michaelis, A. "Otto Jahn." *ADB* 13 (1881) 668–686.

Michaelis, A. and Petersen, E. "Otto Jahns Leben." *Otto Jahn in seinen Briefen.* Edited by E. Petersen. Leipzig, 1913: 1–52.

Mommsen, Theodor. "Otto Jahn." *Archaeologische Zeitung* 27 (1869) 95–96 = *Reden und Aufsätze* (Berlin, 1905): 458–461 = *Briefwechsel,* 362–364.

Pulver, J. "Otto Jahn." *The Musical Times* (1913) 237–239.

Wickert, L. *Theodor Mommsen.* 4 vols. Frankfurt-am-Main, 1959–80.

Wilamowitz-Moellendorff, U. von. *Erinnerungen,* 2d ed. Leipzig, 1929: 84–87.

Letters

Otto Jahn in seinen Briefen. Edited by E. Petersen. Leipzig, 1913.

Theodor Mommsen–Otto Jahn. Briefwechsel 1842–1868. Edited by L. Wickert. Frankfurt-am-Main, 1962. With 21 newly found letters at *Philologus* 127 (1983) 262–283.

In June 1988, an interdisciplinary colloquium on Otto Jahn took place in Bad Homburg v. d. H. (Reimerstiftung). The papers will appear in *Otto Jahn (1813–1869). Ein Geisteswissenschaftler zwischen Klassizismus und Historismus.* Ed. W. M. Calder, III, H. Cancik, and B. Kytzler. *Mnemosyne* Supplementband. Leiden (in press).

R.C. Jebb

27 August 1841 – 9 December 1905

ROGER D. DAWE
Trinity College, Cambridge

My dear Uncle,

I have got a nice set of tools amongst which there is a saw half a yard long.

Such is the first recorded written sentence of Richard Claverhouse Jebb. He was six years old at the time. We see him losing no time in getting to grips with essentials, appreciative of the good things in life, and with an English style capable of combining a note of wonder ("half a yard" is not, except to mathematicians, the same as one foot, six inches) with an awareness of a limitless potential for evil if a useful instrument (like conjectural criticism?) should fall into the wrong hands. This little boy grew up to become a Knight, a holder of the Order of Merit; a member of Parliament, a founding father of the Cambridge Philological Society, the Society for the Promotion of Hellenic Studies, the British School at Athens, and the British Academy; and the recipient of numerous honorary degrees from Universities abroad as well as at home. If ever there was a figure of the establishment it was Sir Richard.

Yet the little boy with the unimpeachable English style, who in another letter speaks of a universal human tragedy with the same economy—"I go to school next Wednesday. It cannot be helped"—an economy that was to become one of the hallmarks of his commentaries, was not extinguished in the later, graver figure whose words were reported in 1893 in such respectful terms as, "The foremost scholar in England urged the paramount importance of an essentially unremunerative branch of learning." Much of his private correspondence is preserved, and from it we form a picture quite different from that of the public figure whose portrait has recently been taken out of store to gaze with some hauteur on those who dine in the Master's Lodge of Trinity College. Those who see the Victorian old duffer on the wall are unaware that he was suffering from hay fever at the time the portrait was painted; nor do they know that Jebb's own comment on it was, "I wish he had made me a more cheerful and spirited-looking chappy."

Richard was one of four children of an Irish barrister and the daughter of a clergyman. He was born very much on the right side of the tracks, for the Jebb family had distinguished itself from the reign of Queen Elizabeth onward, particularly in the literary life of the eighteenth century. He was educated at Charterhouse and entered Trinity. It made quite an impression on him. "Have you ever seen our hall at Trinity during feeding time? If you have not, I will assist your imagination. Fancy a vast hall, traversed lengthwise by narrow tables. Fancy these tables crowded to excess with British youths in every stage of starvation or repletion: some, with the stony look of despairing hunger; some, in whose faces despair has not yet frozen boiling indignation; some, whose countenances express ungrateful content and the peace that is engendered by unctuous pudding. Between these tables, where haggard misery is the neighbour of stolid fatness, fancy a dense tide of slovenly men and dirty old women pushing, wrangling, struggling, for hacked and gory joints, upsetting gravy, dripping dishes, always in a hurry, never attending to one, but always doing to everybody." It is all quite different now, of course.

In his undergraduate career Jebb emerged effortlessly as the best student in his subject. His Latin verses, we are told, "extracted tears from the venerable eyes of Dr. Jeremie," and he maintained that healthy dislike of his subject that is the mark of the true professional: "For years everything conspired to make me think that Greek and Latin were the end of existence. This miserable illusion disappeared when I came up here, and yet I know that my pretensions to any ability whatever rest solely on proficiency in these wretched Classics, which I now almost detest. What I yearn for is a start in the serious business of life, and emancipation from these utterly barren studies. . . ." His widow records that "there had been talk about his going into the Church" but, in her superb phrase, "the claims of an eager vitality were clamouring in his ears too insistently for self-abnegation." He fell passionately in love, but the girl did not reciprocate his feelings. Is it sympathy or satisfaction that we hear in his widow's comment that this was "in the long run an unmixed benefit, keeping him clear of love affairs through the years when a man is most apt to act rashly"?

The letters from these early years at Cambridge are a delight to read; it is clear that Jebb had all the qualities it takes to become a novelist. He speaks of "a group of unmistakeable townsmen carefully got up and smoking questionable cigars" and "mighty Dons in blameless black." A sermon by Archbishop Whately impressed him but did not blind him: "It seemed as if his Mind had come down by train to preach without noticing it had not put on its best Body." This edge to his writing extended into scholarly comment too, when he speaks of "consuls, who, to judge from their universal incapacity, must have been chosen by the Senate of the time simply in the educational interests of posterity." Whether this style rubbed off on his wife, the widow of an American general, or whether she was a kindred spirit, it is impossible to say, but it was in fact Lady Caroline, not Sir Richard, whose testimonial to another scholar reads "Dr. Blackie was an accomplished and amiable man, blessed with a fortunate want of sensitiveness."

From 1863 to 1875 Jebb was one of the classics dons of Trinity, and then, not without much misgiving, he decided to accept the chair of Greek at Glasgow, returning to Cambridge each summer. There is conflicting evidence on Jebb's qualities as a lecturer, but there are at least two enthusiastic testimonials to his teaching as occupant of the Glasgow chair. "I have no hesitation in saying that he was by far the best teacher I ever knew, and that he made his subject real and inspiring as few are able to do." So the Rev. Dr. Denney, who notes, however, that "he could not in any sense fraternise with his pupils." Another clergyman, John Walker, wrote of "your influence over my own mind. My experience is not singular in this; I have heard it expressed very strongly by many others who have been as fortunate as myself in coming through the Greek class in the years they did." A different view was expressed by someone else, describing Jebb's temper as short, bursts of it sweeping the classroom like a storm. We shall not at this distance of time be able to recover a true picture of Jebb the lecturer, but there is one anecdote that bears repetition. John Veitch used to lecture on logic and rhetoric in the room over the one in which the Greek class was held. On one occasion his lecture reached an excited finish and his audience stamped in appreciation across the room and down the stairs. Jebb looked up and observed: "Gentlemen, I fear that my premises will not support Professor Veitch's conclusions."

Various books and articles by Jebb appeared during this period. His *Selections from the Attic Orators*, written, it is said, in a single month, is still in use today. But of Jebb's early works the most startling is one composed before the time of the Glasgow Chair. It is a translation into the metres of Pindar's Fourth *Pythian* of Browning's "Abt Vogler." It was apparently worked out in his mind during a single walk. It is not flawless, and in fact one line is deficient of two syllables. But it is of amazingly high quality. Tyrrell, in his "Memoir of Jebb" in the *Proceedings of the British Academy*, remarked that it was, to him at any rate, far clearer in the Greek than in the English. It shows an intimate understanding of Pindaric style that makes one bitterly regret that Jebb never lived to write the full commentary he hoped to do on this author. The Bacchylides is no substitute, for it has necessarily been overtaken by recent advances, and, in any case, as Jebb sighed, "One does wish that the man were just a little better."

In 1889 Jebb returned to Cambridge as Professor of Greek. The first volume of the seven that comment individually on the plays of Sophocles had appeared two years earlier. *Sophoclis sui interpreti exquisitissimo* says the memorial brass in the chapel of Trinity College, and that is how he is, and always will be, remembered. If we tried a word-association test on classical scholars, asking them whose name came immediately to mind in connection with major Greek authors, we would get a huge diversity of answers for Homer, Pindar, Aeschylus, Euripides, Herodotus, Thucydides, Plato, Aristotle and the rest. But for Sophocles there is, at any rate in the English-speaking world, only one answer, for Jebb's commentaries, dated and flawed in some respects as they may be, remain the yardstick by which all subsequent ones are measured. For a hundred years or so the only criterion of merit for an editor of Sophocles is how far short of Jebb's his performance falls.

This reservation, "in the English-speaking world," is a necessary one, for although Jebb was at pains to acquaint himself with the work of German scholars, the compliment was not reciprocated as heartily as it might have been. Kaibel's over-praised *Elektra*, published not so long after Jebb's edition, shows hardly any awareness of the English scholar at all. The loss is Kaibel's. Continental scholarship may have regarded with amusement Jebb's adherence to the superseded metrical theories of J. H. H. Schmidt when treating the choral passages, and certainly Sir Richard was never a textual critic to set the heart racing. But as the "exquisite interpreter" he has no equal. Perhaps those whose mastery of the English language was incomplete were never able to realize just how exquisite. Wilamowitz partially sensed this deficiency in his fellow countrymen. "With us Sir R. Jebb is known essentially as a commentator on Sophocles, and that too less than he deserves." When he mysteriously added later that "scholarly production was not his field" ("wissenschaftliche Produktion nicht sein Feld war") we have to interpret that remark in the light of others that accompany it. Jebb was not the founder of a method, opening up new avenues of research, surrounded by a faithful clique whose advancement depended on making themselves useful to the great man. He was not a German professor.

It is regrettable that, in his own country, those whose command of Sophoclean Greek has never been put to the test have embarked on a campaign of denigration. C. O. Brink speaks of his "tasteful floating" by comparison with Housman, and H. D. Jocelyn takes his cue and refers to "the superficiality of his [own] scholarship." When it comes to those areas where Housman and Jebb came into direct conflict over matters of Sophoclean interpretation, anyone who wishes to observe the difference can turn to the pages of pedantic ranting that lead often to conclusions which no person in his right mind would accept in Housman's article on *Oedipus at Colonus* (=*Classical Papers* 1:181–208) and compare them with Jebb's own cool concision on the same topics.

Of course fashions change. It is hard for us to believe today that Jebb's translations were once admired as models. Though they never descend to the mindless level of W. S. Barrett's exposition of Euripides *Hippolytus*, lines 545–554: "The Oichalian filly unyoked abed, manless before and unwed, she yoked from Eurytos' house and like a running Naiad or a bacchant, amid blood, amid smoke, in a bloody bridal gave her, did the Cyprian, to Alkmene's child; oh, unhappy in your bridal" (the vintage is 1963), they do nevertheless often provoke a smile today. A few samples from the inexhaustible supply must suffice: "Why is the sailor trafficking with thee about me in these dark whispers?" "In sooth, that is the meed; yet lucre hath oft ruined men through their hopes." "Then do not thou, my son, at pleasure's beck, dethrone thy reason for a woman's sake." "If I am to nurture mine own kindred in naughtiness, needs must I bear with it in aliens." "Then wottest thou of having noted yon man in these parts?" The enlightened teacher of classics today will do all he can to steer his pupils away from this kind of thing, as from Headlam's translation of Aeschylus *Agamemnon*: "Such is the boasting; though brim-full of truth, unseemly, surely for a noble dame to trumpet" (lines 613–614), a nervous oscillation between the language of the King James Bible and that of Damon Runyon.

Sophocles' own diction would not have sounded anything but archaic even to the audiences who first heard the plays, and the simple test of Jebb's admittedly often hilarious versions is, Can you do better? Very often they reveal nuances that it would be ponderous to explain in the running commentary: in a sense they *are* a running commentary, and in the places where, as sometimes happens, translation and notes are at variance, it is more usually the translation that has best captured the truth. If Jebb says "she stood not on denial of aught" the reader may be confident that the original Greek says something grander than "She did not deny anything." Some disrespectful young persons of Trinity College were observed to fall about on finding Oedipus ask the question "Say, am I vile?" But the original does have something, not identical with, but still corresponding with the "say"; and the "vile" is not there to represent the Greek adjective, the ordinary word for "bad" but imparts the nuance of the verb, which means "be" in the sense of "be by nature, by birth." Jebb has got it exactly right. The translations achieve the perplexing feat of being both horrendously awful and superbly right at one and the same time.

In the list of Great Emenders given on pp. 378–380 of this book, Jebb's name appears low on the list, and only for Sophocles. Even so, he scores twice as many points as A. C. Pearson, a Cambridge Greek professor of this century whose three-volume edition of the Sophocles fragments, continuing Jebb's work, is itself a formidable work of technical scholarship. But what distinguishes Jebb from other textual critics is this: the emenders of texts, considered as a special class of human being, are distinguished by the attitude "Of course I am right; it is just that you are too stupid to see it." Jebb took an entirely different line. Of the thirty-two readings that have survived the envious scrutiny of the Teubner editor, a quarter are directly repudiated by Jebb himself, and many of the others are mentioned as the merest possibilities. Jebb knew better than anyone when to stay his hand. As Verrall put it in a first-rate evaluation of his work, printed as an Appendix to the *Life and Letters*, he was not the dupe of his own cleverness.

This restraint may seem a negative virtue, but we shall only appreciate its true value properly if we remember that, at the time Jebb was working, conjectural criticism was at full flood. As the speed with which a man could draw a gun enhanced his prestige among certain communities in the New World, so in the Old the standing of a classical scholar was often determined by the number of notches he could carve onto his texts of ancient authors. It required much sanity and courage to blow the whistle on a game that was getting out of hand. What particularly aroused Jebb's ire was the wanton excision of lines held to be interpolated. "It is to be regretted," he wrote icily, "when a habit of mind such as might be fostered by the habitual composition of telegrams is applied to the textual criticism of poetry,—or, indeed, of prose." In his Preface to *Oedipus at Colonus* his creed is set out at greater length:

> The detection of spurious work has come down from a past age as a traditional exercise for a scholar's acuteness. In Germany, where scholarship is a crowded profession, involving the severest competition, every competitor is naturally and rightly anxious

to prove his originality; and, if the Greek drama is his subject, one of the time-honoured modes of doing this is to discover interpolations. Thenceforth he is a man with a view, and has earned a mention; he is the critic who holds that such or such verses are spurious. English copiers of this fashion are not wanting. It is, however, high time to recognize the fact that the principal classical texts are no longer such as they were found by the scholarship of the sixteenth, or even of the last century. They no longer teem with those rank overgrowths of corruption in which the earlier critics found such ample material. The purification of these texts, though still incomplete, has now reached such a point that, if any real advance is to be made, reserve and delicacy of judgment must be cultivated. Interpretation—of the spirit, as well as of the letter—has a twofold office to perform. It has to aid and control the process of emendation. It has also to defend the text against wanton defacement or mutilation.

. . . It may be permissible to observe, since the practice of classical composition has been subject in late years to some ignorant and silly disparagement, that not a few of the conjectures which we sometimes see put forward are such as could not have been suggested, if their proposers had profited, even a little, by the discipline of Greek verse composition. It is earnestly to be hoped that the day will never come when that exercise,—duly reserved for those to whom it is congenial,—shall cease to have a place among the studies which belong to the English conception of classical scholarship. . . . It helps to educate an instinct which will usually refrain from change where no change is required.

Those who are unable to savor to the full the delights of Jebb's own translations into various Greek metres of famous passages of English poetry would do best to turn, after the Sophocles commentaries, to the *Essays and Addresses*. Oddly enough, the weakest is precisely the one on Sophocles. It may be an early work, or it may be that the Society for Afternoon Lectures on Literature and Art of Dublin, before whom it was delivered, did not bring out the best in him; not but what we learn from another source, of other lectures, "He gave us of his best: a smaller man might have thought us hardly worth the trouble." The Pindar essay is a comprehensive account, useful today as a compendium of everything that you need to know about Pindar unless you are taking a highly specialized examination. The review of Froude's *Caesar* shows us Jebb in an unusual light, as a destructive critic capable of lashing out in unexpected directions, as when he says of Burke, "He first elicits the damning eloquence of facts, and then overlays it with the rhetoric of denunciation." He punctures Mommsen and accuses Froude at one point of "spanning an impassable gulf with a bridge of cobwebs." The Erasmus lecture also has an edge to it. Erasmus' true name was Gerhard Gerhardson: "It was a singular fortune for a master of literary style to be designated by two words which mean the same thing, and are both wrong." In his Thucydides paper Jebb anticipates a famous book by Cornford: "It might not be difficult, with a little adroitness, to represent Thucydides as a conscious dramatic artist throughout his work; and an ingenious writer has actually shown how his History may be conceived as a tragedy cast into five acts" (i.e. Ulrici, *Charakteristik der antiken Historiographie*).

The Delos article shows that Jebb had the same keen interest in archaeology that Sir Denys Page had, and in *Ancient Organs of Public Opinion* we get a passage that might almost have been written by Sir Denys himself:

> Any one who reads the column of Answers to Correspondents in a prudently conducted journal will recognise the principal types of oracle. In truth, the Delphic oracle bore a strong resemblance to a serious newspaper managed by a cautious editorial committee with no principles in particular. In editing an oracle, it was then, as it still is, of primary importance not to make bad mistakes. The Delphian editors were not infallible; but, when a blunder had been made, they often showed considerable resource. Thus, when Croesus had been utterly ruined, he begged his conqueror to grant him one luxury—to allow him to send to Delphi, and ask Apollo whether it was his usual practice to treat his benefactors in this way. Apollo replied that, in point of fact, he had done everything he could; he had personally requested the Fates to put off the affair for a generation; but they would only grant a delay of three years. Instead of showing annoyance, Croesus ought to be grateful for having been ruined three years later than he ought to have been.

In the later pages of the collection we see more of Jebb, the man of affairs. In *Life and Letters* too we begin to lose sight of Jebb the scholar as Jebb the public figure begins to take over. We cannot be sure if he thought his correspondents would be more interested in his political doings than in his academic work, or whether he genuinely believed that what he did as a member of Parliament and member of countless commissions was more important than putting down on paper his thoughts on Sophocles. He may have deluded himself. By all accounts he was not a good extempore speaker in the House of Commons, though outside it, delivering a set piece, he could be magnificent: the speech he made at the inauguration of the Memorial Cloister at Charterhouse in 1903 survives. We must make allowances for the spirit of the times and local loyalties that we may not ourselves share. Once we do, we shall find the speech a perfectly judged piece, which its audience must have found deeply moving. No student of the classics can read it without forming in his mind a tacit comparison with the famous funeral oration put into the mouth of Pericles by Thucydides, and it requires no great imagination to suppose that in Jebb's mind too it was present as a model.

Sir Richard Jebb cannot be assessed as one in the great tradition of classical philologists. He stands to the side of it, apart, a restrained and dignified figure, his warm and boyish humor kept for his family and friends. Classical literature was for him not material on which to practise a brand of pyrotechnics. Someone once said that the difference between Heifetz and Kreisler was that every time Heifetz came on stage it was with the determination to prove once again that he was the greatest violinist in the world; Kreisler came as one to play for a circle of friends. Jebb was a Kreisler.

Books

The Electra of Sophocles: Catena Classicorum. London, Oxford, and Cambridge, 1867.

The Ajax of Sophocles: Catena Classicorum. London, Oxford, and Cambridge, 1868.

Theophrastus, Characters. London, 1870; revised version by J. E. Sandys, 1909.

Translations into Greek and Latin Verse. Cambridge, 1873; 2d ed. (enlarged), 1907.

The Attic Orators from Antiphon to Isaeus. London, 1876; 2d ed., 1893.

Translations. With H. Jackson and W. E. Currey. Cambridge, 1878. (Greek and Latin, verse and prose, into and out of English.)

Xenophon Anabasis III. Glasgow, 1879.

Scriptores Graeci. London, 1880. (Selections from *The Attic Orators.*)

Bentley. London, 1882.

Sophocles Oedipus Tyrannus. Cambridge, 1883; 2d ed., 1887; 3d ed., 1893.

Facsimile of the Laurentian MS of Sophocles. With an introduction by E. M. Thompson and R. C. Jebb. London, 1885.

Introduction to Homer. Glasgow, 1886.

Sophocles Oedipus Coloneus. Cambridge, 1889.

Sophocles Philoctetes. Cambridge, 1890; 2d ed., 1900.

Sophocles Antigone. Cambridge, 1891; 2d ed., 1900.

Sophocles Trachiniae. Cambridge, 1892.

The Growth and Influence of Classical Greek Poetry. London, 1893. (Turnbull Lectures given at the Johns Hopkins University.)

Sophocles Electra. Cambridge, 1894.

Sophocles Ajax. Cambridge, 1896.

Sophocles, Text of the Seven Plays. Cambridge, 1897.

Sophocles Antigone: Catena Classicorum. Cambridge, 1900.

Translation of Sophocles. Cambridge, 1904.

Bacchylides. Cambridge, 1906.

Bacchylides. Cambridge, 1906. (Text only.)

Aristotle Rhetoric. Cambridge, 1909. (Translation.)

Articles (Collected)

Essays and Addresses. Cambridge, 1907. This work includes: 1. The Genius of Sophocles; 2. Pindar; 3. The Age of Pericles; 4. Ancient Organs of Public Opinion; 5. Lucian; 6. Delos; 7. Caesar (review of Froude); 8. Erasmus; 9. The Speeches of Thucydides; 10. Suidas on the Change ascribed to Sophocles in regard to Trilogies; 11. Samuel Johnson; 12. Humanism in Education; 13. On Present Tendencies in Classical Studies; 14. The Influence of the Greek Mind on Modern Life; 15. The Work of the Universities for the Nation, Past and Present; 16. An Address delivered at the Mason College; 17. University Education and National Life.

Besides these there also exist pamphlets relating to a dispute with Mahaffy, speeches delivered by the Public Orator (1875), and the Glasgow Inaugural Lecture of the same year; the address to Bologna University (1888) and a speech at the annual meeting of the central committee of the National Society for Women's Suffrage (1892); a lecture on Macaulay (Cambridge, 1900); two lectures on Modern Greece (1901) and Milton's Areopagitica, privately printed in 1872, published in a fuller version (Cambridge, 1918); and a number of more ephemeral productions.

Sources

Bobbitt, Mary Reed. *With Dearest Love to All: The Life and Letters of Lady Jebb.* London, 1960.

Duff, J. D. "Jebb, Sir Richard Claverhouse." *DNB Supplement 1901–1911*: 366–369. (With the accompanying bibliography.)

Gow, A. S. F. *Letters from Cambridge.* London, 1945: 240. (Highly uncomplimentary remarks on Jebb's lecturing style.)

Jebb, Caroline. *Life and Letters of Sir Richard Claverhouse Jebb.* Cambridge, 1907.

Raverat, Gwen. *Period Piece.* London, 1952. (Interesting sidelights, especially on Lady Caroline.)

Tyrrell, R. Y. "Sir Richard Claverhouse Jebb 1841–1905." *PBA* 2 (1905–6) 443–448.

Karl Lachmann
4 March 1793 – 13 March 1851

WOLFHART UNTE
Freie Universität Berlin

The history of nineteenth-century philology abounds in important names, but Karl Lachmann is without doubt one of its most outstanding figures. Moreover, he achieved greatness in two different fields: classical and older Germanic philology.

Karl Konrad Friedrich Lachmann, the son of a pastor, was born on 4 March 1793, in Braunschweig. He attended the Katharineum Gymnasium in the city of his birth and then in 1809 went to Leipzig to study theology; here, however, he also sat in on a course of lectures in philology given by Gottfried Hermann. After one semester he transferred to Göttingen and devoted himself chiefly to philology. The predominant scholarly tendency at Göttingen, as it was exemplified by Christian Gottlob Heyne—the study of history and of artifacts—had little attraction for him; his gifts and his inclinations led him to linguistic philology and textual criticism. Consequently he attached himself chiefly to Ludolph Dissen, under whose direction he pursued the study of (among other things) rhythms and meter. These studies bore fruit in works that appeared years later: *De choricis systematis tragicorum Graecorum* (1819) and *De mensura tragoediarum* (1822).

Lachmann took his doctorate in 1814 at the University of Halle with an unpublished dissertation, "De critica in Tibulli carminibus recte instituenda." In 1815 he habilitated at Göttingen with a text-critical study on the Latin poets, *Observationum criticarum capita tria*.

After Napoleon's return from Elba, Lachmann—as his American student B. L. Gildersleeve wrote (*Atlantic* 80 [September 1897] 338)—"dropped his Propertius to take up arms for his country" by joining the detachment of volunteer riflemen in Duderstadt, but his unit saw no action.

In 1816 Lachmann went to Berlin. Here he passed the examination to qualify as an upper-level schoolteacher and accepted a position on the staff of the Friedrichs Werdersches Gymnasium. At the same time he habilitated at the University of Berlin with his edition of Propertius and with his famous treatise *Über die ursprüngliche Gestalt des Gedichts von der Nibelungen Noth.*

His stay in Berlin was short; in the same year Lachmann took a position as an upper-level teacher at the Collegium Fridericianum in Königsberg, and in 1818 he became Extraordinarius for Classical and Germanic Philology at the University there. He interrupted his teaching in 1824 with a trip to inspect manuscripts in Wolfenbüttel, Kassel (where he visited the Brothers Grimm), Heidelberg, Munich, St. Gallen, and Eppishausen im Thurgau (where he visited Joseph Freiherr von Lassberg, who was at work on old German manuscripts). This journey laid the foundations for much of Lachmann's later researches.

In 1825 Lachmann was transferred, at his own request, to the Friedrich-Wilhelms Universität in Berlin, where he became Professor Extraordinarius. Thus he moved to the city in which he was to work until his death on 13 March 1851. In 1829 he became Professor Ordinarius and Director of the Latin section of the Philological Seminar; one year later he was named member of the Royal Prussian Academy of Sciences.

When Lachmann came to Berlin his name was already well-known among scholars. Nevertheless, the period of his greatest creativity and importance—his more than twenty-five years in the rising capital of Prussia—was still before him.

Lachmann's sphere of influence was essentially limited to the University. Here, in addition to his teaching and research, he took on administrative duties. He was several times Dean of the Philosophical Faculty, and in 1843–44 he was Rector of the University. Apart from this, however, he was not so involved in administrative and organizational duties as was his colleague August Böckh, nor was he quite so predominant as the latter in the Prussian Academy. Yet Lachmann was one who sought and maintained ties with colleagues and friends. The scholar and teacher who was feared for his stern criticism was a decidedly social man, who always attended the meetings of a large number of clubs and societies. In daily intercourse, too, he appreciated opportunities for intellectual and professional conversation. These contacts were not without effect upon Lachmann's scholarly work.

Two organizations were especially important to him: the Graeca (which was founded at the end of the eighteenth century) and the Gesetzlose Gesellschaft.

In the Graeca, which Lachmann joined in 1824, persons interested in Greek culture—philologists and laymen—met weekly to read a Greek author. The Gesetzlose Gesellschaft was a social club whose members came together to enjoy relaxed, harmonious, intellectual conversation. Philipp Buttmann had founded it; in 1840 Lachmann took the lifetime office of fifth "Zwingherr."

The exchange of ideas with members of these two organizations provided the stimulus for several of Lachmann's scholarly works. Immanuel Bekker and August Meineke, whose influential textual and philological methods were similar to Lachmann's, were especially important in this respect, as was Schleiermacher, who, *inter alia*, took no little interest in Lachmann's researches on the New Testament. Lachmann finally produced his *editio maior* of the New Testament in partnership with

Philipp Buttmann, Jr., whose father had been, until his death in 1829, Lachmann's fellow member of the Graeca and the Gesetzlose Gesellschaft. Lachmann paid a final tribute of friendship to Buttmann, Sr., by producing the fourteenth edition of the latter's *Greek Grammar*, a famous school text. A particularly close relationship was that with Clemens August Carl Klenze, Professor of Jurisprudence at the University of Berlin. Lachmann had been his friend since their student days in Göttingen and, remaining a bachelor, lived as a member of his friend's household until Klenze's death in 1839. This connection with Klenze and with other jurists, such as Johann Friedrich Ludwig Göschen in Göttingen, led to Lachmann's intensive research on Roman legal texts, which produced, among other things, his work on Dositheus (1837) and his edition of Gaius. At Niebuhr's request, Lachmann took part in producing the series of Byzantine writers that Niebuhr had founded, and he brought out the edition of Genesius; again, his edition of the Roman land surveyors went back to a suggestion by Niebuhr.

In this manner Lachmann's contacts with scholars outside his own field often provided the impulse for his scholarly works. During his years in Berlin, these contacts led him especially into work on Latin texts of a historical and antiquarian nature, and Lachmann thereby took up a sort of middle ground in the methodological quarrel between August Böckh and Gottfried Hermann. Even before this, Lachmann had already experimented successfully with scholarly cooperation in his studies of Old and Middle High German poetry.

The methodological and theoretical content of Lachmann's scholarly work can be readily summarized in two expressions: the development of scientific textual criticism and the theory of epic.

His critical examination of ancient and medieval texts came to be called "the Lachmann method." This comprised *recensio*, carried out on scientific principles, i.e., the comparison of the various manuscripts of an author in order to construct the most reliable transmission of the text, by removing all errors, inconsistencies, and later interpolations. *Recensio* became thereafter the basic principle of textual criticism.

This method of critical study of texts on the basis of examining the manuscript transmission was long considered to be Lachmann's innovation; it was in fact a return to principles of textual study that had been advocated and practiced in the past, and a series of scholars took part in resurrecting it in the nineteenth century. Friedrich August Wolf had been the first to call for a return to textual study with the aid of the manuscripts, and scholars such as Karl Gottlob Zumpt, Johann Nicolai Madvig, and Friedrich Ritschl had a large share in its further development. Yet Lachmann's name deservedly remains associated with this renewal, particularly because of the unique energy and passion with which he insisted on returning to the manuscript tradition and sorting and then evaluating its components. As early as 1818, he criticized the neglect of the manuscripts in a review of Gottfried Hermann's edition of Sophocles' *Ajax* (in the Jena *Allgemeine Literatur-Zeitung*, 203 [November 1818] 249–250; reprinted in *Kleine Schriften* [Berlin 1876] 2:2–3.).

Lachmann stated his position yet more clearly twelve years later in his 1830 "Rechenschaft" on the small "stereotype" edition of the New Testament (*Theologische Studien und Kritiken* 3.2 [1830] 817–845; reprinted in *Kleine Schriften* 2:250–272). He called for a text that ceased to rely on the received text and was based instead on "what had really been transmitted." He declared that the philological criticism of the eighteenth century, "with the exception of the solitary and misunderstood figure of Bentley," had been "random and desultory." And, he added, the "mass of common critics" worked in this manner "even today."

Lachmann himself viewed his demands that attention be paid to the textual tradition as a return to principles of philological work that had previously been known and practiced. It was the prime task of *recensio* to establish the text as it had originally been transmitted, without any previous interpretation. In the foreword to his *editio maior* of the New Testament he wrote: "ex auctoribus, quod primo loco posui, id quod recensere dicitur, sine interpretatione et possumus et debemus."

Thus *recensio* laid the foundations for textual criticism by ascertaining and noting agreements and variants in the manuscript transmission. From this beginning one could draw conclusions about the connections and relationships between manuscripts and thus form judgments about errors, inconsistencies, and interpolations in individual passages of the text. *Recensio*, the first step in textual criticism, was followed by *emendatio*—the correction of errors and the restoration of the original text (*originem detegere*) as it had existed in the archetype of the manuscript transmission.

The text-critical work based on these fundamental principles stands at the center of Lachmann's researches. These researches are documented in the scholarly works he left behind, the overwhelming majority of which are editions of texts and discussions of text-critical problems. The Latin authors predominate, and by this preference Lachmann played an essential role in the renaissance of Latin philology in the nineteenth century.

Lachmann quite early (1816) published his first critical edition: the elegies of Propertius. In this edition the beginnings of his text-critical principles are already visible. He set his face against rash *emendatio* and the numerous transpositions and alterations of the text to which it led—though he did not, to be sure, completely avoid falling into the same snares himself, above all in his novel and rather willful division of the books. Yet Lachmann's work was a step forward in that he took as his basis the dependable Wolfenbüttel manuscript and consulted others, though only sporadically and as he saw fit.

After a period in which Lachmann devoted himself with renewed enthusiasm to Old and Middle High German texts, the late 1820s saw further editions of ancient authors, especially of Roman poets.

In 1829 his edition of Catullus appeared, which was unusual in that, contrary to his own principles, he did not go back to the original tradition of the oldest manuscript, the Codex Veronensis, but made do with Renaissance manuscripts. On the basis of these he posited a "line-number theory" and held that each page of the lost archetype of Catullus had contained thirty lines. This theory had great and lasting influence; indeed, Moriz Haupt, in his *Quaestiones Catullianae* (1837), tried to work it out in detail. But subsequent research was obliged to abandon the theory as erroneous.

In the same year Lachmann published editions of the Roman elegiac poets Tibullus and (in an *editio minor*) Propertius; these editions were the products of the continuation of earlier studies. As in the case of Propertius, the new edition of which was based on the results of the edition of 1816, Lachmann founded his work on Tibullus on the manuscript tradition. Although he did not succeed in selecting the best manuscripts of Tibullus, his edition was a considerable advance.

Only two years later followed his *editio minor* of the New Testament (1831), which, however, still leaned quite heavily on the unsatisfactory texts of previous editions. Nevertheless, the new tendency in textual criticism can be detected here as well, especially since, in the above-mentioned (p. 251) essay, "Rechenschaft," Lachmann made fundamental observations on the investigation and significance of the manuscript tradition.

The *editio minor* was for Lachmann only the preliminary result of long years of research. Over a decade later (1842) the first volume of his *editio maior* appeared, and the second volume followed eight more years later (1850). The fundamental principle of his New Testament criticism was the abandonment of the *textus receptus*, the text that had been put together, quite arbitrarily, by Robertus Stephanus and the Elzeviers and that had already been sharply criticized by Richard Bentley. Lachmann's goal was to restore the text of the New Testament as it had existed at the end of the fourth century. His great two-volume edition was an enormous step forward, despite the small number of manuscripts he was able to use.

Besides his edition of the New Testament, he produced in these years a series of other editions, some of them of obscure authors. To a large degree they share the characteristic that the editor was able to make use of only one manuscript for each edition; thus, *recensio* was not possible, and the establishment of the text had to begin with *emendatio*. This was true of the edition (1834) of Genesius' history of the Byzantine emperors, which existed only in a single Leipzig manuscript, and also of the grammatical textbook of Terentianus Maurus (1836); Lachmann based his edition of the latter on Georgio Galbiati's *editio princeps*, which had, in turn, been based on a unique manuscript found in Bobbio and then lost again. It was true as well of the *Institutiones* of Gaius, which are preserved only in a single Verona palimpsest discovered by Niebuhr in 1836. Similarly, a unique manuscript, which had been discovered in a monastery on Mt. Athos, served Lachmann as the basis for his edition (1845) of Babrius, which he produced in conjunction with August Meineke.

His work on Babrius led him to Avianus (1845), another poet of fables. In this case a wealth of manuscripts was available; Lachmann did indeed make use of them, but his handling of the textual transmission was too simplistic, and so the value of the edition, according to S. Timpanaro, resides only in a few good conjectures. The case is quite different in his editions of the Roman land surveyors (1848–52), which he produced together with Friedrich Blume and Adolf Rudorff. Here Lachmann followed the oldest textual tradition to establish the text. His work has not yet been superseded, since the edition begun by Karl Thulin has not been completed.

The high point of Lachmann's text-critical research in classical philology was reached in his studies on Lucretius; these were both his last and his most extensive labors. The edition of the text appeared first (1850); it was followed immediately in the same year by the great commentary. It was in his edition of Lucretius that Lachmann first fully carried through his principle of tracing the textual transmission back to the archetype. In the commentary, his long years of textual study enabled him to trace parallels and echoes in details and to evaluate individual readings—observations that proved to be methodologically paradigmatic. Wilamowitz (*Geschichte der Philologie*; 59) characterized the work in a remark valid for his generation: "From it we have all learned text-critical method." Lachmann's commentary on Lucretius is still held to be an epoch-making masterpiece; though superseded in many respects, it still remains a basic and indispensable resource for classical philology, not only for text-critical method but also for many individual questions of language and meter.

One of Lachmann's most significant accomplishments was his application of the text-critical method of classical philology to Old and Middle High German texts. Here too his progress was not solitary; rather, scientific textual criticism in this area developed into a securely based and systematic method through the labors of four scholars working together: Georg Friedrich Benecke (1762–1844), Jacob Grimm (1785–1863), Wilhelm Grimm (1786–1859), and Lachmann. Their joint researches began long before Lachmann took his lifetime position at the University of Berlin.

In contrast to classical philology, the textual study of Old and Middle High German poetry required preliminary labors. The problem was that the existing editions were based on manuscripts that did not precisely reproduce the language of the authors. Systematically established and strictly observed grammatical and metrical rules did not exist. But such rules had to be the foundation for judging the variant readings, and a comparison and evaluation of these would result in understanding of the genealogical relationships within the manuscript transmission and—the ultimate aim—the establishment of the original text.

Benecke began these preliminary studies, and Lachmann carried on the work by collecting and examining the relevant materials. Through linguistic analysis he recognized the importance of rhymes, which provided insight into accentuation, meter, grammar, orthography, and the linguistic evolution of phonemes. Consequently, he used all available sources to construct an extensive inventory of rhymes as a tool in his researches.

Similarly, he spent years in the study of meter. As the starting point for his researches into Middle High German meter he selected the Old High German Gospel Book of Otfried von Weissenburg, since the textual transmission of this work was relatively pure. Lachmann's extended treatise "Zur althochdeutschen Prosodie und Verskunst," analyzing Otfried's Gospel Book with Jacob Grimm (to whom Lachmann had sent the manuscript in 1824, and who supplied notes, additions, and corrections), remained unpublished. Nonetheless, it laid the foundation for Lachmann's first systematic studies, and provided a basis for his edition of Wolfram von Eschenbach. Despite considerable criticism aimed at the rules he had established, the extensive collection of material that supported these rules made him an authority in this field, and his accomplishment is still acknowledged today.

Lachmann likewise produced significant preliminary work in the area of grammar, but as early as 1819 the appearance of the first volume of Jacob Grimm's German grammar put into his hands a fundamental tool for his researches that made his own systematic studies superfluous. He nevertheless continued to deal with grammatical questions within the framework of his own researches, and he shared his results with Grimm.

After these preliminary studies the ground was prepared for editing works of literature. Beginning in 1825, Lachmann produced a series of editions, one after another. He began with a volume of Old High German selections: *Specimina Linguae Francicae*. In 1826 came the edition of *Der Nibelunge Noth und die Klage*, the poetical work to which he had devoted special attention for more than decade. Here he divided the manuscript transmission into three chief manuscripts (a division still accepted today): "A" (Hohenems/München), "B" (St. Gallen), and "C" (Hohenems/Donaueschingen). His own edition of the text he based on "A," which, in his view, came closest to the original text. In so doing Lachmann deviated from the principle he had himself laid down in 1817 (in the Jena *Allgemeine Literatur-Zeitung*, nos. 132–135; reprinted in *Kleine Schriften* 1:81–114)—namely, to use the existing manuscript tradition to restore the original text or at least a text that closely approached the original, and in his edition he restricted himself to removing scribal errors and blunders and to establishing a consistent orthography.

His edition of the *Nibelungenlied* was followed by editions of other Middle High German poets: Hartmann von Aue, *Iwein* (in conjunction with Benecke, 1827; 2d ed., 1843); the poems of Walther von der Vogelweide (1827; 2d ed., 1843); the works of Wolfram von Eschenbach (1837); Hartmann von Aue, *Gregorius* (1838); Ulrich von Lichtenstein (with notes by Theodor von Karajan, 1841); and an anthology (edited posthumously by Moriz Haupt) of the Middle High German Minnesänger: *Minnesangs Frühling* (1857). He also produced a series of articles and book reviews, which are collected in the first volume of the *Kleine Schriften*.

Lachmann's editions of Middle High German poetry were regarded in their day as masterpieces. Yet they also provoked criticism, especially inasmuch as he did not consistently abide by the principles of textual editing that he had himself established—the restoration of the original text or a close approximation to it. He was also criticized for positing a single fixed archetype at the beginning of a given textual transmission and for basing his editions on a single manuscript—conditions that, in the case of medieval poetry, cannot necessarily be assumed and that, in the case of the *Nibelungenlied*, do not obtain. Despite these too one-sided and (in the modern view) partially false ideas about the genesis and transmission of a text, still, many of his editions of medieval poets have continued to be republished and are in use at the present time. This is true of the *Iwein* and the *Gregorius* of Hartmann von Aue, the poems of Walther von der Vogelweide, and the works of Wolfram von Eschenbach and Ulrich von Lichtenstein.

Lachmann broke completely new ground in his attempt to apply the methods he had developed for the textual criticism of ancient and medieval authors to works of modern German literature, as he did in his edition of Lessing. Although Lachmann could not take into account in his edition the possibilities of autograph, or at least authorized, transmission and thus disregarded essential factors in the textual criticism of modern authors, nevertheless his edition was the first step on the way to scientific textual criticism in this field. Moreover, certain of his principles, such as printing the works in the order of their original publication, are followed to this day.

The powerful influence exerted by Lachmann's text-critical method was virtually equalled by that of his theory of epic, which he developed first for the *Nibelungenlied* and then for the *Iliad*. Lachmann took as his starting point the revolutionary theses of Friedrich August Wolf: that the Homeric epics had originated in a preliterate period, had been composed in the memory, had been transmitted orally, and had received their fixed form only centuries later. The unity of Homer was thus called into question.

Lachmann took up Wolf's theory of the multiple authorship of the Homeric epics and applied it in a modified form to the *Nibelungenlied* in the above-mentioned 1816 treatise *Über die ursprüngliche Gestalt des Gedichts von der Nibelungen Noth*. The novelty in Lachmann's use of Wolf's ideas was that, unlike Wolf, he did not base his discussion on external evidence about the poem's genesis; rather, he detected and analyzed omissions and contradictions in the poetry itself. Such inconcinnities could not go back to the poet himself; Lachmann maintained, therefore, that they were proof that inept adaptors had been at work. According to Lachmann's investigations, the text consisted of "a still visible union of individual ballad-like lays" ("romanzenhafter Lieder"). Lachmann posited twenty of these lays; they had arisen as folksongs in the period 1190–1220 and could still be detected by certain formal, especially metrical, criteria. According to Lachmann, these individual lays had been arranged and suitably joined together by a later "Diaskeuast."

Having first dissected the *Nibelungenlied* into individual lays, Lachmann returned years later to the starting point provided by Wolf: the question of the origin of the *Iliad*. In a study delivered in two parts before the Berlin Academy of Science in 1837 and 1841 (published in 1847 as a single work, *Betrachtungen über Homers Ilias*, with additions by Moriz Haupt), he sought to trace in the epic as we have it inconsistencies, gaps, and seams, and he came to the conclusion that the *Iliad* in its present form consisted of sixteen individual lays, which, even after the redaction under Peisistratus, could still be detected.

Lachmann's analysis of epic poetry, based on Wolf, was closely connected with the thought and feeling of the age. His conception of a poem evolving through the creative energies of the "Volksgeist" was especially influenced by Romanticism.

Lachmann's theory of epic had great influence. There was agreement but also—especially in regard to his dissection of the *Iliad*—passionate rejection. Even such a man as Jacob Grimm, with whom Lachmann worked closely in his studies of medieval poetry, did not accept his analysis of Homeric epic. In the subsequent course of the discussion set in motion by Lachmann, scholars moved further and further away from his ideas—ideas that did not, any more than did the strictly Unitarian position, lead to any ultimate solution.

Nevertheless, the immense influence of Lachmann made itself fully felt only after his death, especially in the predominant position taken thereafter by a philology that restricted itself exclusively to textual researches. The study of artifacts, as practiced by August Böckh and Karl Otfried Müller, was relegated to the background. An essential role in this process, and in the exaltation of Lachmann to his outstanding position, was played by Moriz Haupt, his friend and successor in the Berlin professorship, who displayed admirable devotion in disseminating, expanding, and passionately defending his master's teachings. Haupt agreed with Lachmann in his philological methodology as well as in uniting classical and Germanic philology. This is apparent in the fact that he followed through to press new editions of many of Lachmann's works.

Among Lachmann's successors in Germanic philology, especially deserving of mention is Karl Müllenhoff, who in 1864 became Professor of Older German Philology at the University of Berlin and used Lachmann's methods in his work in this field.

In his *Grundriss der klassischen Philologie*, Alfred Gudeman introduced the section on Lachmann with the words, "One of the greatest textual critics of all time." This judgment, formulated before the turn of the century, was still completely under the influence Lachmann exercised in the second half of the nineteenth century. With the revival of universal-historical *Altertumswissenschaft*—a revival connected with the names of Mommsen and Wilamowitz—textual philology lost its predominant position and became only one branch of a science that aimed at the investigation of classical antiquity in all its aspects. Lachmann thus retreated somewhat into the background, though his accomplishments were never depreciated. Some even gave him historical credit for the fact that the formerly opposed tendencies of Böckh and Gottfried Hermann did come together. In modern discussion, too, Lachmann's significance is undisputed; this is true not only in classical philology but also in older Germanic philology. Thus Karl Lachmann deservedly lives on as one of the heroes in the history of both disciplines.

Translated by Michael Armstrong

Books

Observationum criticarum capita tria. Göttingen, 1815.
Sex. Aurelii Propertii carmina emendavit et ad codd. meliorum fidem et annotavit Carolus Lachmann. Leipzig, 1816.
Über die ursprüngliche Gestalt des Gedichts von der Nibelungen Noth. Berlin, 1816.
Sagenbibliothek des Skandinavischen Alterthums in Auszügen, mit litterarischen

Nachweisungen von Peter Erasmus Müller. Translated from the Danish by Lachmann. Berlin, 1816.

De choricis systematis tragicorum Graecorum. Berlin, 1819.

Shakespeare's Sonnette. Translated by Lachmann. Berlin, 1820.

Auswahl aus den Hochdeutschen Dichtern des dreizehnten Jahrhunderts. Königsberg, 1820.

De mensura tragoediarum. Berlin, 1822.

Specimina linguae Francicae. Berlin, 1825.

Der Nibelunge Noth und die Klage. Berlin, 1826; 2d ed., 1841; 3d ed., 1851; 5th ed., 1878.

Hartmann von Aue. Iwein. Notes by G. F. Benecke, Lachmann, and L. Wolff. Berlin, 1827; 2d ed., 1843; 7th ed. translated by Thomas Cramer. Berlin, 1981.

Die Gedichte Walthers von der Vogelweide. Berlin, 1827; 13th ed. edited by Hugo Kuhn, 1965.

Q. Valerii Catulli Veronensis. Berlin, 1829.

Albii Tibulli libri quattuor. Berlin, 1829.

Sex. Aurelii Propertii elegiae. Berlin, 1829.

Shakespeare's Macbeth. Translated by Lachmann. Berlin, 1829.

Novum Testamentum Graece. Berlin, 1831; 2d printing, 1837.

Wolfram von Eschenbach. Berlin, 1833; 6th ed. edited by Eduard Hartl, 1926; 7th printing, 1952.

Philipp Buttmann, Griechische Grammatik. Enlarged by Lachmann. Berlin, 1833.

Genesius. Bonn, 1834.

Zu den Nibelungen und zur Klage. Notes by Lachmann [Wörterbuch von Wilhelm Wackernagel]. Berlin, 1836.

Terentiani Mauri de litteris syllabis et metris liber. Berlin, 1836.

Versuch über Dositheus. Berlin, 1837.

Gotthold Ephraim Lessings sämmtliche Schriften. Edited by Lachmann. Vols. 1–13. Berlin, 1838–1840.

Gregorius, eine Erzählung von Hartmann von Aue. Edited by Lachmann. Berlin, 1838.

Zwanzig alte Lieder von den Nibelungen. Edited by Lachmann. Berlin, 1840.

Gaii institutionum Commentarii quattuor. Edited by J. F. L. Goeschenii, completed by Lachmann. Bonn, 1841.

Ulrich von Lichtenstein mit Anmerkungen von Theodor von Karajan. Edited by Lachmann. Berlin, 1841.

Novum Testamentum Graece et Latine. Edited by Lachmann and P. Buttmann. Vols. 1–2. Berlin, 1842–1850.

Babrii fabulae Aesopeae Carolus Lachmann et amici emendarunt ceterorum poetarum choliambi ab Augusto Meinekio collecti et emendati. Berlin, 1845.

Aviani fabulae. Berlin, 1845.

Betrachtungen über Homers Ilias. Edited by Lachmann with additions by M. Haupt. Berlin, 1847.

Die Schriften der römischen Feldmesser. Edited by F. Blume, Lachmann, A. Rudorff, et al. Vols. 1–2. Berlin, 1848–1852.

T. Lucretii Cari de rerum natura libri sex. Berlin, 1850.

Carolus Lachmann in T. Lucretii Cari de rerum natura libros commentarius. Berlin, 1850.

Minnesangs Frühling. Edited by Lachmann and M. Haupt. Leipzig, 1857; vol. 1, 38th ed., 1988; vol. 2, 36th ed., 1977; vol. 3, 30th ed., 1950.

Articles (Collected)

Kleinere Schriften. 2 vols. Vol. 1 (German philology), edited by K. Müllenhoff; Vol. 2 (classical philology), edited by J. Vahlen. Berlin, 1876. Vol. 1 reprinted 1969; vol. 2 reprinted 1974.

Sources

Bibliography

Kühnel, J. "Karl Lachmann," *NDB* 13 (Berlin, 1982) 371–374.

Scherer, Karl. "Karl Lachmann," *ADB* 17 (Leipzig, 1883) 471–481.

Biographical

Bornmann, J. "Sui criteri di 'recensio' meccanica enunciati dal Lachmann nel 1817." *Rivista di letterature moderne e comparate* 15 (1962) 46–53.

Ganz, P. F. "Lachmann as an Editor of Middle High German Texts" (1966). Reprinted in *Probleme mittelalterlicher Überlieferung und Textkritik.* Berlin, 1968: 12–30.

Grimm, J. "Erinnerungen an Lachmann" (1852) = *Kleinere Schriften* 7:604f.

Haupt, M. "De Lachmanno critico." *Neue Jahrbücher für das klassische Altertum, Geschichte und deutsche Literatur* 14 (1911) 529–538. (Written in 1854.)

Hennig, U. "Karl Lachmann." *Berlinische Lebensbilder Geisteswissenschaftler.* Edited by M. Erbe. Berlinische Lebensbilder 4. Berlin, 1989: 73–86.

Hertz, M. *Karl Lachmann.* Berlin, 1851; reprinted Osnabrück, 1972.

Leo, F. "Rede zur Säcularfeier Karl Lachmanns am 4. 3. 1893." *Ausgewählte Schriften.* Vol. 2: *Storia e letteratura* 83 (Rome, 1960) 415–431.

Lutz-Hensel, M. *Prinzipien der ersten textkritischen Editionen mittelhochdeutscher Dichtung, Brüder Grimm-Benecke-Lachmann. Eine methodenkritische Analyse.* Philologische Studien und Quellen 77. Berlin, 1975.

Neumann, F. "Karl Lachmanns 'Wolframsreise.' Eine Erinnerung an seine Königsberger Zeit." In *Wolfram von Eschenbach.* Edited by H. Rupp. *Wege der Forschung* 57. Darmstadt, 1966: 6–37. (Written in 1952.)

Pasquali, G. *Storia della tradizione e critica del testo.* Florence, 1952: 1–12.

Pfeiffer, R. *History of Classical Scholarship 1300–1850.* Oxford, 1976: 190.

Sparnaay, H. *Karl Lachmann als Germanist.* Bern, 1948.

Stackmann, K. "Die klassische Philologie und die Anfänge der Germanistik." In *Philologie und Hermeneutik im 19. Jahrhundert*. Edited by H. Flashar, K. Gründer, A. Horstmann. Göttingen, 1979: 240–259.

Timpanaro, S. *Le genesi del metodo del Lachmann*; new ed. revised and enlarged, Padua, 1981. German translation, Hamburg, 1971.

Wilamowitz–Moellendorff, Ulrich von. *Geschichte der Philologie*. 3d ed. Leipzig, 1927: 58–59 = Volume 1.1 of *Einleitung in die Altertumswissenschaft*. Edited by Gercke and Norden.

Eine Wissenschaft etabliert sich. 1810–1870. Edited with an introduction by J. Janota. Texte zur Wissenschaftsgeschichte der Germanistik 3. Tübingen, 1980.

Zacher, K. "Karl Lachmann." *Ersch und Grubers Allgemeine Encyklopädie* II.41 (Leipzig, 1887) 105–126.

Letters

Lachmann, K. *Briefe an Moriz Haupt*. Edited by J. Vahlen. Berlin, 1892.

Briefe an Karl Lachmann. Aus den Jahren 1814–50. Edited with notes by A. Leitzmann. *Abhandlungen der Königlich Preussischen Akademie der Wissenschaften, Philos.–hist. Klasse* 1915 (Berlin, 1915).

Lachmann, K. *Briefe*. Edited by A. Leitzmann. Vol. 1: To Georg Fr. Benecke. *Abhandlungen der Preussischen Akademie der Wissenschaften. Philos.–hist. Klasse* 1942 (Berlin, 1943).

Briefwechsel der Brüder Jacob und Wilhelm Grimm mit Karl Lachmann. Edited by A. Leitzmann, with an introduction by K. Burdach. Two vols. Jena, 1927.

J. N. Madvig
7 August 1804 – 12 December 1886

JØRGEN MEJER
University of Copenhagen

Johan Nicolai Madvig is beyond doubt the greatest Scandinavian Latinist and one of the most prominent Latin textual critics and grammarians of the nineteenth century. In addition, he played an important role in Danish politics and modernized the educational system in Denmark.

Madvig was born on the island of Bornholm in the Baltic Sea but spent most of his life in Copenhagen. When his father died in 1816, Madvig was sent to Frederiksbog Gymnasium, north of Copenhagen, with the support of private benefactors; from there he graduated in 1820 with honors; he studied classics at the University of Copenhagen from 1820 to 1825, won an M.A. in 1826, and got his doctorate in 1828; the same year he was appointed Reader of Latin. Nobody in the university was able to teach him much; he was mainly self-taught, though he gained much from a group of fellow students who also became respected scholars. In 1829 he married, and from 1829 to 1848 he was Professor of Latin; from 1851 to 1879, Professor of Classics at his alma mater. He was never a man of means and supplemented his income with various extra jobs, e.g., as librarian of the University library from 1833–1848. He worked hard and wrote university programs, often more than once a year, between 1829 and 1838, and frequently later (cf. his *Opuscula academica*), and published papers in the yearbook of the Royal Academy of Sciences and Letters, of which he became a member in 1833 (cf. *Kleine philologische Schriften* and *Sprachtheoretische Abhandlungen.*).

His early work is concentrated on textual emendation and editing of Cicero and other Latin authors. His doctoral dissertation on Asconius shows a remarkable knowledge of Latin and a firm grip on the principles of historical and philological methods; this book remained the best account of Asconius until recently. Madvig had a fine stylistic sense and a good ear for the rhythm of a Ciceronian sentence; over the next decade his understanding of the importance of the study of the interrelations of the manuscripts (*recensio*) grew, while he offered many improvements over Orelli to the text of Cicero. His criticism of contemporary and previous Latinists is fierce and direct, since he has no respect for anything but the evidence of the codices (the sixth volume of Baiter and Kayser's edition of Cicero is dedicated to Madvig, "Tullianorum criticorum princeps"). The core of his philological efforts remained conjectural criticism, and many of his emendations have later been confirmed by new manuscript readings. His masterwork in this period is his edition of the *De finibus*, in which he not only offered a text superior to all earlier editions but also provided a comprehensive commentary that demonstrated a thorough knowledge of Cicero's Greek sources. In the preface Madvig examines the manuscripts and lays down the principles of textual criticism. The editor is like a judge who must sort out the value of conflicting evidence and find the truth (cf. F. A. Wolf); he must first identify and explain errors in the text and establish by means of conjecture what the author could have said on the basis of the manuscripts, the meaning, and the style of the author. Madvig returned to these principles in his introduction to the *Adversaria Critica*.

The foundation of all philological scholarship is knowledge of the language, and it was only natural that Madvig should follow up his editorial work with his *Latin Grammar* (1841) and *Greek Syntax* (1846), the more so since he had very definite ideas about general linguistics (cf. *Sprachtheoretische Abhandlungen*). True to his historicism, Madvig dealt in both grammars with the languages only within a definite period (the period from Caesar and Cicero to the early first century A.D.). Both works clear up many problems that had remained unclear for centuries (e.g., about the particle ἄν), and they enjoyed great popularity in schools and among scholars for the rest of the century.

During the first twenty years of his career Madvig stayed within academia, where he became respected by both colleagues and students. The Scandinavian movement, the constitutional debate, and the problem with Schleswig-Holstein in the 1840s moved him to take a more active part in political life; in 1848 he became a member of the Constituent Assembly and from 1848 to 1851 he was Secretary of Education and Culture. After his resignation he returned to the university, but he was a member of Parliament until 1874; he was also Inspector General for the Danish educational system from 1852 to 1874; Vice President of the university several times, and from 1867 to 1886 President of the Academy of Sciences and Letters. Thus he was a prominent public figure; he wrote frequently in the papers about politics and education. He resumed his textual studies, and, with the help of his former student and now colleague, J. L. Ussing, he contributed as much to a better text of Livy as he had to that of Cicero. His many studies of Roman history and law culminated in his two volumes on the Roman constitution and administration (1881–1882), an admirable accomplishment in view of the fact that he was almost blind at the end of his life. As always, Madvig's approach is historical in the tradition of Niebuhr and thus anti-Mommsen: the Roman people and their history are inseparable from their institutions. Madvig has no general theory that must be imposed on the evidence, and he describes the changes and modifications in detail during the Republic and, more summarily, in the Empire. Over 1,100 pages long, this account presents all the evidence then available, and it remains a useful reference work. Madvig's last work, his memoirs, is an important description of intellectual and political life in Denmark in the nineteenth century.

Though textual criticism is Madvig's main contribution to classics, his strictly historical attitude toward the ancient Greco-Roman world, which he viewed with no Romantic idealism, was an important forerunner of the historicism of the late nineteenth century. The ancient world should be studied on the basis of the transmitted texts and monuments and was no more and no less than the foundation of the modern world. Historical knowledge is the basis of our understanding of our own culture, but the study of the ancient world is only valuable when inspired by the contemporary world. He had a firm grip on all the disciplines of classical philology, and he influenced more than one generation of Danish classicists, many of whom concentrated on textual criticism and editions, e. g., J. L. Heiberg (Greek mathematics and medicine), M. Cl. Gertz (Seneca, Medieval Latin), and K. Hude (Thucydides with scholia, Herodotus, Lysias, Xenophon, and Aretaeus).

Books

Epistula Critica ad Virum Celeberrimum Jo. Casp. Orellium de Orationum Verrinarum libris II extremis emendandis. Copenhagen, 1828.

De Q. Asconii Pediani et aliorum veterum interpretum in Ciceronis Orationes commentariis disputatio critica. Diss., Copenhagen, 1828.

M. Tullii Ciceronis Orationes selecta duodecim. Copenhagen, 1830; rev. eds. 1841, 1848, 1858, 1867, 1879, 1885, 1899, 1916.

Opuscula academica. Copenhagen, 1834; *Opuscula academica altera.* Copenhagen, 1842; *Opuscula academica. Ab ipso iterum collecta, emendata et aucta.* Copenhagen, 1887.

M. Tullii Ciceronis de finibus bonorum et malorum libri quinque. Copenhagen, 1839; 2d ed., 1869; 3d ed., 1876 (with important revisions); reprinted Darmstadt, 1963.

Latinsk Sprogløre til Skolebrug. Copenhagen, 1841; revised ed. 1844, 1852; revised and abridged 1862, 1867, 1878, 1882, 1889, 1897, 1907; syntax only 1895, reprinted 1962; German translation as *Lateinische Sprachlehre für Schulen* (Braunschweig, 1844); revised eds. 1847, 1851, 1857, 1867, 1868, abr. ed. 1877, 1884; Dutch translation as *Latijnsche spraakleer voor schoolen* (Amsterdam, 1846); revised eds. 1849, 1858, 1876, 1881; Greek translation 1846; English translation as *A Latin Grammar for the Use of the Schools* (Oxford, 1849); revised eds. 1849, 1851, 1856, 1859, 1863, 1878, 1889; Boston, 1870, 1871, 1873, 1875, 1880, 1892, 1902; Russian translation (Moscow, 1868) 1871; Italian translation as *Grammatica della lingua latina ad uso delle scuole* (Milan, 1867), abridged edition 1970, new translation (Turin, 1894); French translation as *Grammaire latine* (Paris, 1870, 1873, 1881); Portuguese translation as *Grammatica latina para uso das escholas* (Porto, 1872); abridged edition (Lisbon, 1887).

Græsk Ordføiningslære, især for den attiske Sprogform. Copenhagen, 1846; 2d ed.,
    1857; German translation as *Syntax der griechischen Sprache, besonders der
    attischen Sprachform, für Schulen* (Braunschweig, 1847); 2d ed., 1884, re-
    printed Copenhagen, 1968; English translation as *Syntax of the Greek
    Language* (London, 1853); revised editions 1867, 1873, 1880; French
    translation as *Syntaxe de la langue grecque principalement du dialecte attique*
    (Paris, 1884).

Emendationes Livianae. Copenhagen, 1860; 2d ed., 1877.

Titi Livii Historiarum Romanarum libri qui supersunt, Vols. 1–4. Ex recensione Jo. Nic.
    Madvigii ediderunt Jo. Nic. Madvigius et Jo. L. Ussing. Copenhagen,
    1861–1866; 2d ed. (1–2 only), 1872–1875.

Adversaria critica ad scriptores Græcos et Latinos, 1–2. Copenhagen, 1871–1872; vol.
    3: *Adversariorum criticorum ad scriptores graecos et latinos, novas emendationes
    graecas et latinas continens.* Copenhagen, 1884.

Kleine philologische Schriften. Vom Verfasser deutsch bearbeitet. Leipzig, 1875;
    reprinted Hildesheim, 1966.

Den romerske Stats Forfatning og Forvaltning 1–2. Copenhagen, 1881–1882; German
    translation as *Die Verfassung und Verwaltung des römischen Staates,* (Leipzig,
    1881–1882); French translation as *L'état romain, sa constitution et son
    administration* (Paris, 1882–1889).

Livserindringer. Copenhagen, 1887; *Supplementer til Liverindringer af J. N. Madvig.*
    Copenhagen, 1917. (Published by his son.)

Sprachtheoretische Abhandlungen. Edited by K. Friis Johansen under the supervision of
    F. Blatt and Povl Johs. Jensen. Copenhagen, 1971.

Sources

Gertz, M. Cl. [Obituary] BPhW 6 (1887) 189–192 and 7 (1887) 221–224.

Heiberg, J. L. [Obituary] *Biographisches Jahrbuch für Altertumskunde* 9 (1887)
    202–221.

Johan Nicolai Madvig, Et Mindeskrift, 1–2. Copenhagen, 1956. Comprehensive
    studies of Madvig's scholarly, political, and administrative accomplishments,
    by various authors. The section on Madvig as a classical scholar has been
    published separately in French (see next entry).

Jensen, Povl Johs. *J. N. Madvig, Avec une esquisse de l'histoire de la philologie classique
    au Danemark.* Odense, 1981.

Johansen, Karsten Friis. "Einleitung." In *J. N. Madvig Sprachtheoretische Abhand-
    lungen*: 1–46. (On Madvig's linguistic theories.)

Sandys, J. E. *A History of Classical Scholarship.* Cambridge, 1908 3:319–323.

Spang-Hanssen, E. *J. N. Madvig-Bibliografi.* Copenhagen, 1966; with Supplement,
    1971.

Letters

Spang-Hanssen, E. *Under Madvigs Auspicier. Danske Filologers Udvandring til Rusland
    1875, etc.* Studier fra Sprog-og Oldtidsforskning, no. 218 (Copenhagen,
    1952).

Eduard Meyer

25 January 1855 – 31 August 1930

CHRISTHARD HOFFMANN
Technische Universität Berlin

In the annals of ancient studies, the name of Eduard Meyer stands for the bold attempt of a single scholar to construct a comprehensive account of the history of the ancient world from its oriental beginnings down to Roman times, on the basis of his own independent study of the sources. Meyer's concept of a universal history of antiquity was not actually new; new was the intensity with which he succeeded in uniting a broad synchronistic view with the most exact research into details, thus bringing the history of Egypt and the Near East (including Israelite and Jewish history) into the ancient historian's range of vision. When Meyer died in 1930 it was clear to all scholars in his field that, because of the expanding wealth of material and because of the increasing specialization of research, no single historian would probably ever again be able to control so extensive a field of work.

The foundations of Meyer's universal lifework were laid in his parents' home and in school. The son of a scholarly preparatory-school teacher in Hamburg, he grew up in a cultivated atmosphere in which classical German poetry and ancient literature were central. At the age of twelve he wrote a tragedy in five acts: *Brutus oder die Ermordung Cäsars*; the play was inspired by Shakespeare, but its details were based on the author's own study of sources (chiefly Plutarch). The Johanneum in Hamburg—a school designed to educate scholars and at that time a center of research on Thucydides—gave the highly gifted pupil a philological training that was at university level. In particular, the director of the Johanneum, Johannes Classen, a student of Niebuhr, exerted a decisive influence on Meyer by making him familiar with Niebuhr's style of viewing ancient history from the perspective of universal history. While still at school Meyer learned, along with Greek and Latin, Hebrew and the basics of Arabic.

In his first semester, at the age of seventeen, he had his eyes firmly fixed on the goal of his studies. The history of antiquity interested him not because it was to serve as a model for modern civilization nor because of its classicism, but because it was "the first epoch in the evolution of the human spirit" (Hoffmann, *Calder-Demandt*). He sought in antiquity answers to the fundamental anthropological questions that had been raised since Darwin, of the descent and primitive history of man and of the origin of language, religion, culture, and morality. The young Meyer was persuaded that he could use positivistic methods of research to illuminate an area that had hitherto lain in the semiobscurity of religious or philosophical speculation. In conformity with his universalist anthropological approach, Meyer devoted himself during his university studies (one semester in Bonn, five semesters in Leipzig) almost exclusively to the ancient Orient as the earliest form of human civilization. With admirable tenacity and sense of purpose, he studied the most important oriental languages: Arabic, Persian, and Turkish with H. L. Fleischer and O. Loth, Sanskrit with the Indo-Europeanist E. Kuhn, and Egyptian with G. Ebers. He later added a knowledge of cuneiform inscriptions. In addition, he devoted himself—for the most part autodidactically—to studies in the history of languages and religions. The young student's appraisal of religion as "the most interesting part of the history of illusions" is entirely in the tradition of the rationalistic criticism of religion. He attended Christian worship services "as a cultural study" and grew indignant at the "hypocrisy, mendacity, and immorality that religion brought into the human race" (Hoffmann, *Juden und Judentum*: 136 n. 10).

At the early age of twenty he received his doctorate with a thesis directed by Ebers, on the Egyptian god Set-Typhon. Next, as a tutor to the children of the British general consul in Constantinople, Sir Philip Francis, Meyer had the opportunity in 1875–1876 to become acquainted with the Orient by personal observation. In his long wanderings through the city and by means of his contacts with European diplomats Meyer investigated political, social, and religious conditions in the Ottoman Empire, which had been weakened by serious crises. Longer excursions took him also to the ancient sites in Asia Minor, to Bithynia and Troy. As the product of this personal observation, he published in 1877 the short treatise *Geschichte von Troas*, in which he took a critical attitude toward Schliemann's hypotheses.

In 1879 Meyer habilitated in ancient history in Leipzig with a study on the history of Pontus, the foundations for which he had laid in a paper written while he was still a schoolboy. In the same year the twenty-four-year-old *Privatdozent* accepted a proposal from the publisher Cotta to write a *Handbuch* and textbook on ancient history. From now on, the *Geschichte des Altertums* (GdA) was his life's work. The five volumes of the first edition appeared between 1884 and 1902; they covered an expanse of time from the earliest days of Egypt to Philip of Macedon. Meyer modeled the basic plan of his work on the universal-historical conception of A. H. L. Heeren (*Handbuch der Geschichte der Staaten des Alterthums*, 1799), but in the execution of the plan Meyer conformed to the source-critical standards that since Heeren's time had become obligatory for the scholarly writing of history. Detailed chapters on sources and on chronology introduce each book of the history; political history stands in the foreground, but cultural, religious, and economic history is also dealt with. The most significant and generally acknowledged achievement of the GdA is that here the histories of the individual peoples are set free from their isolation and are integrated, on the basis of synchronistic treatment, into the totality of universal history. Thus the epochs of Menes and Hammurabi, of Moses, Homer, and Zoroaster, of Alexander the Great and the Roman empire all appear together as a necessary unity, and the unique characteristics of individual peoples, placed against a background of the universal tendencies and developments that influenced them all, can be portrayed with especial vividness.

Meyer's work was criticized chiefly on points of specialized research, in which the state of knowledge was being rapidly expanded by new excavations and discoveries, and Meyer sometimes passed over such problems with excessive self-assurance. Meyer's decided proclivity toward constructing analogies was also perceived as problematic by his contemporaries, as it is today. For example, to the Homeric and early archaic periods (ca. 1000–650 B.C.) Meyer had attached the name "Greek Middle Ages" in order to denote a specific level of cultural development, and he described Athenian society in the Periclean Age in terms of modern categories and perspectives ("agrarians vs. capitalists"). In his justified attempt to free Greek history from the classicizing aestheticism of an Ernst Curtius and to reveal its true conditions, Meyer emphasized too greatly the "modernity" of antiquity. Finally, objections were raised against the form of the work. Meyer wrote in a dry style that mingled general description and specialized investigation. The "Handbuch" form of the GdA, its division into paragraphs, and the extended discussion in the text of detailed problems, rather than in the footnotes, aimed chiefly at an audience of specialists and lessened the work's popularity among the general public. The judgment of Mommsen, who found the "Handbuch" form scarcely bearable in an historical work, is characteristic: "The narrare breaks down entirely in this book written capitulatim" (Mommsen und Wilamowitz, Briefwechsel 1872–1903, Berlin, 1935: 485–86).

In this same period further important works took shape in connection with the GdA—some as preliminary studies, some as supplements. The Geschichte des alten Ägyptens (1887) was a decisive advance in comparison with previous works, because it went beyond merely enumerating the deeds of particular pharaohs or listing cultural-historical facts and in addition furnished a lively picture of the different epochs of Egyptian history in their historical development.

Meyer's study Die Entstehung des Judenthums (1896) caused a sensation. Here he maintained that the Persian decrees transmitted in Ezra 4–7 are largely genuine; he defended them against the hypercritical objections of contemporary Biblical scholarship and emphasized the decisive importance of Persian religious policies for the growth of postexilic Judaism. Meyer's study brought on a sharp controversy with the grand old man of Protestant Biblical scholarship, Julius Wellhausen, in Göttingen. The ostensible point of dispute was the criticism and use of sources, but more important were the two scholars' differing approaches to the study of Jewish history.

Whereas Wellhausen sought to understand the history of Israel and of Judaism from itself alone and stressed its internal development, Meyer strongly emphasized the external influences that were exerted on the Jewish people by the surrounding oriental nations. On the question of authenticity, scholarship has largely supported Meyer's view (Parente, *Calder-Demandt*). The fragmentary decree of Darius II from the year 419 B.C., discovered among the Elephantine papyri ten years after Meyer's investigation was published, in which the rite of the feast of unleavened bread is made binding on the whole Persian Empire, provided brilliant confirmation of Meyer's main thesis (cf. *Der Papyrusfund von Elephantine*, 1912: 95).

In close connection with the GdA he also published the two volumes of *Forschungen zur alten Geschichte* (1892 and 1899) in which individual problems in Greek history—from the Pelasgians and Lycurgus of Sparta to the history of Attic finances in the fifth century B.C. to the historical works of Herodotus and Thucydides—were subjected to intensive analysis.

Meyer also took part in two important debates within German historiography at the turn of the century. Characteristically, his expressions were more edged and polemical than calm and judicious. In the question as to how economic conditions in antiquity were to be fundamentally evaluated, Meyer (as well as K. J. Beloch) stubbornly opposed the thesis defended by the Leipzig national economist K. Bücher—and before him by J. K. Rodbertus—that autonomous household economies (*Oikenwirtschaft*) had been the predominant economic entity in the ancient world. Meyer, on the other hand, sought by numerous isolated examples to support his contention that the ancient economy was already familiar with well-developed trade, commerce, money economies—even "factories," "division of labor," and "big business" (*Die wirtschaftliche Entwickelung des Altertums*, 1895). Meyer saw a direct parallel between economic development in archaic and classical Greece on the one hand, and early modern Europe on the other; he emphasized that one's view of economic conditions in certain epochs of antiquity (e.g., in Hellenistic times) "cannot be modern enough" (*Kleine Schriften*, 1:141). In opposition to the evolutionist interpretation of ancient economic history, Meyer proposed a cyclical model, according to which economic development proceeds in circular fashion from rather primitive beginnings through highly developed forms of money economy and mobilized labor forces, returning to a natural economy and serfdom at the end of ancient times. The course of the "Bücher-Meyer controversy" was unfortunate in that it led to no more far-reaching scholarly discussion between the two opponents—e.g., on the fundamental problem of applying modern economic theories to the history of the ancient economy or on the differentiation between the too-rigid alternatives of "ancient" and "modern." Meyer's unusually brusque rejection of Bücher's views was largely to blame for this (Schneider, *Calder-Demandt*; on Max Weber's criticisms cf. Deininger, *Ibid.*).

Meyer's treatise *Zur Theorie und Methodik der Geschichte* (1902) was also primarily a polemical attack on contemporary theories—those of Karl Lamprecht and Kurt Breysig, among others—that held that the goal of historical study was analogous to that of the natural sciences and consisted of discovering laws and constructing general models. Meyer maintained that defining historical research as a "science of laws" was utterly mistaken. "History is no systematic science," reads the very first sentence of his treatise, and in support of this proposition he cites the "enormous" importance of chance, of "free will," and of the "power of ideas," which *a priori* exclude any "obedience to law" in the historical process. To Meyer the objective of historiography was not to depict "mass phenomena" or "typical" conditions but to investigate and portray the "individual" event (29). He saw the significance of a historical phenomenon solely in the influence it exerted. "That is historical which is or has been influential" (36). Consequently the historian in his work must start from the historical effect and proceed thence to its causes. The subjective element inherent in this procedure was, in Meyer's view, inescapable. "At all times we can arrive at nothing but our own understanding of history, never an absolute and unconditionally valid understanding" (45). Max Weber, in his *Kritische Studien auf dem Gebiet der kulturwissenschaftlichen Logik* (1906), subjected Meyer's thoughts on the theory of historiography to extensive and suggestive criticism (Deininger, *Calder-Demandt*).

As his scholarly *oeuvre* increased, Meyer's reputation in the academic world grew. His career took him to Breslau (1885) and Halle (1889), and in 1902 he was called to the University of Berlin, after he had declined invitations from universities outside Prussia (1887 to Tübingen, 1900 to Munich). He taught in Berlin, as a colleague of Otto Hirschfeld, Hermann Diels, and Ulrich von Wilamowitz-Moellendorff, until his retirement in 1923. In contrast to Wilamowitz's concept of a universal *Altertumswissenschaft* that united the fields of classical philology and ancient history in the Institut für Altertumskunde, Meyer always stressed that ancient history, because of the questions that it posed and the methods that it employed, belonged rather to the general field of history and at best ought to be connected with classical philology for purely pragmatic reasons (e.g., a common library). (On the difference between the views of Wilamowitz and Meyer, see Calder, *Calder-Demandt*.) During his years at Berlin, Meyer's academic influence grew as he became a member of the Akademie der Wissenschaften, the Deutsche Orientgesellschaft, the board of directors of the Deutsches Archäologisches Institut, and later the Notgemeinschaft Deutscher Wissenschaft as well. Nevertheless, his scholarly productivity suffered no ill effects because of his new duties nor because of social obligations, which in Berlin, the capital, were much more numerous than in Breslau or Halle. A series of specialized studies from this period deserves mention: *Ägyptische Chronologie* (1904), *Die Israeliten und ihre Nachbarstämme* (1906), *Theopomps Hellenika* (1909), and *Der Papyrusfund von Elephantine* (1912).

In Berlin Meyer also continued to work on the GdA, but he did not, as many readers had hoped, bring the work down to Hellenistic and Roman times. Rather, he undertook a fundamental revision of the first volume. This had become necessary because the scholarly picture of the eastern Mediterranean world and the Near East in the third and second millennia B.C. had been fundamentally altered since the appearance of the first edition by archaeological discoveries and the growth of knowledge. The first volume appeared in reworked form in 1909 (in final form in 1913); it contains, in a scant thousand pages, the history of the Near Eastern and Mediterranean world down to the sixteenth century B.C. Meyer had prefaced the volume with a half-volume methodological introduction to historiography in general and to prehistory and early history in particular (*Elemente der Anthropologie*, 1907). This book—a remarkable production for a historian—documents Meyer's intensive preoccupation, dating from his student days, with questions of anthropology, ethnology, and the comparative study of religions. But aside from its impressive display of the author's knowledge of the subjects, it also exhibits doctrinaire traits—for example, in the exaggerated thesis, which goes back to Aristotle, that the state, as the pre-condition for all human development, "is in its origin older than the human race" (11) or in the "consistent style of imperturbable certainty" with which Meyer sets forth his pronouncements, whether they are based on his own investigations or are taken at second hand or are founded simply on common knowledge (Nippel, *Calder-Demandt*).

In 1904 Meyer was guest professor at the University of Chicago and in 1909–1910 exchange professor at Harvard University. He was quite enthusiastically received by the American scholarly community. Americans called him "the most eminent living historian" (Chambers, *Calder-Demandt*). He got to know the country as he traveled about on extended lecture tours. His stay in America was also productive in a scholarly sense; in 1912 appeared his book *Ursprung und Geschichte der Mormonen*. The ancient historian Meyer found the origin and history of the Mormons of interest, because he hoped to gain insights, by means of the concept of historical analogy, into comparable phenomena in the history of ancient religions, particularly the rise of the prophetic religions Christianity and Islam (Henrichs, *Calder-Demandt*).

The First World War brought about a harsh break in Meyer's life of scholarship. Convinced that the Allies had forced the war on Germany and especially aggrieved by England's entry into the war, he set aside work on the GdA and concentrated on lectures, manifestos, memorials, and pamphlets for "the cause of the Fatherland" (Fischer; Söseman, *Calder-Demandt*). Hitherto Meyer had taken hardly any part in politics, but in the course of the war he increasingly became the convinced champion of expansionist war aims and the embittered critic of the moderate policies of Bethmann Hollweg, especially on the question of submarine warfare. He attributed plans for world domination to England and saw in her Germany's chief opponent; his war writings thus document his attempt "to ideologize the war between Germany and England into a fundamental spiritual and cultural struggle" (Lehmann, 278). Meyer's outlook while he was engaged in his political and publicistic activities was basically pessimistic. The outbreak of the war was for him the end of the modern European world, which had been characterized by fruitful competition and mutual respect between the nations. For the future he now expected the irresistible decline of European civilization, analogous to the "fall" of the ancient world that followed Rome's seizure of unopposed domination throughout the Mediterranean world (on this analogy of Meyer's see Ungern-Sternberg, *Calder-Demandt*). To Meyer, who had been sixteen years old when the German empire was founded and who was always a loyal supporter of the monarchy, Germany's military collapse and the revolution of

1918–1919 was a catastrophe in which he saw the signs of the political, intellectual, and moral collapse of the German people. He rejected the parliamentary democracy of the Weimar Republic, even though he was aware that the monarchy, once toppled, could never again be reestablished. But Meyer looked on parliamentarianism, democracy, and political parties as evils which the victorious powers had imposed on Germany in order to weaken her. As Rector of the University of Berlin, Meyer worked against the existing order, most notably in the Kapp-Lüttwitz *putsch*, in which he was involved, though tangentially. As a protest against the "surrender of war criminals" demanded by the Versailles treaty, Meyer organized a proclamation at the German universities, and he announced publicly that he had torn to pieces the honorary degrees that English and American universities had conferred upon him.

After his turbulent year as Rector, Meyer withdrew more and more from politics. But even in these years of energetic public labors he found the energy for scholarly work. In the spring of 1918 he published the monograph *Cäsars Monarchie und das Principat des Pompeius*. Roman internal policy in the period of transition from Republic to dictatorship to principate was among the subjects that Meyer was able to "really understand" during the years of the World War. Consciously distancing himself from Mommsen and his idealized picture of Caesar, Meyer traced the struggles for power in the late Republic back to a rivalry between three conceptions of the Roman state: the old Republic in the form of senatorial rule, the "absolute monarchy" of Caesar, and the military and political leadership of the state by the Senate's "trusted minister without portfolio," the *princeps*. Pompey, Meyer maintained, had already aimed at the third solution, and thus (the book's central thesis) the "principate of Pompey" was Augustus' model. This equation of Pompey's position, which was based solely on force, and the specific form of Augustus' personal rule, which evolved in the course of a long reign, has generally been rejected by the scholarly world as exaggerated (cf. Stahlmann, *Imperator Caesar Augustus*, 87).

Meyer was also the first to apply the approach and the methods of the ancient historian to the history of Christian origins (*Ursprung und Anfänge des Christentums* I–III, 1921–23). In contradistinction to theological literary criticism of the New Testament, Meyer underscored the relative trustworthiness of the tradition. He believed that one could derive from the Gospel of Mark and the subsequent traditions a dependable picture of the historical Jesus and his goals. In his treatment of the history of Christianity, which also dealt in detail with the evolution of Judaism, Meyer laid stress on the Jewish roots of Jesus' teaching. "Jesus' religious world-view was entirely that of the Pharisees" (II, 245). In his conception of the binding nature of the ritual law, however, Jesus transcended Pharisaism and established a religious ethic that Meyer (here gazing through Kantian lenses) regarded as the high point in the human race's moral development. But toward Christianity Meyer was clearly more critical. He rejected the views of other scholars—e.g., that of Bossuet or Reitzenstein, who emphasized Hellenistic influences on Christianity—and pointed to the popular and mythical character of Christian practices, which had nothing in common with the "Hellenistic Enlightenment." In Meyer's opinion the spread of Christianity was an essential factor in the increasing "Orientalization" of the Western world. Meyer received an honorary doctorate from the theological faculty at Berlin for his three-volume work, but all the same his history of Christianity was criticized, especially by professional theologians. Meyer's analysis of sources was regarded as a step backward in comparison with the contemporary state of New Testament research, because he ignored the question of the synoptic gospels' intentions in their portrayal of Jesus and the influence they aimed to exert on their readers. "For him [Meyer] criticism still means: to reduce the tradition as it stands, by means of operative abridgements, to history, whereas it is far more to the point to recognize the process that is frozen in the tradition" (von Soden: 433). This negative judgment is still current today among theologians (Plümacher, *Calder-Demandt*). But historians judge Meyer's book more positively. Victor Ehrenberg ranks it among the "great creative works" (Ehrenberg: 506), and Momigliano prophesied "that in a not very distant day ancient historians and theologians will make a pilgrimage to the tomb of Eduard Meyer, whom nowadays nobody quotes any longer. He remains after all the only historian of this century who succeeded in producing (*inter alia*) a diptych, however crude, of pre-rabbinic Judaism and New Testament Christianity" (*Sesto Contributo* 2:778).

After his retirement in 1923, Meyer once more devoted himself entirely to the GdA and before the end of his life he was almost able to complete the revision of the second volume, down to the golden age of the new Assyrian empire in the eighth century B.C. After Meyer's death in 1930 the remaining volumes were reworked and republished by Meyer's student Hans Erich Stier, who used Meyer's notes and specialized studies. Nonetheless one must admit that Meyer's monumental universal history of antiquity remained, in the end, a torso.

Meyer's influence as a teacher was incomparably less than that of, e.g., Mommsen. Of the approximately thirty-five doctoral candidates who wrote their dissertations under Meyer only two (Ulrich Kahrstedt and Hans Erich Stier) became professors of ancient history. Arthur Rosenberg was also among the inner circle of Meyer's students. Toward his students Meyer was a tolerant teacher and (in contrast to his attitude in politics) by no means doctrinaire. He did not have the ambition to lead a "school"; rather, he let his students go their own ways in scholarship, just as he had autodidactically found his own way to the universal history of antiquity. Meyer was no great speaker; he influenced his students chiefly through his lively seminars and by his open and friendly nature and his legendary booming laugh.

As for the effectiveness of Meyer's life work, he chiefly influenced the conceptions and the content of the works of those historians who also took the universal-historical approach, e.g., Max Weber, Oswald Spengler (whose *Untergang des Abendlandes* Meyer reviewed critically but quite positively), or Arnold Toynbee. In the study of ancient history Meyer's universalism remained an outstanding and isolated phenomenon, but his insistence that all real historical research must proceed from the universal point of view certainly found imitators (Toynbee). The modern reader is impressed by the total mass of Meyer's scholarly work, which comprises over five hundred titles. To be sure, specialized research has superseded much of it, Meyer's style is bare of ornament and inclines toward stereotypical formulae, his conceptualization is sometimes inappropriately modernizing, his judgments are always a bit too unequivocal, and his appraisals are not seldom distorted by contemporary attitudes and polemical exaggerations. Nevertheless, because of the breadth of his historical perspective, because of his capacity to make the universal visible in and through the particular, and not least because of his insistence on adhering closely to the sources, Meyer's great works continually repay rereading.

Translated by Michael Armstrong

Books

(For complete list see bibliography.)

Set-Typhon. Eine religionsgeschichtliche Studie. Leipzig, 1875.

Geschichte von Troas. Leipzig, 1877.

Geschichte des Königreiches Pontos. Leipzig, 1879.

Geschichte des Altertums. Vol. 1: *Geschichte des Orients bis zur Begründung des Perserreichs.* Stuttgart, 1884; 2d ed. in two parts: Vol. 1.1: *Einleitung. Elemente der Anthropologie.* Stuttgart and Berlin, 1907; 7th ed., 1965. Vol. 1.2: *Die ältesten geschichtlichen Völker und Kulturen bis zum sechzehnten Jahrhundert.* Stuttgart and Berlin, 1909; 8th ed., 1965. Supplement to the first volume: *Die ältere Chronologie Babyloniens, Assyriens und Ägyptens.* Stuttgart and Berlin, 1925; 2d ed. [revised], ed. Hans Erich Stier. Stuttgart and Berlin, 1931.

Geschichte des alten Ägyptens. Berlin, 1887; Italian edition, Milan, 1895; 1896; 1897.

Forschungen zur alten Geschichte. Vol. 1: *Zur älteren griechischen Geschichte.* Halle, 1892.

Geschichte des Altertums. Vol. 2: *Geschichte des Abendlandes bis auf die Perserkriege.* Stuttgart, 1893. 2d ed. completely revised in two parts: Vol. 2.1: *Die Zeit der ägyptischen Großmacht.* Stuttgart and Berlin, 1928; Vol. 2.2: *Der Orient vom zwölften bis zur Mitte des achten Jahrhunderts.* Edited from the *Nachlaß* by Hans Erich Stier. Stuttgart and Berlin, 1931; 4th ed., 1965.

Die wirtschaftliche Entwickelung des Altertums. Jena, 1895.

Die Entstehung des Judenthums. Eine historische Untersuchung. Halle, 1896; reprinted Hildesheim, 1965.

Die Sklaverei im Altertum. Dresden, 1898.

Forschungen zur alten Geschichte. Vol. 2: *Zur Geschichte des fünften Jahrhunderts vor Christ.* Halle, 1899.

Geschichte des Altertums. Vol. 3: *Das Perserreich und die Griechen. Bis zu den Friedensschlüssen von 448 und 446 vor Christ.* Stuttgart, 1901; 2d ed. completely revised: *Der Ausgang der altorientalistischen Geschichte und der Aufstieg des Abendlandes bis zu den Perserkriegen.* Edited by Hans Erich Stier. Stuttgart, 1937; 4th ed., 1965.

Geschichte des Altertums. Vol. 4: *Das Perserreich und die Griechen. Athen vom Frieden von 446 bis zur Capitulation Athens im Jahre 404 vor Christ.* Stuttgart, 1901; 3d ed. in two parts: Vol. 4.1: *Das Perserreich und die Griechen bis zum Vor-*

abend des Peloponnesischen Krieges. Edited by Hans Erich Stier. Stuttgart, 1939; Vol. 4.2: Der Ausgang der griechischen Geschichte. Edited by Hans Erich Stier; 5th ed., 1965.

Geschichte des Altertums. Vol. 5: Das Perserreich und die Griechen. Fourth Book: Der Ausgang der griechischen Geschichte. Stuttgart and Berlin, 1902; 5th ed., 1969.

Zur Theorie und Methodik der Geschichte. Geschichtsphilosophische Untersuchungen. Halle, 1902; Russian edition, Moscow, 1904; Japanese edition, Tokyo, 1924.

Aegyptische Chronologie. Berlin, 1904.

Die Israeliten und ihre Nachbarstämme. Alttestamentliche Untersuchungen. With contributions by Bernhard Luther. Halle, 1906; reprinted Darmstadt, 1967.

Theopomps Hellenika. Mit einer Beilage über die Rede an die Larisäer und die Verfassung Thessaliens. Halle, 1909.

Kleine Schriften zur Geschichtstheorie und zur wirtschaftlichen und politischen Geschichte des Altertums. Halle, 1910.

Der Papyrusfund von Elephantine. Dokumente einer jüdischen Gemeinde aus der Perserzeit und das älteste erhaltene Buch aus der Weltliteratur. Leipzig, 1912.

Ursprung und Geschichte der Mormonen. Mit Exkursen über die Anfänge des Islams und des Christentums. Halle, 1912.

Reich und Kultur der Chetiter. Berlin, 1914.

England. Seine staatliche und politische Entwicklung und der Krieg gegen Deutschland. Stuttgart and Berlin, 1915.

Nordamerika und Deutschland. Berlin, 1915.

Weltgeschichte und Weltkrieg. Gesammelte Aufsätze. Stuttgart and Berlin, 1916.

Der amerikanische Kongreß und der Weltkrieg. Berlin, 1917.

Caesars Monarchie und das Principat des Pompeius. Innere Geschichte Roms von 66 bis 44 vor Christ. Stuttgart and Berlin, 1918; 3d ed., 1922; reprinted Darmstadt, 1963.

Die Vereinigten Staaten von Amerika. Geschichte, Kultur, Verfassung und Politik. Frankfurt-am-Main, 1920.

Ursprung und Anfänge des Christentums. Vol. 1: Die Evangelien; vol. 2: Die Entwicklung des Judentums und Jesus von Nazaret. Stuttgart and Berlin, 1921; vol. 3: Die Apostelgeschichte und die Anfänge des Christentums. Stuttgart and Berlin, 1923; vols. 1–3 reprinted Darmstadt, 1962.

Kleine Schriften. Vols. 1 and 2. Halle, 1924.

Blüte und Niedergang des Hellenismus in Asien. Berlin, 1925.

Articles (Selected)

(A selection of articles not included in Forschungen zur alten Geschichte or in the Kleine Schriften; for a complete list see bibliography.)

"Über einige semitische Götter." Zeitschrift der deutschen Morgenländischen Gesellschaft 31 (1877) 716–741.

"Bevölkerung des Altertums." *Handwörterbuch der Staatswissenschaften*. Jena, 1891, 2:443–456; 2d ed. (1899) 2:674–689; 3d ed. (1909) 2:898–913.

"Homerische Parerga." *Hermes* 27 (1892) 363–380.

"Griechische Finanzen." *Handwörterbuch der Staatswissenschaft. Supplement*. Jena, 1897, 2:448–461; 2d ed. (1900) 3:936–949; 3d ed. (1909) 4:134–146.

"Sumerier und Semiten in Babylonien." *Abhandlungen der Königlich Preussischen Akademie der Wissenschaften* 3. Berlin, 1906.

"Über die Anfänge des Staats und sein Verhältnis zu den Geschlechtsverbänden und zum Volkstum." *Sitzungsberichte der Königlich Preussischen Akademie der Wissenschaften*. Berlin, 1907: 508–538.

"Die ältesten datierten Zeugnisse der iranischen Sprache und der zoroastrischen Religion." *Kuhns Zeitschrift für vergleichende Sprachwissenschaft* 42 (1908) 1–27.

"Untersuchungen über die älteste Geschichte Babyloniens und über Nebukadnezars Befestigungsanlagen." *Sitzungsberichte der Königlich Preussischen Akademie der Wissenschaften*. Berlin, 1912: 1062–1108.

"Die Gemeinde des neuen Bundes im Lande Damaskus. Eine jüdische Schrift aus der Seleukidenzeit." *Abhandlungen der Preussischen Akademie der Wissenschaften. Philologisch–historische Klasse* 9. Berlin, 1919.

"Spengler's *Untergang des Abendlandes*." *Deutsche Literaturzeitung* 45 (1924) 1759–1780. (Review.)

Sources

Bibliography

Marohl, Heinrich. *Eduard Meyer Bibliographie*. Mit einer autobiographischen Skizze Eduard Meyers und der Gedächtnisrede von Ulrich Wilcken. Stuttgart, 1941.

Biographical

Calder, William M. III. " 'Credo gegen Credo; Arbeit gegen Arbeit; Anschauung gegen Anschauung.' Ulrich von Wilamowitz-Moellendorff contra Eduard Meyer." *Calder-Demandt* (see below).

Calder, William M. III and Alexander Demandt, eds. *Eduard Meyer—Leben und Leistung eines Universalhistorikers*. Leiden (forthcoming).

Canfora, Luciano. "Die Kritik der bürgerlichen Demokratie durch Eduard Meyer." In *"Klassische" Antike und moderne Demokratie—Arthur Rosenberg zwischen alter Geschichte, Politik und politischer Bildung*. Edited by R. W. Müller and G. Schäfer. Göttingen and Zürich, 1986: 46–58.

———. "Eduard Meyer zwischen Kratippos und Theopomp." *Quaderni di storia* 27 (1988) 93–99.

Chambers, Mortimer. "The 'Most Eminent Living Historian, the One Final Authority': Meyer in America." *Calder-Demandt*.

Christ, Karl. *Von Gibbon zu Rostovtzeff. Leben und Werk führender Althistoriker der Neuzeit*. 2d ed. Darmstadt, 1979: 286–333.

Deininger, Jürgen. "Eduard Meyer und Max Weber." *Calder-Demandt.*

Ehrenberg, Victor. "Eduard Meyer." *Historische Zeitschrift* 143 (1931) 501–511.

Finley, Moses I., ed. *The Bücher-Meyer Controversy.* New York, 1979.

Fischer, Kurt. *Die politische und publizistische Tätigkeit Eduard Meyers im ersten Weltkrieg und in den ersten Jahren der Weimarer Republik.* Sonderdruck [typescript]. Potsdam, 1963.

Henrichs, Albert. "Alte und neue Propheten als Stifter von Offenbarungsreligionen: Der Ursprung der Religionen nach Eduard Meyer." *Calder-Demandt.*

Hoffmann, Christhard. *Juden und Judentum im Werk deutscher Althistoriker des 19. und 20. Jahrhunderts.* Leiden, 1988: 133–189.

———. "Die Selbsterziehung des Historikers. Zur intellektuellen Entwicklung des jungen Eduard Meyer (1855–1879)." *Calder-Demandt.*

Jantsch, Johanna. *Die Entstehung des Christentums bei Adolf von Harnack und Eduard Meyer.* Diss., Marburg, 1988.

Lehmann, Gustav Adolf. "Eduard Meyer." *Berlinische Lebensbilder.* Vol. 4. Geisteswissenschaftler. Edited by M. Erbe. Berlin, 1989: 269–285.

Liebeschütz, Hans. *Das Judentum im deutschen Geschichtsbild von Hegel bis Max Weber.* Tübingen, 1967: 269–301.

Mazza, M. "Meyer vs. Bücher: Il dibattito sull' economia antica nella storiografica tedesca tra otto e novecento." *Societa e storia* 29 (1985) 508–546.

Momigliano, Arnaldo. "Premesse per una discussione su Eduard Meyer." *Rivista Storica Italiana* 93 (1981) 384–398.

———. *Sesto Contributo alla storia degli studi classici e del mondo antico.* Rome, 1980: 845–860.

Nippel, Wilfried. "Prolegomena zu Eduard Meyers Anthropologie." *Calder-Demandt.*

Otto, Walter. "Eduard Meyer und sein Werk." *Zeitschrift der Deutschen Morgenländischen Gesellschaft* 85 (1931) 1–24.

Parente, Fausto. "*Die Enstehung des Judenthums*: Persien, die Achämeniden und das Judentum in der Interpretation von Eduard Meyer." *Calder-Demandt.*

Plümacher, Eckhard. "Eduard Meyers *Ursprung und Anfänge des Christentums.* Verhältnis von Fachwissenschaft und Zeitgeist." *Calder-Demandt.*

Schmidt-Phiseldeck, Kay Frederik. *Eduard Meyer og de historiske Problemer.* Aarhus, 1929.

Schneider, Helmuth. "Die Bücher-Meyer Kontroverse." *Calder-Demandt.*

Soden, H. von. "Die Anfänge des Christentums in der Darstellung Ed. Meyers." *Zeitschrift für Kirchengeschichte* 43 (1924) 429–440.

Sösemann, Bernd. " 'Der kühnste Entschluß führt am sichersten zum Ziel.' Eduard Meyers Vorstellungen zu partei- und weltpolitischen Entwicklungen." *Calder-Demandt.*

Stahlmann, Ines. *Imperator Caesar Augustus. Studien zur Geschichte des Principatsverständnisses in der deutschen Altertumswissenschaft bis 1945.* Darmstadt, 1988: 67–90.

Tenbruck, Friedrich H. "Max Weber und Eduard Meyer." In *Max Weber and his*

Contemporaries. Edited by W. J. Mommsen and J. Osterhammel. London, 1987: 234–267.

Toynbee, A. "Die 'Alte Geschichte' und die Universalhistorie." *Saeculum* 21 (1970) 91–105.

von Ungern-Sternberg, Jürgen. "Politik und Geschichte. Der Althistoriker Eduard Meyer im Ersten Weltkrieg." *Calder-Demandt.*

Letters

Audring, Gert, Christhard Hoffmann, and Jürgen von Ungern-Sternberg, eds. *Eduard Meyer und Victor Ehrenberg. Ein Briefwechsel (1914–1930)*. East Berlin and Stuttgart (forthcoming).

Polverini, Leandro. "Il carteggio Beloch-Meyer." In *Die Antike im neunzehnten Jahrhundert*. Edited by Karl Christ and Arnaldo Momigliano. Berlin, 1988: 199–219.

Papers

Akademie der Wissenschaften der DDR, Zentrales Akademiearchiv, Berlin/DDR. Nachlaß Eduard Meyer (the major part of the Nachlaß).

Staatsbibliothek Preussischer Kulturbesitz, Berlin (West): Manuscript Department. Nachlaß No. 213: Eduard Meyer. (A small but important collection.)

Staats- und Universitätsbibliothek Hamburg, Manuscript Department. Nachlaß Eduard Meyer. (A small collection.) See "Ein Orientalist, der auch am Ilissus und am Tiber heimisch ist," ed. Edgar Pack, *Der Teilnachlaß des Althistorikers Eduard Meyer in der Staats- und Universitätsbibliothek Hamburg*. Cologne, 1989.

Arnaldo Momigliano

5 September 1908 – 1 September 1987

KARL CHRIST
Philipps-Universität Marburg

On 1 September 1987, Arnaldo Dante Momigliano—Alexander White Visiting Professor at the University of Chicago, Professore Ordinario di Storia Romana in Soprannumero of the Scuola Normale Superiore di Pisa, and former Professor (1951–1975) of Ancient History at University College, London—died in a London hospital, a few days before completing his seventy-ninth year.

Born in Caraglio (Cuneo), he was of a Jewish family that can be traced back to the fourteenth century in Piedmont and Savoy, and he was proud of this heritage. "In a sense, in my scholarly life I have done nothing else but try to understand what I owe both to the Jewish house in which I was brought up and to the Christian-Roman-Celtic village in which I was born"—thus he himself described the powerful influence exerted on him by his place of origin (*Contributi alla storia degli studi classici e del mondo attico*, vol. 8, Rome, 1987, 432). His studies at the Universities of Turin and Rome brought him into the orbit of Gaetano De Sanctis and Augusto Rostagni; later he owed much to Giovanni Gentile and Benedetto Croce. By 1932 he had already been appointed Professore Incaricato di Storia Greca at the University of Rome, and in 1936 he became Professore Titolare di Storia Romana at the University of Turin. Thus, early in his life an outstanding academic career seemed to lie open to him.

Then began the bitterest period of his existence. Momigliano lost his position on ethnic grounds, and while he himself was able to continue his scholarly work in Oxford (thanks chiefly to the help of Hugh Last and Isobel Henderson), both his parents were put to death in a German extermination camp, a fate shared by nine others of his relatives.

After the war, although professorships were offered him in his homeland, first in Turin and later in Pisa, Momigliano remained in Great Britain. From 1947 to 1949 he worked as Lecturer, from 1949 to 1951 as Reader in Ancient History at the University of Bristol, and after 1951 he was Professor of Ancient History at University

College, London. Yet his teaching soon found an even wider audience. In rapid succession prestigious guest professorships and lectureships were offered to him in both Europe and America. Momigliano taught in Israel and at the École Normale Supérieure in Paris, at Chicago, and at Harvard. But it was above all in Italy that he won outstanding recognition through his yearly seminars at the Scuola Normale Superiore di Pisa.

Meanwhile, his influence and his work were being acknowledged with the highest academic honors. Momigliano was an honorary Knight of the British Empire; member of the Accademia dei Lincei, the British Academy, the Accademia delle Scienze di Torino, the Arcadia, the Istituto di Studi Romani, the Istituto di Studi Etruschi, the Royal Dutch Academy, the American Academy of Arts and Sciences, the Institut de France, and the Deutsches Archäologisches Institut; and an honorary member of the American Historical Association. Venerable universities of Europe, the United States, and Israel awarded him honorary doctorates, as did the Fachbereich Geschichtswissenschaften of the Philipps-Universität Marburg in 1986. Momigliano was also awarded the Kenyon Medal of the British Academy, the Premio Feltrinelli, the Premio Cantoni of the University of Florence, the Kaplun Prize of Hebrew University (Jerusalem), the Premio Sila, the Premio Viareggio Internazionale, a grant from the MacArthur Foundation, and many other honors.

This glory is the visible reflection of an impressive scholarly lifework. His essays, addresses, and reviews (a collection of specialized studies that is characteristic of Momigliano's work) are available now in the eleven volumes of the eight-part *Contributi alla storia degli studi classici e del mondo antico*. The bibliographies of his oeuvre (*Quarto Contributo . . .*, Rome, 1969: 669–719; *Sesto Contributo . . .*, Rome, 1980: 845–860; *Ottavo Contributo . . .*, Rome, 1987: 435–449) list over seven hundred titles, up to July 1986, in the most important languages of the Western world. Momigliano's researches and his contributions to scholarship extend over widely disparate fields. They include investigations on the sources of ancient history in the broadest sense of the word; historical interpretations; above all, works on ancient and modern historiography; his *Sommario di storia delle civiltà antiche*, a widely used Italian textbook; and, not least, his stimulating reviews, such as have appeared in *Gnomon* and elsewhere. All this can be described only briefly here.

With his Turin *tesi di laurea*, *La composizione della storia di Tucidide* (1930), which was published by the Turin Academy in its series *Memorie*, Momigliano dealt with the question, then under lively discussion, of the genesis and construction of Thucydides' history. He regarded it "as an honor" to be in essential agreement with Wolfgang Schadewaldt. If his choice of theme here was rather conventional, the *Prime linee di storia della tradizione Maccabaica*, which was published in the same year (1930) and later reprinted, first testified to his never-flagging interest in the problems of Jewish tradition and history. The unique character and the chronology of the First Book of Maccabees, the problem of the doublets in the Second Book, the question as to the use of Jason of Cyrene, and finally the legend of a relationship between the Jews and the Spartans were the major subjects of these learned philological and historical researches. As in several later studies on Philo and Flavius Josephus or in the work on the oriental factors in post-exilic Hebrew and in Greek historiography, Momigliano was less interested in isolated source-critical analysis of individual authors than in illuminating the interrelations between oriental, Hebrew, Greek, and Roman forms of thought.

His interest in interrelations led him next to the long-neglected Greek historians of the fourth, third, and second centuries B.C., to Ephorus, Theopompus, and Timaeus of Tauromenium, and to Polybius. But he was also led back to Herodotus, and Momigliano's Herodotean studies are characteristic of his prioritites as well as of his methods. Momigliano was fascinated with Herodotus' contribution to the development of historiography, especially because this historian, above all, had recourse to the oral tradition and because he sought to acquire on his travels ethnographic and historical information about the lands of the Persian Empire. In order to gain a balanced total picture of the author, Momigliano not only analyzed all the ancient reproaches against Herodotus but also investigated the critical response to his work from the fifteenth century to the present. He justified his method as follows: "The history of Herodotus' posthumous struggle against his detractors is a significant chapter in the history of historical thinking; it is also, in my opinion, an important key to the actual understanding of Herodotus" (in *Herodot*, ed. W. Marg, Darmstadt, 1962, 139).

The monograph *The Development of Greek Biography* was judged by F. W. Walbank in 1973 to be "easily the most important contribution to the subject since Leo." This superbly written small work, which also drew upon all modern discussions of the role of biography, dealt chiefly with the connections and differences between biography and history. In contrast to Leo, who had tied Greek biography firmly to the Peripatetic school, and in contrast to Dihle, who had underscored the connection with the Socratics, Momigliano reached back to the preliminary stages of biography and to oriental influences in the fifth century B.C. He thus attempted to sketch out a complex total picture while yet laying primary stress on the influential works of the fourth century B.C.

Momigliano turned to the problem of the sources for the history of late antiquity only after the Second World War. But his first contribution to the study of this epoch, "An Unsolved Problem of Historical Forgery: The *Scriptores Historiae Augustae*" (1954), was to prove one of the most stimulating works in this field. It was followed by studies on Cassiodorus and the Italian culture of his time, on the Anicii and the Latin historiography of the sixth century, and finally on Ammianus Marcellinus. His 1981 essay on Greek historiography, contributed to the volume *Griechische Literatur* edited by E. Vogt for the *Neues Handbuch der Literaturwissenschaft*, restored a personal balance to work on this strand of the ancient tradition.

At the center of Momigliano's historical interpretations stood the following group of subjects: the history of the Hellenistic Age, the early Roman Republic, the Principate in the first century A.D., and late antiquity. The 1934 monograph *Filippo il Macedone. Saggio sulla storia greca del IV secolo a. C.* was Momigliano's first great contribution to the study of Hellenistic history in the broader sense. The book was not a biography of Philip II; rather, it dealt primarily with the intellectual history and the political conceptions of his age, and it was animated as much by Momigliano's disagreements with Isocrates as by those with Droysen.

In 1935 he began his great inquiry into the historical origin and the modern meaning of the concept of the Hellenistic Age, and further studies on this topic followed. They culminated in the monograph *Alien Wisdom: The Limits of Helleniza-tion* (1975), which was published in German translation in 1979 (*Hochkulturen im Hellenismus*). This was Momigliano's most original and most personal book. Here he investigated the cultural, and especially the religious, connections between the Greeks on the one hand and the Celts, Jews, Romans, and Persians on the other, and in this connection he expressed parenthetically his own conviction: "The triangle Greece-Rome-Judaea is still at the centre and is likely to stay at the centre as long as Christianity remains the religion of the West" (11).

The problems of the early Roman Republic had occupied Momigliano as early as the nineteen-thirties, when he sought to understand the individual Roman magis-tracies, the *comitia centuriata*, such figures of Roman mythology as Tanaquil, Gaia Cecilia, Acca Larenza and Thybris Pater, and key Republican concepts such as "Terra marique" and "Camillus and Concord." Then, after the Second World War, renewed interdisciplinary and international discussion on the origins of Rome called him back to the field. A fundamental *Forschungsbericht* (1963) was followed by specialized studies on patricians and plebeians, the *rex sacrorum*, the *praetor maximus*, and the origins of the Republic, as well as on Greeks, Trojans, and Romans.

The results of these individual researches were finally brought together in "The Origins of Rome," Momigliano's great contribution to the seventh volume of the second edition of the *Cambridge Ancient History* (= *Settimo Contributo . . . .*, Rome, 1984: 379–436). In an impressive examination of the results of archaeological, philological, religious-historical, ethnological, and historical researches, Momigliano here laid great stress on the Greek influences, direct or indirect, on early Rome. At the same time, however, he underscored the significance of the Romans' conscious decision to follow a middle way between the Greeks and the Etruscans, a choice that he found was documented symbolically in Rome's connection with Troy.

The 1932 monograph *L'opera dell' imperatore Claudio*, which appeared two years later in English translation, depicted above all the scholarly character of Clau-dius. (Perhaps a certain inner affinity to this *princeps* was at work here.) The work impressively displayed the knowledge of history and the will to reform, but also the religious policies and the "politica di accentramento," of this Roman ruler who had long been discredited by biased judgment. For Momigliano's basic understanding of the Roman imperial period, the monograph *La formazione della moderna storiografia sull' impero Romano* (1938) was even more important. Momigliano's fundamental conviction here was that the customary absolute separation between a profane his-tory, as it were, of the *Imperium Romanum* and the history of Christianity and of the Christian Church was dangerous. He insisted instead that both entities be conceived as parts of a unified historical process and that their interconnections be duly taken into account. To illustrate the necessity of doing so he persuasively (cf. W. Enßlin, *Gnomon* 19 [1943] 61–62) sketched the development of the modern conception of the Roman Empire from Lenain de Tillemont to Ranke. The collection *The Conflict between Paganism and Christianity in the Fourth Century*, which Momigliano edited in 1963, along with several specialized investigations show that he himself lived up to his own demands.

Momigliano's strongest influence was in the field of the history of historiography. His works on the history of scholarship were, at first, part of a complex process of research, but after the Second World War they advanced ever farther into the foreground. His London inaugural lecture of 1952 on "George Grote and the Study of Greek History" was in this case exemplary. Momigliano showed how greatly Grote's life, his values, and his liberal political ideas influenced his judgments on Greek history, and he also determined Grote's place in a total overview of the conceptions of Greek history in the framework of the European tradition.

Whether in extensive *Forschungsberichte*, in original insights, such as those in "Ancient History and the Antiquarian" (1950), in studies on the critical response to individual ancient authors, or in his many smaller papers and essays on the foremost representatives of historiography and *Altertumswissenschaft* from the days of the Renaissance humanists to the present, Momigliano was always intent on stimulating and deepening our understanding of the history of these disciplines. He was intent on comprehending the modes of thought, the judgments, and the methods of individual scholars not only from the point of view of the genealogy of their particular disciplines; specifically, he sought to take into account the leading ideas of their times and the nature of their own lives. In all this he insisted on well-grounded knowledge and the highest standards of accuracy. To him it was self-evident that the student of the history of historiography must also be familiar with the sources upon which the authors whom he studied had built. Since he kept a critical eye on all new developments and all new tendencies in the whole range of humanistic studies, he ultimately felt called upon to defend the objectivity of historical research against tendencies to distort history with ideology or rhetoric.

Numerous collections of Momigliano's shorter works have brought them to a wide audience. To name only a few: *Studies in Historiography* (1966); *Essays in Ancient and Modern Historiography* (1977); *Problèmes d'historiographie ancienne et moderne* (1983); *Sui fondamenti della storia antica* (1984); *Tra storia e storicismo* (1985); *Storia e storiografia antica* (1987); *Pagine ebraiche* (1987). A similar collection in German does not yet exist. The scholar who did so much to carry on the classic German tradition of scholarship, who, in spite of all he had gone through, aided German colleagues and students in a magnanimous and unrestrained manner, who, as late as the fall of 1986, gave an Italian-German seminar on antiquity in the nineteenth century at the Istituto Storico Italo-Germanico in Trento—this scholar is known in German-speaking countries almost solely among specialists. His work deserves to gain there at last the recognition that it has long enjoyed in other countries.

Momigliano's personality was many-faceted. He was obsessed with the mission to pass on the ancient as well as the modern tradition and to preserve the highest scholarly standards. Thus he could become authoritarian and scathing when he saw incompetence and mere rhetoric putting on airs. Even the pictures of him as a youthful scholar reveal his extraordinary strength of will. But in addition to all this, he was also at the end a wise patriarch, in every sense of the word, as well as warm-hearted and kind. Social reserve he abhorred: even those who had the opportunity to speak with him for several hours were never released from intense scholarly intimacy. Here his knowledge of ancient and of the latest literature was incomparable. He was familiar with the most recent trends in American theology as well as with those in German or Italian philosophy. One could not read a paper or a review by him without encountering the latest, hitherto unknown works.

Aside from his strictly logical analysis, his precise criticism, and a unique erudition, as well as an extraordinary ability to synthesize, Momigliano, like Droysen, was a historian who put his heart into his subject and knew how to arouse strong feelings. His famous feuds (for example, that with Piero Treves) sometimes attained a virtually Old Testament level of virulence. Yet he also possessed "friends" throughout the world, and also, as he ironically said, "friends of his friends"—friends who, despite passing irritations, admired and honored him and were grateful to have encountered in him one of the most fascinating personalities of our time in the fields of history and ancient studies.

His intellect and his whole personality enabled Momigliano to keep seminars and large audiences in a state of great intellectual excitement; even listeners who at first had been reserved came completely under his spell. The well-known American sociologist Edward Shils thus described his influence in Chicago: "In a gloomy time in the life of universities, Arnaldo Momigliano stood before us as the embodied ideal of what a university is when it is at its best and what the best professor in that ideal university would be" (Memorial Service for Arnaldo Momigliano, Chicago, 22 October 1987).

Momigliano's entire life was pervaded with the will to work and pervaded too by constant restlessness. This restlessness increased in his old age. It was exciting to see how this small, personally quite modest man hurried from country to country, from congress to seminar, from university to institute in order to chair a conference, give a lecture, and meet with friends, colleagues, and publishers. As many of his letters and many of his final utterances reveal, he had lived, since the onset of serious heart disease in July 1985, in the awareness that death might soon come upon him. In accordance with his wishes, he was buried on 7 September 1987 in the little Jewish cemetery in Cuneo.

Translated by Michael Armstrong

Books

La composizione della storia di Tucidide. Tesi di laurea, Turin, 1930; published Turin, 1933.

Sommario di storia delle civiltà antiche. 2 vols. Florence, 1934 with many reprints.

The Conflict between Paganism and Christianity in the Fourth Century. Edited by Momigliano. Oxford, 1963. Italian translation by Anna Davies Morpurgo as *Il conflitto tra paganesimo e cristianesimo nel secolo IV.* Turin, 1968.

Studies in Historiography. London and New York, 1966.

The Development of Greek Biography: Four Lectures. Cambridge, MA, 1971.

Introduzione bibliografica alla storia greca fino a Socrate. Florence, 1975.

Alien Wisdom. The Limits of Hellenization. Cambridge, 1975; German translation as *Hochkulturen im Hellenismus: Die Begegnung der Griechen mit Kelten, Juden, Römern und Persern.* Munich, 1979.

Essays in Ancient and Modern Historiography. Oxford, 1977.

Problèmes d'historiographie ancienne et moderne. Paris 1983.

Sui fondamenti della storia antica. Turin, 1984.

Tra storia e storicismo. Pisa, 1985.

Storia e storiografia antica. Bologna, 1987.

Pagine ebraiche. Turin, 1987.

On Pagans, Jews, and Christians. Middletown, CT, 1987.

Saggi di storia della religione romana. Brescia, 1988.

Monographs

Prime linee di storia della tradizione Maccabaica. Rome, 1930; 2d ed., Turin, 1931; 3d ed., Rome, 1968.

L'opera dell' imperatore Claudio. Florence, 1932; English translation by W. D. Hogarth as *Claudius: the Emperor and his Achievement.* Oxford, 1934; 2d ed., 1961.

Filippo il Macedone. Saggio sulla storia greca del IV secolo a. C. Florence, 1934; 2d ed., 1987.

La formazione della moderna storiografia sull' impero Romano. Turin, 1938.

George Grote and the Study of Greek History. An inaugural lecture delivered at University College, London, 19 February 1952. London, 1952.

Cassiodorus and the Italian Culture of His Time. London, 1956. Orig. published PBA 41 (1956) 207–245.

Jacob Bernays. Amsterdam and London, 1969.

Second Thoughts on Greek Biography. Amsterdam and London, 1971.

Articles (Collected)

Contributi alla storia degli studi classici e del mondo antico. Thus far, 8 parts in 11 volumes. Rome, 1955–1987.

Articles (Selected)

"Ancient History and the Antiquarian." *JWI* 13 (1950) 285–315.

"An Unsolved Problem of Historical Forgery: The *Scriptores Historiae Augustae*." *JWI* 17 (1954) 22–46.

"An Interim Report on the Origins of Rome." *JRS* 53 (1963) 95–121.

Sources

Ampolo, C. et al. "Arnaldo Momigliano e la sua opera." *Rivista Storica Italiana* 100 (1988) 283–446.

Enßlin, W. *Gnomon* 19 (1943) 61–62.

Walbank, F. W. Review of *The Development of Greek Biography*. *History and Theory* 12 (1973) 230–240.

Theodor Mommsen

30 November 1817–1 November 1903

ALEXANDER DEMANDT
Freie Universität Berlin

In the history of German *Altertumswissenschaft*, the achievement of Theodor Mommsen was epoch-making in three respects: First, contrary to the fixation of German classicism's philhellenic humanism on Greek culture, he gave the Romans an independent and equal position in the total picture of antiquity; second, in his scholarly career, Mommsen completed the transition from the aesthetic and literary historiography of the eighteenth and nineteenth centuries to a strictly scientific, detailed discipline of research oriented toward data and sources; and third, Mommsen applied to *Altertumswissenschaft* the concept of organized "big business," employing state resources and numerous workers. These three achievements took place within the framework of a shift from classicism's aesthetic and absolute estimate of antiquity to the historical and relativistic evaluation of historicism. Mommsen saw this transformation accomplished in his lifetime. Let us first take a look at the man himself.

Mommsen was born on 30 November 1817, at Garding in Schleswig-Holstein. Like so many great minds of the nineteenth century—e.g., Droysen (born 1808), Burckhardt (born 1818), Schliemann (born 1822), and Nietzsche (born 1844)—he was the son of a Protestant pastor. To be sure, Mommsen gave up his Protestantism along with his Christianity, but he always retained a fundamentally Protestant attitude. From 1838 to 1843 Mommsen studied history and law at the University of Kiel, which was then subject to the King of Denmark. At the age of twenty-five he took his doctorate with a dissertation on Roman law and then, with the help of a Danish research stipend, traveled to France and Italy. (The Danish crown, of course, played Maecenas to many German scholars and artists; the most famous among them are Klopstock, Schiller, and Hebbel.) In Italy Mommsen devoted himself, under the influence of Borghesi, to the Roman inscriptions in the Kingdom of Naples; for this work the Berlin Academy, at the end of 1844, put an initial 150 taler at his disposal. During the Revolution of 1848 he was editor of the

Schleswig-Holsteiner Zeitung. Like Johann Gustav Droysen and Theodor Storm, Mommsen worked against the dynastic ambitions of the Danish king Frederick VII, who was attempting to incorporate Schleswig-Holstein, the majority of whose population was German, into Denmark. In the autumn of 1848 Mommsen became Professor of Jurisprudence at Leipzig, but he lost his position in 1851 when he joined Otto Jahn and Moriz Haupt in protesting against the constitution imposed by the Saxon king. The law under which Mommsen was dismissed dated back to 1580. He was called to Zürich in 1852, to Breslau in 1854, and in 1858 to the Berlin Academy.

The signature of Friedrich Wilhelm IV on Mommsen's appointment to a research professorship at the Berlin Academy on 27 October 1857, was one of the dying Prussian king's last official acts. That Mommsen had been removed from his post as a political dissenter did not disturb Friedrich Wilhelm; he had already taken in other scholars dismissed for political reasons—e.g., the Brothers Grimm and Moriz Haupt. On the advice of Alexander von Humboldt he had even accepted into the Academy a scholar of the Jewish faith. The king wanted to get on with the work on the inscriptions.

Mommsen as Historian

Mommsen devoted all his energy to the Academy; the University played a comparatively small role in his life. He had intended to habilitate at Kiel, but he had given up this plan while in Rome in 1847 in preference to the inscriptions. As a member of the Academy he received a call to Bonn in 1861 and rejected it in favor of a professorship of Roman Antiquity at the Friedrich Wilhelm University in Berlin. He also declined calls to Göttingen in 1868, to Strassburg in 1872, and to Leipzig in 1874; the last he rejected after his election as a Secretary of the Academy. In 1874–75 he was Rector of the University. In 1885 he was released from teaching duties, and after that he appeared only sporadically in the course catalogue—for the last time in 1887.

Mommsen's teaching duties normally comprised four hours of lecturing and a two-hour reading class. While the theme of the latter was not, as a rule, listed, the lectures completely avoided Mommsen's actual field, the Roman Republic. Most often, Mommsen lectured on the Roman Empire—twenty times in all. Half of these lectures dealt with the period after Diocletian. Aside from the fact that such specialization in instruction was unusual and did not become the rule after Mommsen's time, the choice of subject is surprising in that Mommsen excluded the Imperial period from his *Römische Geschichte* (RG), and an extensive literature exists on the question of why that work's fourth volume, which was to have dealt with the Imperial period, did not appear. We possess remarks of Mommsen that testify to his distaste for the history of the Empire. Academic teaching occupied Mommsen only incidentally; his contemporaries' judgments on his rhetorical capabilities are quite contradictory. Sebastian Hensel was fascinated by Mommsen, but Friedrich Althoff called him "a poor lecturer." He always excited interest when he pronounced judgment on a sinner like

Constantine and tore him to shreds before his audience's eyes. In any case, Mommsen founded a significant school of ancient historians. Among them are such scholars as Hirschfeld, Dessau, Domaszewski, Seeck, Ludo Hartmann, and Ulrich Wilcken.

Zangemeister lists 262 publications up to the year of Mommsen's call to Berlin; among them the most important work is the *Römische Geschichte* (to 46 B.C.; vol. I, 1854; vol. II, 1855; vol. III, 1856). At first the work provoked widespread indignation—for example, from D. F. Strauss, J. J. Bachofen, Camille Jullian, Ferdinand Gregorovius, Friedrich Ritschl, and others. Mommsen's style was perceived as "journalism of the worst sort," and his pronouncements met with detailed criticism. Yet Mommsen's work meanwhile went through sixteen editions and was translated into many languages—Italian in 1857, Russian in 1858, English in 1862, French in 1863, Polish in 1867, Hungarian in 1874, Spanish in 1875. In 1902 the *Römische Geschichte* brought its author the Nobel Prize for Literature; he was the first German and has been the only historian to win the prize, except for Winston Churchill.

Mommsen's obvious sympathy with Rome stands in contrast to the older humanistic tradition in Germany. An elective affinity with the ancient Greeks had existed since the sixteenth century. In Winckelmann, Goethe, and Schiller, in Herder, Hölderlin, and Humboldt, the love for Hellenism predominated, while they maintained a distant, indeed dismissive, attitude toward the Romans. For this there were several reasons. The Reformers Luther and Melanchthon looked on the popes as the successors of the Roman emperors, and their abandonment of Catholic Rome was also an abandonment of ancient Rome. From the eighteenth century onwards, Germany was endeavoring to develop a "national culture," for which the ancient Greeks provided a model. Whereas Roman culture was merely secondary, derived from the Greek, the literature, philosophy, and art of the Greeks themselves seemed, so to speak, autochthonous, original. Politically, on the other hand, ancient Greece was just as splintered as was the German people under its countless princes. And so in Germany "philhellenism" was fostered, while invoking Rome was left to the "Welsch"—the Italians and the French. Louis XIV, Robespierre, and Napoleon, in their several ways, made use of it.

The French Revolution and the struggle against Napoleon awakened in Germany a national consciousness and the desire for a unified state. The Romantic movement developed the concepts of "Volksgeister," "Völkerfamilie," "Völkerfrieden"—the earth was to become, as it were, a "Völkergarten." These were Mommsen's ideas as well. For him, culture no longer held primacy over politics; his ideal of man was the *homo politicus*, and the aim of writing history was "political pedagogy."

Pedagogy always requires models, and such a model Mommsen discovered in Republican Rome. The Roman community is for Mommsen an ideal: "a free people, which knew how to obey, in clear renunciation of all mystical priestly fraud, in unconditional equality before the law and among themselves, bearing the distinct stamp of their own nationality" (*Römische Geschichte* 1:80). Unique among the civilized nations of antiquity, the Romans had succeeded in realizing a national unity;

they had found the mean between liberty and discipline, between equality and order, between individualism and citizenship. Greece was the prototype of cultural development, Rome of national development. After Germany had gone to school in Greece and found its national culture, it must now go to school in Rome and create a unified state. It was in this spirit that Mommsen wrote his *Römische Geschichte*.

In the broad context of cultural history, Mommsen describes the migration of the Indo-Europeans into Italy, the Latins' annexation of territory, and the beginnings of the city of Rome. The sagas of Romulus and Remus, appropriately, are relegated to mythology; they are mentioned only in passing, as is the entire annalistic tradition of the early period, which Barthold Georg Niebuhr (1776–1831) had already recognized as legendary. Mommsen highly esteemed his countryman Niebuhr, seeing in him the founder of critical historiography.

Mommsen placed special emphasis on constitutional law. Occasionally it is described too starkly in the rational categories of the nineteenth century—for example, in the assumption that, from the very beginning, "the Roman citizen community, just like the German and presumably the most ancient Indo-European community, was the true and ultimate repository of the idea of the sovereign state" (RG 1:72). Here, once more, we see Mommsen's Romans portrayed in their capacity as models.

Mommsen describes Rome's subjugation of Italy from the viewpoint of national unification, parallel to the conception of an Italy unified by Piedmont or a Germany unified by Prussia. Mommsen placed the highest value on national unity; for its sake, he felt, even military force was justified, in contemporary Germany as much as in ancient Italy (*Reden und Aufsätze*, 318).

This defense of Rome's Italian policies was justly attacked by Eduard Meyer (1855–1930), for, though one could point, in the case of the modern unification of Germany or Italy, to the existence of a German or an Italian people, the ancient Romans first compelled the ethnically and culturally heterogeneous Etruscans, Samnites, Greeks, Celts, etc. into a political unity; a preexisting feeling of community cannot be demonstrated. Strabo (6.4.2) accurately describes how the *Imperium* grew up out of the *urbs Romana*. The notion of a *populus Italicus* was unknown to antiquity.

On the other hand, Meyer was in agreement with Mommsen's judgment on the development that followed. Rome's reaching out beyond the borders of Italy seemed to both authors a betrayal of the national principle. Mommsen declared that "conquest, so long as it consolidates the nation, is self-preservation; similarly, it becomes self-annihilation when it steps beyond national boundaries" (RA, 318ff.). The latter contingency befell the Romans contrary to their expectations. "The free Latin nation, to its own horror, found itself once more the jailer of the bordering nations, entangled in the snares of so-called world domination."

Mommsen condemns any policy aiming at hegemony or imperialism—not only with respect to the protected and obedient peoples, but equally in regard to the protecting and ruling people. The switch to imperialism had a devastating effect on Rome. A sound peasantry, the pillar of the state, had been replaced by a capitalistic economy of *latifundia* with their hordes of slaves. This economy had withdrawn the social basis of the Republic (*RG* 2:380). The monetary system and mercantile interests had spawned an upper class that was oriented toward profit. The resulting social tensions shattered the Republican constitution.

Following Hegelian dialectic, Mommsen maintained that Rome had created in the conquered peoples its own antithesis, and in Herder's language he mourns the balance of peoples that Rome had destroyed. Expansion is healthy until it reaches the national borders; beyond this point it becomes "unnatural" (*unnatürlich*) and suicidal (*RG* 2:379). "It is the fate of those political entities which detach themselves from the concept of nationality to recognize no further limits" (*RA*, 321). Faced with the rising might of the generals, the "sun of freedom" set and the state was internally dead.

With this idea Mommsen closely approaches the argumentation of Montesquieu in the ninth and tenth chapters of his *Considérations sur les causes de la grandeur des Romains et de leur décadence* (1734). Montesquieu too saw in the expansion of the *Imperium* beyond the sea and the Alps the reason for the loss of the sense of citizenship, the growth of the prosperity that undermined morals, and the might of the generals. But Montesquieu's argument is concerned only with the immoderate size of the Roman hegemony and not with the foreign nations within Rome's sphere of dominance. And even Montesquieu, of course, had not invented the idea. One may trace it back to the younger Scipio, who inserted into the Roman state prayer the plea that the gods might not make the Roman state any greater; it was big enough as it was (Valerius Maximus 4.1.10). Amid the ruins of Carthage (the city he had himself destroyed) Scipio had before his eyes the fall of Rome (Polybius 38.22). Even if he expected this fall too to be an act of God, God's means were moral corruption that arose from the power that created luxury.

We find in Mommsen a very similar fusion of guilt and fate. Although he condemns the expansion of Rome on moral and political grounds, he describes that expansion in terms of a destiny that is also visible in his numerous metaphors from nature. Again and again he uses the images of sunset, autumn, old age to describe Rome's situation at the end of the Republic. The course of history thus takes on a fateful necessity that reduces all moral judgments on Roman politics to the level of mere stylistic ornamentation.

The synchronization of two planes, this drama on the double stage of historical fatalism and political morality, grants Mommsen the freedom to make value judgments independently of context, particularly in his characterization of great men. This is clearest in the contradictions in his picture of Caesar. The "democratic king" Caesar, the utterly perfect man, of the sort that appears "once every thousand years," before whose greatness the historian must be dumb with reverence (*RG* 3:468)—to this Caesar all is permitted. The liberal Mommsen pardons Caesar for the establishment of the absolute military dictatorship that put the seal on decadence (*Abriss des römischen Staatsrechts*, 276); the nationalist Mommsen excuses the subjugation of Gaul.

To be sure, by describing the Gauls as Rome's "ancestral enemies" whom Caesar vanquished, he did open up the possibility of a defense; but Mommsen well knew that this defense was irrelevant. To save Caesar, Mommsen changes his values. The free Roman people were no more; but men need ideals for which they can sacrifice themselves, and these were now to be found in a glorious policy of conquest by "not only a standing, but a victorious, army" (RA, 324). "Caesar had realized this when he taught his nation to conquer," when he set up the absolute monarchy—which Augustus then watered down into the defensive dyarchy.

Mommsen had defended himself against the charge of Caesarism. Yet his Caesar recalls the interpretations that were made of Napoleon's actions, e.g., by the Comte de Segur: "L'éstablissement d'un gouvernment militaire vigoureux est un remède funeste pour la civilisation, mais le seul pourtant qui puisse rendre la vie à un peuple tombé dans l'anarchie" (Pensèes, 1823, CCXVIIII).

Caesar, in Mommsen's work, takes the necessary steps without mercy. He unites in his own person the managing director of the Hegelian Weltgeist with the instrument of higher requital in Herder's sense. Caesar's greatness as general of a popular army and democratic king lies in his having drawn the logical conclusions from the loss of freedom, nation, and fatherland and having established a dictatorship that transcended nations and subjugated nations. He brought to the Gauls the blessings of a higher civilization; he liberated the Italians from the rule of a corrupt aristocracy. The arrogance of the Junker class (i.e., the senators) and the plutocracy of the capitalist class (i.e., the equites) were gone. The remède funeste was unavoidable. "Indubitably, the more quickly and thoroughly a despot cleared away all the debris of the old liberal constitution, the better for Rome" (RG 2:380). Caesar, the despot of genius, brought about in Rome the "curse of absolutism" and imperialism in order to achieve, through the "catastrophe" of monarchy, the rebirth of the deeply divided nation. Mommsen's Caesar is exalted above all human criteria; he was taken over by Bernard Shaw.

Mommsen's Römische Geschichte ends with Caesar's final victories. Mommsen never completed the work. The fifth volume, which appeared in 1885, was devoted to the provinces under the emperors. It is written in a cooler, more matter-of-fact tone, without the fire of the first three volumes, and it achieved only a succès d'estime with the public. Mommsen never gave up his plans to write the fourth volume, and it continued to be expected up to the time of his death. A sort of substitute for the missing volume on the Imperial period may be the still unpublished lecture notes of Paul and Sebastian Hensel for the years 1882–1886 that came to light in 1980. These notes confirm Mommsen's loathing for the period that followed Caesar: "leaden tedium" (RA, 352); "dreary desolation of the absolute monarchy" (RA, 342); "centuries of a decaying culture" (Wucher, 126); "deeply degenerate age" (Hensel 3:227); "complete intellectual marasmus" (Hensel 1A:72). The flourishing economy, the increasing sophistication of the law, the evolution of city life—all this was far removed from what Mommsen—or "the angel of the Lord"—would find today in the Mediterranean countries (RG 5:5). Yet Augustus' monarchy, according to Mommsen, was founded on the "complete bankruptcy—political, military, economic, and moral—of the civilization of the day" (RA, 107). The pax Augusta was "the peace of the grave—the quiet of the graveyard" (RA, 142).

The concept of decadence is Janus-faced, and a present that is degenerate in comparison with the sublime past can yet be praised as a still-fortunate period in relation to the ever-degenerating future. The depth of the descent is limitless, and thus Mommsen can trace further steps into the abyss beyond the nadir reached under Augustus. Roman Imperial history was, for Mommsen, a step-by-step decline.

With the beginning of the monarchy, the internal death of the community was complete. Augustus halted the process to a certain degree, but after the Servian dynasty ended in 235, "the Roman empire fell apart" (Abriss, 275). Gallienus annihilated the "dyarchy of the Principate" (Ibid., 276), but it was left to Diocletian to give the Empire an "Indian summer" (Herbstfrühling) (Ibid., 278) by "once more simultaneously regenerating and destroying the state of Augustus" (RA, 109). In constitutional terms, Mommsen places a deeper gap between the Principate of Augustus and the Dominate of Diocletian than between the Republic and the Principate, because even the Principate is for him a constitutional entity based on the sovereignty of the people. The princeps is still a magistrate; the dominus is not. From the Republic to the dyarchy of the Principate and on to the pure monarchy of Diocletian, the res publica consolidates itself on progressively lower levels. The Germanic states established on the soil of the Empire are yet a step lower. Each founder of a state administers the estate of the bankrupt who preceded him.

Rome's demise is revealed externally in the failure against the Germanic peoples. Mommsen posits three turning points. The first is the clades Variana, A. D. 9, which, "after the flood tide, marks the beginning of the ebb in Rome's foreign policy" (RA, 341; RG, 5:53). The second crisis is the war against the Marcomanni, from A. D. 166 on. "Here the die is indeed cast. After Trajan the Empire was old, to be sure, but not yet senile. But this is extinction" (Hensel 1:241). Mommsen hears the knell for the third time in the year 376. "We are standing before the great catastrophe, which we may well call the end" (Hensel 3:209). Mommsen is thinking of the battle of Adrianople in 378. "With the loss of the Danube frontier, the die is cast for Rome, and to trace the agony further would be distasteful and superfluous. The advantage now lies with the Germanic peoples" (Hensel 3:221). The Eastern Roman Empire merely puts forth "blossoms in winter"; Byzantium for Mommsen—as for Gibbon, Herder, and Burckhardt before him—is nothing but the protracted wasting away of Roman history (RA 176), just as the Imperial period is only the gradual extinction of the Republic.

Mommsen repeatedly emphasized that Rome met its end not from without but by an "internal disease," by "inner putrescence" (Abriss: 275, 289). The Germanic nations merely performed the "execution" of the Empire (Hensel 3:223), merely carried out the sentence of fate. Alaric in 410: "The Gothic tempest burst over Italy—richly merited by the grievous guilt of the government and the yet more grievous guilt of the nation." It was Alaric's destiny "to destroy the thousand-year city, its incomparable splendor together with its incomparable vileness" (RA, 321ff.).

With this appeal to fatalism Mommsen had no desire to free the Germanic peoples from the reproach of having barbarously destroyed a superior culture. Mommsen did not share his age's tendency to apotheosize the ancient Germans. He disparages the Germanic tribal kings as nothing but "brigand chieftains" (Hensel 3:206); Alaric is a captain of bandits (227); the Germanic kingdoms are merely "the rubble of the crumbling Roman Empire" (*RA*, 141). The product is, to be sure, a "wonderful semi-culture" (Hensel 3:240).

Nevertheless, the Germanic peoples were for Mommsen, as for many others in his day, the ancient Germans, and if Felix Dahn and Friedrich Engels lauded them for precisely this reason, Mommsen castigated them for this same reason. For even then they possessed the German national vice: factionalism. Even under Augustus, "Germans helped foreigners to open up Germany" (*RA*, 332), and this internal strife of German against German runs through Mommsen's depiction of Roman Imperial history. For example, the accession of Magnentius in A. D. 350: "Germans stood there and decided against Germans, as so often in history" (Hensel 3:155).

Mommsen maintains the same reserve in the face of the second victorious power, Christianity. The pastor's son who in his youth described himself as *homo minime ecclesiasticus* and preferred to be called Jens rather than Theodor (for example, in the correspondence with Theodor Storm) was perhaps not exactly an atheist but had no understanding of religious questions.

Mommsen viewed Christianity as the product of resignation. The idealistic quality of life, he felt, had retreated into religion (Hensel 3:156). In his speech on the catacombs of Rome he said, "The union of devotion with burial, the evolution of the grave to the cemetery, the cemetery to the church, is thoroughly Christian—one might perhaps say that it is Christianity itself" (*RA*, 300–301). The *pax Augusta* was to him the peace of the graveyard, and the graveyard was the emblem of Christianity. Christian teaching itself he declared to be "simple faith" (*Köhlerglauben*) the only excuse for which lay in the mentality of the times; it was a *Köhlerglauben* for counts and barons (Hensel 3:109) and historically significant for just that reason. It was precisely because of the irrational element in Christianity that people had found it attractive; thus the more rational Arianism had been vanquished by orthodoxy.

In Mommsen's work the struggle between pagans and Christians has a social aspect. He equated paganism with the literary culture of the upper classes and, contrasting it with Christianity, described the latter as a "plebeian religion," the tone of which consequently remained plebeian (Hensel 3:104). The principle of Roman religion was toleration; religious intolerance had been brought into the world by the Jews (105) and taken over by the Christians. "With the Christian hierarchy arises a principle ominous in the highest degree to the state," a "state within the state" (107, 130ff.); against this principle an emperor like Diocletian would have been obliged to defend himself, even if he had been an enlightened, religiously indifferent man like Cicero or Marcus Aurelius. But Diocletian was no such thing; according to Mommsen, he believed in the gods whom the Christians branded as devils, and thus he was forced to intervene.

If Mommsen's sympathies lie with Diocletian rather than with Constantine, he is influenced in part by the parallel between these two on the one hand and Caesar and Augustus on the other, but the religious question is no doubt decisive. Neither in his religious policy nor in his founding of Constantinople did Constantine possess breadth of vision, according to Mommsen; success lay beyond all calculations (129). The sectarian struggles of the Christians were now, of course, a burden to the state. With Athanasius begins the conflict of church and state. Mommsen sees this as presumption (Hensel 3:159). When Mommsen goes so far as to maintain that religion brought on Rome's final catastrophe (Hensel 3:212), he is following Gibbon.

However much Mommsen deplored the "abdication" (*Abriss*: 281) of the late Roman state and the supremacy of the Church, he considered them unavoidable. "Polytheism had outlived itself" (Hensel 3:70). Constantine and Constantius, in their efforts to promote religious unity, did what was necessary. Julian, whom Mommsen found essentially more sympathetic as a human being, misread the situation. He ought to have known that it was all up with the old faith (Hensel 3:179), that the state now had to promote a general orthodoxy rather than cling to the outmoded idea of toleration (182). Nothing could be accomplished by a policy of indifference. Mommsen praised Ammianus Marcellinus for his "man of the world's contempt" for religious strife (Hensel 3:157)—and here Mommsen is characterizing his own relationship with the "Wonderland of religion."

Mommsen viewed Roman history as "the last act in the great historical drama" staged for us in the evolution of ancient civilization. For him it represents a self-contained cultural cycle that is paradigmatic for all of history. Its unity is expressed in metaphors of youth, maturity, and senility, of morning, noon, and evening, of spring, summer, and autumn. Modern history appears to him as just such another cycle, connected of course to the preceding cycle but presumably destined to end in a similar manner, through the "drying up of the creative energies in glutted satisfaction at the attainment of the goal" (*RG* 1:4). But history will not end there; every goal is transitory and points to a new and a higher goal. Roman history leads into an expanse of rubble, "but new life sprang up out of the ruins: the Latin race appeared, the Roman character permeated with the German; in metamorphosis, in solution the Roman character lived on, and from the ancient stem burst forth, in a happier age, fresh blossoms." The heirs of Alaric "continue in vigorous life even today" (Hensel 3:241). These formulae are familiar to us; we have seen them at the end of the third volume of the *Römische Geschichte*: after the "long historical night" of the Middle Ages, the European nations spring up out of the seed that Caesar had sown.

Mommsen considered the "ethical and political tendencies" of his historiography to be more important than its scholarship, since he was concerned above all with "political pedagogy." And so he wrote consciously *cum ira et studio*. His "political" history has been juxtaposed with the cultural-historical orientation of a Jakob Burckhardt; his subjectivity has been contrasted with Leopold von Ranke's calm, deliberate objectivity; his hope for progress in world history has been derived from the Hegelian tradition; his insight into the cyclic nature of world history has been traced to Romanticism; and his anachronism and modernizing have been repeatedly assailed. In this last point he was criticized not only by Karl Marx in *Das Kapital* (MEW 23, 182; 25, 339 and 795) but also by Friedrich Nietzsche in the 1873 "Bayreuther Horizontbetrachtungen" (*Musarion-Ausgabe* 7:235), written in 1873: "The author who seeks to make Roman history come alive by loathsome references to the paltry views of modern political parties and their ephemeral configuration commits a yet greater sin against the past than does the mere scholar who leaves everything dead and mummified (e.g., an historian much talked of at present, Mommsen)." Nevertheless, Marx and Nietzsche were in fundamental agreement with Mommsen: "Whatever has no value for life is not true history" (Nietzsche, *Ibid.*). It merely depends on how one goes about rendering the past usable to the present.

During his years in Berlin Mommsen produced his *Römisches Staatsrecht* (vols. I–III, 1871–1888), in which he discusses the *Institutiones* of the Empire in systematic form. The work as a whole has not yet been superseded; as is common in the case of a pioneering and fundamental work, criticism has been directed at its concepts. Influenced by Herder's idea of the fixed character of a people, Mommsen conceived of the Roman state, from the days of the kings to late antiquity, as a systematic unity. He thought of even the Emperor as a magistrate—in contradiction to the sources, in which the Emperor is never called a magistrate; in the popular mind he had received his legitimation by the will of the gods, as revealed in his nomination by his predecessor, his ratification by the Senate, and the army's acclamation. Mommsen knew that every monarchy, in the last analysis, is based on the grace of God, but in the case of Rome he managed to avoid drawing the logical consequences from this by conceiving of the Principate as a dyarchy, a double rule by Emperor and Senate. Scholarship has justly rejected this thesis; it has also disallowed Mommsen's assumption that the Roman constitution rested on the sovereignty of the people. This hypothesis is vulnerable even in the case of the Republic. But these objections aside, the *Staatsrechte* offers such a wealth of information that it has remained an indispensable tool.

Mommsen's works on chronology, coinage, and Roman criminal law also laid the foundations for further research, as did his rich essays on late antiquity, which are still the best gateway to the subject for the beginner. Altogether, Zangemeister and Jacobs's 1905 bibliography (which is incomplete) lists over 1,500 publications by Mommsen. Since Mommsen took into consideration and superseded practically all previous scholarship in the field of Roman history, it is usually sufficient to consult the works that have appeared since his day; one does not, as a rule, reach back beyond Mommsen. Since he seldom cites the books from which he has learned, he forms a barrier in the history of scholarship—a barrier it is occasionally worthwhile to pass.

Mommsen as Organizer

Not only were Mommsen's achievements as an historical researcher outstanding; he also did pioneering work in the organization and politics of scholarship. Adolf von Harnack justly regarded Mommsen's entry into the Academy as epoch-making. With Mommsen, writes Harnack, the Academy became truly acquainted with the "big business" of scholarship.

Mommsen had been a corresponding member of the Academy since 1853; the proposal that he be made a regular member came from the archaeologist Eduard Gerhard and the Egyptologist Richard Lepsius. Mommsen was admitted on 27 April 1858. At that time (although it soon grew larger) the Academy had forty-six ordinary members, equally divided among the mathematical and physical section and the philological and historical section. In 1874 Mommsen succeeded Moriz Haupt as one of the four secretaries of the Academy and remained in this position until 1895; he was succeeded by Hermann Diels. During this period he exercised considerable influence on the destiny of the Academy.

Mommsen's most important task at first was the work on the *Corpus Inscriptionum Latinarum* (CIL). After numerous fruitless attempts had been made at a comprehensive collection of inscriptions, Olaus Kellermann (a Dane) had undertaken the project; but he died of cholera only two years later. In 1847 Mommsen had sent his long memorandum to the Academy from Rome. But seven years of effort on the part of Eduard Gerhard were required before the Academy, over the objections of August Böckh, agreed to undertake the project. It was to cost 20,000 taler—the Academy's largest expenditure to date. Mommsen insisted that all previously published inscriptions be checked against the actual inscriptions in stone, and the funds for travel costs thus devoured were great. He gained support from the jurist Friedrich Karl von Savigny for this, "the Academy's greatest, most fruitful, and most brilliant undertaking" (Harnack)—on which it had spent, by 1900, over 400,000 gold marks. Director of the *CIL* after 1853, Mommsen did a great part of the work himself; he carefully selected the scholars who worked on this international project and—as his correspondence demonstrates—gave them indefatigable support. At his death fifteen of the sixteen volumes had appeared, and the *Corpus* was all but complete. Five volumes bear Mommsen's name.

Mommsen provided the impetus for the founding of the journal *Hermes*, which has appeared since 1866. The *Ephemeris Epigraphica*, of which Mommsen was joint founder, served for the publication of new discoveries; it appeared from 1872 to 1913. The *Année épigraphique* (Paris) now fulfills this task. Less successful was the *CIL*'s sister project, the *Corpus Inscriptionum Graecarum*. It was edited from 1825 to 1859 by the Prussian Academy and was then replaced by the *Inscriptiones Graecae* (IG), but this work is not yet completed.

The beginnings of the corpus of Latin inscriptions are intimately connected with the Deutsches Archäologisches Institut (DAI) in Rome. Founded in 1829 by Eduard Gerhard as the Istituto di corrispondenza archeologica, the Institute occupied the Palazzo Caffarelli on the Capitoline Hill (then still called Monte Caprino). It was at first an international center for archaeological research but enjoyed the patronage of the Prussian king, Friedrich Wilhelm IV, whose contributions provided the Institute's financial basis. The Palazzo Caffarelli had been the starting place of Mommsen's career when he arrived in Rome on 30 December 1844, and entered into a lifelong friendship with the Institute's secretaries Wilhelm Henzen and Heinrich Brunn.

In his post at the Berlin Academy, Mommsen took great interest in the growth of the Institute, as his letters to Henzen, Brunn, and Helbig testify; he even dealt with such questions as whether Italian scholars should receive the third or the fourth class of the Order of the Crown. Mommsen's own attitude toward such honors is revealed in a letter of 14 April 1860, to Henzen: "So I too have received the tiresome légion d'honneur—that is, it was sent to my address by our Minister to France; I will neither refuse it nor wear it, since I don't care to play Don Quixote and find it simplest just to lock the rubbish up in my closet." Mommsen recognized the purpose of this award: they were trying to woo him to be a collaborator in Napoleon III's researches on Caesar. Mommsen allowed himself to accept the star of the Order of the Crown, second class, but in 1897 he declined the title "Excellency," although Wilhelm II had already signed the patent.

The year 1859 marked a turning point in the history of the Archaeological Institute. Mommsen became a member of the board of directors, which consisted for the most part of members of the Academy, and he quickly became "one of the most active members of the Institute and of its board of directors" (Schmidt-Ott). He worked with energy to make the Institute an agency of the Prussian government, with assured financial support. By degrees he was successful. In April 1859 the Prussian *Abgeordnetenhaus* approved an increase in contributions from 1,340 to 4,500 taler for the next five years.

In his long letter of 5 June 1859, Mommsen explained to Brunn the new situation regarding the position of the two secretaries, the finances for research projects, travel grants (which were awarded on a regular basis after 1860), publications, and the problematic position occupied by the board of directors between the Institute and the Foreign Office. Mommsen was delighted to see the Institute developing more and more into the "succursal of German scholarship."

The transformation of the Roman Institute into a government agency was completed in 1871. On 2 March—the day after peace was concluded between Germany and France—Wilhelm I, on the advice of Bismarck, signed the document approving the takeover; the Institute's finances were secured and its ties to the Academy strengthened. On 16 May 1874, the Royal Prussian Institute became the German Imperial Institute, and the newly revised charter came from Mommsen's pen. In the same year (it had been approved a year earlier) the branch office in Athens was founded, and German excavations were begun in Olympia under Ernst Curtius, the tutor of Friedrich III. Curtius had been calling since 1852 for the excavation to begin, and now he wanted "a genuine work of peace" to match the triumph of German arms. In 1878 Carl Humann began excavations on the citadel of Pergamon with Prussian funds; he, too, enjoyed Mommsen's support.

On the other hand, attempts to improve relations with France and to establish a young archaeologist in Paris as representative of the Roman Institute met with no success. Because of his political letters *agli Italiani* during the Franco-Prussian war, Mommsen had been expelled from the Société Nationale des Antiquaires de France (but not, however, from the Académie des Inscriptions et Belles Lettres).

Among the Roman Institute's scholarly projects after 1859, besides collaboration on the *CIL* and the publication of smaller sets of monuments, was a "great museographical repertorium." This project is mentioned often in Mommsen's letters. Its subject appears from an address given by Mommsen on 18 March 1880: "a complete and systematic publication of ancient art-works, divided into categories and, within the categories, classified by period and locality" (RA 99). Mommsen had been inspired by Eduard Gerhard's collection of Etruscan seals and had conceived of a complete index of all portable antiquities. Such a gigantic project could not be realized. But the idea remained alive after Mommsen's death, and certain subdivisions of ancient art have been catalogued—for example, the corpus of vases, the corpus of sarcophagi, and the corpus of Mycenaean seals.

In 1884 Mommsen resigned from the board of directors of the DAI. His statements during this period are full of deep despondency. "I have long been sick to death of this whole board of directors, with its mixture of bureaucracy and archaeology, to the detriment of both, and of this mish-mash of opposing and incongruous interests." Yet he continued to take a lively interest in the problems in Rome. The language question is evidence of this. In the Institute, Italian, French, and Latin were spoken and written, and this persisted as late as 1879. The German scholars, as their national consciousness grew and their knowledge of Italian dwindled, naturally opposed this state of affairs. The thing became a public scandal, and on 9 May 1885 Bismarck, as the Institute's presiding officer, made continual financial support conditional on the future use of German in publications and proceedings.

Mommsen had proudly remarked in 1874 that "our neighbors are now reluctantly compelled to learn our language; difficult as it is, it has become indispensable." But in 1885 he felt that Bismarck had ruined the Institute. In the DAI's new bylaws of 1885 he missed the old spirit. The trouble here lay, of course, not merely in the altered conditions; the observer too had changed. Though Mommsen had once worked to secure a solid financial basis for the DAI, now he feared that it was developing into a "veritable government agency . . . with a few jobholders living on their pension, some temporary and some for life."

The third great project that owed its existence and growth largely to Mommsen was the Römisch-Germanische Kommission (RGK). After Mommsen's great services to archaeology in classical lands, he wanted to set in motion research into the remains of the Roman provinces that had existed in Germany. This research was then in the hands of local organizations and amateurs. "Might it not be possible," he asked in 1890, "to call into existence, on German soil, an institute for Roman-German antiquities, since we have Imperial Archaeological Institutes in Rome and in Athens?"

Mommsen had presented such a plan to the Prussian Ministry of Culture in 1874. Now he wanted a military man to be in charge of the work on the *limes*—no less a man than the former chief of the Prussian General Staff, Count Helmuth von Moltke, who "was passionately interested in the matter." Von Moltke had been a member of the Academy since 1860, he had been of service in advancing knowledge of historical topography in Italy and Asia Minor, and in his letters from Turkey

(1835–1839) he had revealed an amazing knowledge of the ancient authors. After exhaustive negotiations with the Ministry of the Interior on the subject of finances, Mommsen's plan was rejected in 1890 because of Bismarck's objections. But Mommsen was stubborn. His letters to Brunn allow us to follow the project in all its phases. "The old hot blood and the fever of the Gründerjahre will not let up yet," he wrote to Brunn on 1 December 1890, and in the same year, at the Winckelmann anniversary celebrations, he lamented that the *limes* had not yet been declared a national monument and placed under the protection of the Empire. Mommsen succeeded in winning the support of Wilhelm II, whom he greatly esteemed, for the reconstruction of the *castellum* of Saalburg near Frankfurt. The Emperor's patronage is epigraphically commemorated on the Mommsen monument there:

> THEODORO MOMMSEN
> SCRIPTORI RERUM ROMANARUM
> INTER OMNES PRINCIPI
> CUIUS IMPULSU ATQUE CONSILIO
> LIMES IMPERII ROMANI
> PATEFACTUS EST.
> GUILELMUS II IMPERATOR GERMANORUM.

For directing work on the *limes* Mommsen considered the "constant collaboration of a trained officer a scholarly necessity." In place of von Moltke, who celebrated his ninetieth birthday on 26 October 1890—Mommsen penned the Academy's official address of congratulation—the retired Bavarian Major-General Karl Popp (1825–1905) offered his services, but his military superiors refused to approve the appointment. Yet Bavaria and Württemberg were insisting on having a South German officer in charge, because otherwise "the project would be un-German." And so a general from Württemberg, cousin of the Württemberg Minister of Culture, was named as candidate for the provisional directorship of the undertaking; Mommsen mistrusted him on scholarly grounds.

These intrigues were the source of political headaches for Mommsen. His dream was of a Ministry of Culture for the German Empire as a whole, and he placed his talents in scholarly organization, as well as his writing of history, at the service of national political pedagogy. He was proud of the contributions made by the DAI and the *Monumenta Germaniae Historica* (MGH) to a national consciousness that would transcend the boundaries of the individual German states, and this spirit was lacking in the *limes* project. Mommsen was not satisfied with the German Empire of 1871. He called the "wretched patchwork of Anno 71 a political fiasco." It called forth from Mommsen a gloomy prognosis: "Our poor fatherland, despite its apparent unification, is so fragmented. . . . Our children will have to pay the price."

Mommsen had had in mind Felix Hettner, the director of the Trier Museum, to be archaeological director of the *limes* project, and he accepted the assignment. Members of the Berlin Academy as well as representatives of the five German states that were involved in the project met at Heidelberg in December 1890 for the first *limes* conference. In 1892 the Reichslimeskommission began its work, which has been continued, since 1901, by the Römisch-Germanische Kommission, based in Frankfurt. It could not be organized from Berlin, as Mommsen well knew: "Berlin is built on non-classical soil." The most significant result of these efforts is the monumental fourteen-volume *Der obergermanisch-raetische Limes des Römerreiches* (ORL) by E. Fabricius, F. Hettner, and O. v. Sarvey (1894–1938).

After smaller preparatory studies, Mommsen's history of Roman coinage appeared in 1860. He called for a *corpus nummorum*, which remains a desideratum even today, as does his projected *corpus papyrorum*. Mommsen at least opened the way for the publication of the Berlin papyri, and he was one of the founders of the Archiv für Papyrusforschung. Likewise uncompleted is the atlas of the ancient world, "long desired" by Mommsen and others. Substantial portions of this work were produced after 1893 by the Kieperts, Sr. and Jr., under the auspices of the Academy.

Ultimately successful was the idea of a *prosopographia imperii romani*. In 1874 Mommsen proposed an alphabetical catalogue of the personages (mentioned chiefly in inscriptions) of Roman history. But the work made slow progress; it has now reached the letter M. Mommsen also called for a catalogue of known persons of historical significance in late antiquity. This work was taken over in 1901 by the Kirchenväterkommission but got no further than the index-card stage. Not until 1957, when John Morris brought the material from East Berlin to Cambridge "on loan," did the work move forward. *The Prosopography of the Later Roman Empire* (vol. I, 1971; vol. II, 1980), edited by John Martindale with the support of numerous British scholars, has become a standard work.

The Monumenta Germaniae Historica (MGH)—"the greatest undertaking of our nation and of its best man," as Mommsen wrote to his son-in-law Wilamowitz on 30 March 1887, referring to the Freiherr vom Stein—did not actually lie within Mommsen's bailiwick. Nevertheless, after Haupt's death he handled the negotiations that turned the Gesellschaft für die ältere deutsche Geschichtskunde into a subsidiary project of the Academy. At this time the publication of the *Auctores Antiquissimi* (vital for the study of German history) was also decided on, and Mommsen took it under his wing. He himself edited Eugippius, Jordanes, Cassiodorus, and—indispensable for the study of late antiquity— the *Chronica Minora*, collating the most important manuscripts in Germany, France, England, and Italy. The first part of the *Gesta Pontificum* in the MGH is also his.

Among the other pioneering accomplishments that we owe to Mommsen as editor are the digests in the *Corpus Juris Civilis* and (in conjunction with Paul Krüger and Paul Martin Meyer) the *Codex Theodosianus*. Neither of these works has yet been superseded. He was the moving spirit behind the *Vocabularium Jurisprudentiae Romanae*, the first volume of which is dedicated to him. Mommsen was a member of the *Thesaurus Linguae Latinae* and also—like "Saul among the prophets," as he himself put it—of the Kirchenväterkommission for the editing of the Greek Christian authors of the first three centuries, which was founded in 1891 and financed by the Wentzell-

Heckman foundation. These two projects are not yet completed; the latter remained under the auspices of the Academy of the German Democratic Republic, while the *Thesaurus* moved to Munich and has now progressed to the letter *P*.

For the *Thesaurus* Moritz Hertz arranged collaboration between the academies of Berlin, Munich, and Vienna. Working with Friedrich Althoff, Mommsen expanded the idea and sketched out the statutes of a cartel involving the academies of all the German-speaking countries. In January 1893 the representatives met in Leipzig. From this meeting grew a plan for an international organization of the academies of all countries. At the first general convention at Paris in 1901, Mommsen represented the Prussian Academy. He was primarily concerned with the *corpus nummorum*. Mommsen always viewed scholarly cooperation as a means, on the one hand, to transcend the hostilities of races and nations, and on the other hand, as a necessary condition for any great scholarly accomplishment. The basic idea behind this policy was formulated by Mommsen on the occasion of Harnack's admission to the Academy on 3 July 1890: "Scholarship too has its social dimension; like great powers in politics and large-scale operation in industry, large-scale scholarship—not pursued, but directed, by a single man—is a necessary element in our cultural evolution, and its proper representatives are—or ought to be—the academies."

Mommsen as Politician

Though it was of secondary importance to him, national politics always retained Mommsen's passionate interest, and this interest did not wane after his political activities in Rendsburg during 1848 and during 1850 in Leipzig. From 1863 to 1866 he was a member of the Prussian Abgeordnetenhaus, in which, after his election by the city of Halle and the Saale district, he joined the liberal German Progressive Party. Mommsen opposed Prussian annexation as a means of solving the German question and advocated the creation of a German Parliament modeled on the Pre-Parliament in the Paulskirche in Frankfurt in 1848. He supported the war of 1870–71, but he did so hesitantly in view of the destruction of international scholarly cooperation, and later, in 1900, he recommended the abolition of Sedan Day, the extremely popular holiday commemorating the victory over France. His attitudes here contrast favorably with the passionate patriotism of men like Eduard Meyer during the First World War, to say nothing of the frigid ideological conformity of men like Wilhelm Weber in the Second World War. From 1873 to 1879 he represented Kottbus-Spremberg-Kalau in the Prussian Landstag, and from 1881 to 1884 he was member of the Reichstag for Coburg.

Mommsen delivered five speeches in the Abgeordnetenhaus. They dealt with university issues, the improvement of foreign language instruction in the schools, a nonsectarian policy in the secondary schools, easier access to the libraries of Berlin, and the modernization of museums. Mommsen insisted that Germany's political achievements should now be matched by corresponding advances in the field of scholarship.

Mommsen's political activities repeatedly made headlines—as for example, in the anti-Semitism quarrel of 1879–80. Mommsen had close relations with Jews. The publisher Salomon Hirzel had urged him to write the *Römische Geschichte* and the *Staatsrecht* (see above). It is not surprising, therefore, that Mommsen opposed the famous historian and orator Heinrich von Treitschke. After the Jews had been granted legal equality in Prussia in 1869, there arose fears of an influx of Jews from Eastern Europe and irritation at the involvement of Jews in financial scandals. In the November 1879 issue of the *Preussische Jahrbücher* Treitschke published his article "Our Views," in which he gave expression to these anxieties. "They must become Germans, must feel themselves to be Germans, as far as may be—without prejudice to their faith and their ancient sacred memories, which we all respect." Treitschke opposed the "spirit of arrogance" in certain Jews; it was due to this spirit that "today we hear it spoken, as if with one voice: 'The Jews are our misfortune!' "

This article unleashed a far-ranging controversy, in which Mommsen became the spokesman for the opponents of Treitschke. Much light is cast on the two adversaries by their correspondence with Herman Grimm. As the son of Wilhelm Grimm, the author of fairy tales, Herman Grimm was the friend of both scholars. On the Jewish question he leaned toward Treitschke but nonetheless stood godfather to one of Mommsen's children and was a frequent guest in the Mommsen household.

Grimm first expressed his satisfaction at the fact that discussion had begun. "Because almost the whole of the public press is in Jewish hands," the issue, he felt, had been artificially suppressed. "The Jews ought to be glad that these things are being debated at a time when they still can be debated"; otherwise the tension between German idealism and Jewish realism would have "burst forth in a tremendous explosion." Grimm lamented their "open arrogance," their "feeling of apartness as Jews," their exploitation of their "double position" and oppression for "shameless demands" of a pecuniary nature. Thus he wrote to Treitschke on 10 December 1879. On the day before Christmas Grimm prophesied incalculable consequences, which he traced to the two peoples' irrepressible growth in national consciousness, and on 28 December he expressed once more his relief at being able to speak: "A service, in fact, has been done the Jews, for which they will one day thank the care of Providence."

On 28 January 1880, Treitschke asked Grimm to open negotiations with Mommsen. On the same day Grimm promised, "I will do what I can with Mommsen, but it would be the first time I had succeeded in directly compelling him to give in." On 1 February Grimm visited Mommsen and wrote the next day of his "frightful outbursts and the cannon-blasts that shot from his eyes." Since Mommsen, "like all Schleswig-Holsteiners, was christened in the milk of infallibility," he would probably "snap right back to his former position." Mommsen reproached Treitschke with having published something that would have been "proper and permissible" as a chapter in his historical works but was not suitable as a newspaper article. Grimm, on the other hand, declared to Mommsen—without contradiction—that Treitschke was right in the matter.

At the beginning of November 1880 appeared the "Declaration of the Seventy-five." The signatories, Mommsen among them, expressed their opposition to Stöcker and Treitschke, although they named neither of them. In fact, Treitschke did not at first feel that reference was being made to him, as appears from his letter to Grimm on 15 November 1880. This is what he wanted to ascertain. "I cannot take such defamation lying down; I owe it to my students, at least, to protest."

Before he replied, Grimm sketched out an extensive rough draft of his answer. "The Jews are essentially different from the Germans." A clear-headed German who said this, he maintained, was only doing what clear-headed Jews had always done. "And this fact is in no way due to the unjust treatment with which we have oppressed the Jews through the centuries." Grimm spoke of an agreement to stem the rising tide of Jewish influence—an agreement that must remain tacit. "As soon as one feels compelled to admit that it is in fact a question of race, one would—perhaps quite innocently—conjure up monstrous misfortune." Grimm feared an uprising of the working class against Jewish wealth, because it would threaten non-Jewish prosperity, too. "I confess that I have presentiments of great social upheavals of this sort, and the thought of what might come of them weighs upon me sometimes like an oppressive dream." Grimm warned Treitschke that if he should issue a statement, "every word you speak in public will be misunderstood and will be exploited in the most ruinous manner by people with whom you wish to have nothing to do." Such were Grimm's ideas.

The answer that Grimm sent on 17 November 1880, was much shorter. He admits that Treitschke is in the right but begs him not to stir up the controversy any further, because he fears that a pogrom mood may develop. "Our role will begin when there is actual need to protect the Jews. It would be a great misfortune if it should prove impossible to offer this protection, for we all know how much we owe the Jews, and it would be a national misfortune to be deprived of this element as a partner." Here Grimm thinks just as Mommsen does.

On the same day Treitschke published a request to be informed whether the "Declaration of the Seventy-five" had been directed at him; on 19 November Mommsen's "Jawohl!" appeared in the *Post*. Grimm now took his place at Treitschke's side and wrote that the Seventy-five had "unleashed the spirits that will rise up out of the depths." Thereupon Mommsen wrote his pamphlet "Auch ein Wort über unser Judenthum," which included a warning against a "Jewish war." Mommsen was no more uncritical toward the Jews than toward his Christian countrymen, but "the thousand-year oppression of German Semites by German Christians, equally ruinous to both," had to cease. Providence had done well in adding "a few percent of Israel to the fashioning of German metal."

Mommsen sent this article to Grimm on 10 December 1880, with the words: "Dear Grimm, what I send you will not have your applause, and *unus ex paucis* is always in a bad way. But that's why I am sending it to you; for if I cannot have your praise, I can put up with scolding. . . . Let us remain on the same old footing, in good times as well as in bad. Yours, Mommsen."

On 11 December Grimm replied: "Dear Mommsen, when I finished reading your article, I had the strange feeling that you have said nothing but what Treitschke has said or what I myself would have said." In Grimm's view, Treitschke had done good service in opening the debate and getting in ahead of the Social Democrats, from whom Grimm expected the real protest against the Jewish financiers. "We in Germany demand, above all freedoms, the freedom to criticize"; yet he looked on the "Declaration of the Seventy-five" as a breach of courtesy between colleagues.

With this indiscretion on Mommsen's part one might compare, first, Treitschke's resorting to the public press and, second, his involving his students in the affair; this, too, broke the rules of the academic game. Treitschke, who had not signed the Zöllner-Förster petition against the Jews, accepted the homage of the anti-Semitic students with mixed feelings, but he could not free himself from the suspicion of having summoned up the spirits that thereafter he could not exorcise. Such at least was Mommsen's reproach. On 12 December he wrote to Grimm that quite possibly there were reasons for anti-Jewish feelings, but he accused Treitschke of having secretly welcomed the student demonstrations. Again and again, questions of protocol predominate over more substantive issues. Mommsen privately expressed himself about the Jews quite in Treitschke's vein. How widespread this feeling was is clear from the anti-Semitic remarks of Ranke and Jacob Burckhardt's invectives against the "almighty Jewish press" in his letters to Preen.

In his answer on December 13, Grimm agreed with Mommsen about the damage that had been done but thought that the Seventy-five bore the greater share of the blame. "For the matter was not flagrant, since Treitschke's article was a year old and since there was no mention of these things in his lecture hall." Grimm clings firmly to the belief in an irremovable racial difference between Jews and Germans and doubts that the Jews have the desire to assimilate. Here he differs from Treitschke. He noted in his diary on 25 June 1882: "When Mommsen (from sincere conviction) preaches to the Semites about liberty and equality, he reminds me of the owner of a stud farm who thinks that with the proper fodder and handling he can persuade jackasses to become horses."

Although our basic sympathies surely lie with Mommsen in this affair, still we cannot overlook the fact that here—as later, when he was prosecuted by Bismarck—he had recourse to sophistical ambiguities. The passage most often quoted on the Jews in Mommsen's writings is in the *Römische Geschichte* (3:549f.). Here he is dealing with the question of why Caesar assigned to the Jews—along with the "two nations destined for joint rule," the Romans and the Greeks—a certain position of eminence above the other nations within the Empire. Mommsen's answer: "In the ancient world as in the modern, Jewry constituted an active ferment of the cosmopolitanism and national decomposition" upon which Caesar's multinational state was based. From the viewpoint of Caesar the imperialist, this was an advantage; in the eyes of any nationalist, on the other hand, it was a reproach. To Mommsen, Jewry was "not the pleasantest element" in Roman history; he speaks of the "peculiar antipathy of the Occidental toward this race which is fundamentally so Oriental." Mommsen's verdict on the Jews is as full of contradictions as is his picture of Caesar, which, brilliant though it is, cannot alter the fact that Caesar brought to an end what Mommsen considered "real" Roman history.

In his first answer to Mommsen, Treitschke quoted his opponent's own words: "I do not share the pessimistic views of my colleague Mommsen, that everywhere in the world 'Jewry constitutes an active ferment of cosmopolitanism and national decomposition;' rather, I live in the hope that complete emancipation will be followed, in the course of time, by internal amalgamation and reconciliation." Rather deftly, Treitschke had turned the tables.

Mommsen acknowledged his own words, but applied them to the present in a different manner from Treitschke. "Just as the Jews, in the Roman state, were a factor making for national decomposition, so in Germany they are doubtless a factor in the decomposition of the principalities." It was for this reason that there were so many Jews in Berlin. Mommsen construes the movement for German unification as a "process of decomposition" of the principalities and the individual German states; he even mourns for his own homeland Schleswig-Holstein, its national consciousness dissolved or submerged in the Reich! That was dishonest, for, though he viewed the transition from a unified Italian nation-state to the *Imperium Romanum* as a step into the abyss, he saw the coalescence of the German states into a national Empire as a step forward, which had never before elicited from him any tears for his lost "childhood happiness." His criticism of the founding of the Empire cited above is a criticism of its defective unity.

In his reply Treitschke disputed this reinterpretation of the passage from the *Römische Geschichte*. He denied that the presence of Jews in Berlin was evidence for a national consciousness that transcended the German states and promoted "reconciliation between the Saxons, the Suabians, the Franconians, etc." "These elements in Jewry are hostile to all that is truly German," he claims; they embody "a cosmopolitanism that knows no home." Georg von Below saw that the Jews' "dissective" function, which Mommsen emphasized in his *Römische Geschichte*, supported Treitschke's political position rather than Mommsen's. Of course Treitschke was now withdrawing from his original faith in the incorporation of the Jews into Germany. Although Mommsen and Treitschke stubbornly insisted that each maintained his original position, this is only half true for both of them.

As we saw, Mommsen sent his pamphlet against Treitschke to Grimm, and Grimm, in his reply of 11 December, discussed the quotation from the *Römische Geschichte*. "Since you permit me to criticize, I would like to point out a weakness in your interpretation of 'decomposition.' When an Empire is put together out of provinces, one cannot, in my opinion, speak of decomposition, a word that implies only putrescence and not a new creation rising out of chaos." Here Grimm lays his finger on the flaw in Mommsen's overdrawn parallel between the Roman and the German Empires.

Mommsen replied on 12 December: "Your remarks on 'decomposition' are, I think, incorrect. Putrescence, to be sure; but does not putrescence always mean new creation? Diocletian's constitutional reforms, Ammianus' conception of history (which is greater than that of Thucydides) are founded on decomposition. Our own is pretty putrid—*vide* certain Berlin literati. But it also contains hope for the future." Mommsen was not reconciled to Treitschke. "For me, the figure of Treitschke gives proper expression to the ethical brutalization which is calling our civilization into question"; Treitschke is "the father of modern anti-Semitism." When Treitschke's admission to the Academy could no longer be prevented, Mommsen took the opportunity to resign his position as secretary. "I cannot remain with him there," he wrote to his wife on 15 May 1895.

Just as Mommsen had in the Jewish question opposed discrimination on genealogical or religious grounds, he protested against such grounds being used as an excuse for preferential treatment in the Spahn affair. In November 1901 Spahn was granted a professorship of modern history in Strassburg because he was a Catholic. But sectarianism, Mommsen maintained, was the mortal enemy of all that a university was meant to be; a university's very mainspring was investigation free from all preconditions of this sort. A demand for "Catholic professorships" would benefit only the creatures of mediocrity and would be a betrayal of the idea of a university. In this one instance Mommsen found himself in opposition to Friedrich Althoff, Under Secretary in the Prussian Ministry of Culture, who was one of Mommsen's closest friends. In 1894 Mommsen had interceded on behalf of the Jewish physicist Dr. Arons, who as an active Social Democrat was threatened with expulsion from the faculty.

Mommsen's political mood grew increasingly gloomy after 1880. Even then he was complaining publicly about the "moral pestilence" that was taking hold with "epidemic violence" and about the "process of ethical disintegration." On 10 December 1881, he commented in a letter to Helbig on misunderstandings with Italy, "But on the whole this is only one more instance of that process of political self-annihilation which now marks us and which is probably unexampled in history. . . . I am writing during the Socialist debates in the Reichstag; this is another of those cases in which our protectors are more dangerous than our enemies." The slander action brought against him by Bismarck, the "greatest of all opportunists," called forth pessimistic remarks from him—which may be due in part to the fact that he could not conduct his defense without some loss of self-respect. For he was probably wrong in claiming that his charges on 24 September 1881, about a "politics of swindle," had not been leveled at specific persons. The court could not—or would not—prove the contrary, and he was acquitted.

Expressions of national self-hatred—Treitschke calls them *Maulgrillen* ("grumbling") (20 July 1880)—begin around 1880. In line with them is his complaint against Henzen on 8 September 1884—"The Germans simply have no backbone"—and they end with the gloomy clause in his will: "In Germany the individual, even the best, can do no better than serve in the ranks or practice political fetishism." Mommsen deplored blind discipline in one case and blind wishful thinking in the other.

Yet Mommsen's mood was never entirely dark. He remained an optimist on the subject of scholarship. During the Leibnitz anniversary celebrations in 1895 he said, "Scholarship, indeed, is making enormous and irresistible progress" (RA 196). The same was true of political developments in general; he spoke of "the increase in humanitarianism, the spreading of civilization" (RA 197). This might well call to mind the Roman Imperial period, but Mommsen would not hear of such an analogy. The "generally peaceful and amicable coexistence of the several nations, which seems to be the goal of modern political evolution, is foreign to antiquity" (RG 1:664).

Even as late as the year of his death, Mommsen felt that the best possible future was the "holy alliance of the nations" (1903); the worst possible prospect, on the other hand, was a world-state in the Roman style. According to the parallels that Mommsen (like Eduard Meyer and Oswald Spengler after him) saw between the course of ancient and modern history, another *Imperium* might be expected sooner or later, which would find a political solution in the civilizing economic rapprochement of the European or Europeanized peoples. Mommsen feared this development (RA 142), but he hoped that it might perhaps lie far in the future. Unlike Eduard Meyer, Mommsen did not dread a *pax Anglo-Americana*. His feelings toward America were expressed in a poem written in the 1850s for the historian George Bancroft, who was American ambassador in Berlin from 1867 to 1874:

> Wir sind vom selben Schlage,
> Uns hebt dieselbe Flut.
> Ihr braucht die alte Sage,
> Wir brauchen frisches Blut.
> Des Einen Volks Begründung,
> Das war, das ist uns Rom.
> Vertiefung und Verbündung
> Schafft jetzt am Völkerdom.
> So klingt hier die Parole,
> Sie klingt auch drüben wohl:
> Vom alten Kapitole
> Zum neuen Kapitol!

Translated by Michael Armstrong

Books (Selected)

Römische Geschichte I–III. Berlin, 1854–56; V, 1885. (Volume IV never published.)
Römisches Staatsrecht. Leipzig, 1871.
Abriss des römischen Staatsrechts. Leipzig, 1893; reprinted 1974.
Römisches Strafrecht. Leipzig, 1899.
Reden und Aufsätze. Berlin, 1905.
Gesammelte Schriften I–VIII. Berlin, 1905–1913.
Briefwechsel 1872–1903. With Ulrich von Wilamowitz-Moellendorff. Berlin, 1935.

Sources

Bibliography

Zangemeister, Karl, und Emil Jacobs. *Theodor Mommsen als Schriftsteller.* Berlin 1905.
(Bibliography of Mommsen's works in chronological order.)

Biographical

Bohlich, Walter. *Der Berliner Antisemitismusstreit.* Sammlung Insel 6. Frankfurt,
1965; paperback edition, 1988.

Brocke, Bernhard vom. "Hochschul- und Wissenschaftspolitik in Preussen und im
Deutschen Kaiserreich 1882–1907: Das 'System Althoff.' " In *Bildungspolitik
in Preussen zur Zeit des Kaiserreichs.* Edited by Peter Baumgart. Stuttgart,
1980: 9–118.

Christ, Karl. *Von Gibbon zu Rostovtzeff: Leben und Werk führender Althistoriker der
Neuzeit.* Darmstadt, 1972.

———. *Römische Geschichte und deutsche Geschichtswissenschaft.* Darmstadt, 1982.

———. ". . . die schwere Ungerechtigkeit gegen Augustus." *Augustus, Mommsen
und Wilamowitz. Tria Corda: scritti in onore de Arnaldo Momigliano.* Edited
by E. Gabba. Como, 1983: 89–100.

Croke, Brian. "Mommsen and Byzantium." *Philologus* 129 (1985) 274–285.

Demandt, Alexander. *Der Fall Roms. Die Auflösung des Römischen Reiches im Urteil
der Nachwelt.* Munich, 1984.

———. "Alte Geschichte an der Berliner Universität." In *Berlin und die Antike:
Architektur, Kunstgewerbe, Malerei, Skulptur, Theater un Wissenschaft vom 16.
Jahrhundert bis Heute.* (Aufsatzband zur Ausstellung.) Edited by Willmuth
Arenhövel and Christa Schreiber. Berlin, 1979: 69–97.

———. "Mommsens ungeschriebene Kaisergeschichte." *Jahrbuch der Berliner
Wissenschaftlichen Gesellschaft 1983* (Berlin, 1984) 147–161.

———. "Die Hensel-Nachschriften zu Mommsens Kaiserzeit-Vorlesung." *Gymnasium* 93 (1986) 497–519. Plates XVII–XXIV.

———. "Mommsen in Berlin." In *Wissenschaftspolitik in Berlin: Minister, Beamte,
Ratgeber. Berliner Lebensbilder.* Edited by W. Treue and K. Gründer. Berlin,
1987: 3:149–173.

Fowler, W. Warde. "Theodor Mommsen: His Life and Work." In *Roman Essays and
Interpretations.* Oxford, 1920: 250–268. (Written in 1909.)

Galsterer, H. "Theodor Mommsen." *Berlinische Lebensbilder Geisteswissenschaftler.*
Berlin, 1989: 175–194.

Grau, Conrad. *Die Berliner Akademie der Wissenschaften in der Zeit des Imperialismus,
t. 1: Von den neunziger Jahren des 19. Jahrhunderts bis zur Grossen Sozialistis-
chen Oktoberrevolution.* Studien zur Geschichte der Akademie der Wissenschaften der DDR 2. Berlin, 1975.

Harnack, Adolf. *Geschichte der königlich preussischen Akademie der Wissenschaften zu
Berlin. Band 1: Darstellung* (cited by pages). *Band 2: Urkunden und
Actenstücke* (cited by numbers). Berlin, 1900.

Hartmann, Ludo Moritz. *Theodor Mommsen. Eine Biographische Skizze.* Gotha, 1908.

Hensel, Paul. "Theodor Mommsen. Römische Kaisergeschichte von Caesar bis Vespasian." Unpublished lecture notes. Berlin, Winter-semester, 1882–83. (Cited as Hensel 1.)

Hensel, Sebastian. "Theodor Mommsen. Römische Kaisergeschichte von Vespasian bis Diocletian." Unpublished lecture notes. Berlin, Summer-semester 1883. (Cited as Hensel 2.)

―――. "Theodor Mommsen. Römische Kaisergeschichte von Diocletian bis Honorius." Unpublished lecture notes. Berlin, Summer-semester 1886. (Cited as Hensel 3.)

Heuss, Alfred. *Theodor Mommsen und das 19. Jahrhundert.* Kiel, 1956.

Hirschfeld, Otto. "Gedächtnisrede auf Theodor Mommsen." In *Otto Hirschfeld, Kleine Schriften.* Berlin, 1913: 931–965. (Written in 1904.)

Hoffmann, Christhard. "Juden und Judentum im Werk Deutscher Althistoriker des 19. und 20. Jahrhunderts." *Studies in Judaism in Modern Times 9.* Edited by Jacob Neusner. Leiden, New York, Copenhagen, Cologne, 1988: 87–132.

Imelmann, T. "Mommsen über Gibbon." *Der Tag* 12 November 1909. Illustrierte Unterhaltungsbeilage 266: 4.

Johne, Klaus-Peter. "100 Jahre Prosopographia Imperii Romani." *Klio* 56 (1974) 21–27.

Kirsten, Christa. *Die Altertumswissenschaften an der Berliner Akademie. Wahlvorschläge zur Aufnahme von Mitgliedern von F. A. Wolf bis zu G. Rodenwaldt 1799–1932.* Berlin, 1985.

Liebeschütz, Hans. "Treitschke and Mommsen on Jewry and Judaism." *Yearbook VII of the Leo Baeck Institute.* 1962: 153–182.

Liebeschütz, Hans. *Das Judentum im deutschen Geschichtsbild von Hegel bis Max Weber.* Tübingen, 1967.

Mey, Hans-Joachim. "Herman Grimm, eine biographische Skizze." *Hessische Blätter für Volks- und Kulturforschung.* Neue Folge 18 (1985) 162–170.

Michaelis, Adolf. *Geschichte des Deutschen Archäologischen Instituts 1829–1879.* Berlin, 1879.

Reich, Emil. "Theodor Mommsen." *Monthly Review* (London) 13 (Oct.–Dec. 1903) 74–84.

Rodenwaldt, Gerhart. *Archäologisches Institut des Deutschen Reiches 1829–1929.* Berlin, 1929.

Sachse, Arnold. *Friedrich Althoff und sein Werk.* Berlin, 1928.

Sartori, Franco. "Theodor Mommsen radiato dalla Socété des Antiquaires de France." In *Xenia. Scritti in onore di Piero Treves.* Edited by F. Broilo. Rome, 1985: 183–190.

Schmidt-Ott, Friedrich. *Erlebtes und Erstrebtes 1860–1950.* Wiesbaden, 1952.

Treitschke, Heinrich von. *Briefe.* Edited by M. Cornicelius. Band 3, Teil 2 (1871–1896). Leipzig, 1920.

Wickert, Lothar. *Beiträge zur Geschichte des Deutschen Archäologischen Instituts 1879–1929*. Mainz, 1979.

––––––. *Theodor Mommsen. Eine Biographie*. Frankfurt-am-Main. Vol. 1, 1959; vol. 2, 1964; vol. 3, 1970; vol. 4, 1980.

Wilamowitz-Moellendorff, Ulrich von. *Erinnerungen 1848–1914*. Leipzig, 1928.

Winkelmann, F. *Prosopographia Imperii Romani saec. IV, V, VI. Sitzungsberichte der Akademie der Wissenschaften*. Berlin, 1980: 29–34.

Wucher, Albert. *Theodor Mommsen. Geschichtsschreibung und Politik*. Göttingen, 1956; 2d ed., 1968.

Papers

Major Mommsen collections are held in East Berlin by the Akademie-Archiv and the Staatsbibliothek der DDR. Smaller collections are in the Schiller-National-museum in Marbach, in the Universitätsbibliothek Kiel and in the Staatsbibliothek, West Berlin.

Gelehrten- und Schriftsteller-Nachlässe in den Bibliotheken der DDR. Edited by Hans Lüfling. Vols. I–III. Berlin, 1959–1971.

Die Nachlässe in den Bibliotheken der Bundesrepublik Deutschland. Edited by Ludwig Denecke and Tilo Brandis; 2d ed., Boppard am Rhein, 1981.

Karl Otfried Müller

28 August 1797–1 August 1840

WOLFHART UNTE
Freie Universität West Berlin

Among the names of the great sons given to nineteenth-century scholarship by the eastern German province of Silesia, that of Karl Otfried Müller possesses unique resonance. Classical scholars, ancient historians, and archaeologists alike count him among the great masters of their fields. In all these disciplines, Müller's influence is felt to the present day; Karl Kerényi has recently described him as "one of the best representatives of classical studies at the end of the age of Goethe." To Müller's personality, as well as to his life and work, clings an aura of genius and of great good fortune—and of tragedy too, when we consider his premature and unexpected death, at the zenith of his influence and creativity, in Hellas, the land of his longing.

Karl Müller (who later assumed the pen name Karl Otfried Müller on the advice of Philipp Buttmann, one of his teachers in Berlin) came from the family of a Silesian clergyman; he was born in Brieg on 27 August 1797, the oldest of four children—three sons and a daughter—of Pastor Karl Daniel Müller. Karl Otfried Müller spent his school days in Brieg, even after his father had exchanged his pastorate with that in Ohlau. Thus Ohlau became the site of the family home for Karl and for his two younger brothers, Julius, the famous theologian, and Eduard, who was later director of Gymnasia in Ratibor and Liegnitz; Ohlau was the domestic refuge to which they all eagerly returned, again and again, even in later years, when they practiced their professions far from home. In the surviving letters to his parents, Müller often expresses the attachment he feels for his father, mother, brothers, and sister, as well as for his home.

Even during his school days in Brieg, Müller revealed intellectual abilities far above the average in his original compositions, both in prose and in verse, and he distinguished himself in valedictory addresses for the graduates. He matriculated in the newly founded Schlesische Friedrich-Wilhelms-Universität in Breslau in Spring

1814. At first his studies were general, for he had broad interests in the humanities and the natural sciences, but he felt increasingly drawn to philological subjects. His chief teacher here was Friedrich Heindorf, who had been transferred from Berlin to Breslau in 1811 and who, in Berlin, had been one of the circle of Niebuhr, Buttmann, and Schleiermacher. Müller always recalled Heindorf with great gratitude, and it was he who encouraged the young student to read Niebuhr's *Römische Geschichte*. The reading of this work made a lasting impression on Müller, and it was the decisive factor in his resolve to devote himself entirely to philological and historical studies. Consequently he undertook a history of the Roman king Numa Pompilius and a study of the most ancient Roman poetry. In his philological method he was even then an adherent of an all-encompassing historical view of classical antiquity, as it was being advocated at this time by Friedrich August Wolf and by his student August Böckh in Berlin.

So in Spring 1816 Müller transferred to Berlin to continue his studies. Here he attended lectures by Schleiermacher and by Schelling's student Friedrich Solger, whose aesthetics were not without their effect on him. Wolf was a member of the Berlin Academy of Sciences and thus gave lectures at the University, but he found less acceptance here than in Halle because of his intolerant manner, and Müller found him repellent. All the greater was the effect on Müller of Philipp Buttmann and, especially, of August Böckh. Buttmann was then writing his *Mythologus*, and the intensive exposure to questions of mythology and history of religions that Buttmann gave him was of great significance for Müller's later scholarly work. But even more decisive was his encounter with August Böckh, the chief representative of the historical and antiquarian trend in *Altertumswissenschaft*, which contrasted with the more grammatical and text-critical school led by Gottfried Hermann in Leipzig. Under Böckh's direction Müller pursued the study of an all-embracing view of antiquity and thereby laid the foundation for his later position as the greatest representative of philological-historical research in his time, surpassing even his teacher Böckh in universality.

The rising scholar's years in Berlin were characterized by a unique and indefatigable zeal for work and a passion for research. We are told that he could work as much as sixteen hours a day without exhaustion—a phenomenon that later contributed to his great scholarly accomplishments. As the subject of his dissertation he chose the island of Aegina and set himself the task of portraying its history from every angle. In October 1817 he received his doctoral degree with the Latin dissertation "Aegineticorum liber scripsit Carolus Mueller Silesius." Because of the work's completely novel methodology—the historical consideration of the theme from all perspectives, taking into account all factual details (in his knowledge of which the author revealed a much-admired erudition)—it quickly became well-known among scholars of *Altertumswissenschaft* and had widespread influence.

After completing his studies Müller accepted, at the beginning of 1818, a position as gymnasium teacher at the Magdalenäum in Breslau. But this period as gymnasium teacher in Breslau gave him little satisfaction; he found contentment here only in scholarly activity. He was then working on his *Orchomenos und die Minyer*, which was intended to continue the portrayal of individual Greek states that he had begun in the "Aeginetica." It was all the more important, therefore, that he maintain scholarly contact with Berlin—especially with Böckh, who continued to take a lively interest in Müller's personal and professional future and was trying to advance him. And it was Böckh who, in reply to a query from Göttingen, was able to recommend Müller as successor to Friedrich Gottlieb Welcker, who had transferred to Bonn, as Professor of Classical Philology and Archaeology.

In the fall of 1819 Karl Otfried Müller—just turned twenty-two—became Professor Extraordinarius at the Georgia Augusta University in Göttingen. Since the duties of his position included the archaeology of art—a Göttingen tradition that went back to Christian Gottlob Heyne—the Hanoverian government granted Müller supplementary funds for a two-month stay in Dresden, where he would be able to deepen his knowledge by personal examination of the *objets d'art* in the collections of antiquities. Müller later attested to the special importance of personal examination of ancient monuments for his scholarly work; as is well-known, he often used the periods when he gave no lectures to visit collections in Europe.

In his new location Müller, with characteristic energy, became deeply involved in research and teaching and also in university administration. Despite his youth he already, at the beginning of his teaching career, lectured on a great variety of subjects, and this variety increased over the years. As early as 1821 the Hanoverian government rewarded his success as an academic teacher (especially as an interpreter and explicator of ancient art-works, of which he had plaster casts made as visual aids) by approving a more extensive tour, in France and England, for the study of art history. Academic promotion also came quickly: in 1823 he was named Professor Ordinarius and was appointed member of the Göttingen Society of Sciences. In the same year Böckh arranged to have him called to the Friedrich-Wilhelms-Universität in Berlin—however, he did not accept. He felt obligated to the Hanoverian government, and besides, he had come to feel at home in Göttingen; after his marriage in 1824 to Pauline Hugo, daughter of the famous Göttingen jurist Gustav Hugo, he became even more closely attached to the city. Yet his attachment to Göttingen did not mean that he felt any weakening of ties to his Silesian homeland and to his parents' house in Ohlau; during the 1820s he traveled to Silesia each year during the autumn vacation. That he always retained Silesian traits in his personal manner is suggested too by the jocose remark of friends about the house that he designed and constructed in Göttingen: it was built, they said, in the "Silesio-Hellenic style."

Müller's academic career in Göttingen was crowned with outstanding success. The essential factor in this success—much more significant even than his university teaching—was the number of his scholarly publications, which documented his pioneering research in the most various fields of *Altertumswissenschaft* and acquired for him a reputation as one of the most brilliant and most versatile classical scholars of the nineteenth century. He had already made a name for himself among classical scholars with his dissertation, for in this work he had used an extensive knowledge and evaluation of all available sources concerning the island of Aegina to sketch a full picture of its history from the beginnings to Frankish times. His investigations had embraced topography and geography, commerce, coinage, navigation, demography and social structures, constitutional law, national customs, and art. Under the influence of Romantic thought, Müller had, already in this work, used myth and saga as historical sources; he had tried to extract from them the kernel of historical fact about the shadowy early history of Aegina and had attempted to illuminate, on the evidence of sacral cult sources, the idiosyncrasies of individual Greek peoples and their relations to each other. With this multi-faceted portrayal of one Greek community, Müller gave methodological direction to the historical study of antiquity; his encyclopedic examination of one Greek people became the model for many other histories of peoples and cities.

Müller's plan was to investigate the history of individual Greek peoples and communities in order to derive from this mosaic a comprehensive history of the entire Greek nation, and he pursued his aim still further. While in Breslau as a Gymnasium teacher he occupied himself (as mentioned above) with the history of the Boeotian city Orchomenos and with the legendary race of the Minyae, who are connected with the place; he strove to disentangle their early history from the North Greek myths. His work appeared in 1820 under the title *Orchomenos und die Minyer*; it was the first volume of a multivolume work with the programmatic title *Geschichte der hellenischen Stämme und Städte*. Yet Müller did not envisage his work as a final history of the Greek peoples but only as a series of preliminary studies. In this connection he discussed his much-criticized principle of evaluating myth and saga as source material for early Greek history. He called attention to his strict and careful distinction between the "historical" and the "symbolic," the genuine content of the sagas and their poetic elaboration. Only when this distinction had been made might one proceed to compare the similarities and differences in the transmission of the saga among other peoples; this comparison would lead finally to "the basis and common theme of old sagas."

Continuing the *Geschichte der hellenischen Stämme und Städte*, he produced perhaps his richest work, *Die Dorier* (2 vols., 1824). Here he followed the same principles to portray the history, the religion, the politics, and the culture of this great Greek people, which he found especially attractive. Müller distinguished the Dorians rather too starkly from the other Greeks; for example, he attributed solely to the Dorians cultic and mythic elements, such as the cult of Apollo, which were common to all or to several Greek peoples. The just reproach of one-sidedness is still heard today. However, there is evidence for the supposition that Müller would have revised his views on the basis of what he learned on his later trip to Greece, especially on his visit to Athens and Attica, and that he would have granted to the Ionian-Attic people the place they deserve.

The critics of his *Geschichte der hellenischen Stämme und Städte* took issue above all with his practice of deriving evidence for early Greek history from myth and saga, and these criticisms moved Müller to produce a basic work on this theme: the

Prolegomena zu einer wissenschaftlichen Mythologie (1825). In this book he developed a definition of myth and described its characteristic traits; moreover, he described the origins and dissemination of myth. In his opinion, myths had been based on historical events and had been developed among the various peoples as national sagas; they had then been disseminated by migration and colonization. These sagas are, according to Müller, characteristic of a particular people, and from them one can draw several conclusions as to its original location and its wanderings. But along with this aspect of myth, Müller described the symbolic dimension of many myths. He paid less attention to the myths of the gods and mythic elements in cult, and Welcker was one of the first to reproach him for this. Though the objection may be valid that his view was perhaps somewhat one-sided, yet Müller's researches into myth constituted fundamental progress, and their effects are still felt today; Martin P. Nilsson, for example, one of the foremost modern scholars of Greek religion, justly characterized Müller as a "pathfinder in the labyrinth of the myths."

Shortly after the publication of the *Prolegomena*, Müller entered an entirely different field of *Altertumswissenschaft*. A prize offered by the Berlin Academy of Sciences for a work on the history of the Etruscans called forth his two-volume book on this enigmatic people. Müller won the prize and received it on 3 July 1826; his work was published in 1828. The methodology of the work, like that of his other histories of peoples, followed the universal-historical principle. As regards the content, Müller (as he himself remarked) restricted himself to linguistic questions and was able to discuss artistic monuments only incidentally. Despite this self-imposed limitation, Müller's work was the first comprehensive description of the Etruscans and on the whole has remained a basic work of Etruscology down to the present time.

The archaeological instruction that had been assigned to him in Göttingen bore fruit in numerous publications on archaeology, which he likewise produced from a universal historical-philological perspective on antiquity. An immediate product of his stay in Dresden, before he assumed his post at Göttingen, was the Latin treatise *De tripode Delphico* (1820), which discussed the famous candelabra base in Dresden portraying the theft and reconsecration of the tripod. In a Latin treatise written in the same period, *Minervae Poliadis sacra* (1820), Müller discussed the cult of the city-goddess Athena and the site and construction of the Erechtheion on the Athenian Acropolis. A few years later he published *De Phidiae vita et operibus commentationes tres* (1827), a biographical study of the great Greek artist, which dealt especially with the artistic ornamentation of the Parthenon, including the fragments brought to the British Museum by Lord Elgin.

Müller crowned his archaeological researches with his *Handbuch der Archäologie der Kunst*—once more, the first comprehensive treatment of a field of research—which first appeared in 1830. This *Handbuch*, which has remained a model work to the present day, took as its aim "to sum up previous scholarly work" in the field. In very compressed and strictly articulated form Müller here described the evolution of art in antiquity as well as providing a geographical conspectus of the monuments of ancient art and a systematic overview of the individual subdivisions within the subject—e.g., architecture, painting, sculpture, and vase-painting, as well as "artistic form" and artistic motifs. The *Handbuch* found widespread acceptance; a second edition appeared within five years. Further reprints followed, as well as translations into English and French. Müller continued his series of archaeological publications with the major "Übersicht der Griechischen Kunstgeschichte von 1829–1835" in the Halle *Allgemeine Literaturzeitung*.

Also worthy of mention is his topographical treatise *De munimentis Athenarum* (1836), in which he described the fortifications of Athens and their construction in the time of Demosthenes. Much earlier, at the beginning of his Göttingen period, he had published topographical investigations on Athens and Attica, producing, in the article "Attika" in Ersch und Gruber's *Allgemeine Realencyclopaedie*, the first German scholarly work on this subject; he also wrote for this encyclopedia the articles "Böotien," "Eleusinien," and "Pallas Athene." Topographical researches were also published in his Latin work *Antiquitates Antiochenae* (1839), in which he gave a geographical description of the city of Antioch on the Orontes in Syria and a history of architectural structures there from the founding of the city to the Middle Ages. Especially in this final archaeological publication Müller displayed his astonishing ability to gather information from all available sources on the monuments and to sketch as authentic a picture of the city as if he had engaged in archaeological fieldwork on the site. Some one hundred years later the book was used as a guide by the American excavators of Antioch. Müller was their Pausanias.

In the field of philology in the stricter sense, Müller produced a Greek-German edition of Aeschylus' *Eumenides*, which grew out of a lecture. The main goal of the edition was to interpret the drama by means of a literal translation that would yet reproduce the drama's poetical content. In the notes and appendices Müller gave valuable descriptions of artifacts, especially those connected with the Greek stage; he also discussed blood revenge and its expiation in the cult of Apollo. With his edition of the *Eumenides* Müller came into close contact with the area of work of Gottfried Hermann, the chief representative of the school of research that concentrated on philology and textual criticism, and a remark in Müller's preface (made more for the sake of his colleague in Göttingen, Ludolph Dissen) about "deeper questions than pedantry (*Notengelehrsamkeit*) can answer" ignited a violent feud. With this polemic and the self-vindications that followed from both sides, Müller entered the front ranks in the methodological quarrel between the schools of Hermann and Böckh. Müller recognized the necessity and importance of philological textual criticism, although it was not among his own favorite areas of work. He was not himself one of the classical scholars who, directing their researches toward history and antiquities, underrated text-critical study, but he was just as disinclined to exalt textual criticism as an end in itself. He viewed it rather as one area in a comprehensive and universal investigation of antiquity.

Müller first turned to editing and textual criticism in his edition of M. Terentius Varro's *De Lingua Latina* (1833). Yet the purpose of his work on Varro was not primarily to produce a critical edition of the text; his investigations proceeded rather from his researches on the Etruscans and from questions on the history of the Latin language, which he dealt with especially in his lectures. A role was also played by the influence of the two most significant representatives of the newly founded science of comparative linguistics, Franz Bopp and Jacob Grimm, with whom Müller was in personal and scholarly contact in Göttingen. As a preliminary to source analysis on the evolution of the Latin language, it was necessary to produce a usable text of Varro's important source work. Müller's edition contained numerous valuable additions to the important earlier work of Leonhard Spengel. Nevertheless, as Müller himself noted in the "Praefatio" to his edition, many important questions remained open.

Further work on the Latin grammarians led Müller to S. Pomponius Festus' incompletely preserved extract from the *De Verborum Significatione* of M. Verrius Flaccus, a lexical work from the age of Augustus that explained archaic and obsolete expressions and thus offered rich sources of antiquarian knowledge. But, here, too it was first necessary to produce a readable text in order to evaluate these sources. Müller's edition, which appeared in 1839, contained a precise description of the manuscripts, much factual explanation, and an investigation into the original work of Verrius and Festus' handling of it. Müller was the first to recognize the two layers of Verrius and Festus, and the thoroughness of his researches began a new era in the study of this Roman grammatical work.

Müller's last great project, which remained unfinished, was his *Geschichte der griechischen Literatur bis auf das Zeitalter Alexanders*. The incitement to begin the work came from an external source: it was commissioned by the London Society for the Diffusion of Useful Knowledge. From 1836 on, Müller worked at this task. A first part appeared in 1841, in English translation. When he departed on his trip to Italy and Greece, he left behind an uncompleted manuscript, which his brother Eduard published posthumously in 1841. Of the individual literary genres, only the section on the development of Greek poetry was completed; on philosophical literature, the chapters on Anaxagoras and Empedocles; on historiography, Herodotus and Thucydides; of the orators, Lysias and Isocrates. Müller did not plan a literary history complete with scholarly apparatus, but rather an extended and comprehensive account for young readers. His basic scheme in this work, as before, was to begin with the division of the Greek nation into various peoples and with the characteristics of these peoples. Müller's *Geschichte der griechischen Literatur*, despite its fragmentary condition, probably exercised greater influence than any other in the previous century, and Wilamowitz could still declare that it was "not only the most readable, but the only real, history."

To a degree attained by very few classical scholars of the nineteenth century, Karl Otfried Müller realized in his scholarly work the ideal of an all-encompassing view of antiquity. His ability to differentiate clearly between the essential and the less significant enabled him to arrange the multiplicity of separate facts and insights into a coherent system of *Altertumswissenschaft*. This breadth of vision made it possible for him, in the little more than two decades of his scholarly life, to create fundamental comprehensive surveys in various fields of *Altertumswissenschaft*—in several cases, the first such surveys made up to that time. In this way Müller was not only a pioneer for his own time, opening up many hitherto unknown aspects of antiquity; on the contrary, many of the results of his researches have become and remain common property to this day, and others provided the impetus to further investigation. Methodologically too, Müller laid the groundwork for the posing of problems in *Altertumswissenschaft* beyond his own time, particularly in that he regarded personal examination of ancient monuments as the foundation of research—a thought that was less well-defined in Böckh. Many of Müller's ideas prepared the way for the new concept of a total *Altertumswissenschaft* as it was sketched out by Theodor Mommsen and Ulrich von Wilamowitz-Moellendorff in the second half of the nineteenth century and determined the course of research in the twentieth.

In the late summer of 1839 Karl Otfried Müller was able to realize his long-cherished plan of visiting the ancient sites of Greece and Italy. The journey was intended to lay the foundations for his lifework, the great *Geschichte Griechenlands*, for which he regarded all his previous works as preliminary studies. Fate decided otherwise: Müller did not return from his great journey. Almost at the end of his visit to Hellas, which had proved so productive of scholarly results, the great god of Delphi struck him down with his death-bringing arrow in his holy temple. With his indefatigable passion for research and characteristic energy, Müller had copied, in the broiling sun, the inscriptions he had discovered near the temple terrace in Delphi. This exertion, though he was otherwise so resilient, proved too much for him. He contracted a severe fever; on the journey back to Athens he collapsed on the first stage to Kasa, the pass of Eleutherai. He was brought with difficulty to the then new capital of Greece. But help came too late. There he died on 1 August 1840. He was buried on the hill of Kolonos in north Athens, on the spot where Oedipus found his redemption, as Sophocles has described. The deme of Kolonos was also the home of the great tragic poet, who, according to ancient tradition, reached an extreme old age in the greatest serenity and yet as a poet had an unrivalled ability to depict human suffering. This union of radiant happiness and deep tragedy is mirrored in the brief life of Karl Otfried Müller, a scholar who was one of the most brilliant figures in the *Altertumswissenschaft* of his age and whose influence, as evidenced by scholarly interest in him, continues to the present day.

Translated by Michael Armstrong

Books

Aegineticorum liber. Berlin, 1817.
Geschichten hellenischer Stämme und Städte. Vol. 1: *Orchomenos und die Minyer.* Breslau, 1820; 2d ed., 1844; vols. 2–3: *Die Dorier.* Breslau, 1824; English translation as *The History and Antiquities of the Doric Race.* Oxford, 1830.
Minervae Poliadis sacra et aedem in arce Athenarum illustravit. Göttingen, 1820.
De tripode Delphico. Göttingen, 1820.

Die Etrusker. 4 vols. Breslau, 1823; new ed. edited by W. Deecke, Stuttgart, 1877.

Prolegomena zu einer wissenschaftlichen Mythologie. Göttingen, 1825; new ed. with foreword by Karl Kerényi, Darmstadt, 1970.

Über die Wohnsitze, die Abstammung und die ältere Geschichte des Makedonischen Volkes. Eine ethnographische Untersuchung. Berlin, 1825.

De Phidiae vita et operibus commentationes tres. Göttingen, 1827.

Commentatio qua Myrinae Amazonis, quod in museo Vaticino, signum Phidiacum explicatur. Göttingen, 1832.

Aeschylus, Eumeniden. Göttingen, 1833. (Greek and German with an explanatory essay.)

M. Terenti Varronis de Lingua Latina. Leipzig, 1833.

Handbuch der Archäologie der Kunst. Breslau, 1835; corrected and enlarged by F. G. Welcker, Breslau, 1848; 2d printing 1878.

Denkmäler der alten Kunst. Plates by Carl Oesterley. Continued by Friedrich Wieseler. 2 vols. Göttingen, 1835–1836; 4th ed. revised and enlarged, Leipzig, 1899–1903.

De munimentis Athenarum quaestiones historicae et tituli de instauratione eorum perscripti explicatio. Göttingen, 1836.

Antiquitates Antiochenae. Göttingen, 1839.

S. Pompei Festi de verborum significatione. Leipzig, 1839.

A History of the Literature of Ancient Greece. London, 1840. Continued after the author's death by J. W. Donaldson. 3 vols. London, 1858.

Geschichte der griechischen Literatur bis auf das Zeitalter Alexander's. Edited from the author's manuscript by Eduard Müller. 2 vols. Breslau, 1841; 3d ed. with notes and emendations by Emil Heitz; 2d vol, 1875; 4th ed. continued by Emil Heitz, Stuttgart, 1882–1884.

Archäologische Mitteilungen aus Griechenland. Edited by Adolf Schöll. I. Athens Antiken-Sammlung. Frankfurt-am-Main, 1843.

Articles

German articles and reviews (*Abhandlungen, Aufsätze, Rezensionen*) are found in *Kleine deutsche Schriften über Religion, Kunst, Sprache und Literatur, Leben und Geschichte des Altertums.* Edited by Eduard Müller. 2 vols. Breslau, 1847–1848; reprinted Hildesheim, 1979. Writings in Latin and German on ancient art and archeology are found in *Kunstarchäologische Werke.* 5 vols. Berlin, 1873 = *Calvary's philologische und archäologische Bibliotheken,* vols. 8–12.

"Attika." In *Allgemeine Encyclopädie der Wissenschaften und Künste.* Edited by Ersch and Gruber. Sect. 1. vol. 6:215–259.

"Böotien." *Ibid.,* Sect. 1, vol. 11:252–274.

"Eleusinien." *Ibid.,* Sect. 1, vol. 33:268–296.

"Pallas Athene." *Ibid.,* Sect. 3, vol. 10:75–120.

"Übersicht der Griechischen Kunstgeschichte von 1829–1835." *Allgemeine Literaturzeitung* 97–110 (1835) = *Kleine deutsche Schriften* 2:638–751.

Sources

Böckh, A. *Briefwechsel mit C. O. Müller.* Leipzig, 1883.

Baumeister, A. "Karl Otfried Müller." *ADB* 22:656–667.

Bleicken, J. "Die Herausbildung der Alten Geschichte in Göttingen: Von Heyne bis Busolt." In *Die Klassische Altertumswissenschaft an der Georg-August-Universität Göttingen, Eine Ringvorlesung zu ihrer Geschichte.* Edited by C. J. Classen. Göttinger Universitätsschriften. Series A: Schriften, Bd. 14. Göttingen, 1989: 98–127.

Borbein, A. H. "Tektonik. Zur Geschichte eines Begriffes der Archäologie." *Archiv für Begriffsgeschichte* 26 (1982) 60–100.

Bravo, B. *Philologie, histoire, philosophie de l'histoire. Etude sur J. G. Droysen.* Breslau, 1968.

Burkert, W. "Griechische Mythologie und die Geistesgeschichte der Moderne." *Les Etudes classiques aux XIXe et XXe siècles: leur place dans l'histoire des idées.* Entretiens sur l'Antiquité classique 26 (1980) 159–207.

Bursian, C. *Geschichte der classischen Philologie in Deutschland.* Volume 19 of *Geschichte der Wissenschaft in Deutschland.* Munich, 1883: 1007–1028.

Curtius, E. "Zum Gedächtnis von K. O. Müller." *Altertum und Gegenwart.* 2d ed. Berlin, 1882. 247–260.

Dilthey, C. "Karl Otfried Müller. Rede zur Säcularfeier am 1. Dezember 1897." Göttingen, 1898.

Döhl, H. "Karl Otfried Müller." *Archäologenbildnisse. Porträts und Kurzbiographien von Klassischen Archäologen deutscher Sprache.* Edited by R. Lullies and W. Schiering. Mainz, 1988: 23–24.

———. "Karl Otfried Müllers Reise nach Italien und Griechenland 1839/40." In *Die Klassische Altertumswissenschaft an der Georg-August-Universität Göttingen, Eine Ringvorlesung zu ihrer Geschichte.* Edited by C. J. Classen. Göttinger Universitätsschriften, series A: Schriften, Bd. 14. Göttingen, 1989: 51–77.

Donaldson, J. W. "On the Life and Writings of Karl Otfried Müller." In K. O. Müller, *A History of the Literature of Ancient Greece.* Continued after the author's death by John William Donaldson. 3 vols. London, 1858, 1:xii–xxxi.

Foerster, R. "Otfried Müller. Rede zum Antritt des Rektorats der Universität Breslau." Breslau, 1897.

Fuchs, W. "Kunstphilosophie und Kunstarchäologie. Zur kunsttheoretischen Einleitung des Handbuchs der Archäologie der Kunst von K. O. Müller." *Boreas* (1984) 269–294.

Gudeman, A. *Grundriss der Geschichte der klassischen Philologie.* Leipzig and Berlin, 1909: 230–231.

Hertz, M. "De Carolo Odofredo Muellero ex actis Universitatis Vratislaviensis excerpta." *Index lectionum univ. Vratisl.* (Summer 1884.)

Hillebrand, K. *Unbekannte Essays.* Edited by H. v. Uhde-Bernays. Bern, 1955: 184–241.

Kerényi, K. "Foreword" to K. O. Müller, *Prolegomena zu einer wissenschaftlichen Mythologie.* Darmstadt, 1970: v–xx.

Kroll, W. "Carl Otfried Müller." *Schlesische Lebensbilder*, vol. 1. Breslau, 1922; reprinted Sigmaringen, 1985: 42–45.

Lücke, F. *Erinnerungen an Karl Otfried Müller.* Göttingen, 1841.

Müller, E. "Biographische Erinnerungen an K. O. Müller." In K. O. Müller, *Kleine deutsche Schriften.* Breslau, 1847, 1: vii–lxxviii.

Nickau, K. "Karl Otfried Müller, Professor der Klassischen Philologie 1819–1840." In *Die Klassische Altertumswissenschaft an der Georg-August-Universität Göttingen, Eine Ringvorlesung zu ihrer Geschichte.* Edited by C. J. Classen. Göttinger Universitätsschriften, series A: Schriften, Bd. 14. Göttingen, 1989: 27–50.

Pfeiffer, R. *History of Classical Scholarship 1300–1850.* Oxford, 1976: 186–187.

Pflug, G. "Methodik und Hermeneutik bei Karl Otfried Müller." In *Philologie und Hermeneutik im 19. Jahrhundert.* Edited by H. Flashar, K. Gründer, A. Horstmann. Göttingen, 1979: 122–140.

Ranke, F. "C. O. Müller. Ein Lebensbild." *Programm der königlichen Realschule.* Berlin, 1870.

Sandys, J. E. *History of Classical Scholarship.* Cambridge, 1920. 3.213–216.

Selle, G. von. *Die Georg-August-Universität zu Göttingen.* Göttingen, 1937: 251–254.

Wegner, M. *Altertumskunde.* Volumes 1 and 2 of *Orbis Academicus.* Freiburg and Munich, 1951: 199–205.

Wilamowitz-Moellendorff, U. von. *Geschichte der Philologie.* Volume 1.1 of *Einleitung in die Philologie.* Edited by Gercke and Norden, 3d ed. Leipzig, 1927: 57–58.

See also the Anthology in the *Annali della Scuola normale superiore di Pisa. Cl. di Lett. e. Filos.,* series III, vol. 14.3 (Pisa, 1984). It contains contributions by G. Arrigoni, E. Campanile, R. di Donato, F. Ferrari, G. Gambiano, A. Momigliano, M. M. Sassi, S. Settis, A. Wittenberg, and P. Zanker.

Letters

Müller, K. O. *Briefe aus einem Gelehrtenleben, 1797–1840.* Edited by K. Svoboda. 2 vols. Berlin, 1950.

———. *Ein Lebensbild in Briefen an die Eltern.* Edited by O. and E. Kern. Berlin, 1908.

Gilbert Murray

2 January 1866 – 20 May 1957

ROBERT L. FOWLER
University of Waterloo

Gilbert Murray, OM, FBA, Regius Professor of Greek in the University of Oxford 1908–1936, was widely regarded as the leading English Hellenist of his day. For the educated public, on whom he had an impact such as few scholars ever have, he was synonymous with the English tradition of humane letters and scholarship in the service of the cultured life. His impassioned vision of ancient Greece enabled him to bring its literature alive again in vivid and realistic detail, particularly in his translations and interpretations of Greek drama; he almost single-handedly resuscitated Euripides' fortunes in England, and must be given a large part of the credit for the continued vitality of Greek studies in his country throughout the early decades of the twentieth century. His power of bringing past life alive sprang from the intensity of his involvement in modern life; he was committed with a religious devotion to the ideals of Gladstonian Liberalism, which he tirelessly promoted in a great many capacities, but mainly in connection with the League of Nations. These ideals he saw as the driving force of both Victorian England and Periclean Athens: the ideals of progress, rationalism, and freedom, which he tended to sum up with the single word "civilization." Very few of his writings were addressed to the professional scholar, and not much of his scholarly work retains its validity today; but his influence on his contemporaries was so diffuse that its effects must still be felt in a thousand undetected ways. And even when the reverberations of his personal influence are no longer felt, he will still be the best example of a certain kind of scholarship that will always have something of value and should never be forgotten.

George Gilbert Aimé Murray was born in Sydney, Australia, into a family of mixed Irish, Welsh, and English heritage. His Irishness, particularly as embodied by his father, was a point of pride, and the origin of his radicalism in politics and skepticism in religion. His childhood experiences in Australia, although undoubtedly romanticized by him in later life, also accounted for certain traits of character such as his resilience and inner strength of purpose; his schoolboy experiences with bullying induced a keen aversion to cruelty in any form. His father died when he was seven; in January 1877, when he was eleven, his mother took the family back to England.

Beginning in the autumn of 1878 Murray was a day-boy at Merchant Taylors' School, his entrance made possible by a scholarship. The evidence for these years, slight though it is, is sufficient to show a precocious boy hard at work, learning and loving his classics, and coming to conclusions at an early age on life's great questions. He discovered Mill and Shelley (especially the *Prometheus Unbound*, whose spiritual values he imbibed unmixed); other influences were Tennyson, Swinburne, Rousseau and Comte. His special aptitude for Greek poetry, encouraged by his teacher Francis Storr, was evident from the start. At the age of fifteen he turned parts of the *Prometheus Unbound* into Greek verse, and he was awarded spectacular marks on the examination for the scholarship to St. John's College, Oxford, whither he duly went in autumn 1884.

During the summer he spent a month with the celebrated teacher J. Y. Sargent, whose coaching in Latin composition helped him win the Hertford Scholarship during his first year for accomplishment in the art ; more impressively, he also won the Ireland Scholarship for Latin and Greek (competition for which was open to all undergraduates, not just those in the first two years). It was a feat seldom achieved before or since; and in an age when classical education consisted almost entirely in prose and verse composition, it must be evidence of an astonishing aptitude for the ancient languages. To later generations the emphasis on verse composition in Victorian education has seemed grossly exaggerated; but it could encourage the kind of familiarity with the ancient texts that has always been the foundation of the greatest English scholarship. Murray not only knew large tracts of Greek poetry by heart, he was gifted with literary understanding and a measure of historical insight; he understood that such a skill was only the beginning, not the end, of classical scholarship.

Murray's star continued to shine at Oxford throughout the following four years. He took the Gaisford prizes for Greek prose and verse composition and the Chancellor's prize for Latin verse composition. The teachers he most loved were T. C. Snow at St. John's and Arthur Sidgwick at Corpus Christi, the former a classic Oxford eccentric, the latter the guru of Greek composition; both reinforced the tendency of Murray's previous education and kept him away from such tentative influences of German scientific scholarship as were to be found in the Oxford of the day. The Arabist D. S. Margoliouth, the Latinist Robinson Ellis, and the High Churchman Charles Gore of Pusey House were further influences; the latter cured him of his anticlericalism, although he failed to persuade him of the truth of Christianity. In his leisure hours Murray began to speak out in favor of Radical Liberal causes, and showed the first signs of his literary aspirations by writing an adventure novel entitled *Gobi or Shamo*. The book, which was eventually published, requires no special discussion here; but it is notable for its theme of civilization surrounded by seas of barbarism, already a leading idea in Murray's humanistic philosophy.

Immediately after finishing his undergraduate degree Murray was elected a Fellow of New College, Oxford. He was not to stay there long; in July 1889 he was the surprise choice for the chair of Greek at the University of Glasgow, recently vacated by Richard Jebb's promotion to Cambridge. The income enabled him to marry Mary Howard, eldest daughter of the (soon to be) Earl of Carlisle. With her he began a lifelong love affair of Shelleyan proportions, not without its trials to keep the thing in perspective. With her too he began his crusadelike work in Liberal causes, for she was a believer like the rest of her family—in particular her imperious mother, the Countess of Carlisle, a formidable figure intimately bound up with Murray's public activities from this time until her death in 1921. But at first the young professor had little time for such things. At Glasgow he had to contend with large audiences of demanding students, as well as the hostility of a Conservative establishment and a faculty resentful of so young an incumbent of the prestigious chair. But he set to work with zest, and soon won converts, particularly among the students. They warmed to the dramatic style and lively re-creations of his lectures, delivered in unfaltering, rhythmically beautiful prose and an enviably melodious voice.

He published nothing at first; but in 1897 the first edition of *A History of Ancient Greek Literature* appeared, covering the period from Homer to Demosthenes. It is a peculiar work, uncertain of its audience and uneven in content. That Murray thought he could write it at all, as his first book at the age of thirty-one, tells us as much about the standards of contemporary scholarship as it does about Murray. He admits in the preface that he was unhappy with the balance of what he calls "the scientific and aesthetic sides" of his subject. The clash is most obvious in the first chapter on Homer; he wrote the book with the professed aim of communicating the importance of ancient poetry for modern life, but instead of beginning with the poetry of the epics he plunges into the thickets of the Homeric question and barely emerges from them in time for chapter two. Yet the book is not without value or interest; at least it was fairly well accepted by the reading public, being reissued as late as 1966. The Homeric chapter, despite its inadequacy, contains the germ of *The Rise of the Greek Epic*; the Euripidean chapter contains the germ of *Euripides and His Age*. The preface has biographical interest: it trumpets the gospel of the Greeks as real people, not classical abstracts or "fleshly" aesthetes who need to be re-created by an effort of historical imagination; already this is the keynote of his approach, sounded again (for example) in his Oxford inaugural lecture of 1909. The preface also mentions, in connection with the search for realism, the "Greek of the anthropologist," providing an early reference to Murray's absorption with this branch of study; and it acknowledges as his two main "teachers" T. C. Snow and "Professor Ulrich von Wilamowitz-Moellendorff of Göttingen, whose historical insight and singular gift of imaginative sympathy with ancient Greece seem to me to have changed the face of many departments of Hellenic study within the last fifteen years." Wilamowitz was Murray's hero in scholarship all his life. Here he calls him his "teacher," although at that time he knew him only from his books and a correspondence just three years old. Wilamowitz's commentary on Euripides' *Herakles* (1889) had overwhelmed Murray when he first read it at Glasgow; he was dazzled by the range, depth, and focus of its learning, and especially by the way it brought the Greeks alive. This ability lay at the heart of both men's scholarship, so Murray's attraction to Wilamowitz and his friendly reception by him are no surprise.

In 1896 Murray was invited by the Oxford University Press to produce an edition of all the plays of Euripides. He had been planning a series of editions of individual plays in collaboration with other scholars, as well as a Euripidean lexicon. He had written to Wilamowitz for advice on these projects in 1894; with the change in plans he wrote again for information on the manuscripts. Wilamowitz responded with copies of his own collations and advice about where to find others; he was later involved at all stages of production, contributing many notes and conjectures and reading the proofs. Murray was almost entirely dependent on this help for his knowledge of the manuscripts; only after the first volume appeared in January 1902 did he do any extensive collating of his own. Well-read though he was in the works of Wilamowitz and other German scholars, and much as he drew inspiration from them, Murray never learned the secret of their professionalism, and his previous training left him poorly qualified for the technical aspects of editing a classical text. Yet the edition was a success, not only because of Wilamowitz's cooperation. Murray's sure sense of Euripidean idiom enabled him to produce a more sensible text than that of many previous editors who were inclined to irresponsible meddling. It became the standard text of Euripides in English-speaking countries for seventy-five years; the third volume is still in use.

Murray worked incredibly hard at Glasgow, with eventual cost to his health. He felt obliged to resign his chair in 1898. For the next seven years he and his family lived in Surrey, supported mainly by his mother-in-law. He continued his work of editing Euripides, wrote regularly in the liberal press, and toyed with the idea of running for Parliament. He also entered the world of letters with two original plays, *Carlyon Sahib* and *Andromache* (a revision of the old legend for modern times); in spite of some clear merits, they were not commercial successes. Two other original plays never reached the stage. But these failures, besides introducing him to certain leading figures such as William Archer and Bernard Shaw, gave him invaluable practical experience in the theater and turned him from original composition to translation, where his real talent lay. In 1902 the first of his famous translations of Euripides appeared. Over the next fifty years he was to translate nine plays of Euripides, four of Sophocles, all seven surviving of Aeschylus, three of Aristophanes, and two of Menander; they were reprinted many times and sold hundreds of thousands of copies. They often provided the text for professional productions; indeed the first performance of a Murray translation, the *Hippolytus* in 1904, was a hit. Famous theater people like Harley Granville Barker and Dame Sybil Thorndike were eager promoters of this newly discovered drama; Max Reinhardt mounted an extravagant production of *Oedipus Tyrannus* at Covent Garden in 1912. Professional performances were not infrequent during the next fifty years; they were greatly outnumbered, however, by amateur stagings. Dramatic societies found the Greek drama affordable to produce, with its few main characters to be costumed and its sparse sets, and the Murray idiom rolled easily and beautifully from the lips of less-than-talented actors. The style of the translations has been severely criticized, most famously by T. S. Eliot; the density of facile devices and the use of rhyme did not recommend the poetry to his fastidious taste. In not much time, many people agreed with Eliot; today his blank verse translations in the *History of Greek Literature* seem much more effective. But when they first appeared the translations perfectly suited the age, and whatever one may think of them, their technical mastery and their languorous beauty cannot be denied.

Murray was sufficiently famous in the London theater world to be recognized by audiences as the subject of Shaw's entertaining caricature in *Major Barbara* (1905), where he is Adolphus Cusins; other members of the Murray family figure as the title character (Lady Mary) and Lady Britomart (The Countess of Carlisle). But the life of a literary lion was not for Murray in the end; he longed to return to academic life, and in 1905 an opportunity arose to return to New College, Oxford. Three years later he was appointed to succeed Ingram Bywater as Regius Professor of Greek, an appointment he held until succeeded by E. R. Dodds in 1936. Most of his major works were written during this period, in spite of the great amount of time he spent on political causes. *The Rise of the Greek Epic* arose from a series of lectures at Harvard University; it is probably his best book. It tried to reconcile the conflicting views of analysts and unitarians by using the concept of the "traditional book" (on the analogy of the Old Testament); it is largely successful in this aim, although most of its discussion has now been superseded by the discoveries of Milman Parry. It includes a great wealth of material on almost anything remotely connected with Homeric studies; but all this information is marshalled together and made to move forward in a clear and focused manner. Murray also succeeds in creating a vivid sense of the historical context in which the Homeric epics are to be understood. For these qualities the book greatly impressed his contemporaries; it provided them through all its four editions with a convenient orientation in Homeric problems and is still a useful guide to the state of the Homeric question at the time. From a biographical point of view the book is significant for the theme of Greek literature as an example of progress; for Murray, the epics represented the first great step forward toward high civilization. The morally improving qualities of the poem are what interested him; but in this connection the gods of Homer posed certain difficulties that Murray was hard put to solve. For romantic reasons he wanted the gods to be real and supposed they were real enough at some point before Homer; but he cannot take Homer's gods seriously and imposes the same attitude upon the poet himself. The unworthy crudities and moral shortcomings of the gods are not Homer's doing; they are unfortunate remnants of the "primeval slime" clinging to one only recently emerged from it. He heralds Homer's religious enlightenment; yet he argues that Homer's "scepticism" meant death for the old gods. The tragedians, Murray continues, fortunately understood the better side of the Homeric gods and resuscitated them in even more glorious form; but as pure symbols they could have no reality whatsoever.

Of course, hardly anybody in Murray's day would take the Greek gods totally seriously. Murray at least wanted to take them somewhat seriously. The basic weakness in understanding springs from the pervasive influence of Christianity in his society, not from Murray himself. It is evident again in a book devoted purely to the subject, *Four Stages of Greek Religion* (later *Five Stages* when a chapter on the philosophical schools was added). This book, in its first form a series of lectures at Columbia University, was a reaction to Jane Harrison's exaltation of the chthonic spirits in *Prolegomena to the Study of Greek Religion* and *Themis* (books that Murray nevertheless greatly admired and contributed to). Murray wished to show that the enlightened Olympian ideals of the fifth century B.C. represented the very best of Greek civilization. The preceding stage of religion out of which the Olympian splendor emerged is described in terms favored by the anthropology of the day; "*mana*" is the central concept. This, incidentally, reveals the main reason he was so intrigued by the new science: to understand civilization one must understand where it came from, and anthropology provided the key. Murray's interest was first excited by the writings of Andrew Lang; his active promotion of anthropology and the classics made him the only outside member of the "Cambridge Group" of Jane Harrison, James Frazer, F. M. Cornford, and A. B. Cook. Great advance as it was, however, the Olympian religion failed in the end, partly because the superstitious substratum was too well-established at the popular level, partly because it failed to reach monotheism (here the modern prejudice is plain), and partly because the collapse of the polis created new needs. In the new climate the Greeks experienced a "failure of nerve" in which they turned to the mystery religions for salvation. Murray regarded Christianity as one of these; the influence of Richard Reitzenstein is explicit. For Murray, religion was mostly superstition, Christianity not excepted; agnostic himself, he believed only in what he called the "great unknown" or "uncharted" regions of life to which one must necessarily have a relation, but a relation to be kept enlightened and rational at all costs. It was congenial to him to believe the latest discoveries that Christianity was just a religion like any other. (He was, it should be added, very sympathetic to the general moral teaching of Christianity, greatly admiring St. Paul; he preferred Stoics to Epicureans; and he often used the terms "Christian" and "Hellenic" civilization as equivalents, stressing the supposed identity of their ideals and joint role in the formation of modern Europe.)

In 1913 Murray published his most famous book, *Euripides and His Age*. Produced for the Home University Library of which he was an editor, it was a small book intended for the general reader; its Wilamowitzian purpose of putting Euripides in historical context was, however, identical with that of *The Rise of the Greek Epic*, and audiences of all kinds responded warmly. Blessed with a clear, novel, and convincing thesis, which was presented moreover in memorable prose, the book set out an interpretation of Euripides that was to be canonical for decades. Murray portrayed Euripides as a rational critic of tradition, a progressive promoter of social causes, and a wise agnostic in religion. Some important influences on Murray's criticism deserve recognition, in particular the Cambridge scholar Arthur W. Verrall;

but it must be pointed out that Murray made important modifications to Verrall's at times preposterous picture of "Euripides the Rationalist." Jane Harrison's idea of the year-spirit was, however, accepted wholeheartedly, and championed by Murray to the end of his days; he thought that certain standard plots of tragedy and comedy (even Menander!) derived from the old chthonic religion and retained their ritual significance for the audience. Apart from this aberration, however, Murray's conception won wide assent. Nowadays it seems obvious that he read too much of his own day into Euripides; he made him a social critic in the manner of Ibsen, who was translated into English by his friend Archer (Murray drew the parallel himself often enough). Yet our Euripides—an existentialist reflector of humanity in all of its horrors and sublimities, scarcely to be credited with a consistent philosophy from one moment to the next—is suspiciously appropriate to our milieu; if we blame Murray too quickly for seeing himself in his ancient brother, we must be prepared to answer a charge of pot and kettle. In fact, both views have their strengths, and Murray even now cannot be dismissed out of hand.

The war years and the 1920s saw Murray increasingly occupied with public duties, which it is impossible to treat adequately here. The list of his offices is impressive enough: Chairman of the Executive of the League of Nations Union (1918–1919), Vice Chairman (1919–1922), Chairman (1922–1938), joint President with Lord Robert Cecil from 1938 (at its height the organization numbered over 600,000 members); Chairman of the League of Nations Committee for Intellectual Cooperation from 1928 until its absorption by UNESCO in 1951; joint President with Lord Lytton of the United Nations Association (1945–1947); sole President (1947–1949); joint President with Dame Kathleen Courtney (1949–1957). In these capacities Murray showed an extraordinary flair for diplomacy and practical organization, surprising to many who judged him by his serene, unworldly exterior and the idealism of his writings. In fact he possessed clear vision and a keen sense of people; his political skill saw the LNU and the League itself through many anxious moments. It can be argued that his most important work for humanity was done here.

At a quick glance it might appear that Murray tried to have two rather incompatible careers. It seemed so to one Vice Chancellor of the University of Oxford, who became anxious that the Regius Professor might be neglecting his academic duties. Murray was not neglecting them and saw no conflict between his two spheres of activity. The ideals of Hellenism and liberalism were identical for him; and as a rationalist, a conviction that a cause was right meant he was obliged to take action in its favor. The possibility of progress had only once before in history been truly understood; tragedy had averted its realization, but after many centuries the same spark had kindled new flame. It was his duty to tend the flame however he could.

Murray's convictions informed everything he did in life. His purpose was ultimately one of gospel spreading; like Wilamowitz, he conceived his function as a professor exclusively in terms of teaching, not research. Hence the conscious amateurism of his work. Even in the book with the most technical stuff, *The Rise of the Greek Epic*, the learned details are always subordinate to his didactic purposes. In large stretches of it, indeed, he is merely dependent on his favorite authorities; he does not really go behind them to the manuscripts, scholia, and monuments as a professional would. Murray was not interested in the cold facts for their own sake; they had to be made warm in an historical context so that one could understand their real significance and extract lessons from them for the modern age. If the lessons were not communicated to one's pupils—among whom Murray could count the general public—Greek literature could no longer be a living influence on contemporary society. He rightly saw that technical research does not contribute directly to this effort. It is remarkable that the Regius Professor hardly ever wrote an article in a professional journal.

The essential continuity of ancient and modern literature, and the half-forlorn hope that the amateur might be given pride of place in talking about it, formed the basis of Murray's Norton lectures of 1926, which were published the following year under the title *The Classical Tradition in Poetry*. The book's principal aim was to illustrate how the forms and qualities of ancient literature have survived in the poetic tradition; if Murray had confined himself to this, it would have been a diverting catalogue of a highly cultivated man's mental treasures. He also tried, however, to show his readers what good poetry ought to be (mostly, he says, it ought to be beautiful); Murray's remarks on this subject are amateurish in a bad sense and came in for some criticism. In his next two books, *Aristophanes: A Study* and *Aeschylus, The Creator of Tragedy*, Murray stuck to Greek subjects. Once again the amateur is unrepentant: the preface of the latter states that it is "not, in the stricter sense, learned," while the preface of the former opens with the startling words, "There is little or no research in this book." Like most of his works they were intended to demonstrate the existence of liberal ideas in the ancient poets; with Euripides Murray may have had a case, but not with these two. The failure is particularly embarrassing in Aristophanes, whose crudity and ruthlessness are not to be argued away.

In the same decade Murray produced his Oxford text of Aeschylus, whom he edited along the same lines as Euripides; but the standards of the day would no longer tolerate it, and the edition has never been highly regarded, not even after revision in 1955. Murray was by now getting old; his political ideals had long been superseded, and his style of scholarship seemed dated. But he lost none of his vigor, his essential happiness, or his strength of conviction. He continued to write prolifically in the name of his great causes; *Stoic, Christian and Humanist* (1940; rev. ed. 1950) and *Hellenism and the Modern World* (1953) are buoyant expressions of his faith. He carried on to the day he died his constant run of lectures, letters to the press, addresses, and broadcasts, all bearing his message to the multitudes. His liberalism was no vague sense of do-goodism, but an intelligent acceptance of the Gladstone system; nor did it turn into socialism at any point. At its heart was the belief in the progress of humanity toward an ideal civilization. Sometimes his actions seemed to other liberals to be inconsistent with this goal, as when, in 1914, he supported the war effort (he broke with his wife's cousin, Bertrand Russell, over the issue); but given a choice, as he saw it, between peace and civilization, Murray could only choose the latter. When, in his last years, he astonished everyone by voting conservative and supporting Prime Minister Anthony Eden in the Suez crisis, he was being perfectly consistent in refusing to condone ochlocracy or the treatment of barbarians on an equal footing with the civilized.

Murray's ability to curb his will to the dictates of reason was only one aspect of his remarkable character. Those who knew him refer consistently to his charm, courtesy, hospitality, and wonderful talk. He was blessed with a developed sense of the absurd, which not only produced many moments of the most delightful whimsy in his writings and conversation but kept his puritanical tendencies more or less in their place. His evident happiness and serenity seemed won by inner self-discipline, and were therefore the more to be admired. He and Lady Mary were angels of mercy to the refugees and needy of war-torn Europe. His courtesy even to his rudest adversaries never failed; but his gentle exterior concealed an ardent soul fired by the noblest passions. He was a stranger to academic pettiness; he was the kind of person humanistic scholarship ought to produce but so rarely does in spite of its fine talk. When he died on 20 May 1957, he had won the reputation of a secular saint. His ashes were placed in Westminster Abbey.

Books

Gobi or Shamo, A Story of Three Songs. London, 1889; New York, 1978.

A History of Ancient Greek Literature. London, 1897; New York, 1966; 2d ed., London, 1898; 3d ed. entitled *The Literature of Ancient Greece.* Chicago, 1956; Spanish translation as *La Historia de la Literatura del Griego anciana,* (Buenos Aires and Mexico City, 1944).

Andromache. A Play in Three Acts. London, 1900; Portland, ME, 1913; 2d ed., London, 1914, 3d ed., London, 1931.

Carlyon Sahib. A Drama in Four Acts. London, 1900.

Euripidis Fabulae, Vol. I. Oxford, 1902; with many reprints.

Euripides, Translated into English Rhyming Verse. Athenian Drama, Vol. 3. London, 1902; 2d ed., 1904; 3d ed., 1906; 4th ed., 1908.

Euripidis Fabulae, Vol. II. Oxford, 1904; with many reprints.

The Electra of Euripides, Translated into English Rhyming Verse, with Explanatory Notes. London, 1905; with many reprints.

The Trojan Women of Euripides, Translated into English Rhyming Verse, with Explanatory Notes. London, 1905; with many reprints.

The Rise of the Greek Epic. Oxford, 1907; 4th ed., London, 1934; 1949; 1960.

Euripidis Fabulae. Vol. III. Oxford, 1909; rev. ed. 1913.

The Iphigenia in Tauris of Euripides, Translated into English Rhyming Verse, with Explanatory Notes. London, 1910; with many reprints.

The Medea of Euripides, Translated into English Rhyming Verse, with Explanatory Notes. London, 1910; with many reprints.

Sophocles. Oedipus King of Thebes, with Explanatory Notes. London, 1911.

Four Stages of Greek Religion. New York and London, 1912; rev. ed. entitled *Five Stages of Greek Religion*. Oxford, 1925; with many reprints.

Euripides and His Age. London, 1913; with many reprints; Spanish translation by A. Reyes as *Euripides y su época* (Buenos Aires and Mexico City, 1951), reprinted as *Euripides y su tiempo*, 1966; Italian translation by N. Ruffini as *Euripide e i suoi tempi* (Bari, 1932); German translation by G. & E. Bayer as *Euripides und seine Zeit* (Darmstadt, 1957).

The Rhesus of Euripides, Translated into English Rhyming Verse, with Explanatory Notes. London, 1913; with many reprints.

The Alcestis of Euripides, Translated into English Rhyming Verse, with Explanatory Notes. London, 1915; with many reprints.

Faith, War and Policy. Lectures and Essays. Boston and London, 1918.

The Agamemnon of Aeschylus, Translated into English Rhyming Verse, with Explanatory Notes. London, 1920.

Essays and Addresses. London, 1921; reprinted as *Tradition and Progress*, Boston and New York, 1922.

The Choephoroe of Aeschylus, Translated into English Rhyming Verse. London, 1923.

The Eumenides of Aeschylus, Translated into English Rhyming Verse. London, 1925.

The Classical Tradition in Poetry. The Charles Eliot Norton Lectures. London, 1927; Cambridge, MA, 1927; New York, 1957; 1968.

The Suppliant Women, Translated into English Rhyming Verse, with Introduction and Notes. London, 1930.

Prometheus Bound, Translated into English Rhyming Verse, with Introduction and Notes. London, 1931.

Aristophanes. A Study. Oxford, 1933; New York, 1964.

The Seven against Thebes of Aeschylus, Translated into English Rhyming Verse, with Introduction and Notes. London, 1935.

Aeschyli septem quae supersunt tragoediae. Oxford, 1937; rev. ed. 1955.

Liberality and Civilization. Lectures given at the invitation of the Hibbert Trustees at the Universities of Bristol, Glasgow and Birmingham. London and New York, 1938; New York, 1979.

The Persians of Aeschylus, Translated into English Rhyming Verse, with Preface and Notes. London, 1939.

Aeschylus, the Creator of Tragedy. Oxford, 1940; London, 1978; Spanish translation by A. Reyes as *Esquilo, el creador de la tragedia* (Buenos Aires and Mexico City, 1943); German translation by S. Melchinger as *Aischylos* (Velber, 1969).

Stoic, Christian and Humanist. London 1940; Boston 1950; rev. ed. London, 1950; Freeport, NY, 1969.

Sophocles. Antigone, Translated into English Rhyming Verse, with Introduction and Notes. London, 1941.

The Rape of the Locks. The Perikeiromene of Menander. The Fragments Translated and the Gaps Conjecturally Filled In. London, 1942.

The Arbitration. The Epitrepontes of Menander. The Fragments Translated and the Gaps Conjecturally Filled In. London, 1945.

Greek Studies. Oxford, 1946; Spanish translation (Madrid, 1962).

The Wife of Heracles. Being Sophocles' Play The Trachinian Women, Translated into English Rhyming Verse, with Explanatory Notes. London, 1947.

Sophocles. Oedipus at Colonus, Translated into English Rhyming Verse, with Introduction and Notes. London, 1948.

From the League to U.N. London, 1948.

Aristophanes. The Birds, Translated into English Rhyming Verse, with Introduction and Notes. London, 1950.

Hellenism and the Modern World. Six Talks. London, 1953; Spanish translation by J. M. Gimeno as *Grecia clásica y mundo* (Madrid, 1962); German translation by K. Nicolai as *Hellas und die Welt von heute* (Darmstadt, 1966).

Euripides. Ion, Translated into English Rhyming Verse, with Explanatory Notes. London and New York, 1954.

Aristophanes. Knights, Translated into English Rhyming Verse, with Introduction and Notes. London, 1956.

Humanist Essays. London, 1964.

Articles, Addresses, and Pamphlets

"The Place of Greek in Education." *Inaugural Address Delivered before the University of Glasgow, 6 November 1889.* Glasgow, 1889.

"The Exploitation of Inferior Races in Ancient and Modern Times. An Imperial Labour Question with a Historical Parallel." In *Liberalism and the Empire. Three Essays by Francis W. Hirst, Gilbert Murray and J. L. Hammond.* London, 1900: 118–157.

"Critical Appendix on the Orphic Tablets." In J. E. Harrison, *Prolegomena to the Study of Greek Religion.* Cambridge, 1903; 3d ed. 1922: 660–674.

"Critical Note on Thucydides 2.15.3–6." In J. E. Harrison, *Primitive Athens.* Cambridge, 1906: 159.

Wilamowitz-Moellendorff, U. von. *Greek Historical Writing and Apollo. Two Lectures Delivered before the University of Oxford, June 3 and 4, 1908.* Translated by Gilbert Murray. Oxford, 1908.

"Anthropology in the Greek Epic Tradition outside Homer." In *Anthropology and the Classics. Six Lectures Delivered before the University of Oxford by Arthur J. Evans, Andrew Lang, Gilbert Murray, F.B. Jevons, J. L. Myres, W. Warde Fowler.* Edited by R. R. Marett. Oxford, 1908: 66–92.

"The Interpretation of Ancient Greek Literature." *Inaugural Address Delivered before the University of Oxford, 27 January 1909.* Oxford, 1909.

"The Hymn of the Kouretes." *ABSA* 15 (1908–1909) 357–365.

"Excursus on the Ritual Forms Preserved in Tragedy." In J. E. Harrison, *Themis.* Cambridge, 1912; rev. ed. 1927: 341–363.

"How Can War Ever Be Right?" (London, 1914). Translated into German, French, Italian, Spanish, Swedish, Dutch, Arabic, etc. London, Paris, etc., 1915.

"The Stoic Philosophy." *Moncure Conway Memorial Lecture, 16 March 1915.* London, 1915; 1918.

The Foreign Policy of Sir Edward Grey 1906–1915. Oxford, 1915.

The Way Forward. Three Articles on Liberal Policy by Gilbert Murray, with a Preface by the Right Hon. Viscount Grey of Fallodon. London, 1917.

"*Religio Grammatici.* The Religion of a 'Man of Letters'." *Presidential Address, Classical Association, 8 January 1918.* London, 1918.

The League of Nations and the Democratic Idea. London, 1918.

The Problem of Foreign Policy. A Consideration of Present Dangers and the Best Methods for Meeting Them. London and New York, 1921; German translation (Stuttgart and Berlin, 1922).

"The Value of Greece to the Future of the World." In *The Legacy of Greece.* Edited by R. W. Livingstone. Oxford, 1921; 1937; 1969: 1–23.

"Hymn of the Kouretes." In *New Chapters in the History of Greek Literature.* Edited by J. U. Powell, E. A. Barber. First Series. Oxford, 1921: 50–53.

"Jane Ellen Harrison." *An Address Delivered at Newnham College, 27 October 1928.* Cambridge, 1928.

The Ordeal of this Generation. The War, the League and the Future. Harley Stewart Lectures. London, 1929.

"Pagan Religion and Philosophy at the Time of Christ." *The History of Christianity in the Light of Modern Knowledge.* London and Glasgow, 1929: 42–82.

"Menander." In J. U. Powell, E. A. Barber, *New Chapters in the History of Greek Literature.* First series; 2d series. Oxford, 1929: 9–34.

"The Trojan Trilogy of Euripides (415 B.C.)." *Mélanges G. Glotz.* Vol. 2. Paris, 1932: 645–656.

"Aristophanes as a Critic of Athens." PCA 29 (1932) 33–51.

"Then and Now. The Changes of the Last Fifty Years." *The Romanes Lecture Delivered in the Sheldonian Theatre, 14 June 1935.* Oxford, 1935.

"The Anchor of Civilization." *The Philip Maurice Deneke Lecture Delivered at Lady Margaret Hall, Oxford, 24 November 1942.* London, 1943.

"Ritual Elements in New Comedy." CQ 37 (1943) 46–54.

"Myths and Ethics, or Humanism and the World's Need." *Moncure Conway Memorial Lecture, 19 March 1944.* London, 1944.

Humanism. Three B.B.C. Talks by Dr. Julian Huxley, Prof. Gilbert Murray, O. M., Dr. J. H. Oldham. London, 1944.

"Reactions to the Peloponnesian War in Greek Thought and Practice." JHS 64 (1944) 1–9.

"Victory and After." *The Third Montague Burton Lecture on International Relations Delivered at the University of Leeds, 1 June 1945.* Leeds, 1945.

"The Future of Greek Studies." Presidential Address, Society for the Promotion of Hellenic Studies, 1946. JHS 65 (1945) 1–9.

"What is Liberalism? A Re-Statement of Fundamentals." *World Review* n. s. 12
  (February 1950) 7–14.

"Advance under Fire." *The Ramsay Muir Memorial Lecture Delivered at the Debating
  Hall, Oxford Union Society, 22 July 1951.* London, 1951.

" 'Dis Geniti.' " *JHS* 71 (1951) 120–128.

"Europe and the Classical Tradition." In *English Studies Today.* Edited by C. L.
  Wrenn and G. Bullough. First Series. Papers Read at the International
  Conference of University Professors of English, Magdalen College, Oxford,
  August 1950. London, etc., 1951: 1–10.

"Are Our Pearls Real?" Presidential and Jubilee Address, The Classical Association.
  PCA 51 (1954) 7–22; reprinted separately, London, 1954.

"Memoirs of Wilamowitz." *A & A* 4 (1954) 9–14.

Sources

Autobiography and Biographies

Murray, Gilbert. *An Unfinished Autobiography.* With contributions from E. R. Dodds,
  J. Smith, Isobel Henderson, Sybil Thorndike, Salvador de Madariaga,
  Bertrand Russell. London, 1960.

West, Francis. *Gilbert Murray: A Life.* London and Canberra; New York, 1984.

Wilson, Duncan. *Gilbert Murray OM 1866–1957.* Oxford, 1987.

Bibliographies

Gongoll, Ward E. "Bio-Bibliography of George Gilbert Murray 1866–1957."
  Master's thesis, Catholic University (Washington, DC) 1967. (Incomplete
  and often erroneous.)

Patry, Madeleine. "A Bibliography of the Works of Gilbert Murray, O.M., D. C. L.,
  Litt. D., LL. D." Diss., University of London, 1950.

Biographical

Ackerman, Robert. "Euripides and Professor Murray." *CJ* 81 (1985/1986) 329–336.

Bowra, C.M. "Gilbert Murray." *Atlantic Monthly* 201 (May 1958) 71–76.

Dodds, E. R. "Gilbert Murray." *Gnomon* 29 (1957) 476–479 = An Unfinished
  Autobiography, 13–19.

Highet, Gilbert. "Gilbert Murray." *The Immortal Profession: The Joys of Teaching and
  Learning.* New York, 1976: 145–176.

Essays in Honour of Gilbert Murray. London, 1936.

"Dr. Gilbert Murray." Unsigned obituary. *New York Times* 106 (21 May 1957) 35.

"Dr. Gilbert Murray, OM." Unsigned obituary. *Times* (London) (21 May 1957) 13.

Greek Poetry and Life. Essays Presented to Gilbert Murray on his Seventieth Birthday.
  Oxford, 1936.

Henderson, M. I. "George Gilbert Aimé Murray." *Dictionary of National Biography
  1951–1960.* Edited by E. T. Williams and H. M. Palmer. London, etc.,
  1971: 757–761.

Lloyd-Jones, Hugh. "Gilbert Murray." *American Scholar* 51 (1982) 55–72 = Lloyd-

Jones, *Blood for the Ghosts. Classical Influences in the Nineteenth and Twentieth Centuries*. London, 1982: 195–214.

Thomson, J. A. K. "Gilbert Murray." PBA 43 (1957) 246–270.

Papers

The Gilbert Murray Papers are housed in the Modern Manuscripts Reading Room, Bodleian Library (New Building), Parks Road, Oxford.

Martin P. Nilsson

12 July 1874 – 7 April 1967

JØRGEN MEJER
University of Copenhagen

Martin P. Nilsson is perhaps the greatest of all modern scholars in the field of Greek religion, though his influence extends into many other areas of classical scholarship. No other modern Scandinavian classicist has done more to promote the study of Greco-Roman antiquity.

Nils Martin Persson Nilsson was born in southern Sweden of peasant parents, and he never lost touch with his agricultural background. He studied the classics at the University of Lund from 1892 to 1895; he also obtained his doctorate there in 1900 with his book on the Attic Dionysiac festivals. His most important teachers were Sam Wide (Lund), Jacob Wackernagel (Basel), and Ulrich von Wilamowitz-Moellendorff (Berlin); he is comparable to the latter in his catholic interests, his prolific publications and his long scholarly career, covering seven decades. He was Reader of Greek at Lund from 1900 to 1909; Professor of Classical Archaeology and Ancient History at Lund from 1909 to 1939; in addition to being President of that university from 1936 to 1939, he held many other academic and administrative positions and he was behind the establishment of the Swedish Academy in Rome in the 1920s.

The first decade of Nilsson's scholarship demonstrates his unusually wide learning and untiring energy: while struggling for both personal and professional recognition, he published two books on Greek religion, of which *Griechische Feste* from 1906, with its comprehensive research has remained a cornerstone, one book on the history of Epirus, one on Rhodian amphoras found during the Danish excavations of 1905–1907 in which he participated, and two books on Greek and Latin linguistics, besides many scholarly and popularizing articles on innumerable topics, reviews, and travel reports. Though his scholarship from the beginning focused on the history of Greek religion, his interests remained catholic, and quite often he dealt with other problems that came up in his work on Greek religion in separate books and papers.

Thus, between 1911 and 1920, his publications cover Scandinavian religion and folklore, time reckoning, calendar studies, and the Greek alphabet. A projected lexicon on Greek and Roman religion in cooperation with other scholars came to nothing because of the First World War, but it is a clear indication of his international recognition at that time. Many of his subsequent books and papers were based on his lectures around Europe and the United States; he was elected member of many academies and received several honorary doctoral degrees. He was editor of *Archiv für Religionswissenschaft* from 1923 to 1939.

By 1920 Nilsson began to reap the fruit of his many special studies in more comprehensive books on Greek religion and ancient history. While his survey of Greek myths (*Olympen*, 1918–19) never became known outside Scandinavia, his *History of Greek Religion* (1921) remains a standard work. His work on this subject is based on no monolithic theory about religion; he once wrote: "The key which opens all locks is usually a picklock." He had little patience with the approaches of W. F. Otto or with Freudian analysis. Some basic principles are evident in all his works: a conviction that prehistoric religion is animistic and has left traces in Greek religion of the historical period, that Greek religion is intimately connected with the calendar and practices of an agrarian culture, and that the study of Greek religion must be based on cult and ritual, while myths to a large extent are independent of religion and should be studied within the framework of folklore, folktale, and literature. Even so, his chapter on "The Origins of Greek Mythology" is one of the most concise and illuminating treatments of Greek myths.

In 1927 came his masterly examination of the Minoan-Mycenean religion and its survival in Greek religion, followed by his Sather lectures, *The Mycenean Origin of Greek Mythology* (1932) and his *Homer and Mycenae* (1933), lectures originally delivered at University College, London, in 1929. The combination of archaeological and literary evidence is stunning, his analyses and interpretations subtle and much more open-minded than previous scholarship (e.g. Evans), and many of his observations have since become generally accepted, e.g. on the variety of cults in the Minoan-Mycenean age, the significance of the Mycenean world for Greek religion, the correspondence between the geography of the Mycenean world and the locations of Greek heroic myths, the reflection of the Mycenean society in the organization of the Olympian gods, or on the oral nature of Homeric poetry (this before the work of Milman Parry became known). Besides these monumental contributions to the study of Greek religion, Nilsson in the 1920s also published one major study of the Roman empire and two volumes on Greece and Rome in a Swedish world history.

Nilsson continued his studies of special topics in Greek religion and history during the 1930s, and with his retirement in 1939 he was ready to launch a series of major books on Greek religion: *Greek Popular Religion* (lectures originally delivered in the United States in 1939 and 1940), *Geschichte der griechischen Religion 1–2* (in Iwan Müller's *Handbuch der Altertumswissenschaft*), and *Greek Piety*, all of which are still indispensable tools for the study of Greek religion. Both volumes of *GGR* consist of a ("static") description of certain key concepts, rites and practices, and a ("dynamic") historical account of the development of Greek religion beginning with the Minoan-Mycenean period, and of the cult(s) of the individual deities; the emphasis is on the presentation and analysis of the monumental and philological evidence. Greek religion is always seen against the background of history and politics. Mythology is only discussed when needed to explain a cult or deity, and the personal convictions of the Greeks about their gods are deliberately given a rather brief mention. Nilsson was sceptical of the possibility of identifying a specific, general Greek belief in the gods, since different beliefs belong to different social groups. He did, however, deal with this subject in *Greek Piety*, in which he concentrated on the beliefs rather the cults, while his *Greek Popular Religion* deals more with popular cults and practices.

During his long retirement Nilsson continued his research on many individual topics (e.g. *Cults, Myths, Oracles, and Politics in Ancient Greece* and *Die Hellenistische Schule*), but he also published a number of papers that revealed his more general convictions about the development of religion and its role in human life (see vol. 3 of his *Scripta Minora*), e.g., "Religion as man's protest against the meaninglessness of events," and "The High God and the Mediator," the latter describing the development towards monotheism and how the increased remoteness of the cosmic high god required a mediator; the Christians fulfilled that need by means of Jesus, whose help and comfort to all mankind made Christianity victorious in the struggle among the religions of late antiquity. The rationality of man, the first sign of which Nilsson saw already in the anthropomorphism of Homeric poetry, plays a crucial role in this development. In his retirement he also published many studies of local Swedish history, and because of his longevity it fell upon him to write the obituaries of a number of his contemporaries. He also reviewed a considerable number of books.

Nilsson's scholarship is a towering example of a historical approach to religion and to classical antiquity in general. He was as much an archaeologist as he was a historian of religion. He called himself an evolutionist; his approach to historical scholarship was eclectic. While his interpretations may be challenged, his presentation of the evidence is unsurpassed. His books are well organized and elegantly written; translations into numerous languages have ensured his widespread influence for more than fifty years. No books on Greek religion can be written for a long time to come without taking the results of Nilsson's research into account.

Books

Though the majority of Nilsson's books are listed below, the bibliography is very selective. His complete bibliography contains 1,000 items, without counting his many contributions to lexica.

Studia de Dionysiis Atticis. Lund, 1900.

Griechische Feste von religiöser Bedeutung mit Ausschluss der attischen. Leipzig, 1906; reprinted Stuttgart, 1957; Milan, 1975.

Die Kausalsätze im Griechischen bis Aristoteles. 1. Die Poesie. Würzburg, 1907.

Studien zur Geschichte des alten Epeiros. Lund, 1909.

Timbres amphoriques de Lindos. Publiés avec une étude sur les timbres amphoriques rhodiens. Académie royale des sciences et des lettres de Danemark. Extrait du Bulletin de l'année 1909 nos. 1 et 4. Copenhagen, 1909.

Primitiv religion. Stockholm, 1911: reprinted 1923, rev. ed. 1934; German translation as *Primitive Religion* (Tübingen, 1911); Danish translation as *Primitiv Religion* (Copenhagen and Kristiania, 1912).

Die volkstümlichen Feste des Jahres. Religionsgeschichtliche Volksbücher für die deutsche christliche Gegenwart R. 3. 17–18. Tübingen, 1914; Danish translation as *Aarets Folkelige Fester* (Copenhagen and Kristiania, 1914); Swedish translation as *Årets folkliga fester* (Stockholm, 1915); rev. ed. 1936.

Daimon, Gudemagter og Psykologi hos Homer. Studier fra Sprog– og Oldtidsforskningen 111. Copenhagen, 1918.

Die Entstehung und religiöse Bedeutung des griechischen Kalenders. Lunds universitets årsskrift 14: 2, 21. Lund and Leipzig, 1918; 2d ed. revised.

Scripta Minora Regiae Societatis Humaniorum Litterarum Lundensis 1960–61. Lund, 1962.

Die Übernahme und Entwicklung des Alphabets durch die Griechen. Det Kongelige Danske Videnskabernes Selskab. Historisk-filologiske Meddelelser, 1, 6. Copenhagen, 1918.

Olympen. En framställning av den klassiska mytologien. Stockholm, 1918–19; reprinted 1964, 1968; Danish translation (Copenhagen, 1923); reprinted 1966.

Primitive Time-reckoning. Acta soc. hum. litt. Lund. 1. Lund, 1920; reprinted 1960.

Den grekiska religionens historia. Stockholm, 1921; English translation as *A History of Greek Religion* (Oxford, 1925; 2d. ed. 1949; rev. ed. 1952; reprinted New York, 1964; Westport, CT, 1980); German translation as *Die Religion der Griechen* (Tübingen, 1927); Spanish translation as *Historia de la religiòn griega* (Buenos Aires, 1961).

Die Anfänge der Göttin Athena. Det Kongelige Danske Videnskabernes Selskab. Historisk-filologiske Meddelelser. 4, 7. Copenhagen, 1921.

Den romerska kejsartiden 1–2. Stockholm, 1921; English translation of vol. 1 as *Imperial Rome* (London and New York, 1926; reprinted 1936; reprinted New York, 1962; Chicago, 1974).

Primitiv kultur. Stockholm, 1924; reprinted 1926; Danish translation as *Primitiv kultur* (Copenhagen, 1925).

Festdagar och vardagar. Uppsatser om folkseder och kalender. Stockholm, 1925.

The Minoan-Mycenean Religion and Its Survival in Greek Religion. Acta Reg. soc. hum. litt. Lund. 9. Lund, 1927; 2d ed. revised, 1950; reprinted New York, 1971.

Hellas och de hellenistiska rikena. Nordstedts Världshistoria 2. Stockholm, 1928.

Rom och det romerska riket. Nordstedts Världshistoria 3. Stockholm, 1929.

The Mycenaean Origin of Greek Mythology. Sather Classical Lectures 8. Los Angeles and Cambridge, 1932; reprinted New York, 1963; 1969.

De arkeologiska upptäckterna i den klassiska södern och den forna orienten. Stockholm, 1933.

Homer and Mycenae. London, 1933; reprinted New York, 1968; Philadelphia, 1972.

Straff och sällhet i den andra världen i förkristen religion. Stockholm, 1937; reprinted as *Helvetets Förhistoria* (Stockholm, 1963).

Greek Popular Religion. New York, 1940; reprinted 1947 as *Greek Folk Religion.* Philadelphia, 1961; Gloucester, MA, 1971; French translation as *La religion populaire dans la Grèce antique* (Paris, 1954).

De grekiska tyrannerna. Svenska humanistiska förbundets skrifter nr. 52. Stockholm, 1941.

Geschichte der griechischen Religion l. Die Religion Griechenlands bis zur griechischen Weltherrschaft. Handbuch der Altertumswissenschaft 5. 2, 1 Munich, 1941; 2d ed. revised, 1955, 3d ed. revised, 1967.

Grekisk religiositet. Stockholm, 1946; 2d ed., 1960; English translation by H. J. Rose as *Greek Piety* (Oxford, 1948; reprinted New York, 1969); Italian translation by C. Diano as *Religiosità greca* (Florence, 1949); German translation by B. Christ *Griechischer Glaube* (Bern and Munich, 1950; reprinted 1959); Spanish translation as *Historia de la religiosidad griega* (Madrid, 1953); French translation *Les croyances réligieuses de la Grèce antique* (Paris, 1955).

Geschichte der griechischen Religion 2. Die hellenistische und römische Zeit. Handbuch der Altertumswissenschaft 5. 2. 2. Munich, 1950; 2d ed. revised, 1961.

Cults, Myths, Oracles, and Politics in Ancient Greece. Skrifter utg. av Svenska Institutet i Athen, 8.1. Lund, 1951.

Opuscula selecta linguis anglica, francogallica, germanica conscripta 1–2. Skrifter utg. av Svenska Institutet i Athen 8.2: 1–2. Lund, 1951–52 ; Vol. 3, Skrifter utg. av Svenska Institutet i Athen 2:3. Lund, 1960. (Volumes 1–2 contain a large selection of papers and reviews from 1905 to 1939; vol. 3 contains similar work from 1939 to 1958).

Die hellenistische Schule. Munich, 1955.

The Dionysiac Mysteries of the Hellenistic and Roman Age. Skrifter utg. av Svenska Institutet i Athen. No. 5. Lund, 1957; reprinted New York, 1975.

Articles (Selected)

"ΚΑΤΑΠΛΟΙ. Beiträge zum Schiffskataloge und zu der altionischen nautischen Litteratur." *RhM* 60 (1905) 161–189.

"Studien zur Vorgeschichte des Weihnachtsfestes." *ARW* 19 (1916–1919) 50–150.

"Der mykenische Ursprung der griechischen Mythologie." ΑΝΤΙΔΩΡΟΝ *Festschrift Jacob Wackernagel.* Göttingen, 1923: 137–142.

"Die Religion in den griechischen Zauberpapyri." *Kungl. human. vetenskapssamfundet i Lund. Årsberättelse* 1947–1948: 59–93.

"Letter to Professor Arthur D. Nock on Some Fundamental Concepts in the Science of Religion." *HThR* 42 (1949) 71–107. Italian translation by G. Pasquali as *Fondamenti di scienza delle religioni* (Florence, 1950).

"Second Letter to Professor Nock on the Positive Gains in the Science of Greek

Religion." *HThR* 44 (1951) 143–151.

"Religion as Man's Protest against the Meaninglessness of Events." *Kungl. Human.*
Vetenskapssamfundet i Lund. Årsberättelse (1953–1954): 25–92.

"The High God and the Mediator." *HThR* 56 (1963) 101–120.

Sources

Gjerstad, E. "Martin P. Nilsson in Memoriam" In *Scripta Minora Regiae Societatis*
Humaniorum Litterarum Lundensis 1967–1968 1. Lund, 1968. Gerstad's
memoir is more or less the same as the one printed in *Gnomon* 40 (1968)
100–103.

Hanell, K. "Martin Persson Nilsson." In *Vetenskaps-Societeten i Lund Årsbok 1968*,
143–154.

Nilsson, M. P. "Lebenslauf." In *Scripta Minora* 3:ix–xi.

Bibliography

Knudtzon, E. J. and Callmer, C. "A Complete Bibliography." In *Scripta Minora*
Regiae Societatis Humaniorum Litterarum Lundensis 1967–1968 1. Lund, 1968.

Papers

The University Library, Lund, contains his *Nachlaß* and a large collection of letters.

Eduard Norden

21 September 1868 – 13 July 1941

BERNHARD P. P. KYTZLER
Freie Universität Berlin

When visiting Harvard University on the occasion of its tercentenary cele-bration in 1936, Eduard Norden was greeted by the University's President, James B. Conant, who conferred upon him an honorary doctorate, as "the most famous Latinist in the world." When Norden died only five years later, the leading Latinist had lost his library and his home, his professorship and his citizenship. The bitterness of exile broke his heart. He was forced to leave Berlin and Germany in 1939 for no other reason than having been born a Jew—no matter that he had been baptized a Protes-tant more than half a century earlier at the age of seventeen on 13 December 1885. In these dark years it no longer mattered that he had directed more than fifty disserta-tions, had served his University as Rektor and in many other positions, nor that he had broken the ground in a field that is still discussed in his terms, after the *Antike Kunstprosa*. That he had written the model for all Latin commentaries in the twenti-eth century, *Aeneis VI*, was now forgotten; even his two books on old Germania could not save their author from the hate of an irrational persecution.

Norden came from the north of Germany. He was born in Emden as the child of a medical doctor, Geheimer Sanitätsrat Dr. Carl Norden, and his wife Rosa, née Hamburger. All his life long he felt lasting ties with his home province. In 1933 he called his forthcoming book on old Germania "a testimony of a man of Frisian origin for his German native country." In a similar way, he felt attached to his alma mater in Bonn and to his teacher Franz Bücheler, to whom he dedicated in 1898 his first great book, the *Antike Kunstprosa*, and in 1939 his last work, *Aus altrömischen Priesterbüch-ern*. At the end of the preface to *Kunstprosa*, Norden explains why he feels that his time in Bonn will be sacred to him for all his life: "That Latin literature is the product of the Greek, that the two literatures lack chronological limits, that the ancient authors have to be felt to be understood—these are the ideas with which we were educated at Bonn, where I enjoyed the greatest years of my life." In a similar way, Norden analyzed the influence of Bücheler on him and his work in his inaugural speech at the Berlin Academy in 1913, naming also Usener and Mommsen as his most important teachers and models.

Norden was only twenty-three years old when in 1891 he submitted his dissertation, "In Varronis saturas Menippeas observationes selectae." How the difficult text of this author fascinated him through all his years is documented in the preface to *Priesterbücher*: "Since that time I have never ceased to pay attention to the text . . . the terror that once seized the youth vibrates still in the old man and may have helped him—utinam quidem—to understand the verses rightly."

With the streams of Norden's important publications came the sequence of calls to more and more important universities: 1895 to Greifswald, 1899 to Breslau, 1906 to Berlin. This *cursus honorum* was completed in 1913 with membership in the Berlin Akademie der Wissenschaften. One may add the Rektorat already mentioned, participation in the work of the *Thesaurus Linguae Latinae*, membership in the directorium of the Deutsches Archäologisches Institut. But it was his contributions to classical scholarship more than such honors as these that made Norden famous and influential.

Die Antike Kunstprosa covers in about 1,000 pages almost 2,000 years of literary history, "from the VI. century B.C. to the time of the Renaissance," as the subtitle explains. This breathtaking survey examines theory and praxis in Greek and Roman, pagan and Christian, classical, medieval, and humanistic rhetoric. It is still, today, the basic book about the art of eloquence, its means and methods. Despite its enormous size, the book is not meant as a handbook to consult here and there; rather, it is conceived as a work to be read in its entirety. "If someone would read what I have to say about Thucydides, Plato, Cicero, Seneca or Tacitus without connection to the pertinent theory discussed before, he would not understand the position which I give them in the course of the development," explains the preface. Even if these directions were more often than not neglected, the influence of Norden's history of style in antiquity and later ages can hardly be overestimated. The book has remained the standard investigation and the foundation for all similar undertakings in this century.

"Virgilstudien" were published as early as 1893. A decade later Norden brought out his masterpiece, the great commentary on the sixth book of the *Aeneid*, again a model for all comparable undertakings in the twentieth century. All aspects of the philological treatment that an important text might receive are masterly displayed here in about 500 pages. These elucidations are not lost in the context but are pointed out to readers and users alike in the famous Register, including "Topics" (from "Agonistik" to "Zauberliteratur"), "Mythology, Religion, Philosophy" (from "Aberglaube" to "Wintersonnenwende"), "Grammar and Lexicography," "Metre and Prosody," "Rhetoric," and finally, an index of passages. This plain enumeration might already make clear what an enormous amount of learning is condensed in these pages. Perhaps more characteristic is another feature: Norden prints next to his Latin text a German translation, which, with the help of an often-changing rhythm, aims at conveying to the modern reader the flow of the original hexameter. But the most important point was expressed by the aged Mommsen, as Hermann Diels tells us: "A few days before his end I found him bent over your Virgil commentary looking at the lines with his half blind eyes. 'Oh yes, the youth,' he sighed, 'they have a better stand. What we old ones have tried in vain, this they handle with courage and with excellence: the religious question.' "

Indeed, Mommsen's dictum is the best evalution of Norden's achievements. It is the "philology of religion," quoted by Norden as A. D. Nock's definition, to which he confessed himself with all his strength.

This holds true for two other great works also. *Die Geburt des Kindes* treats in 171 pages only sixty-three Latin verses: the fourth Eclogue of Virgil. The subtitle, "History of a Religious Idea" indicates that this is not so much a running commentary (as his *Aeneis VI*) but rather a general introduction to one of the most disputed, most difficult—and most beautiful—poems of the Latin language. Perhaps one should better say: a general introduction to the world of this poem, its thoughts, themes, and traditions. They comprise "Egyptian theologoumena" as well as "gospel criticism." And they must be seen in connection with Norden's book published in 1913, eleven years earlier, under the title *Agnostos Theos*. Here the subtitle is "Investigations concerning the History of Religious Speech." It is easy to see that the two main fields of Norden's interest, history of rhetorical forms and patterns of religious ideas, are combined here in an extraordinary sequence of interpretations and elucidations. The author brings into comparison Hellenica (Horace's ode for Messala), Judaica (including Babyloniaca and Egyptiaca for the origin of certain stylistic forms) and Christiana. He sets out to explain the twenty-one lines of Acts 17 that give the famous Areopagus speech of Paul in order "to find out first, what is the material in thoughts and forms that the author has taken over, and second, how has he adapted this material to a certain situation."

It is not difficult to see the themes and topics to which Norden dedicated his main interests and his major works. On the one side, there is his restless search for what he, following Michelangelo, calls the "immortale forma": the figures of speech and thought; on the other side, there is his deep dedication to religious questions: it is certainly a meaningful day when he dates the second edition of *Geburt* with "Christmas 1930"; he also asserts in the preface to *Agnostos Theos* that this "is a work on which I certainly did not work with my intellect only." It should not be forgotten that it was Virgil—the deeply religious poet—to whose works Norden turned in his two great books on *Aeneid* 6 and *Eclogue* 4 and also in more than half a dozen other minor works (*Kleine Schriften*: 358–532; *Hermes* 28 (1893) 360–406 and 501–521), to which one may add *Ennius und Vergilius. Kriegsbilder aus Roms großer Zeit* (Leipzig; Berlin, 1915). And to name a last field: two investigations treat problems connected with the early history of Germany. *Die germanische Urgeschichte in Tacitus Germania* (1920) analyzes the style of Tacitus, thus explaining the relation of traditional *topoi* to reality in this work. *Alt-Germanien. Völker- und namensgeschichtliche Untersuchungen* (1934) deals with a number of special questions; Heinz Haffter's *bon mot* rightly says it should be entitled *Alt-Germanien, Alt-Gallien, Alt-Italien.*

In his study "Lessing als klassischer Philologe" Norden enumerates the prerequisites, the items of "Philologischer Hausrat" that he finds in the great German poet of the age of Enlightenment—we may safely call them his own philological creed. He begins with "the solid knowledge of both the ancient languages," he adds "precision" and "sensitivity for stylistic nuances" ("Stilgefühl") and ends with "the gift to see problems and the dedicated endeavour to solve them." And as a corollary: "Without a more or less considerable library one cannot even think of working in the humanities ("Geisteswissenschaften")."

To complete this list of "philologischer Hausrat": In his foreword to a new edition of Usener's *Götternamen* Norden explains that he counts among the strongest impressions during his time as a student Usener's inexorable search for truth, which led this professor to confess in front of his students that he felt compelled to give up his former positions on certain questions. Such a modesty was shared by Norden. It might be significant that he insisted on avoiding exclamation marks but recommended the use of question marks, "the truly scientific punctuation." This information tallies with his soft voice in private conversations, a certain shyness, which disappeared during his lectures: "Again and again I had the impression that each of his lecture classes, setting aside the value of its information, presented itself as a perfect rhetorical performance constructed carefully to the last detail."

The center of his teaching was thus defined by Werner Jaeger: "The experience of form was the first; the second step the attempt to support this newly awakening sense by the use of observation and parallels."

It was certainly not overly pretentious when Norden was hailed in Harvard as the most famous Latinist in the world. In his generation, during the first half of this century, there was indeed no greater scholar in Latin studies than he. The development of ancient style and rhetoric is still today seen with his eyes, understood along his lines as pointed out in *Kunstprosa*. The comprehension of Virgil in this century is based on his commentaries and analyses. The "philology of religion" was inaugurated by him and carried on by many others. Among his students, such names appear as Werner Hardtke and F. W. Lenz, Erich Pertsch, the lexicographer, and Alfred Kurfess, the Sallust editor. All his great books have been reprinted in the second half of this century; they will certainly remain standard works even after the end of this millennium.

Books

Die antike Kunstprosa vom VI. Jahrhundert v. Chr. bis in die Zeit der Renaissance. 2 vols. Leipzig and Berlin, 1898; 3d printing 1915.

P. Vergilius Maro: Aeneis Buch VI Erklärt. Leipzig, 1903; 4th ed. Stuttgart, 1957.

Die lateinische Literatur im Übergang vom Altertum zum Mittelalter. In *Die Kultur der Gegenwart.* Vol. 1. Leipzig and Berlin, 1905: 374–411; 3d ed. enlarged 1912.

Die römische Literatur. In *Einleitung in die Altertumswissenschaft.* Vol. 1. Leipzig, 1910.

Die römische Literatur. Mit Anh.: Die lateinische Literatur im Übergang vom Altertum zum Mittelalter (s.o.). 6th ed. enlarged, Leipzig, 1961.

Agnostos Theos. Untersuchungen zur Formengeschichte religiöser Rede. Leipzig and Berlin, 1913.

Ennius und Vergilius. Kriegsbilder aus Roms großer Zeit. Leipzig and Berlin, 1915.

Die Geburt des Kindes. Geschichte einer religiösen Idee. Leipzig and Berlin, 1924; 3d printing 1958.

Alt-Germanien, Völker- und namensgeschichtliche Untersuchungen. Leipzig and Berlin, 1934.

Aus altrömischen Priesterbüchern. Lund and Leipzig, 1939.

Articles (Collected)

Kleine Schriften zum klassischen Altertum. Edited by B. Kytzler. Berlin, 1966.

Sources

Bibliography

Kytzler, B. In Norden's *Kleine Schriften zum klassischen Altertum.* Berlin, 1966: 683–690. (Includes a list of dissertations directed by Norden.)

Biographical

Abel, W. *Gymnasium* 91 (1984) 449–484.

Dessoir, M. *Buch der Erinnerung.* Stuttgart, 1946: 183–187.

Haffter, H. "Eduard Norden." *Neue Zürcher Zeitung.* No. 3897 (September 1963) 29 = *Maia* 17 (1965) 241–247 (Italian version).

Kytzler, B. *Praefatio* to *Kleine Schriften,* v–ix.

———. "Eduard Norden." *Berliner Lebensbilder Geisteswissenschaftler.* Berlin, 1989: 327–342.

Lenz, F. W. In A & A 7 (1958) 159–171. Cf. W. Theiler, *Gnomon* 31 (1960) 390–1.

———. "Eduard Nordens Leistung für die Altertumswissenschaft." *Das Altertum* 6 (1960) 245–254.

Letters

Abel, W. *Gymnasium* 92 (1985) 526–532.

Kytzler, B. (see above).

Mensching, E. In *Latein und Griechisch in Berlin = Mitteilungsblatt des Landes Verbandes Berlin im Deutschen Altphilologenverband (DAV)* 27 (1983) 54–56; 29 (1985) 88; 31 (1987) 117–128.

Skutsch, O. "Wilamowitz an Norden über dessen 'Ennius und Vergilius.'" A & A 29 (1983) 90–94.

William Abbott Oldfather

23 October 1880 – 27 May 1945

JOHN BUCKLER
University of Illinois
   at Urbana-Champaign

There was nothing simple about William Abbott Oldfather, as his career amply demonstrates, but much that was fruitful. The very variety of his scholarly interests, achievements, and experiences is itself remarkable. Perhaps Richmond Lattimore put it best, when he rhetorically asked in his poem, "Memory of a Scholar (W. A. O.)": "How shall I shape the wind that / once was you?"

The poem was published in both *The New Republic* (13 November 1961) and *CJ* 57 (1962) 271–272. Of course, the thing is impossible, but the effort reveals much about the man and his enormous and diverse impact on the world of classical scholarship. Although it was not unusual in the nineteenth century for young Americans to complete their formal education at the great universities of Germany, Oldfather was one of the first American classicists to make his own research felt in both Europe and America. He thereby gave added stimulus to classical studies in the United States, and his efforts to introduce German principles of higher education influenced not only his own University of Illinois but also the general development of modern American education. He was hearty and friendly, a bit too forthright for some, but a man who made many friends. He tempered his intense research with intense outdoor exercise. In both he excelled, for he was equally at home with an ancient text or a baseball bat. His presence in the classroom was one of brilliance, inquiry, and grandeur, and his courses were among the most popular on campus.

Oldfather was born on 23 October 1880 in Urumiah, Persia (now Rezaieh, Iran) of Presbyterian missionary parents. On his paternal side he traced his origins to Austria, where the family name was Altvater, while on his maternal side he counted the American frontiersman Daniel Boone among his ancestors. The family proved to be academically gifted. His sister, Helen, founded the Deaf Oral School in Tokyo, and was the mother of Edwin O. Reischauer, who later became a distinguished professor of

Japanese history at Harvard University and United States ambassador to Japan. Oldfather's younger brother, Charles Henry, both taught ancient history at the University of Nebraska and served there as dean of the graduate school. He also translated the first fourteen books of Diodorus Siculus for the Loeb Classical Library.

Upon its return from Iran, the family settled in Hanover, Indiana. There Oldfather attended Hanover College, his two most influential teachers being Joshua Bolles Garritt and John Livingston Lowes. After receiving a B.A. in 1899, he attended Harvard College, where he studied with the great philologists William Watson Goodwin, Charles Burton Gulick, and Herbert Weir Smyth, the latter of whom greatly stimulated his studies in classical antiquity. From Harvard he received a second B.A. in 1901 and his M.A. in 1902, after which he became an instructor at Northwestern University and so steeped himself in German that he became bilingual.

A momentous change in his life occurred in October, 1906, when he entered the University of Munich to pursue graduate work and thereupon stepped into the world of international scholarship. In the early twentieth century, few universities in the world rivalled Munich in the field of classical studies. In Germany he worked most closely with Otto Crusius in Greek, who did much to further his scholarship, and with Friedrich Vollmer in Latin. Robert von Pöhlmann stimulated his interest in ancient history and Adolf Furtwängler in archaeology. During these years he developed a lasting appreciation of and respect for German scholarship and a love of German culture that two world wars could not diminish. He became and remained a scholar whose outlook was international.

After receiving his doctorate from the University of Munich (1908) under Crusius, Oldfather returned to Northwestern University to serve as Assistant Professor of Latin, but in 1909 he moved to the University of Illinois in Urbana. There his career blossomed until his premature death. He was not only promoted to Associate and later to Professor of Classics, but he also guided his department as its head from 1926 to 1945. These years saw him, together with a few others, transform a land-grant institution into a major university. He was the champion of his own department and of the humanities in general, and his battles in these causes won him enemies as well as friends. An enduring contribution was his support of the classics library, which he made the third best among American universities. He did so in part by acquiring the private libraries of the great German scholars Wilhelm Dittenberger and Johannes Vahlen and by purchasing various manuscripts of ancient and medieval authors. For over twenty-five years he also found time to edit the *University of Illinois Studies in Language and Literature*. Not one to remain in the library, he spent many summers on the Continent and in Greece in order to undertake extensive topographical work, notably in the little-known region of Locris, one result of which was the publication of many new inscriptions.

Oldfather wished to institute at Illinois the German concept of large, joint academic endeavors. He organized the Illinois Greek Club and launched numerous bibliographical programs, including word indices to Seneca's tragedies, Apuleius' works, and Cicero's *Letters* and *Rhetoric* and the still unpublished "Classica Americana," which noted the publication of Americans in classical scholarship and of foreigners who published their work in the United States. He guided the research of forty-six doctoral students, including J. B. Tischener (1923), Aubrey Diller (1930), Kenneth M. Abbott (1933), Richmond Lattimore (1934), and Revilo P. Oliver (1940).

His impact on the development of the American university extended far beyond his own institution. As early as 1911 Oldfather discussed the relative values of the elective system and traditional requirements for students (*Educational Review* [Nov. 1911] 367–375), in which he made a stirring defense of liberal education, especially the study of languages and mathematics. In the dark days after World War I he made vigorous pleas for American support of the *Thesaurus Linguae Latinae* (*CJ* 18 [1922] 45–54) and of *Bursian's Jahresbericht* (*AJP* 47 [1926] 104). He argued in favor of individuality and democracy in the functioning of the graduate curriculum (*CW* 30 [1937] 259–260) and the place of the dissertation in graduate study (*CW* 32 [1939] 231–233). He often insisted upon the significance of Greek and Latin for a full appreciation of the English language in particular and Western culture in general. He also described the concept and working of Illinois's executive committee system of university administration as a model for other institutions (*AAUP Bulletin* 27 [1941] 1–16).

Oldfather also played a major role in professional organizations, and his unceasing energy and vision won him many honors. Chief among them was the Sather Lectureship (1934), in which he spoke on "The Decline of Culture in the Roman Empire." He was president of the American Philological Association in 1937–1938, member of the American Academy of Arts and Sciences, Linguistic Society of America, and the National Research Council. The result of this gigantic effort was the "Oldfather School," which can be defined as the total integration of all facets of ancient life in order to draw a complete picture of antiquity. To that end he employed paleography, textual criticism, bibliography, history, topography and archaeology, philosophy, and numismatics. In 1943 his "school" honored him with a *Festschrift* of classical studies.

Oldfather was also involved in one of the ugliest episodes in the history of the University of Illinois. On Halloween night in 1917, he came to the defense of several colleagues who had been summoned by a federal agent to the Urbana City Hall. Victims of a wave of war hysteria, they all, Oldfather included, were informally but publicly charged with pro-German sentiments and disloyalty to the United States. One of their principal accusers was one Mary E. Busey, a prominent local banker, trustee of the University, and an officious bigot. Oldfather demanded and received a public hearing, in which he proved that the accusations were baseless. In this atmosphere of bile and intimidation, Oldfather defended the culture and the character of the German people, but nevertheless the University subsequently suspended within its walls freedom of speech, the principle of neutrality, and academic freedom for the duration of the war.

Oldfather remained staunchly pro-German throughout his life, which gained him a great deal of animosity during the World Wars, yet he was adamantly democratic in politics and philosophy. His love of Germany never embraced Nazism, and he early warned of the dangers of fascism. He urged the adoption of conscription as early as 1928 and argued against isolationism. Nevertheless, when, on 27 May 1945, he died while canoeing near Urbana, the accident was ascribed by some to his despondency over the German military surrender some twenty days earlier and even to suicide. The verdict of the coroner of Champaign County, Illinois, reports accidental death by drowning.

In addition to his books, Oldfather wrote some 207 articles and reviews and over 500 articles in German for Pauly-Wissowa, many of the latter treating the history, topography, religion, mythology, culture, dialects, and prosopography of eastern and western Locris. Here he was a pioneer in areas still not well studied today and in a region still not yet adequately excavated. This is especially true of western Locris, which even the indefatigable Pausanias did not visit, and which Strabo describes scantily and not from autopsy. Oldfather began his work with his dissertation, *Lokrika*, in which he discussed Homeric knowledge of early Locris. Firmly in command of the literary sources, he walked the Locrian countryside in order to find physical remains that could identify ancient sites. The work in western Locris was especially demanding, both in terms of available literary and archaeological evidence and also in the physical demands that the terrain made on the topographer. In this instance, Oldfather's love of strenuous physical exercise and his sturdy endurance were as useful to him as his familiarity with ancient sources. He found, especially in western Locris, a scholar's challenge and an outdoorsman's delight. Wilamowitz singled out his article on Locris in the Pauly-Wissowa for special praise as an example of the ideal of a total, systematic study of the topic, and Oldfather himself once remarked: "If anyone should ask whether I ever did any really careful research, tell him it was on the topography of Locris" (CJ 41 [1945–1946] 9). He was intellectually honest enough to admit when he had failed to put an ancient name to a site, but nevertheless he reported many theretofore undiscovered remains and numerous inscriptions. Of particular use to the historian is his identification of Locrian sites in the Thermopylae corridor, an area significant in ancient history from the time of Leonidas and Themistocles to the age of Justinian. More importantly, his treatment of the entire area went so far beyond the work of topographers like William Martin Leake and geographers like C. Bursian as to point the way to the modern study of ekistics. A lasting result of his endeavors is the preservation by means of acute, diligent, and informed observation of much evidence that has subsequently been lost owing to the modern development of Greece. Although he has very occasionally been criticized for his topographical research in Locris, the work of his critics has never measured up to his standards, and indeed would have been virtually impossible without his trail blazing. In fact, he did more than any of his predecessors or successors to bring this neglected area back into the light of modern scholarship. His article "Lokroi" in the Pauly-Wissowa, treating the

Greek colony in southern Italy, is another example of his total and thorough approach to a place, its inhabitants, their culture and history.

The outbreak of World War I nonetheless encouraged Oldfather to turn his attention to military affairs. He and Howard Vernon Canter began with an analysis of the impact of Varus' defeat in A.D. 9 upon the way in which Augustus and his successors considered the problem of defending the northern frontier of the Roman Empire. From this study, Oldfather concluded that Roman policy aimed basically at creating a "buffer state" there to protect the Empire. Early in 1917 the war prompted him and some colleagues who constituted the Illinois Greek Club to examine Greek military writers, some of whom were readily available only in the German translation of W. Rüstow and H. Köchly, *Griechische Kriegsschriftsteller*, 3 vols. (Leipzig 1853–1855). As usual, Oldfather began with exhaustive textual studies of the manuscripts before he and his colleagues produced their translation for the Loeb Classical Library (1923). He also explored various aspects of military and naval warfare and ancient seafaring in subsequent publications.

Philosophically inclined and always the democrat, Oldfather was attracted by the Stoic philosophy of Epictetus, the emancipated slave. Once again, Oldfather began his study of the subject with textual criticism of the manuscripts and extensive bibliography, the latter of which appeared separately as the magisterial *Contributions toward a Bibliography of Epictetus* (1927). One mark of his work on Epictetus was his proclivity to discover in various places previously unrecognized manuscripts of authors, both ancient and medieval, whose writings elucidated the manuscript tradition. The fruit of his varied labor was the translation in two volumes of Arrian's reports of Epictetus' thought published in the Loeb Classical Library in 1926–1927. Oldfather's other philosophical interests ranged from Pythagoras, to whose thought he drew analogies to the totalitarian propaganda of the day, to Plato, Seneca, and even to Nietzsche's use of Greek literature and rhetoric in the formation of that philosopher's thought.

Oldfather devoted considerable attention to Greek and Latin literature, the results of which he sometimes applied to modern letters. He was always concerned with the relation of the classics to the cultural inheritance of Western civilization. His interests in these areas were far-reaching, extending among the ancients from Homer through Old Comedy, Plato, and Apuleius to Tacitus. While his emphasis was usually on the text, he never failed to appreciate the literary message and style of the author. The results of his approach varied. Sometimes they led to the purely grammatical, as in his examination of the objective genitive in Greek and Latin (e.g., in *Donum Natalicum Schrijen* [Utrecht, 1929] 624–634) or Caesar's grammatical theories (*CJ* 23 [1928] 584–602) and at other times to a historical reexamination of the trial of Socrates (*CW* 31 [1938] 203–211) or a discussion of Tacitus' knowledge of early German history (*CJ* 19 [1924] 458–461). At other times, he drew various threads together in more general studies, as with his discussion of the historical and cultural significance of Roman comedy (*CW* 7 [1914] 217–222) and the impact of the classics on such modern authors as John Milton and Gerhart Hauptmann. In general terms, he made a fertile contribution to American classical studies by his frequent comments upon and reviews of German scholarship.

Given his interest in religion and texts, Oldfather was not surprisingly drawn to patristics, especially the study of the church father Jerome, whose own similar research had led to a reliable text of the Bible. Oldfather directed the dissertations of six doctoral students who explored the manuscript traditions and the contents of several of Jerome's lesser-known *Lives* of early Christian saints. He also applied himself to Jerome's text of the *Lives of the Fathers*, to the topic of classical quotations in the Pastoral Epistles, and the *Homilies* of Paul the Deacon. From late antiquity he moved easily into medieval studies. He commented upon the Urbana manuscript of Syntipas, the Byzantine historian of philosophy, the Fleury text of the late Roman fabulist and poet Avienus, and, among other things, the text of the *Excidium Troie*, a medieval account of the fall of Troy. From the Middle Ages it was a short step to the early modern period and his translations of some of the important writings of the humane and liberal Samuel Pufendorf, who, like John Locke, examined the nature of the social contract, and the purely scientific theories of Leonhard Euler's *Concerning Elastic Curves*.

In sum, Oldfather helped substantially to make Illinois a major university, one better known in Europe than the vast majority of other American institutions. He introduced to the American educational system the finest fruits of German scholarship, which included an ideal that encouraged scholars to examine every aspect of antiquity systematically in order to understand the past. He demanded rigorous method when dealing with the sources, and careful, thoughtful reading in every relevant language of the secondary material. Bibliography preserved the results. During his lifetime, the mark of respect for and appreciation of his learning and vision can most easily be demonstrated by the high reputation that he enjoyed both in the United States and on the Continent. Even today, much of his work has yet to be surpassed, and no one with a serious interest in such diverse topics as Locris or Epictetus can do more than build upon the pioneer's work.

Books

Lokrika, Sagengeschichtliche Untersuchungen. Diss., Tübingen, 1908 = *Philologus* 67 (1908) 412–472.

The Defeat of Varus and the Frontier Policy of Augustus. With H. V. Canter. Urbana, 1915.

Index Verborum in Senecae Fabulis necnon in Octavia praetexta reperiuntur. Edited with A. S. Pease, H. V. Carter. Urbana, 1918.

Ysopet-Avionnet: the Latin and French Texts. Edited with K. McKenzie. Urbana, 1919.

Aeneas Tacticus, Asclepiodotus, Onasander. Translated and edited with members of the Illinois Greek Club. Loeb Classical Library. Cambridge, MA, 1923.

Epictetus. 2 vols. Loeb Classical Library. Cambridge, MA, 1926–1927. (Translation.)

Contributions toward a Bibliography of Epictetus. Urbana, 1927.

S. Pufendorf, *Elementorum Jurisprudentiae Universalis*. Oxford, 1931; reprinted New York, 1964. (Translation.)

Leonhard Euler's Elastic Curves (De Curvis Elasticis). Translated and edited with C. A. Ellis and D. M. Brown. Bruges, 1933.

S. Pufendorf, *De Jure Naturae et Gentium*. Translated with Charles Henry Oldfather. Oxford, 1934.

Index Apuleianus. Edited with H. V. Canter, B. E. Perry, et al. Middletown, CT, 1934.

Index Verborum Ciceronis Epistularum. Edited with H. V. Canter, K. M. Abbott, et al. Urbana, 1938.

Cherf, Father John Frank, et al. *Studies in the Text Tradition of St. Jerome's Vitae Patrum*. Edited with others. Urbana, 1943.

Index Verborum in Ciceronis Rhetorica. Edited with H. V. Canter and K. M. Abbott. Urbana, 1964. (Posthumous.)

Articles

"Lokris." *RE* 13 (1926) 1135–1288.

"Lokroi." *RE* 13 (1927) 1289–1363.

"Terence's Phormio and Adelphi." In *Latin Literature in Translation*. Edited by K. Guinagh et al. New York and London, 1942. (Translation.)

Sources

Biographical

Calder, W. M., III. "Ulrich von Wilamowitz-Moellendorff to William Abbott Old-father: Three Unpublished Letters." *CJ* 72 (1976–1977) 115–127.

Daley, L. W. "Oldfather." *DAB* Supp. 3, 1941–1945 (New York, 1973) 571–572.

Forbes, C. A. "William Abbott Oldfather." *CJ* 41 (1945) 8–11.

Griffiths, S. N. "Doctoral Dissertations Completed at the University of Illinois under William Abbott Oldfather." *CJ* 74 (1978–1979) 149–153.

Pease, A. S. "William Abbott Oldfather." *TAPA* 76 (1945) xxiv–xxvi.

Papers

The principal *Nachlaß* is at the library of the University of Illinois, Urbana-Champaign. Oldfather's letters to A.S. Pease are at the Houghton Library, Harvard.

D. L. Page

11 May 1908 – 6 July 1978

ROGER D. DAWE
Trinity College, Cambridge

Denys Lionel Page's father achieved two distinctions not granted to ordinary mortals: he became Chief Engineer for the Great Western Railway Company, and he lived to celebrate his hundredth birthday, surviving Denys, the third of his five children. Originally from South Wales, the family moved to Berkshire, and Page's education in the classics began at Newbury Grammar School, to such good effect that the boy won a scholarship to Christ Church, Oxford. There were three scholars in classics of that vintage, 1926–1930. The two others were Donald Allan, who went on via Balliol and Edinburgh to hold the chair of Greek at Glasgow. The other was a man who was to become a lifelong friend, Quintin Hogg (Viscount Hailsham). Page's undergraduate life was not focused solely on the study of antiquity any more than Jebb's had been. He had sporting ambitions, including, *mirabile dictu*, that of playing cricket for England, and oral tradition still speaks with awe of him as a fast bowler. While Hailsham busied himself with undergraduate politics, Page and Allan were occupied in lifting various University prizes. Hailsham remembers at a distance of some sixty years how he and Page both attended a dinner at the time of their final examinations "when we conversed solely in inappropriate Latin: mainly imprecations of which I only remember 'pereant examinatores; morbum obscoenum capiant examinatores,' none of which happily came to pass."

All three obtained first class degrees, and Page went on to spend a year in Vienna before returning to become a classics don at Christ Church. In those days no person with an Oxbridge Fellowship would do anything as vulgar as writing a Ph.D. dissertation, but it was still necessary to establish oneself. In Page's case this objective was attained in one leap with the publication of *Actors' Interpolations in Greek Tragedy*, studied with special reference to Euripides' *Iphigenia in Aulis*. It is still indispensable for those who have protracted dealings with that play. In later life Page had some of Jebb's reluctance to excise from tragedy lines that others might have thought spurious, perhaps in reaction against his own youthful work. But there was nothing in this first book that the mature scholar need have deplored. Page was now seen to be a young man with a brilliant mind and a command of his subject. But the world is full of young men with brilliant minds and a command of their subjects, and most of them sink from sight after a few years. Was *Actors' Interpolations* to be a springboard, or was it to be the once-and-for-all passport to the comfortable life of an Oxford don? With the publication of the *Medea* edition the answer seemed to be taking shape. Many years later Page confided to a friend that the whole thing needed doing again, thinking perhaps of advances made by others that ought to be incorporated. Even so, it remains a worthy contribution to what has proved to be a distinguished series, and the many who use it will include among their reasons for gratitude its moderate compass. Editions tend to get ever bigger, in obedience to the tacit law, which we all recognize, that classical books exist not to serve the reader but to parade the erudition of their authors. Page did not parade his erudition, but it was beyond even his powers to conceal it.

It has been said, by one who is not a member, that there are three ways into the British Academy (of which Page was later to be President): sodomy, papyrology, and treason. Page was qualified only in the second of these, developing an interest in the subject long before it became fashionable. This interest brought him into contact with Edgar Lobel, a scholar for whom he had the very highest regard, and led to the next book, an unpretentious-looking volume in the Loeb library series, now going under the unexciting title *Select Papyri iii*. It was devoted to fragments of Greek poetry and gave Page the chance to deploy his ever-increasing skills to fill out the gaps in the texts. In the preface, he writes, "I began eager to fill every gap with flawless fragments of my own composition; I ended with the desire—too late—to remove all that is not either legible in the papyrus or replaceable beyond reasonable doubt. At the eleventh hour, indeed, I expelled handfuls of private poetry. . . ." At least one reviewer expressed his regrets at the probable loss to scholarship brought about by this unhappy access of modesty.

By now it was wartime. Page became part of the not-quite-as-secret-as-it-ought-to-be Intelligence department located at Bletchley, and then ended his military service in a coordinating capacity in the Far East. A large slice had been taken out of his life, and on his return to the academic world he renewed his studies with an intensity all the greater. He was soon to be rewarded, for in 1950 he was elected to the Cambridge Chair that he was to hold with such distinction for a quarter of a century. It was an inspired choice, based on academic merit, assessed for once by the scholar's contribution to his subject rather than by the loudness of his voice, *Salonfähigkeit*, or a sustained record of boats left unrocked. The removal from his shoulders of the weight of undergraduate teaching enabled him to romp ahead, and as Jebb said of Porson, "he served the true purpose of his chair, as few have served it, by writings which advanced the knowledge of his subject." In 1951 was published the edition of Alcman's *Partheneion*, a wonderful clarifier of the mind. Anyone familiar with the problems of the poem will understand that it is no disparagement to say that it was more successful on such matters as the rigorous classification of evidence for the dialect used by Alcman than in its explanation of what exactly is going on, and when he writes of one problem, "It must surely seem surprising that the lucid evidence of the text should ever have been misunderstood" and the adoption of a hypothesis not favored by him would lead to a state of affairs where "instantly chaos and confusion obnubilate the scene" we may feel that he is pressing ahead too hard; yet we remain grateful for a trail blazer whose combative methods so often yielded greater rewards than ever fall to the lot of the mildly judicious. As was remarked at his farewell dinner, Page was a fast bowler in Greek studies too.

Three years later appeared the standard commentary on Sappho and Alcaeus, with the same mastery of technical detail. Those who envied Page his superlative professional competence felt it necessary to detect some weakness, and his apparent preference for the more versatile Alcaeus over the sacred cow, Sappho, provoked sneers in certain quarters. (One may be confident that if "Twinkle, twinkle, little star" had been preserved as a papyrus fragment and attributed to Sappho, in those same quarters ecstasy would have prevailed.) The *Poetarum Lesbiorum Fragmenta*, being devoid of literary judgments, could not be similarly assailed, but *The Homeric Odyssey*, being full of them, could be, and was. It was a very necessary book, for the English had been sheltered for too long from the chill blasts of Homeric analysis. It met with a virulent response from some reviewers but was read with delight by the audience for whom it was intended. The charm of the exposition was backed up by deep erudition resting in the notes. Possibly the most curious feature of the book is the debt it owes to Adolf Kirchhoff. The debt was openly and frequently acknowledged, yet somehow one never quite believed that Page, the original thinker *par excellence*, would be relaying the views of others with so little alteration. Only when one reverts to Kirchhoff himself does one see that the extent of the borrowing is indeed as great as Page had said it was. But if Kirchhoff had got it right, why interfere? *The Homeric Odyssey* is Page's most enjoyable book. There is a light touch to the rhetorical style. The ability *ridentem dicere verum* comes over beautifully on p. 85:

There follows at once an omen: a hawk was observed holding a dove in its talons, plucking it and shedding its feathers to the ground, midway between Telemachus and his ship. Theoclymenus accepts the challenge to his professional skill, and interprets the omen as follows (first calling Telemachus to stand apart from his companions, nobody knows why). "Telemachus, not without divine agency came the bird on our right; I knew, when I looked full upon it, that it was a bird of omen" (so far, it needed no prophet come from Argos to tell us this). Now the interpretation: "Among the people of Ithaca there is no race more kingly than yours, but you are supreme forever." That is not the work of a man who has gone far in his profession; he might, without excessive intellectual effort, have interpreted the killing of a dove by a hawk as symbolising the killing of the Suitors by Odysseus. That is presumably what the hawk had in fact intended: away it flies, disgusted by this drab *non sequitur*.

In 1957 appeared another book that annoyed a lot of people. "I warn my students against it" said one Scandinavian professor. It was the *Agamemnon* edition, which had been begun by Page's old teacher, J. D. Denniston. Page lectured on the play at the same time as finishing the written version. To one undergraduate who had read through Fraenkel's three volumes twice before coming to the University and thought them the ultimate in scholarship, Page's lectures seemed shocking to the point of sacrilege, and he fumed righteously as Fraenkel's shortcomings were exposed to the undiscerning merriment of the youthful audience. G. T. Griffith, wisest of men, on learning of these outraged feelings suggested with an evanescent smile that the two should meet, and Page's Introduction, with its cross-examination of Aeschylus, was the direct result of refuting ideas that the Fraenkel-indoctrinated undergraduate put forward at that meeting. In sessions of this kind, given in what Americans call "office hours," Page would effortlessly win every argument with his younger antagonists; but he never did so by crushing them under a weight of superior learning. It was on commonsense reasoning and the use of knowledge that both parties shared that he relied. The *esprit de l'escalier* was a frequent visitor to the minds of those who emerged dazed from these encounters, but they had been enriched by an exhilarating intellectual experience.

Page understood as well as Cicero the different requirements of lecturing before a large or a small audience, and he understood better than most scholars of his eminence what the intellectual capacity was of the average undergraduate. Before large audiences he practiced the technique that Harold Macmillan said had been recommended to him by an old hand after his maiden speech in the House of Commons: say one thing, or two, and say it in as many ways as you like; but do not try to cover every aspect of the topic under debate. Page would hammer home just one or two great verities. The technique was successful, as one examiner can attest. Page had been lecturing on *Oedipus Rex*. Early in the play the blind prophet Teiresias blurts out the whole truth, and the play then continues as if nothing had happened. Page several times in his exposition used the phrase, "He has let the cat out of the bag." It found its way into so many essays that when the weary examiner went at the end of the day into a fitful sleep he had visions of countless cats jumping out of bags beyond number. But from that one phrase many people had learned something very important about the structure of a masterpiece. It was all done with great good humor, and generations of Cambridge men will remember Page as the funniest, as well as the most interesting, lecturer in an admittedly subfusc department: funny for his entirely conscious exaggerations as he piled a semitheatrical contempt on those who had incurred his intellectual displeasure. It was all without malice, and he knew perfectly well that what he represented as black and white was often in reality a lighter or darker shade of grey. But he knew too that only in this way would he keep the interest of those young men and women for whom the delights of exercising the mind generally came a poor second to those of the body.

Before small audiences he was different. The final-year students who had textual criticism as their speciality approached the subject with much *Angst*. They were swiftly reassured, as after some introductory lectures that spoke of manuscript descent, types of error ("the jollity of Percy is not strained"), etc.—all very much cut and dried—he embarked on textual exegesis. One who attended his lectures on *Philoctetes* remarked that the professional expertise shown would have been worthy of someone who had devoted his whole life solely to that one topic. But the expertise was always the servant of common sense, and the sometimes complex chains of reasoning were made easy to remember by the genial lucidity of the lecturer. Perhaps the most important general lesson he imparted was this, and it is one of wide applicability: first define your difficulty with the utmost possible precision; the solution will then often present itself.

With his research students, too, Page gave the impression of total professional competence in their own specialized fields. Cambridge professors do not found schools, and one hardly knows whether to say that it is by accident or example that, if we confine ourselves to Greek tragedy, the standard texts of Aeschylus, Sophocles, and Euripides are either the product of Page himself or of one or the other of his pupils leaning heavily upon his advice. He also saw through the dissertation that has made it an eccentricity to regard *Prometheus Vinctus* as the work of Aeschylus. How many other books and articles he improved before publication it is impossible to say. What is certain is that any assessment of Page's written contribution to scholarship that considers only the books published under his own name will fall a long way short of the truth.

In 1959 another Homer book appeared, this time on the *Iliad*. Like the *Odyssey* volume of four years earlier it was the outcome of a series of invited lectures delivered in America, his Berkeley Sathers. Its dealings with the notorious Catalogue of Ships have not passed unchallenged, but the Appendix on Multiple Authorship should be required reading for any student approaching the *Iliad* who feels that Marzullo's pronouncement, 'Il problema omerico e morto,' is a premature obituary. More than any other book, this one gave Page the chance to indulge his passion for archaeology. And it was a passion: he once confessed that he would have found archaeology an attractive alternative career (exactly how he would have fitted it in with playing cricket for England and exercising command on the high seas—another of his passions—we had better not enquire). It might have been a dangerous one: Marinatos, the Greek Director of Archaeological Services, almost literally died in Page's arms on a site in Santorini, and an almost identical accident there a year or two later left Page himself badly bruised. It was not, however, his own health that preoccupied him, but that of his wife, who had a serious heart condition, making it necessary for the scholar to discharge many of the duties that normally fall to the distaff side. This lady, an American whom he met on a cruise, had been Miss Katherine Dohan, the daughter of an archaeologist mother who had excavated in Crete and written about Etruscan tomb groups. Their marriage produced four daughters, whose interests range from medical research to Assyriology, and from vegetarian cooking and bereavement (any connection?) to bringing up five children.

In the same year as the appearance of the *Iliad* book Page accepted the invitation to become Master of Jesus College. In reply to a congratulatory letter he wrote that he had no intention of giving up Work: the capital letter indicating a proper understanding of priorities. All the time articles were flowing from his pen, but the next major work was the *Poetae Melici Graeci*, the standard edition of the major lyricists not already dealt with in the edition of the Lesbian pair. It was a book of over six hundred pages, calling for the highest professional competence. Only a year later a volume in the *Oxyrhyncus Papyri* series came out under his name. Thereafter and until the end of his life the greater part of his academic energies—apart from such chores as being President of the British Academy, which he did not particularly enjoy—went into the Greek Anthology. In collaboration with the crusty old Trinity don A. S. F. Gow, the fearsomely austere editor of Theocritus, he produced *Hellenistic Epigrams* and the *Garland of Philip*, Gow's role in the latter being comparatively slight. But these four large volumes were not the end; besides a small separate edition of Rufinus, there was the huge posthumous collection called, for want of a better name, *Further Greek Epigrams*. Just about everything in the Greek Anthology down to A.D. 50 was thus covered. When one thinks of Page's name, this work on the Anthology is not what springs first to mind, though in bulk it is his biggest contribution to Greek scholarship: the Anthology is not a fashionable area of study at the moment, and Page's distinctive humorous style is only occasionally given the opportunity to surface.

For all his amazing productivity the impression Page made on others was not that of an academic wrapped up in his work. As Master of Jesus he would watch his College teams playing cricket or rugby, and he was valued by students who had no idea of his academic stature as a friendly old soul with a genuine interest in their welfare. He could talk to anyone about anything. From newspapers and television he followed the fortunes of tennis players around the world, and his pronouncements on their merits and defects—less reliable than his pronouncements on matters of scholarship, e.g., he had a quite irrational dislike of the charming Miss Chris Evert—were delivered with his customary air of authority. One of his less probable enthusiasms was for naval strategy. Once he found himself explaining to another apparent enthusiast whom he had just met how some great battle—perhaps the battle of Midway—could have been better conducted, only to find as the other left that he had been lecturing the Commander-in-Chief. Refighting these battles was a hobby that he put to good use. Page had one massive blind spot: music was a totally closed world to him. Duty once called him to a concert. A friend expressed surprise at finding him there. "Scarcely had the opening bars died away," he was told, "than the low grey hulls slipped from their moorings. . . ." But if music was a closed world, the literature of Europe was not. This side of Page's life was not disclosed to public view and does not find frequent expression in his books. But it is not every Greek scholar who reads *Faust* half a dozen times in the original. Those who seek to find some weakness in the apparently impregnable fortress of his scholarship make patronizing remarks about Page as not really a cultured man—the implication being that no textual critic or metrician could be at the same time actually cultured—should know that he was a voracious reader of French, German, and Russian novels. How he found the time to pursue these interests on top of his other duties is a mystery; but so are those other duties themselves, for whenever one saw him his desk seemed to be clear of anything that spoke of work in progress.

In 1973, one year after the Aeschylus edition, appeared a third book on Homer, again from an invited series of lectures in America. The *Aeschylus* and *Folktales* stand at opposite ends of the Page spectrum: exact textual criticism, of a type that some would call arid, coming from the same pen as the good-humored romp through that part of the *Odyssey* that is concerned with the hero's wanderings into the lands of ogres and enchantresses. Some scholars are noted for their versatility, others for the penetration of their minds; Page's combination of these qualities is rare.

He retired a year or two before the statutory time and moved to as remote a part of England as it is possible to imagine, to a place in Northumberland, marked only on maps of the largest scale, where there was, as one wit unkindly put it, nothing beyond the baaing of a few sheep to remind him that he had ever presided over the Fellows of Jesus. Here he was visited once by a former student and his family and delighted the young children by acting the role of busy traffic policeman as he ushered them out into a road that seemed never to have had wheeled traffic on it in its life. It was a very peaceful existence, but with the shadow of his wife's illness hanging over it all the time. In fact, he predeceased her.

Honors had been showered on him in plenty, including a knighthood and an honorary doctorate from Oxford. Trinity College, which had conducted open warfare against Richard Bentley, dishonored an understanding to give Porson a lay fellowship and elected some inferior candidate to a fellowship for which Jebb was a candidate, continued its campaign against Greek scholars—still vigorous as I write today—by refusing Page a memorial brass in the Chapel; though it did at least have the grace to elect him to an honorary fellowship. During his tenure of office, the Faculty of Classics at Cambridge had been perhaps the best in the world, and he its brightest star. Whether one takes written contributions to scholarship as the criterion, or the whole range of duties that fall to a professor in the encouragement of his subject, Page was the best Professor of Greek that Cambridge has had in the four centuries since the chair was founded. "My memories of him," Lord Hailsham writes, "was of a friend without blemish, in whom learning was an ornament and never dull." With an epitaph like that, memorials made of brass are perhaps neither here nor there.

Books

(The list given below is confined to his books; see below for bibliography.)
Actors' Interpolations in Greek Tragedy. Oxford, 1934.
Euripides Medea. Oxford, 1938.
Greek Literary Papyri (=*Select Papyri iii*). Loeb Classical Library. Cambridge and
    London, 1941.
Alcman: The Partheneion. Oxford, 1951.

Corinna. London, 1953.

Sappho and Alcaeus: An Introduction to the Study of Ancient Lesbian Poetry. Oxford,
1955.

The Homeric Odyssey. Oxford, 1955.

Aeschylus Agamemnon. With J. D. Denniston. Oxford, 1957.

History and the Homeric Iliad. Sather Lectures 31. Berkeley, 1959.

Poetae Melici Graeci. Oxford, 1962.

The Oxyrhynchus Papyri xxix. London, 1963.

The Greek Anthology: Hellenistic Epigrams. With A. S. F. Gow. Cambridge, 1965.

Lyrica Graeca Selecta. Oxford, 1968.

The Greek Anthology: the Garland of Philip and Some Contemporary Epigrams. With A.
S. F. Gow. Cambridge, 1968.

Aeschyli Septem Quae Supersunt Tragoediae. Oxford, 1972.

Folktales in Homer's Odyssey. Cambridge, MA, 1973.

Supplementum lyricis Graecis. Oxford, 1974.

Epigrammata Graeca. Oxford, 1975.

The Epigrams of Rufinus. Cambridge, 1978.

Further Greek Epigrams. Cambridge, 1981. (Posthumous.)

Sources

Bibliography

A full Bibliography of Sir Denys may be found in *Dionysiaca, Nine Studies in Greek
Poetry by Former Pupils presented to Sir Denys Page on his Seventieth Birthday.*
Cambridge, 1978.

Biographical

P. H. J. Lloyd-Jones. "Denys Lionel Page." PBA 65 (1979) 759–769.

Letters from Lord Hailsham.

Personal knowledge.

Milman Parry

20 June 1902 – 3 December 1935

CHARLES ROWAN BEYE
Lehman College/Graduate Center
City University of New York

Milman Parry revolutionized the criticism and scholarship of the Homeric texts by demonstrating that the manner of composition of these narratives was both coherent and unlike subsequent literary texts. He gave substance to the idea that these were the products of oral poets living in a preliterate age. His researches made clear that generalizations about Homer must rest on statistics and that the comparative study of similar narratives from other cultures had much to tell Homerists. He turned the subsequent study of the *Iliad* and *Odyssey* by American scholars away from content toward the mechanics of style. His approach to the poems influenced a generation of classical scholars in the United States to look at ancient literature as a historical phenomenon, as a product of a culture with all the inherent limitations and parochialisms more than or rather than the beginnings of a continuum extending into the present day.

Milman Parry was born in Oakland, California, the fourth child and only son of Isaac Milman and Alice (Emerson) Parry, whose antecedents were Welsh, Scotch, and English. The family were Quakers. He went through the Oakland public schools and then in 1918 entered the University of California at Berkeley, intent on finding a major field in the natural sciences. There his interest turned to classical literature. Herbert Weir Smyth, then a visiting professor from Harvard, was so impressed with Parry when he taught him that years later he remembered the man when it was time to make a new appointment at Harvard. Parry received the B.A. degree in the spring of 1922 and in the subsequent academic year wrote his Master of Arts thesis with the Homerist George Calhoun, entitled "A Comparative Study of Diction as One of the Elements of Style in Early Greek Epic Poetry." In this study Parry has already identified the distinguishing feature of Homeric verse construction in singling out the repeated epithets, their position in the line, and their juxtapositions. He labels them "traditional," and distinguishes this use of epithets from that found in later epic poets. This work also reveals the considerable knowledge and strong interest that the young Parry had in literature and art in general. He considers the repetition of epithets principally as a matter of aesthetic interest.

In 1924 Parry went to Paris to study at the Sorbonne. Parry's decision was forced upon him when he was denied scholarship money for advanced study in the United States. In May 1923 he had married his college classmate, Marian Than-houser, a German Jewish woman from Milwaukee, who accompanied him to Paris along with their six-month-old daughter, Marian. In Paris Parry became father to a second child, a son named Adam Milman, and also acquired the degree Docteur ès lettres, awarded in 1928 for two *thèses*, or dissertations, which he wrote in the comparatively brief time of four years under the direction of Aimé Puech. (He benefited as well from his teachers Antoine Meillet and Maurice Croiset.) French professors, by contrast, customarily took considerable time writing their *thèses* and received the Docteur ès lettres well into their academic career, as a kind of a capstone to it rather than its foundation.

The first and more important of these dissertations, *L'Épithète traditionelle*, consists of a statistical analysis of repeated epithets in combination with names and a few common nouns (sea, ships, etc.). The statistics are used to demonstrate that the poet built his dactylic hexametric lines from phrases with fixed metrical shape, almost none of which overlap in meaning. These phrases then function exactly as individual words do in the normal speech act. Parry thus argued that the poet had the components of verse narrative in his memory just as ordinary persons have words, in a sense that Homeric diction functions as another language. The other dissertation, *Les Formules et la métrique*, demonstrated that the presence of hiatus throughout the Homeric poems reveals an accommodation by the poet to the inevitable juxtaposition of vowels when two formulaic phrases were matched. This suggested to Parry that the maintenance of the formulaic phrase system was all-important to the poet, being the building blocks of his narrative just as individual words function for the later epic poet or prose writer. The importance of these dissertations was that they created a solid theoretical basis for a belief in the unity and integrity of the Homeric poems. Homeric criticism in the previous two centuries had rested upon the belief that these poems derive from a period of illiteracy in which no poet could carry in his head anything so grand. Hence, the problem of the composition of the *Iliad* and *Odyssey* became the preoccupation of Homeric scholarship. (The introductory chapter to A.B. Lord's *Singer of Tales* [Cambridge, MA, 1950] is probably a good example of the way Parry conceived of the "Homeric problem" as it lay waiting for his solution.) Parry's work received an immediate, thorough, perceptive, and sympathetic appraisal from Pierre Chantraine in the form of a review article (*Revue de philologie* 3 [1929] 294–300).

Parry then returned to his first teaching post at Drake University in Des Moines, Iowa, for the 1928–1929 academic year. By all accounts he found the place as uncongenial as the institution found him. After this year he was appointed to the faculty of Harvard University as an Instructor. The quality of his teaching there has been caught in a brief memoir by his student Harry Levin ("Portrait of an Homeric Scholar," *CJ* 32 [1937] 259–66), who describes how Parry was able to make the necessarily mechanical learning of ancient languages part of a greater whole with his constant classroom allusions to literature, to the civilizations of the past, to contemporary American culture. In sum, in a field that all too frequently casts up a species of pedantic drudge he was that rarity: a cultivated, engaged man of the world.

His immediately subsequent research was designed to show that certain "problems" in Homeric narrative would vanish if approached as aspects of a traditional style. His essay on glosses, for instance, demonstrates that the poet no longer understood the meaning of certain ornamental epithets because they were embedded in traditional, fixed phrases in which the noun carried the operative meaning. His two essays in *Harvard Studies in Classical Philology* were the means whereby he conveyed to the English-speaking world the results of his French dissertations. Parry enlarged his conception of formula in these pieces, developing the argument for creation by analogy that helped to extend the definition of traditional phraseology to a considerably higher percentage of the lines of the poems.

The refinements and advances in argument in these pieces convinced Parry that the Homeric poems were the product of an oral poetic tradition, as the title of the second of these two articles indicates ("Homeric Language as Language of Oral Poetry"). Arguments for orality made the old Homeric problem finally irrelevant, since what Parry was theorizing was an entirely different way of creating and maintaining a narrative. It was not that no one had ever entertained the notions Parry was now advancing; rather, his work was the first to present a closely reasoned, statistically detailed study that tries to offer conclusive proof.

In the absence of ancient evidence Parry decided that determining the orality of Homeric poetry could only finally be achieved by comparative study with a living oral tradition. Influenced by Mathias Murkos's *La Poésie populaire épique en yougoslavie ou début du XXᵉ siècle* (Paris, 1929) he spent the summer of 1933 in Yugoslavia investigating the local singers. The following June he embarked with his family for Yugoslavia, where he settled into Dubrovnik for the academic year 1934–1935. He was accompanied on this longer trip by his graduate assistant, Albert Bates Lord. The two men proceeded to take from dictation and then, with the new recording technology that had become available, to record, the spontaneous performances of a number of professional singers. Parry learned Serbo-Croatian (his son, Adam, attended the local school) the better to understand the songs and to integrate himself into the community of singers. The material he collected was vast: more than 12,000 texts, some 3,500 recordings on 12-inch aluminum disks. These constitute the nucleus of the collection named after him in Harvard's Widener Library. The immediate result of this field trip was the article "Whole Formulaic Verses in Greek and Southslavic Heroic Song." He was gathering material for a book to be entitled *Cor Huso: A Study of Southslavic Song*, largely concerned with Serbo-Croatian poems. At the same time he was taking notes for a book to be entitled *The Singer of Tales*. Albert Bates Lord quotes the opening pages of the latter in his "Homer, Parry, and Huso" (*AJA* 52 [1948]

34–44), which is a memoir of this time in Parry's life. *The Singer of Tales* is itself the title of Lord's own study (the title as well of his doctoral dissertation) in which the research of his teacher and himself is brought together to advance the argument that oral poetic technique is universal and not culture-bound. In the fall of 1935 Parry returned to Harvard, where he had been promoted to Assistant Professor in 1932. On 3 December 1935, in a Los Angeles hotel room, Parry died of wounds from a gun he had in his possession. Despite the academic world's persistent determination to see this as suicide on the theory that Parry was denied tenure at Harvard, there is no evidence that he would not have been promoted (he had just been reappointed to a second three-year term as Assistant Professor in the summer of 1935), and the physical circumstances of his death argue against suicide.

In the posthumous publication of "About Winged Words," an answer to his old teacher Calhoun's arguments against the idea that ornamental epithets have no meaning for the auditor, Parry sets forth what has always been one of the more difficult of his ideas for critics of the Homeric poems. He always insisted that "[Homeric poetry] . . . is filled with phrases emptier of meaning than any in Pope or Falconer." (*Collected Papers* 37). After his flirtation with aesthetics in his M.A. thesis, Parry, once in France and under the influence of Marcel Jousse and Meillet, was at pains to keep aesthetics out of his theorizing. He emphasized the *mechanics* of oral versemaking: language was a tool, ornamental epithets without semantic value, the bard or singer no more than an anonymous cog in the vast machine of oral poetic creation whose individual contribution was scarcely to be noticed. In defense of the clichés of English Augustan poetry, and, by analogy, Homer, Parry could say ". . . what the words lost in meaning they gained in charm of correctness" (*Ibid.*). However vague "charm of correctness" may be, Parry hit upon one of the most important aesthetic principles and habits of mind of that early culture, one that explains so much of ancient Greek conservatism, their tragic sense of life, their infinite capacity for irony, their obsession with stereotypes. Parry's writings again and again demonstrate him to have anticipated what is now contemporary literary critical theory, that is, that the style of the narrative is as much the content as the so-called story line. Parry's theme and formulae are thus in a sense Homer's story, as his son Adam brilliantly demonstrates in "The Language of Achilles" (*TAPA* 87 [1956] 1–7).

Parry had no chance to revise his theory over a lifetime of investigation and reflection. The romance of his youthful death contributed to its rapidly hardening into an orthodoxy; the theory's adherents could be divided into those who insisted both upon the truth of Parry's statistical analyses and the implications he outlined for them and those who accepted that Parry had conclusively demonstrated that the Homeric texts reveal a system of composition but were still investigating the nature of this system and its implications.

His son, Adam Parry, who followed in his father's footsteps as a promising classical scholar, also died prematurely in an accident, but left an excellent overview of his father's contribution and limitations in the introductory chapter in *Collected Papers*. The chapter on formulae in Norman Austin's *Archery at the Dark of the Moon*

(Berkeley, 1975) offers fundamental criticisms of Parry's use of statistics as well as of the literary critical theory upon which his work rests, arguing for a poet who consciously manipulates his language. Austin's emphasis upon the formula in context is an important modification of Parry's view. More recently, David Shive, in *Naming Achilles* (Oxford, 1987), has subjected Parry's statistics in the *Iliad* to review and found them certainly in need of revision, if not fundamentally flawed. Needless to say, the definition of a formula is arguable. Hainsworth's *The Flexibility of the Homeric Formula* (Oxford, 1968) is a basic rethinking of some of Parry's assumptions (see especially chapter three, "What is a Formula?"). The early revisionists of the Parry-Lord orthodoxy get an important rejoinder from A. B. Lord in "Homer as an Oral Poet" (*HSCPh* 72 [1967] 1–46).

R. H. Finnegan's *Oral Poetry: Its Nature, Significance and Social Context* (Cambridge, 1977) shows the great influence Parry has had on the study of oral poetry in general since the days of H. M. and N. K. Chadwick, whose monumental *Growth of Literature* (Cambridge, 1932–1940), encyclopedic as it may be, seems nowadays very limited without the Parry perspective on orality. Nonetheless, Finnegan's researches show that facts gathered from the field over a wide spectrum of cultures will challenge many of Parry's assumptions, e.g., the inevitability of the bard's illiteracy, the lack of individuality in the oral performer's style, etc. Gregory Nagy, linguist and Homerist, whose work in oral studies proceeds from the Parry-Lord orthodoxy with ever new modifications and original insights, offers important new definitions in "Oral Poetry and the Homeric Poems: Broadening and Narrowing of Terms" (*Critical Exchange* 16 [1984] 32–54).

Furthermore, orality itself as a concept and field of study owes enormously to Parry's work; Eric Havelock has written extensively on the fundamental differences to be found in ancient Greek culture as the population changed from a preliterate or oral state to that of a literate mentality. His most important work, *Preface to Plato* (Cambridge, MA, 1963), is deeply indebted to Parry's theories and insights. Walter Ong has studied the phenomenon in a wider context, the results of which are embodied in his *Orality and Literacy* (London, 1982), which is underlaid with an initial conceptual framework that derives from Parry.

Parry's early death made little impression on the world. His work had not received its due recognition; he had not created a host of acolytes. It was only thirty-six years later that the papers of this man, so important for classicists, comparativists, linguists, and anthropologists were finally published. Nonetheless, however research into oral poetry, the Homeric texts, or orality moves away from the theories originally promulgated by Milman Parry, it is certain to be the case that scholars and critics will continue to address the questions and opinions offered so many years ago by this man while still in his youth.

Books

L'Épithète traditionelle dans Homère: Essai sur un problème de style homérique. Paris, 1928.

Les Formules et la métrique d'Homère. Paris, 1928.
The Making of Homeric Verse. The Collected Papers of Milman Parry. Edited by Adam Parry. Oxford, 1971.

Articles

"The Homeric Gloss: A Study in Word Sense." *TAPA* 59 (1928) 233–47.
"The Distinctive character of Enjambement in Homeric Verse." *TAPA* 60 (1929) 200–20.
"Studies in the Epic Technique of Oral Verse-Making. I. Homer and the Homeric Style." *HSCPh* 41 (1930) 73–147.
"Studies in the Epic Technique of Oral Verse-Making II. The Homeric Language as the Language of Oral Poetry." *HSCPh* 43 (1932) 1–50.
"The Traditional Metaphor in Homer." *CP* 28 (1933) 30–43.
"Whole Formulaic Verses in Greek and Southslavic Heroic Song." *TAPA* 64 (1933) 179–97.
"The Traces of the Digamma in Ionic and Lesbian Greek." *Language* 10 (1934) 130–44.
"About Winged Words." *CP* 32 (1937) 59–63.
"On Typical Scenes in Homer." (Review of *Die Typischen Scenen bei Homer* by Walter Arend.) *CP* 31 (1936) 357–60.

Sources

Boedeker, Deborah. "Amerikanische Oral-Tradition-Forschung. Eine Einführung." *Colloquium Rauricum 1 Vergangenheit in mündlicher Überlieferung*. Edited by Jürgen von Ungern-Sternberg and Hansjörg Reinau. Stuttgart, 1988: 34–53.
Bynum, David. *Four Generations of Oral Literary Studies at Harvard University*. Center for the Study of Oral Literature. Cambridge, MA, 1974.
Gulick, C. B., Greene, W. C., Finley, J. H., Jr. [necrology]. *Harvard University Gazette* (15 February 1936) 22–23.
Levin, Harry. "Portrait of an Homeric Scholar." *CJ* 32 (1937) 259–266.
Lord, A. B. "Homer, Parry, and Huso." *AJA* 52 (1948) 34–44.
The Making of Homeric Verse. The Collected Papers of Milman Parry. Edited by Adam Parry. Oxford, 1971. Introduction: i-lxii.

Papers

Unpublished papers of Parry and the recordings made by Parry are to be found in the Milman Parry Collection of Oral Literature and James A. Notopoulos Collection, Room C, Widener Library, Harvard University, Cambridge, MA 02138. 617-495-1550 (admission by appointment).

Giorgio Pasquali

29 April 1885 – 9 July 1952

LUCIANO CANFORA
Università di Bari

The lesson that Giorgio Pasquali taught Italian classical philology (a lesson heard far outside the boundaries of that field) was to think about every scholarly problem, whether textual, literary, or historical, in terms of the history of tradition. His teaching has been important not only for students of texts but also for students of history. Since this *forma mentis* came to Pasquali from his congenial understanding of the work of Eduard Schwartz, Wilamowitz, and Friedrich Leo, and from a fruitful contact with these teachers' students, we can say in a certain sense—even though the expression might appear reductionist—that Pasquali was an important intermediary between German philology and Italian culture. He brought the seed of renewal. Those aspects of Italian philology that have not undergone his influence bear the unmistakable mark of backwardness.

Born to a family of the Roman *buona borghesia*, he grew up "in the gentlemanly environment of the learned professions," as he himself put it (*Storia dello spirito tedesco*: 8). (His father, Gustavo Pasquali, was a lawyer, as was his brother Alberto.) Pasquali describes his own origins in a *curriculum vitae* penned 15 December 1911, in support of a request of a *venia legendi* at the University of Göttingen, which has recently been published (*Belfagor* 39 [1984] 686–7). It furnishes the following facts: 27 June 1907, degree in Greek Literature from the University of Rome with a thesis, *Sulla commedia mitologica e i suoi precedenti nella letteratura greca*; 1908–1909, two semesters of study in Germany (Winter-semester at Berlin, Summer-semester at Göttingen); April 1910, *libera docenza* (officially approved tutor) in Greek Literature at the University of Rome. While at Rome he was the student of Nicola Festa, who had himself studied under Girolamo Vitelli, but Pasquali felt no true affinity with Festa's temperament. In his *curriculum* Pasquali announces his desire to live in Germany, at Göttingen, the city he called "the scholarly capital of Europe." It was a statement about the kind of life he wanted and a symptom of his intolerance of the intellectual climate of the Italian university, from which he had received some initial disappointments. In 1908 he had emerged from a competition for a position as Extraordinarius with words of praise that were strong, but for the very purpose useless. (Among the members of the committee were Girolamo Vitelli and Ettore Romagnoli.) After another failure, he became Professor of Greek Literature in 1920 and taught first at Messina and, from 1921, at Florence.

Before that came the year that Europe broke apart spiritually, 1914. That year also decided, definitively, the individual fate of Pasquali, who was "restored" to Italy in the spring of 1915 following Italy's unexpected declaration of war on Austria and Germany. (On 11 July 1915 Kurt Sethe, Dean of Göttingen's Philosophical Faculty, annulled Pasquali's *venia legendi* on the grounds that he was the citizen of a hostile country.) "Restored" against his will, he was by no means happy with the turn of events, since his own stance was favorable to Italian neutrality. (The evidence includes his letter to the "Giornale d'Italia" of 17 September 1914 and the articles from Berlin for Cesare De Lollis's magazine, *Italia Nostra*, in the early months of 1915.) He returned to Italy for good, since renewed contact with his old adopted fatherland after the war never achieved a complete restoration of the original harmony. A kind of veto against calling Pasquali to a German university was posted at least twice by Wilamowitz, in February 1914 (Calder, MH 43 [1986] 259) and January 1931 (Wilamowitz, *Selected Correspondence*, ed. W. M. Calder III [Naples 1983] 110–111). In his private correspondence Wilamowitz demonstrated intolerance towards Pasquali (*Ibid.*, 171, 193); in January 1931 he wrote to Eduard Fraenkel: "To call Pasquali to a chair in Germany would be really unforgivable" (*Ibid.*, 110–111). The years 1908–1914 constitute Pasquali's "German Period." He works and expresses himself in German, in German presses and reviews: in 1908 a Teubner text of Proclus's commentary on Plato's *Cratylus*, long articles in *Hermes*—the prestigious review founded by Mommsen and Kirchhoff and directed in Pasquali's German years by Carl Robert and Friedrich Leo—as well as in Göttingen's *Nachrichten* and *Gelehrten Anzeigen*, and finally his first real book, published by the Göttingen university press, *Quaestiones Callimacheae*.

The first books that Pasquali published in Italy all came out in 1920. All three can be seen as the final issue of all his previous experience: *Socialisti tedeschi, Orazio lirico, Filologia e storia*. The first came out in a tentative edition at the end of 1919, and in a complete edition in 1920. Well-informed, based on a wide use of the daily prints, it attempts, among other things, to be a true history of the majoritarian Socialist Party (SPD). It demonstrates Pasquali's lively interest in German politics. Even in this area Germany is the country to follow. The book also shows that at this time his sympathies are with the moderate Socialists: such was, in his youth, Pasquali's friend, Ludwig Curtius, archaeologist and later director of the Deutsches Archäologisches Institut in Rome. In the Germany of the years before 1914, home of the largest, most authoritative, and most academic Socialist party, Pasquali must have liked and been acquainted with some men who, as old as he, were sympathizers of the Socialist movement. (This attitude certainly would not have increased Wilamowitz's sympathies for him.) Pasquali's judgment of 1920 on German affairs is relevant: "The Socialists are not the majority and do not have the power to impose themselves on the other parties. I am convinced that, despite multiple attempts, the parties of the right will not succeed in bringing back the Hohenzollern to the throne. I am just as certain that the republic, even with Socialist leadership, even adopting certain reforms that could certainly be called Socialist, will remain for now bourgeois and will continue the traditions of the Empire" (*Socialisti tedeschi*, Appendix, dated 13 March 1920). Pasquali wrote this with political acumen, while his teachers (Schwartz, Wilamowitz, etc.) were maintaining an attitude of prejudice and negativity toward the Weimar republic.

Orazio lirico is Pasquali's first book of substantial length on antiquity. It arises happily from an area of research very much alive in German *Altertumswissenschaft*: the unity of Hellenistic-Roman literature, according to the teachings of Wilamowitz in the last pages of his *Geschichte der Philologie*. In that sense Pasquali's book has a "parallel" in *Plautinisches im Plautus* (1922) by his contemporary and friend, Eduard Fraenkel. Two central themes of *Orazio lirico* deserve to be emphasized. One is the notion of *aemulatio* in respect of Greek models. The Greek poems taken as models by Horace represent for him only the starting point. They are assumed as an initial "motto" rather than as the object of pedantic transposition. This concept of *aemulatio* would have its own original and autonomous development in the 1942 article, "Arte allusiva," which refers back explicitly to *Orazio lirico*. The second theme of *Orazio lirico* is the determining influence of Hellenistic poetry (as opposed to archaic lyric) as the source of the inspiration of Horace's lyric poetry. The book also contains an analysis of the genuinely Roman elements in Horace, that is, the "Roman Odes," but without the conservatism and nationalism with which scholars such as Heinze and Reitzenstein approached those difficult texts. Unluckily, the book appeared in Italy in the middle of a polemic between philologists and antiphilologists, which had already begun during the war but had grown more fierce later on. The philologists were represented by Vitelli (a polemicist free from incivility); their opponents by Romagnoli (a virulent anti-German nationalist, despiser of the philological method with which he had no familiarity, a crude and insolent polemicist, in that respect truly *anima naturaliter fascist*). It was a polemic in which hatred of philology and venomous hatred of Germany were, and were intended to be, synonymous. In that climate, *Orazio lirico* could only appear German *par excellence*. The most violent attack came from Corrado Barbagallo ("Un libro sbagliato sulla poesia di Orazio," ["A Mistaken Book on Horace's Poetry"], *Nuova rivista storica* 6 [1922] 479–485); La Penna properly called it "a horrifying hodge-podge of Crocean idealism and anti-German hatred" (preface to the new edition of *Orazio Lirico*: xvii). The historian Adolfo Omodeo wrote in defense of Pasquali in Giovanni Gentile's journal (*Giornale critico della filosofia italiana* 3 [1922] 417–420). Gentile had himself reviewed the volume on its appearance. The situation in Germany was completely different. There, along with important praise, the criticism expressed reservations on the merit of the research, especially the failure to establish Horace's place in the development of Latin poetry (F. Jacoby, *DLZ* 42 [1921] 48).

With the small volume *Filologia e storia*, Pasquali entered directly into the contemporary polemic and faced the encounter with intellectual honesty and a desire to be understood. He was fighting at its roots the fallacious reasonings with which the antiphilologists confused critical editions with diplomatic editions or placed translation above every other critical and exegetical activity. Above specific arguments, however, there is, in the preface and reappearing here and there in the text, an antiracist position that deserves reflection. Pasquali understood that idolatry for the "Latin Genius" and hatred of Germany are in reality forms of racism, and for that reason he takes a position against racial prejudice. He will return to this theme with some difficulty in the Fascist era. Admittedly, the antiphilologists had no intention of debating but of rioting, and the pointless insults continued, until, years later, the narrow-minded nationalists like Romagnoli, turned into Fascists in the meantime, found themselves facing the embarrassing philo-German policy of the Fascist regime.

With the March on Rome (28 October 1922) and the formation of Mussolini's first government, Giovanni Gentile became Minister of Public Instruction. He nominated Giorgio Pasquali, for whom he nourished a deep esteem and authentic admiration, for membership in the Consiglio Superiore della Pubblica Istruzione. There is evidence for the seriousness with which Pasquali took the problems of schooling in the pamphlet *L'università di domani*, written in collaboration with Piero Calamandrei. The theme of the politics of school and university is one to which Pasquali will return in the coming years, even after the Second World War. On the personal level the nomination by Gentile was an important recognition, but in the political and cultural area it was no small embarrassment. Pasquali soon (spring 1925) found himself in a striking contradiction. He enjoyed Gentile's support (who, among other things, hoped for his full involvement in the *Enciclopedia Italiana*), but meanwhile he signed the "Manifesto" of the anti-Fascist intellectuals who had gathered around Benedetto Croce. That gesture did not fail to have some effect on the future public career of Pasquali, whose march toward Fascism was slow and winding, never amounting to a profound commitment, and was crowned much later with his promotion to membership in the Accademia d'Italia almost on the eve of the fall of Fascism.

In the years to come Pasquali moved from the study of important moments and forms of literary tradition to the full study of tradition as an historical problem. This phase of his research culminated in 1934 in the book that is justly his most famous and still without an equal, *Storia della tradizione e critica del testo*. Pasquali's own expression is often repeated: "This book is born from a book review" (*Storia della tradizione*: ix). It was a book review of the first edition of Paul Maas's *Textkritik* (Leipzig, 1927), which appeared in the German journal *Gnomon* 5 (1929) 417–435, 498–521. The fact is interesting not only as a paradoxical curiosity (the review is forty-two pages long, while the book under review had only eighteen pages) but above all as an aid to chronology. (The seven years from 1927 to 1934 were almost exclusively consecrated by Pasquali to the maturing of *Storia*.) It also helps to measure the difference between the abstract undertaking codified in Maas's pamphlet and the effort of historical reconstruction poured out by Pasquali, generally with success. The *Textkritik*, in its original form to which Pasquali's review refers, omits completely one essential preliminary part, what is known as "stemmatics" (the theory that helps individualize the genealogical connections between manuscripts). Paradoxically, that missing part, developed later by Maas in the form of an article (*ByzZ* 37 [1937] 289–294), was added by him as an appendix to the second edition (1950), a disturbing and illogical juxtaposition. Pasquali's book, on the other hand, represents an imposing exemplification of concrete stemmatics, a series of histories of individual texts. The analysis in each case tends to include, on the one hand, the oldest phases and the oldest testimonies on the history of the text and, on the other, the most recent witnesses, in the documented conviction that the latter *might* preserve, especially in the Latin tradition, good independent tradition ("*recentiores non deteriores*").

It is difficult to estimate the value of so rich a book. Pasquali himself tried in the "dodecalogue" that introduced the first (1934) and second editions (1952). Let us note here three formulations of innovative importance for method: a) "It is a prejudice to believe that the tradition of ancient authors is always mechanical; it is only mechanical when the scribe resigns himself to not understanding"; b) "It is a prejudice to believe that the transmission of texts is uniquely vertical; it is often horizontal or transversal, and in texts that are much read and in school texts one can say always so"; c) "As in linguistics . . . so also coincidence of a reading in manuscript copies in areas far from the center of the culture and far from one another constitutes a presumption for the genuineness of that reading. . . . Often there is formed from much-read texts, whether in antiquity or the Middle Ages, a vulgate that, as with a fashion, progresses from a center towards the periphery" (*Storia della tradizione*: xvii).

As is clear, a text-critical problem for Pasquali always becomes an historical and cultural problem. This way of viewing tradition was extended by Pasquali to what is apparently the most technical discipline, paleography, in an essay contemporary with the *Storia della tradizione*: "Paleografia come scienza dello spirito," an essay in which, in the wake of Traube and Schiaparelli, the problem of writing and the problem of culture blend together. From this nonmechanical vision of the acts of writing and of copying follows a proper devaluation of the so-called criterion of "paleographical probability," about which Pasquali talks in the second appendix of the *Storia della tradizione*.

We can ask ourselves whether Pasquali's teaching in this field might have or has had paralyzing effects on the text-critical activity: that is, whether the effort spent on reconstructing the history of a tradition, pushed to the extreme, does not put off *sine die* the attempt to give a critical edition. Timpanaro objected to Pasquali (*La genesi del metodo del Lachmann* [Florence, 1963] 91 = [Padua, 1985] 102): "There is still the practical need not to put off forever certain critical editions in order to study the history of the tradition in all its smallest details, not to immerse oneself so deeply in the study of medieval and humanist culture so as to forget to return to textual criticism." The objection does not appear completely convincing. The imperative, nevertheless, is not to get up new critical editions but rather to produce them now only when they will be truly innovative (in those cases the complete reconsideration of the history of the text is essential) and then to publish real progress. The impact of the *Storia della tradizione* has not been equal to its admittedly great prestige. (One finds it now present in the bibliographies of many critical editions.) In the *postilla* to the third edition of his *Textkritik* (1957), Maas thinks he can liquidate with a summary polemic Pasquali's reflections on the attention that needs to be paid to "deteriores" and concludes with an angry outburst, recalling Cobet: "*comburendi [recentiores], non conferendi!*"

That the most important theme of Pasquali's thinking concerned the history of texts is shown by the fact that after the difficult parenthesis of the years 1943–1947, characterized by powerful political and existential traumas, Pasquali picked up the thread of his own work with the "Preghiera" of 1947 (*SIFC* 22 [1947] 261), where he asked scholars for proposals and objections to consider while writing a new, completely recast edition of the *Storia della tradizione*. That edition never appeared. The edition of 1952 was furnished with new appendices, one of which was a review from *Gnomon* 1951 (=*Storia della tradizione*, 469–480) that demonstrates appreciation for the work of Alphonse Dain and his teacher Desrousseaux. It was a recognition, admittedly somewhat belated, of the validity of the orientation of French classical studies. Pasquali's positive evaluation was in clear distinction from the studied contempt for French scholarship exhibited by Wilamowitz and his orthodox students. It was only natural that Pasquali, with his positive attitude toward "recentiores," had much in common with Dain, a student of manuscripts as concrete realities, which had their own trials and tribulations, but who was also alert to the most remote phases of the history of their texts.

After the conclusion of the long work on the *Storia della tradizione* (1934), the second half of the thirties was characterized by the reemergence in Pasquali of interests in the Roman world on the one hand, and by a laborious reconsideration of the Platonic Epistles on the other.

Pasquali had already shown some interest in archaic Rome, for example, in the introductory essay for an Italian translation of Fustel de Coulanges's *Cité antique* (1924), where among other things he recognized the importance of Arthur Rosenberg's research on the government of the early Italici, as well as in a review of Meillet's *Esquisse d'une histoire de la langue latine* (*Pegaso* 2 [1930]). His most important work in this area, however, is *Preistoria della poesia romana* (1936), along with the contemporary essay on *La grande Roma dei Tarquini*. The book develops a theory according to which the Saturnian is the fruit of an "original Roman synthesis" of Greek *cola*. "But the book's value is not tied to that hypothesis. Linguistics, archaeology and history compete to reconstruct the culture of archaic Rome and the Greek influences on it" (Gennaro Perrotta, "Intelligenza di Giorgio Pasquali," *Primato* 1 [1943] 6). S. Timpanaro, in the introduction to the new edition of 1981, page 59, went along with that judgment: "The historical and cultural part of the volume . . . has turned out to be truer and more vital than the strictly, technically metrical part." When he collected his "Roman" writings of 1936–1941, Pasquali announced, "I have not lost all hope of being able to finish, before my death, a history of the idea of Rome in antiquity, to which these essays are preliminary sketches." The project, however, never developed beyond the article "Idea di Roma" in the *Enciclopedia Italiana* (39 [1936] 906–916).

The book on Plato's Letters began as seminars held at Florence and at the Scuola Normale at Pisa in 1931–1932. Pasquali was following in the footsteps of Eduard Meyer, who had argued for the authenticity of the Epistles against a scholarly consensus that had denied their authenticity. Unlike Meyer, Pasquali accepted only VII and VIII as genuine. In the "Preghiera" of 1947, where he also says he would get up a new edition of the Letters, Pasquali criticized himself: "I think I know now that there are quite a few other letters which are genuine besides the two I defended fourteen years ago." As had happened to Wilamowitz's book on Plato, Pasquali's book found less success than he had hoped for. G. Pugliese Carratelli wrote in the introduction to the reprint of 1967, "Today the debate on the authenticity has begun again, even for the Seventh Epistle." More recently Jaap Mansfeld denies the authenticity of the entire corpus.

In his last years (1948–1952) Pasquali felt called upon to intervene again in the problems of school and university. This renewed engagement was brought about by the new political situation in Italy, characterized by conservative drives of a clerical nature, to which Pasquali's *laicismo* reacted critically. His research turned toward an interest in Italian linguistics, even though he still wrote admirable essays on the ancient world, such as "Il proemio dell' Odissea" (1951). His last work (*Storia dello spirito tedesco*) was a long reflection on the memoirs of his old friend, Ludwig Curtius, which appeared in 1950 (*Deutsche und antike Welt*). Pasquali reveals the desire to write his own autobiography. "I will explain this better," he writes at a certain point, "if my life should last long enough to allow me to write my own memoirs, which ought to prove of some interest for the history and the culture of the Roman middle class of the end of the last century." The title was in no way pretentious. Pasquali really was an historian of the German "Geist," since he composed "portraits" of the greatest figures of a crucial discipline, classical philology. He wrote of Wackernagel, Hulsen, Warburg, Wilamowitz, etc. The high point of his reflections is perhaps his essay on "Theodore Mommsen's Will," which concentrated on the self-critical torment, the anguish of "seeming rather than being," that undermined the apparent arrogance of the great historian.

When Pasquali was named to the Italian Academy, Gennaro Perrotta wrote for the journal *Pegaso* the portrait we mentioned above. It begins with the aspect that seemed to Perrotta most important in Pasquali's personality: that of the teacher. Pasquali was an innovator in Italian university instruction. He introduced into Italy the German-style seminar. The place from which his instruction spread its influence was the Seminar for Classical Philology of the Scuola Normale at Pisa (which today bears his name). It was Giovanni Gentile, for many years the school's diligent director, who brought Pasquali there. There Pasquali's influence was felt not only by the most important figures of the next generation of Italian classical philology but also by students of the Renaissance, Italian language and literature, and by modern historians.

Translated by E. Christian Kopff

Books

Quaestiones callimacheae. Göttingen, 1913; revised with corrections in *Scritti filologici*. Edited by F. Bornmann, G. Pascucci, and S. Timpanaro. Florence, 1986. 1:152–301.

Socialisti tedeschi. Politica ed economia; later in the series Biblioteca di cultura moderna. Bari, March 1920 [but 1919 on the frontispiece].

Orazio lirico. Studi. Florence, 1920; reprinted with introduction, indices, and a bibliographical update by A. La Penna. Florence, 1964.

Filologia e storia. Bibliotechina del saggiatore. No. 2. Florence, 1920; reprinted with a foreword by A. Ronconi and an appendix. Florence, 1964.

L'Università di domani. In collaboration with P. Calamandrei. Foligno, 1923; re-printed in *Scritti sull'Università e la Scuola*. Edited by M. Raicich. Florence, 1978: 1–296.

Pagine stravaganti di un filologo. Lanciano, 1933; reprinted with two new chapters and the title *Vecchie e nuove pagine stravaganti di un filologo*. Turin, 1952; re-printed in *Pagine stravaganti*. Edited by G. Pugliese Carratelli. Florence, 1968: 1:1–240.

Storia della tradizione e critica del testo. Florence, 1934; reprinted with a new preface and three appendices, Florence, 1952; reprinted in the collection Oscar Studio, Milan, 1974.

Pagine meno stravaganti. Florence, 1935 = *Pagine stravaganti* 1:241–400.

Preistoria della poesia romana. Florence, 1936; reprinted with an introduction by S. Timpanaro, Florence, 1981.

Le lettere di Platone. Florence, 1938; reprinted, ed. G. Pugliese Carratelli. Florence, 1981.

Terze pagine stravaganti. Florence, 1942 = *Pagine stravaganti* 2:1–270.

Università e scuola. Florence, 1950 = *Scritti sull'Università*, 297–378.

Stravaganze quarte e supreme. Venice, 1951 = *Pagine stravaganti* 2:271–474.

Storia dello spirito tedesco nelle memorie di un contemporaneo. With a preface by G. Devoto. Bibliotechina del saggiatore. No. 10. Florence, 1953.

Conversazioni sulla nostra lingua. With a preface by E. Cecchi. Turin, 1953.

Lingua nuova e antica. Edited by G. F. Folena. Bibliotechina del saggiatore. Florence, 1964.

Rapsodia sul classico. Edited by *Enciclopedia italiana*. Rome, 1986.

Scritti filologici I–II. Edited by F. Bornmann, G. Pascucci, S. Timpanaro. Florence, 1986.

Books (Edited)

Procli Diadochi in Platonis Cratylum commentaria. Leipzig, 1908.

Teofrasto, I caratteri. Florence, 1919; new ed. edited by V. De Falco, Florence, 1956; Milan, 1979.

Gregorii Nysseni Opera VIII, 2: *Epistulae.* Berlin, 1925; new ed. edited by W. Jaeger, Leiden, 1959.

Articles

"Sui *Caratteri* di Teofrasto." *Rassegna italiana di lingue e letterature classiche* 1 (1918) 73–79, 143–150; 2 (1919) 1–21.

"Mimnermo." *SIFC* n.s. 3 (1923) 293–303.

"La scoperta dei concetti etici nella Grecia antichissima." *Civiltà moderna* 1 (1929) 343–362.

"Paleografia quale scienza dello spirito." *Nuova Antologia* 277 (1931) 342–354.

"I purosangue." *Pan* 1 (1933) 57–62.

"Omero, il brutto e il ritratto." *La Critica d'Arte* 5 (1940) 25–35.

"Arte allusiva." *L'Italia che scrive* 25 (1942) 185–187.

"Il testamento di Teodoro Mommsen." *RSI* 61 (1948) 337–350.

Sources

Bibliography

Grassi, E. and S. Timpanaro. *Per Giorgio Pasquali.* Pisa, 1972: 149–181. Supplements by C. F. Russo, *Belfagor* 31 (1976); 33 (1978); 39 (1984); 40 (1985).

Biographical

Per Giorgio Pasquali. Edited by Lanfranco Caretti. Pisa, 1972. (With an essential list of studies on Pasquali by S. Timpanaro.)

"Giorgio Pasquali." *Enciclopedia Italiana* 36 (1935), with a supplement on his life and writings in Appendix 3 (1949–1960).

A lively discussion on Pasquali took place between Timpanaro and Ranuccio Bianchi Bandinelli in *Società* (1952) 564–565, 704–705. It started up again after the appearance in *Quaderni di storia* 3 (1976) of "Discussione sul classicismo nell'età dell'imperialismo." Cf. L. Canfora, *Ideologie del classicismo* (Turin, 1980) 49–52, 83–89, 113–119, as well as Timpanaro's preface to the new edition of *Preistoria della poesia romana* (Florence, 1981) (along with some polemical intemperance).

Richard Porson

25 December 1759 – 19 September 1808

ROGER D. DAWE
Trinity College, Cambridge University

"The study of Porson's life and work is neither an easy nor a pleasant task" said Sir Denys Page in one of his most polished performances, a lecture delivered before the British Academy. Perhaps it would be better to say that the evaluation of Porson's life and work is neither an easy nor a pleasant task; for the study of it has been made easy for us by an admiring circle of worshipers who treasured the words that dropped from his lips and collected the very scraps of paper he wrote on. The element of unpleasantness may be quickly disposed of: it resides principally in the distress any right-minded person must feel at watching a fine intelligence being undermined by alcoholism; though we may remark that Housman's attempted witticism to the effect that Cambridge had seen many strange things—it had seen Wordsworth drunk and Porson sober—loses much of its force when we remember that Byron, no friend of Porson, tells us that he was never seen drunk on such relatively public occasions as dining in the full company of his colleagues.

Our difficulties revolve around this one problem: how are we to reconcile the extravagantly favorable verdict passed on Porson by those who knew him personally and by posterity alike with the evidence of his intellectual abilities as we see it before our eyes today? The myth seems indestructible. In his own day Villoison, an honored name in Homeric studies, called Porson "le plus savant et le plus justement célèbre du pays où la Littérature grecque est le plus cultivée." Twenty-five years after Porson's death J. W. Donaldson delivered a Latin eulogy that contained the words "I say with the utmost emphasis that knowledge of the Greek language and the esoteric science of textual criticism has progressed further in the last thirty years than in the preceding thirty centuries put together, and this benefit is to be attributed, either solely or very largely, to the authoritative example set by Porson." In 1867 H. L. Luard opined, "The great glory of Porson's is his power of emendation—the one in which he far excelled all his predecessors, even Bentley." In our own time a paper notable as much for the apparent total absence of proofreading as for the truculent iconoclasm of some of its judgments still sings in perfect harmony: "He possessed a genius for conjecture arguably as acute as Bentley's and certainly better disciplined" (H. D. Jocelyn, *Liverpool Classical Papers*, no. 1). Trevelyan, with the distortion permitted to historians and Masters of Trinity, wrote, "Bentley is the king of English classical scholars, but Porson, in the estimation of those able to judge, holds the next place."

Porson's own estimate of himself, reflected in his famous saying that he would be content if he was remembered in three hundred years' time as someone who had done a good deal for the text of Euripides, besides being less extravagantly phrased, comes much closer to the truth. How close? Porson's work was not confined to Greek tragedy, but neither was the work of his competitors who strove in the same battlefield. In the hopes of injecting a note of objectivity into estimates of Porson, I have, from "an excess of curiosity or even an abuse of leisure"—terms applied, as I discovered too late, by Page to his own limited exercise of comparing in the same way the records of Porson with those of Hermann and Elmsley—gone through the critical texts of Greek tragedy taken as standard today, i.e. Page for Aeschylus, Dawe for Sophocles, Diggle for Euripides volumes I and II, and Murray for volume III, noting down every place where a scholar is cited as proposing a conjecture either actually accepted by the editor into his text or deemed worthy of serious consideration for such an elevation. I have corrected false attributions where these are known to me, but it has to be said that there remains a certain gray area that makes it unlikely that anyone else who is misguided enough to attempt to duplicate my results will arrive at the same figures. For example, if a scholar says that the right way to spell a certain word is such-and-such, and the spelling is corrected accordingly in four different places, does that constitute one emendation or four? If Murray says, "I have written after Verrall," does that mean the credit belongs to Verrall or to Murray? (In such instances I have incorporated both names.) If two corrections are embodied in one line and one is not required by the other but is all the more plausible for it, does that add up to one conjecture or two? Special problems are posed by the article of M. McCall in *TAPhA* 111 (1981) 111–134. It discloses numerous errors of ascription or unjustifiable silences in the standard edition of Aeschylus for one play. It is unlikely that errors are confined to that play, and it is probable that Tournebou does not receive the recognition he should in the list now given. On the other hand, McCall plainly does not himself fully understand what guidelines Page had set himself for corrections that come almost into the proofreading category. There are further difficulties and refinements with which I will not bore the reader; suffice it to say that I have by and large taken things very much at their face value: what an editor puts down as a correction is taken to be precisely that, one correction. The figures that are of the greatest relevance to us are so huge that these minor reservations cannot dim their message, especially when we remember that the same treatment has been accorded equally to all the scholars cited. Here, then, is a list of all scholars whose work has stood the test of evaluation by others, and whose names appear in our standard texts twenty or more times. What verdict posterity will pass on Page's own emendations on Aeschylus, Dawe's on Sophocles, and those in Murray's volume III, time alone will tell. The figures are cited but not included in the totals. It is certain, too, that the name of Diggle would appear in this list if it had been compiled thirty years from now; he has so far advanced over three hundred conjectures on Euripides.

Total	Name	Aesch.	Soph.	Eur.	
975	Hermann	220	188	567	
561	Elmsley	43	131	387	
482	Musgrave	17	78	387	
398	Nauck	5	88	305	
367	Dindorf	68	114	185	
354	Wecklein	24	43	287	
338	Reiske	0	58	280	
322	Porson	93	49	180	
317	Blaydes	37	230	50	
312	Wilamowitz	32	12	268	
267	Bothe	51	48	168	
255	Kirchhoff	13	0	242	
243	Heath	42	38	163	
233	Hartung	35	46	152	
231	Seidler	12	20	199	
227	Canter	50	12	165	
217	Scaliger	31	8	178	
214	Markland	1	1	212	
203	Brunck	10	133	60	
202	Turnebou	177	25	0	
180	Herwerden	10	40	130	
178	Dobree	11	32	135	
172	Weil	72	0	100	
167	Barnes	0	0	167	
148	Musurus	0	0	148	
131	Wakefield	15	66	50	
126	Burges	33	21	72	
122	Matthiae	0	5	117	
122	Paley	36	4	82	
119	Valckenaer	13	11	95	
116	Blomfield	70	3	43	
115	Badham	0	3	115	
108	Schuetz	108	0	0	
104	Monk	2	6	96	
102	Murray	14	0	88	(+182)

101	Etienne	9	6	86
96	Vettori	25	0	71
96	Tyrwhitt	9	8	79
93	Meineke	26	66	1
87	Erfurdt	7	62	18
84	Bergk	4	64	16
83	Page	(111)	24	59
75	Lenting	0	0	75
74	L. Dindorf	0	2	72
74	Dorat	67	7	0
74	Pierson	2	8	64
72	Pauw	72	0	0
64	Robortello	64	0	0
64	Schaefer	0	26	38
59	Cobet	4	6	49
58	Casaubon	51	1	6
58	Heimsoeth	23	14	21
55	Stanley	53	2	0
55	Wunder	1	51	3
54	F. W. Schmidt	1	25	28
53	Brodeau	0	0	53
53	Portus	27	0	26
50	Headlam	36	1	13
50	Jackson	0	8	42
45	Jacobs	2	2	41
42	Schneidewin	3	37	2
40	Camper	0	0	40
39	Fix	1	0	38
34	Verrall	6	0	28
33	Dawe	21	(188)	12
32	Bruhn	0	3	29
32	Jebb	0	32	0
32	Reisig	3	21	8
29	Lachmann	17	4	8
29	Tucker	23	0	6
28	Enger	17	10	1
27	Bamberger	26	0	1
26	Barrett	0	0	26
26	Butler	26	0	0
26	Lobeck	4	10	12
26	Naber	4	6	16
26	Seyffert	0	25	1
25	Vitelli	0	0	25

25	I. Pearson	15	0	10
24	Madvig	1	5	18
24	Wieseler	13	9	2
23	Mekler	0	12	11
23	Vauvilliers	0	23	0
22	Broadhead	9	3	10
22	Kvíčala	0	3	19
21	Abresch	20	0	1
21	England	0	0	21
21	Fritsche	0	0	21
20	Schenkl	0	1	19

The reader may care to know that there are some outstanding cases of uneven distribution: thus, the vast majority of Badham's emendations concern *Iphigenia in Tauris* (27), *Ion* (46), and *Helen* (28); England's *Iphigenia in Aulis* (15); Markland's the same play (69), *Iphigenia in Tauris* (73), and *Suppliants* (55); Vettori's *Electra* (50); and Reisig's *Oedipus at Colonus* (18).

Porson, it appears at once, did indeed do a good deal for the text of Euripides. Who was he, and where did he come from?

This hero of Cambridge University folklore was a local lad, born in Norfolk; his father was a parish clerk and his mother the daughter of a shoemaker. He had two younger brothers, one of whom, according to Luard, died "of a decline" at the age of thirty-four and the other even more prematurely "of a rapid decline" at the age of twenty-two. Porson's own health was never good; he suffered all his life from asthma, and the charitable may like to suppose some link between his illnesses and his weakness for the bottle. Besides these short-lived brothers there was a sister, with characteristics much like Richard's (Watson: 392); she married a brewer.

His earliest education was with a schoolmaster called Summers, and then with the curate of his village, a Mr. Hewitt, who had four sons who became Fellows of Colleges; a fifth died, no doubt of a decline, as an undergraduate. Later he came to the notice of Norris, the founder of a Cambridge divinity professorship, and when plans to get the boy into Charterhouse, the school that was later to produce Sir Richard Jebb, failed, he was sent to Eton. When Norris died three years later, Sir George Baker arranged for financial provision to continue. The world of classical scholarship owes much to the enlightened patronage of those who, recognizing Porson's academic promise, dipped into their own pockets to help him fulfill it. But to what extent the boy's career at Eton justified their faith in him is unclear, for accounts vary. Reading between the lines as well as on them, we may conclude that he did not stand out among his contemporaries at school as a major intellectual force, though he was well liked on the social level. Eton's reputation is secure enough for it to be able to ride with a pained smile the blow represented by Porson's verdict on his time there: the only thing he remembered with pleasure, he said, were the rat hunts in the Long

Chamber. From these days at the institution "where grateful science still adores / Her Henry's holy shade" is preserved the "Tragi-Comi-Operatical Farce" he wrote, in which the author himself played Punch. At the end of Act 1, Punch delivers the patter:

> If a Master you have he's the Plague of your Life
> For with him you've nought but contention and strife:
> Go as fast as you can, he would have you go faster
> Oh what a plague is a whimsical Master!

We are not far here from Jack Point, a hundred years before his time.

After Eton, Porson entered Trinity College, where he had already been introduced to the Professor of Greek. He won a number of University distinctions for classical undergraduates and was elected into a fellowship in 1782, which lapsed in 1791. "A lay-fellowship, to be sure, might have secured his services to the cause of Letters; but the disingenuous conduct of an individual withheld from him that resource" is how his obituary in the *Gentleman's Magazine* put it. The individual was the Master.

This episode rankled more than one might expect, for Porson was never one of those dreary dons who are tied by an invisible umbilical cord to their colleges; in fact, from the age of twenty-five onward he had chosen to make his home in London, in the Middle Temple, earning his living by journalism, much of it anonymous. But the unfortunate interlude that followed the expiry of his fellowship was not to last long, for at the age of thirty-three Porson was unanimously elected to the Chair of Greek, which carries with it the right to a Trinity fellowship. As Professor he had intended to break with tradition and deliver lectures, but in practice he undertook few duties beyond examining. Not for nothing did Winstanley, a historian of the University, describe the Chair of Greek as a "sinecure of trifling value." (Its value was in fact £40 a year, as compared with the £200 Porson was to receive after 1806, when he became Librarian—a negligent one at that—to the recently established London Institute, with his own rooms and servant provided.)

Two things had drawn the attention of the learned world to Porson's scholarship: his supplementary work on Toup's edition of the medieval Greek lexicon known at the time as Suidas, and what remains to this day his masterpiece, the *Letters to Archdeacon Travis*. These first appeared individually in the *Gentleman's Magazine*, and then, revised and collected, in book form. Everyone who mentions this book finds it necessary to add that it contains 400 pages, and so it does. But the pages are of small format, and the print is large. If the book came from a modern publishing house, it would not need to occupy more than 200 pages, for it is of some 80,000 words, the size of an average novel of today. Nor did it need to be so big. The topic itself did not merit such extensive discussion, and the style did not need to flow so amply, even in the eighteenth century; for what Porson is doing is, in essence, describing a family tree and adding copious comment, instead of drawing it and adding pithy footnotes. The members of this family tree are manuscripts, and the point in question is whether the passage on the Three Heavenly Witnesses in Chapter V of St. John's First Epistle (vv. 7–8) is authentic or spurious. Erasmus had mistakenly added it to the third edition of his authoritative text, believing it had some manuscript support. Isaac Newton was only one of those who had written to disprove its authenticity, and his contemporary at Trinity, the great classical scholar Bentley, had delivered a public lecture on the subject. More recently Gibbon had treated the passage as spurious, and it was this that prompted Travis to write three letters to the *Gentleman's Magazine* urging that it was authentic. Porson leapt to Gibbon's defense, though not without a dig that must have made him wince. It comes in a sentence early in the book, a sentence too good to suppress here, for all that it has been quoted by others: ". . . he pleads eloquently for the rights of mankind, and the duty of toleration; nor does his humanity ever slumber, unless when women are ravished, or the Christians persecuted." The very next sentence is almost as good. "Mr. Gibbon shews, it is true, so strong a dislike to Christianity, as visibly disqualifies him for that society, of which he has created Ammianus Marcellinus president." After quoting *Love's Labour Lost* to the effect that he "draws out the thread of his verbosity finer than the staple of his argument"—a charge that applies to his own treatise all too often—Porson indulges himself to the point of saying of the man he plainly admired, and in support of whom he is writing, ". . . I should guess that these disgraceful obscenities were written by some debauchee, who having from age, or accident, or excess, survived the practice of lust, still indulged himself in the luxury of speculation."

If the point of the rapier was the right weapon with which to nick the flesh of the consummate historian and stylist (when Gibbon and Porson later met, the former mildly remarked, "I must think that occasionally, while praising me, you have mingled a little acid with the sweet"), the hapless Travis deserved cruder weapons and was belabored with the bludgeon. In one of his countless errors Travis had, by selective quotation, misrepresented the views of a certain Zoellner. "Let any man believe Mr. Travis hereafter when he talks of his own truth, candour, charity, and upright intentions, or when he is angry with others for their deficiency in those qualities. Whenever I hear such zealous sticklers for truth, they bring to my mind those undetected females who rail with all the bitterness and insolence of conscious virtue against the frailties of their less prudent sisters." All good rollicking stuff, and there is plenty more where that came from. Those who have met with it during the course of their academic lives will particularly treasure the phrase "malignity under the mask of moderation."

In his *Letters to Archdeacon Travis* Porson was using a steamroller to crack a nut that informed opinion had agreed was cracked already. But he did more: he drove his steamroller over it repeatedly and from every possible angle; and with glee. It could all have been done with the concision that marks Porson's prefaces and commentaries on Euripides, or his notes on Aristophanes and others. A few more paragraphs like the following would have done the trick:

In short, when we consider that these seven manuscripts of Stephens, on the one supposition give a reading which has never been found in any manuscript, Greek or Latin; that they destroy the antithesis between *heaven* and *earth*, which the context, if the verse were genuine would plainly demand; that Stephens often misplaced his marks; that no manuscript can now be found in the library to which Stephens returned his manuscripts that exhibits this reading; while on the other hand, if we only suppose a single semicircle wrong placed, we shall have a text agreeing with all the other Greek manuscripts, or at least with more than one hundred; when we add to this, that Wettstein found at Paris five manuscripts, which agreed with five of Stephens's manuscripts in other places, but here contradicted his margin, none will hesitate to pronounce, that Stephens's copies followed the herd, and omitted the seventh verse, except only those, who by a diligent perusal of Tertullian have adopted his maxims of reasoning, and measure the merits of their assent by the absurdity of the proposition to be believed.

What was uppermost in Porson's mind cannot have been the mere refutation of a textual error. Certainly, the destruction of humbug was always congenial to him. But the true reason for the *Letters* can only have been to establish Porson once and for all as England's foremost Greek scholar. In achieving that end it was successful. To those of us who think of Porson as he wished to be thought of, as an editor of Euripides, the *Letters* come as a revelation. Their author gives the impression of knowing every page of the Christian fathers as if they were indexed and capable of flashing up before him on a computer screen whenever needed. And in a manner of speaking they were. Anecdotes from several different sources attest to what we should nowadays call his photographic memory, and to that memory was committed not only classical and post-classical Greek and Latin literature but a wealth of English and some French literature as well, to which his own writings contain a host of often fleeting allusions. The spectacle of a Porson entirely at home with Emanuel Caleas (mid-fourteenth century) and Joseph Bryennius (early fifteenth) is more daunting than Porson the emender of texts, and once we have witnessed it we feel no surprise at finding that the sale catalogue of Porson's books, not including those bought in by Trinity for a thousand guineas, listed 1,391 items.

The *Letters* and the work on Suidas secured election to the Cambridge Chair after the formality of the required public lecture. This was composed in two days and consists of an elegant Latin essay on Euripides. Porson's own verdict at the end of his lecture is just: "What I promised at the outset I have performed—namely that I would not advance anything new or recondite." The only signs of a scholar wrestling with his subject come when he tries to assess the difficulties Euripides caused for himself by having the action of his *Hecuba* take place now in Thrace, now in Troy. The expenditure of a mere two days exemplifies in practice the attitude that, on a more theoretical level, Porson expounded in the following words:

> I cannot indeed but think, that the judgement of the Public, upon the respective merits of the different classes of Criticks, is peculiarly partial and unjust.

Those among them who assume the office of pointing out the beauties, and detecting the faults, of literary composition, are placed with the orator and historian in the highest ranks; whilst those, who undertake the more laborious task of washing away the rust and canker of time, and bringing back those forms and colours, which are the subject of criticism, to their original purity and brightness, are degraded with the index-maker and antiquary, among the pioneers of literature, whose business it is to clear the way for those who are capable of more splendid and honourable enterprises.

But, nevertheless, if we examine the effects produced by those two classes of Criticks, we shall find that the first have been of no use whatever, and that the last have rendered the most important services to mankind. All persons of taste and understanding know, from their own feelings, when to approve, and disapprove, and therefore stand in no need of instructions from the Critick; and as for those who are destitute of such faculties, they can never be brought to use them; for no one can be taught to exert faculties which he does not possess. Every dunce may, indeed, be taught to repeat the jargon of criticism, which of all jargons is the worst, as it joins the tedious formality of methodical reasoning to the trite frivolity of common-place observation.

Washing away the rust and canker of time gave Porson plenty to do, and most of his conjectural criticism was of this mechanical kind. None of his conjectures on tragedy exudes the quality of a laserlike mental penetration. One constantly feels that if Porson had not made a particular emendation that goes under his name, someone else would have soon enough. Fraenkel, in the preface to his three-volume edition of Aeschylus's *Agamemnon*, selects for praise the conjecture on line 1052 of the next play, *The Offering at the Tomb*; but many do not accept it. He mentions *Agamemnon* 850; but does it really require a genius to change "rout the disease of harm" to "repel the harm of the disease?" And thirdly, 1391–1392—hardly more than a redivision of words, and even so not certainly right. M. L. Clarke in his biography of Porson also draws attention to *Agamemnon* 1391–1392 and adds two others. One is Euripides *Helen* 751, where for "at least nothing" Porson writes "Nor Helenos," i.e., οὐδ᾽ Ἕλενος for οὐδέν γε. This is not a feat of brilliant intuition or a scientific assessment of the likely corruption of word shapes or sounds. We have had the name of one prophet and now we need the name of another, and the immediately obvious candidate is Helenos, so in he goes, whether paleography approves or not. The other correction is much more impressive: at *Ion* 1115 the manuscripts throw in the sponge: "We have been fairly judged, and in the extremity of evil." Some judicious redivision of letters, the diagnosis of a phonetic confusion, and a little bit of extra tweaking of the text will give us what Porson did give us: "You have got it right: you will not be among the last to have your share in misfortune": (from ἐγνώσμεθ᾽ ἐξ ἴσου· κέν ὑστάτοις κακοῖς to Ἔγνως· μεθέξεις οὐκ ἐν ὑστάτοις κακοῦ.). Here for once is something for us to admire, but it was not often that Porson raised his head so high over the parapet. More than one critic has cited Euripides *Medea* 1015, where the manuscripts give: "Don't worry: you are victorious, you too, by your children yet," and Porson changed the nonsensical "You are victorious" to "You will be restored from exile": (κρατεῖς changed to κάτει). But as Porson himself acknowledged—for he was always just to those to whom he owed a scholarly debt—the true sense had already been seen by his predecessor Musgrave, and someone with Porson's memory would have had no difficulty in recalling the *mot juste*, since a good deal of play is made with this particular word in this particular meaning by Aristophanes, one of his most favorite authors. For the most part this hero of English scholarship did little but restore the right dialects, switch little words to eliminate metrical abnormalities, and in general tidy things up. In this he is neither a novel nor an exceptional figure: Elmsley, who was not even a Professor of Greek but of ancient history, was doing the same thing at the same time, and doing it more productively and with no less insight.

There are times when Porson falls short of his objective. When reviewing Weston's *Hermesianax* he comes to a passage in Theocritus (*Id.* 8.53) "May I not have golden talents" (i.e. of money), and expresses admiration for Pierson's "May I not have the talents of Croesus" (χρύσεια changed to Κροίσοιο). But why no word on Κροίσεια, giving the same sense, a slighter and more elegant change, made by Jortin? Why, when discussing a metrical problem in Sophocles's *Oedipus at Colonus*, does Porson do everything except actually propose one form of "as" for another, when this would remove the difficulty? The corruption would be one more of a type he exemplifies in the very paragraph that discusses the line, but in the critical notes of today the credit for the actual alteration has to go to Wilamowitz, working a hundred years later. In his *Letters to Archdeacon Travis*, at one point Porson is faced with a Greek note saying that something had been "taken out" by Areios. He proposes "rubbed out," i.e., for ἐξελήφθη read ἐξηλείφθη. But the normal Greek would be "ejected," ἐξεβλήθη. More revealing than any of these is something in the preface to the first edition of *Hecuba*. He toys here with four different ways of emending a line in Sophocles's *Ajax*. None is right, and in his second edition he has to take notice of the true reading, which in the meantime had been published from a manuscript by Hermann. He covers his embarrassment with "I would not stop you accepting it" (*Non equidem intercedam, quo minus hoc adoptes*).

Not infallible then; but with a quick eye for merit in others, even if he does sometimes exaggerate the differences between those he likes and those he does not. He goes out of his way more than once to praise Valckenaer and scorn Pauw, to extol Dawes and depreciate Barnes. But when he is reading Weston's *Hermesianax*, his steadily lowering opinion of it does not mask from him the appeal of an emendation made on Xenophon: "They sat down just as they were" for "They sat down, *as you would expect*" or "as was probable, reasonable," an expression that had occurred a few lines earlier. The change is from εἰκός to εἶχον, and deserves the approval Porson bestows on it. The standard editions of today ignore it, since for all the lip service paid to Porson, few actually read him; yet, if the experience of one editor of Sophocles is anything to go on, we ought to: the *Adversaria* would have saved him from two false attributions of conjectures, which are assigned there to the right authors. The last words of the following extract from a review of Dr. Edwards's edition of Plutarch *On the Education of Children* reproach him from the grave:

> What! are we to give every man, who sets up for a critic, an unlimited right of correcting ancient books at his pleasure? Not at his pleasure, but in conformity to certain laws well known and established by the general consent of the learned. He may transgress or misapply these laws, but without disowning their authority. No critic in his senses ever yet declared his resolution to put into the text what at the time he thought a wrong reading; and if a man, after perusing the works of his author perhaps ten times as often as the generality of readers,—after diligently comparing MSS. and editions,—after examining what others have written relative to him professedly or accidentally,—after a constant perusal of other authors, with a special view to the elucidation of his own,—if, after all this, he must not be trusted with a discretionary power over the text, he never could be qualified to be an editor at all. Whatever editor (one, we mean, who aspires to that title,) republishes a book from an old edition, when the text might be improved from subsequent discoveries, while he hopes to show his modesty and religion, only exposes his indolence, his ignorance, or his superstition.

A noble clarion call; yet it was not Porson, but Elmsley, who took the trouble to make use of what is the oldest and best manuscript of Aeschylus and Sophocles. It is noticeable, too, that many of Porson's own writings teem with misprints, as if he had never troubled to correct the proofs.

Porson put beyond doubt that Fourmont's inscriptions were bogus, and in another place correctly argued that the Parian marble was genuine. Yet a man so methodical in the deployment of such technical evidence as the shapes of letters at particular times in particular places was content to believe that the tragic poets allowed themselves to elide the final iotas of dative cases, and to withhold credence from the frequent observance of the letter *digamma* by Homer, a letter absent from our written texts but pronounced at a formative time in the poems' composition. This is the odder in that the discovery, if one may so call it, of the Homeric *digamma* was one of the feats of the scholar whom Porson esteemed above all others, Richard Bentley. But there is one triumph for which Porson's methodical approach is still remembered today: his "Law" relating to the permissible length of the syllable preceding the last three syllables of the line in the iambic trimeter, the metre in which most of the speeches in Greek tragedy are written. It is true that anyone who spent a wet afternoon looking at the word divisions and the length of syllables in Euripides might very well come to suspect the existence of this law by tea-time; and it is true that laws of much greater subtlety have been discovered in profusion in more recent times. But honor is due to pioneers, and here at any rate Porson qualifies for that title.

Whether he qualifies for the title of the founder of a school of critics is more doubtful, though as early as 1857 one had been fathered on him by Paley: "It will hardly be denied that the Porsonian school of critics, much and justly as we admire their varied learning and ingenuity, have been the means of introducing into our schools a somewhat dull and dry kind of annotation useless to the mere beginner, often tiresome even to the advanced student, and fitted only for professed critics." Whether of his "school" or not, those who knew him for the most part fell under his spell. A man who did not possess the highest intellectual gifts and what some now call charisma could never have inspired such feelings of veneration in the minds of such persons, formidable enough in their own right, as Monk, Blomfield, and Dobree. Their devotion outweighs the evidence of those who were stupid, like Travis, or who lacked the bond of a common professional interest, like Byron: "Of all the disgusting brutes, sulky, abusive and intolerable, Porson was the most bestial as far as the few times that I saw him went. . . . I saw him once go away in a rage because no one knew the name of the 'Cobbler of Messina,' insulting their ignorance with the most vulgar terms of reprobation. He was tolerated in this state amongst the young men for his talents, as the Turks think a madman inspired and bear with him. He used to recite or rather vomit pages of all languages. . . ."

Even such unflattering contributions as these to the hagiography of Porson help to ensure that he will be remembered. We are presented with a fascinating enigma: the "dull and dry" annotator of whom Paley speaks turns into the Mr. Hyde of Byron; the fastidious student of versification talks with bargees and with *filles de joie* who stray into his rooms; the scholar who is furious at being passed over for a fellowship prefers in any case to live in London; the man who enjoys conversation with his friends far into the night discourteously omits to acknowledge gifts of books from foreign scholars paying tribute to him. In Cambridge the legend lives still. Porson's picture looks down on the fellows of Trinity at their dessert every evening; a copy of it is a few feet to the left of me as I type this chapter, part of a prize still awarded at Cambridge, funded by monies raised for him when he lost his fellowship. Two hundred of the three hundred years that Porson asked for have passed, and so far the verdict, right but for the wrong reasons, has not been overturned. The lumpish boy from the obscure village in Norfolk, who grew into an asthmatic alcoholic, valuing truth and honesty above all things, acquired a fame that went beyond the limits of his subject. It looks like going far beyond the limits of three centuries.

Books

Items marked with an * appeared anonymously; those marked with a † are posthumous.

Letters to Mr. Archdeacon Travis. London, 1790.
*Aeschylus. Edited by Foulis. Glasgow, 1795.
*Euripides Hecuba. London, 1797; 2d ed., 1802.
*Euripides Orestes. London, 1798.
*Euripides Phoenissae. London, 1799.
Euripides Medea. Cambridge, 1801.
*Aeschylus, Tragoediae Septem cum versione Latina. London, 1806.

†*Adversaria.* Edited by J. H. Monk and C. J. Blomfield. Cambridge, 1812.

†*Tracts and Miscellaneous Criticisms.* Edited by Thomas Kidd. London, 1815.

†*Ricardi Porsoni Notae in Aristophanem.* With a critical edition of *Plutus.* Edited by P. P. Dobree. Cambridge, 1820.

Other

1. The Appendix to Toup's *Emendationes in Suidam.* Oxford, 1790.

2. Collation of the Harleian MS of the *Odyssey* in the Homer edition of T. Grenville, R. Porson, W. Cleaver, etc. Oxford, 1800–1801.

3. *Transcript of the Photius Lexicon. Edited by P. P. Dobree. London, 1822.*

Sources

There is a mass of memoirs, anecdotes, etc., that can be found listed at the end of Jebb's article on Porson in the *DNB* 16:154–163 and M. L. Clarke's *Porson* (Cambridge, 1937). To these could be added notices in *The Morning Chronicle*, 6 October 1808, and *The Courier*, 7 October 1808, and William Norris, *An Account of the Last Illness of Richard Porson* (London, 1808).

From more recent times we may cite:

Brink, C. O. *English Classical Scholarship: Historical Reflections on Bentley, Porson and Housman.* Cambridge, 1986.

Jocelyn, H. D. *Liverpool Classical Papers*, no. 1 (1988).

Katz, S. A. "Even Classicists Are Odd." *CJ* 43 (1947–1948) 411–415. (Merely repeats old gossip.)

Page, D. L. "Richard Porson (1759–1808)." A lecture given before the British Academy. *PBA* 45 (1959) 221–236.

The Correspondence of Richard Porson M.A. Formerly Regius Professor of Greek in the University of Cambridge. Edited for the Cambridge Antiquarian Society by Henry Richards Luard M.A. Cambridge, 1867.

Readers with a taste for the macabre may like to know that one of Porson's biographers, the Rev. J. S. Watson, murdered his wife and died in Parkhurst prison as a result—if the inquest verdict is to be believed—of striking his head on the floor after falling out of his hammock.

Friedrich Ritschl

6 April 1806 – 8 November 1876

ERNST VOGT
Universität München

Friedrich Ritschl was one of the most prominent philologists and most influential academic teachers of the nineteenth century, a pioneer in the field of Old Latin and, particularly, Plautine studies.

Friedrich Wilhelm Ritschl was born on 6 April 1806 at Groß-Vargula near Erfurt, son of a Protestant clergyman and eldest of three siblings. After completing his preparatory education in Erfurt and Wittenberg, where his most important teachers were Franz Spitzner and Gregor Wilhelm Nitzsch, he began his study of philology in 1825 at the University of Leipzig with Gottfried Hermann, who at that time was at the height of his powers. After two semesters Ritschl transferred to Halle, which seemed more congenial to him than Leipzig, in order to study with Hermann's brilliant pupil Carl Reisig. Ritschl in turn would become Reisig's most distinguished pupil. Later, in brief sentences he wrote an impressive evaluation of the personality and work of his teacher. In the summer of 1829 Ritschl took his doctorate at Halle with the dissertation *Schedae criticae* (Reisig had died unexpectedly earlier that year in Venice at the age of thirty-six), and several months later he habilitated there with the monograph *De Agathonis vita*. In the winter semester of 1829–30, Ritschl began his teaching career at Halle, which, from the start, he pursued with the greatest success. In 1832 his influence was recognized when he was awarded the title Professor Extraordinarius.

In 1833 Ritschl was appointed salaried Extraordinarius at Breslau, where in autumn 1834 he was promoted to Ordinarius (i.e., full professor). For the year 1836–37 he was granted a traveling fellowship to Italy that was of decisive importance for his subsequent scholarly work. He chiefly visited Milan, Florence, and Rome, and in the libraries of these cities he engaged in intensive manuscript study. At Milan he met, among others, Alessandro Manzoni.

A full year after his return Ritschl was appointed the successor of August Ferdinand Naeke at Bonn. Here, in the following twenty-six years (1839–1865), he achieved unique eminence and produced a large number of remarkable students. Among them one may recall Georg Curtius, Heinrich Brunn, Jacob Bernays, Otto Ribbeck, Johannes Vahlen, Franz Bücheler, Adolf Kießling, Hermann Usener, Friedrich Blass, Erwin Rohde, and Friedrich Nietzsche. In 1842, along with Friedrich Gottlieb Welcker, he founded anew the *Rheinisches Museum* and turned it into an organ for publication of outstanding articles that pointed the way to future research. He edited the journal until his death. In 1854 he succeeded Welcker as head librarian of the Bonn University Library, which he reorganized from the ground up and for which he continually performed a lasting service.

In 1865, as a result of a disagreement concerning the appointment of a new colleague, an unpleasant quarrel arose between Ritschl and his *collega proximus*, Otto Jahn, which separated into two hostile camps not only faculty and university but the whole of Bonn, as well as the scholarly public. Because of this, Ritschl accepted an appointment at the Saxonian University of Leipzig. A number of his students, among them Erwin Rohde and Friedrich Nietzsche, sided with him. For eleven years more, in spite of increasing illness and the infirmities of old age, he was able to work successfully. The most important students of the Leipzig period were Wilhelm Roscher, Friedrich Schöll, Georg Goetz, Paul Cauer and Otto Crusius. He died in Leipzig during the night of 8–9 November 1876. He was also the cousin of Albrecht Ritschl (1822–1889), one of the leading Protestant theologians of his time.

As a student of Gottfried Hermann and Carl Reisig, Ritschl began with contributions to the field of Greek philology. His dissertation, *Schedae criticae*, offers a series of critical contributions mainly to Greek authors and already reveals the young scholar's analytical gift and his vast erudition in ancient literature from its beginnings down to late antiquity. The *Habilitationsschrift* on Agathon, which appeared in the same year as the *Schedae*, was part of a comprehensive monograph on the life and work of this Greek tragedian. In broad investigations, starting in the footsteps of Scaliger, Ritschl determined there with methodologically strict proofs the place of Agathon in the history of Greek literature, faithful to his proud motto, "nil tam difficilest quin quaerendo investigari possiet" (Ter. *Heaut.* 675). His edition of Thomas Magister, *Ecloga vocum Atticarum* (1832), has retained its importance until the present day. Similarly his study *De Oro et Orione* (1834), which Ritschl in his subtitle called *Specimen historiae criticae grammaticorum Graecorum*, laid the groundwork for later concern with these grammarians. His comprehensive monograph, *Die Alexandrinischen Bibliotheken unter den ersten Ptolemäern und die Sammlung der Homerischen Gedichte durch Pisistratus* (1838) yielded important results *inter alia* concerning the chronology of the first Alexandrian librarians as well as stichometry in antiquity. It started off from a scholiast's note in a fifteenth-century parchment manuscript of Plautus in the library of the Collegio Romano.

At this time, and for many years previously, Ritschl's attention was attracted strongly to the Plautine comedies. The first fruits of this interest were an edition of *Bacchides* (1835) and a comprehensive monograph, *Ueber die Kritik des Plautus*, which contained a complete survey of the manuscripts and editions up to that time. Now that poet was to enter into the center of Ritschl's lifework and gain for him the honorable title of *sospitator Plauti*. In 1815 Angelo Mai had announced the discovery of the Plautus palimpsest he had found in Milan. The careful utilization of this find during his time in Italy led Ritschl to his insight into the regularity of the structure of Plautine verse, whereby suggestions of Richard Bentley and Gottfried Hermann were brilliantly confirmed. A flood of further studies, among them on the name, lifetime, and theatrical activity of Plautus, followed and were first brought together in *Parerga zu Plautus und Terenz* (1845). In 1848 Ritschl's Plautus edition began to appear. By 1854 nine plays had been edited. The edition placed scholarly attention to the poet on a totally new foundation. With the help of Ritschl's pupils Gustav Loewe, Georg Goetz, and Friedrich Schöll, the work was later published in revised form and brought to completion.

After Plautus, Terence and Varro had chief claim on the penetrating researches of Ritschl. His treatment of the *Seven against Thebes* of Aeschylus, on the other hand, was not consistently happy. There the assumption of a strict parallelism in the seven pairs of speeches led to a series of arbitrary attacks on the text that caused Wilamowitz to speak of the "tyrannical dialectic of Ritschl."

Ritschl's concern with Plautus aroused his interest in the collection and editing of archaic Latin inscriptions. They seemed to him essential for a more precise understanding of the history of the Latin language. The preparatory work of many years led in 1862 to the monumental publication of *Priscae Latinitatis monumenta epigraphica*, with numerous lithographs elegantly inserted and the inclusion of exemplary indices. The importance of this volume for research in the history of the Latin language can scarcely be overestimated and has certainly benefited the understanding of archaic literary Latin.

The philological works of Ritschl are accompanied by a lifelong concern with the goals and methods of philology. Already in his lectures on meter at Halle in winter semester 1831–32 he had concerned himself with this theme. In a contribution to the third volume of the *Conversations-Lexikon der neuesten Zeit und Litteratur* that appeared in 1833, he defined the task of philology as "the reproduction of the life of antiquity through research on and intuition of its essential manifestations." In summer semester 1835 at Breslau, for the first time he delivered lectures on the encyclopedia and methods of philology, which, along with a similar one on philological hermeneutics and criticism, he held again and again later in revised forms. A planned publication, "On the Method of Philological Study," never went beyond fragments and aphorisms, first published from his literary remains in the fifth volume of his *Opuscula philologica*. His "Ten Commandments for Classical Philologists" composed with Karl Lehrs give an idea of how he wanted the activity of the philologist to be seen.

1. Thou shalt not parrot.
2. Thou shalt not steal.
3. Thou shalt not fall down on thy knees before manuscripts.
4. Thou shalt not take the name of Method in vain.
5. Thou shalt learn to read.

6. Thou shalt not gather Sanskrit roots and reject my manna.

7. Thou shalt learn to distinguish intellects.

8. Thou shalt not believe that Minerva is blue haze and a humbug: she has been ordained Wisdom for you.

9. Thou shalt not believe that ten bad reasons are equal to one good one.

10. Thou shalt not believe what several of the pagans have said: "Water is the best."

The importance of Ritschl lies in the brilliant handling of the critical and exegetical method perfected by him and in the consequent historical exploitation of the material studied by him. With this way of working, not least because of the great number of his students, he essentially determined the further development of philology. Obviously not all the results that he reached in this way have lasted permanently, but, on the other hand, what is offered in opposition to him could not, as Wilamowitz remarks in his *Geschichte der Philologie*, have been attained without him. Friedrich Nietzsche in *Ecce Homo* called him the only genius in the world of learning whom he had personally met.

Translated by William M. Calder III

Books

Thomae Magistri sive Theoduli Monachi Ecloga vocum Atticarum. Halle, 1832.

De Oro et Orione: Specimen historiae criticae grammaticorum Graecorum. Breslau, 1834.

Die Alexandrinischen Bibliotheken unter den ersten Ptolemäern und die Sammlung der Homerischen Gedichte durch Pisistratus, nach Anleitung eines Plautinischen Scholions. Breslau, 1838; reprinted Amsterdam, 1970.

Parerga zu Plautus und Terenz. Leipzig, 1845.

T. Macci Plauti Comoediae. Vols. 1–3. Bonn, Elberfeld, and Leipzig, 1848–1854.

Aeschyli Septem ad Thebas. Elberfeld and Leipzig, 1853; 2d ed., Leipzig, 1875.

Priscae Latinitatis monumenta epigraphica ad archetyporum fidem exemplis lithographis repraesentata. Berlin, 1862.

Neue Plautinische Exkurse. Sprachgeschichtliche Untersuchungen. Leipzig, 1869.

T. Macci Plauti Comoediae. Posthumously completed by Gustav Loewe, Georg Goetz, Friedrich Schöll. Vols. 1–4. Leipzig, 1878–1894.

Articles (Collected)

Opuscula philologica. Vols. 1–5. Leipzig, 1866–1879; reprinted Hildesheim and New York, 1978.

Sources

Bibliography

Opuscula philologica. Leipzig, 1879: 5:725–766.

Biographical

von Bezold, Friedrich. *Geschichte der Rheinischen Friedrich-Wilhelms-Universität von der Gründung bis zum Jahr 1870.* Bonn, 1920: 313–314; 386–389; 503–512.

Bickel, Ernst. *Friedrich Ritschl und der Humanismus in Bonn.* Bonn, 1946.

Buecheler, Franz. In *Kleine Schriften.* Leipzig, 1927: 2:427–429.

Bursian, Conrad. *Geschichte der classischen Philologie in Deutschland von den Anfängen bis zur Gegenwart.* Munich, 1883: 812–849.

Calder, William M., III. "Karl Lehrs' Ten Commandments for Classical Philologists." CW 74 (1980–81) 227–228.

Gildersleeve, Basil L. "Personal Reminiscences of Friedrich Ritschl." *PAPA* 8 (1877) 14–15.

———. "Friedrich Ritschl." *AJPh* 5 (1884) 339–355.

Herter, Hans. "Aus der Geschichte der Klassischen Philologie in Bonn." In *Kleine Schriften.* Edited by Ernst Vogt. Munich, 1975: 648–664.

Hübinger, Paul Egon. "Heinrich v. Sybel und der Bonner Philologenkrieg." *HJ* 83 (1964) 162–216.

Jensen, Christian and Bickel, Ernst. "Das Philologische Seminar." In *Geschichte der Rheinischen Friedrich-Wilhelm-Universität zu Bonn am Rhein.* Vol. 2. *Institute und Seminare 1818–1933.* Bonn, 1933: 187–210.

Mansfeld, Jaap. "The Wilamowitz-Nietzsche Struggle: Another New Document and Some Further Comments." *Nietzsche-Studien* 15 (1986) 41–58, especially 52–55.

Mueller, Lucian. *Friedrich Ritschl. Eine wissenschaftliche Biographie.* Berlin, 1877; 2d ed., 1878.

Prete, Sesto. "Gli inizi della critica Plautina (F. Ritschl)." In *Convivium, Raccolta nuova* 1 (1947) 759–769.

———. "Zwei unbekannte Briefe von Friedrich Wilhelm Ritschl." *RhM* 115 (1972) 363–370.

Ribbeck, Otto. *Friedrich Wilhelm Ritschl. Ein Beitrag zur Geschichte der Philologie.* Vols. 1 and 2. Leipzig, 1879–1881.

———. "Ritschl: Friedrich Wilhelm," *ADB* 28: 653–661.

Rohde, Erwin. "Friedrich Ritschl." In *Kleine Schriften.* Tübingen, 1901: 2:452–462.

Sandys, John Edwin. *A History of Classical Scholarship.* Cambridge, 1903–1908: 3:138–142.

Schmid, Wolfgang. "Aus der Geschichte der klassischen Philologie vor Usener und Bücheler. Friedrich Ritschl und Jacob Bernays." In *Ausgewählte philologische Schriften.* Edited by Hartmut Erbse and Jochem Küppers. Berlin, 1984: 695–717.

Vogt, Ernst. "Nietzsche und der Wettkampf Homers." A&A 11 (1962) 103–113, especially 108–111.

———. "Der Methodenstreit zwischen Hermann und Böckh und seine Bedeutung für die Geschichte der Philologie." In *Philologie und Methodologie der Geisteswissenschaften*. Edited by Hellmut Flashar, Karlfried Gründer, Axel Horstmann. Göttingen, 1979: 103–121, especially 119–120.

Wilamowitz-Moellendorff, Ulrich von. *Geschichte der Philologie*. Leipzig, 1921: 60–61.

Erwin Rohde

9 October 1845 – 11 January 1898

HUBERT CANCIK
Universität Tübingen

The life and works of Erwin Rohde are of particular significance for three areas of scholarship. His detailed and imaginative studies of the Greek love-romance and Greek beliefs about the soul (eschatology) are important for the history of scholarship. His place in intellectual history derives from his relations with Friedrich Nietzsche, Franz Overbeck, and Richard and Cosima Wagner; he thus exemplifies the connection between classical philology and anti-modernistic cultural criticism. For social historians he is significant as a representative of the educated bourgeois class and its movement away from liberalism in the era of Bismarck (who died in 1898).

In all three of these fields the sources for the life of Rohde are quite rich, easily accessible, and untapped. The genesis of his great works can be traced from his readings as a schoolboy on through his student notebooks all the way to his scholarly notations and corrected proofs. An extensive correspondence and personal *Nachlaß* provide a wealth of gossip and information about Rohde's friendships and love-life, his travels and his illnesses. This sedentary intellectual's bodily history, with its afflictions of bowels, stomach, heart, eyes, and head, tells us much about the costs incurred by one privileged to spend his life in thinking. The study of Rohde's life was obstructed by the biography that Otto Crusius—Rohde's successor, but not his student, at Tübingen and Heidelberg—rapidly put together in 1902, bedizening it with all the brilliant colors of the Wilhelmine age, in his capacity as admirer of Nietzsche, of his sister, and of her Nietzsche Archive.

Erwin Rohde was born on 9 October 1845 in Hamburg; he was the second of four children. His father, Adolph Rohde, M.D. (1813–1866), the first member of the family to attend a university, was a general practitioner. Rohde's mother Bertha, née Schleiden (1813–1883), was an educated woman from a large family whose members had been successful in politics and science. M. J. Schleiden, Professor of Botany at

Jena (until 1862), persuaded the parents to send their shy and refractory boy to the modern pedagogical institute in Jena that had been founded by K. V. Stoy in 1844; here he spent the years from 1852 to 1859. Looking back on those seven years, the successful scholar declared that they had given him "complete unhappiness for my entire life" (Rohde to Anna Brandt, 14 October 1886). After 1860 Rohde attended the highly respected Johanneum in Hamburg, which, by means of its extensive and ambitious program of study in ancient languages, surpassed the classical grammar school ("Gelehrtenschule") and the academic gymnasium and allowed its pupils to pass without break or hesitation into university studies. The city of Hamburg, open to the world and rich in traditions, left its mark on Rohde's life. Also influential were his connections with a hard-working and ambitious educated bourgeois class (doctors, lawyers, apothecaries, professors), the advances and the losses involved in the Industrial Revolution, and the rise of Prussia to the status of a great German power in its wars with Denmark (1864), Austria (1866), and France (1870–1871).

In May 1865 Rohde became a student of philology at Bonn, one semester later than Friedrich Nietzsche (15 October 1844–25 August 1900). Like Nietzsche, Rohde transferred in the fall of 1865 from Bonn to Leipzig, where he worked under Ritschl, Curtius, and Tischendorf. The preliminary studies for a "Culturhistorie antiker Erotik" and his book on the Greek novel became gradually more and more coherent and precise ("Philologische Adversaria" 8:325–430). Rohde is first mentioned in a letter of Nietzsche in July 1866 (F. Nietzsche to Mushake, 11 July 1866); for so long the two had passed each other by. The intensive phase of their friendship lasted only one year; in the fall of 1867 Rohde registered at the University of Kiel. Here he encountered two of his future mentors, the liberal historian Alfred von Gutschmid and Otto Ribbeck, whose lectures on Greek tragedy he attended. Rohde received his doctorate on 9 March 1869 with a dissertation on ancient writers on the Greek theater. The career toward which Rohde had been moving even as a schoolboy went forward without a pause: after the obligatory trip to Italy and Rome, Rohde habilitated at Kiel, and in the winter semester of 1870 he began teaching as a Privatdozent with a lecture, before five students, entitled "The History of Grammatical and Philological Studies among the Greeks."

The friendship with Nietzsche is one of the unsolved problems in Rohde's life. How much, how long, and in what direction did Nietzsche influence his life, his thought, and his writings? Rohde owed to Nietzsche his immersion in Schopenhauer's philosophy; pessimism that has cast off all illusions, denial of the will, opposition to Christianity, and the religion of art remained Rohde's world-view long after Nietzsche had gone beyond Schopenhauer. He owed to Nietzsche his personal acquaintance with the church historian Franz Overbeck and with Richard and Cosima Wagner, as well as the intoxication he and Nietzsche found together in Wagner's music; Bayreuth remained holy ground for Rohde long after Nietzsche had been excommunicated from the Wagnerite congregation.

But after the brief noontide of their friendship in Leipzig came separation, which was seldom interrupted, followed by alienation (by 1875 at the latest), and finally the breach, which was painful for them both. While Rohde grew ever more firmly rooted in family, university career, and professional scholarship, Nietzsche detached himself more and more from all three. Rohde rejected Nietzsche's critical philosophy and supposed that he had been led astray to it by Paul Rée; later, he searched the text of *Also Sprache Zarathustra* for signs of madness. Nietzsche's lasting influence on Rohde lay in the connection he had established between philhellenism on the one hand and Schopenhauer's philosophy and Wagner's music on the other, as well as his program for a conservative reform of German culture: "we may yet hope for a reawakening of Hellenic antiquity of which our fathers never dreamed" (F. Nietzsche to R. Meister, 14 July 1871). It was for this reason that Rohde defended Nietzsche's manifesto (*Geburt der Tragödie aus dem Geiste der Musik*, 1872) against the silence of professional classicists and the attacks of the young Ph.D. Ulrich von Wilamowitz-Moellendorff (*Zukunftsphilologie!* 1872) in the form of an "open letter to Richard Wagner" (*Afterphilologie* 1872).

The Wagner circle, to which the authors of *Geburt der Tragödie*—with a *Vorwort an Richard Wagner*—and of *Afterphilologie: Sendschreiben eines Philologen an Richard Wagner* (1872) both belonged, associated the attacks on Nietzsche and Rohde with its old bugbear, the Jews (R. Wagner, *Das Judentum in der Musik*, 1850). In the criticisms of the Wagnerians, Wilamowitz, of all people, became the agent of "literary Jewry" at Berlin (C. v. Gersdorff to F. Nietzsche, 31 May 1872; Gersdorff to Rohde, 31 May 1872). In Rohde's published writings this hostility toward the Jews (which around 1880 was crystallized in the expression "antisemitism") has no place. In letters and personal notes, however, Rohde projected onto the Jews his revulsion toward modernity, toward industry and capitalism, which were destroying the world he knew, and toward Christianity. As a student he had informed his mother that the belief in progress and the soft optimism of so-called Christianity was only "the Jewish, actually quite heterogeneous part of Christianity" (E. Rohde to Berta Rohde, 30 June 1866). After all, Schopenhauer had said "that one day Europe too will be cleansed of all Jewish mythology" (*Paralipomena*, 115). But now—after the emancipation of the Jews (in 1869 in northern Germany) and with their advance particularly in the newly rising professions (the press, medicine, art, finance)—Rohde was anxious: "And it is this nation to which our people and our future are falling victim" (Rohde, *Cogitata* 18 [D.], probably 1870). Genuine "Christianity" and "Judaism" could produce "no plastic art" (Rohde, *Cogitata* 31 [D.], dated "9 August 70"): "Who has heard of a Jewish sculptor, who a Jewish dramatist?" The mysteries of Hellenic education, genius, and creativity, the tragic and the plastic, are inaccessible to Jews and Jewish Christians. This prejudice, metaphysically developed and supported by such authorities as Schopenhauer, Wagner, and Lagarde, is maintained without contradiction into Rohde's maturity. But the sources have not yet been examined, interpreted, and evaluated. To be fully understood they must be brought into connection with other standard questions in social psychology—questions as to Rohde's mother and wife, friends and children—and be compared with the positions of Overbeck and Nietzsche, Treitschke and Harnack. Such an investigation would be of some importance for an anthropological theory of antisemitism and philhellenism.

Contrary to the various fears of the Wagners and of Rohde's friends in Basel, his advocacy of Nietzsche's manifesto did him no harm professionally. In 1872 he became *extraordinarius* at Kiel, and in 1876 *ordinarius* in Jena. This position of security made it possible for him to begin a family and by 17 July 1876, Rohde was engaged to Valentine Framm (1859–1901), daughter of an attorney in Rostock. Unlike Nietzsche, Rohde was anchored firmly in the social order of the Bismarck period by his professorship (which gave him the status of a government official), his marriage (August 1877), his children (Bertha, Franz Erwin Otto, Anna, Hans Adolph), and his ownership of property—and this despite the fact that he passionately rejected the spirit of his age in art (except for Wagner), technology, and scholarship. Nietzsche, by contrast, remained without wife and children, without a fixed residence; he retired early with a small pension and lived as a writer, and his income was always uncertain. The ever-increasing divergence of their life-styles, their work, and their experiences hastened the alienation between the Leipzig Dioscuri.

When Rohde received the call to Jena, the first of his two masterpieces was in the press. At Easter 1876, Breitkopf und Härtel in Leipzig published *Der griechische Roman und seine Vorläufer*; the work was dedicated to the author's "teacher and friend Otto Ribbeck." The work's origins can be traced far back into Rohde's student days, even to his schooldays (MS, Heidelberg 1997, from the winter semester 1867–68, with plans for "Lucius oder der Esel"). In his diary one can see how erotic experiences and Schopenhauer's philosophy came together in a question on the history of literary genres (*Cogitata*: 2 [Cr.; October 1867; supplements after the manuscript]; cf. Rohde, *Roman*: 179 [Schopenhauer on the novel]). How can literature with its fixed types and genres (novel, drama) grasp "life," "the whole," the "incalculable and individual," "the play of shadows on the wall, whose brief life exists precisely in the eternal flux of gay colors"? The question that was then occupying his friends in Leipzig and would soon fascinate the church historian Franz Overbeck (1837–1905; after April 1870 in Basel) was: whence does literature arise, and how does life, the true, unique, subjective life—for Rohde, inner life, psychology (*Roman*: 129)—relate to its representation in the dead monuments of literature? In response to questions such as these Nietzsche investigated the birth of tragedy from cult, play, and music, while Overbeck drew a boundary between the primitive history of the Christian church, its cult, and its original texts ("Urliteratur"), on the one hand, and its literary treatment in Church historiography and patristic literature, on the other. Rohde, too, was interested in origins; it was no accident that the "forerunners" of the Greek novel appear in the very title of his book. Their subject, however, and their place in life, which Rohde was seeking, was love. Thus his definition reads: ". . . this Greek novel [is] essentially nothing but narrative love-poetry" (*Roman*: 10; cf. Cancik, "Typus" ¶3.2.2: "Urgeschichte und Literaturbegriff").

More recent research has overturned Rohde's chronology. Chariton dates not from the fifth or the sixth century A.D. (*Roman*, 520ff.) but from the first or the second century. Modern scholarship has a new conception of the significance of rhetoric and historiography for the history of the genre, and it has attempted to relate the novel's religious language and allusions to the "new" Hellenistic religions. Rohde's first masterwork remains important as a stage in the study of the novel and in the writing of the history of literature, as a document of its age because of its connection with Schopenhauer and with Rohde's friends in Basel, and because it deals with the question that occupied them all, the origin of literature from life.

In the summer of 1878 Erwin Rohde was called from the kingdom of Saxony to the University of Tübingen in the kingdom of Württemberg. He succeeded Wilhelm Sigmund Teuffel (1820–1878), who, together with Ernst C. Walz (1802–1857), had succeeded in freeing philological studies in Württemberg from their theological and philosophical yoke. Only since 1838 had the University of Tübingen possessed a philological seminar, thus making it possible for a student to enter the teaching profession without having studied theology. But Württemberg clearly clung much longer than all the other German states to the connection of the clerical office with the teaching profession. Rohde thus found in the university community of Tübingen, a "moss-grown" university in which the Protestant seminary and the theological faculties exerted a strong influence while the neo-humanistic movement was a late and feeble arrival. Here Rohde worked with unspectacular but long-continued success from 1878 to 1886; in the last year he was dean of the philosophical faculty. He turned with renewed energy to "cultural history" and the history of religions, and he began collecting the materials that would finally weigh "like a nightmare" on his breast: the preliminary studies for *Psyche* (E. Rohde to F. Overbeck 20 December 1886; cf. E. Rohde to F. Overbeck 9 December 1883).

His transfer to Leipzig, the university of Ritschl and the scene of his youthful friendship—a transfer which Otto Ribbeck and Nietzsche had encouraged and which everyone awaited with the highest hopes—was a catastrophe. His attempt to renew his ties with Nietzsche failed. The stress of living in a large city, the pace of Saxon industry, and the presence of jealous colleagues drove Rohde and his family back to the river Neckar. As early as the autumn of 1886 Rohde accepted a call to Heidelberg. He became director of the philological seminar, senator, dean, and finally (1894–1895) pro-rector of the University. He bought a home in Neuenheim, on land the Romans had settled. He had reached the high point in his professional career and his family happiness.

While working on his study of the novel Rohde had already conceived of a "book about the vicissitudes of the belief in immortality." He found a point of approach in the contradictory pronouncements given by the various religions and philosophies concerning the soul and its manner of existence post-mortem, the "next world," and the compensation to be granted in another life for unhappiness and injustice in this life. Rohde compared the heroic solution to these questions in Homer with the Buddhist's expectation of complete annihilation and the short-sighted thoughtlessness of the rabble: "What would be left for one who despises this? What would be left for a whole people that has lost its faith? Here is a looming question for the future" (*Cogitata* 53 [24 January 1874]).

More than fifteen years later Rohde published an answer: *Psyche. Seelencult und Unsterblichkeitsglaube der Griechen*. This book of nearly eight hundred pages was also stylistically ambitious, and it sold well. Rohde investigated the popular and philosophical conceptions of the soul, the spirits of the dead, the beyond, and immortality, as well as the religious realization of these concepts in the cults of the dead, of heroes, and of chthonic deities in the classical mystery religions, in the cult of Dionysus, and among the Orphics. His discussion, which carefully and clearly organizes a wealth of material, gives a thematic cross-section of the whole range of the history of Greek religion, the main lines of which Rohde briefly summarized once more in his inaugural address as pro-rector ("Die Religion der Griechen," 1895). Thus Rohde's *Psyche* became, especially in educated circles, the authoritative history of Greek religion, after F. G. Welcker's *Griechische Götterlehre* (1857). Only around 1930 was Rohde's book superseded by the works of Walter F. Otto (*Die Götter Griechenlands*, 1929; *Dionysos*, 1933) and Ulrich von Wilamowitz-Moellendorff (*Der Glaube der Hellenen*, 1931–32). Rohde writes as a layman, a rationalist, and a free-thinker, sober and pious, vehemently rejecting clerical profundity and fanaticism while retaining a deep respect for the simple piety of the people, which endures forever in the same forms. This is Rohde's answer to the "looming question." He still retains full confidence in the "spirit of Hellenism": "But it never runs dry; it vanishes to return, it conceals itself to re-emerge" (*Psyche*, 10th ed., 1925: 2:404).

Rohde's history of religion, like his book on the novel, is "modern." The title points intentionally to psychology; the new theories of ethnology and the study of religions are critically accepted—e.g., evolutionism, animism. An important element in his religio-historical analysis is Dionysos. In his cult asceticism, dance, narcotics, and possession are used; from these arose, Rohde maintains, the belief in an immortal soul and the desire for union with the deity. But Dionysos, according to Rohde (and in this point Wilamowitz follows him) is an alien, non-Greek god. Dionysian mysticism and the belief in the soul's immortality are the consequences of a collective spiritual malady. The contrast with Nietzsche's Dionysian psychology is evident. To him Dionysos was heightened life, and even Dionysian madness was a "neurosis of health" (Nietzsche, "Versuch einer Selbstkritik" [1886] cap. 4). Modern research has refuted the essential points in Rohde's analysis: Dionysos is an ancient god in Hellas, and the belief in the soul's immortality cannot be derived from a single source.

While Rohde was preparing his *Psyche* for the press, his friend Nietzsche fell ill. On 7 January 1889 Rohde received a note from Turin in which Nietzsche dared "to translate [him] to the plane of the gods"; Nietzsche signed himself "Dionysos" (F. Nietzsche to E. Rohde, 3–4 January 1889). Afterward Rohde reread Nietzsche's *Zarathustra* (E. Rohde to F. Overbeck 4 April 1889) and detected in it "the deeply melancholy echo of a great soul's descent into the abyss" (E. Rohde to F. Overbeck 17 May 1892). But he did not see his friend again until 1894—"he obviously feels nothing anymore" (E. Rohde to F. Overbeck 27 December 1894). Rohde had traveled to Naumburg to advise the philosopher's sister in setting up her Nietzsche Archive. A second meeting between Rohde and Elisabeth Förster-Nietzsche, supposedly in the winter of 1896–1897 in Frankfurt, is probably a fiction invented by the archive's directress; it bears witness, however, to the prestige that Rohde's name lent to the Archive (cf. E. Förster-F. Nietzsche to E. Rohde, 28 June 1897).

A meeting with Frau Cosima Wagner in Heidelberg induced Rohde to publish in the *Bayreuther Blätter*, despite his earlier refusals to do so; he had a slightly abridged version of his address on the religion of the Greeks reprinted in the Wagnerian journal. Thus at the end of his life, apparently by chance, Rohde appears in a group portrait that recapitulates his beginnings, ignores contradictions, and overemphasizes the antimodernistic points of agreement: Wagner, Nietzsche, Rohde—the composer of genius, the philosopher marked by fate, the conscientious scholar. It was in this configuration that Rohde exerted his influence on the Wilhelmine period.

Completion of *Psyche*, renewal of old ties with Naumburg and Bayreuth, numerous honors as a mark of his success, and the birth of his second son (Hans Adolph, 1 July 1895), opened up new prospects, or so it seemed. A charming short work on Friedrich Creuzer (1771–1858) and Karoline von Günderode (1780–1806) testifies to his attachment to Heidelberg. But exhaustion, general depression, and grief for the death of his young son (December 1896) exacerbated the symptoms that Rohde had been noting for decades in his letters: stomach pains, constipation, compression in the chest, loss of appetite, nervous palpitations of the heart, and shortness of breath. His doctors could make nothing of the symptoms from which the sedentary intellectual suffered; the usual cures at Marienbad and Meran were unsuccessful. In the night of 10–11 January 1898 Erwin Rohde died at his home in Heidelberg. The exact cause of death is unknown.

His one-time rival, the future historian of Greek religion, Ulrich von Wilamowitz-Moellendorff, in a letter to Otto Crusius defined his attitude toward the dead man. "Rohde's death moved me deeply, of course, since he was an irreplaceable power in scholarship. I have seldom felt more vividly how the immanent evolution of scholarship leads the most different men, by the most different paths, to the same goal than in the case of the attitude toward religion that he and Diels and I (in contrast to Usener, for example) gradually adopted; but in addition I have never learned so much on the subject from any living scholar as from Rohde" (Wilamowitz to Crusius, 24 February 1898; transcript by W. M. Calder, III, quoted in Henrichs, *Der Glaube*, 285 and n. 109).

In the "autobiographical notes" of Overbeck the configuration of persons takes firm shape: "In this sense I sincerely and heartily loved them all, most of all that one among them with whom I advanced least far in the intimacy of our relations, Rohde. But this was in any case at least partly because our relations, once we had at length come together, were never able to continue for long at a time. For this reason his premature death (1898) fell as an insupportable blow on my heart more heavily than that of Treitschke or Nietzsche. And that not merely because the last-named friends, for different reasons, were both dead to me before their deaths" (Overbeck, *Nachlass* Basel A 267e: "Meine Freunde" [written 1901] p. 2).

Translated by Michael Armstrong

Books

De Iulii Pollucis in apparatu scaenico enarrando fontibus. Accedit de Pollucis libri secundi fontibus epimetrum. Leipzig, 1870.

Afterphilologie. Zur Beleuchtung des von dem Dr. Phil. Ulrich von Wilamowitz-Möllendorff herausgegebenen Pamphlets: "Zukunftsphilologie!" Sendschrieben eines Philologen an Richard Wagner. Leipzig, 1872.

Der griechische Roman und seine Vorläufer. Leipzig, 1876; 2d ed. 1900; 3d ed. 1914; 3d ed. reprinted with a preface by K. Kerényi, Leipzig, 1974.

Psyche. Seelencult und Unsterblichkeitsglaube der Griechen. Freiburg, Vol. I, 1890; Vol. II, 1893–94; 2d ed. 1897; 3d ed. 1903; 4th ed. 1907; 9th and 10th eds. 1925, with an introduction by Otto Weinreich. English translation from the 8th edition by W. B. Hillis as Psyche: The Cults of Souls and the Belief in Immortality among the Greeks, London and New York, 1925; reprinted, New York, 1966.

Friedrich Creuzer und Karoline von Günderode. Briefe und Dichtungen. Edited by Erwin Rohde. Heidelberg, 1896.

Articles (Collected)

Kleine Schriften. Edited by Fritz Schöll. Tübingen and Leipzig, 1901. Includes bibliography.

Articles (Review)

"Die Geburt der Tragödie aus dem Geiste der Musik. Von Friedrich Nietzsche." Norddeutsche Allgemeine Zeitung, 26 May 1872.

Sources

Bibliography

Kleine Schriften. Edited by Fritz Schöll. Tübingen and Leipzig, 1901.

Biographical

Bernoulli, C. A. Franz Overbeck und Friedrich Nietzsche. Eine Freundschaft. Two volumes. Jena, 1908.

Burkert, Walter. "Griechische Mythologie und die Geistesgeschichte der Moderne." Entretiens sur l'antiquité classique 26 (1980) 159–199.

Calder III, W. M. "The Wilamowitz-Nietzsche Struggle: New Documents and a Reappraisal." Nietzsche-Studien 12 (1983) 214–254.

Cancik, Hubert. "Erwin Rohde—Ein Philologe der Bismarckzeit." In: Semper Apertus. Sechshundert Jahre Ruprecht-Karls-Universität Heidelberg 1386–1986. Festschrift in sechs Bänden. Berlin, Heidelberg, New York, and Tokyo, 1985: 2:436–505.

———. " ' . . . die Befreiung der philologischen Studien in Württemberg.' Zur Gründungsgeschichte des Philologischen Seminars in Tübingen 1838." *Tübinger Universitätszeitung* 37 (1989) 8–11.

——— and Hildegard Cancik-Lindemaier. "Der 'psychologische Typus des Erlösers' und die Möglichkeit seiner Darstellung bei Franz Overbeck und Friedrich Nietzsche." In *Franz Overbecks unerledigte Anfragen an das Christentum.* Edited by R. Brändle and E. Stegemann. Munich, 1988: 108–135.

Crusius, Otto. *Erwin Rohde. Ein biographischer Versuch.* Tübingen and Leipzig, 1902.

Gründer, Karl, editor. *Der Streit um Nietzsches "Geburt der Tragödie." Die Schriften von E. Rohde, R. Wagner, U. von Wilamowitz-Moellendorff.* Hildesheim, 1969.

Henrichs, Albert. " 'Der Glaube der Hellenen': Religionsgeschichte als Glaubensbekenntnis und Kulturkritik." In *Wilamowitz nach 50 Jahren.* Edited by W. M. Calder III, H. Flashar, and Th. Lindken. Darmstadt, 1985: 263–305 (especially pp. 280ff.: Rohde and Wilamowitz).

McGinty, P. *Interpretation and Dionysos: Method in the Study of a God.* Religion and Reason 16. The Hague, Paris, New York, 1978.

Overbeck, Franz. "Erinnerungen an Friedrich Nietzsche." Edited by C. A. Bernoulli. *Die Neue Rundschau* 1 (1906) 209–330. Reprinted (slightly abridged) in C. A. Bernoulli. *Franz Overbeck und Friedrich Nietzsche.* 2:157–161. (See below.)

Silk, M. S., and J. P. Stern. *Nietzsche on Tragedy.* Cambridge, 1989.

Wagner, Cosima. *Die Tagebücher.* Edited with commentary by M. Gregor-Dellin and D. Mack. Vol. 1: 1869–77. Vol 2: 1878–83. Munich, 1976, 1977.

Letters

Däuble, Hedwig. "Friedrich Nietzsche und Erwin Rohde. Mit bisher ungedruckten Briefen." *Nietzsche-Studien* 5 (1976) 321–354.

Nietzsche, Friedrich. *Nietzsche: Briefwechsel. Kritische Ausgabe.* Edited by Giorgio Colli and Mazzino Montinari. Berlin and New York, 1975.

———. *Briefwechsel mit Erwin Rohde.* Edited by Elisabeth Förster-Nietzsche and Fritz Schöll. Leipzig, 1923.

Franz Overbeck—Erwin Rohde. *Korrespondenz.* Edited with commentary by A. Patzer [*sub prelo*].

Ribbeck, Emma. *Otto Ribbeck. Ein Bild seines Lebens aus seinen Briefen 1846–1898.* Edited by Emma Ribbeck. Stuttgart, 1901.

Die Briefe des Freiherrn Carl von Gersdorff an Friedrich Nietzsche. IV. Teil: Ergänzungsband: *Ausgewählte Briefe Gersdorffs über Nietzsches Leben und Werk an Erwin Rohde, Richard Wagner, und Carl Fuchs aus den Jahren 1872–1903.* Edited by Erhart Thierbach. Gesellschaft der Freunde des Nietzsche-Archivs 8–11. Nietzsche-Archiv Weimar 1937; reprinted Nendeln, Liechtenstein, 1975 (Gersdorff to Rohde, 1–21).

Papers (*Selection; mostly unpublished*)

Basel. Universitätsbibliothek. (*Nachlaß* of F. Overbeck, C. A. Bernoulli.)

Bayreuth. Archiv der Richard-Wagner-Gedenkstätte/National-Archiv Bayreuth. (Correspondence from and to Rohde; books donated by Rohde.)

Bonn. Universitätsbibliothek. (Correspondence of Franz Rühl; Rohde to Usener.)

Frankfurt. Schopenhauer-Archiv. (Rohde's copy of Ed. v. Hartmann. Philosophie des Unbewussten, with marginalia by Rohde.)

Heidelberg. Universitätsbibliothek. (Scholarly and personal Nachlaß of E. Rohde, O. Ribbeck, F. Schöll.)

Karlsruhe. Generallandesarchiv. (Official school reports, inspection reports.)

Karlsruhe. Private possession. (Personal Nachlaß; correspondence.)

Munich. Bayrische Staatsbibliothek. (Nachlaß of Otto Crusius and W. Krumbacher, with letters by and about Rohde.)

Stuttgart. Württembergische Landesbibliothek. (Student notes of Rohde's lectures at the University of Tübingen.)

Tübingen. Universitätsbibliothek. (Official proceedings of the Dean's office, reports on promotion and hiring of faculty, students' notes of lectures, letters.)

Weimar. Goethe- und Schiller-Archiv. (Contents of the former "Nietzsche-Archiv." Correspondence of Friedrich Nietzsche, Elisabeth Förster-Nietzsche.)

M. Rostovtzeff
10 November 1870 – 20 October 1952

J. RUFUS FEARS
Boston University

Michael Rostovtzeff was the most significant ancient historian of the first half of the twentieth century. In his methodological innovations and range of knowledge, he can be compared to Theodor Mommsen and Eduard Meyer. In his comprehensive vision of a major theme of ancient history and his ability to translate this into sustained literary production, he is the peer of George Grote and Edward Gibbon.

Mikhail Ivanovich Rostovcev—Michael Rostovtzeff—was born in Russia, in the town of Zhitomir in the Ukraine. The vicissitudes of his life as well as the cosmopolitan character of his scholarship are reflected in the variant spellings which his name assumes in his publications. Rostovtzeff was the form which he habitually used in the last thirty years of his life, after his emigration from Russia. His family was Russian and is attested as early as the reign of Catherine the Great in the person of Pavel Rostovcev, a *meschanin* ("lower-class townsman") and *kupec* ("merchant") (Wes: 207). Both Rostovtzeff's grandfather (Yakov Pavlovich) and father (Ivan Yakovlevich) were educators. His father rose from being a teacher of Latin and Greek at the gymnasium in Kiev (1853) to the position of curator, the chief educational official, of the district of Orenburg (1890–1904). To him Rostovtzeff owed his sound philological training, his interest in classical antiquity, and perhaps also an appreciation for the bourgeoisie as the most progressive and supportive element in an enlightened monarchical system, a concept which would loom large in Rostovtzeff's historical thinking about the ancient world.

After studies at the classical gymnasium in Kiev and briefly at the University of Kiev, Rostovtzeff entered the University of St. Petersburg in 1890. His teachers included Peter V. Nikitin, Victor Jernstedt, Theodor T. Sokolov, Thaddeus Zielinski, and Nikodeme P. Kondakov. Entries on several of Rostovtzeff's teachers in the Russian encyclopedia, *Russkiy Entsiklopedicheskiy Slovar* (St. Petersburg, 1890–1907) (cited as *Slovar*), give useful summaries of their achievements at the time Rostovtzeff was studying with them. Sokolov was an ancient historian, who published on Greek political and diplomatic history (*Slovar* 30: 736; for one of his contributions, see *Bibliotheca Philologica Classica* 24 [1897] 166). Jernstedt was a Hellenist, who, among other contributions, prepared an edition of Antiphon. His *Opuscula* (St. Petersburg, 1907) contains a list of publications (*Slovar* 11: 677). Nikitin was a textual critic, who also wrote on Greek drama, including a study in Russian of *The History of the Dramatic Competition in Athens* (St. Petersburg, 1882) (*Slovar* 21 [1897] 81). Jernstedt, Nikitin, and Sokolov all published largely in Russian and consequently were known primarily in Russian academic circles. By contrast, as the author of *Cicero im Wandel der Jahrhunderte* (1897), the Pole Zielinski (1859–1944) had a European reputation. Among these teachers, it was probably Kondakov who had the most seminal influence on the young Rostovtzeff. He directed Rostovtzeff's attention to the monuments of South Russia, took the young student on a tour of Spain, and must have been instrumental in giving Rostovtzeff that critical appreciation of art history and the monuments as a historical source which distinguished him among ancient historians of his own and subsequent generations (see the entry on Kondakov in *Slovar* 15 [1895] 927). Rostovtzeff himself presented appreciations of three of his teachers, Zielinski, Nikitin, and Kondakov (see items 399–403, 405 in Welles 1: 379–80).

In 1892, Rostovtzeff took his first university degree with a thesis on Pompeii "in the light of new excavations." In 1898 he received the master's degree with a thesis on the history of tax-farming (farming out of tax-collecting rights to publicans) in the Roman empire, later published in a German version under the title *Geschichte der Staatspacht in der römischen Kaiserzeit bis Diokletian*. His doctoral dissertation, submitted in 1903, was the basis for his 1905 German monograph *Römische Bleitesserae: Ein Beitrag zur Sozial- und Wirtschaftgeschichte der römischen Kaiserzeit*. His teaching career began in 1892 with a three-year stint at the prestigious gymnasium at Tsarkoe Selo. In 1898 he began teaching Latin at the University of St. Petersburg and ancient history at the Women's College in the same city. In 1901 he married one of his students, Sophia M. Kulchitski. A formidable personality in her own right, she would share the trials of his life and assist his scholarly vocation in a variety of ways, including preparing the indices to his books.

The formative event in this period of Rostovtzeff's academic training were the three years 1895–1898, that he spent on a traveling fellowship in Europe and the Near East. Intensive visits to sites in the classical lands were complemented by periods of study in Vienna, in the collections of the Cabinet des Médailles in Paris and the British Museum in London, and at the German Archaeological Institute in Rome. In 1900, he visited Austria for the first time, studying archaeology and epigraphy in the Vienna seminars of Otto Benndorf and Eugen Bormann. Under the guidance of Bormann, a pupil of Mommsen, Rostovtzeff began work on an inscription from Halicarnassus, which would lead to his master's thesis on tax-farming. Under the guidance of Ernest Babelon and with the collaboration of Maurice Prou, he carried out that detailed catalogue and analysis of Roman lead tokens which would serve as his doctoral dissertation. With August Mau he deepened his knowledge of Pompeii; in 1911, *Römische Mitteilungen* served as a vehicle for Rostovtzeff's major study, "Die hellenistisch-römische Architekturlandschaft." Under the influence of Ulrich Wilcken and his approach to the social and administrative history of the Roman empire, Rostovtzeff began the papyrological researches into Roman agrarian history which would achieve fruition in his *Studien zur Geschichte des römischen Kolonates* (1910), a major contribution which made Rostovtzeff's reputation. That same year, he received his first honorary degree, a doctorate from the University of Leipzig.

Thus, by the outbreak of the First World War, the forty-four-year-old Michael Rostovtzeff was a scholar of international distinction. Thoroughly grounded in the major ancillary disciplines of archaeology, epigraphy, numismatics, and papyrology, and with a profound knowledge of the monumental sources, his research and writing were fully abreast of those innovative scholarly currents which were giving new scope, definition, and importance to the social and economic history of the Greco-Roman world. His scholarship was cosmopolitan, and he had published works in German, French, and Italian as well as in his native Russian. His scholarship was not only learned and exacting but also bold. He was audacious enough to sketch in four pages so controversial a topic as the origin of European serfdom or to state that "the history of the *tesserae* reflects the whole development and gradual establishment of the Roman Empire" (*Römische Bleitesserae*: 39). Rostovtzeff's European standing is suggested by the fact that in 1914, Wilamowitz and Eduard Meyer invited him to write a social and economic history of the Hellenistic and Roman world. In his own country, he was reaching the pinnacle of his profession. Professor of Latin at the Imperial University of St. Petersburg and Professor of Ancient History at the St. Petersburg College for Women, he would become in 1916 a member of the Imperial Academy of Sciences.

Rostovtzeff was and remained throughout his life a Russian patriot, "deeply attached" to his country. When the exigencies of war limited his access to western Europe and the classical lands, he "plunged into a detailed investigation of . . .[the] antiquities of South Russia in order to better understand the peculiar aspect which Greek art and life assumed in South Russia" (Rostovtzeff cited in Welles 3: 130–31). He was completing a major multi-volume work on Scythia and the Bosporus when the Bolsheviks seized power, and he felt compelled to emigrate in 1918.

Rostovtzeff was among the founders of the Constitutional Democratic Party. As a Liberal, he had welcomed the first stages of the Russian Revolution, which promised to bring constitutional government to Russia. For Rostovtzeff, "the ideals of our intelligentsia have always been democracy and freedom" ("Why the Russian Intelligentsia is Opposed to the Bolshevist Regime": 793). He saw the Kerenski government as working to preserve cultural institutions "built up by centuries of creative work" ("Proletarian Culture in Bolshevist Russia": 459). Rostovtzeff aided in the cultural task of bringing liberal government to Russia and he wrote a small volume on *The Birth of the Roman Empire* for the Kerenski government. The collapse of the Provisional Government and the Bolshevik seizure of power made his situation in

Russia intolerable. His abhorrence for Bolshevism was total. The Bolsheviks were "a regime of violence, bloodshed, dictatorship, slavery, and enmity towards true culture" ("Why the Russian Intelligentsia . . .": 793). For Rostovtzeff, as a result of Bolshevism "Russia is completely enslaved, liberty is dead, culture and religion are being exterminated, all morality is being driven out of the souls of our children" ("Should Scientists Return to Russia?": 372). In these and similar essays written immediately after his emigration, Rostovtzeff describes the intellectual and political devastation of Russian educational life which forced him to leave the "terrifying realities" and to escape imprisonment. Prison was not the most serious of fates awaiting Rostovtzeff had he remained in Russia; according to his figures, seventeen of his colleagues in the Russian Academy of Sciences died in 1918 ("Proletarian Culture in Bolshevist Russia": 486).

His flight from Russia cost him his library and the manuscript of his book *Scythia and the Bosporus*. In 1925 a portion of this was published by Soviet scholars without consulting Rostovtzeff. He himself would supervise the subsequent German translation of this work, published in 1931 as *Skythien und der Bosporus*. In the meantime, Rostovtzeff had become an American academic.

After leaving Russia in 1918, Rostovtzeff spent two years at Oxford, where he was associated with Queens College and lectured on the social and economic history of the Hellenistic and Roman world. He had the admiration and assistance of scholars like J. G. C. Anderson and Sir Ellis Minns, who were capable of appreciating the range of his learning; and the Clarendon Press would become his publisher. But he failed to become Camden Professor or even to receive a permanent appointment. Thirty years later Hugh Last still felt compelled to explain why Rostovtzeff was unsuited to Oxford and was better off in America: Apparently, Rostovtzeff had too thick an accent, knew too much, and did not keep his knowledge to himself (*JRS* 43 [1953] 133–134). Rostovtzeff may also have irritated British intellectuals by seeking to destroy with facts their Pollyannish views of the Bolsheviks ("Proletarian Culture": 459).

In 1920, at the urging of W. L. Westermann, Rostovtzeff received a one-year appointment as professor of history at the University of Wisconsin; in the next year, it was made permanent. In the preface to his *A History of the Ancient World*, he spoke of his deep gratitude to the University of Wisconsin, which "in the darkest hour of my life made it possible for me to resume my learned studies and to carry them on without interruption." In 1925 he became Sterling Professor of Ancient History and Archaeology at Yale University. In 1928 he also assumed the position of Director of the Yale University Expedition at Dura-Europos. After his retirement from the Sterling Chair in 1939, he served as director of Archaeological Studies until 1944. Following the massive task of researching and writing *The Social and Economic History of the Hellenistic World* in 1941, nervous exhaustion and depression began to incapacitate Rostovtzeff. This condition was aggravated by his preoccupation with the Second World War and contemporary events, especially the murder of Leon Trotsky. Finally a lobotomy left Rostovtzeff incapable of carrying out sustained intellectual efforts for some years before his death at New Haven in 1952.

The years in America saw Rostovtzeff achieve the summit of scholarly achievement and recognition. He was a member of almost every relevant European learned academy; to his honorary doctorate from Leipzig were added degrees from Oxford, Cambridge, Athens, Harvard, Chicago, and Wisconsin. He declined offers of chairs from the University of Berlin and from Harvard. In 1935 he was President of the American Historical Association.

This recognition was based upon a record of remarkable scholarly productivity in the period from 1920 to 1941. His studies of South Russia led him further afield to problems of Aryan art, including a monograph, *The Animal Style in South Russia and China*. Numerous articles and notes explored specific questions of Hellenistic and Roman social and economic history. Already in 1922, his papyrological studies led to the publication of the monograph *A Large Estate in Egypt in the Third Century* B.C.: *A Study in Economic History*, a work "no less astonishing for its diligence in collecting together so large and dispersed a mass of documents as it is for its imaginative handling of that material" (Bowersock 2: 396). Rostovtzeff's powers of synthesis are nowhere shown to better effect than in the seven chapters which he contributed in this period to various volumes of *The Cambridge Ancient History*. Although he excluded a systematic study of religious developments from his major books on the Hellenistic and Roman world, Rostovtzeff was himself deeply interested in ancient religion. His Colver Lectures, published under the title *Mystic Italy*, were an essay in understanding the religious evolution of the early Roman empire, the process by which religion and mysticism triumphed over science and materialism, giving birth to Christianity. Among his immediate predecessors as Colver Lecturers were the Harvard medievalist Charles Homer Haskins, the jurist Roscoe Pound, and the Supreme Court Justice John H. Clark. Rostovtzeff addressed his lectures to a broader audience and his other writings from this period, such as his *Iranians and Greeks in South Russia* and *Caravan Cities* attest to his desire to bring the results of his scholarship to a broader educated public. As a teacher of large undergraduate lecture courses, he produced in two volumes *A History of the Ancient World*, which remains the most thoughtful and stimulating textbook ever written in the field.

His great contributions, however, were his two magisterial books, *The Social and Economic History of the Roman Empire* (1926) and *The Social and Economic History of the Hellenistic World* (1941), and the excavations at Dura-Europos.

Both histories, that of the Roman Empire and that of the Hellenistic World, were immediately recognized as masterpieces of scholarship. Of *The Social and Economic History of the Roman World*, Tenney Frank wrote that "it is safe to say that no single volume dealing with the Roman Empire exists that is at the same time so full of stimulating suggestions, so packed with important details, so penetrating in its interpretations, so original, so scholarly as this (*AJP* 47 [1926] 290). Frank then went on to compare Rostovtzeff to Gibbon, Grote, and Mommsen. W. W. Tarn called *The Social and Economic History of the Hellenistic World* "a very great book, alike in its vast learning, in the ease with which the author handles his huge and complex mass of often very refractory material, in the closeness of its reasoning, and in the sanity of its judgements" (*JRS* 31 [1941] 165).

The Social and Economic History of the Roman Empire was much the more controversial of the two great books. Its preface boldly stated the thesis that the evidence of the book was marshaled to support (xii–xiii, xv–xvi):

The constitutional monarchy of the Antonines rested on the urban middle class throughout the empire and on the self-government of the cities. Despite his autocratic power, the monarch was regarded as the chief magistrate of the Roman people. At his side, as an advisory council, stood the Senate which represented the municipal *bourgeoisie*. The imperial bureaucracy and the army were coordinated with the self-governing bodies in Italy and the provinces. This adaptation of the Constitution of the Empire to the leading social forces had one weak point. The foundation of the Empire, the urban middle class, was not strong enough to support the fabric of the world-state. Resting as it did on the toil of the lower classes—the peasants of the country and the proletariat of the cities—the municipal *bourgeoisie*, like the imperial aristocracy and bureaucracy, was unwilling to open its ranks to the lower orders. All three groups became more and more exclusive, and the society of the Empire became more and more divided into two classes or castes: the *bourgeoisie* and the masses, the *honestiores* and the *humiliores*. A sharp antagonism arose and gradually took the form of an antagonism between the country and the cities. The emperors sought to remove this hostility by promoting urbanization and by supporting the peasants in the country and the workmen in the cities. The effort was in vain. It was this antagonism which was the ultimate cause of the crisis of the third century, when the aspirations of the lower classes were expressed by the army and countenanced by the emperors. After the failure of the Severi to establish a *modus vivendi* between the two classes, the struggle degenerated into civil and social war and the political anarchy of the second half of the third century A.D. The *bourgeoisie* and the upper class of society were destroyed, and there arose a new form of government which was more or less suited to the conditions: the oriental despotism of the fourth and fifth centuries, based on the army, on a strong bureaucracy, and on the mass of peasants. . . . The spiritual, intellectual, and artistic life of the Empire developed along the same lines as its economic and social life. The late Republic and the early Empire created a refined, delicate, highly aristocratic civilization, foreign alike to the urban middle class and to the masses. The same is true of the lofty philosophic religion of the higher classes. As time passed, this high civilization was gradually absorbed by the growing middle class and adapted to their standards and requirements. In becoming so widely diffused, the delicate creation of the first century was bound to become more and more simplified, more and more elementary, more and more materialistic. Even this civilization, however, remained foreign to the lower classes, and it was finally destroyed by them in their onslaught on the cities and the city *bourgeoisie*.

The book and its thesis bore the impress of the Russian Revolution. Already in "Proletarian Culture," one of the essays written for the émigré journal *Struggling Russia*, Rostovtzeff drew a parallel between the rise of Bolshevism and the forces which destroyed ancient civilization. A more developed scholarly statement of his thesis was then published in his article "La crise sociale et politique de l'empire romain au IIIe siècle." The genesis of *The Social and Economic History of the Roman Empire* is a model instance of Arnold Toynbee's theory of challenge and response. The shattering of Rostovtzeff's Russian academic career forced him to write the great book in order to gain academic security in his new world. The events of that revolution, superimposed upon the Roman world, provided his theme.

By the time he published *The Social and Economic History of the Hellenistic World*, Rostovtzeff had academic security and fame. More than one friendly critic has regretted that the volumes on the Hellenistic world lack the fire of Rostovtzeff's treatment of the Roman Empire (Heichelheim: 129–30; Momigliano: 101); and it is generally conceded that the volumes on the Hellenistic world were far more carefully researched and written. Rostovtzeff himself agreed that his treatment of the Hellenistic world was far more exhaustive of its topic. But he saw the two books as complementary; and there was no backing away from the fundamental thesis of his study of the Roman Empire. For Rostovtzeff, the most momentous development of the Hellenistic period was the consolidation of the Greek *bourgeoisie*, which became the pivot of the social system of the Greek cities in the Hellenistic period. It was a legacy of Hellenism to the Roman emperors, who chose to make the Greek *bourgeoisie* the pillar of their rule over the provinces of the empire (2:1304–06).

While researching and writing his history of the Hellenistic world, Rostovtzeff was simultaneously engaged in another major project, the excavations at Dura-Europos. The site had been briefly explored in two seasons, 1922 and 1923, by Franz Cumont and the French Academy. Learning that the excavations were not to be continued, and with the full support and cooperation of Cumont, Rostovtzeff began to plan a joint French-American expedition at Dura. "Here, as a result of the conquest of the Persian Empire by Alexander, several great civilizations of the past were brought into closer contact than under the Persian rule. I refer to the Greek civilization of the conquerors, the Iranian civilization, the civilization of India, that of Babylonia and Mesopotamia, and those of the western Semites and the Arabs and the Anatolians . . .The uniting link between these was the Greek civilization, spread by Alexander and his successors, especially the Seleucids, over the whole of the former Persian Empire and part of India" (*Dura-Europos and Its Art*: 5–6).

The interests which led Rostovtzeff to Dura were already reflected in his work on South Russia, where the currents of Greek and oriental cultures met. "In Dura he recognized a rare opportunity to explore two of the fields in which he was most interested: the synthesis of Eastern and Western art in the classical period, and the contribution that parchments and papyri might make in a region where none had been previously found" (Hopkins: 25). Moreover, as Clark Hopkins notes, Rostovtzeff was also "eager to make a truly significant contribution to American universities," to repay, in a sense, Wisconsin and Yale for having made possible in a new world a new life of study and teaching about the Old World.

Rostovtzeff may have been "more at home in armchair archaeology than with roughing it in the field" (Hopkins: 29), but he had the genius to recognize the possibilities of Dura, the energy to organize the expedition and get it funded, and the managerial ability to guide ten seasons of one of the most significant archaeological achievements of the twentieth century. "Today hardly a book that touches on the ancient Eastern Mediterranean sphere, on the history of religion or art in the Orient, is without reference to the spectacular find of the painted Christian chapel of Dura, or the astonishing revelation of a standing Jewish synagogue whose four walls had been covered with paintings drawn from the Old Testament" (B. Goldman in Hopkins: xv).

The Social and Economic History of the Roman Empire, *The Social and Economic History of the Hellenistic World*, and Dura-Europos were each a domineering scholarly achievement. The personality of the author of these works was no less domineering. More than one photograph captures the aggressive pose and fierce blue eyes of "a man of great physical strength and exceptional memory, passionate and egotistical, capable of lecturing in six languages and of quarreling in as many" (Momigliano: 91). He was, on occasion at least, as audacious in his private life as in his scholarship. He reportedly accepted his position at Wisconsin without ever having heard of the place. When his visa was held up by the State Department, he sailed to New York without passport or visa and simply walked off the boat unmolested and made his way to Madison (Bowersock 2: 392, 394–95).

Rostovtzeff had observed at first hand the brutalities of the Russian Revolution, and for several years after his emigration from Russia he contributed passionate pieces to various émigré journals, including a call to the American government to render "all possible assistance to General Wrangel" ("Memorandum": 283–85). He did not allow a lost cause to consume his life but retained an abiding interest in contemporary politics; his 1935 Presidential Address to the American Historical Association, "The Hellenistic World and Its Economic Development," begins with a reference to the current world economic crisis. He was himself not unshrewd in economic matters, and he quickly learned how to manipulate the American academic system. At a time when $3,500–4,000 was a good salary for a university professor in America, the jobless Rostovtzeff came to Madison at a salary of $5,000. Within three years he had managed to raise it to $6,500, with every sixth semester off at full pay. Two years later he went to Yale at a still higher salary. It should equally be noted that he was very active in efforts to assist refugee scholars in finding positions. With his colleagues he was perhaps better received by historians than classicists. He was a member of the History Department at Wisconsin, and his contacts with the Classics Department were minimal. Initially, his colleagues in the classics department at Yale sought to have Rostovtzeff placed in another department, fearing rightly that he would change the direction of their department away from literature and philology to history and archaeology. His presidency of the American Historical Association was not reciprocated by a similar office in the American Philological Association, and he was never even considered for the Sather Lectureship (Dow).

His eagerness for research semesters notwithstanding, Rostovtzeff was also a dominating personality as a teacher. He taught his share of basic courses, not only a large undergraduate survey of ancient history but even a course on Russian architecture. The Wisconsin undergraduates called him "Rough Stuff," and he "loved it" (Hopkins: 25). The preface of his *History of the Ancient World*, written for undergraduates, speaks with affection of his Wisconsin students. One of his advanced students from the days in Russia, Elias Bickerman, emigrated to America and became a distinguished historian in his own right. Rostovtzeff and the excavations at Dura-Europos trained a generation of scholars, including Alfred Bellinger, F. E. Brown, Leroy Campbell, R. O. Fink, Frank Gilliam, Clark Hopkins, J. H. Oliver, Henry Rowell, Prescott Townsend, and C. Bradford Welles. Several of these became not only significant scholars but also figures of major influence in the profession. At their best, like Rostovtzeff, their excellence as epigraphers, papyrologists, or archaeologists was grounded in a sound historical knowledge of the ancient world and motivated by a deep appreciation of the languages, literature, and culture of classical antiquity.

From Hugh Last's snide review of *The Social and Economic History of the Roman Empire* in 1926 to the present day, Rostovtzeff has never lacked critics. His theory of the decline and fall of the Roman Empire was an easy target (see Demandt). It may continue to be excerpted in textbooks of sources and problems (e.g. Kagan). However, Rostovtzeff's view of the collapse of the Roman Empire "became and remains a curiosity" (Bowersock 1:19). A less kind recent critic has simply called it "nonsense" (Ferrill).

Much more difficult to shake were the factual foundation and methodological structure of *The Social and Economic History of the Roman Empire* and, more particularly, *The Social and Economic History of the Hellenistic World*. At the zenith of Rostovtzeff's influence, in 1946, Meyer Reinhold published an extremely perceptive analysis of the methodological and conceptual deficiencies of Rostovtzeff's work. But certainly *The Social and Economic History of the Hellenistic World* held sway as the definitive book in the field until well into the second half of the twentieth century. Surveying scholarship in Roman history from 1911 to 1960, Chester Starr called *The Social and Economic History of the Roman Empire* the most famous but not the most important book published in that period (Starr: 151).

Aspects of Rostovtzeff's vision of the ancient world and its economy continue to be of scholarly interest. His view of late antiquity will probably always be able to inspire controversy (see Heuss). Comparison of his views with those of one of the dominant economic and social historians of the late twentieth century, M. I. Finley, can be fruitful (see D'Arms). But the presence of Rostovtzeff is much diminished in the study of social and economic history. The most influential school of ancient economic history, that of M. I. Finley, is fundamentally at odds with Rostovtzeff, and Finley's *The Ancient Economy* is a skillful attack upon Rostovtzeff's basic assumption that the difference between the ancient and modern economies is quantitative rather than qualitative. Finley rejects Rostovtzeff's conceptual framework and is not above calling specific aspects of Rostovtzeff's detailed analysis "imaginative fiction" (*Ancient Economy*: 194 n. 57). The general feeling is that study of the ancient economy has moved beyond Rostovtzeff. In a review essay, aptly titled "Afscheld van Rostovtzeff," H. W. Pleket summarized the importance of three recent books on ancient economic history—Finley, *The Ancient Economy* (1973); Ramsay MacMullen, *Roman Social Relations, 50 B.C. to A.D. 284* (1974); and R. Duncan-Jones, *The Economy of the Roman Empire* (1974)—"With these three books, we say good-bye to Rostovtzeff, not in his capacity as a collector of material or as a 'synthesizer' but rather in his role as the provider of an interpretative framework for the study of the ancient economy" (Pleket: 284).

Not everyone is convinced, however, that Rostovtzeff has departed the scene. Chester Starr is critical of the current disparagement of Rostovtzeff's achievement. "Nowadays . . . it is not considered proper to praise Rostovtzeff, whose conceptual framework is considered weak, leading to 'vagueness' and 'inadequacy' in the treatment of the Hellenistic peasants [the reference is to Finley]. The trouble rather is the fact that he brought with him to the United States 'bourgeois' attitudes fostered in Czarist St. Petersburg that are now out of favor; but the greatness of his work on the Hellenistic era cannot be denied. He was master of as great a range of material as anyone who has worked on the period, visible not only in the notes which occupy his third volume but also in the commentary on the plates—and those illustrations, we must remember, were not incidental decorations of the text but fundamental supports to his arguments" (Starr: 27).

Rostovtzeff's presence is now perhaps more to be noted among Marxist historians who, both in the East and West, continue to feel the need to critique his economic and social views (Várady; de Ste. Croix; Kreissig). In his native Russia, discussion of Rostovtzeff was for some time either "discouraged or controlled" (Momigliano: 93), but the third edition of the *Great Soviet Encyclopedia* gives a balanced appraisal: "Rostovtzeff's overall conception of the Greek and Roman world's development, as set forth in his general works on the socioeconomic history of Hellenism and Rome, is one of modernization. It is built on a recognition of the existence in antiquity of capitalism, an entrepreneurial Greek and Roman bourgeoisie, and proletarian revolutions. Still, the huge mass of factual synthesis of this material, and a number of the conclusions he draws are of great scholarly interest" (Kuzishchin: 292).

Rostovtzeff best summarized his own achievement. It was to describe the society and economy of the Hellenistic world and the Roman Empire as a historical phenomenon, "to follow the trend of evolution, to deal with the social and economic phenomena in the light of the general political, constitutional, and cultural developments of the time, . . . to present the social and economic features of human life not as dry abstractions, in the form of statistics and tabulations, but as living dynamic phenomena, indivisible from and closely related with other equally important features of that life" (*Social and Economic History of the Hellenistic World*: viii). Rostovtzeff undoubtedly learned from the school of German economic and social historians, encouraged by the work of Max Weber and led by Ulrich Wilcken. But it was Rostovtzeff who wrote the big books. After Rostovtzeff it was no longer possible to approach the society and history of the Greco-Roman world from that antiquarian perspective which characterized much of the scholarship of the nineteenth century.

Rostovtzeff's analysis, with its emphasis on tracing the process of historical development, was equally a departure from the more static delineation that Mommsen adopted in describing the Roman legal system or which Wissowa took in his treatment of Roman cult. Methodologically, Rostovtzeff built upon the achievements of Mommsen, Wilcken, and others, fully integrating the inscriptions, coins, papyri, and monuments into his work. But in his range and expertise in the historical use of these sources, he remains unequaled. He is unequaled as well in following his own admonition that we must learn to write history with the aid of archaeology. We are the poorer for the refusal of more recent students of social and economic history to adopt his format of lavish use of plates, richly and minutely described, to buttress and expand the argument of the text.

Rostovtzeff has been called the last of the nineteenth-century historians (Bowersock 1:23). Like Grote and Mommsen, he chose a great theme. But more than that, he shared with them a commitment to liberal values. As another who shared that commitment, Arnaldo Momigliano, has said of Rostovtzeff, "Those who have known him have known greatness. They will cherish the memory of a courageous and honest historian to whom civilization meant creative liberty" (Momigliano: 104).

Books (Selected)

"Pompeii in the Light of New Excavations." Thesis, St. Petersburg, 1892 (published in Russian in the *Journal of the Ministry of Education*, Series IV, no. 291 [1894] 45–101).

Geschichte der Staatspacht in der römischen Kaiserzeit bis Diokletian (German version of St. Petersburg master's thesis). *Philologus* Ergänzungsband 9 (1902) 331–512.

Tesserarum Urbis Romae et Suburbi Plumbearum Sylloge. St. Petersburg, 1903.

Römische Bleitesserae: Ein Beitrag zur Sozial- und Wirtschaftsgeschichte der römischen Kaiserzeit. Klio Beiheft 3. Leipzig, 1905; reprinted Aalen, 1963. (Drawn from St. Petersburg dissertation.)

Studien zur Geschichte des römischen Kolonates. *Archiv für Papyrusforschung* Beiheft 1. Leipzig and Berlin, 1910; reprinted Stuttgart, 1970.

Proletarian Culture. Russian Liberation Committee Series 11. London, 1919.

A Large Estate in Egypt in the Third Century B.C.: *A Study in Economic History*. University of Wisconsin Studies in Social Sciences and History 6. Madison, 1922; reprinted Rome, 1967.

Iranians and Greeks in South Russia. Oxford, 1922; reprinted New York, 1969.

Scythia and Bosporus. Published in Russian. Russian Academy of the History of Material Culture. Leningrad, 1925; German translation by E. Pridik as *Skythien unde der Bosporus. Kritische Übersicht der schriftlichen und archäologischen Quellen*, Berlin, 1931.

A History of the Ancient World. Written in Russian, translated from the Russian by J. D. Duff. Vol. I: *The Orient and Greece*; vol. II: *Rome*. Oxford, 1926–1927; *Greece*, ed. E. Bickerman, New York, 1963 (a slightly revised reprint of chapters I–II, parts of VI and VII, chapters XII–XXVI of the 2d ed. [1930] of

The Orient and Greece); *Rome*, ed. E. Bickerman, New York, 1960 (reprint of the second corrected impression [1928] of *Rome*); both reprinted Westport, CT, 1971; Bulgarian translation (1932, 1937); German translation by H. H. Schaeder as *Geschichte der alten Welt*, Wiesbaden, 1941–1942; reprinted 1955; Dutch translation (1955); Italian translation as *Storia del mondo antico* Florence, 1965.

The Social and Economic History of the Roman Empire. Oxford, 1926; 2d ed., rev. by P. M. Fraser, 1957; German translation (1931); Italian translation by G. Sanna (preface by G. de Sanctis) as *Storia economica e sociale dell' Impero romano*, Florence, 1933; Spanish translation by L. López-Ballesteros as *Historia social y económica del Imperio romano*, Madrid, 1937.

Mystic Italy. Colver Lectures. New York, 1927.

The Animal Style in South Russia and China. Princeton and London, 1929.

Caravan Cities. Translated by D. and T. Talbot Rice. Oxford, 1932; reprinted New York, 1971; Italian translation by C. Cortese de Bosis as *Città carovaniere*, Bari, 1934.

Dura-Europos and Its Art. Oxford, 1938.

The Social and Economic History of the Hellenistic World. 3 vols. Oxford, 1941; 2d ed. with additions and corrections by P. M. Fraser (1953); German translation by G. and E. Bayer as *Die hellenistische Welt: Gesellschaft und Wirtschaft*, Stuttgart, 1955–1956; Italian translation by M. Liberanome and G. Sanna as *Storia economica e sociale del mondo ellenistico*, Florence, 1966.

The Excavations at Dura-Europos Conducted by Yale University and the French Academy of Inscriptions and Letters. New Haven, 1929 et seqq. (Rostovtzeff edited ten volumes of the *Preliminary Report* [1929–1952] and six volumes of the *Final Report* [1943–1949].)

Articles

Welles' bibliography (see below) lists 444 titles of books, monographs, articles, notes, and reviews arranged under the following headings: Archaeological News; The Tesserae; Serfdom; The History of South Russia; The Monuments of South Russia; The Art of Asia; Decorative Wall Painting; Problems of the Roman Empire; Problems of the Hellenistic East; History of the Ancient World; *The Cambridge Ancient History*; "Out of the Past"; Religion; Caravan Cities; Dura; Miscellaneous; Reviews; Personalia; Russian History; Modern Russia. I list here only those articles mentioned in the text.

"Die hellenistisch-römische Architekturlandschaft." *Römische Mitteilungen* 26 (1911) 1–185; reprinted as a monograph in the series Mitteilungen des Kaiserlich deutschen archaeologischen Instituts. Römische abteilung. Vol. 26 fasc. 1–2. Berlin, 1911.

"Why the Russian Intelligentsia is Opposed to the Bolshevist Regime," *Struggling Russia* 1 (1919–1920) 792–795.

"Proletarian Culture in Bolshevist Russia," *Struggling Russia* 1 (1919–1920) 459–462, 484–487.

"Memorandum," *The New Russia* 3 (1920) 283–285.

"Should Scientists Return to Russia?" *The New Russia* 2 (1920) 370–372.

"La crise sociale et politique de l'empire romain au IIIe siècle." *Musée Belge* 27 (1923): 233–242.

"The Hellenistic World and Its Economic Development." *American Historical Review* 41 (1936) 231–252 (AHA presidential address).

Sources

Bibliography
Welles, C. Bradford. "Bibliography–M. Rostovtzeff." *Historia* 5 (1956) 351–388 (Welles 1).

Biographical
Borodin, I. *Uchenye zaslugi M. I. Rostovtseva.* Moscow, 1915.

Bowersock, G. W. "The Social and Economic History of the Roman Empire by Michael Ivanovitch Rostovtzeff." *Daedalus* 103 (1974) 15–23 (Bowersock 1).

———. "Rostovtzeff in Madison." *Daedalus* 55 (1986) 391–400 (Bowersock 2).

Christ, Karl. *Von Gibbon zu Rostovtzeff.* Darmstadt, 1972: 334–349.

D'Arms, J. "M. I. Rostovtzeff and M. I. Finley: The Status of Traders in the Roman World." *Ancient and Modern: Essays in Honor of Gerald F. Else.* Ed. J. D'Arms and J. Eadie. Ann Arbor, 1977: 159–179.

Demandt, A. *Der Fall Roms: Die Auflösung des römischen Reiches im Urteil der Nachwelt.* Munich, 1984: 452–454.

Dow, S. *Fifty Years of Sathers.* Berkeley, 1965: 47.

Ferrill, Arthur. *The Fall of the Roman Empire: The Military Explanation.* [London, 1986]: 16.

Frank, T. Review of *Social and Economic History of the Roman Empire.* AJP 47 (1926) 290–92.

Heichelheim, F. M. Review of *Social and Economic History of the Hellenistic World.* JHS 63 (1943) 129-130.

Heuss, A. "Das spatantike römische Reich kein 'Zwangsstaat'? Von Herkunft eines Historische Begriffes." *GWU* 37 (1986) 603–618.

Hopkins, Clark. *The Discovery of Dura-Europos.* Ed. Bernhard Goldman. New Haven, 1979.

Jones, A. H. M. "Michael Ivanovitch Rostovtzeff 1870–1952." *PBA* 38 (1952) 347–361.

The End of the Roman Empire: Decline or Transformation. Ed. D. Kagan. 2d ed. Lexington, MA, 1978: 3–6, 91–102, 180.

Kreissig, H. "Der Hellenismus und die Epochen der ökonomischen Gesellschaftsformen." *EAZ* 23 (1982) 45–50.

Kuzishchin, V. I., "Rostovtzeff, Michael Ivanovich." *Great Soviet Encyclopedia: A Translation of the Third Edition*. New York, 1979: 22:292.

Last, Hugh. Review of *Social and Economic History of the Roman Empire*. JRS 16 (1926) 120–128.

———. "Obituary: Professor M. I. Rostovtzeff." *JRS* 43 (1953) 133–134.

Momigliano, Arnaldo. "M. I. Rostovtzeff." *The Cambridge Journal* 7 (1954) 334–346; reprinted in Momigliano, *Contributo alla Storia degli Studi Classici*. Rome, 1955: 341–54 and in Momigliano, *Studies in Historiography* London, 1966: 91–104. (This is the reprint cited in the text.)

Pleket, H. W., "Afscheld van Rostovtzeff," *Lampas* 8 (1975) 267–284.

Préaux, C., "Michel Rostovtzeff." *Chronique d'Egypte* 29 (1954) 179–190.

Reinhold, M., "Historian of the Classic World: A Critique of Rostovtzeff." *Science and Society* 10 (1946) 361–391.

de Ste. Croix, G. E. M. *The Class Struggle in the Ancient Greek World from the Archaic Age to the Arab Conquests*. Ithaca, NY, 1981: 463–65.

Starr, Chester, "The History of the Roman Empire 1911–1960." *JRS* 50 (1960) 149–160.

———. *Past and Future in Ancient History*. Publications of the Association of Ancient Historians 1. Lanham, MD, 1987: 27.

Tarn, W. W. Review of *Social and Economic History of the Hellenistic World*. *JRS* 31 (1941) 165–171.

Várady, L. *Die Auflösung des Altertums*. Budapest, 1978: 54–57.

Vernadsky, G. V. "M. I. Rostovcev." *Seminarium Kondakovianum* 4 (1931) 239–252.

Welles, C. Bradford. "Michael I. Rostovtzeff." In *Architects and Craftsmen in History: Festschrift für Abbot Payson Usher*. Ed. Joseph Lambie. Tübingen, 1956: 55–73 (Welles 2).

———. "Michael Ivanovich Rostovtzeff." *The Russian Review* 12 (1953): 128–133 (Welles 3).

Wes, Marinus. "The Russian Background of the Young Michael Rostovtzeff." *Historia* 37 (1988) 207–221.

Papers

The major collections of Rostovtzeff's papers are currently at Duke University, Durham, NC, and Yale University. The Duke collection is in the possession of the American Society of Papyrologists, consists primarily of letters to Rostovtzeff. The material in the Sterling Memorial Library at Yale consists primarily of manuscripts of published books and articles, lectures and research notes. Material relating to the Dura expedition is in the Yale Art Gallery. Some items also relating to Rostovtzeff's tenure at the University of Wisconsin are in the University of Wisconsin library.

I am grateful to Alan Samuels and John Oates for supplying biographical information as well as information about the Rostovtzeff collections at Yale and Duke.

Wolfgang Schadewaldt

15 March 1900 – 10 March 1974

HELLMUT FLASHAR
Universität München

After Ulrich von Wilamowitz-Moellendorff and Werner Jaeger, Wolfgang Schadewaldt was the twentieth century's most important German Hellenist. Not only did he do pioneering work as a scholar (especially in his work on Homer) but his potent influence extended beyond scholarly circles into the sphere of the greater public, to whom he brought the words and thoughts of the Greeks in various forms. His merits were accordingly rewarded by membership in academies (Leipzig, Berlin, Vienna, Heidelberg, Darmstadt) and by honors of many different kinds (the Grand Cross of Merit with the Star of the Federal Republic of Germany, the Austrian Medal for Science and Art, the Orden pour le Mérite für Wissenschaften und Künste).

Schadewaldt was brought up "in the old Berlin style," as he himself said. He was deeply influenced as a schoolboy by his encounter with the thought and poetry of Goethe and after early attempts at the art of sculpture he turned to the study of classical philology, archaeology, and German literature at the University of Berlin. His teachers were Ulrich von Wilamowitz (already emeritus but still active in teaching) and Wilamowitz's successor, Werner Jaeger, whose endeavors to give new and modern horizons to the subjects of his study were fascinating to students.

Both teachers determined the course of Schadewaldt's entire philological endeavor. The presence of each is palpable in their student's combination and integration of, on the one hand, the manner of approaching the text through careful observation and, on the other, the attempt to combine the methods of traditional philology with newer humanistic and philosophical categories.

His dissertation, "Monolog und Selbstgespräch," already displayed the twenty-six-year-old scholar's complete mastery of the subject. The work deals with monologues, monodies, and soliloquies in tragedy. The lengthy treatment of Euripides would not have been possible without the work of Wilamowitz, who was the first to rehabilitate this poet among scholars. And it is with Wilamowitz that Schadewaldt, young as he was, again and again takes issue. That the seventy-eight-year-old Wilamowitz reviewed this book, the author's first work, is astounding; even more astounding is the remark (which has since become famous) in Wilamowitz's review: that he is "always ready to learn anew" (*umzulernen stets bereit*) (*Deutsche Literaturzeitung* 47 [1926] 854 = *Kleine Schriften* 1:466).

Two years later Wilamowitz refers to "my colleague Schadewaldt" in the edition with commentary of Hesiod's *Erga* (Berlin, 1928), a work that was the product of a joint seminar conducted by the two unequal partners.

His *Habilitationsschrift*, "Der Aufbau des pindarischen Epinikion," which was kept within a decidedly brief compass, was dedicated to Wilamowitz on the occasion of his eightieth birthday, yet it breathes an entirely different spirit from that of the master's massive biographically oriented book on Pindar (1922). Schadewaldt's aim is to isolate the conventional parts of the victory ode that come together to form the so-called "programme" and thereby to grasp the way the poet includes objective givens in his finished art. His results are still valid today.

This is not true to the same degree of his book *Die Geschichtsschreibung des Thukydides*, in which Schadewaldt searched for new criteria for a division of Thucydides' history into two layers, a division that is not tenable in this manner. In general, his early works, which were written under the influence of Werner Jaeger and in which Schadewaldt aimed at a more elevated style, have not remained so persuasive as have the later works. This is particularly true of the essay, which Schadewaldt later regarded as superseded and did not reprint, contributed to *Das Problem des klassischen und die Antike* (1933), a collection edited by Werner Jaeger, which comprised the papers delivered at the famous 1930 Naumburg Congress for Classical *Altertumswissenschaft*. "We follow Werner Jaeger, who, in his profound and original reflections on the meaning of the concept of culture and the allied concept of classicism, has shown us the way," he states in this essay (18). And Schadewaldt, pursuing this course, concludes (31): "Classicism is nobility of intellectual and spiritual humanity elevated to the law of form." In a famous reply to Schadewaldt, who had sent him a copy of the paper, Wilamowitz vigorously rejected the whole notion of classicism.

A series of smaller works on early Greek lyric, on the beginnings of historiography, and on Greek tragedy was followed by the real breakthrough of the *Iliasstudien*, in which Schadewaldt gave the deathblow to Homeric "analysis" in the old style. This work, which attained a level since unsurpassed in Homeric studies, used precise interpretation to reclaim the *Iliad* as a unified and organically developed poem. In the following years, work on Homer occupied the foreground of his studies, until the chaos attendant on the end of the war (including the burning of Schadewaldt's library in an air raid) caused a hiatus.

The postwar years, which in Berlin were especially rich in deprivations, brought with them a new beginning in many respects. This was a time of planning, during which arose the project of producing a Goethe lexicon, a work that began to appear very much more slowly than originally hoped. Furthermore, in studies on Winckelmann, Goethe, and Hölderlin and their attitude toward the Greek spirit,

Schadewaldt sought a new personal access to Hellenism by immersing himself in the thoughts of others.

The book on Sappho, written in Berlin, remained incomplete, since the appendix, announced in the book, which was to contain references, notes, and the Greek text, never appeared; thus his new textual readings and restorations of lacunae must be understood through his translation (with a new but unfortunately unusable enumeration of the fragments). Immediately after the book appeared, the twenty-first volume of the Oxyrynchus papyri appeared (1951) that, with its new Sappho discoveries, brought forth so much additional material that considerable revision and correction to Schadewaldt's book would have been necessary; but his temperament was not suited to such work.

His Tübingen period (after 1950) was a time of largely untroubled work and influence, the scope of which was broadened to embrace the public at large. The basis for this was his feeling of security in the small university town, which had remained undamaged during the war. Thanks to a far-sighted policy of higher education, which in the early years received consistent support from the French military authorities, Tübingen in the postwar period managed to attract important scholars. Schadewaldt lived here as in an intimate *polis*, but he remained to the bottom of his heart a Berliner. His splendid essay "Lob Berlins" ("In Praise of Berlin," 1961; reprinted in *Hellas und Hesperien*, 2d ed.: 787–808) is decisive proof of this.

The breadth and fullness of his activities is reflected in *Hellas und Hesperien*, expanded to two volumes in its second edition. Its numerous chapters range over topics from Greek poetry and thought to Shakespeare, Gerhart Hauptmann, T. S. Eliot, Carl Orff, and Ingeborg Bachmann and to questions of modern technology and atomic physics.

A further major dimension of Schadewaldt's public influence was his translations, which he himself justly described as an "integration of the entire business of philology" (*Hellas und Hesperien*, 2d ed.: 781). After his masterly prose translation of the *Odyssey* it was above all his translations of dramas that found a wide audience in radio, television, and the theater. Great directors like Gustav Rudolf Sellner, Günther Fleckenstein, and Hansgünther Heyme staged his translations in Darmstadt, Göttingen, Wiesbaden, Cologne, Stuttgart, and elsewhere. Especially with Heyme the most modern ideas of staging were united with the "documentary" style of translation (as Schadewalt called it), which, preserving the greatest possible literalness, makes no concession to easy understanding (and is similar in this to the translations of Hölderlin) and lays no small demands on the actors. Schadewaldt took an active part in the work of the theater; he was regularly present at rehearsals to discuss his concept of translation.

He was also actively engaged in Carl Orff's musical settings of Greek tragedies (*Antigone*, *Oedipus Rex*, *Prometheus Bound*) and in their stage performances. In this way he became acquainted with Wieland Wagner, who invited him to Bayreuth, where, in the context of the festival performances, he delivered his important lectures "Richard Wagner und die Griechen" (1961–65; printed first in the performance programs and reprinted in *Hellas und Hesperien*).

All the while Schadewaldt clung firmly and with iron energy to philological scholarship. His works on the Aristotelian theory of tragedy as well as several works on the *Odyssey* are in the central tradition of philological research. To be sure, his analysis of the *Odyssey* has not met with acceptance. It was difficult to understand how the scholar who had impressively demonstrated the poetic unity of the *Iliad* now embraced arguments that, in the case of the *Iliad*, he had criticized and opposed and who insisted on viewing the *Odyssey* as the epic composition of two poets—namely Homer, the poet of the *Iliad*, from whom (he maintains) the nucleus of Odysseus' homecoming is derived, and a poet "B," who composed the *Telemachy* and various additions throughout the epic.

As a result, one feels all the more grateful that it was granted to Schadewaldt to translate the *Iliad* and to complete his masterly book *Der Aufbau der Ilias* as his last works. His name thus will be forever linked with the study of the great Homeric epic.

Schadewaldt's academic career was a steep and rapid ascent. After his Habilitation in Berlin (1927), he was immediately called to Königsberg (1928) as Professor Ordinarius; only a year later he accepted a call to Freiburg; then in 1934 he transferred to Leipzig; his call to Berlin in 1941 would have been, under normal circumstances, the summit of a career in philology. The peculiar political situation of the divided Berlin (the old University of Berlin lies in the city's eastern sector) impelled him to accept a call to Tübingen in 1950; he declined a further call to Basel in 1951. Thereafter he looked on Tübingen as his home, and it is in the Tübingen Waldfriedhof that he is buried.

Schadewaldt was never interested in founding a "school." However, he did influence several well-known scholars. After his first period in Berlin, the important Homer scholar Wolfgang Kullmann (now Professor in Freiburg) was among his students, while his most outstanding students in Tübingen, Konrad Gaiser (Schadewaldt's successor at Tübingen, who died in 1988) and Hans Joachim Krämer (now Professor in Tübingen) gave new directions to the study of Plato, a field in which Schadewaldt was never involved. Hellmut Flashar (now Professor in Munich) was his student both in Berlin and in Tübingen.

Translated by Michael Armstrong

Books

Monolog und Selbstgespräch. Untersuchungen zur Formgeschichte der griechischen Tragödie. Diss., Berlin, 1926. Berlin, 1926; reprinted Berlin and Dublin, 1966.

Der Aufbau des Pindarischen Epinikion. Schriften der Königsberger Gelehrten Gesellschaft, geisteswiss. Klasse 5 (1928), Heft 3. Simultaneous publication: Halle 1928; reprinted Darmstadt, 1966.

Die Geschichtsschreibung des Thukydides. Berlin, 1929.

Iliasstudien. Abhandlungen der Sächsischen Akademie der Wissenschaften, phil.-

hist. Klasse 43, 6. Leipzig, 1938; 2d ed., Leipzig, 1943 (burned in the
    publishing house); 3d ed., Darmstadt, 1966.

Von Homers Welt und Werk. Aufsätze und Auslegungen zur homerischen Frage.
    Leipzig, 1944; 2d ed., Stuttgart, 1951; 3d ed., 1959; 4th ed., 1965. (Each edi-
    tion was expanded by the addition of further material.)

Legende von Homer dem fahrenden Sänger. Potsdam, 1947; reprinted Zürich, 1959.

Sappho—Welt und Dichtung. Dasein in der Liebe. Potsdam, 1950.

Griechische Sternsagen. Frankfurt, 1956. Danish and Japanese translations, 1963.

Antike Tragödie auf der modernen Bühne. Heidelberg, 1957. Originally: Sitzungsber-
    ichte der Heidelberger Akademie der Wissenschaften, Jahresheft 1955–56.

Homer: Odyssey. Translated into German prose. Hamburg, 1958; 2d ed. revised,
    Zürich, 1966.

Hellas und Hesperien. Gesammelte Schriften zur Antike und zur neuen Literatur.
    Zürich, 1960; 2d ed. (greatly expanded and in two volumes), 1970.

Goethestudien. Natur und Altertum. Zürich, 1963.

Griechisches Theater. Frankfurt, 1964. (Contains translations of Aeschylus *Persians*,
    Seven against Thebes; Sophocles *Antigone*, *Oedipus Rex*, *Electra*; Aristophanes
    Birds, *Lysistrata*; Menander *Epitrepontes*.)

Der Aufbau der Ilias. Strukturen und Konzeptionen. Frankfurt, 1975.

Homer: Iliad. Frankfurt, 1975 (translation).

Articles (Collected)

Most of Schadewaldt's more than 150 articles are reprinted in *Von Homers Welt und
    Werk*, *Goethestudien*, and *Hellas und Hesperien*.

Sources

Calder, William M., III. "Ulrich von Wilamowitz-Moellendorff toWolfgang
    Schadewalt on the Classic." *GRBS* 16 (1975) 451–457.

Flashar, H. "Wolfgang Schadewaldt." *Gnomon* 47 (1975) 731–736.

Gaiser, K. [Obituary.] *Jahrbuch der Heidelberger Akademie der Wissenschaften* (1975)
    92–97.

Lesky, A. *Orden pour le mérite für Wissenschaften und Künste. Reden und Gedenkworte*
    12 (1974–75) 115–123.

Schadewaldt, W. "Lebensgang" and "Antrittsrede." (1943) for the Preußische
    Akademie der Wissenschaften zu Berlin; "Antrittsrede" (1958) for the
    Heidelberger Akademie der Wissenschaften. All three documents are
    reprinted in *Hellas und Hesperien*, 2d ed.: 780–787.

Festschriften

Synusia. Festgabe für Wolfgang Schadewaldt zum 15. März 1965. Edited by H. Flashar
    and K. Gaiser. Pfullingen, 1965.

Das Altertum und jedes neue Gute. Für Wolfgang Schadewaldt zum 15. März 1970.
    Edited by K. Gaiser. Stuttgart, 1970.

Heinrich Schliemann

6 January 1822 – 26 December 1890

DAVID A. TRAILL
University of California, Davis

The excavations of Johann Ludwig Heinrich Julius Schliemann rank among the most important in the history of archaeology. By demonstrating that an impressive settlement had existed at Hisarlik from a date far earlier than the Trojan War, he seemed to settle once and for all the long-simmering controversy over the site of Troy. His excavation of Mycenae uncovered an astonishing array of gold objects and other precious artifacts, showing that civilization on the Greek mainland had attained a remarkable degree of wealth and sophistication a thousand years earlier than anyone had imagined. His spectacular discoveries at these and such other sites as Tiryns and Orchomenos, combined with his flair for publicity, gave a tremendous boost to archaeology, making it a subject of general interest. To the general public and even to a great many scholars his work seemed to confirm the essential historical truth of Homer. He has been called the Father of Mediterranean Archaeology. His name remains probably the most widely recognized of all those who have contributed to classical studies. Recent research, however, has indicated that he had a penchant for fraud and deceit. How far these tendencies compromised his archaeological work is still unclear, but that to some extent they did so is no longer in doubt.

Heinrich Schliemann was born in Neubuckow, Mecklenburg-Schwerin, where his father was a Lutheran pastor. In 1823 the family moved to Ankershagen, where Heinrich lived until he was nine. In later life Heinrich sometimes stated, even in official documents such as passports, that Ankershagen was his birthplace, though he was fully aware that he had been born in Neubuckow. He had an unsettled childhood. His mother died in 1831 shortly after giving birth to her ninth child. His father engaged in activities normally considered unsuitable for a man in his position. He carried on an affair with the maid and beat his wife. He may also have misappropriated church funds. His failings were reported to church authorities shortly after the death of his first wife, and he was forced to resign his post in 1832.

Understandably, these unpleasant details are glossed over in Schliemann's autobiographical introduction to *Ilios*, where the successful archaeologist is at pains to point out that "the pickaxe and spade for the excavation of Troy and the royal tombs of Mycenae were both forged and sharpened" in Ankershagen. Schliemann tells us of the rich tradition of Ankershagen folk tales and legend that had a formative influence on him as a young boy and how he longed to dig up the remains of the notorious Baron Henning, whose leg was believed to sprout so mysteriously from his grave in the churchyard, or to search for the golden cradle buried in a hillock or the silver basin that was supposed to lie at the bottom of the pool behind his father's house.

For Christmas 1829, we are told in *Ilios*, Heinrich received a copy of G. L. Jerrer's *Die Weltgeschichte für Kinder*, which contained an engraving of Aeneas escaping from blazing Troy with Anchises and Ascanius. The engraving made a deep and lasting impression on him. He informed his father, who dismissed the picture as fanciful, that traces of the massive city walls must still exist "hidden away by the dust of ages." Father and son agreed that when Heinrich grew up he would excavate Troy. From that day on he never lost sight of his childhood resolve. This wonderful story, which has endeared Schliemann to millions of readers, is unfortunately untrue. Quite apart from the sheer implausibility of an eight-year-old boy possessing an awareness of archaeological realities that most scholars then lacked, no trace of interest in excavating Troy has been found in any of Schliemann's voluminous letters or diaries prior to 1868. Moreover, the inscription "Heinrich Schliemann" on the title page of Schliemann's copy of Jerrer's book appears to have been written by an adult.

In 1831 Heinrich was sent to Kalkhorst to stay with his uncle Friedrich, who also was a pastor. Here he was tutored by Carl Andress. In 1833 he started at the Gymnasium in Neustrelitz, but after one term, apparently because of his father's financial difficulties, he was transferred to the Realschule in the same building. His school record was surprisingly undistinguished, even in foreign languages (French, English, and Latin), for which he later showed an extraordinary aptitude.

In 1836 he became an apprentice grocer in Fürstenburg. It was here that he gained his first practical business experience. It was here too that he later claimed to have had a memorable experience that had a lasting effect on his life. One evening a young miller's apprentice, Hermann Niederhöffer, came into the shop. He was drunk but could still recite a hundred lines of Homer that he had learned by heart. Among the barrels of butter, herrings, and potato-whisky Schliemann listened, entranced. Though he could not understand a word of the Greek, he was captivated by the sound of the language and the melodious rhythm of Homer's verses. He plied young Niederhöffer with drink and had him repeat the lines three times over. "From that moment," he tells us, "I never ceased to pray God that by His grace I might yet have the happiness of learning Greek."

His employment in Fürstenburg came to an end in 1841 when he burst a blood vessel in his lungs, lifting a heavy cask of chicory. His plans to sail to the New World in late July were aborted when his father refused to give his permission. He moved to Rostock to learn double-entry bookkeeping, a crucial but perhaps rather unromantic fact that is excluded from his autobiography. He completed the course by mid-September and then looked for employment in Hamburg. Finding nothing satisfactory, he set sail for La Guaira, Colombia, in November 1841, where he had been told a good job awaited him. The ship was wrecked off the island of Texel on the Dutch coast in a violent storm. With the help of various people he obtained a position as a clerk in Amsterdam. To improve his prospects he studied in his spare time calligraphy and foreign languages (English, French, Dutch, Spanish, Italian, and Portuguese). Finally, in March 1844 he was hired as correspondent and bookkeeper in the trading house of B. H. Schröder & Co. Seeing the advantages of a knowledge of Russian in his new position, he set about learning that language too and in January 1846 was sent to St. Petersburg as Schröder's agent.

In St. Petersburg Schliemann quickly made a name for himself as a highly successful dealer in commodities—saltpeter, sugar, wine, tea, coffee, and, above all, indigo. Though he always remained Schröder's agent, he soon established an independent business for himself. In the summer of 1850 he learned that his brother Ludwig, who had been drawn to California by the gold rush, had died at the age of twenty-seven in Sacramento. Accordingly, in December 1850 he sailed to America to see to Ludwig's estate. The diary he kept of this trip records details of personal interviews with the presidents of the United States and Panama en route, but these have now been exposed as fictitious. In California he found no trace of his brother's wealth but erected a tombstone over what he believed to be his grave. From September 1851 to April 1852 he operated a bank in Sacramento and bought gold dust from the miners. His precipitous departure from California in April 1852 was not due to a third bout of fever, as he alleges in his diary, but appears to have been connected with a disastrous breakdown in his relations with his San Francisco banking associate, B. Davidson. Davidson accused Schliemann of repeatedly sending him short-weight consignments of gold dust. Schliemann closed his bank and returned promptly to St. Petersburg.

Shortly before his return to Russia he proposed by letter to two women in St. Petersburg simultaneously. In 1852 he married Katerina Lyshin, by whom he had a son and two daughters. The marriage, however, was not a success and Schliemann continued to devote most of his energies to enhancing his fortune. He astutely exploited the business opportunities presented by the Crimean and American Civil Wars. He also returned to his study of languages and learned modern and ancient Greek and improved his knowledge of Latin. Though he was not yet forty, the prospect of retirement now began to figure more prominently in his thoughts. Among various alternatives he saw himself as a landowner in Mecklenburg or running a literary salon in Athens. Significantly, there is still no talk of excavating Troy either in his diaries or in his correspondence. Moreover, in his 1858–59 travels to Egypt, the Near East, and Greece, he made no attempt to visit Homeric sites. In *Ilios* he states that in the summer of 1859 he was on the point of visiting Ithaca when he was recalled from Athens to St. Petersburg, where Solavieff, a business associate, had filed a lawsuit against him for fraudulent business practices. When, however, a few weeks later, he was free to leave St. Petersburg for a further six weeks of touring, it was not to Homeric sites that he went but to Spain. All mention of this Spanish tour is suppressed in the autobiography.

Winning the lawsuit on appeal, Schliemann embarked on a trip around the world (1864–66): Tunis, Carthage, Egypt, India, Ceylon, Singapore, Java, Saigon, China, Japan, California, Nicaragua, New York, Cuba, Mexico, Paris. His itinerary still shows no sign of a particular interest in Homeric or even Greek sites. As always when he traveled, he kept a detailed diary of his experiences. On his trip from Yokohama to San Francisco, which lasted fifty days, he reworked his China and Japan entries for publication.

After his trip around the world, "in the spring of 1866," Schliemann tells us in *Ilios*, he "settled down in Paris to study archaeology, henceforth with no other interruption than short trips to America." This is partly misleading and partly untrue. It is misleading in that it suggests that by this time Schliemann's interest was focused on archaeology, whereas Meyer's biography informs us that in February 1866 Schliemann enrolled at the Sorbonne in the following eight courses: 1) sixteenth- century French poetry; 2) Arabic; 3) Greek philosophy; 4) Greek literature: Sophocles' *Ajax*; 5) Petrarch and his travels; 6) Comparative grammar; 7) Egyptian philology and archaeology; 8) modern French language and literature. These choices suggest that at this stage Schliemann was more interested in philology than archaeology. His claim that his studies were interrupted only by short trips to America is simply false. By 7 March he was in Moscow, where he resumed his business activities. He stayed there until July, when he set out once again for France, traveling through Russia, Germany, and Switzerland and not reaching Paris until October.

At least part of the reason for his return to Russia in March seems to have been to effect a reconciliation with his wife. In this he was unsuccessful. When he left St. Petersburg in July 1866, he began to liquidate his assets and in the following winter invested heavily in rental property in Paris. Though Schliemann was continuously resident in Paris for the academic year 1866–67, there is no sign in the extant correspondence that he was taking courses in archaeology or other academic subjects at this time. Much of his business correspondence has to do with the managing and renting of the apartments, which Schliemann seems to have handled himself at this stage. His personal correspondence is preoccupied with attempts to persuade his wife to bring the children and join him in Paris or, if she preferred, in Dresden. His wife seems to have been concerned that if she joined him in Dresden she would be forced to move to Paris. She was obviously unimpressed by his repeated promises and required a written legal guarantee that this would not happen. This Schliemann was not prepared to give, and negotiations finally broke down amid threats that he would seek an American divorce (July 1867). Throughout this period, it should be noted, and throughout his life, he kept up child-support payments. From October to the end of January 1868 he was on a trip to the United States and Cuba, assessing the prospects of various corporations, particularly railroad companies, in which he had made or planned to make investments.

When he returned from the United States, his correspondence immediately showed signs of an active interest in archaeology and allied subjects. From 11 February onward he wrote enthusiastically to a number of correspondents about the courses he was taking at the Sorbonne, the Collège de France and the Bibliothèque Impériale and about the meetings of the societies of geography, ethnography, American archeology, and oriental archeology. Nonetheless, so acutely did he miss his children that he had made up his mind that he would give up these attractions of Paris and return to St. Petersburg and resume his business activities there. This was his intention as late as 4 April 1868, when he wrote to his son Serge outlining his planned trip through Switzerland, Italy, and then via Ithaca, Corfu, Corinth, Athens, the Dardanelles, the "battleground of Troy," Constantinople, Odessa, Kiev, Moscow, to St. Petersburg, which he hoped to reach by the end of May. It is clear that at this stage he had no intention of conducting any excavations or even of examining the sites carefully with a view to future excavations. A few days later, however, his plans changed rather abruptly. He learned from sources in St. Petersburg that the widow of Solavieff and others were preparing to file a lawsuit against him on some other aspect of the Solavieff affair. On 13 November he wrote to a friend in St. Petersburg about these developments, concluding that he would not return to St. Petersburg unless he heard more reassuring news about the threatened lawsuit.

In a letter of 27 April 1868 to his son he indicated that on his trip he was particularly interested in seeing the recent archaeological discoveries in Rome and Pompeii. Nonetheless, he spent four weeks in Rome (5 May–6 June) and more than three weeks around the Bay of Naples (7–30 June), visiting for the most part the standard sights recommended by the guidebooks. He went to Pompeii twice. He admired the wall-paintings there but was not very impressed with the speed of Fiorelli's excavations, noting that they scarcely uncovered one house in two weeks. Even in Corfu (6–7 July) and Ithaca (8–17 July), where he devoted most of his time to finding Homeric sites, he could hardly be said to have departed radically from the itineraries and preoccupations recommended by J. Murray's *Handbook for Travellers in Greece*.

On his arrival in Ithaca he promptly examined the Cave of the Nymphs near Vathy and then climbed Mt. Aetos and inspected the ruins traditionally identified as those of Odysseus' palace. He then visited different villages of the island, acquiring antiquities as he went. He purchased a particularly rich collection of pieces from a villager, Loizos, who was excavating tombs in a collapsed cave on the shore of Polis Bay. It was only after these purchases and not before, as he recounts in his published account, that he excavated the supposed site of Odysseus' palace on the summit of Aetos. It is therefore possible that the twenty or so small vases, the broken sword, and other pieces he claims to have found in a round hole there, when the workmen were working in another part of the site, are in fact these purchased items. Though unsure of the date of the pottery, he reckoned it to be very early and even speculated that the white powder found in the vases might well be the calcified bones of Odysseus and Penelope! On 20 July he moved to Athens, putting up at the Hotel Grande Bretagne in Syntagma. The next few days he went sightseeing in Athens after a daily morning swim at the Piraeus. On 25 July he met the German architect Ernst Ziller, "who gave me useful information about the Troad, where he discovered the walls of the Pergamos." Ziller had excavated at Balli Dag above Pinarbasi (Bunarbashi) with J. von Hahn in 1864. This conversation apparently filled Schliemann with enthusiasm for finding Troy at Pinarbasi, for, a few days later, he tried to book a passage to the Dardanelles on the next French steamer, but, finding that it reached that port at night and could not disembark passengers, he decided to visit Corinth, Mycenae and Argos instead. On 30 July he climbed Acro-Corinth and admired the panoramic view. The next day he visited Mycenae. His diary account of this visit draws heavily on Murray's *Handbook*. Practically the only original detail is his observation that the large number of sherds to be found at the site makes it probable that this was Agamemnon's capital. Schliemann returned to Athens and soon set out for the Troad.

After a brief visit to Hisarlik, which he seems not to have seriously considered as a candidate for Troy, he dug at Balli Dag with one workman for half a day and with two workmen on the next day and concluded that it could not have been the site of Troy. On leaving the Troad he was persuaded by Frank Calvert (1830–1908) that Hisarlik was the real site of Troy, and he resolved to return next year and excavate there.

In Paris he devoured all the relevant scholarly literature that he could lay his hands on and wrote up a more polished version of his trip, entitling it *Ithaque, le Péloponnèse et Troie*. Comparison of the diary with the published book shows that Schliemann made substantial alterations to the facts of this trip. For instance, regarding his visit to Ithaca, besides altering the date of his excavations on Mt. Aetos as noted above, he moved his visit to Mycenae to 19 August, *before* his arrival in Athens. Moreover, there are least two fictitious incidents in the Ithaca section: his encounter with the hostile sheep dogs, which is a close adaptation of a passage in Murray's *Handbook*, and his visit to the small island of Dascalia, which some scholars identified with Asteris, where the suitors lay in wait for Telemachus. Schliemann's reason for the latter addition is clear. He was committed to identifying Mt. Aetos with the site of Odysseus' palace. One of the best arguments against Mt. Aetos and in favor of Polis Bay was the location of Dascalia/Asteris. It is too far north of Aetos to be suitable for ambushing someone sailing from the Peloponnese. To dispose of this argument Schliemann invented a visit to the island in which he determined from autopsy that it did not conform to Homer's description.

The chapter on Mycenae is noteworthy chiefly for his insistence that the tombs of Agamemnon and his companions mentioned by Pausanias (2.16) must refer to tombs located within the visible city walls rather than to the beehive tombs outside, as almost all scholars then believed. What led him to this important conclusion is unclear. The diary entries give no inkling. They show no interest in the location of the heroic tombs or even an awareness that Pausanias had referred to them. Since Schliemann saw signs within the citadel of what was fairly obviously clandestine excavation to a depth of six meters (*Ithaque*: 100), a reasonable hypothesis is that local sources informed him that there were rumors of rich burials inside the visible city walls.

In the section on the Troad the book makes it seem as if Schliemann had decided when he first saw Balli Dag that it could not be the site of Troy. He carefully marshalled the arguments against Balli Dag put forward by G. von Eckenbrecher and others, recasting some of them as his own personal experiences. For instance, he claims that he personally took the temperature of the forty springs at Bunarbashi, finding none that could truly be called hot or cold, and tried in vain to run around the site, as Hector and Achilles had done. There is no mention of these activities in his diary. His excavations at Balli Dag, which he expanded from two and a half to fifteen man-days, he claims were conducted simply to confirm his conclusion that it could *not* be the site of Troy. He placed his visit to Hisarlik *after* his excavations at Balli Dag and *before* his interview with Frank Calvert and stated that, as soon as he saw Hisarlik, he realized that Troy had to be here. These alterations had the effect of making Schliemann seem more diligent and perceptive than had actually been the case.

He had his old tutor Carl Andress translate the work into German and submitted both French and German editions, additional Greek and Latin versions of the *vita*, and *La Chine et le Japon* to the University of Rostock in support of his candidacy for a doctorate. The reviewing board thought little of Schliemann's views on Mycenae and Troy and even less of his ability to write ancient Greek. They were sufficiently impressed, however, with his discussion of the topography of Ithaca to award the degree, unaware, apparently, that most of the ideas and many of the arguments put forward by Schliemann as his own were in fact drawn from Murray's *Handbook*. The doctorate was duly awarded in the spring of 1869.

In March 1869 Schliemann set out for America to obtain a divorce from his Russian wife. He gained his American citizenship in New York by persuading someone to swear that he had been living in New York State for the preceding year and in the United States for the preceding five years. Later, in the autobiographical introduction to *Ilios*, he stated that he obtained his U.S. citizenship simply by being present in California when it was admitted to the Union in 1850. He resorted to this untruth in order to conceal the fact that his citizenship and, consequently, his divorce had been obtained by fraud. At that time Indiana had the most liberal divorce laws in the United States, but even there a year's residence was required before a divorce petition could be filed. With the help of two separate legal firms in Indianapolis, Schliemann filed the petition within a week of his arrival in the state and then found someone to give perjured testimony about his residence. To establish grounds for divorce he submitted doctored translations of his wife's letters. While waiting for his divorce he asked Theokletos Vimpos, Archbishop of Mantinea, for help in finding him a Greek wife. Vimpos obliged by suggesting, among others, his niece, Sophia Engastromenos.

Schliemann won his divorce in June 1869, married Sophia Engastromenos in Athens in September, and returned to Paris in October. In February 1870 he came back to Athens with his wife, eager for news that Frank Calvert had been successful in obtaining a *firman* (permit) for him to dig at Hisarlik. Meanwhile, he set out on 27

February on a tour of ancient sites in the Cyclades: Delos, Rhenea, Paros, Santorini (Thera), Therassia. Using the information in Murray's *Handbook* and the resources of his own sharp and inquiring mind, Schliemann turned this trip into a practicum in archaeology. On Delos he saw a wide variety of Greek ruins, primarily of the classical period. Therassia was particularly instructive. There he saw the remains of ancient houses and their contents that had been buried by the great eruption of Thera, then dated ca. 2000–1800 B.C. (now dated ca. 1500 B.C.). He noted the varying strata clearly visible in the cliff face and speculated whether they were all of volcanic origin and about the implications they had for the dating of the prehistoric remains some twenty meters below the surface. Probably Schliemann learned more about archaeology from this trip to the Cyclades than he ever learned in Paris.

After his return to Athens on 20 March, Schliemann won permission from the Greek government to start excavating at Mycenae on 25 April. On 10 April, tired of inactivity, Schliemann sailed off to the Troad and began excavating at Hisarlik, though he lacked a *firman* from the Turkish government and the permission of the owners. Employing about fifteen workmen, Schliemann excavated two trenches, each thirty meters long, at the western end of the ridge. On 17 April he visited the nearby village of Neochorion, where he purchased three inscriptions and several coins. On 20 April he was forced by the Turkish owners of the site to close his excavations. Though the significance and date of the ruins he had discovered at Hisarlik were far from clear, he announced to the world in the Augsburg *Allgemeine Zeitung* (24 May 1870) that he had uncovered the walls of a palace or temple on the Pergamus of Priam.

Schliemann returned to Athens shortly after a number of foreigners had been murdered by a gang of brigands near Athens. Consequently, he abandoned his plans for excavating Mycenae until public safety could be assured in the Greek countryside. Throughout the period of the Franco-Prussian War (July 1870 until February 1871) Schliemann was acutely concerned about the safety of his property in Paris. The war, his wife's health, and his plans for further excavation in Greece all combined to make Athens seem a more sensible choice for his permanent home than Paris. He set about drawing up plans for building an elaborate house on a plot of land he had purchased on a prime site between the palace and the University.

Meanwhile, negotiations were resumed with the Turkish authorities for a *firman* to renew excavations at Hisarlik. Schliemann was obliged to apologize for his illegal behavior of 1870. These negotiations dragged on interminably and were finally resolved, thanks to the intervention of the American diplomat John Brown, only in October 1871.

The 1871 season at Hisarlik lasted from 11 October until 24 November. Despite Schliemann's published assertions that his wife was "present at the excavations from morning to night" (*Troy and its Remains*: 62), Sophia remained in Athens throughout the 1871 season. Schliemann had commissioned Brockhaus of Leipzig to publish the results of his excavations. Periodically, he sent them drafts of reports on his progress. These draft reports, subsequently revised, became the chapters of his book *Trojanische Alterthümer*. Interim reports were also sent to the Greek and German press. It stands to Schliemann's credit that he soon found himself nonplussed by the confusing stratification of Hisarlik. At this stage, however, he was convinced that Homeric Troy was to be found at the lowest occupation level. With excessive zeal he had his workmen dig quickly down through the upper levels. Among the most important discoveries of this season, reported in the first few days of excavation, were three Greek inscriptions. However, since we know (see below) that Schliemann on occasion purchased inscriptions and then claimed to have discovered them in his own excavations, there must remain a suspicion that these are the three inscriptions purchased in Neochorion in 1870.

During the winter of 1871–72 he read several works of the oriental scholars Max Müller and Eugène and Emile Burnouf. Their influence on him can be seen in his subsequent preoccupation with the significance of the swastika and other symbols he found engraved on Trojan pottery. The 1872 season lasted from 1 April to 13 August. Though Schliemann states in *Troy and its Remains* (98) that Sophia was with him on Hisarlik from the beginning, his correspondence reveals that she arrived only on 24 May and departed on 27 June. In this season he started an immense cutting from the north side of the ridge, removing everything above the lowest occupation level, an estimated 78,500 cubic yards of material. This entailed removing the foundations of the great Hellenistic temple of Athena. The major find of this season, which was made on the northeastern section of Hisarlik on land belonging to Frank Calvert, was the Helios metope from that temple, now in the Pergamon Museum in East Berlin. Schliemann identified the figure riding the chariot as Apollo and concluded that the temple was dedicated to that god. He purchased Calvert's half-share in the find for £40, swearing on his word of honor that it was not worth a penny more. With the help of the Calvert brothers he smuggled the metope out of Turkey to Athens. The following spring, when Calvert learned that the market value of the piece was at least £400 and that Schliemann was boasting to friends that it was worth £2,500, relations between Schliemann and the Calverts deteriorated considerably. In 1872 Schliemann found masses of Early Bronze Age and Hellenistic pottery, some bronze weapons and tools, and two small finds of jewelry. The first of these ("Treasure N" of Schmidt's catalogue) comprised three bracelets, a gold earring, and two bunches of electrum and silver earrings corroded together. The second ("Treasure R") was all of gold pieces, including a finger ring, three earrings, a pin, beads, and an oval ring. In *Troy and Its Remains* Schliemann reports finding this second treasure near the skeleton of a woman. However, his diary makes it clear that the skeleton and jewelry were found two months apart and in different locations.

The third season at Troy began on 1 February and lasted until 15 June 1873. The discovery of the "Apollo" metope on the northern slope of Hisarlik had convinced Schliemann that the foundations he was excavating there must be those of the Temple of Apollo, and his interest shifted more to the southern slope, where he expected to discover traces of the Temple of Athena. There he seems to have come across a number of rich finds in March and April. On or close to the complex of walling that he called the "Tower" he found a number of early houses and what appears to have been an early cemetery. He reported finding numerous cinerary urns, a great quantity of human bones, and two more or less complete adult skeletons. To the west of the "Tower" he uncovered a city gate in the wall of Troy II and pronounced it the "Scaean Gate," and just north of this gate a large building, which he quickly identified as "Priam's Palace." As he followed the course of the circuit wall northwest of the gate he came across a large collection of objects in gold, silver, and bronze—"Priam's Treasure."

It is now clear that Schliemann's published account of this incident, in which he claims that he and his wife alone excavated the treasure at the end of May, is fraudulent, for Sophia went back to Athens at the beginning of May and did not return to Troy. Furthermore, there are grounds for believing that the treasure itself is a composite of a substantial find of mainly bronze pieces excavated on 31 May and gold and silver objects from earlier finds that went unrecorded in his diary. Some scholars, however, still hold that the treasure is indeed a single find as reported by Schliemann. On his return to Athens Schliemann tried to find a goldsmith in Paris who would make duplicates of the gold and silver objects from "Priam's Treasure" and whose discretion could be relied upon. There is no evidence that Schliemann ever had these duplicates made. It remains possible, however, that the treasures found in 1878 and 1879, which contain many pieces identical to pieces in "Priam's Treasure," are contaminated with fakes.

Schliemann returned to Athens in mid-June and spent most of the rest of 1873 preparing the German (*Trojanische Alterthümer*) and French (*Antiquités troyennes*) editions of his excavation reports. These were published simultaneously in January 1874. Reviews began to appear even before the book was officially published. While the signal importance of Schliemann's work in bringing to light an ancient civilization on a site that had an excellent claim to be that of Homer's Troy was almost universally recognized, his naïve enthusiasm for attributing to Priam the treasure and principal building he had uncovered were just as widely criticized. There were also complaints about the book's arrangement, for Schliemann had simply strung together his periodic reports to Brockhaus with only minimal editing. Thus, initial opinions that were later discarded, such as, for instance, his early belief that the Homeric level must be the lowest, remained in the text without proper warning being given to the reader that his opinion changed later. While we are today grateful for Schliemann's innovative (though not unprecedented) use of photographs to illustrate his finds and trenches, it was this aspect of his work that met with the severest criticism from his contemporaries. The criticism, moreover, was just. Little consideration had been given to presenting the artifacts in a coherent or even an aesthetically pleasing manner. In addition, the quality of execution of the photographs, even judged by contemporary standards, was often poor and sometimes execrable. The unfortunate result of these criticisms was that Schliemann illustrated his subsequent works with engravings and never again with original photographs.

Immediately after the publication of *Trojanische Alterthümer*, Schliemann began negotiations with the Greek authorities for permission to excavate at Mycenae and Olympia. Without waiting for this permission to be granted, he set off for Mycenae at the end of February. With the aid of local workmen he sank some thirty-four shafts at various locations on the site. The shafts went deepest in the area now known as Grave Circle A; some, at twenty feet, must have reached the level of the top of the shaft graves. Though these illegal preliminary soundings were abruptly terminated by the outraged authorities in Athens, the permission to excavate at Mycenae was nonetheless granted in March. In the meantime, however, the Turkish government filed suit against Schliemann in the Greek courts for recovery of their half-share of "Priam's Treasure" as provided by the terms of the contract. The litigation, which lasted for more than a year, forced him to postpone excavation at Mycenae. To prevent sequestration of "Priam's Treasure," Schliemann hid it, apparently in the French School at Athens. The dispute was finally settled in April 1875, when Schliemann agreed to pay the Turkish government the sum of 50,000 francs (£2,000) in return for their renouncing all claims to "Priam's Treasure."

After the settlement Schliemann spent most of 1875 travelling in northern Europe. He lectured on his discoveries and learned more about archaeology and, in particular, prehistoric archaeology, by visiting museums in Paris, London, Leiden, Copenhagen, Stockholm, Mainz, Rome, and Naples. He excavated briefly at Alba Longa and Motya in October. Meanwhile, his Trojan discoveries were meeting with a more sympathetic reception in Britain than in Germany or France, thanks to the influence of Charles Newton of the British Museum, who was among the first to realize their importance, and W. E. Gladstone, whose effusive writings on Homer Schliemann assiduously praised and claimed to have vindicated.

The first half of 1876 was consumed in negotiations with the Turkish government for permission to resume excavations at Hisarlik. Though he eventually obtained a *firman* from Constantinople, he was blocked from beginning excavation by the obstructionist tactics of the governor of the Dardanelles. Meanwhile, he had also applied for permission to excavate Tiryns and Mycenae. When news that this permission had been granted, he promptly returned to Athens. After a few trial trenches at Tiryns, Schliemann conducted full-scale excavations at Mycenae from 7 August till 4 December. He excavated at the Lion Gate, on the site of what proved to be Grave Circle A and the immediately adjoining buildings to the north and south, and at the Tomb of Clytemnestra. He employed about a hundred workmen, the exact number varying considerably from day to day, was assisted by his wife, who directed the workmen at the Tomb of Clytemnestra, and was supervised by Panagiotis Stamatakis, who represented both the government's Archaeological Service and the Greek Archaeological Society. Whenever Stamatakis tried to exercise his authority—for example, by restricting the number of workmen employed or by attempting to restrain Schliemann's eagerness to remove, without taking time to record, anything blocking access to the prehistoric remains—frequent and bitter altercations arose.

Schliemann discovered five shaft graves (subsequent excavation by Stamatakis in 1877 revealed a sixth) within the grave circle. These were all furnished with rich grave goods. The quantity and range of gold objects (belts, breastplates, buttons, crowns, cups, cutouts, diadems, discs, earrings, goblets, greave ornaments, masks, necklace pieces, scabbard bosses, seal rings, vases and other vessels, etc.) astonished the world. Graves III, IV, and V proved particularly spectacular, accounting for 13.4 kilograms of the approximately 14 kilograms of gold found in the six tombs. It is clear that Schliemann uncovered other burials within the grave circle, which he apparently failed to recognize. His dramatic accounts of these excavations were published periodically in the London *Times* from 27 September 1876 to 12 January 1877, arousing enormous interest worldwide. Immediately after the excavation of Grave V the excavations were closed rather abruptly on 4 December, and Schliemann returned to Athens.

He remained in Athens until mid-March 1877, transforming his series of reports to the *Times* into book format and having photographs made of the principal finds. Then he moved to London and Paris to work closely with his publishers and to give lectures on his discoveries. In London the Schliemanns were fêted like conquering heroes. In some ways this was the high point of Schliemann's career.

The English edition of *Mycenae* appeared in December 1877. Easily Schliemann's most readable book, *Mycenae* is also arguably his best. The narrative is clear and detailed and the provenance of the finds more consistently given. Doubtless, the short season, the distinguishing features of the site (Lion Gate, Grave Circle, etc.), and the concentration of practically all the important finds in a few graves all help. The book is lavishly illustrated with excellent engravings.

In the February 1878 issue of *Fraser's Magazine* there appeared an article by William C. Borlase (1848–1899) that was highly critical of Schliemann's excavations at Troy. Borlase had visited Troy in August 1875 and had learned from eyewitnesses that Sophia had not been present when "Priam's Treasure" had been discovered at the end of May 1874. Nicholas Yannakis, Schliemann's personal servant, had witnessed the discovery, but his account of it differed substantially from Schliemann's. Borlase also pointed out that the building Schliemann identified as "Priam's Palace" actually blocked passage from the "Scaean Gate" into the city and consequently could not be contemporary with it.

In late August and early September of 1878 Schliemann excavated at several sites on Ithaca: Polis Bay and the School of Homer in the north and on the upper slopes and col of Mt. Aetos, in the Cave of the Nymphs, at Paleachora and among the "sties of Eumaeus" on the Plain of Malathri in the south. Results were everywhere disappointing. On the upper slopes of Mt. Aetos, however, where he excavated for two weeks with thirty workmen, he claimed to have found traces of 190 houses. The few sherds he found were unlike Mycenaean pottery but similar, he thought, to that of Troy I and II. A summary account of his excavations in Ithaca was included in *Ilios*.

Excavations at Troy were resumed in late September 1878 and lasted for two months. They were continued in the spring of 1879. In 1878 Schliemann concentrated on the palace. He quickly set about refuting Borlase's criticisms by claiming that the palace "wall" apparently blocking the entrance through the Scaean Gate was merely "a huge mass of wood ashes." Officers of H.M.S. *Pallas*, who examined the structure, were said to be able to confirm this finding. Witnesses, in fact, whose absence at the discovery of "Priam's Treasure" Borlase had deplored, are now to be found in abundance. The discovery of Treasure D on 21 October 1878 was witnessed by the officers of H.M.S. *Monarch*; in 1879 Treasures H and J were discovered in the presence of Emile Burnouf (1821–1907) and Rudolf Virchow (1821–1902). The suspicion that some of these finds were stage-managed to counteract Borlase's criticisms finds support in the clear evidence that among the pieces excavated in 1878 in the presence of the naval officers was a particular bunch of earrings and bracelets corroded together that had actually been found in 1872 (*Ilios* no. 861 = *Atlas* no. 2078). If it was found as Schliemann reports, it must have been planted.

In 1879 he concentrated on uncovering the circuit wall of Troy II (which, along with the burnt "Homeric" stratum, he now attributed to Troy III) and houses of the same date lying between the "Tower" and the northern section of the circuit wall. He also went on a tour of the Troad with Virchow and excavated a number of the tumuli, notably those of Besik Tepe and Üvecik Tepe.

Rather than publish the results of 1878–79 excavations as a supplement to his first work on Troy, Schliemann decided to write a composite work that would summarize the course of all his excavations at Troy and then give a detailed account of the finds made in each stratum. This decision has led to a certain lack of clarity in *Ilios*, for Schliemann frequently fails to mention where or in what season a given object was found. The book was conceived and executed on a grand scale. Longer than *Mycenae* and *Troy and its Remains* combined, it is illustrated with some 1,500 engravings. Nine appendices by R. Virchow, Frank Calvert, J. P. Mahaffy, A. H. Sayce, and others were added on such topics as the local flora, Calvert's excavation of Hanay Tepe, and Troy's relations with Egypt. Schliemann prefaced the work with an extended autobiographical sketch and a summary account of his excavations in Ithaca.

Work on the English and German editions of *Ilios* occupied the rest of 1879 and most of 1880. In the summer of 1880 articles by L. Stephani and E. Schultz started a heated but short-lived scholarly battle. They argued that the objects in the tombs at Mycenae were of much later date than Schliemann believed and had probably been deposited by marauding northern tribesmen in the third century A.D. For a while, their arguments won over some distinguished adherents, but the weight of evidence favoring an early date for the tombs was soon acknowledged to be overwhelming.

As soon as work on *Ilios* was completed, Schliemann set off in mid-November of 1880 to Orchomenos to begin excavations there. He seems to have expected the major finds there to be made in the cemetery, where he was supervising, but it was the tholos tomb, where Sophia was in charge, that provided the most spectacular discovery—the richly decorated ceiling of the side chamber. When he returned to

Athens about 8 December, he found a letter waiting for him from the Director of the South Kensington (now the Victoria and Albert) Museum in London, where a selection of his most important finds from Troy had been on display since December 1877. Since the museum wished to use the space for another exhibit, the director asked Schliemann to remove his collection. Schliemann set off at once for London. He stopped at Berlin on his way and arranged to transfer the Trojan collection to that city. Virchow persuaded him to give the collection to the German people. In return, it was agreed that Schliemann would be made an honorary citizen of Berlin.

Back in Greece, Schliemann visited the excavations at Olympia in mid-March 1881, where he was shown around and duly impressed by the able young architect in charge of the technical side of the excavations, Wilhelm Dörpfeld (1853–1940). In April Schliemann, accompanied by the Oxford Assyriologist, A. H. Sayce (1846–1933), returned to Orchomenos for a further two weeks of excavation. After writing up his report on the two seasons work at Orchomenos, Schliemann toured the Troad from 10 to 23 May in search of other sites that might be worth excavating. In June, at a gala banquet in the Berlin Rathaus, he was made an honorary citizen. He stayed in Berlin till mid-July, supervising the setting up of his Trojan collection in the Kunstgewerbemuseum (in 1885 the collection was moved to the new Museum für Volkerkunde). The transfer of the collection from London to Berlin seemed to be paralleled by a shift in his reputation in the two countries. In August Schliemann complained to Percy Gardner, the editor of the *Journal of Hellenic Studies*, when Gardner politely indicated that Schliemann's account of his trip to the Troad was unsuitable for the journal, that he was now held of no account in England, for his *Ilios* had been scorned by the reviewers there, whereas in Germany it had been hailed as a masterpiece.

The 1882 season at Troy lasted from the beginning of March till 21 July. This time Schliemann took two architects with him, W. Dörpfeld and J. Höfler. Unfortunately, they were prohibited from taking measurements and making plans by the Turkish overseer, who suspected or at any rate claimed to suspect that they were really trying to make plans of the Turkish fortress at Kum Kale, some five miles distant. Eventually, after the excavations were closed, permission was obtained and the plans made.

Troja, on which Schliemann worked for a month in the following summer in his childhood home in Ankershagen, appeared in the fall of 1883. It is perhaps Schliemann's least successful book. After the brilliance of the discoveries in the 1873, 1878, and 1879 seasons the new finds seem meager and rather routine. Even Schliemann's usually lively style is smothered under technical detail. The "burnt stratum" containing Homeric Troy is reassigned to Troy II. The most significant discoveries, attributable to the discerning eyes of Dörpfeld, were the floor plans of two buildings of the megaron-type, though at this stage they were identified as temples. Another positive feature of the book is the space given to the more interesting Roman and Hellenistic sculpture. Also included are further excavations of various tumuli and other sites in the region, and Schliemann's trip to the Troad in May 1881.

In the following winters there were brief excursions from Athens to conduct excavations at Thermopylae (1883) and Marathon (1884). The attempt to find the burial place of the Spartans at Thermopylae proved fruitless. Before cutting into the mound at Marathon Schliemann was convinced that it was far too early to be the burial mound of the one hundred ninety-two Athenians. He found nothing but sherds of pottery, which he dated to the ninth century B.C. or earlier. Unfortunately, because of the high water-table, he was able to dig to a depth of only one meter below ground level. A few years later, Stais dug one meter deeper and discovered the bodies of the Athenians.

Dörpfeld was again employed to assist in the excavation of Tiryns. The season ran from mid-March to the end of May, 1884. Dörpfeld returned in mid-April of 1885 for a further two months. The floor plan of the palace was soon uncovered. It was seen to incorporate at its center a structure bearing a remarkable resemblance to "Temple A" at Troy. Dörpfeld identified this architectural form with the Homeric megaron. Another major advance was the discovery of Mycenaean wall-paintings.

While Dörpfeld was conducting the second season at Tiryns, Schliemann was hard at work with his publishers and a whole team of editors and translators. On 10 November 1885 he achieved the remarkable feat of bringing out simultaneously in London, New York, Leipzig, and Paris, the British, American, German, and French editions of *Tiryns* and the huge French edition of *Ilios*, which incorporated *Troja*.

Schliemann's contributions to *Tiryns* were mainly confined to the pottery and other small finds. These, however, had been disappointing and added little of much significance. It is Dörpfeld's chapters on the architecture and wall-paintings that have proved the most valuable. Also useful was the perceptive prefatory essay by Dörpfeld's teacher and father-in-law, J. Friedrich Adler.

Schliemann naturally liked to spend his winters in warm climates. Usually, he made a point of being in Athens. In late November 1885, exhausted from his labors in seeing five books through the press simultaneously, he had decided to recuperate with a trip up the Nile. A few days later he was off to Cuba, leaving Sophia cold and miserable in Lausanne to keep an eye on their daughter, Andromache, who was attending school there. Why he changed his mind so suddenly is unclear. It seems to have had something to do with his investments in Cuban railways. Perhaps he saw that the abolition of slavery there (1886) was imminent and wished to assess for himself the impact that this would have on the Cuban economy.

In the spring of 1886 Schliemann and Dörpfeld excavated briefly at Levadia, where they searched in vain for the site of the oracle of Trophonius, and once more at Orchomenos. There Schliemann looked unsuccessfully for signs of a Mycenaean palace near the tholos tomb, while Dörpfeld cleaned out and drew up a more accurate plan of the tomb. For a few days in May he and Dörpfeld visited Crete. It had been obvious for some years that there was an important site at Knossos. Schliemann was anxious to secure permission to excavate there. However, the owners would only sell the land outright and at a price (100,000 francs) Schliemann considered far too high.

Meanwhile, an article had appeared in the London *Times* by the American journalist W. J. Stillman (1828–1901). He reported that he had visited Tiryns with F. C. Penrose (1817–1903) and two American archaeologists and that it was the unanimous opinion of the party that the building identified by Schliemann as the prehistoric palace was in fact of Byzantine date. A lively series of exchanges in the *Times* prompted a special meeting of the Hellenic Society on 3 July to discuss the matter. Schliemann and Dörpfeld traveled to London to attend the meeting and successfully defended their theories.

Schliemann spent the next two winters in Egypt. Both times he sailed all the way up the Nile to Wadi Halfa, visiting the standard sites along the way. On 17 February 1887 during his visit to the Valley of the Kings he noted on a wall-painting in the tomb of Rameses III (reign 1182–1151 B.C.) a vase of the Mycenaean stirrup-jar type. In February 1888 he excavated in Alexandria near the station for Ramli in the hope of finding Cleopatra's palace and perhaps a portrait bust of the famous queen. After a week Virchow arrived. Schliemann immediately abandoned the excavation and set off with him up the Nile. At the end of March he learned from Flinders Petrie in the Fayoum that the Mycenaean stirrup-jar first makes its appearance in Egyptian graves in the reign of Rameses II (1279–1212 B.C.). Once back in Athens, he announced that during his excavations in Alexandria he had in fact found what appeared to be a portrait bust of Cleopatra. Grave doubts have been raised recently about Schliemann's truthfulness in this account. These doubts are strengthened by the consideration that several of the Attic inscriptions that Schliemann published in the *Athenische Mitteilungen* for 1888, claiming to have found them while excavating in his garden in Athens, are now known to have been purchased.

Since 1883 Captain Ernst Bötticher had been publishing a series of articles in which he argued that Hisarlik was not the site of an ancient city but rather a necropolis, where people from the surrounding countryside cremated their dead. This theory, while certainly wrong, is not quite so absurd as has generally been believed. It drew some plausibility from Schliemann's own observation that he had found "a vast number of funeral urns, containing human ashes, in the third and fourth cities" (*Ilios*: 39). Schliemann's later claims that he was simply wrong in seeing these as funeral urns have been rendered less convincing by the recent discovery at Besika Bay of cremation urns dating to 1300 B.C.

Because Bötticher presented his arguments in such an unscholarly and disorganized manner, little attention was paid to his theory. Bötticher could not be shaken off, however, and kept bringing his views before the scholarly public and embarrassing Schliemann at conferences. Finally, Schliemann decided to resume excavations at Hisarlik and to invite Bötticher to see for himself that his theory was impossible. Excavations were accordingly resumed at Troy in early November 1889 and lasted for a month. From 1–6 December Bötticher inspected the site in the presence of Schliemann, Dörpfeld, G. Niemann, and H. Steffen. It was clear that Niemann and Steffen were siding with Schliemann. When they tried to draw up a protocol of the conclusions reached, Bötticher refused to sign and promptly departed.

The 1890 season ran from 1 March to 28 July. A second Hisarlik Conference was held at the end of March, to which eight eminent scholars were invited, including R. Virchow, K. Humann, O. Hamdy Bey, Charles Waldstein, and C. Babin. They issued a formal protocol confirming Schliemann's interpretation of the ruins.

The use of tramways now facilitated the removal of excavated soil. The most significant development of this season was the excavation of an untouched section outside the walls of Troy II. Here, where the strata had not been disturbed by the Roman rebuilding, substantial remains of Troy VI and VII were found for the first time. Sherds of Mycenaean pottery, including stirrup-jars, were found in association with a megaron. The conclusion was clear: it was Troy VI (or VII), not Troy II, that must be the Troy of the Trojan War. Schliemann, however, an eyewitness reports, "looked balefully at each succeeding stirrup-jar that emerged." He was reluctant to consign his "Priam's Palace" and "Priam's Treasure" to some shadowy past unilluminated by the lines of Homer and insisted until his death that Troy II was Homeric Troy.

Throughout his adult life Schliemann periodically experienced pain in his ears. In his last years, increasingly, this pain was accompanied by temporary deafness. In April 1890 during a trip to Mt. Ida with Virchow, he suffered a particularly severe attack. Virchow diagnosed exostosis (bony growth) in the auditory canal and advised that it could only be remedied by a serious operation involving the complete removal of the ear muscle. Schliemann stayed in Troy until the excavations closed at the end of July. When acute pain in the ears returned in November he decided to leave Athens at once and have the operation done by the best ear specialist in Germany, Professor Schwartz of Halle.

The operation took place on 12 November. Schliemann recuperated for a month and was released on 12 December. In the next few days, he visited his publisher in Leipzig, inspected with Virchow the new arrangement of the Schliemann Collection in the Museum für Volkerkunde in Berlin, and went on to Paris. There he visited an ear specialist who removed a "mass" of bone material from the left ear. He was eager, however, to set off for Naples to see the most recent discoveries from Pompeii. On the afternoon of Christmas Day he collapsed, unconscious, on a street in Naples. He died the next day. A few days later Dörpfeld arrived and escorted the body to Athens. He was buried in a splendid mausoleum, which he had had Ernst Ziller design for him. It is placed in a prominent position in the First Cemetery of Athens. The beautifully sculpted friezes show scenes from the *Iliad* on one side and Heinrich and Sophia supervising excavations at Troy on the other.

Schliemann had completed work on the *Bericht* of the 1890 excavations before his death. It is prefaced with an account of the 1889 conference at Hisarlik and the protocol of the 1890 conference. Schliemann wrote the general account of the excavations and Dörpfeld dealt with the architecture. Schliemann reported that for the first time iron had been found in a prehistoric level. He also referred *en passant* to the major find of the season, four beautiful stone axes. Greater precision in identifying the strata had been obtained. For instance, Troy II, still identified as Homer's

Troy, was now seen to comprise three periods. Emphasis was placed by both Schliemann and Dörpfeld on facts that refuted or worked against Bötticher's thesis.

There is no doubt that Schliemann's contribution to Mediterranean archaeology was of enormous and lasting importance. Unquestionably, he opened up a whole new world for archaeology. Even today his discoveries still lie at the very core of what we know about the prehistoric Aegean. Compared with the magnitude of his achievements, the few misrepresentations of which he has been proved guilty are indeed trivial. It is the nature of these misrepresentations, however, that gives us pause. Schliemann bought pieces and passed them off as excavation finds—certainly in the case of the Attic inscriptions, almost certainly in the case of the Cleopatra head, and probably in the case of several Trojan inscriptions and coins. In 1872 he combined objects found on different occasions and in different parts of the site to create larger, more dramatic finds. "Priam's Treasure" is almost certainly one of these composite finds. In 1878 at Troy he planted pieces he had brought with him and then excavated them in front of witnesses. Given Schliemann's skills and character, it would be naïve to suppose that the only times he resorted to fraudulent behavior in his excavations are those that we have been, or even will be, able to detect. It is clear that all of his work needs to be reassessed carefully. Ironically, Schliemann's motive for enhancing his genuine finds with fraudulent additions seems to have been to make them more striking and thereby secure his fame. His work is bound to remain of crucial importance; so his fame is unassailable. Our admiration, however, must now be tempered by doubt.

Books

La Chine et le Japon. Paris, 1867; German ed., *Reise durch China und Japan im Jahre 1865*, Konstanz, 1984; Japanese ed., *Nihon Chugoku ryokoki*, Tokyo, 1982 = *Shin ikokou sosho*, series 2, vol. 6.

Ithaque, le Péloponnèse, et Troie. Paris, 1869; German ed., Leipzig, 1869; reprinted Darmstadt, 1984.

Trojanische Alterthümer. With accompanying *Atlas* of photographs. Leipzig, 1874; French ed., *Antiquités troyennes.* With *Atlas.* Paris, 1874; English ed. [incorporating many of the *Atlas* photographs as engravings], *Troy and its Remains*, London, 1875; New York, 1876; reprinted New York, 1976.

Mycenae. London, 1878, 1880; New York, 1878, 1880; reprinted New York, 1976; German ed., *Mykenae*, Leipzig, 1878; French ed., *Mycènes*, Paris, 1879.

Ilios. London, 1881; New York, 1881; New York, 1976; German ed., Leipzig, 1881, French ed. [incorporating *Troja*], Paris, 1885.

Orchomenos. Leipzig, 1881; English ed. in *JHS* 2 (1881) 122–163.

Reise in der Troas im Mai 1881. Leipzig, 1881; English ed. in *Troja* (see below).

Troja. London, 1884; New York, 1884; reprinted New York, 1976; German ed., Leipzig, 1884.

Tiryns. New York, 1885; London, 1886 <1885>; reprinted New York, 1976; French ed., Paris, 1885; German ed., Leipzig, 1886 <1885>.

Bericht über die Ausgrabungen in Troja im Jahre 1890. Leipzig, 1891; shortened
    English version appended to Carl Schuchhardt, *Schliemann's Excavations.*
    See Sources below.

Sources

Autobiographies

Calder, William M., III. "Heinrich Schliemann: An Unpublished Latin *Vita.*" CW
    67 (1973–1974) 271–282 (cf. CW 69 [1975-1976] 117–118).

Schliemann, H. "Autobiography of the Author." *Ilios.* London, 1881: 1–66.

———. *Selbstbiographie, bis zu seinem Tode vervollständigt.* Edited by Sophia Sch-
    liemann and Alfred Brückner. Leipzig, 1892; 2d to 10th ed. edited by Ernst
    Meyer, 1936–1968.

Bibliographies

Korres, G. Βιβλιογραφία Ἑρρίκου Σλῆμαν . Athens, 1974.

Schindler, Wolfgang. "Heinrich Schliemann: Leben und Werk im Spiegel der
    neuen biographischen Forschungen." *Philologus* 120 (1976) 271–289.

Myth, Scandal and History (See Calder and Traill, below): 261–263. Supplements
    Korres.

Biographical

Bloedow, Edmund F. "Schliemann on his Accusers." *Tyche* 1 (1986) 30–40.

———. "Schliemann on his Accusers II: A study in the Re-use of Sources." AC 57
    (1988) 5–30.

Bölke, Wilfried. *Heinrich Schliemann und Ankershagen: Heimat, Kindheit und El-
    ternhaus* = *Mitteilungen aus dem Heinrich-Schliemann-Museum* 2 (1988).

Borlase, William C. "A Visit to Dr. Schliemann's Troy." *Fraser's Magazine* n.s. 17
    (February 1878) 228–239.

Calder, William M., III. "Schliemann on Schliemann: A Study in the Use of
    Sources." *GRBS* 13 (1972) 335–353.

———. "Wilamowitz on Schliemann." *Philologus* 124 (1980) 146–151.

———. *Myth, Scandal, and History: the Heinrich Schliemann Controversy and a First
    Edition of the Mycenaean Diary.* Edited by William M. Calder III and David
    A. Traill. Detroit, 1986.

———. "A New Picture of Heinrich Schliemann." *Myth, Scandal, and History*
    17–47.

Calvert, Frank. "Trojan Antiquities." *Athenaeum,* nos. 2454 and 2455 (7 and 14
    November 1874) 610–611 and 643–644.

Cobet, Justus. "Das erfundene Troja." *Frankfurter Allgemeine Zeitung* (29 April
    1987) 36.

Dickinson, O. T. P. K. "Schliemann and the Shaft Graves." *G&R* 23 (1976)
    159–168.

Döhl, Hartmut. "Schliemann the Archaeologist." *Myth, Scandal, and History:*
    95–109.

Dörpfeld, W. "Geleitwort." In Schliemann's *Briefe*: 7–16.

Easton, Donald F. "Schliemann's Discovery of 'Priam's Treasure': Two Enigmas." *Antiquity* 55 (1981) 179–183.

———. "The Schliemann Papers." *BSA* 77 (1982) 93–110.

———. "Schliemann's Mendacity—a False Trail?" *Antiquity* 58 (1984) 197–204.

———. "Priam's Treasure." *AnatSt* 34 (1984) 141–169.

Finley, Moses I. "Schliemann's Troy—One Hundred Years After." *PBA* 60 (1974) 393–412; reprinted in his *The World of Odysseus*, 2d ed., Harmondsworth, 1979.

Gardner, Percy. "Henry Schliemann." *MacMillan's Magazine* no. 3781 (April 1891) 474–480.

Goessler, Peter. *Wilhelm Dörpfeld: ein Leben im Dienst der Antike.* Stuttgart, 1951: 65–83.

Grimm, Hans. "Heinrich Schliemann und Rudolf Virchow in heutiger Sicht." *Mitteilungen aus dem Heinrich-Schliemann-Museum. Ankershagen* 1 (1987) 10–19.

Isserlin, B. S. J. "Schliemann at Motya." *Antiquity* 42 (1968) 144–148.

Komnos, S. "Hissarlik and Mycenae." *Athenaeum* no. 2441 (8 August 1874) 178–179.

Korres, Georgios S. "Ἐπιγραφαὶ ἐς'Αττικῆς εἰς κατοχὴν Ἑρρίκου Σλῆμαν." *ΑΘΕΝΑ* 75 (1974–75) 54–67 and 492 (French résumé).

———. "Τὸ ‹Ἰλίου Μέλαθρον› ὡς ἔκφρασις τῆς προσωπικότητος καὶ τοῦ ἔργου τοῦ Ἑρρίκου Σλῆμαν." In G. Korres, Ἀναδρομαὶ εἰς τὸν Νεοκλασσικισμόν. Ατηενσ, 1977: 75–169.

———. "Ἡ συλλογὴ νομισμάτων τοῦ Ἑρρίκου Σλῆμαν καὶ ὁ κατάλογος αὐτῶν ὁ ουνταχθεὶς ὑπὸ τοῦ Ἀχιλλέως Ποστολάκκα." *ΔΕΛΤΙΟΝ* 29 (1977) 245–269.

———. "Das Mausoleum Heinrich Schliemanns auf dem Zentralfriedhof von Athen." *Boreas* 4 (1981) 133–173.

Kyrieleis, Helmut. "Schliemann in Griechenland." *Jahrbuch des Römisch-Germanischen Zentralmuseums Mainz* 25 (1978) 74–91 and Pl. 11.

Michaelis, Adolf. *A Century of Archaeological Discoveries.* London, 1908: 215–222.

Niederland, W. G. "An Analytic Inquiry into the Life and Work of Heinrich Schliemann." In *Drives, Affects, Behavior.* Edited by Max Schur. New York, 1965: 2:369–396.

Reinach, Salomon. "Henri Schliemann." *RA* sér. 3, v. 16 (1890) 416–419.

Richter, Wolfgang. "Heinrich Schliemann und die Stadt Rostock." *Wissenschaftliche Zeitschrift der Wilhelm-Pieck-Universität Rostock* 33 (1984) 40–49.

Schindler, Wolfgang. "Schliemann's Cleopatra," *Myth, Scandal, and History* 81–94.

———. "Rudolf Virchow und Schliemanns Kleopatra." *Mitteilungen aus dem Heinrich–Schliemann-Museums Ankershagen* 1 (1987) 43–54.

Schuchhardt, Carl. *Schliemann's Ausgrabungen.* Leipzig, 1890; English translation by E. Sellers as *Schliemann's Excavations.* New York, 1891; reprinted Blom,

1971; later reprinted as *Schliemann's Discoveries of the Ancient World*. New York, 1979.

Scott, John A. "Ludwig and Schliemann." *CJ* 27 (1931) 15–22.

Stark, B. Review of *Trojanische Alterthümer* in *Jenaer Literaturzeitung* (1874) 347–351.

Steinart, Harald. "Die Legende vom Schatz des Priamos." *Frankfurter Allgemeine Zeitung, Feuilleton* (30 April 1984) 25.

Traill, David A. "Schliemann's Mendacity: Fire and Fever in California." *CJ* 74 (1979) 348–355.

———. "Schliemann's American Citizenship and Divorce." *CJ* 77 (1982) 336–342.

———. "Schliemann's Discovery of Priam's Treasure: A Re-examination of the Evidence." *JHS* 104 (1984) 96–115. (Contains new letter by Heinrich to Sophia Schliemann.)

———. "Further Evidence of Fraudulent Reporting in Schliemann's Archaeological Works." *Boreas* 7 (1984) 295–316.

———. "Schliemann's 'Dream of Troy': The Making of a Legend." *CJ* 81 (1985) 13–24.

———. "Schliemann's Mendacity: A Question of Methodology." *AS* 36 (1986) 91–98.

———. "Schliemann's Acquisition of the Helios Metope and his Psychopathic Tendencies." *Myth, Scandal, and History* 48–80. (Contains new letters between Schliemann and Frank Calvert.)

———. " 'Priam's Treasure': Schliemann's Plan to Make Duplicates for Illicit Purposes." *Myth, Scandal, and History* 110–121. (Contains new letter from Schliemann to P. Beaurain.)

———. "Bloedow on Schliemann's Accusers." *Tyche* 3 (1988) 235–239.

———. "Hisarlik, 31 May 1873, and the Discovery of 'Priam's Treasure'." *Boreas* 3 (1988) 235–239.

———. "How Schliemann Smuggled 'Priam's Treasure' from the Troad to Athens." *Hesperia* 57 (1988) 273–77. (Contains new letter of Schliemann.)

Virchow, Rudolf. "Gedächtnisfeier für Heinrich Schliemann." *Zeitschrift für Ethnologie* 23 (1891) 42–58.

Wace, Elizabeth French. "Schliemann on the Pottery from Mycenae." *Atti e Memorie del 1° Congresso Internazionale di Micenologia, Roma 27 Septembre–3 Ottobre 1967*. Rome, 1968: 170–175.

Witte, Reinhard. "Virchows Parteinahme für Heinrich Schliemann im Spiegel seiner Veröffentlichungen." *Mitteilungen aus dem Heinrich-Schliemann-Museum* 1 (1987) 20–27.

Zimmermann, Konrad. "Mecklenburg in den Selbstdarstellungen Heinrich Schliemanns." *Rostocker Wissenschaftshistorische Manuskripte* 13 (1986) 11–16.

Biographical Fiction

Beye, Bruno. *Schliemann, épisodes ignorées.* (Play) Paris, 1982.

Stoll, Heinrich A. *Der Traum von Troja: Lebensroman Heinrich Schliemann.* Leipzig, 1956.

Stone, Irving. *The Greek Treasure: A Biographical Novel of Henry and Sophia Schliemann.* New York, 1975.

Biographies

Brustgi, Franz G. *Heinrich Schliemann.* Munich, 1971.

Burg, Katerina von. *Heinrich Schliemann: For Gold or Glory?* Windsor, England, 1987.

Deuel, Leo. *Memoirs of Heinrich Schliemann: A Documentary Portrait Drawn from His Autobiographical Writings, Letters, and Excavation Reports.* New York, 1977.

Döhl, Hartmut. *Heinrich Schliemannn: Mythos und Ärgernis.* Munich, 1981.

Faure, Paul. *Henri Schliemann: une vie d'un archéologue.* Paris, 1982.

Herrmann, Joachim. *Heinrich Schliemann: Wegbereiter einer neuen Wissenschaft.* Berlin, 1974.

Ludwig, Emil. *Schliemann of Troy: the Story of a Goldseeker.* Translated by D. F. Tait. London, 1931; Boston, 1931.

Meyer, Ernst. *Heinrich Schliemann: Kaufmann und Forscher.* Göttingen, 1969. (The standard biography.)

Payne, Robert. *The Gold of Troy: The Story of Heinrich Schliemann and the Buried Cities of Ancient Greece.* London, 1959; New York, 1959.

Poole, Lynn and Gray. *One Passion, Two Loves: The Story of Heinrich and Sophia Schliemann, Discoverers of Troy.* New York, 1966; London, 1967.

Exhibition Catalogues

Troja: Heinrich Schliemanns Ausgrabung und Funde. Ausstellung des Museums für Vor- und Frühgeschichte, etc. Berlin, 1981.

Troja und Thrakien: Ausstellung Berlin-Haupstadt der DDR und Sofia. Berlin, 1982.

Troy: Heinrich Schliemann's Excavations and Finds. Exhibition staged by the Greek Ministry of Culture, etc. Athens, 1985.

Letters

Briefe. Edited by Ernst Meyer. Berlin, 1936.

Briefwechsel. Vols. I and II. Edited by Ernst Meyer. Berlin, 1953, 1958.

Abenteuer meines Lebens. Edited by Heinrich A. Stoll. Leipzig, 1960; 1982. (Letters to W. Rust.)

Arndt, K. "Schliemann's Excavation of Troy and American Politics." *Yearbook of German-American Studies* 16 (1981) 1–8.

Korres, G. S. "Ἐπιστολὴ Ἑρρίκου Σλῆμαν πρὸς Ἐρνέστον Κούρτιον ." *ΠΛΑΤΩΝ* 28 (1976) 32–36.

Lilly, Eli. *Schliemann in Indianapolis.* Indianapolis, 1961.

Luce, J. V. "Five New Schliemann Letters in Belfast." *Hermathena* 132 (1982) 8–14.

Marinatos, S. and Mylonas, G. "Περὶ τῆς Προσωπικότητος καὶ τοῦ Ἔργου τοῦ Ἑρρίκου Σλῆμαν ." *ΠρακΑκΑθ* 47 (1972) 212–238.

Meyer, E. "Schliemann's Letters to Max Müller in Oxford." *JHS* 82 (1962) 75–105.

————. "Schliemanns erste Briefe aus Troja." *Ruperto-Carola* 17, Bd. 37, (1965) 77–80.

Mylonas, G. "Ἀνέκδοτος ἐπιστολὴ τοῦ H. *Schliemann* καὶ ὁ <θησαυρὸς τοῦ Πρία-μου>." *ΠρακΑκΑθ*61 (1986) 154–174.

Richter, W. "Ein unveröffentlicher Brief Heinrich Schliemanns aus dem Jahre 1869." *Wissenschaftliche Zeitschrift der Wilhelm-Pieck-Universität Rostock* 29 (1980) 55–64.

Some new letters of Schliemann are included in several articles by D. Traill; see above.

Papers

The major deposit of Schliemann papers is in the Gennadius Library, American School of Classical Studies, Athens. There are significant collections of letters written by Schliemann in the British Library; the Bodleian Library, Oxford; J. Murray, publishers, London; Brockhaus Verlag, Leipzig; the Heinrich-Schliemann-Museum, Ankershagen. For further details, see Easton, "The Schliemann Papers" (above).

Paul Shorey

3 August 1857–24 April 1934

E. CHRISTIAN KOPFF
University of Colorado

Paul Shorey was the proponent of a famous theory of Plato, helped found and was managing editor of *Classical Philology* (1908–1934), was an able theorist and practitioner of the pedagogy of the Greek and Latin languages and was a well-known social and cultural conservative and nationalist. As the first Professor of Greek at the University of Chicago from 1892–1927, he directed over fifty dissertations and was an important influence in the development of classical philology in the United States from a philo-Germanic bias to a pro-English attitude.

Paul Shorey was born in Davenport, Iowa, on 3 August 1857. His family moved to Chicago, Illinois. Although Shorey traveled as student and lecturer over much of Europe and the United States, he lived most of his life in Chicago and died there on 24 April 1934. Shorey's father, Daniel Lewis Shorey, was a prominent Chicago lawyer with a taste for the classics, and a member of the Board of Trustees of the University of Chicago. Daniel and his wife, Maria Antoinette (Merriam), were not conventional Midwesterners. Shorey remembered, "Instead of prescribed Josephus or Fox's *Book of Martyrs*, I read *The Origin of Species* aloud to my mother at the age of nine." A youthful radical, he refused to attend even "a left-wing Unitarian Sunday school." At his graduation from Chicago High School, the text for his commencement address was Shelley's "Happiness and Science dawn, though late, upon the earth." He went on to study at Harvard, where he was graduated with an A.B. in 1878. It was while at Harvard that reading Plato freed him from the influence of Herbert Spencer. Harvard, "that hotbed of infidelity, destroyed my faith" in Spencer, Shelley, and evolution.

Shorey returned to Chicago to work at his father's law firm and was admitted to the Illinois bar (1880). The law, however, was not his vocation, and he went to Europe to study at the Universities of Leipzig (1881–82) and Bonn (1882) and the

American School of Classical Studies in Athens (1882–83). He then went to Munich, where his dissertation (1884) was directed by Wilhelm Christ, who mentioned Shorey in his *Platonische Studien* (Munich, 1885: 3–4). Shorey had already begun his dissertation before going to Christ and was thoroughly at home in the classics, especially in the writings of Plato. Shorey's phenomenal memory and his nearly total recall of Plato's writings impressed the German scholar.

Shorey was among the faculty (which also included Woodrow Wilson) called by M. Carey Thomas (1857–1935) to teach at Bryn Mawr College. While at Bryn Mawr (1885–1892) he became friends with Basil Lanneau Gildersleeve (1831–1924) of Johns Hopkins University, who became his model and living proof that an American might hope to attain great things in classics. Shorey taught philosophy and Latin as well as Greek and worked on a school text of Horace's *Odes*, which he finished during his early years at Chicago (1898; often reprinted). The edition devotes much room to parallels not only from the poet himself but from English poetry. The assiduous collection of parallels reflects Shorey's wide reading and his pedagogy. "In no other way can the right atmosphere for the enjoyment of the *Odes* be so easily created. . . . The student should be taught to distinguish carefully conscious imitation, interesting coincidences, and the mere commonplaces of poetic rhetoric and imagery." The text received a favorable review from J. P. Postgate (*CR* 15 [1901] 230). When coeditor Gordon J. Laing removed some of the parallels from the revised edition of 1910, Basil Gildersleeve devoted a memorable "Brief Mention" to praise of Shorey and the first edition (*AJP* 31 [1910] 485–6). Already at Bryn Mawr, Shorey was impressing and terrifying students with his vast recall of the poetry of Greek, Latin, French, and English. He insisted on command of meter and the value of reading aloud.

In 1892 Shorey returned to Chicago as first Professor of Greek at President William Rainey Harper's (1856–1906) University of Chicago. He spent the years until 1903 developing a short but significant essay, "The Unity of Plato's Thought." To appreciate his insight, a little background is needed. Stylistic analysis, beginning with the great Scottish scholar Lewis Campbell, had been able to establish three main periods in Plato's voluminous writings. It rather naturally became the fashion to analyze Plato's own intellectual development as falling into those three periods. There are, however, problems with stylistic analysis based on this division. Some individual dialogues are hard to place, and the culmination of the second period, the *Republic*, begins with a book that is placed by stylistic criteria in the middle of the first period. Shorey burst into the (largely Germanic) scholarly discussion like a bull into a china shop. In his own words, "My thesis is simply that Plato on the whole belongs rather to the type of thinkers whose philosophy is fixed in early maturity (Schopenhauer, Herbert Spencer), rather than to the class of those who receive a new revelation every decade (Schelling). And I have tried to show that the method which proceeds on the contrary assumption leads to misinterpretation of his writings." (Shorey had said this already in *AJP* 9 [1888] 276, and it also forms the basis for his discussion of Plato in his dissertation.) Although the idea of Plato's gradual evolution remains the dominant one in Platonic studies, Shorey's case (which resembles the views of Schleiermacher) has always won a minority assent, including that of such important scholars as Hans von Arnim and Werner Jaeger (see Jaeger's *Paideia* [New York, 1943] 2:77–106, with favorable reference to Shorey on page 385, note 52).

Most of Shorey's scholarly publications are devoted to Plato and most of the rest to Aristotle, his commentators, and other ancient philosophers. He did discuss over a period of years the change in metrical scholarship from the musical or rhythmical views of Rossbach, Christ, and Schmidt to the metrical views of Wilamowitz and Maas. The Rossbach view of ancient meter can still be met with in the metrical analyses of choral lyrics in Jebb's Sophocles and Gildersleeve's Pindar. They have disappeared from modern texts. The greatest American metrician, Shorey's contemporary John Williams White, converted from the one system to the other. Shorey remained loyal to the system of Jebb and Gildersleeve for reasons he discussed in "Choriambic Dimeter and the Rehabilitation of the Antispast" (1907) and "The Issue in Greek Metric" (1924) as well as his reviews of White's *Verse of Greek Comedy*, (1913), his response to White's reply in the same volume (217–220) and his review of Wilamowitz's *Griechische Verskunst* (1922). Shorey felt that it was not physically possible for human beings to pronounce verse without recourse to stress accent and metrical ictus. He denies Hephaestion's authority over modern observation. ("I would accept no authority, and least of all that of Hephaestion, against a physiological and psychological necessity," he tells White.) He insists that no one can read Greek verse with feeling and intelligence with the "New Metric," while it is possible with the system of Rossbach and Schmidt. The last point should not be undervalued. Shorey was a teacher, and he was impatient with learning that was intelligible only to self-appointed experts. He notes with satisfaction that Murray and Wilamowitz read with a rhythmic stress. Shorey was again in a minority, but the debate is not yet over. W. S. Allen has defended the existence of the ictus in Greek poetry in *Accent and Rhythm* (Cambridge, 1972), while Günther Zuntz has argued that we can pronounce Greek verse with a musical and not a stress accent in "Drei Kapitel zur griechischen Metrik" (Vienna, 1984).

In another area Shorey was on the cutting edge of change. It was H. Meuss, in "Thukydides und die religiöse Aufklärung" (*Neue Jahrb. fur kl. Philol.* 146 [1892]), who first presented a Thucydides who rejected traditional morality and the gods (N. Marinatos, *Thucydides and Religion* [Königstein 1981] 1–16). Shorey's article "On the Implicit Ethics and Psychology of Thucydides" (1893), argued that the two chief aspects of Thucydides' criticism of life are 1) ethical positivism and 2) intellectualism. This is a cynical Thucydides, for whom the ethical, the social and the religious are "sheath after sheath of decorous pretence" wrapped around the harsh reality "that the nature and conduct of man are strictly determined by his physical and social environment and by a few elementary appetites and desires." Written with conviction and intelligence, the article still influences even those who have never read it. It was relevant to his Platonic studies. Shorey calls the society against which Plato is reacting "Thucydidean Athens," e.g. in "The Idea of the Good in Plato's Republic," (1895).

Shorey also published extensively in nonprofessional journals on pedagogical, social, and cultural issues. He felt especially strongly on the subject of the weakening role of the humanities and the classics in education. His essay "The Assault on Humanism" which appeared initially in the *Atlantic* in 1917 and was published as an "Atlantic Monograph" that same year, concludes by predicting that the disappearance of Latin is only the first step to the elimination of reading the Great Books. A prophecy that must have seemed hysterical in 1917 has been fulfilled in the new Stanford "Culture, Ideas, Values" curriculum. His essay "The Case for the Classics" (1910) was often republished. He appeared frequently on the conservative side in social and educational debates, even defending William Jennings Bryan in "Evolution: A Conservative's Apology" in the *Atlantic* (1928). "I preached conservatism mainly because, though the ordinary Main Street American does not yet vote red, all intellectual America reads and talks pink" (*The Creative Intelligence and Modern Life*: 172).

"I have but twice had the good fortune to speak on the popular side of any question," was Shorey's ironic boast. One occasion was his support for United States entry into World War I and the accompanying anti-German and pro-English sentiments. Shorey's attitude was rooted in his scholarly positions as well as his nationalism and conservatism. Germany was the prime mover behind the scholarship that taught Homeric analysis, the development of Plato, and the (literally unspeakable) New Metric. Germany was the home of the progressive in scholarship, theology, and philosophy. Shorey expressed his views in "American Scholarship" (1911). America suffers from "the divorce of our scholarship and our science from culture. . . . The chief cause, perhaps, is the fact that our professional scholarship has been in the past an importation . . . from Germany." Not only is German culture not American, but German scholars do not know what German culture there is. "They do not know their own literature as Frenchmen and Englishmen know theirs. . . . The consequent crudity and amateurishness of their criticism of life and letters is their misfortune and not their fault." Further, German obsession with originality in scholarship leads to narrow specialization and a contempt for the truth. "The chief objection to hunting for mares' nests is that you are sure to find them. But the quest itself impairs the reasoning powers. . . . The big ambitious books of the Nordens, the Heinzes, the Reitzensteins, the Joels, the Dümmlers, the Hirzels, the Wendlands, and even, alas! of the Wilamowitzes cannot be trusted."

The editor of *The Nation* was a man of letters and a classicist, Paul Elmer More (1864–1937), who was later to teach in the departments of Philosophy and then of Classics at Princeton University and write a multi-volume study of *The Greek Tradition from Socrates to the Council of Chalcedon* (Princeton, 1921–1931). This work, a sensitive mixture of translation and interpretation of the development of the Socratic tradition and its influence on early Christianity, is marred by outbursts of irritation aimed at German culture, philosophy, and scholarship. More, with his Harvard classmate, Irving Babbit (1865–1933), and their disciples, was one of the leaders of the conservative intellectual movement of the twenties known as The New Humanism.

Although on the cutting edge of intellectual movements in his own country, his article was less popular in Germany, where a spiteful colleague broadcast word of it after Shorey was named Theodore Roosevelt Exchange Professor at the University of Berlin for 1913. The part of the exchange program that involved Shorey was managed by the German Ministerialdirektor of the Prussian Kulturministerium and the President of Columbia University, Nicholas Murray Butler (1862–1947). Both men worked hard to smooth over the tempest in a teapot caused by Shorey's piece, "the little paper that first established my war record three years before the war and got me into hot water in Germany" ("Fifty Years of Classical Studies in America," 34). Shorey was to give a series of lectures on American culture in German and a seminar on a Classical subject. His suggestions of Plato's *Republic* and Pindar's *Odes* were vetoed by the Professor of Greek at Berlin, Ulrich von Wilamowitz-Moellendorff (1848–1931). Shorey's term in Berlin changed his mind on nothing, from the New Metric to the arrogance of German *Kultur* and its advocates. Nearly twenty years later Shorey's student, President George Norlin of the University of Colorado, spent a term as Visiting Professor at the University of Berlin and like Shorey returned to the United States committed to a campaign to alert the American people of the dangers of Germany.

After his retirement in 1927, along with many articles and reviews, both scholarly and popular, Shorey published the first volume of a text and translation of Plato's *Republic* in the Loeb series. The text is conservative and the translation never burkes a difficulty. The second volume appeared in 1935 (edited by Stella L. Lange). His lively summary with notes of Plato's Dialogues appeared in 1933 with the pugnacious title, *What Plato Said*. The battles with Wilamowitz continue and the notes are often worth consulting. Shorey's last Sather lectures, *Platonism Ancient and Modern*, were published in 1938, edited by Procope S. Costas of Whitman College. Although a tribute to Shorey's phenomenally wide reading, they are not generally considered one of the more important contributions to the Sather series.

Shorey received eleven honorary degrees, including one from the Université de Liège in Belgium, 1924, where he gave a series of lectures. He was later elected Associé de l'Académie Royale de Belgique (1929). Among his activities in professional organizations, he was President of the American Philological Association in 1910; Professor of Greek at Chicago from 1892 and head of the Greek Department from 1896; and managing editor of *Classical Philology* from 1908–1934. He retired from his professorship in 1927 but continued to teach until the summer term of 1933. He was Annual Associate Director of the American School of Classical Studies in Athens in 1901–1902 and Roosevelt Exchange Professor in 1913. He delivered the Harris lectures at Northwestern University, the Lowell Lectures at Boston, and the Sather Lectures at Berkeley in 1916–17, 1918–19 and 1928–29.

Shorey married a graduate student in Latin at Chicago, Emma L. Gilbert, in 1895. They had no children.

Paul Shorey was a significant figure in the creation of Bryn Mawr College and the University of Chicago. He founded a major graduate program at Chicago and a very important scholarly journal. His ideas are still taken seriously, as the reprinting of his minor writings (1980) and translation of his dissertation (1982) indicate. Several of his books are still in print. He took an important part in the educational and cultural debates of his time. In his conservatism and his creativity he was a worthy peer of Basil Lanneau Gildersleeve and William Abbot Oldfather.

Books

"De Platoni idearum doctrina atque mentis humanae notionibus commentatio." Diss., Munich, 1884 = *Selected Papers*, 253–313. Translated as "A Dissertation on Plato's Theory of Forms and on the Concepts of the Human Mind" by R. S. W. Hawtrey; preface by R. K. Sprague. *Ancient Philosophy* 2 (1982) 1–59.

Horace. Odes and Epodes. Boston, 1898; revised with G. J. Laing, 1910.

The Unity of Plato's Thought. Chicago, 1903; reprinted New York, 1968; New York, 1980.

The Creative Intelligence and Modern Life. Boulder, CO, 1928.

What Plato Said. Chicago, 1933

Plato. The Republic. 2 vols. Loeb Classical Library. Cambridge, MA, and London, 1930 and 1935.

Platonism, Ancient and Modern. Berkeley, 1938.

Selected Papers in Two Volumes. Edited by Leonardo Tarán. New York, 1980.

Articles

"On the Implicit Ethics and Psychology of Thucydides." *TAPA* 24 (1893) 66–68.

"The Idea of the Good in Plato's Republic." *University of Chicago Studies in Classical Philology* 1 (1895) 214–215.

"Choriambic Dimeter and the Rehabilitation of the Antispast." *TAPA* 38 (1907) 57–88.

"The Case for the Classics." *School Review* 18 (1910) 585–617.

"American Scholarship." *Nation* 92, no. 2393 (11 May 1911) 466–469.

Review of White's *Verse of Greek Comedy, CPh* 8 (1913) 99–104.

"The Assault on Humanism." *Atlantic Monthly* 119 (June 1917) 793–801 and 120 (July 1917) 94–105. Published separately as an *Atlantic* Monograph in 1917.

"Fifty Years of Classical Studies in America." *TAPA* 50 (1919) 33–61.

Review of Wilamowitz's *Griechische Verskunst, CPh* 17 (1922) 150–153.

"The Issue in Greek Metric." *CPh* 19 (1924) 169–174.

"Evolution: A Conservative's Apology." *Atlantic Monthly* 142 (October 1928) 475–488.

Sources

Bibliography

Latimer, John Francis. "Paul Shorey: A Bibliography of his Classical Publications," *CPh* 81 (1980) 1–31. Latimer numbers Shorey's total publications at 833.

Biographical

Diès, A. "Un platonisant d'Amérique: Paul Shorey." *BAGB* 24 (1929) 1–21.

Kopff, E. Christian. "Wilamowitz and Classical Philology in the USA: An Interpretation." In *Wilamowitz Nach 50 Jahren*. Edited by W. M. Calder III et al. Darmstadt, 1985: 558–580, esp. 569–576.

Laing, Gordon J. "Paul Shorey." *DAB* 9 (1935–1936) 125–6.

Obituary in *CPh* 29 (1935) 185–88, followed by George Norlin on Shorey as a teacher: 188–91.

Putnam, Emily James. *Atlantic Monthly* 161 (June 1938) 795–804.

The quotations on Shorey's early life and other unattributed quotations come from *Atlantic Monthly* 142 (1928) 475–476.

Lily Ross Taylor

12 August 1886 – 18 November 1969

T. ROBERT S. BROUGHTON
University of North Carolina

Lily Ross Taylor, Professor of Latin at Bryn Mawr College, was a brilliant teacher, scholar, academic administrator, and public servant, who received international recognition for her studies in Roman religion, history, and institutions. She was a person of wide interests, with a gift for friendship, whose unflagging energy and whose vivid and outgoing personality won an immediate response from people of widely varying interests, young and old alike.

She was born in Auburn, Alabama, on 12 August 1886, of old Southern stock, and retained vivid memories of her childhood there, still having to face problems of the postbellum South. She attended the University of Wisconsin, where her father was Professor of Railway Engineering. A course on Lucretius with Professor M. S. Slaughter led her to change her major from mathematics to classics, which became the field of her scholarly career. Receiving her A.B. in 1906, she came to Bryn Mawr College and studied Latin literature and Roman history with Professors Arthur Wheeler and Tenney Frank. A year (1909–1910) at the American School of Classical Studies in Rome initiated her into the study of Roman topography, antiquities, and religion and aroused her lifelong love of Rome and Italy. Her Ph.D. dissertation on *The Cults of Ostia* (1912), begun in Rome at the suggestion of Jesse Benedict Carter and completed at Bryn Mawr under the direction of Tenney Frank, provided a firm beginning for further study of Roman religious institutions and of the people they served.

Appointed to the faculty of Vassar College (1912–1927), she rose from Instructor to Professor of Latin, in the meantime holding fellowships at the American Academy in Rome (1917, 1919–1920). During and immediately after the First World War she served with the Red Cross in Italy and Yugoslavia. In 1927 she moved to Bryn Mawr as Professor of Latin and chairman of the department, and from 1942 until her retirement in 1952 she was Dean of the graduate school. During this period she returned for a year (1934–1935) to the American Academy as acting Professor in charge of the Classical School, was President of the American Philological Association (1942), was appointed a Trustee of Wellesley College (1943–1949), served during the Second World War as Principal Social Science Analyst in the Office of Strategic Services in Washington (1943–1944), and was Sather Professor of Classics at the University of California at Berkeley (1947).

Retirement merely initiated a still greater variety of services. She returned for three years (1952–1955) to the American Academy as Professor in charge of the Classical School, was appointed National Lecturer for Phi Beta Kappa (1956–57), delegate to the National Committee of UNESCO (1958–1959), Visiting Professor of Latin at Harvard University (1959), and Member of the Institute for Advanced Studies in Princeton (1959). She was also Visiting Professor of Latin at Bryn Mawr College (1960–1961), Visiting Professor of Classics at the University of Wisconsin (1962–1963), and Jerome Lecturer at the American Academy in Rome and the University of Michigan (1964–1965). She died in a motor accident near her home in Bryn Mawr on 18 November 1969, at the age of eighty-three, in full possession of her physical and intellectual powers, and still an actively productive scholar.

Many honors expressed the respect and admiration felt for her in this country and abroad. Listed in *Life* magazine as one of America's great teachers, she also received from Bryn Mawr College the Lindback Award for distinction in teaching. She was awarded many honorary degrees: D. Litt. from Wilson College, Mills College, The University of Wisconsin, Columbia University, and Smith College. She held Guggenheim Fellowships in 1952 and 1960. She received the Achievement Award from the American Association of University Women (1952), the Goodwin Award of the American Philological Association for her book *The Voting Districts of the Roman Republic* (1962), and in the same year the award of the Medaglia d'Oro of the Cultori di Roma recognized her achievement in Roman studies. She was elected a member of the American Philosophical Society; Fellow of the American Academy of Arts and Sciences; Honorary Member of the Society for the Promotion of Roman Studies; and Corresponding Member of the British Academy, of the Pontificia Accademia di Archeologia, and of the Bayerische Akademie der Wissenschaften.

Her published works include seven books, over seventy articles, and more than sixty reviews. As a whole they show a wide range of interests and are witness also to a consistent development, closely connected with the advances in Roman studies in her time. Mommsen's *Römisches Staatsrecht* had laid a firm basis for the study of Roman public institutions, and the vast collections of the *Corpus Inscriptionum Latinarum* provided a great mass of evidence, official and private, that touched upon the interests and concerns of human beings, great and humble alike, of every class. Her work in Rome and on the cults of Ostia brought her into contact with this evidence at a time when Lanciani, Hülsen, Platner, and Ashby renewed the study of Roman topography and monuments, while Wissowa, Warde Fowler, and Cumont were doing the same for the religions and religious rites of Rome and the communities of the Empire. Tenney Frank and Rostovtzeff were soon to direct interest toward social and economic history. These influences, combined with her love of Latin literature (she could recite long passages from Lucretius, Horace, and Virgil from memory) and her enthusiasm for Rome and Italy laid the foundation for a consistent scholarly achievement, which was characterized throughout by an insistent emphasis on how institutions work and how people function in them. She admired Mommsen's work greatly (the *Staatsrecht* was the reading she chose when confined for a time in hospital with a broken ankle), but this emphasis places her firmly in the generation of his successors.

After her study of Ostia, it was natural for her to share in the American Academy's plan for a series of regional studies of the cults of Italy in ancient times. Her book on *Local Cults of Etruria* (1923) was in its time a significant contribution to knowledge of that mysterious land and people, most notable perhaps for her personal knowledge of the land, for the careful collection of the evidence, and for the demonstration that in religious matters little that was purely Etruscan survived.

Meantime, studies of the history and culture of the Hellenistic East were drawing attention to the ideas and the rituals connected with the cult of kings as gods of the state, though with less interest in its appearance in Rome. The problem of the influence of the Hellenistic ruler cult in Rome and the Roman adaptation, processes that became evident with the deification of Caesar and Augustus' gradual acceptance of worship of himself, had been brought into sharp relief in 1919 by Eduard Meyer in *Caesars Monarchie und das Principat des Pompeius* with a full presentation of his controversial view that the acts of Caesar and the honors that he accepted during his dictatorships looked toward establishing him as a divine monarch in Rome. Miss Taylor discussed aspects of the problem in several preliminary articles: "The Worship of Augustus in Italy in his Lifetime" (1920); "The Altar of Manlius in the Lateran" (1921); and "Tiberius' Refusals of Divine Honors" (1929). Her book *The Divinity of the Roman Emperor* (1931) arose directly out of this controversy. Accepting Meyer's thesis ("Caesar," she wrote, "was the first divine ruler in Rome, and Augustus gave the divinity of the ruler the form under which it was destined to endure for three centuries"), she approached the problem as a study also of Roman background and of stages in the development of the feelings and ideas of the people until Augustus, *princeps*, as he claimed, of a restored *res publica*, was deified and enshrined in a public cult. This work was the first comprehensive investigation of the subject that took the whole body of varied evidence into account, and it has been reprinted and kept available as a basic study. But once the cult had become a formal convention, used by courtiers for flattery, and for some emperors a source of delusion, even though it was a symbol of imperial unity and a recognition of the emperor's providence, Miss Taylor lost interest: "I have no interest," she said, "in cataloguing the forms of flattery," and "I abandoned the study of ruler cult when it was in danger of affecting my sanity."

Roman religious institutions are so essential to Roman political life that the transition to studies of Roman politics was easily made. She herself was interested all her life in social and political movements, ancient and modern, and in Rome of the late Republic there was besides the dominating figure of Caesar. Hence a series of articles: "Caesar's Early Career" (1941); "Caesar's Colleagues in the Pontifical College" (1943); "The Election of the Pontifex Maximus in the Late Republic" (1942), as Caesar had won it in a surprising electoral upset in 63; and "Caesar and the Roman Nobility" (1942), her address as President to the American Philological Association. These were, in effect, preliminary studies for her next major work, *Party Politics in the Age of Caesar.*

In the background of this work two factors deserve special mention. The first was the discovery, made independently by her and by Attilio Degrassi, that the Capitoline Fasti, the Augustan lists of the higher magistrates from the beginning of the Republic, and the triumphators, had been displayed on the arch that Augustus erected in the Forum to celebrate the return of the standards captured by the Parthians. These lists, and Degrassi's splendid publication of them, no less than her own papers, drew special attention to the long parade of names, patricians and plebeians, families ennobled for generations and new men, that represent here, as in Livy's *History,* the governing class of the Roman Republic. The second was the better understanding of the composition and relationships of that class attained when Matthias Gelzer, going beyond Mommsen's description of political and constitutional forms, asserted that these forms become understandable only through understanding of the society that used them. His discovery that the term *nobilis* referred only to consuls and descendants of consular families revealed more clearly the meaning of rivalries for office, and helped to create the picture of an aristocratic society in which the winning of support and the attainment of power depended on such personal relationships as *amicitia,* performance of *officia, fides, patrocinium,* and *clientela,* and *hospitium* (*Der Nobilität der römischen Republik,* 1912, published in English translation by Robin Seager, 1969). Building on Gelzer's work, Friedrich Münzer in *Adelsparteien und Adelsfamilien* (1920) found evidence of political combinations, often lasting ones, in intermarriage of prominent families and in collegiality or succession in office. He applied these criteria too rigidly, as Gelzer was one of the first to point out, but his work remains important because it is soundly based on the structure of Roman society. Syme's use of the new approach in *The Roman Revolution* (1939) provided a convincing, and for its time somber, account of the formation of the personal parties of Pompey, Caesar, and Augustus. In this context, the story of Caesar's rise to power demanded a fresh analysis, a challenge that Miss Taylor accepted in her Sather Lectures. Robin Seager, in the introduction to his translation of Gelzer's monograph, cites this work as the one in which "the lessons to be learned from *Nobilität* were first applied on a large scale in English to the Republic."

To this task she brought her skill in recreating the feelings and atmosphere of a time when older structures, though still functioning, were breaking down under the impact of the extension of citizenship to the whole of Italy and of the vast followings of the great military leaders, while political attachments and expediency often clashed with the claims of family solidarity and personal loyalty; and she brought also her insistence on seeing just how things functioned. Some of her contributions may be briefly summarized. An analysis of the complex systems of voting in different assemblies showed more clearly why elections and legislative programs had so little relation to each other. Elections to the higher magistracies continued to take place in the *comitia centuriata* with personal followings prominent, but without emphasis on programs. Legislation was usually introduced by the tribunes of the plebs, now the most active legislative magistrates, to the tribal assembly of the plebs, where within the tribe one man's vote was as good as another's. The campaign for a measure, unlike that for election, consisted largely of speech-making at public meetings (*contiones*). "The popular tribune and his associates," she wrote, "would declare that this measure would liberate the people from slavery to an oligarchy, and opposing optimates that the popular group was setting up a monarchy." Modes of opposition and delay, manipulation of the state religion for political purposes, and the use of the courts for personal and political advancement were all freshly interpreted. Against this background she set a historical review of three major contrasts: first, Cato against Pompey, Caesar, and Crassus, who used popular leadership to overcome the Senate; second, the optimates against the dynasts, while they were fomenting divisions that led to the civil war; and third, the political ideals that set Caesarism against Catonism. "My subject in this chapter," she wrote, "is the ideal of the Republic that became associated with Cato's name, the conflict of that ideal with Caesarism, and the manner in which Augustus resolved that conflict by laying claim to the republicanism of Cato." Thus, by using the new approach to Roman social and political problems, and the material provided by prosopography, she made a special contribution to the understanding of the political structures and the modes, propaganda, and ideologies of the Late Republic and the Augustan Age.

Study of party politics led almost inevitably to a study of the basic component of the Roman assemblies, the territorial tribe, the unit in which every citizen had to be registered. There had been no comprehensive study since the treatise by Kubitschek, *Imperium Romanum tributim descriptum*, published in 1889, although Fraccaro had contributed individual items. Masses of new evidence had become available. The inscription on the bronze tablet from Heba, found in 1947 and published in 1949, showed how tribal groups could be combined to form centuries, while the irregularities in the distribution of the tribes again raised questions regarding their origin and their extension on the map of Italy. In *The Voting Districts of the Roman Republic* (1960) her detailed knowledge of the land of Italy was combined with her study of practical political forces to produce a full scale history of the tribes from their origin until the whole of Italy had been registered in them, along with an interpretation of their expansion in terms of political and military history, and a reassessment of the recurrent disputes about the registration of freedmen in the four urban tribes. There is presented the first full list of the senators whose places of origin and whose tribes are known. Extensions of Roman citizenship and changes in the tribal registration of senatorial families appear as responses to changing political forces and needs.

Roman Voting Assemblies, the Jerome Lectures published in 1966, was also a response to the discovery of new evidence. In the splendid new edition (1960) of *La*

Pianta Marmorea di Roma Antica the Saepta Iulia, the major voting area built by Caesar, and the Diribitorium, where the votes were counted, had been precisely identified, thus making possible a new study of the voting arrangements. At the same time the identification of the Comitium and the Curia at Cosa by analogy threw fresh light on the relation between Comitium, Curia, and Forum in Rome. The inscription on the bronze tablet of Heba had revealed how tribal units could have been combined to form voting centuries in the *comitia centuriata* and illustrated the working of the lot to determine combinations of units and order of voting. Other details were supplied by the Spanish municipal charters and by scenes on coins. Miss Taylor's aim was to present, in the light of the new evidence, a precise description of the procedures in the different assemblies as they performed their elective, legislative, and judicial functions. Characteristically, as questions arose she turned to modern analogies. The shape and dimensions of the voting area provided a reason for visiting the British House of Commons in order to see and feel the effect of an oblong space too small to hold all the members. Colleagues at the American Academy in Rome shared amusedly with her the fun of testing the working of the lot by drawing wooden lots from jars of water themselves. Among her contributions are the noting of the distinction between the procedures in public meetings for speeches (*contiones*) and those in the voting itself, the definition of the use and working of the lot, and the demonstration that the plebeian tribal assembly (*concilium plebis*), presided over by the tribunes of the plebs, remained distinct from the tribal assembly of the people as a whole (*comitia tributa*), presided over by consuls and praetors. There had not been such a description of the assemblies in action before. She was planning a study of the Roman Senate at the time of her death, but only a preliminary study of "Seating Space in the Roman Senate and the Senatores Pedarii," prepared with the collaboration of Professor Russell T. Scott, was available for publication.

A stately series of articles and reviews illustrates the breadth of her interests in literature, history, and education. They range from datings of various letters of Cicero (*CPh* 32 [1937] 228–40; 44 [1949] 217–21), to "The Opportunities for Dramatic Performances in the Time of Plautus and Terence" (1937); "New Indications of Augustan Editing in the Capitoline Fasti" (1951); "On the Chronology of Caesar's First Consulship" (1951); "Lucretius on the Roman Theater" (1952); "Freedmen and Freeborn in the Epitaphs of Imperial Rome" (1961); "Forerunners of the Gracchi" (1962); and "Republican and Augustran Writers enrolled in the Equestrian Centuries" (1968). On the contemporary scene, "Objectives of the Graduate School (1952) is a statement of her educational creed, and "In Praise of Curiosity" (1959) is a defense of the grant of free play to the desire to know. These, like all the rest of her works, make evident the energy and zest, power of analysis, and combination of knowledge and imagination that made her a great and inspiring teacher for whom teaching and research went hand in hand, supporting each other. "My aim as a teacher," she often said, "is to make my students feel that they are walking the streets of Rome, and seeing and thinking what Romans saw and thought." Even in her eighties she could establish immediately a sympathetic and understanding relationship with students and young scholars, and colleagues from all over the world turned to her for advice and help. Her interest in events of the modern world never flagged, and she eagerly participated in the duties and demands of citizenship.

Books

The Cults of Ostia. Diss., Bryn Mawr, 1912. Bryn Mawr College Monograph Series II (1912).

Local Cults in Etruria. Papers and Monographs of the American Academy in Rome 2 (1923).

The Divinity of the Roman Emperor. Philological Monographs 1, American Philological Association (1931).

General Index, An Economic Survey of Ancient Rome. Edited by Tenney Frank with T. R. S. Broughton, A. A. Boyce, and others. Vols 1–5. Baltimore, 1940.

Party Politics in the Age of Caesar. Sather Classical Lectures 22. Berkeley and Los Angeles, 1949.

The Voting Districts of the Roman Republic: The Thirty-five Urban and Rural Tribes. Papers and Monographs of the American Academy in Rome 20 (1960).

Roman Voting Assemblies from the Hannibalic War to the Dictatorship of Caesar. Jerome Lectures, Eighth Series. Ann Arbor, 1966.

Articles (Selected)

"The Worship of Augustus in Italy in his Lifetime." *TAPA* 51 (1920) 116–133.

"The Altar of Manlius in the Lateran." *AJA* 25 (1921) 387–395.

"Tiberius' Refusals of Divine Honors." *TAPA* 60 (1929) 87–100.

"The Opportunities for Dramatic Performances in the Time of Plautus and Terence." *TAPA* 68 (1937) 284–304.

"Caesar's Early Career." *CPh* 36 (1941) 113–32.

"Caesar's Colleagues in the Pontifical College." *AJPh* 63 (1943) 385–412.

"The Election of the Pontifex Maximus in the Late Republic." *CPh* 37 (1942) 421–24.

"Caesar and the Roman Nobility." *TAPA* 73 (1942) 1–24.

"New Indications of Augustan Editing in the Capitoline Fasti." *CPh* 46 (1951) 73–80.

"On the Chronology of Caesar's First Consulship." *AJPh* 72 (1951) 254–68.

"Lucretius on the Roman Theater." In *Studies in Honour of Gilbert Norwood,* Toronto, 1952: 147–155.

"Objectives of the Graduate School." *Journal of Higher Education* 23 (1952) 18–23.

"In Praise of Curiosity." *Boston University Graduate Journal* 8 (1959) 35–43.

"Freedmen and Freeborn in the Epitaphs of Imperial Rome." *AJPh* 82 (1961) 113–32.

"Forerunners of the Gracchi." *JRS* 52 (1962) 19–27)

"Republican and Augustran Writers Enrolled in the Equestrian Centuries." *TAPA* 99 (1968) 466–86.

"Seating Space in the Roman Senate and the Senatores Pedarii." *TAPA* 100 (1969) 529–82.

Sources

Broughton, T. Robert S. "Lily Ross Taylor." *Studi Romani* 10 (1962) 369–72.

———. "Lily Ross Taylor." *The Year Book of the American Philolosophical Society* (1970) 172–79.

———. "Lily Ross Taylor." Gnomon 42 (1970) 734–35.

Hermann Usener
23 October 1834 – 21 October 1905

JAN N. BREMMER
Rijksuniversiteit Utrecht

Hermann Usener was among the greatest German classical scholars of the last decades of the nineteenth century. His writings covered most aspects of the whole period of classical antiquity, reaching even into the earlier Middle Ages, and opened up new vistas in many different areas, such as Greek rhetoric, Epicurean philosophy, classical folklore, the continuity between pagan and Christian religions, and Greek mythology. Moreover, with his colleague Franz Bücheler (1837–1908), he attracted to Bonn the great majority of those students who would establish Germany as the leading country in classical scholarship in the first half of this century.

Hermann Carl Usener was born in Weilburg, in the then still independent Herzogtum of Nassau, in 1834. His father, Georg Usener (1789–1855), occupied the position of *Landoberschultheiss*, a high position in the administration of the duchy. In 1844 Usener entered the Landesgymnasium, where he received his instruction in Greek from Rudolf Krebs (1804–1881), for whom he would arrange an honorary doctorate in Bonn in 1876, and in Latin from Alfred Fleckeisen (1820–1899), the later editor of the so-called *Fleckeisen's Jahrbücher für Philologie und Pädagogik*, who roused his enthusiasm for the classics and remained a lifelong fatherly friend after Usener opened up his heart to him at the age of fourteen (Mette, 17–18). It was probably under the influence of Fleckeisen, a pupil of the Latinist Friedrich Ritschl (1806–1876), that Usener graduated with an "excellent" in Latin and a "very good" in Greek. At school Usener had already shown his varied interest by Latin orations on "The reason for the decline of the Latin language after the Augustan age" and "Niebuhrius exemplum adolescentibus studiosis propositum," his *Abiturientenrede* (cf. Schnell).

Equally important for his later development were the holidays with his half-brother Carl, a pastor. In the preface to his *Weihnachtsfest* (below), which he dedicated to his brother, Usener recalls how he walked with his rucksack along the river Weil to the old vicarage in Laucken. There, in his brother's theological library, he found the writings of the critical Tübingen school, which gave him the idea that "the history of religion must become my life's task" (vii); the main influence being the writings of the young Eduard Zeller (1814–1908), who had started his career as *Privatdozent* in theology in Tübingen, as Usener repeatedly acknowledged in (unpublished) letters to Zeller (cf. Bibliography). Notebooks preserved in the Bonn library show that at the age of eighteen he had already read Grimm's *Märchen*, Creuzer's *Symbolik*, and Lobeck's *Aglaophamus*.

In the summer of 1853 Usener moved to Heidelberg, where he attached himself especially to K. L. Kayser (1806–1872), whose posthumous *Homerische Abhandlungen* (1881) he would later edit in exemplary fashion. Kayser evoked in Usener an interest in rhetoric and referred him therefore to Munich, to Leonhard Spengel (1803–1880), the foremost authority in this field. Having arrived in the winter of 1853, he stayed only two semesters in Munich and spent the next year at home. In the summer of 1855 he took up his studies in Göttingen, where, around the following New Year's, philologists Karl Friedrich Hermann (1804–1855) and Friedrich Schneidewin (1810–1856) both suddenly died. The seminar dedicated to their memory resulted in Usener's first work, *Quaestiones Anaximeneae* (1856), a fruit really of his Munich stay and the first of a series of studies on ancient rhetoric. In the later 1860s he conceived the plan of a complete edition of the rhetorical works of Dionysius of Halicarnassus (cf. *Aspetti*: 107) and published many preparatory studies (*Vorarbeiten*) for this project, but in the end only cooperated with his pupil Ludwig Radermacher (1867–1952) in the first volume of the Teubner edition of Dionysius' *Rhetorica* (1899), the history of religion having gradually become his main focus of attention (see below). It is still the standard edition, despite the fact that, as Wilamowitz points out in his *Sappho und Simonides* (1913, 80–81, note also 154–55), the inscriptions had been neglected in the constitution of the text.

In the autumn of 1857 Usener moved to Bonn, where at the time the best classical scholars of Germany were teaching. Friedrich Welcker (1784–1868) was still working on his *opus magnum*, *Griechische Götterlehre* (3 vols., 1857–63), and although Usener did not become his pupil in the strict sense of the word, he seems to have been indebted to him in his attention to the relation of myth and ritual, the continuity of ancient religious usages in Christianity, and his openness to the comparative method (cf. Henrichs, 1986: 223–229). Contrary to Welcker, Usener rarely worked intensively with archeological materials, except for coins, which he knew well through his friendship with the great numismatist Friedrich Imhoof-Blumer (1838–1920). In the one case where he did so—in a stupendously learned discussion of the comparison in *Il.* 11.473ff—he ventured only to add a word to Welcker's discussion *veneratione tanto viro debita* (first published in 1875 = *Kleine Schriften* [KS] 3:446). Even when, in a memorable autobiographical passage in his *Götternamen*, Usener rejected Welcker's *Urmonotheismus*, he still spoke of him as "he who is the teacher of us all, even of those who do not know it" (273).

Of the other professors, Otto Jahn (1813–1869) did not make much impact on Usener, but he was attracted to Ritschl, who admitted him to the "Philologisches Seminar." Usener was not particularly interested in archaic Latin literature (KS 2:251), Ritschl's specialty, but in Ritschl's seminar he met Franz Bücheler. In November of the same year they prepared with the other *sodales* a greatly improved edition of the London palimpsest of Granius Licinianus, only a year after the *editio princeps*. The coöperation with Bücheler was so successful that Usener immediately thought of him as Otto Jahn's successor in 1869.

In an unpublished letter of 27 June 1857 to Jacob Geel (1789–1862), the librarian of the Rijksuniversiteit Leiden, Ritschl mentions that he had proposed to Usener as the subject for his thesis *Catalogus criticus librorum a Theophrasto scriptorum* (UB Leiden BPL 2426). But it was C. A. Brandis (1790–1867), the professor of philosophy and author of "Kenner der peripatetischen Lehre" (KS 1:95), who instilled in Usener the love for ancient philosophy, in particular the transmission of philosophical doctrines. Already in March 1858 he submitted his thesis, *Analecta Theophrastica* (KS 1:50–90), which was dedicated to Ritschl, his *Doktorvater*, and Brandis. Despite its small size (fifty pages), the thesis contained pioneer research in the tradition of Theophrastus' writings and the collection of his fragments. It also provided the model for the most impressive studies along similar lines, his own *Epicurea* (1877), Wilamowitz's *Antigonos von Karystos* (1881), H. von Arnim's *Stoicorum Veterum Fragmenta* (1903) and, above all, Hermann Diels' *Doxographi Graeci* (1879) and *Die Fragmente der Vorsokratiker* (1st ed., 1903).

In these years Usener met Wilhelm (1833–1911) and Carl (1839–1907) Dilthey, sons of the court preacher of Nassau, who would remain his lifelong friends. In 1856 Wilhelm had become teacher at the Joachimsthalsche Gymnasium in Berlin, with Wilamowitz's Pforte one of the most prestigious schools of Prussia, and through him Usener was appointed as *Adjunkt* after his doctorate (1858–1861). Both read Plato together, while Usener continued his studies of the Greek philosophers (collected in KS I) and, having already studied the commentaries on Aristotle for his thesis ("*perlegit, non perlustravit*," thus Ritschl in the letter quoted above), he prepared an edition of Syrianus' commentary on Aristotle's *Metaphysics*, which he finally published in 1870 (KS 3:199). In 1860 he pronounced the oration on the occasion of the birthday of Friedrich Wilhelm IV, in which he rejected the rationalistic approach to philology of Gottfried Hermann, Ritschl's model, expressing great admiration for August Boeckh's (1785–1867) "Gesamtauffassung des hellenischen Altertums" (KS 3:215–226). In fact, already in early 1859 Wilhelm Dilthey had noted that Usener no longer was a "Ritschelianer," as he manifested more and more interest in the "Sachlich-historische" (Misch: 77). However, Usener remained an admirer of Ritschl all of his life, and the latter helped him to become Professor Extraordinarius at the University of Berne (1861–1863), an appointment customarily combined with a position at the local Kantonsschule. His stay in Berne enabled him to observe the rich local folklore, which he later boldly, if unnoticed, used to explain the origins of Attic comedy (1873 = KS 3:43).

Despite heavy teaching, Usener started an investigation into the manuscript tradition of Dionysius of Halicarnassus and discovered in the library of Berne various interesting manuscripts, in particular one of Lucan's scholia, which he finally published in 1869 and dedicated to Ritschl; an intended second volume never materialized. The scholia are not particularly important, but for Usener's concept of philology there was *nil in studiis parvum* (1873 = KS 3:23) and, characteristically, he later reproached Cobet for a lack of a "sense of duty" (*Pflichtgefühl*) in having neglected the manuscripts of Simplicius in favor of the Attic orators (1892 = KS 3:198).

In 1863 Usener moved as Ordinarius to Greifswald, where he mainly had to teach Latin, which, together with the support of Otto Jahn, helped him to become Ritschl's successor in Bonn in 1866; at the same time, Jacob Bernays (1824–1881) was appointed Extraordinarius. In his youth Usener had copied out Bernays's articles in order to have a complete collection of them, and after Bernays's death he would edit in exemplary fashion his *Gesammelte Abhandlungen* (1885, 2 vols.). The admiration is not surprising, as they had much in common: interest in early Christian literature and the recovery of the lost writings of ancient philosophy. In the same year, 1866, Usener married Lilly Dilthey (1846–1920), the sister of his friends; she gave him four children and provided him with the right atmosphere for his studies.

Still, the first years in Bonn were not easy. The fateful quarrel between Jahn and Ritschl, which had led to Ritschl's departure to Leipzig with Erwin Rohde and Friedrich Nietzsche (1844–1900), had poisoned the atmosphere, and Usener had not yet established himself in the eyes of the students. The situation greatly improved after Jahn's death in 1869, even though Bonn lost again some of its brightest pupils: Wilamowitz, who left immediately for Berlin, and Carl Robert (1850–1922), who followed him after the Franco-Prussian War of 1870. Usener now managed to have his old friend Bücheler appointed, whose arrival, besides clearing the atmosphere, had one other important effect. Commenting on Usener's appointment, Mommsen (*Theodor Mommsen—Otto Jahn Briefwechsel 1842–1868*, edited by L. Wickert [1962] 349–350) had written: "Usener is, to be sure, a good fellow and also quite intelligent, but he is hardly equal to this position and especially weak in *Latinis*. But you will certainly have a good colleague in him, I believe"; indeed, the volume with the *Latina* is the least impressive of his *Kleine Schriften*. After 1870 Usener wrote only occasionally on Latin literature. Bücheler's specialization in this area had made the way free for more pressing interests.

Usener now dedicated all his energy to teaching in the Philologische Seminar, which at the time counted ten members. His pupil Hans Lietzmann (1875–1942; cf. KS 3:342–45 = *Wesen un Rang der Philologie*: 57–59) has given a lively sketch of the impression his appearance made on the students: "The broad-shouldered figure with the powerful head, from which two bright eyes flashed forth beneath bushy eyebrows, evoked in everybody the feeling that he was standing before a prince in the realm of scholarship." His (Latin!) lectures were not so much appreciated for their delivery—Usener often spoke jerkily and in anacoloutha—as for their insights and the problems they raised. His "cool dignity" (*kühle Vornehmheit*) and "sober matter-offactness" (*nüchterne Sachlichkeit*) (Lietzmann) at first intimidated students, but to those who opened up to him he would show permanent friendship. Bücheler's more accessible personality and livelier teaching complemented Usener in a fortunate way. Together they would make Bonn famous and attract the best students of Germany for over 30 years. Among Usener's own pupils were Hermann Diels (1848–1922; thesis, *De Galeni historia philosopha*, 1870, dedicated to Usener), Georg Kaibel (1849–1901; *De monumentorum aliquot Graecorum carminibus*, 1871), Friedrich Leo (1851–1914; *Quaestiones Aristophaneae*, 1873), Eduard Schwartz (1858–1940; *De Dionysione Scytobrachione*, 1880), and Albrecht Dieterich (1866–1908; *Papyrus magica musei Lugdunensis*, etc., 1888)—to mention only the most famous.

In the later 1860s Usener published a variety of mainly critical notes covering an extremely wide field from Hesiod until Eustathius, if not always convincingly. As Jahn observed, sharply but not without reason: "Unfortunately, the gods have denied his erudition the gift of probability" (quoted by Wilamowitz, *Erinnerungen*, 92). Important for Usener's development was the publication of his *Kallone* (1868 = KS 4:1–93), in which he started from a passage in Aristophanes to end up, totally unconvincingly, in lunar myths. Methodologically, this first attempt at Greek mythology is indebted to the ruling paradigm that explained everything in terms of the natural phenomena ("Alles sollte Lichtgott sein," Wilamowitz, *Ibid.*), and Usener would never completely abandon this approach. Evidently he now felt ready to teach Greek religion, and the next winter he announced as his program *Religionis Graecorum historiam mythologiamque exponet quater*. Unfortunately, Hermann Diels's copy of these lectures, most copies of other lectures by various pupils, and Usener's own notes were lost in a bomb attack on Bonn in October 1944.

In 1873 Usener lectured on Greek and Italic mythology, the fruits of which appeared in an uncommonly rich article on Anna Perenna and Mamurius Veturius (1875 = KS 4:93–143). Basing himself on a very wide reading of European folklore, he argued that these minor Roman mythical figures were really ancient *Jahresgötter*. The study also shows his first wrestling with the problem of the relationship between myth and ritual—a problem so prominent in modern discussions. Very perceptively he already distinguished between the "Formula of myth" ("Anna finds her end in the river") and the "Formula of ritual" ("Anna or her image is thrown into the river": 120), and noted that "myth can proceed in a somewhat more drastic and free way than custom." (142). Yet it remains the main weakness of his method that virtually until the end of his life he always assigned mythology priority, although on occasion he realized the truth: the Kouretes "have been transferred from cult into myth" (1894 = KS 4:190).

In 1876 Usener published a small treatise demonstrating the dependence of Byzantine astronomy on Persian doctrines (KS 3:247–371), soon followed by various editions of Stephanus Alexandrinus' astronomical work (1879; 1880 = KS 3:247–322). An unpublished letter to W. G. Pluygers (1812–1880), Geel's successor as librarian in Leiden, shows that already in 1872 he was working on the astronomical work of Theon (23 February, UB Leiden BPL 2432), which he would finally edit for Mommsen's

Chronica Minora III in 1898. Through these studies Usener became interested in astrology, in which he saw a "truly etymological way of thinking" that gave insight into the "motivepowers and spiritual events of pre-historical and pre-scientific thought" (1901 = KS 3:375). His investigations helped to inspire scholars such as Franz Boll (1867–1924) and Franz Cumont (1868–1947), and the latter thanked Usener in the preface of the first volume of the *Catalogus codicum astrologorum Graecorum* (1898) as *horum studiorum veteranus*. Usener's interest in astronomy was closely related to his interest in calendrical matters, through which he hoped to penetrate into early Greek history. A manuscript "full of laborious and complicated calculations about calendrical problems" (Brinkmann: 10) perished in the fire of Mommsen's library on 12 July 1880.

The next year (1877) saw the appearance of the *Anecdoton Holderi*. Long before this Usener had shown interest in a small Latin fragment discovered by Alfred Holder (1840–1916) in a manuscript (Karlsruhe Augiensis 106), that was once part of the famous monastic library of Reichenau. When he finally edited the text, he was able to show that the fragment was an extract from a family history composed by Cassiodorus around A.D. 530, providing indispensible information about Symmachus, Cassiodorus himself, and Boethius, whose theological treatises it definitively authenticated. In two ways this still valuable book is characteristic of Usener's way of working. First, although he soon lost interest in the project, he did not withdraw his promise to publish the text and labored on it for many years. Second, the book was written in the period from August to September 20, as he noted in his *Handexemplar*. The only other *Handexemplar* that survived the 1944 bombing, that of the *Altgriechischer Versbau*, mentions that it was written in 1885 from 17 October to 3 December, and from letters to Fleckeisen (29 October 1894, quoted by Kany [1987] 79) and his pupil Alfred Körte (1866–1946; 23 October 1894, unpublished, UB Bonn S 2109, 2) it appears that *Götternamen* was written within a year. Although Usener apparently took a very long time—sometimes too long—mentally to prepare his writings, he put his thoughts onto paper surprisingly quickly.

The *Anecdoton* had been an offering to the Philologenversammlung in Wiesbaden in 1877. As Usener presided, he took the opportunity to invite Wilamowitz for one of the main lectures—a great honor for the young professor of Greifswald. The lecture was so badly received that Wilamowitz did not return to the conventions until 1921, but during the meeting Usener and Wilamowitz began a friendship that, with vicissitudes, survived until Usener's death. In the following years they carried on an animated correspondence, and Wilamowitz dedicated to Usener his *Antigonos von Karystos* (1881). In 1880 and 1890 Usener unsuccessfully tried to have Wilamowitz appointed in Bonn; in an unpublished letter to Georg Kaibel in 1890 (14 December, UB Bonn S 2109, 2) he even mentioned Kaibel and Wilamowitz as the guides for the coming generations. Yet Wilamowitz always kept a certain distance, and Usener well realized the great difference between him and his younger colleague: "You look for the creations of willpower in history, I for the spontaneous, unconscious coming-into-being" (letter, 20 September 1877, *Briefwechsel*, no. 5). When Usener concentrated more and more on the history of religion, the relationship lost its warmth. In his memoirs Wilamowitz has few good words left for Usener (*Erinnerungen*, 91–92, 167–168, 209) and in his Latin autobiography, written at the end of his life, Usener occupies the first place among those *quibus nihil debeo* (*Antike und Abendland* 27 [1981] 48).

During the next few years Usener edited the collected papers of Kayser (1881) and Bernays (1885), and in 1882 he gave his famous rectoral speech *Philologie und Geschichtswissenschaft* (= *Vorträge und Aufsätze* [VA]: 3–35), a unique nineteenth-century reflection on the role of philology and, to a certain extent, a reversal of his 1860 oration. He now distanced himself from Boeckh and indicated sympathy for Hermann by propagating philology as the key to a more comparative and comprehensive approach to antiquity.

At the end of 1886 he published his *Altgriechischer Versbau*. He had already noted in his 1882 oration (above) that metrics also belong to those aspects of ancient Greece that cannot be studied in isolation, as the existence of an Indo-European *Urvers* had been demonstrated by R. Westphal (1826–1892) (*Kuhn's Zeitschrift für Vergleichende Sprachforschung* 9 [1860] 437–438). It is therefore rather paradoxical that he proceeded to reconstruct this ancestor of the Greek hexameter by basing himself solely on the Greek material without adducing the archaic Indian and Irish parallels. This methodological error invalidates the book, even though the most convincing modern reconstruction of the hexameter (N. Berg, "Parergon metricum: der Ursprung des griechischen Hexameters," *Münch. Stud. z. Sprachw.* 37 [1978] 11–36) also takes its departure from the original Indo-European eight-syllable line, but, unlike Usener, with a catalectic variant.

In 1887, after long tribulations—the work was almost completely printed in 1881—Usener finally published his *Epicurea*, which he dedicated to Bücheler; additional studies on Epicurus and Epicureans appeared during the next few years (*KS* 1:297–325, 362 and 3:188–192; *RhMus* 47 [1892] 414–467). The edition of Epicurus and its *subsidium interpretationis* testified to massive learning and definitively established Usener's international reputation. Curiously, though, Usener nowhere indicates any deep interest in Epicurean doctrines, and the whole work very much looks like a philological *Pflichtarbeit*, which probably originated from his early interest in Diogenes Laertius in connection with his thesis. This would also have been the reason why he never completely finished the *Glossarium Epicureum*, which was not published until 1977 (cf. Gigante; Schmid: 1980). The appearance in the following years (1892–1896) of new editions of Philodemus by his pupil S. Sudhaus (1867–1914) must have meant a delay, but Usener never shrank from hard work. The fact that his attention was taken up more and more by his theological interests meant that other subjects had to take second place.

Amazingly, the following year he again brought out a masterwork, *Das Weihnachtsfest*, his most popular book. In a very learned, if meandering, discussion Usener showed that the celebration of Christ's birth on 25 December was not introduced before the fourth century and was meant to compete with the festival of

Sol invictus. The study opened up virtually unexplored territory, it being the first profound attempt at explaining the origins of Christianity in an historical approach, as against a theological one. Understandably, the book caused much commotion, and the leading church historian Adolf von Harnack (1851–1930) reviewed it highly critically (*Theol. Lit.- Zeit.* 14 [1889] 199–212). Indeed, it is vulnerable in many details, but its main conclusions have stood the test of time. The book also attracted Hans Lietzmann as a student to Bonn; he not only published the second edition but also carried on the interests of his "incomparable teacher" (letter of 9 February 1940, Aland, no. 1136) in this field; he shared these interests with Arthur Darby Nock (1902–1963), who wrote to him: "If I had a *lararium*, it would contain two images of scholars, his [Usener's] and Mommsen's" (9 June 1937, Aland, no. 1010). In Germany, this tradition came to an abrupt end when Lietzmann's brightest pupils were killed in action during Germany's invasion of Russia (Aland, no. 153).

The analysis of the origin of Christmas was not Usener's first study of early Christianity. In 1871 he had already collected the most important remains of the ancient menologies in order to publish them in a reliable edition (unpublished letter to W. G. Pluygers of 21 October 1871, UB Leiden BPL 2432). The plan was never carried out, but from the later 1870s he began to publish a series of lives of early Christian saints and martyrs. The most famous are those on Sancta Pelagia of Antioch (1877) and Saint Tychon of Cyprus (1907), in which he tried to prove that Pelagia was the transformation of Aphrodite and Tychon the transformation of Priapus. Although these editions are still valuable for their observations on early Byzantine Greek, their main theses were soon refuted. The great Bollandist Hippolyte Delehaye (1857–1941) rightly emphasized that the legend of Pelagia was rooted in the church of Antioch (H. D., *Les légendes hagiographiques*, 1905) and Paul Maas (1880–1964) showed that Usener had overlooked a version of Tychon's life that established the bishop's historicity (1907 = Maas, *Kleine Schriften*, ed. W. Buchwald [Munich, 1973]: 454–9; note also Delehaye apud Aland, no. 185; Kany [1988]). Usener's interest in this literature was such that he even published his own version of a saint's life under the pseudonym of E. Schaffner (1894 = VA: 233–259).

Why was he so interested in the continuity of pagan elements in early Christianity? In a letter accompanying his *Weihnachtsfest* to the (excommunicated) Catholic theologian Ignaz von Doellinger (1799–1890), Usener wrote that he aimed to contribute toward the future unification of the church (Mette, 65). As he explained in the preface, he hoped to achieve this by separating that which had only temporary value from the "inalienable eternal content of our religion." In 1904 he told the Basel church historian Franz Overbeck (1837–1905) that his main interest in his studies of ancient religion was "to prove its paganism to the Roman Catholic church" (Overbeck, *Christentum und Kultur* [Basel, 1919] 195–196). In the same year he stated that the aim of mythology as he saw it was "to carry out the purification and elucidation of our religious consciousness" (VA: 65).

Momigliano (1982) has raised the question, which he felt unable to answer, as to whether these attempts at purification resulted in Usener's abandoning the Christian faith. Fortunately, we can let him speak for himself in this matter. When, in 1902, the theological faculty of Bonn presented Usener with an honorary doctorate, he replied in a letter of which only a draft survives (unpublished, UB Bonn S 2109, 3), the original being lost in the war. It explains his position with clarity: ". . . much as some results of my works, to my own greatest regret, distanced themselves from the faith of my youth, I still feel one with you all in the strictly Protestant spirit, which guides me in the investigation of the ideas and institutions of the ancient church. This sounds like a hackneyed sentence: but its application and carrying through means, as I am convinced, the purification and elucidation of the life of our church. Basically, everything that an inner impulse tells me to show is implied in the word of the apostle: 'Now we see through a mirror in a riddle'; only that I would like to say it in a more pointed way: man is able to see God and the divine only in images (*im bilde*)." There is plenty of evidence, therefore, that the researches of Usener's later years were dominated by a commitment to the future of the Christian faith. Wilamowitz sharply commented on this development in a letter to G. Wissowa (1859–1931): "It is more and more evident that he practices theology" (1904 = Henrichs [1985] 282).

But how could Usener distinguish between "temporary" and "permanent" values in Christianity? He presented a first approach to this question in 1896 with the publication of *Götternamen*, a book that he called in a letter to Fleckeisen (29 October 1894, quoted by Kany [1987] 79) "my life's work." Usener thought he could penetrate into the origin of polytheism by analyzing the names of the gods, the oldest witnesses of religious conceptualization. Going back in time, he found older, less personal types of gods in the Roman *indigitamenta*, which he called *sondergötter*, a term he owed to the historian of religion Edward Lehman (1862–1930, cf. L. Deubner, *Kleine Schriften zur Klassischen Altertumskunde* [Königstein, 1981]: 329); he discovered parallels in ancient lists of Lithuanian gods. Even older types of gods, at least from a logical point of view, were the *augenblicksgötter*, gods who owed their existence to those moments when early mankind experienced something divine. A fine illustration of his theory is a later article on Zeus Keraunos (1905 = KS 4:471–497). For primitive people, lightning itself is a god; subsequent reflection raised the lightning to a *sondergott*, Keraunos, who was finally incorporated in Zeus, a personal god. It is, however, only when the original term for the *sondergott* has developed into a proper name that it can become the subject of myth, cult, and poetry. Finally, the polytheism of the personal gods culminated in monotheism through a revelation from Galilee, as Usener stated in only one, hardly satisfactory, page (348). In an unposted answer to Wilamowitz' reaction to the book, he explained that he had wanted to investigate the laws of religious development in order "to distinguish between the passing and lasting in sacred history and dogma" (Mette, 81–83). In Usener's opinion, then, only a knowledge of mankind's religious development could result in a Christianity purified from all pagan motifs.

Usener dedicated *Götternamen* to Carl and Wilhelm Dilthey; the latter in turn dedicated his *Das Erlebnis und die Dichtung* (1905) to Usener. Was Usener perhaps influenced by Dilthey's views? The answer seems to be: not very much.

Admittedly, the Dilthey terminology of *Geschichte-Leben-Nachempfinden* can be found in Usener's work, but on the whole the differences are considerable. It is rather Vico's views of man's infancy in his *Scienze nuova* and the nineteenth-century fascination with etymology that are the main influences behind the book (cf. Kany [1987]). Unfortunately, Usener had not kept up with contemporary linguistics (Mette, 82), as was immediately noticed by Hermann Diels, who also rejected Usener's belief in the power of names (a survival of Wilhelm von Humboldt's [1767–1835] theories). Erwin Rohde observed another methodological failure. As was the case with the book on metrics, Usener had based his theories mainly on the classical material without paying attention to the comparative evidence. Finally, Wilamowitz rejected the book for its many wrong etymologies but also, even if more subjectively, because it went straight against his own idea of Greek religion: "Gefühl is alles, Name ist Schall und Rauch" ("Feeling is everything, names are sound and smoke"). (All reactions quoted by Mette, 79–90.)

Despite these criticisms, Usener's book has not been without influence. Historians of Roman religion especially, but also the great French Sinologist Marcel Granet (1884–1940, cf. Bremmer), have used his insights in their analyses of the Roman and Chinese pantheon. On the whole, however, modern opinion can only agree with Usener's critics. The main theses of the book are unprovable and its methods antiquated. Still, it contains a highly interesting program for the reconstruction of archaic Greek religion by studying the various calendars (hence the interest in astronomy), archaic customs such as human sacrifice, and the religion of neighboring peoples such as the Thracians and Macedonians (274–275). Moreover, there are numerous fine observations on all kinds of mythological figures, and the attention to onomastics as a source for Greek religion is still highly modern. The book is also a delight to read. Like many nineteenth-century scholars, Usener was highly interested in reconstructing prehistory. "Relics," "ruins," and "palimpsests" were his favorite words to denote survivals of the hoary past (cf. Kany [1987] 123). He paid therefore constant attention to the smallest details—an approach that greatly influenced his sometime student Aby Warburg (1866–1929), the art historian (cf. Gombrich; Kany 1989), witness his famous dictum "Der liebe Gott steckt im Detail" (cf. Sassi in *Aspetti*, 86–87). This attention has the effect that the reader sometimes feels himself carried along in a kind of scholarly investigation: one might note a connection in that Usener was a contemporary of Sir Arthur Conan Doyle (1859–1930).

Between the *Weihnachtsfest* and the *Götternamen*, Usener had continued to work on ancient philosophy and the Christian literature of late antiquity, but his most innovative article in this period is *Über vergleichende sitten- und rechtsgeschichte*, a subject he had lectured on in 1871, 1881, and 1891 (VA, 103–157). By comparing the Greek ephebes, Italian *iuvenes*, and German *Burschenschaften*, Usener was able to point to striking resemblances that he traced back to a communal background. Ten years later Heinrich Schurtz (1863–1903) used this classical material in his epochal study of the phenomenon of age groups, *Altersklassen und Männerbünde* (1902), laying the foundation for the many modern studies of ancient initiation. Usener's article shows a great erudition in the field of folklore, but he published only once more in this area in which he had long been interested. In a letter dated 18 October 1868 to Karl Halm (1809–1882) (*Aspetti*: 107–108) he mentioned that he had collected much material on popular justice, and some years later Max Bonnet (1841–1917) answered queries on *charivaris* in Switzerland (unpublished letter of 26 December 1872, UB Bonn S 2101). Usener, however, made no use of this material in 1901 when he brilliantly showed that Mommsen, to whom he had dedicated his article, had neglected popular forms of justice in ancient Rome in his *Römisches Strafrecht* (*KS* 4:356–381). Usener's fortuitous application of modern folklore to ancient customs was continued by Albrecht Dieterich and his pupils, such as Ludwig Deubner (1877–1946), Hugo Hepding (1878–1959), and Otto Weinreich (1886–1972). This tradition proved to be very productive until the Nazis monopolized German *Volkskunde* in the late 1930s.

In the autumn of 1896, Usener fell from the steps in his library and developed an eye infection. Doctors forbade him to read, and for months he had to lie in the dark, while his students read aloud to him texts, preferably the Church Fathers, and also helped him to write. He recovered but remained blind in one eye and was no longer allowed to read by artificial light. The short-sightedness offers us a rare glimpse into Usener as a man. In an unpublished letter of 30 October 1900 to his brother Carl, he writes that during a lecture he realized that there were female students in the audience. Although he could not distinguish their faces but only see their contours, he immediately became distracted: "Disgusting . . . at my age" (UB Bonn S 2109, 2).

Despite his near-blindness, his scientific production hardly flagged. In 1899 he issued a study of the Flood, *Sintfluthsagen*, in which he tried to show that myth developed from a single image, in this case from the *Lichtgott* landing on the shore. The book was skeptically received by Wilamowitz (*Briefwechsel*, 59–60) and understandably so. Usener had spoiled his case by his dependence on the antiquated solar mythology and an overly reductionist approach. On the other hand, he was far ahead of his time in looking for one underlying idea in very different myths: a structuralist *avant la lettre*.

In the following years he continued to find pagan motifs in the Christian tradition, such as the use of milk and honey (1902 = *KS* 4:398–417), the stories about Christ's birth (1903 = *VA*: 159–187), and the idea of the Trinity (1903, reprinted 1966). He was now in the zenith of his fame. His writings were extensively reviewed, even in the *Année Sociologique* of the French sociologist Emile Durkheim (1859–1917) and his school (cf. De Donato in *Aspetti*); in America, B. L. Gildersleeve (1831–1924) had become friends with Usener, having been entertained by him in 1880, and he always paid great attention to his works (Briggs, 141–143, 243–245). In 1903 Usener retired, but his seventieth birthday was still an important event at which his pupils, including Wilamowitz, presented him with his bust, now preserved in the Bonn Philologische Seminar.

In 1904 Usener published "Heilige Handlung" (*KS* 4:422–467), in which he analyzed ritual fights between neighborhoods or city quarters. The study made a great impression on the Dutch historian Johan Huizinga (1872–1945) and confirmed him in his idea that culture is based on fights, games, and competition, an idea later elaborated in his famous *Homo ludens* (1938, cf. W. Krul, "Huizinga en de taak der culturgeschiedenis," *Theoretische Geschiedenis* 13 [1986] 149–68, esp. 155, 164–165). The article also raises fascinating questions about the origin of the myth of the Trojan War and shows that Usener had reconsidered the problem of myth and ritual. His conclusion that the "sacramental act" was the "seed" of myths reversed his earlier position and seems to suggest that he had been influenced by the contemporary Cambridge "myth and ritual" school. This is indeed not impossible. He was acquainted with the work of William Robertson Smith (1846–1894) (cf. *Götternamen*, 254), had J. G. Frazer's (1854–1941) *Golden Bough* read out to him by a student (Karo, 33), and Jane Harrison (1850–1928) was the only scholar to be mentioned by him as having "a feeling for mythology" (*Götternamen*: 136). However, he could not explore this new direction any further. After a dangerous attack of appendicitis in the late autumn, he recovered in the spring of 1905, but in the following autumn he fell ill again, and two days before his birthday he quietly passed away (cf. Aland, nos. 119 and 122). On 24 October 1905 he was buried on the "Alte Friedhof" in Bonn.

Usener's spiritual heir, his son-in-law Albrecht Dieterich, immediately decided to write his biography and, as was his method of working, prepared the book in his mind without making many notes. Around the beginning of May 1908, he told his wife, Usener's daughter Marie (1867–1931), that he was ready to write the book and would finish it in the autumn (Aland, no. 176). A few days later he collapsed in front of his students and died on 6 May. The biography was never written.

During Usener's lifetime, his originality, astonishing productivity, loyal and imposing personality, and total dedication to teaching established him as a leading classical scholar of his time. Yet after his death, he was soon replaced by Wilamowitz as the model for the new generation. There are various reasons for this development. Firstly, Usener's reliance on etymologies, his continuing adherence to the nature paradigm in his mythological studies, and his stress on the primacy of myth above ritual soon made him look old-fashioned. Secondly, with the premature death of Albrecht Dieterich, Usener's legacy had lost its most authoritative and versatile steward. Thirdly, Wilamowitz's superior philological skills and powerful personality soon overshadowed Usener's own philological achievements, and his concentration on and identification with ancient Greece were easier to follow than Usener's theological interests and search for pre-historic roots. Only recent studies (*Aspetti*; Kany [1987]) have again recognized Usener as a pioneer in the analysis of folklore, ritual, early Christianity, and the transmission of philosophical doctrines. It remains difficult to present a balanced evaluation of a scholar who so stubbornly clung to antiquated paradigms but also opened up so many new fields. Usener's boldness excites us, his flights of fancy repel us. Indeed, Hermann Usener is a problematic scholar.

Books

Quaestiones Anaximeneae. Göttingen, 1856 = *Kleine Schriften* I:1–49.

Alexandri Aphrodisiensis quae feruntur problematorum liber III et IIII = Jahresbericht über das Königl. Joachimsthalsche Gymnasium, etc. Berlin, 1859.

Scholia in Lucani Bellum Civile I: *Commenta Bernensia.* Leipzig, 1869; reprinted Hildesheim, 1967.

Syriani in metaphysica commentaria. Berlin, 1870; reprinted in *Aristoteles Opera* IV. Edited by O. Gigon. Berlin, 1961.

Anecdoton Holderi: ein Beitrag zur Geschichte Roms in ostgothischer Zeit = Festschrift zur Begrüssung der XXXII Versammlung deutscher Philologen und Schulmänner zu Wiesbaden. Bonn, 1877; reprinted Hildesheim, 1969.

Acta S. Timothei. = Natalicia regis augustissimi Guilelmi imperatoris Germaniae, etc. Bonn, 1877.

Stephani Alexandrini quod fertur opusculum apotelesmaticum. Bonn, 1879.

Legenden der Pelagia = Festschrift für die XXXIV Versammlung deutscher Philologen und Schulmänner zu Trier. Bonn, 1879; the preface is reprinted in *VA* [below]: 189–215.

Acta S. Marinae et S. Christophori. = Festschrift zur fünften Säcularfeier der Carl-Ruprechts-Universität zu Heidelberg. Bonn, 1886.

Altgriechischer Versbau. Ein Versuch vergleichender Metrik. Bonn, 1887.

Epicurea. Leipzig, 1887; reprinted Stuttgart, 1966.

Religionsgeschichtliche Untersuchungen. Erster Teil: Das Weihnachtsfest, Kapitel I bis III. Zweiter Teil: Christlicher Festbrauch. Bonn, 1889; revised and enlarged ed. edited by Hans Lietzmann, Bonn, 1911; reprinted Bonn, 1969; reprinted Hildesheim, 1972 [together with *Sintfluthsagen*].

Dionysii Halicarnassensis librorum de imitatione reliquiae epistulaeque criticae duae = Natalicia regis augustissimi Guilelmi II, etc. Bonn, 1889.

Der heilige Theodosios. Schriften des Theodoros und Kyrillos. Leipzig, 1890

Acta M. Anastasii Persae. Bonn, 1894.

Götternamen. Versuch einer Lehre von der religiösen Begriffsbildung. Bonn, 1896; reprinted with preface by Eduard Norden, 1929; 3d ed. with preface by Martin P. Nilsson, Frankfurt, 1948.

Die Sintfluthsagen. Bonn, 1899; reprinted Hildesheim, 1972 [together with *Das Weihnachtsfest*].

Dionysii Halicarnasei Opuscula. With L. Radermacher. Vol. 1. Leipzig, 1899.

Der heilige Tychon. Edited by A. Brinkmann. Leipzig and Berlin, 1907.

Vorträge und Aufsätze. Edited by A. Dieterich. Leipzig and Berlin, 1907; 2d ed., 1914.

Kleine Schriften I: Arbeiten zur griechischen Philosophie und Rhetorik, grammatische und textkritische Beiträge. Edited by K. Fuhr. Leipzig and Berlin, 1912; reprinted Osnabrück, 1965.

Kleine Schriften II: Arbeiten zur lateinischen Sprache und Literatur. Edited by P. E. Sonnenburg. Leipzig and Berlin, 1913; reprinted Osnabrück, 1965.

Kleine Schriften IV: *Arbeiten zur Religionsgeschichte*. Edited by R. Wünsch. Leipzig and Berlin, 1913; reprinted Osnabrück, 1965.

Kleine Schriften III: *Arbeiten zur Griechischen Literatur-geschichte, Geschichte der Wissenschaften, Epigraphik, Chronologie*. Edited by L. Radermacher, W. Kroll, F. Koepp, and A. Wilhelm. Leipzig and Berlin, 1914; reprinted Osnabrück, 1965.

Dreiheit: ein Versuch mythologischer Zahlenlehre. Hildesheim 1966 = *RhM* NF 58 (1903) 1–48, 161–208, 321–364.

Glossarium Epicureum. Edited by M. Gigante and W. Schmid. Rome and Bari, 1977.

Articles

All important articles, speeches, and small treatises have been incorporated in *Kleine Schriften* (KS) and the collection of Usener's more general articles, *Vorträge und Aufsätze* (VA), except for his biographical sketches of Jacob Bernays and Alfred Fleckeisen, which have appeared in the *ADB* 46 (1902) 393–404 and 48 (1904) 576–583, respectively.

Sources

Bibliography

There is only a bibliography of Usener's work on the history of religion in KS 4, iii–v. Apparently, no bibliography was published in expectation of Dieterich's announced biography (see above).

Biographical

Glanz und Niedergang der deutschen Universität. 50 Jahre deutscher Wissenschaftsges-chichte in Briefen an und von Hans Lietzmann 1892–1942. Edited by K. Aland. Berlin and New York, 1979.

von Arnim, H. [Obituary.] *Almanach der Kaiserlichen Akademie der Wissenschaften* 56 (1906) 335–340.

Aspetti di Hermann Usener filologo della religione. Preface by Arnaldo Momigliano. Pisa, 1982. Contains A. Momigliano, "Premesse per una discussione su Hermann Usener" 9–21; R. Bodei, "Hermann Usener nella filosofia moderna: tra Dilthey e Cassirer" 23–42; G. Cambiano, "Scienza organizzata e scienza 'selvaggia' in Hermann Usener" 43–64; M. M. Sassi, "Dalla scienza delle religioni di Usener ad Aby Warburg" 65–91; B. Scardigli, "Le lettere di Usener nella Staatsbibliothek di Monaco" 93–118; G. Arrighetti, "Gli studi epicurei di Hermann Usener" 119–136; E. Campanile, "La metrica comparativa di Hermann Usener" 137–145; G. Piccaluga, "Attualità dei Sondergötter?" 147–159; F. E. Consolino, "Usener e l'agiografia: *Legenden der Pelagia* e *Der heilige Tychon* 161–180; F. Parente, "Das Weihnachtsfest" 181–228; R. di Donato, "Usener n'habite plus ici" 213–228.

Bickel, E. "Das philologische Seminar unter Usener und Buecheler." In *Geschichte der Rheinischen Friedrich-Wilhelms-Universität zu Bonn am Rhein*. II. Bonn, 1933: 197–210.

———. "Hermann Usener 1834–1905." *Nassauische Lebensbilder* 5 (1955) 245–252.

Boll, F. "Hermann Usener." *Byzantinische Zeitschrift* 15 (1906) 511– 513.

Bremmer, J. N. "*Aspetti*." *Mnemosyne* 39 (1986) 561–564. (Review.)

Briggs, Ward W., Jr. *The Letters of Basil Lanneau Gildersleeve*. Baltimore, 1987: 141–143, 243–245.

Brinkmann, A. [Obituary.] *Chronik der Rheinischen Friedrich-Wilhelms-Universität zu Bonn* 31 (1906) 7–13.

Bücheler, F. "Gedächtnisrede auf Hermann Usener." *Neue Jahrbücher f.d. Klassische Altertum* 15 (1905) 737–743; reprinted in Bücheler's *Kleine Schriften*. Vol. 3. Leipzig and Berlin, 1930: 324–329.

Capasso, M. "Gli studi ercolanesi di Hermann Usener nel suo carteggio inedito con Hermann Diels." In M. Capasso, et al. *Momenti della storia degli studi classici fra Ottocento e Novecento*. Naples, 1987: 105–136.

Clemen, C. "Hermann Usener als Religionshistoriker." *Studi e materiali di storia delle religioni* 11 (1935) 110–124.

Deubner, L. "Hermann Usener." *Biographisches Jahrbuch für die Altertumswissenschaft* 31 (1908) 53–74.

Dieterich, A. "Hermann Usener." *Archiv für Religionswissenschaft* 8 (1905) i–xi. Reprinted in Dieterich's *Kleine Schriften*. Leipzig and Berlin, 1911: 354–362.

Gigante, M. "Il Glossarium Epicureum di Usener." *Rendiconti dell' Academia di Archeologia, Lettere e Belle Arti di Napoli* 52 (1977) 159–164.

———. "Hermann Usener e i testi epicurei nei papiri ercolanesi." In C. Jensen, W. Schmid, M. Gigante, *Saggi di papirologia ercolanese*. Naples, 1979: 45–91.

Gombrich, E. H. *Aby Warburg. An Intellectual Biography*, 2d ed., Oxford, 1986.

Henrichs, A. " Der Glaube der Hellenen : Religionsgeschichte als Glaubensbekenntnis und Kulturkritik." *Wilamowitz nach 50 Jahren*. Edited by W. M. Calder III et al. Darmstadt, 1985: 263–305; for Wilamowitz and Usener see 280–284.

———. "Welckers Götterlehre." *Friedrich Gottlieb Welcker. Werk und Wirkung*. Edited by W. M. Calder III et al. Stuttgart, 1986: 179–229; for Welcker and Usener see 223–229.

Herter, H. "Die klassische Philologie seit Usener und Bücheler." In *Bonner Gelehrte. Beiträge zur Geschichte der Wissenschaften in Bonn*. Bonn, 1968: 164–211, esp. 165–177.

Kany, R. *Mnemosyne als Programm. Geschichte, Erinnerung und die Andacht zum Unbedeutenden im Werk von Usener, Warburg und Benjamin*. Tübingen, 1987.

———. "Dionysos Protrygaios. Pagane und christliche Spuren eines Weinfestes." *Jahrbuch für Antike und Christentum* 31 (1988) 5–23; for Usener's *Der heilige Tychon* see 17–22.

———. *Die religionsgeschichtliche Forschung an der Kulturwissenschaftlichen Bibliothek Warburg*. Bamberg 1989.

Karo, G. *Fünfzig Jahre aus dem Leben eines Archäologen.* Baden–Baden, 1959.

Koepp, F. "Wilhelm Dilthey und Hermann Usener am Joachimstalschen Gymnasium. Ein Gedenkblatt zu Useners Einhundertsten Geburtstag am 23 Oktober 1934." *Der alte Joachimstaler. Vierteljahresblatt der Vereinigung alter Joachimstaler* 7 (1934), no. 28: 39–41.

Körte, A. "Hermann Usener – Ulrich von Wilamowitz–Moellendorff. Ein Briefwechsel." *Die Antike* 11 (1935) 211–235.

Mette, H. J. "Nekrolog einer Epoche: Hermann Usener und seine Schule. Ein wirkungsgeschichtlicher Rückblick auf die Jahre 1856–1979." *Lustrum* 22 (1979–80) 5–106.

Misch, G. *Der junge Dilthey.* Leipzig, 1933; reprinted Stuttgart, 1960.

Momigliano, A. "Premesse per una discussione su Hermann Usener." *RSI* 94 (1982) 191–203. Reprinted in *Aspetti:* 9–21; A. M., *Settimo contributo alla storia degli studi classici e del mondo antico.* Rome, 1984: 201–214; slightly different "Hermann Usener." *History and Theory,* Beiheft 21 (1982): 33–48.

Radermacher, L. "Hans Lietzmann." *Almanach der Akademie der Wissenschaften in Wien* 93 (1943) 269–280 (Lietzmann and Usener).

Scardigli, B. "Lettere inedite di Hermann Usener." *Munus amicitiae. Scritti in memoria di Alessandro Ronconi.* Vol. 1. Florence, 1986: 263–298.

Schmid, W. "Useners 'Glossarium Epicureum' und seine 'Epicurea'." *Würzburger Jahrbücher für die Altertumswissenschaft* 6a (1980) 19–29.

Schnell, A. "In Memoriam Hermann Usener." *Nachrichtenblatt für die Mitglieder der "Wilinaburgia."* 38 (1934) 4–7.

Schwartz, E. "Rede auf Hermann Usener." *Nachrichten von der Kgl. Gesellschaft der Wissenschaften zu Göttingen, Gesellschäftliche Mitteilungen* (1918) 43–70; reprinted in Schwartz' *Gesammelte Schriften.* Berlin, 1938: 1:301–315.

———. "Usener und Wilamowitz. Ein Briefwechsel. Eine Buchanzeige." *DLZ* 55 (1934) 1978–1986; reprinted in Schwartz' *Gesammelte Schriften.* Vol. I. Berlin, 1938: 316–325.

Treves, P. "*Usener und Wilamowitz.*" *La Critica* 33 (1935): 475–478. (Review.)

Wendland, P. "Hermann Usener. Ein Gedenkblatt." *Preussische Jahrbücher* 122 (1905) 373–387.

Wesen und Rang der Philologie. Zum Gedenken an Hermann Usener und Franz Bücheler. Edited by W. Schmid. Stuttgart, 1969.

von Wilamowitz-Moelendorff, U. *Erinnerungen 1848–1914.* Leipzig, 1928; rev. ed., 1929; English translation as *My Recollections,* London, 1930.

Letters

Usener und Wilamowitz. Ein Briefwechsel 1870–1905. Edited by H. Dieterich and F. Hiller von Gaertringen. Leipzig and Berlin, 1934.

Papers

1. UB Bonn: about 200 letters by Usener to family and colleagues (S 2109), diaries and notebooks (S 2160ª), and various other personal papers (S 2109); about 5,000 letters by numerous scholars to Usener (S 2101–2108), cf. Mette:

12–15; a catalogue with the titles of Usener's *Handexemplare* and the notes of his lectures by various pupils which were lost in the war. The *Archiv* of the university preserves the *Akten* of the Faculty regarding Usener's career.

2. Stadtarchiv Bonn: after the completion of my contribution I learned from Dr. K. A. Neuhausen (letter of 12 September 1988) that in the Stadtarchiv Bonn he has just discovered Bücheler's legacy, which also contains a number of letters by Usener.

3. Heidelberg: Hermann Dieterich, the son of Albrecht Dieterich, owns letters by Usener to his father and Wilhelm Dilthey.

4. The fullest survey of the whereabouts of Usener's letters can be found in the Zentralkartei der Autographen, Staatsbibliothek Preussischer Kulturbesitz, West Berlin. I note here the larger collections. East Berlin: the correspondence with Theodor Mommsen, 1861–1901 (Dt. Staatsbibliothek); the Diels-Usener correspondence in the archive of the Academy in Berlin is in press and will be out in 1989–1990, edited by D. Ehlers. West Berlin: there are letters of Usener in the legacies of Ad. Furtwängler, O. Jahn, R. Kekulé v. Stradonitz, and F. Studniczka in the Deutsches Archäologisches Institut. Darmstadt: 28 letters to W. Dilthey, 1874–1903 (Landes- u. Hochschulbibliothek *W. Dilthey 14 g and 14 l and 57*). Heidelberg: 7 letters to Paul Wendland, 1890–1898 (UB Ms. philos. 206: 107–113). Karlsruhe: the correspondence with Alfred Holder, 1868–1899 (Landesbibliothek K 1645). Munich: cf. B. Scardigli in *Aspetti*, 93–118 and Scardigli 1987. Tübingen: 6 letters to E. Zeller, 1879–1891 (UB Tübingen Md 747.780).

5. Halle (DDR): 'Vorlesungs-Nachschriften' in the legacy of Karl Gerhard.

I am very grateful to the Staatsbibliothek Preussischer Kulturbesitz and the Standesamt Weilburg for helpful information; to the staff of the archives and the library of the Rheinische Friedrich-Wilhelms-Universität Bonn, in particular Mrs. C. Weidlich, for their pleasant cooperation; to Dr. R. Kany and Professors William M. Calder III and Albert Henrichs for helpful comments and corrections; and last but not least, to Professor Adolf Köhnken for his hospitality and most helpful discussions during my stay in Bonn.

Jacob Wackernagel

11 December 1853–22 May 1938

RÜDIGER SCHMITT
Universität des Saarlandes

Jacob Wackernagel was one of the most important linguists and Indo-European scholars who ever lived. He was at once a classical scholar as well as a Sanskritist and linguist, and a man of permanent importance as a philological linguist or a "Sprachforscher philologischer Richtung," as he is reported to have called himself. Like the exponents of the so-called "Berlin school," Johannes Schmidt (1843–1901) and Wilhelm Schulze (1863–1935), Wackernagel pursued the sort of language comparison that relied on the reexamination of the textual tradition along philological lines. His studies in historical linguistics do not rely upon the data found in grammars or dictionaries but always upon factual material drawn from the texts themselves, which he interpreted by a fixed method. Wackernagel's recognition of various phenomena in the general field of Indo-European philology caused certain characteristics of the Indo-Iranian languages to be identified as part of a common Indo-European heritage. Thus today's Indo-European linguistics owes to Wackernagel important contributions to Greek grammar, to syntactical studies, and, above all, to the investigation of Old Indo-Aryan, to which field he contributed his fundamental and monumental *Altindische Grammatik*, though this masterpiece (first continued by Albert Debrunner) is even now not complete.

Jacob Wackernagel was born in Basel (Switzerland) on 11 December 1853 to Wilhelm Wackernagel (1806–1869), who was born in Berlin, but from 1833 was Professor of German Language and Literature in Basel, and his second wife, Maria Salome, née Sarasin, of an illustrious old Basel family. The man who stood godfather to the newborn child (*in absentia*) was none other than Jacob Grimm (1785–1863), one of the founders of modern linguistics and of German philology. Grimm was quite delighted to have the little boy named after him and wished that "er möge gedeihen und einmal Ihnen und mir rechte Ehre machen!," and in fact Jacob Grimm's *genanne* did so!

In Basel he attended the Pädagogium, whose teachers included celebrities like the historian Jacob Burckhardt, the Greek scholar Friedrich Nietzsche, and the Germanist Moritz Heyne. After the finest classical education possible, he matriculated in Basel University in 1871, but by autumn 1872 he went abroad to the Georgia Augusta in Göttingen, where he stayed for nearly two years and studied Sanskrit and comparative philology. He was greatly influenced by Theodor Benfey (1809–1881), who taught him Vedic and Sanskrit. It is obvious that this pioneer, who had a more philological proclivity than the other linguists and comparatists of those days, exerted a special attraction for Wackernagel, and as a result Old Indo-Aryan was always the basis of his comparative linguistic studies. Except for this great Sanskritist, influences of his university teachers or of certain schools upon Wackernagel seem to be nearly nonexistent. "He was his own creation" as Von der Mühll put it, especially in his classical scholarship. For the winter term 1874–75 he went up to Leipzig University, where he attended the classes of Ernst Kuhn, Georg Curtius, and August Leskien among others before he returned to Basel to take the doctor's degree in 1875 with a purely philological study of the beginnings of phonology in the ancient Greek grammarians. The oral examination committee comprised Friedrich Nietzsche (Greek philology), Franz Dorotheus Gerlach (Latin philology), Heyne (German philology), and Wilhelm Vischer (history).

From the beginning Wackernagel went his own way, and even in his thesis the remarkable independence of thinking so typical of all his later writings is conspicuous. This booklet, which shows its young author to have familiarized himself thoroughly with the history of ancient linguistics as well as with particulars of the Greek grammarians, proves that the queer doctrine of the πάθη, i.e. the phonetic changes of the words by addition, omission, transposition of sounds, etc., is the invention of the Alexandrian grammarians (presumably Tryphon) and that it had its sources in dialectology. In other words it may be said that present in that "pathology" are the beginnings of a scientific phonology. In a sense this study may be regarded as a program for Wackernagel's entire lifework, i.e., a program for a linguistics based on historical principles and on a philological foundation.

A few months after receiving his doctorate Wackernagel made his habilitation (summer 1876) as a private lecturer (Privatdozent) in Greek philology and Sanskrit at Basel, where a chair in Sanskrit and comparative philology had been established in 1874 (while he was at Göttingen), to which Franz Misteli was appointed. In 1879 Wackernagel was nominated Professor Extraordinarius of Greek Language and Literature to succeed Nietzsche (who had resigned owing to his illness), and he advanced to Ordinarius in 1881; he was thus Professor of Greek at that university where in the age of the Humanists Johannes Reuchlin had for the first time taught the Greek language. By the terms of his office Wackernagel had to lecture on Greek authors for many years, but he alone of his colleagues included lectures on Greek grammar and syntax. In that period he married (23 March 1886) Maria, née Stehlin, with whom he had eight children, among them the sons Jakob (1891–1967), who later was a Basel Professor of law, and Hans Georg (1895–1967), who later was professor of history, also in Basel. In his first term as Rector of Basel University in 1890, Wackernagel gave an interesting outline of the study and investigation of antiquity in Switzerland since the Renaissance in his rectoral address *Das Studium des klassischen Altertums in der Schweiz*.

He declined an invitation to fill Johannes Schmidt's chair at Berlin in 1901, but in the following year he decided to go to Göttingen, succeeding Wilhelm Schulze (who had been called to Berlin) as professor of comparative philology. But he resigned his professorship in this flourishing center of linguistics and philology in 1915 (despite having served as prorector in 1912–13), when the nationalist policy of the Germans in World War I and especially the infringement of the Belgian neutrality had repelled the neutral Swiss professor working at a Prussian university. So he returned to Basel where he held his former chair of Greek until, following Max Niedermann's departure for Neuchâtel, the linguistics chair fell vacant in 1926. Wackernagel, who in the meantime had won manifold recognition, was an honorary doctor of several universities, a member of various academies, and had held the position of Rector a second time for the two difficult years 1918–19. Finally, he retired in 1936, having completed his sixtieth year as a lecturer, and he died on 22 May 1938 in his native town, Basel.

During his first Basel professorship Wackernagel began to collect material for a grammar of Old Indo-Aryan, which was to become the most comprehensive and exhaustive scientific treatment an old Indo-European language has ever received. The surprise was enormous in 1896 when Wackernagel published his first Indo-Aryan study, volume 1 of the *Altindische Grammatik*; in Switzerland the witticism was common that the Zurich Professor of Sanskrit (Adolf Kaegi) wrote a Greek grammar (the famous *Griechische Schulgrammatik*, which has gone through many editions), while the Basel Professor of Greek wrote an Indo-Aryan one. In any case Wackernagel's book presented a fundamental view of the history and comparative grammar of Old Indo-Aryan and became a standard work and an indispensable instrument for every fellow researcher. It is the model of a linguistic handbook, combining both stringent linguistic method and philological accuracy as well as critical insistence and astonishing completeness in facts and bibliography; notable also is the use of the native Indian grammatical writings of Pânini and his followers, which are here fully exploited for the first time.

Volume 1 first presents in the introduction a lucid summary of the history of Old Indo-Aryan language and linguistics, then gives a full and precise description of the language along with an historical and comparative background from the Indo-European mother tongue up to Middle Indo-Aryan (always investigating the development within Indo-Aryan and stressing the primacy of Vedic). Unlike the later volumes, the phonological section is in part outdated, since the young Wackernagel relied too much on his teacher Benfey, whereas he later reveals the influence of the great Vedic scholar and Göttingen colleague (from 1908) Hermann Oldenberg (1854–1920). In this same Göttingen period he began more intensive work at the *Grammatik* and he also began to learn Old Iranian, culminating in a partnership with the Göttingen Iranist Friedrich Carl Andreas (1846–1930) and in the publication of some Zarathustrian *Gâthâs* upon the principles of Andreas's (today refuted) theory about the textual history of the *Avesta*.

Volume 2, part 1 (on word formation) of *Altindische Grammatik* appeared in 1905 (the second half being completed only posthumously by Albert Debrunner) and, in 1930, volume 3, wherein Wackernagel devoted special attention to pronouns and numerals. This one volume, with its astonishing composition and careful exposition both of manifold examples and of the history of former efforts, has become a standard for the historical and comparative treatment of an Indo-European language. It is thus small wonder that Antoine Meillet welcomed the appearance of that book with these enthusiastic words (*BSL* 30, 2 [1929] 66): "Voici qu'on retrouve cette rigueur de méthode linguistique, cette exactitude de philologue parfait, cette critique jamais en défaut, cette pénétration toujours présente, cette production exhaustive et des faits et de la bibliographie, que M. Wackernagel porte avec aisance: on pense à la liberté avec laquelle J. Séb. Bach écrivait des contrepoints compliqués aussi facilement qu'un musicien ordinaire un chant à une voix." Though remaining a torso, the *Altindische Grammatik* is a standard work of such uniqueness that Indian scholars often call its author a "modern Pâṇini."

At Göttingen Wackernagel also wrote *Sprachliche Untersuchungen zu Homer*, which shows his equal mastery of the philological and linguistic methods. The main part of the book deals with Wackernagel's view that the presence of Atticisms in the Homeric poems shows the strong influence of an Attic redaction of the *Iliad* and *Odyssey*. In this connection he resumes the question of the so-called "epische Zerdehnung." In an 1878 article, he had explained forms like ὁρόωντες as subsequent deformations of uncontracted forms like ὁράοντες (as the poet[s] used them) caused by the influence of the later (Ionic or Attic) contracted forms like ὁρῶντες, the placing of which had mutilated the hexametric verses. According to Wackernagel the forms in question therefore have been artificially restored from the contracted ones and in fact had never been spoken in this manner.

Another chapter treats the "gaps" of Homeric Greek, i.e. the intrusion of post-Homeric developments, archaic features foreign to the Aeolic and Ionian dialects that form the basis of the Homeric language, and, finally, vulgar and improper matters that had to be avoided in an aristocratic poetry like the Homeric epics (i.e. verbs like πέρδεσθαι, "to fart," or ὀμείχειν, "to piss," or nouns such as πέος, "penis," ὄρχις, "testicle," ὄρσος, "arse," and the like).

Wackernagel frequently gave a course of lectures on syntax; by popular request he published two of these series, which were to become his best known and most widely read book, the *Vorlesungen über Syntax*. This work begins with an explanation of syntax and treats both general notions like the functions of the various "parts of speech" and categories such as gender, number, person, *genus verbi*, tense, mood, etc. (where needed, also outside the Indo-European field), and it is something absolutely novel. It is full of interesting observations and splendid interpretations of linguistic particularities. Its relative popularity (for a book on linguistics) is attributable above all to its lively presentation of a rather difficult subject matter and its sometimes humorous and appealing style. In these two volumes the reader gains a striking impression of Jacob Wackernagel as a professor and of his didactic skill: He must have been a very versatile and stimulating teacher (on this see especially Rüegg, 9ff.) who had the power to present the subject in such an impressive and suggestive but also charming and thrilling manner that no one could resist him, not even his slightly older contemporary Ulrich von Wilamowitz-Moellendorff (1848–1931), who praised the work as the model of grammatical lectures and wrote in his *Erinnerungen 1848–1914*, that he himself in his old age wished to sit at Wackernagel's feet: "vor ihn möchte ich mich auch heute auf die Bank setzen" (289). In this rather personal book, which is neither a dry grammar nor strives for a systematic interpretation, Wackernagel really seems to speak to us in person, as he reveals through many acutely observed and vividly demonstrated examples the vitality of human speech, so that even nonexperts can understand the phenomena dealt with. Thus one gains much new information and often the solution of syntactic problems scarcely touched upon or even imagined before.

Despite these *Vorlesungen* Wackernagel is reported to have emphasized again and again that he was not interested in general linguistics. Nevertheless, it was he who advanced the discussion of general linguistic problems in a decisive way by his detailed philological studies. That may be why he set a higher value on his articles than on his books. It is these numerous articles (now completely reprinted in the *Kleine Schriften*) that show his efficiency and versatility. His first two papers of virtually comparative character, "Zum homerischen Dual" and "Der griechische Verbalaccent" demonstrate that Homeric Αἴαντε does not mean "the both Ajaxes, i.e. Ajax Telamonius and Ajax Oiliades" (as Homeric scholars had supposed), but stands for "Ajax and his sibling Teucrus" in the same way as we find, e.g., Vedic *Mitrâ* for "Mitra and Varuṇa". This small but brilliant discovery is a good example of Wackernagel's deductive method of stringent argumentation resulting from critical examination of the sources. Likewise he demonstrated that in the finite verb forms, the Greek verbal accent following the law of the three morae is a new formation based on the original Proto-Indo-European state, fully preserved in Vedic, where the finite verb is accentuated only in subordinate clauses, whereas in main clauses it is enclitic. As so often in his studies we find here the characteristic of combining the Greek with the Indo-Iranian evidence, which seems to be, as it were, the secret of his success. Of course Veda and Homer, Old Indo-Aryan and Greek are the keystones of all Indo-European comparative studies, but it is obvious that Wackernagel read these texts more carefully than most of his colleagues. It was he, rather than Wilhelm Schulze, who bound Indo-European studies closely to the data of textual tradition and thus contributed most to that Copernican turn from comparative reconstruction as a goal in itself toward an "Indo-European philology" that takes into account not only the linguistic development of prehistoric times, but chiefly the processes of development in the history of the separate languages, thereby imbuing linguistics with the spirit of history.

All of his great discoveries arise from noticing specific points (as a rule something in Greek, Latin, or Indo-Aryan texts), and move on to conditions that are valid for all Indo-European languages. This holds true, e.g., for his studies: (A) on the placing of enclitics originally in the second position in the sentence, a rule he established in 1892 (in the article entitled "Über ein Gesetz der indogermanischen Wortstellung") on the basis of rich materials (not only Greek, Indo-Iranian, and Latin, for also Germanic and Celtic show traces of that feature), now known as "Wackernagel's law" ("Wackernagel's law I" according to Collinge, 217ff.) and one of only a few generally accepted syntactic basic features of Proto-Indo-European and its earliest descendants; (B) on the Greek perfect (*Studien zum griechischen Perfektum*, 1904) which by sketching the history and showing the semantic structure of that tense, proved that the Greek perfect primarily indicated the achieved state and only later (after Homer) developed the sense of the "resultative perfect," causing Antoine Meillet and some of his students to trace similar aspects in some cognate languages; (C) on *Das Dehnungsgesetz der griechischen Composita* (1889), where the vowel lengthening in the beginning of the second element of Greek compounds like στρατᾱγός from *στρατο-αγός is explained by an earlier Proto-Indo-European contraction (treated as "Wackernagel's law II" by Collinge, 238–239), from which it has widely spread, however; (D) on "Wortumfang und Wortform" (1906) showing the reluctance of several Indo-European languages to employ verbal and nominal short monosyllables (becoming evident, e.g., in the use of the augment and in avoiding a monosyllabic form like σχέ alongside ἔσχε); and (E) on "Genetiv und Adjektiv" (1908) connecting the Latin genitive in -î with the corresponding Old Indo-Aryan adverb of formations like *mithunî bhû* "to become paired, to copulate" (of the type the Indian grammarians label *cvi*) and combining all that with Latin constructions such as *lucrî facere* "to make a profit."

Among the students of Wackernagel are the linguists Max Niedermann and Albert Debrunner as well as the Greek scholars Giorgio Pasquali and Peter Von der Mühll. Dissertations directed by him include those of Hans Barth, *De Coorum titulorum dialecto* (Basel, 1896), Theophil Gubler, *Die Patronymica im Alt-Indischen* (Basel, 1902; printed Göttingen, 1903), and Herman Lommel, *Studien über Indogermanische Femininbildungen* (Göttingen, 1912).

Jacob Wackernagel, whose characteristics were an intimate knowledge of the sources, encyclopedic learning, fine attentive observation, a brilliant memory, and a feeling for the smallest detail, never lost the ground under his feet and was free of speculations and fancies, so that Von der Mühll (13–14 = Von der Mühll, *Ausgewählte Kleine Schriften*, 539) could say, that there will be only few people ever, "who made so few mistakes as Wackernagel." He proceeded upon the principle written down in the draft for the unfinished third series of *Vorlesungen über Syntax* (quoted by Lohmann, 58) that "besser als von vorgefaßten Theorien lassen sich von der Betrachtung des Ererbten aus die in einer Sprachgeschichte wirksamen Tendenzen erfassen." So we understand that Wackernagel never engaged in the discussion about the then burning question of the ways to reconstruct the Indo-European protolanguage and about the still more disputed problem of the principle of phonetic laws without exceptions, as it was postulated above all by the Leipzig school of the so-called Neogrammarians. Wackernagel was independent from the linguistic theories of his age (including those of Ferdinand de Saussure) but rather argued for the philological foundation of all linguistic research. Such an attitude on the part of linguists greatly benefited philology by interpreting, correctly understanding, or even emending passages in ancient texts. That is what we can learn best from Jacob Wackernagel even today.

Books

De pathologiae veterum initiis. Diss., Basel, 1876 =*Kleine Schriften* 3: 1427–1486.

Das Dehnungsgesetz der griechischen Composita. Dem Basler Gymnasium zur Feier seines dreihundertjährigen Bestehens gewidmet von der Universität Basel. Basel, 1889 = *Kleine Schriften* 2: 897–961.

Das Studium des klassischen Altertums in der Schweiz. Basel, 1891.

Beiträge zur Lehre vom griechischen Akzent. Programm zur Rektoratsfeier der Universität Basel. Basel, 1893 = *Kleine Schriften* 2: 1072–1107.

Altindische Grammatik. I. Lautlehre. Göttingen, 1896; *Introduction générale* [new ed. of Vol. 1] by Louis Renou, 1957. *Band I: Lautlehre*, reprinted 1957; *Nachträge zu Band I* by Albert Debrunner, 1957. *Band II, 1: Einleitung zur Wortlehre–Nominalkomposition*. Göttingen, 1905; reprinted 1957; *Nachträge zu Band II 1* by Albert Debrunner,1957.*Band III: Nominalflexion–Zahlwort–Pronomen* by Albert Debrunner und Jacob Wackernagel. Göttingen, 1930; reprinted 1975. *Band II, 2: Die Nominalsuffixe* by Albert Debrunner. Göttingen, 1954.

Vermischte Beiträge zur griechischen Sprachkunde. Programm zur Rektoratsfeier der Universität Basel. Basel, 1897 = *Kleine Schriften* 1: 764–823.

Studien zum griechischen Perfektum. Ad praemiorum publicam renuntiationem invitatio Universitatis Georgiae Augustae. Göttingen, 1904 = *Kleine Schriften* 2: 1000–1021.

Hellenistica. Ad praemiorum publicam renuntiationem invitatio Universitatis Georgiae Augustae. Göttingen: Vandenhoeck et Ruprecht, 1907 = *Kleine Schriften* 2: 1034–1058.

Über einige antike Anredeformen. Ad praemiorum publicam renuntiationem invitatio Universitatis Georgiae Augustae. Göttingen, 1912 = *Kleine Schriften* 2: 970–999.

Sprachliche Untersuchungen zu Homer. Göttingen, 1916; reprinted 1970; pages 1–159 first published in *Glotta* 7 (1916) 161–319.

Vorlesungen über Syntax mit besonderer Berücksichtigung von Griechisch, Lateinisch und Deutsch. Erste Reihe. Basel, 1920; 2d ed., 1926; reprinted 1950. *Zweite Reihe*. Basel, 1924; 2d ed., 1928; reprinted 1957.

Articles (Collected)

Kleine Schriften. Akademie der Wissenschaften zu Göttingen. 2 Halbbände. Göttingen [1955]; reprinted 1969. *Dritter Band.* Edited by Bernhard Forssman. Göttingen, 1979.

Articles

"Zum homerischen Dual." ZVS 23 (1877) 302–310 = *Kleine Schriften* 1:538–546.

"Der griechische Verbalaccent." ZVS 23 (1877) 457–470 = *Kleine Schriften* 2:1058–1071.

"Die epische Zerdehnung." *Beiträge zur Kunde der indogermanischen Sprachen* 4 (1878) 259–312 = *Kleine Schriften* 3:1512–1565.

"Zum Zahlwort." ZVS 25 (1881) 260–291 = *Kleine Schriften* 1:204–235.

"Miszellen zur griechischen Grammatik." ZVS 27 (1885) 84–92, 262–280; 28 (1887) 109–145; 29 (1888) 124–152; 30 (1890) 293–316; 33 (1895) 1–62 = *Kleine Schriften* 1:564–741.

"Über ein Gesetz der indogermanischen Wortstellung." IF 1 (1892) 333–436 = *Kleine Schriften* 1:1–104.

"Über Bedeutungsverschiebung in der Verbalkomposition." *Nachrichten von der Königlichen Gesellschaft der Wissenschaften zu Göttingen* (1902): 737–757 = *Kleine Schriften* 1:127–147.

"Sprachtausch und Sprachmischung." *Nachrichten von der Königlichen Gesellschaft der Wissenschaften zu Göttingen.* Geschäftliche Mitteilungen (1904): 90–113 = *Kleine Schriften* 1:104–127.

"Die griechische Sprache." *Die Kultur der Gegenwart.* Edited by Paul Hinneberg. Teil I, Abteilung VIII: Die griechische und lateinische Literatur und Sprache. Leipzig, Berlin, 1905: 286–312; 2d ed., 1907: 291–318; 3d ed., 1912: 371–397 = *Kleine Schriften* 3:1676–1702.

"Wortumfang und Wortform." *Nachrichten von der Königlichen Gesellschaft der Wissenschaften zu Göttingen* (1906): 147–184 = *Kleine Schriften* 1:148–185.

"Zu den lateinischen Ethnika." *Archiv für lateinische Lexikographie und Grammatik* 14 (1906) 1–24 = *Kleine Schriften* 2:1322–1345.

"Genetiv und Adjektiv." *Mélanges de linguistique offerts à M. Ferdinand de Saussure.* Paris, 1908: 123–152 = *Kleine Schriften* 2:1346–1373.

"Akzentstudien. I–III." *Nachrichten von der Königlichen Gesellschaft der Wissenschaften zu Göttingen* (1909): 50–63; (1914): 20–51, 97–130 = *Kleine Schriften* 2:1108–1187.

"Indoiranica." ZVS 43 (1910) 277–298; 46 (1914) 266–280 = *Kleine Schriften* 1:262–298.

"Indoiranisches." *Sitzungsberichte der Königlich Preußischen Akademie der Wissenschaften* (1918): 380–411 = *Kleine Schriften* 1:299–330.

"Über einige lateinische und griechische Ableitungen aus den Verwandtschaftswörtern." *Festgabe Adolf Kaegi* (Frauenfeld, 1919): 40–65 = *Kleine Schriften* 1:468–493.

"Griechische Miszellen." *Glotta* 14 (1925) 36–67 = *Kleine Schriften* 2:844–875.

"Kleine Beiträge zur indischen Wortkunde." *Beiträge zur Literaturwissenschaft und Geistesgeschichte Indiens. Festgabe Hermann Jacobi* (Bonn, 1926): 1–17 = *Kleine Schriften* 1:417–433.

"Conubium." *Festschrift für Paul Kretschmer. Beiträge zur griechischen und lateinischen Wortforschung* (Vienna, Leipzig, and New York, 1926): 289–306 = *Kleine Schriften* 2:1280–1297.

"Indoiranica." *ZVS* 55 (1928) 104–112; 59 (1932) 19–30; 61 (1934) 190–208; 67 (1942) 154–182 = *Kleine Schriften* 1: 331–398.

"Zur Wortfolge, besonders bei den Zahlwörtern." *Festschrift Gustav Binz* (Basel, 1935): 33–54 = *Kleine Schriften* 1:236–256.

"Indogermanische Dichtersprache." *Philologus* 95 (1943) 1–19 = *Kleine Schriften* 1:186–204; *Indogermanische Dichtersprache*. Edited by Rüdiger Schmitt (Darmstadt, 1968): 83–101.

"Graeca." *Philologus* 95 (1943) 177–192 = *Kleine Schriften* 2:876–891.

Sources

Bibliographies

A full list of Wackernagel's writings (including reviews, editorial activities, and contributions to the writings of other authors) is to be found in the following:

Debrunner, Albert. "Nachtrag zum Verzeichnis der Schriften Jacob Wackernagels, zusammengestellt von Mathilde Probst." *Indogermanisches Jahrbuch* 23 (1939) 447–451.

Forssman, Bernhard. "Zweiter Nachtrag zum Verzeichnis der Schriften Jacob Wackernagels." *Kleine Schriften* 3:xx–xxvi.

Probst, Mathilde. "Verzeichnis der Schriften Jacob Wackernagels." In *ΑΝΤΙΔΩΡΟΝ. Festschrift Jacob Wackernagel zur Vollendung des 70. Lebensjahres am 11. Dezember 1923*. Göttingen, 1923: 354–361.

Biographical

Collinge, N. E. *The Laws of Indo-European*. Amsterdam and Philadelphia, 1985: 217–219 ("Wackernagel's Law I"); 238–239 ("Wackernagel's Law II").

Debrunner, Albert. "Zum 70. Geburtstag Jacob Wackernagels. 11 Dezember 1923." *Indogermanisches Jahrbuch* 9 (1924) 264–269.

———. "Jacob Wackernagel." *New Indian Antiquary* 1 (1938–39) 601-608.

Hermann, Eduard. "Jacob Wackernagel." *Nachrichten von der Gesellschaft der Wissenschaften zu Göttingen. Jahresbericht* 1938/39 (1939) 76–89.

His, Eduard. "Jacob Wackernagel-Stehlin 1853–1938." Eduard His, *Basler Gelehrte des 19. Jahrhunderts* (Basel, 1941): 340–349.

Kretschmer, P. "Jakob Wackernagel." *Almanach der Akademie der Wissenschaften in Wien* 88, 1938 (1939) 354–356.

Lohmann, Johannes. "Jacob Wackernagel *11. Dezember 1853 Basel, †21. Mai

1938 Basel." *Jahresbericht über die Fortschritte der klassischen Altertumswissenschaft* 280 (1942) 57–70.

Von der Mühll, Peter. "Jacob Wackernagel 11. XII. 1853–22.V.1938." *Zur Erinnerung an Prof. Jacob Wackernagel–Stehlin* (Basel, 1938): 11–16; reprinted in Von der Mühll's *Ausgewählte Kleine Schriften* (Basel, 1976): 537–541.

———. "Jacob Wackernagel †." *Gnomon* 14 (1938) 526–528.

Pasquali, Giorgio. "Ricordo del linguista Jacob Wackernagel." *Letteratura* 2, 3 (1938) 6–15.

Schwyzer, Eduard. "Jacob Wackernagel †." *Forschungen und Fortschritte* 14 (1938) 227–228.

Renou, Louis. "Jacob Wackernagel et les études indiennes." *JA* 230 (1938) 279–286.

Rüegg, August. "Jacob Wackernagel 1853–1938." *Basler Jahrbuch* (1939): 7–17.

Sommer, Ferdinand. "Jacob Wackernagel (*11.12.1853, †22.5.1938.)." *Sitzungsberichte der Philosophisch-historischen Abteilung der Bayerischen Akademie der Wissenschaften zu München* 1939, Heft 11: 23–26.

Letters

Briefe aus dem Nachlass Wilhelm Wackernagels. Edited by Albert Lietzmann. Leipzig, 1916: esp. 27, 30.

Papers

The papers of Jacob Wackernagel are preserved partly in the Öffentliche Bibliothek der Universität Basel (the scientific bequest including collections of material, the manuscripts of his books and lectures as well as annotated copies of his own, and other writings used by him) and partly in the Staatsarchiv des Kantons Basel-Stadt (personal file, deeds and documents, an autobiography of 1936–37, letters, speeches, notebooks, etc.).

Ulrich von Wilamowitz-Moellendorff

22 December 1848 – 25 September 1931

ROBERT L. FOWLER
University of Waterloo

Ulrich von Wilamowitz-Moellendorff is commonly called, with justice, the greatest Hellenist of modern times. This appellation is not granted merely because of the staggering range of his activities and his sheer philological power, impressive as these are, and unequalled in anyone else since Bentley; it is granted because he transformed the whole discipline and brought it from the nineteenth century into the twentieth. When he came to the subject, it was in danger of death due to specialization. Philologists, historians, archaeologists, art critics, and philosophers all went their own ways. Greek philology was informed by the spirit of Gottfried Hermann, who was a very great scholar indeed but a *Wortphilolog* who firmly restricted his activity within certain bounds. Students of literature saw their highest task in conjectural criticism. For Wilamowitz, interpretation of the literature was the pinnacle of philological activity; emendation was only one part of it. If a text was to be fully understood, it had to be placed in its original context; the philologist would need to know everything about the historical, cultural, and intellectual milieu in which the work was created. Wilamowitz therefore insisted that the barriers between the various departments of classical scholarship be knocked down, and the true unity of the subject restored. This was the ideal of *Altertumswissenschaft*, "the science of antiquity," already enunciated by F. A. Wolf, August Böckh, and F. G. Welcker, but for many reasons the ideal had been lost sight of. In part, the time was not ripe; in part, energies had been diverted elsewhere; perhaps most importantly, the necessary material was not at hand, particularly of the archaeological sort. By temperament, talent, education, and place in time, Wilamowitz was ideally suited to bring about a revitalization of classical studies. By the end of his long life he had made contributions of fundamental importance across the whole spectrum of the discipline; his impact was not confined to the Greek sphere alone. Through his books and his students, his influence is still very much alive; in the everyday work of the classicist, the writings of Wilamowitz are, or should be, constantly at hand.

Ulrich Friedrich Wichard von Wilamowitz-Moellendorff was born the third child of his parents in the family home at Markowitz in the Prussian colonial province of Posen, now part of Poland, on 22 December 1848. His ancestry was predominantly Prussian and aristocratic (his father, Arnold, bore the title Freiherr). Certain aristocratic habits of mind are traceable in Wilamowitz and set him off from other scholars, who tended to be pastors' or teachers' sons: his easy assumption of superiority; his unhesitating honesty in judging character and ability; his refusal to be bound by the conventions of the scholarly bourgeoisie; and, on a more positive note, his genuine magnanimity. His simple and austere tastes were characteristic of the Prussian aristocracy in particular. He was fiercely loyal to his king, and, after 1871, the empire. In spite of his birth, however, he turned his back on a military and diplomatic career, a decision for which his father never forgave him. His mother, Ulrike (née von Calbo), after whom he was named, was the real influence on his early life. She saw to his early schooling in both literature and religion. Not many important lessons were learned on the former head, but valuable introductions were made to Homer, Shakespeare, and the German classics; in religion, Wilamowitz acquired the undogmatic, theistical, anti-institutional attitude that found fullest expression in the last book of his life. His devotion to his mother was profound and forms the subject of some moving pages in the *Erinnerungen*.

The greatest service she did her son was to send him for serious schooling at age thirteen to Schulpforte, near Naumburg. This school, founded in an old Cistercian monastery in 1543, was the alma mater of many famous scholars and an ideal choice for the young Wilamowitz. Being entirely surrounded by an academic environment awakened his scholarly instincts. The teachers were sympathetic and, if not all of them were really learned, they were capable of inspiring their charges with enthusiasm for learning. And some, such as August Koberstein, Wilhelm Corssen, Karl Steinhart, and Karl Peter, were learned enough to rival or outperform Wilamowitz's later teachers at university. Latin was stressed more than Greek, in particular Latin prose and verse composition; Wilamowitz became a master in this art and rightly appreciated its usefulness to the scholar. He transferred the skill to Greek, where plenty of opportunity existed for keen students to study on their own. He learned English, French, and some Hebrew; Italian was acquired in voluntary evening lessons. He excelled in mathematics. When he left the school his sense of indebtedness was overwhelming. He swore to dedicate his first great book to it, as he did when he published his commentary on Euripides' *Herakles*. To his teachers he dedicated his *Reden und Vorträge*, the preface of which contains an impassioned encomium of them and their calling. Most beloved of all was the Rector, Karl Peter, in whose house Wilamowitz lived while attending the school as a day-boy, and who was clearly a substitute father for him. His doctoral dissertation was dedicated neither to his parents nor any professor, but to Rector Peter *"pietatis ergo."*

One day at Pforte Wilamowitz read Plato's *Symposium*, which proved to be an experience of religious dimensions; as he tells us many years later at the end of *Platon* and again in his memoirs, he then learned the purpose of life: to search unceasingly for knowledge, inspired by Platonic Eros with the love of the eternal world of God. In his valedictory address to his teachers and fellow pupils, the eighteen-year-old Wilamowitz declared that he would be a "disciple of scholarship"; he explicitly renounces "the supposedly higher circles into which I was born." He goes on to quote verses 673ff. of Euripides' *Herakles*, a passage on lifelong service to the Muses that provided him with his motto; the words appear on the dedication page of his edition of the play and again in the *Nachwort* to the second volume of *Platon*, written during the darkest hours after World War I, when life seemed almost pointless.

Wilamowitz graduated from Schulpforte 9 September 1867 and matriculated at Bonn in October of the same year. Not all his professors were up to the job of teaching him. Hermann Usener had the ability, but Wilamowitz conceived an antipathy to his speculative scholarship; he later realized his mistake and paid full homage to Usener's stimulative genius, although their approaches remained irreconcilable. With Otto Jahn, however, he formed a warm personal relationship, and learned much from him about art history and the Hellenistic age. Jacob Bernays made a strong impression; so did Anton Springer and Reinhard Kekule. In the autumn of 1869, following Jahn's death, he transferred to Berlin; of his teachers there the Aristotelian Hermann Bonitz had the greatest effect on him. He heard Ernst Curtius and Adolf Kirchhoff but was not much impressed with either; he respected Moriz Haupt, the nominal director of his dissertation, but they met only a few times to discuss it. He was to learn more from editing Haupt's *Opuscula* than from Haupt himself. Theodor Mommsen was not much at Berlin in 1869–1870. Wilamowitz's main instruction, indeed, came from the books of scholars dead or all but dead: Porson, Elmsley, Hermann, Welcker; in the years after promotion he added Böckh and Müller. From the first three he learned the central importance to the classical scholar of wide and exact linguistic knowledge; from the last three, Welcker in particular, he acquired the *Totalitätsideal* and a great deal about religion, mythology, archaeology, and art. He was also an enthusiastic devotee of Lachmann in these days, whose work aroused his intense interest in the problems of textual transmission; however, he soon realized the narrowness of Lachmann's approach.

His great friendships were formed in his student days or shortly afterward and should be mentioned here, since it is with these scholars that Wilamowitz was to inaugurate the new age in classical studies. Carl Robert and Hermann Diels he met at Bonn; Georg Kaibel too, although they did not become close friends until 1872 in Rome. Friedrich Leo was added to the group in Rome in 1873. It was a happy coincidence that these like–minded men lived and studied together at the formative point of their careers. Robert, Kaibel, and Leo were thoroughly under the guidance of Wilamowitz; Diels had somewhat different interests, but they complemented rather than contradicted those of Wilamowitz. They made a perfect pair together at Berlin from 1897 on. With respect to the early years, it is interesting that Wilamowitz in his memoirs twice acknowledges that Diels was ahead of him in scholarly accomplishment, although they were the same age. Not a member of this close group, but a good friend of Wilamowitz, was the first secretary of the Deutsches Archäologisches Institut in Athens, the archaeologist and diplomat Otto Lüders.

The dissertation dealt with selected critical problems in Greek comedy. There are enough lasting results for it to find frequent citation in the latest edition of the Greek comic poets, for example in an emendation of Aristophanes fr. 415 (Kassel-Austin). It was a good start to his career; his examiners knew his talents well enough and hardly bothered to read the dissertation before passing it.

Following graduation Wilamowitz spent a year as a grenadier in the Franco-Prussian War of 1870–1871; he then embarked on his *Wanderjahre* in Italy and Greece. Before he departed there occurred the celebrated incident of *Zukunftsphilologie!*, Wilamowitz's attack on Nietzsche's *Die Geburt der Tragödie*. His two pamphlets earned Wilamowitz the scorn and slander of Nietzsche's later apostles, from whom, one suspects, more people have derived their image of Wilamowitz than from the man himself. With regard to the main facts of the issue under dispute, Wilamowitz was absolutely right. Moreover, the work masqueraded as a work of historical interpetation and deserved to have its errors exposed. On the other hand, it was something other than philology; Wilamowitz later realized this and expressed regret in his memoirs for the intemperance of his polemic. His original motives in writing were not blameless; Nietzsche had been an earlier favorite of Rector Peter at Pforte, and a protégé of Ritschl, the archenemy of Wilamowitz's teacher Jahn. By the time he wrote his memoirs, he had recognized Nietzsche's greatness, but he remained profoundly out of sympathy with his thinking.

For the next two years, from 1872 to 1874, Wilamowitz lived in Italy; a little over two months in the winter of 1873 were spent traveling in Greece—a vital pilgrimage for any young Hellenist, but especially for one with Wilamowitz's taste for historical actualization. "Attica was no longer the fairyland of poetry, but a living reality," he says of this trip in his memoirs; he felt able for the first time really to understand Hellenic history and people, "and above all their gods." By a marvelous chance the letter Wilamowitz wrote to his parents on this occasion survives; it mingles the excitement of immediacy with the expected touch of awe and an unexpected touch of youthful irreverence. Many scholars have had similar experiences, but few had them when archaeology was in its youth, and the feeling was abroad that antiquity was really being discovered for the first time; nor did they all have Wilamowitz's sense of what could be done with the new discoveries.

He returned to Italy in May 1873 and "entered the service of Mommsen." Confident of superiority to a fault, the young Wilamowitz nonetheless wanted an authority figure. The *Römische Geschichte* was well-known to him from his school days, and Wilamowitz had met Mommsen in Berlin, but the close contact and influence dates from this period. Mommsen's historiography, instead of concentrating on the great protagonists and the great writers of history for protreptic purposes, made its object the full complexity of human life, and therefore made use of every primary source available, particularly inscriptions. The vibrant realism of his work appealed directly to Wilamowitz. Mommsen taught him many lessons: the importance of understanding institutions and the evolution of societies; epigraphy and the use of sources; the greatness of Rome and Italy; the indissoluble unity of Greco-Roman civilization. He inspired him with his boundless learning, his energy and devotion, and his ability to make the ancients come alive through historical imagination. Wilamowitz had already formed the view that all aspects of a culture—literature, art, history, philosophy, society—must be treated together if they were to be adequately understood; so these lessons fell on willing ears. Mommsen widened his horizons to the whole of the Greco-Roman world and gave him practical signposts along the road he already knew he must travel.

From autumn 1874 to Easter 1876 Wilamowitz was Privatdozent at Berlin. During the summer of 1874 he wrote his *Habilitationsschrift, Analecta Euripidea*. Much of it was written at the family home in Markowitz, without books—a regular habit of his, which is quite disconcerting to scholars of ordinary intelligence who can scarcely credit the fabulous capacity and precision of his memory. The reason for choosing Euripides as the subject of his habilitation was not a particular love of that author, whom in his valedictory essay he called "a middling poet and a poor tragedian"; it was that he had had enough of the canonized Sophocles. "Nothing distorts the image of a man more than his apotheosis," he later wrote. Vague enthusiasm about the beauties of form in Sophocles only served to remove him from the realm of reality. Wilamowitz's strong sense of the Greeks as real people made him reject the prevailing image of them as classical abstracts. Throughout his life he decried the classicistic approach as unhistorical. It is probably the most prominent theme in his works; he plainly regarded classicistic prejudice as the most serious obstacle to truth. In its place he substituted his "historicism," the art of seeing the Greek world as the Greeks saw it. This entailed seeing the ugly bits too. From the start he showed a tendency to seize on the irregular, the imperfect, the abnormal as a better handle on the realities of life. Not that he found second-rate art congenial, but he held that the great works had first to be understood in their original contexts if we wished to extract what was truly valuable, eternal, and "classic" from them. Euripides was an ideal author with whom to start this program, since everyone, even Mommsen, despised him because he was not "classical" enough.

Analecta Euripidea is dedicated to Mommsen in an emotional preface; the subject matter was not exactly Mommsenian, but Wilamowitz wanted to declare his allegiance. The first part of the book discusses the vexed problem of the relation of manuscripts L (C) and P; Wilamowitz's careful work and sharp eyes dragged a good deal more out of the old books than his predecessors had done, and he put the whole problem on a new basis. His hypothesis that P is not a copy of L, but was copied from the same source as L, is now rejected; but the solution of this exceedingly difficult problem was not reached until 1965. On the basis of his reconstruction, Wilamowitz provides an edition of the *Supplices*. He explains that *recensio*, not *emendatio*, is his main purpose, although, he adds, he cannot shirk his duty where he sees that a corruption can be healed. The edition contains not a few convincing conjectures and is competent enough for its time, but Wilamowitz later thought that he had attempted it too early. For one thing, he had not yet begun his original study of meter. The *apparatus criticus* is notable for its simplicity, omitting all quisquiliae; Wilamowitz more than anyone else found ways of making the apparatus both compendious and truly indicative of the textual tradition. More important than the text were the beginnings of certain lines of inquiry that were completed in later years, most notably in the *Herakles* commentary. Wilamowitz has realized that the story of a book must be told from the autograph on, not just from the archetype of the medieval manuscripts. In other words, he wants to go beyond the point at which a Lachmannian inquiry would stop. The evidence lay in scholia, lexica, and grammatical treatises—difficult and abstruse sources. The twenty-six-year-old author already shows a solid grasp of this material. Thinking about scholia and transmission led him to notice that the titles of Euripidean plays without scholia were in alphabetical order; he inferred rightly that a single volume of a collected, uncommented edition had been separated from its fellows and subsequently copied. The commented plays, by contrast, implied sustained interest and therefore unaccidental preservation. In another place he observes that most of the major corruptions in tragic texts occurred before the days of Lycurgus in the fourth century B.C.—a thesis amply confirmed since by the papyri. These observations were the first of many. By going beyond the Lachmannian archetype, Wilamowitz brought to light a vast area of knowledge of the utmost importance to textual criticism and the history of scholarship. The magnitude of this change in perspective is hard to overestimate.

Early in 1876 Wilamowitz gained his first appointment: a chair in the windy city of Greifswald. During the next four years, he spent most of his time acquiring the knowledge he needed for his great projects, in addition to facing the pressures of any new teacher. The preparation of Haupt's *Opuscula* cost him a good deal of labor. Nevertheless, his output and range of activity in these years are notable: Menander, manuscripts, pseudo-Ovid, history of Greek language, epigraphy, Hellenistic poetry, etc. "Commentariolum grammaticum I" and "Parerga" (1879) inaugurated a long series of *miscellanea critica* which in themselves would be enough to establish Wilamowitz as a great scholar. As a teacher he was an instant success. Students no longer heard morally satisfying lectures on Demosthenes; they heard of tinkers and sawyers and cobblers and harlots, of politicians' accounts and grammarians' corner-humming, of stage props and rhapsodes, of saga and belief. In time they came from farther afield, men of promise such as Hans von Arnim, Bruno Keil, Wilhelm Schulze, Eduard Schwartz, Ludwig Traube, and Friedrich Spiro. Among his colleagues Wilamowitz numbered Adolf Kießling, to whose edition of Horace he made vital contributions and, more importantly, Julius Wellhausen. Wilamowitz was attracted by his historical criticism of the Old Testament, and the two men enjoyed a fruitful exchange of ideas. *Homerische Untersuchungen* used methods for Homeric research similar to Wellhausen's and is dedicated to him. The material for the fine portrait drawn by Eduard Schwartz of this great man in the first volume of his *Gesammelte Schriften* was mostly provided by a letter of Wilamowitz, since discovered and published.

In 1880 *Aus Kydathen* appeared, a book of Attic history and topography with a chapter contributed by Carl Robert. The opening section is an expanded version of an address delivered on the Kaiser's birthday in 1877, entitled "On the Splendor of the Athenian Empire." It is obvious enough that the author sees a parallel in the splendor of the German empire; he admits as much on page 45, and is unapologetic about his use of modern terminology to describe the ancient institutions. This habit of his (and Mommsen's) could be overdone, but it was all part of making the ancients come alive again. The assumption is that they were pretty much the same as we are today. Later generations, whose sense of continuity with the past was forever broken by the events of the twentieth century, tended to stress the differences; Wilamowitz's contemporaries were prepared to believe in the similarities.

In *Aus Kydathen* and many other books, one has the impression of being given a guided tour by a native inhabitant of old Greece. One reason for the immediacy is Wilamowitz's habit of working only from the primary sources. He knew the secondary literature very well but had the knack of bypassing it without ignoring it. The facts lived again in his mind in a recreation of past life; his books merely tell what he sees within. This skill is granted to few; Uvo Hölscher called it "half his genius." In this connection the antipositivist manifesto at the end of the book is highly interesting. In it Wilamowitz argues that Athenian greatness did not come about through a mechanical or automatic process, like a plant growing from seed, owing to the accidental combination of certain historical factors; rather, it was the work of the unique Athenian spirit, their *daimon*—a quality of soul, in other words, and not something material or contingent. Athens first showed the world how to transcend its temporal limitations. Those who associate Wilamowitz with positivism would do well do contemplate this passage. Certainly his methods owed something to positivism, but he always looked for eternal values in the literature of antiquity and was well aware of his own subjective involvement in his historical reconstructions. If you are going to describe yesterday as if it were today, you are bound to stress what you think is important in your own society. A certain amount of distortion is inevitable as ancient and modern terms mix. But this is not to say that deliberate falsehood is permitted. The whole effort is based on a wide and exact knowledge of the primary sources, and conscious imposition of modern preconceptions is avoided. Wilamowitz, indeed, excelled precisely at identifying anachronistic interpretations. At bottom the exercise is one of translation, which in a famous essay Wilamowitz calls "metempsychosis." The ancient writer must be made to speak in a modern tongue and call forth the same reactions as the ancient reader once had. To achieve this result the translator must first have thought himself into the mind of the ancient writer. An attempt to remain "objective" would be as lifeless as a slavishly literal translation. In another famous passage, Wilamowitz declares that the ghosts of antiquity will not speak until we give them our own blood; but that very act, he adds, imports something alien, which must be cast out in the name of truth. It is a difficult business to do these contradictory things at once, but it can sometimes be done by the right person.

In *Aus Kydathen* Wilamowitz was finally able to show how Mommsen's lessons could be relevant to the study of Greek literature. The Mommsenian slant of his approach is explicit on page 5, where we are told how new methods, beginning from a juristic standpoint, had revolutionized Roman history—"the proudest triumph of classical studies our age has seen." Only the name Mommsen is missing. Wilamowitz hopes that someday the same methods will be applied to Attic history. Obviously his little book is meant to be a model. It is stuffed with details of imperial administration, trade, finance, military service and the like. But toward the end of the opening essay it becomes clear that everything has been only background to what really matters: the cultural achievements of Athens. The two generations who created the Athenian empire did not worship Mammon; they created the right climate for the arts, literature, science, and philosophy—the truly immortal things. The greatest Greek literature was in a real sense the literature of the empire and could only be understood by one who knew literature and empire well. Here was the reason why the young philologist had so puzzled his contemporaries by writing articles on Thucydides and Boeotian epigraphy. For him it was all the same subject.

Wilamowitz's connections with Mommsen had taken an even closer form when he married his daughter Marie on 20 September 1878. After *Aus Kydathen*, however, there is not much by Wilamowitz that owes its specific inspiration to Mommsen. There are exceptions (*Aristoteles und Athen* and *Staat und Gesellschaft*), and the general inspiration abided; but Wilamowitz was after all a philologist, not an historian. The relationship was not all one of taking on Wilamowitz's part; he made decisive contributions to the fifth volume of the *Römische Geschichte* and the third volume of *Römisches Staatsrecht*. Indeed, these books would not have been written without Wilamowitz's help and encouragement. In time certain differences asserted themselves—personal, political, scholarly; one can even speak of alienation. But Wilamowitz never doubted Mommsen's greatness and asserted in 1910 that the philologist who had not learned from him did not count.

The year after *Aus Kydathen* was published, *Antigonos von Karystos* appeared, dedicated to Hermann Usener. The book was a reaction to the treatise of one of Wilamowitz's earliest and most loyal pupils, Ernst Maas, *De biographis Graecis quaestiones selectae* (Philologische Untersuchungen 3, 1880). As he tells us in the preface to *Hellenistische Dichtung*, his interest in the Hellenistic period had already been awakened; it was a natural part of his anticlassicistic program. He also felt the need to improve his knowledge of ancient philosophy, Bernays's subject. Furthermore, Antigonos (or rather, the three Karystians of that name, who he argued were identical) made a good case study in the problems of source criticism. Wilamowitz saw that such issues were not settled until all the rivulets had been traced to their ultimate source and, more importantly, it had been shown how and under what circumstances the stream had been divided. He had already demonstrated his grasp of a basic truth about ancient biography, that it is normally based on inferences from the authors' own works, in an influential article of 1877, "Die Thukydideslegende." A recent spur to write on the subject was Hermann Diels's masterpiece, *Doxographi Graeci* (1879). Wilamowitz wanted to broaden and extend its principles, for biographical traditions were more complex than the doxographic, which sprang from a single book of Theophrastus. In the course of his reconstruction he gives a characteristic sketch of the age in which Antigonos lived, and has much to offer on the philosophical schools of the third century B.C. His investigation also had important results for the source criticism of Diogenes Laertius (on whom, incidentally, Nietzsche had written). Only recently has attention been directed to this subject, and the book must still be consulted.

In autumn 1883 Wilamowitz was appointed Ordinarius at the Georgia Augusta University of Göttingen, a far more prestigious post than Greifswald. The next fourteen years were in many ways the most productive, and certainly the happiest, years of his life. The year 1884 saw the publication of a major book, *Homerische Untersuchungen*. The bulk of it is taken up with dissection of the *Odyssey* according to now-outdated analytical assumptions, building on foundations laid by Adolf Kirchhoff. The details of the analysis need not concern us now, but it was influential until superseded by Wilamowitz's own second effort in 1927 (*Die Heimkehr des Odysseus*), which is in many ways merely a refinement of the first. His effort to understand the character of the poets behind the poems is worth comment, however. It ran counter to the Romantic tendency to think of the poems as "folk poetry," a series of lays not really the property of any one creator. For Wilamowitz, this vague appeal to the Greek "people" as if they were the same everywhere at every time was simply unhistorical. Each stage of the poem's creation could be tied to specific times and places of Greek history and culture. This idea would find fuller expression in *Die Ilias und Homer*. It is also significant that he looks for the individual creators of the poem, whom he tries to revivify. His scholarship had a strong biographical bent; figures of genius form the titles of most of his books, reflecting his view of what is important in history and how it works. No Hegelian he.

Of more lasting importance than the analysis are the chapters on a variety of Homeric topics, including the Peisistratid recension, Lycurgus, the supposed rewriting of the poems into a different alphabet, and the epic cycle. Discussion revolves around problems such as the orthography of early texts, their transmission, early corruptions, the international book trade, the history of dialects, the use of inscriptions as evidence for these questions, and the results for textual criticism. The ground broken in *Analecta Euripidea* and *Antigonos von Karystos* was beginning to yield rich fruit, and the way was prepared for the full harvest of *Herakles*. The book is still consulted for many details. Wilamowitz's discussion of the epic cycle is worth particular mention, for it was the single most important contribution after Welcker's and, with the possible exception of the work of Wilamowitz's pupil Erich Bethe, dominated subsequent research until A. Severyns's thorough examination of the whole subject in 1963.

In 1885 Wilamowitz published a text and translation of Aeschylus' *Agamemnon*, the first substantial evidence of his consuming interest in this author and the first public proof of his prowess as a translator. When the *Agamemnon* and other plays were published in two volumes as *Griechische Tragödien* in 1899–1900, they were immediately popular and remained so for half a century or more. A vigorous and idiosyncratic style challenged prevailing notions of classical tragedy and gave the plays a direct and realistic appeal. Producers found them eminently produceable, and a flurry of performances followed closely on their appearance. In November 1900 the first production of the *Oresteia* ever seen in Germany—and, with one apparent exception, the first production of any Aeschylean tragedy—was put on by Hans Oberländer in Wilamowitz's translation and enthusiastically received. Wilamowitz must be given a great deal of the credit for the revival of interest in ancient drama among the educated public of his country.

One day in 1885 Wilamowitz read in the latest issue of the Greek journal *Ephemeris Archaiologike* a few poems by one Isyllus uncovered by archaeologists in the sanctuary of Asclepius at Epidaurus. A few months later (14 October 1885) he had finished a monograph, which was published early the following year; nearly forty years later he pronounced himself still pleased with this amazingly rapid production. The conjunction of archaeology and literature was exactly the sort of thing to fire Wilamowitz. By drawing on a wide store of learning, he wrings the full significance out of the dumb stones; he gives them a context and makes the reader feel as if he shares the perspective of an educated ancient counterpart. A few baffling scribbles turn out to have religious, historical, mythological, and literary importance. The book is a good example of what Gilbert Murray meant when he said that many other scholars might competently edit a papyrus or inscription, but Wilamowitz asked questions the others never dreamed of.

Trying to reconstruct the thoughts of the original reader or audience was the cornerstone of Wilamowitz's method of interpretation; it was not so naive as twentieth-century hermeneutics now makes us think. His approach is most famously illustrated in his commentary on Euripides' *Herakles*, which he published in his fortieth year, the peak of life according to ancient views. It is his greatest work, variously and rightly called the foundation of modern classical scholarship, the first modern commentary on a Greek tragedy, the one book every classical scholar must know. It made an epoch in textual criticism and the history of texts, meter, literary history, and the study of myth and religion. Even now that a great deal of the material in the first volume, *Einleitung in die attische* (or *griechische* in the separate edition) *Tragödie*, has been superseded, it is still constantly read, for it is the background of all subsequent discussions; and in the commentary, it need hardly be said, the individual notes are an inexhaustible fund of knowledge. Wilamowitz's mastery of Greek, which lay at the heart of his scholarship, is first visible here in all its range.

As early as January 1877 he had formed a plan to edit the play, and two years later he had completed a text and translation, which was privately printed as a gift for the Mommsens' silver wedding. We have already discussed his reasons for studying Euripides at this stage of his career, but what attracted him to this play is not clear; it had provided him with his motto as early as his school days, but one passage does not seem enough to explain attachment to the whole play. A better clue is offered by the strong sympathy Wilamowitz felt for the hero. Self-identification with his subject is not confined to this book; the portrait of Hippolytus in his edition of the play (1891) as an idealistic youth who attempted too much and whose father could not understand him is strongly reminiscent of the young Wilamowitz, and in his old age, as is well known, he put a great deal of himself into *Platon*. The portraits never match perfectly, and one must be careful of mistaking a good actor's imaginative impersonation for self-portraiture; but in *Herakles*, the personal commitment is unmistakeable. Ultimately Wilamowitz fathers his own values upon the ancient hero. The Dorian, aristocratic, duty-bound, hardworking Herakles ("You want life: so work," is the summation of the creed in vol. 2, p. 41) is Prussian enough. "Born a man, become a god; labors borne, heaven won," runs the summation in another place (38): Christian enough. Wilamowitz later abandoned the thesis of Herakles as the Dorian hero *par excellence* (and one must not think that Wilamowitz overestimated the importance of Dorian values in Greece; in *Isyllos von Epidauros* he criticized K. O. Müller for his exaggerations and repeatedly stated that the Ionian contribution, as tempered by the Dorian, was the real source of Athenian greatness). More important than the thesis itself is the passionate revival of Müller's method of interpreting the Greek legends, with the history of the tribes at the center. The advance of archaeology seemed to confirm Müller's insights, and Wilamowitz showed how much further they could be taken. The inspiration of Friedrich Gottlieb Welcker must be mentioned in the same connection. Wilamowitz was an unrepentant adherent of this school all his life, even after it was long out of date. In 1889 he was in the forefront; his methods, providing as they did a great many new, sensible, and convincing insights, constituted a great advance over the ridiculous allegorizing of a Max Müller.

The introduction also contains famous sections on the origin of tragedy and comedy and the history of the text. On the former topic, Wilamowitz's discussion remained the starting point for forty years and still exercises recent authors. Again more important than the actual thesis is the perspective. The section sets out to answer the simple question, "What is an Attic tragedy?" Already the form of the question—not "what is Attic tragedy (in essence)" but "what is *an* Attic tragedy"—suggests that the answer will be empirical and realistic, describing what we actually have, rather than a few plays that we think embody the true nature of tragedy according to some aesthetic theory. His purely historical answer has often been quoted: "An Attic tragedy is a self-contained piece of heroic legend, poetically re-worked in elevated style for dramatic presentation by a chorus of Attic citizens and two or three actors as a part of public worship in the sanctuary of Dionysus." On the history of texts, Wilamowitz can still form the starting point in spite of new discoveries. The masterful overview of all the relevant materials, presented with clarity and concision, gives a history not only of Euripides' text, but, in essence, of all Greek texts; the implications for editorial practice are constantly brought forward. What was possible in this field had already been hinted at in earlier works, but this book contained the fully matured version and would find a broader readership. To many these revelations came as a complete surprise. Dozens of possibilities for new research were suddenly created.

Wilamowitz presented Euripides himself as a restless child of the Sophistic age, a changeling, a thinking dramatist, a realist, a critic of tradition who nonetheless saw much truth in it, if expressed in new terms. He did not make him a progressive liberal in the manner of Murray's Euripides, nor again a rationalist in Verrall's sense; he was stimulated by Verrall's views but in time came to see their folly. The general outline of his portrait did not change much through the years, as can be seen from the discussions in *Euripides Hippolytos griechisch und deutsch* (1891), *Die griechische Literatur des Altertums* (1905, 1912), and *Griechische Tragödien* 4 (1923). Wilamowitz has been accused in this respect once again of importing modern notions into ancient drama, seeing in Euripides the counterpart of the realistic drama of his own day. In this case one can only be grateful, for it is of course true that Euripides was the most realistic of the dramatists—and the most mannered, as Wilamowitz also knew. His interpretation of the poet was decisive in Germany for decades and exerted great influence abroad as well. For the young Gilbert Murray, professor in Glasgow, reading this book was a change of life.

On pages 254ff. of volume 1, Wilamowitz concludes a section on the history of modern criticism with a discussion of the tasks facing contemporary philology. Here may be found the clearest and most forceful statement of his aims and beliefs. All of the leading notes had been sounded in earlier publications, as we have noted above: the central importance of language ("Our first and noblest task is to learn as much Greek as Hermann and Elmsley knew"), the new historical perspective of philology, the necessity of integrating all aspects of classical studies ("Tragedy is the poetry of the Athenian Empire"), the importance of approaching historical situations empirically and not forcing the untidy facts of real life to fit *a priori*, logical constructions. These ideas need no further comment here, except to draw attention to their succinct expression in a very significant place.

If *Herakles* is Wilamowitz's greatest work, *Aristoteles und Athen* is not far behind it. The publication of Aristotle's *Constitution of Athens* in 1891 was followed closely by a joint edition by Wilamowitz and Georg Kaibel, then two years later by this weighty two-volume monograph on the historical problems. The appearance of such a mass of new evidence left most historians dazed and uncertain as to how it fitted in with known sources; but the philologist Wilamowitz stepped forward with his usual assurance to clear away the confusion. The speed of production was astonishing; he started to write in late 1891, was forced to suspend work because of his duties as Prorektor of the University of Göttingen, and resumed again in late 1892 to finish 22 May 1893. Yet, writes Mortimer Chambers: "In originality, breadth, and detailed observation it is one of the jewels of all modern work on Greek history. All scholars who work on any topic that he covers in the 800 pages of this study constantly cite it. Indeed, one may suspect that it is the most quoted of all Wilamowitz' many books." It would be impossible here even to list the many topics he covers, much less follow the fortunes of his discussions. Of some biographical interest, however, is the obvious influence of Mommsen's theory about the origins of Roman historiography on Wilamowitz's theory about the beginnings of the Atthis. The putative involvement of the exegetai was eventually disproved by Felix Jacoby, but it took one of his stature to do it, in a long and careful discussion. As so often, even when Wilamowitz's own answer to a question is now rejected, one still learns from the terms in which the question was put.

The first reaction to these two great works was not always favorable and was often at least ambivalent. To some contemporaries, Wilamowitz seemed to be attempting too much. He seemed restless, impatient, inconsistent, careless. His professional manners, particularly in the early days, could seem offensive. It is well known that he can contradict himself in his books, print poor Greek, or translate inaccurately. Those whose toes were trodden on when he was alive, like those who now resent his apotheosis, were more inclined to base their judgments on these faults than to applaud his merits. But these were recognized by some people, among them the powerful and autocratic Minister of Culture, Friedrich Althoff, who overcame Wilamowitz's own reluctance and the opposition of nay-sayers to arrange his transfer to the Friedrich-Wilhelms-Universität, Berlin, in 1897.

Nominally, Wilamowitz was the successor of Ernst Curtius as Professor of Rhetoric. The older Johannes Vahlen and Adolf Kirchhoff were still there as the Ordinarii of Classical Philology. Wilamowitz would work alongside his friend from student days, Hermann Diels; together they started a "Proseminar" (as opposed to the Seminar of the senior professors) in which the students were exposed to the new philology. With the arrival of Eduard Norden in 1906 the triumvirate was in place. At Wilamowitz's instigation they established an Institute of Classical Studies, a single building uniting the philological, historical, and archaeological branches of the discipline, with library and seminar facilities. The plan became a model for Germany and beyond.

In the beginning Wilamowitz had many tasks to attend to, sometimes at the behest of Althoff, sometimes for the Academy, of which he was a corresponding member since 1891, and a regular member since 1899. He was unable to devote himself wholly to research of personal choosing for sixteen years. All the books he published in this period were either the completion of earlier promises or tasks put in his hands by others. (His articles continued unabated, among them the *Lesefrüchte* and the famous "Asianismus und Atticismus," which threw floods of light on the whole history of rhetoric; when one speaks of a reduction of research in Wilamowitz's case, one speaks in relative terms.) Work for the *Textgeschichte der griechischen Lyriker* (1900) had begun with an earlier promise to edit the fragments of the lyric poets; his *Textgeschichte der griechischen Bukoliker* (1906) was done in conjunction with his edition of the bucolic poets for the Oxford Classical Texts, a commission he felt unable to decline in the interests of international cooperation. Both these textual histories are special studies in the general field of textual history, "a field of which he had a unique mastery," as A. S. F. Gow puts it, editor of the now-standard text of Theocritus. Every page of Gow's preface shows the extent of his debt, and all students of archaic poetry must still be closely familiar with the lyric book.

Wilamowitz's *Griechisches Lesebuch* (1902) arose from a promise given in connection with Althoff's educational conference of 1900. Interestingly, this book cost him more pains than any other. He wanted to include as wide a variety of texts as possible in order to counteract the classicizing tendencies of schoolmasters, but then he found he could not print texts without editing them properly for himself. The book did not have the impact Wilamowitz hoped it would, but it has enjoyed a long-term success among scholars rather than students; the brief notes included by way of commentary often contain gems of learning and insight. It has been translated into Dutch, English, and Italian.

Timotheos: Die Perser (1903) arose from his work on the many unpublished papyri in the Royal Museums of Berlin that he saw it as his duty to edit. It too is an important contribution to the study of lyric poetry, particularly of dithyramb and citharody. Two longer works were written for the series *Die Kultur der Gegenwart: Die Griechische Literatur des Altertums* (1905) and *Staat und Gesellschaft der Griechen* (1910). He tells us that he allowed himself to be talked into writing the first because it could be done quickly without much research. Perhaps also he felt some responsibility, as a teacher, to contribute to this series of educational works for the general public. The book is saved from the usual faults of its genre by its liveliness and is filled with typical *bons mots* and useful insights (the summation of Euripides on pages 80–81 of the third edition seems particularly brilliant); but Wilamowitz himself was not happy with the general arrangement of the content even after some radical additions (in the third edition of the host volume; in the second edition Wilamowitz's contribution was unchanged). *Staat und Gesellschaft*, on the other hand, is thoroughly satisfactory, but perhaps the most neglected of Wilamowitz's books. This neglect is undeserved, for it is a clear and compendious treatment of the whole of Greek history and society, full of facts and beautifully written. It is a kind of superior version of the ubiquitous modern civilization course and might be consulted by teachers who are able to identify what is no longer true. Alfred Zimmern's *The Greek Commonwealth*, a book with a long and useful record, affords a good comparison in spite of its very English perspective; in tone and content it is quite Wilamowitzian, and not surprisingly evoked a good review from him.

Other tasks that robbed Wilamowitz of time included his membership of the Academy's *Kirchenväterkommission*, which oversaw the edition of the Church Fathers; similar involvement with the production of the *Corpus Medicorum Graecorum*; and work for the German Archaeological Institute. Papyri and the Institut für Altertums-kunde have already been mentioned. Most time-consuming of all was the direction of *Inscriptiones Graecae*, a project that lay in utter disarray and required Wilamowitz's personal scrutiny of the texts. He had already contributed much to earlier volumes edited by Georg Kaibel and Friedrich Hiller von Gaertringen, and had clear views on how the series ought to be produced. His many innovations put the whole science of editing inscriptions on a new footing, and it is difficult to think what might have happened to these fundamental documents without Wilamowitz's self-sacrificing intervention. The theatrical productions of his translations also occupied him, and he had much work to do for the international meeting of historical societies in Berlin in 1908. As always, he gave generous help to anyone who asked; the "Mitarbeiter" sections of the *Wilamowitz-Bibliographie* amount to a life's work in themselves. Eduard Fraenkel remarked that Wilamowitz gave more time to others' works than most scholars give to their own.

In 1913 he was able to return to a work of his own choosing, *Sappho und Simonides*; even so, the book was not exactly as he would have liked. The plan to edit the lyric poets had been abandoned by now; he offered as a settling of the debt this book and his earlier *Textgeschichte*. *Sappho und Simonides* consists of a series of essays on lyric subjects, in some respects a miscellany of unconnected pieces, but for all that covering the ground quite thoroughly. A main purpose of the essay on Sappho was to save her honor against the lascivious suggestions of a certain French book that would now be quite forgotten had not Wilamowitz mounted his horse and tilted against it. We smile at his chivalry, and tend to think he was blind to the facts, but forget his frankness, quite unusual for the time; one may compare the discussion of pedophilia in *Staat und Gesellschaft* and the straightforward treatment of sexual matters in his edition of Aristophanes' *Lysistrata*. He hated prudery. Of lasting importance in this book is the demonstration, in Welcker's footsteps, that the popular tradition about Sappho was decisively influenced by the wilful misrepresentations of comedy. The essay on the dialect of Lesbian lyric forms the background to the later work of Edgar Lobel and Denys Page; the chapter on Solon contains some of the best interpretation ever written of the long, difficult elegy fr. 13 West. Two concluding chapters discuss the influence of archaic Greek lyric on Latin poetry, a most fruitful subject scarcely explored in those days; Eduard Fraenkel found the essay on Horace a masterpiece, from which one could learn more about Latin poetry than from many books devoted exclusively to the subject.

The following year saw the publication of Wilamowitz's text of Aeschylus and a book of interpretations to go with it. These works were the product of lifelong engagement with the poet, his favorite tragedian. The text alone, with its superior analysis of the manuscripts, typically incisive and circumspect apparatus, and many important conjectures, constituted a major advance. Innovative sections at the foot of the page entitled "Actio" show how Wilamowitz constantly thought of the text as a dramatic script—a radical departure from previous critical practice. The book of interpretations is somewhat selective and leaves many topics untouched; gaps often can be filled from *Griechische Tragödien* and the important commentary on the *Choephoroe* (1896). One topic treated for every play is the previous state of the myths; these discussions are still required reading, for only a handful of scholars have ever possessed Wilamowitz's mastery of the whole mythographical tradition. The general literary interpretations are often rejected now (in particular the thesis, repeated from *Aristoteles und Athen*, that Aeschylus maintained a scrupulous neutrality in the *Eumenides*, seems untenable), but discussions of individual passages are, as ever, enlightening. In 1982 it was still possible for a distinguished critic to write that ". . . his feeling for poetry and the dramatic skill of Aeschylus was such that . . . *Aischylos-Interpretationen* remains the primer to which all critics of Aeschylus must turn."

The book ends with a passage of autobiographical intensity. Aeschylus' religion, says Wilamowitz, was one of true piety and reliance upon God; it was perfectly compatible with traditional cults, which even Plato retained, not out of superstition but because he recognized "the one God in the gods of others, so long as he is alive in them." Wilamowitz's own undogmatic religion allowed him to believe in the gods of others too; he thought this empathy was essential for understanding Greek religion. For Wilamowitz, scholarship and poetry alike served the eternal world of God, each in its own way attempting to glimpse and communicate some of that reality; he found this Goethian idea incarnate in the greatest Greek poets, Aeschylus in the forefront, and, of course, in Plato. The attraction to Aeschylus was at bottom religious. In this light we can understand the rest of his summary: Aeschylus was a thinker who saw the symbolic meaning of myths and from them extracted a belief in a divine ruler who reveals himself in the justice of the world order; he was a patriot who kept above party strife and only taught the moral qualities that made Athens great; he was a poet who created tragedy out of Homer's stuff and never ceased improving his art; he was a craftsman in language who wrote the first great Attic works and made the rest of the world read them. We know little of his person, but that was only a mortal body; from the plays arises the specter of the poet's immortal soul, "which even today forces us to our knees before this man and the God he reveals to us."

A book of not much less passion is *Die Ilias und Homer* (1916). The war had turned his thoughts to the poet, as they turned Eduard Schwartz's to Thucydides; both men lost sons in the war, and Wilamowitz's work is dedicated to his beloved Tycho (killed 15 October 1914), a promising scholar whose influential book, *Die dramatische Technik des Sophokles*, was finished by his father. Like almost everyone else in his day, Wilamowitz accepted the Analytical premise that the *Iliad* had begun as a very much smaller epic, to which additions and alterations had been made in the course of time. Debate revolved around the precise arrangement of the layers, and the role of Homer himself in the evolution of the poem. Many scholars tended toward the extreme position that the *Iliad* was a patchwork quilt of many different songs, not very competently put together by an editor of the sixth century B.C.; if Homer had anything to do with this at all, he would have been the author of one of the earlier songs, but he existed before the time of writing and was really only a figure of legend. Wilamowitz argued that this purely mechanical view of the poem's composition was as unhistorical as the Unitarian position, which believed in the miraculous composition of the whole by one great poet. The poem's evolution was at once more simple and more complex than the Analysts had believed; the number of hands involved in its creation was smaller, but the amount of intelligent reworking was greater. For all their analysis, he says, they had ignored the poem itself, which obviously contains a certain degree of artistic integrity. The result of his analysis was to place Homer toward the end of the *Iliad*'s evolution and make him responsible for a substantial part of it; the main post-Homeric additions were books 8–10 and 24 (most of books 18–20 was also reworked).

Homer himself was a Smyrnean of about 750 B.C. Nowadays this book is commonly dismissed in English-speaking countries as the main example of the much-derided Analytical school. It is not realized that it in fact represented a very large step in the direction of the Unitarians, precisely on aesthetic grounds. There are very strong words about this on page 20; learning is misplaced, says Wilamowitz, if it treats the poem only as an object of cold research. A poem is a poem, and the real purpose of learning is to help the reader appreciate its beauty and extract its truth. Of course, there remains much over which one shakes the head; in particular, Wilamowitz could not see that books 9 and 24 lie at the very heart of the poem's artistic conception. But it is wrong to blame him for views that seemed self-evident to his contemporaries almost without exception, and one must acknowledge the strong influence this book exerted on such scholars as C. M. Bowra, Wolfgang Schadewaldt, and Karl Reinhardt, whose books on Homer are still widely read. E. R. Dodds, surveying in 1956 the Homeric scholarship of the previous fifty years, called it "one of the great books on Homer."

Platon (1919) is Wilamowitz's act of homage to the Greek author he loved most, and the one who provided him with his religion. The autobiographical aspects of the book were noticed immediately; the portrait of the lover of knowledge estranged from his own time but devoted to the eternal world of learning bore obvious resemblances to Wilamowitz himself, particularly after the war. For all its passion, however, it was the least well received of all Wilamowitz's books. His aim was to restore "Plato the man" to the world; he wanted to write his biography by going behind the works to the author himself. This was the same task he set himself in all his works of interpretation. In a way, the work of art mattered less than the artist, because art, as Goethe held, was the personal expression of a creative individual to whom some eternal truth had been vouchsafed. Wilamowitz sometimes seems impatient to peel off the layers of art, as if they were so much clothing, to get at the artist's personality. He has been fairly criticized for paying insufficient attention to how the art itself works, seeming to think that poems consisted only in coded statements of personal views. In the case of Plato, he deliberately avoided purely philosophical discussion, for which he had no inclination. Philosophers derided his amateurishness; nowadays they mostly ignore the book. In the opening pages Wilamowitz tries to defend his practice, arguing that the tasks of the philologist and philosopher are different; the philologist/biographer proceeds from work to work, interpretation to interpretation, until the individual details fall together into a convincing portrait of the whole man, and then willingly steps aside for the philosopher to criticize the man's thoughts. Reviewers rightly pointed out that the first activity cannot be done independently of the second. They also noted that Wilamowitz had to assume as settled many controversial details regarding the order of the dialogues and the data for Plato's life if he was going to write his biography. Although Wilamowitz did not completely avoid discussion of these problems, the foundations of his book must be as shaky as the evidence is inconclusive. All this admitted, however, Wilamowitz's argument is correct, that Plato is not a philosopher like a modern one, for whom philosophy is almost all *theoria* and no *praxis*; for the ancient philosopher, *praxis* meant a good deal, and the experiences of Plato's life had a strong impact on his thinking. His biography is relevant to his philosophy, and in that respect Wilamowitz has done more than any other writer. The opening chapter on Plato's youth also provides a unique sketch of the intellectual milieu of contemporary Athens, which no one was better qualified to write than he. The many translations in the first volume (which contains no Greek) ought to be constantly consulted by philosophers, for none of them knows Greek as he did. Even Greek scholars who know their business will consult these—to say nothing of the textual criticism in volume 2; Plato's Greek is much more difficult and subtle than its brilliantly clear patina suggests.

Platon appeared at the very end of the Great War, an event that broke the pattern of Wilamowitz's life as it did that of so many others. The agonized *Nachwort* in which he weeps for the "self-emasculation" of his country was added shortly after the German surrender and dated to his seventieth birthday. For an old man of Prussian honor, he says, there was nothing to do but die away. During the war, particularly in 1915–1916 when he was Rector of the University, Wilamowitz had spoken out on public affairs as never before; he correctly perceived the threat that defeat posed to German culture, and took an uncompromisingly conservative stand on war policy. But even he could not foresee the extent of the catastrophe. The old world was destroyed forever, and all that he had worked for seemed in vain. Politically, Germany was a madhouse; in scholarship, the younger generation was beginning to find him distinctly old-fashioned. His forced retirement in 1921 contributed to his sense of isolation. But he persevered all the same, finding consolation in work and reminding himself of the promise given to "dear mother Pforte" to serve the world of Forms as long as he drew breath.

Thus the final decade saw an increase in an already astonishing rate of production. Practically every year a stately volume appeared, none of them showing any diminution of mental powers. Partly, of course, he had more time owing to retirement. Some of the books were written for the same reason as his others—merely as things came into his hands, or as he perceived the need. In the preface to the edition of Hesiod's *Works*, for instance, he tells us that he noticed while teaching the poem how much remained to be done for it. (He continued teaching without interruption until winter semester 1927–1928, as always selecting new or long-neglected topics—a habit, incidentally, which helps to explain how he learned so much.) On the other hand, there is a sense of urgency about his later work, and one has the impression, as Calder observes, of a desperate attempt to record knowledge that could never be duplicated. His four commentaries (Menander's *Epitrepontes*, 1925; Euripides' *Ion*, 1926; Aristophanes' *Lysistrata*, 1927; Hesiod's *Works*, 1928) are quite compendious and selective, but they record what was essential in Wilamowitz's view and are on that account precious; the work on comedy and Hesiod in particular has been recognized as fundamentally important by recent experts. There is also a programmatic aspect to these commentaries: they illustrate the true method of interpretation against the increasingly popular emphasis on the aesthetics of the poetry, an approach that in Wilamowitz's view was as unhistorical as the criticism of the eighteenth century. (See, for example, the preface to *Hesiodos Erga*.) Only by careful, unprejudiced reading of verse by verse could one build up a picture of the whole. Bringing preconceptions about the nature of poetry to a text, he argued, only leads to the imposition of alien views on it. It must have irked Wilamowitz to be told, in effect, that he did not know what poetry was. His greatest love was poetry; it won him for scholarship. But what he understood best about poetry was what a philologist understands, the words. On the level of *Stilgefühl*, he had no equal; his ability to think in the Greek of different styles and periods was legendary. He could and did charge his critics with ignorance. But they might reply that an "unprejudiced" reading is impossible, and that poetry is much more than a philologist thinks it is. Ideally, of course, one ought to use the best of both ways, but in practice, the philological and the aesthetic approaches tend to find champions in persons of very different character. In Wilamowitz and his later critics we see the beginnings of an argument that is still unresolved, and has, one could maintain, played more mischief with classical studies than any other issue.

Griechische Verskunst (1921) is the book with the least outdated material, even though some important parts of it were published much earlier ("De versu Phalaeceo" in *Mélanges Weil*, 1898; the two *Commentariola metrica* in 1895; "Choriambische Dimeter" in *SPAW* for 1902). Wilamowitz tells us in the preface that it was a duty to produce the book; his views about meter had long been partly explained, but a full account was required. Ideally he would have rewritten everything, he says, and he is keenly aware that he had not provided a systematic treatise; but building a theoretical system was after all never his aim, only understanding the poetry. There is, in fact, a coherent system underlying the book (it was expounded by Paul Maas), and the treatment of the major species of rhythm in part II is thorough enough; but one sees what he means: all his metrical thinking was from the start conditioned by the texts in which the rhythms occurred, and it was impossible for him to divorce discussion of theory from discussion of practice. When he began the serious study of meter, the elaborate theories of R. Westphal and J. H. H. Schmidt were widely approved, but Wilamowitz perceived that there must be something wrong with these wonderfully complicated schemes if they could be made to work for even the most corrupt texts. Textual criticism and metrical study, he argued, must proceed together. Metrical rules may be developed only from the strictest empirical inferences. The ancient handbooks can provide the names of the basic cola, but we are no more bound by their strange metrical theories than we are by their primitive grammar. In addition to this strong dose of common sense, Wilamowitz added, as might be expected, a historical perspective. He insisted that any rhythm had to be understood in context; one had to know how any poet's practice differed from that of his predecessors and successors. Wilamowitz effected a revolution in metrical studies that has not yet run its course; the latest handbook of Greek meter still works within the Wilamowitzian framework. Only in very recent years has the use of linguistics opened up lines of inquiry wholly unthought of by Wilamowitz, and even these are not incompatible with his; they try to explain the reasons for the rules whose existence he established.

In the same year Wilamowitz wrote an eighty-page outline of the history of classical scholarship for the series *Einleitung in die Altertumswissenschaft*. No one but Wilamowitz had the comprehensive experience to write the book—not only in philology but also in general European culture. One of the work's virtues is its constant awareness of the context of classical scholarship within the history of the various nations; Wilamowitz was well read in, and spoke, the languages of a great many countries. And only he could present so many facts in such a finely judged, easily absorbed, witty and incisive survey. There is no point denying his occasional unfairness or glossing over his prejudices, which are as frank as ever; but the book remains unique in its genre for balance and concision.

Pindaros appeared in 1922. The aristocratic Dorism of the poet had always appealed to Wilamowitz, for all that his "heart belonged to the Athenians." As usual, he set himself the task of discovering the man behind the works. The issue of the philological or biographical versus the aesthetic approach is at its most acute in this book, or at least has become so in the light of subsequent research. Pindar has always seemed obscure; in Wilamowitz's day it was natural to attribute this obscurity to the character of the poet and to assume that his darker utterances were personal statements motivated by something in the circumstances of the poem's composition. As a result of ground-breaking discoveries by E. L. Bundy in 1962, we now understand the conventions of the epinician genre much better and can use them to explain many difficult passages. Wilamowitz's book, until then a standard, has come to be regarded as the extreme example of "historico-biographical" criticism. Certainly it seems odd to begin a book on Pindar with a long chapter on life in Boeotia. But once again the thing must be put in perspective. Before Wilamowitz, the search for unity in Pindaric odes had led to the invention of some absurd schemes according to which Pindar was supposed to have composed them. These must have seemed to him as foolish as the metrical schemes he had rejected in *Griechische Verskunst*. In turning away from these notions to seek the unity of the poems in the poet, Wilamowitz was not being obtuse. Moreover, he occasionally saw the literary point of a gnomic passage in which others had found an historical allusion; A. B. Drachmann, a respectable authority, drew particular attention in his review to Wilamowitz's good sense about this. Other reviewers declared themselves unable to measure the advance Wilamowitz had achieved with this book. Of course, the book is filled, as usual, with valuable textual criticism, metrical observations, and interpretations of individual passages, for which it is continually cited.

Hellenistische Dichtung in der Zeit des Kallimachos (1924) is arguably the great book of his old age. Wilamowitz had always had the taste for Hellenistic poetry denied to his classicizing contemporaries, and he was uniquely fitted to work in a field where a great deal of rarefied learning must be kept constantly on call yet the temptation avoided of calling it in at the wrong time. His program of rehabilitating Hellenistic literature was begun early in his career at Jahn's stimulus, and found vigorous expression at the midpoint in *Die griechische Literatur des Altertums. Hellenistische Dichtung* is the last word. The amount of new territory mapped out by Wilamowitz over the course of his career allows comparison only with great pioneers like Bentley or Scaliger.

Typically, *Hellenistische Dichtung* opens with a survey of the Hellenistic world, but if one wonders about the relevance of such a survey in *Pindaros*, it is obvious here. For most students, because of the emphasis still prevailing in school and university, the writers of the Hellenistic age seem to swim in a timeless sea without shores. The Classical Ages of Greece and Rome are terra firma somewhere on either side. The links between the different periods are forged with difficulty, if at all, by the student in private study; the task is not made easier by the fragmentary nature of the sources. Readers would be saved a lot of trouble if they started with Wilamowitz. The chapter on the Hellenistic world is followed by one on the revolution in poetry in the later fourth century; the first volume concludes with a look forward to Roman literature and a sketch of the intellectual climate of the second century. These chapters are excellent examples of Wilamowitz's wonderful powers of combination and historical reconstruction, the ability that Eduard Fraenkel singled out as his salient characteristic. The second volume contains discussions of many individual poems, including all the hymns of Callimachus (edited four times by Wilamowitz between 1882 and 1925) and seven poems of Catullus. Rudolf Pfeiffer, a pupil of Wilamowitz and the greatest master of the Hellenistic age after him, drew attention in his review to the countless ways this book improved our understanding of the age and its poetry.

Mention should be made of the seminal address of 1925, "Storia italica," in which Wilamowitz expounded a favorite thesis, that Roman history was really Italian history. Over sixty years later, the present writer heard the distinguished Roman historian E. T. Salmon, reviewing a life of work in the field, begin his remarks by stressing the importance of this article. In 1927 *Die Heimkehr des Odysseus* was written in reaction to Eduard Schwartz's *Die Odyssee* (1924); it was highly influential in the short term on Analytical criticism, but has now been mostly superseded along with other works of the school. Apart from the immortal *Erinnerungen*, the remaining years of his life were taken up with the composition of *Der Glaube der Hellenen*. Wilamowitz's interest in Greek religion goes back as far as *Isyllos von Epidauros*, and he had written and taught much on the subject since; three important articles on mythography in 1925–1926 indicate his increasing preoccupation with the subject in his last decade. Greek religion was a natural choice for his last book, not because an old man tends to think a lot about religion, but because the whole thrust of his career demanded it. Interpretation was the highest philological activity, according to Wilamowitz; as we have seen, "interpretation" meant extracting the ideas and beliefs of the artist from his creation. Wilamowitz had spent his life interpreting one artist after another; a book about Hellenic belief in general was an appropriate conclusion, particularly when this belief was his own.

A book called "The Belief of the Greeks"—or let us translate it rather as "The Faith of the Greeks"—implies already a certain perspective. "Faith" has unavoidable

Christian overtones of a personal creed and relationship to God such as can hardly be documented in Greek culture apart from a few thinkers or some cults (e.g., Orphism) traditionally regarded as foreign. Even in a Greek mystery cult like that of Eleusis, where parallels to Christianity have often been sought, the term "faith" would scarcely be used by scholars now without careful qualification. It would seem that Wilamowitz is claiming for the Greeks a kind of religion that is atypical of most of them. Despite his protests to the contrary, he does not succeed in keeping Christian preconceptions out of his discussion. But the attempt is not wholly misconceived. Wilamowitz argued that one must distinguish the higher and lower aspects of Greek religion. The cults of the masses belonged to the latter, the religion of an Aeschylus or a Plato to the former. One studies the cults, to be sure, but only in order to understand the gods worshiped in them; in other words, to articulate and intellectualize the collective impulse of the worshipers in terms a thinking person can accept. The true—that is, the best—belief of the Hellenic people will be found, in this view, in the greatest writers, and in the body of heroic legend that provided their subject matter. In adopting this approach, which was that of Müller and Welcker, Wilamowitz was deliberately turning his back on the advances of religious studies in Germany and England since the turn of the century. In *Isyllos von Epidauros* and *Euripides Herakles* he stood on firm ground, for the validity of the new science was very uncertain. In 1931, indeed, he still had many discoveries to reveal; *Der Glaube der Hellenen*, as all experts readily admit, is an inexhaustible treasury of notes, suggestions, source criticism, and so on. But in 1931 it was more difficult to ignore the new school, which had achieved many positive results; it has achieved many more since. One can argue further: even accepting Wilamowitz's sharp dichotomy of higher and lower, of true religion and "superstition," his understanding of the higher aspect is at fault; what is most truly Greek is not the mystical otherworldliness of Plato but the pessimistic realism of a Homer or Sophocles as understood by followers of Nietzsche—Wilamowitz's old adversary, inventor, in his words, of an "irreligious religion."

The circumstances of his last decade naturally reinforced Wilamowitz's conservative tendencies. His intellectual world was formed in the 1860s on the basis of German thought of the late eighteenth and early nineteenth centuries; throughout his life he never found anything better. His consistency demands respect; the heroic and defiant struggle with death to complete *Der Glaube der Hellenen* demands unconditional admiration. Even after he was confined to bed and in great pain from kidney disorders, he continued to dictate page upon page, eventually reaching the penultimate chapter, the proofs of which arrived the morning of the day he died.

Summation of Wilamowitz's achievement is next to impossible. He would prefer to be remembered first as a teacher. In his memoirs he makes the claim—remarkable in view of his huge output—that for a German professor teaching was more important than research. This may not have been true of everyone, but it was true of him. Many of his books have a sustained didactic tone, omitting the ordinary apparatus of footnotes and breathing the spirit of a man with a message. In the lecture hall he could be transported by his material and give the impression of a preacher before a mob of determined heathens. His sparkling performances two evenings a week in Berlin became social events that attracted huge audiences. At the University, he always had time for his students and was indulgent to beginners. His seminar could be poorly prepared and somewhat disorganized, but more important than the content of the lessons was the stimulation he imparted. Students were infected by his enthusiasm; many fine minds were won by him for the classics. The list reads like a roster of the modern discipline's founding fathers: Hans von Arnim, Erich Bethe, Wilhelm Crönert, Paul Friedländer, Johannes Geffcken, Rudolf Keydell, Günther Klaffenbach, Walther Kranz, Ludolf Malten, Werner Peek, Max Pohlenz, Karl Reinhardt, Hans Wegehaupt, to mention only a few of the eighty-nine whose dissertations he directed; to them must be added men who studied under him in different capacities, such as the students from Greifswald days mentioned above, and others like Eduard Fraenkel, Hermann Fränkel, Felix Jacoby, Werner Jaeger (his successor at Berlin), Friedrich Klingner, Paul Maas, Hans-Joachim Mette, Giorgio Pasquali, Rudolf Pfeiffer, Otto Regenbogen, Wolfgang Schadewaldt, Friedrich Solmsen, Konrat Ziegler, Friedrich Zucker, and Günther Zuntz. Many of these men made enormous contributions, although confining themselves to only one part of their teacher's universal activity. No student of his could ever wholly escape his influence, even those who held radically different views about the Greeks. Those who differed most, Reinhardt and Friedländer, felt most keenly the need to come to terms with him. Their generation bridges the gap to the present day; if they were so exercised by Wilamowitz, it is a good argument for us to be.

In the various activities of traditional philology Wilamowitz's status is beyond contention. As a textual critic alone his achievement is monumental. His editions of Aeschylus, Callimachus, Theocritus, and of selected works of Euripides, Aristophanes, Hesiod, and Menander, in addition to many shorter editions and the textual notes scattered throughout his *oeuvre*, are a body of work of the highest significance. In a private letter A. E. Housman, the greatest English textual critic since Porson, said he was "a very great man, the greatest now living and comparable with the greatest of the dead." The judgment is significant, for Wilamowitz was guilty of some of the faults that most aroused Housman's wrath (haste and carelessness). Housman placed him in a category by himself, beyond such criticism. As an explicator of texts he will be consulted, like the great scholars of past centuries, as long as classical philology survives.

As an interpreter of antiquity Wilamowitz might seem dated. He was, after all, a man of the nineteenth century, a fact perhaps most evident in the attempt to master the whole of the discipline. He was the last one to try. The burgeoning of knowledge now makes the attempt impossible, but more than this, the infinity of questions to be asked of the individual facts makes it seem naive. "Fully" understanding even a single text is not humanly possible. Wilamowitz's notions of literature and society now seem superficial and jejune. On the other hand, it is significant that people still argue about the validity of his approach. This attests the continuing attraction of his work. Reading contemporaries of his like Murray or Verrall, we do not expect to be taught;

we still expect insights from Wilamowitz and slip easily into the trap of judging him by present-day standards. The reason for his continuing immediacy may lie in the central goal of his work: "wieder lebendig zu machen," to make the past come alive again. He can still make us see ancient life directly. Of course, there is some naïveté here too; one has to ask what "alive" means. We tend to give a very complicated answer nowadays, conditioned by all kinds of considerations—psychological, sociological, philosophical. But complexity is not always better. Technicality makes a subject more and more esoteric; we begin to teach only our fellow experts. For ordinary folk, life is lived intuitively, and even for not-so-ordinary folk more depends on character than intellect. Philosophy has too few answers, theology has too few questions; most ethical decisions are based on neither but on an ad hoc calculation of the most advantageous course. The great people of history make these calculations better than others. In the end, a book written about such people by such a person has a better chance of providing lasting inspiration than a book with the most brilliant theoretical basis. It is on the intuitive, ordinarily human level that Wilamowitz speaks to readers.

That a talent of Wilamowitz's proportions should find common lodgings with an admirable character almost defies the laws of probability. But this was the case. Arrogance is the chief fault with which he is charged, justly to some extent; but only a saint could combine humility with intelligence like his. And if he never concealed his contempt for certain types of scholars, he never bragged about his own accomplishments or put on false airs; he never placed any artificial barriers between himself and his colleagues or students; he was always ready to forgive and was extraordinarily open to justified criticism. When he suffered from insomnia, stress, or grief, he hardly ever gave those around him the slightest evidence of it, except in the early 1920s. This is only a small example of his Prussian sense of duty and honor, which forbade him to put personal convenience ahead of responsibility; the greatest example is his acceptance of the call to Berlin. He remarks about this in his memoirs, that "man is not here to be happy, but to do his duty." Every minute of his waking time (which was probably about eighteen hours a day, if not more) was efficiently used to maximize work; he rarely went out in the evenings, because it robbed him of time. His stature naturally tended to isolate him from his fellows, and, though he was by no means reclusive and opened his house once a week to students, he was not markedly gregarious. He had few close friends, and in private could exhibit a pronounced streak of melancholy. Yet he was anything but glum; on the contrary, he was filled with the joy of life, perhaps deeper than ordinary gaiety precisely because he strongly sensed the world's sorrows. Everything fascinated him, from the plants of his beloved garden (Norden reports his tears for a favorite tree destroyed by a freezing rain; it was the "nymph" of the garden) to the sublime thoughts of Aeschylus.

Eduard Fraenkel likened the job of one who would give a complete picture of Wilamowitz to that of an artist required to depict the Battle of Waterloo on a piece of jewelry. A great deal has to be omitted; it may be doubted that anyone can do an adequate job. But all who seriously study the life and works of this complex man must admit that he was a genius of the first rank, one of the great glories of his discipline and of his country.

Books

Observationes criticae in comoediam Graecam selectae. Dissertatio inauguralis . . . in alma litterarum universitate Friderica Guilelma ad summos in philosophia honores rite capessendos. Berlin, 1870.

Analecta Euripidea. Inest Supplicum fabula ad codicem archetypum recognita. Berlin, 1875; reprinted Hildesheim, 1963.

Mauricii Hauptii opuscula. 3 vols. Leipzig, 1875–1876; reprinted Hildesheim, 1967.

Euripides Herakles als Manuskript gedruckt. Berlin, 1879.

Aus Kydathen. Philologische Untersuchungen 1. Edited by A. Kießling and U. von Wilamowitz-Moellendorff with C. Robert. Berlin, 1880.

Antigonos von Karystos. Philologische Untersuchungen 4. Edited by A. Kießling and U. von Wilamowitz-Moellendorff. Berlin, 1881; reprinted Berlin and Zürich, 1965. Pages 185–186, 194–197, 263–272, 279–288 translated in *La scuola dei filosofi.* Edited by C. Natali. L'Aquila, 1981: 29–45.

Callimachi hymni et epigrammata. Berlin, 1882; 2d ed., 1897; 3d ed., 1907; 4th ed., 1925; 1958; 1962.

Homerische Untersuchungen. Philologische Untersuchungen 7. Edited by A. Kießling, U. von Wilamowitz-Moellendorff. Berlin, 1884; 1914.

Aischylos Agamemnon. Griechischer Text mit deutscher Übersetzung. Berlin, 1885; 1940. Translation reprinted in *Griechische Tragödien,* vol. 2. Berlin 1900; 1901; etc.

Isyllos von Epidauros. Philologische Untersuchungen 9. Edited by A. Kießling, U. von Wilamowitz-Moellendorff. Berlin, 1886; reprinted Dublin, 1967.

Euripides Herakles erklärt. Vol. 1: *Einleitung in die attische Tragödie.* Vol. 2: *Text und Kommentar.* Berlin, 1889. Vol. 1 chapters 1–4 reprinted as *Einleitung in die griechische Tragödie.* Berlin, 1907; 1910; 1921, etc.; reprinted Darmstadt, 1959; 1981. Vol. 1, chs. 5–6, Vol. 2 revised and reprinted in 2 vols. as *Euripides Herakles;* 2d ed. Berlin, 1895; 1909, etc.; reprinted Darmstadt, 1959; 1981.

Aristotelis ΠΟΛΙΤΕΙΑ ΑΘΗΝΑΙΩΝ. With G. Kaibel. Berlin, 1891; 2d ed., 1891; 3d ed., 1898.

Euripides Hippolytos griechisch und deutsch. Berlin, 1891. Translation reprinted in *Griechische Tragödien,* vol. 1. Berlin, 1899; 1900; etc. Preface "Was ist Übersetzen?" reprinted with revisions in *Reden und Vorträge,* Editions 1–4.

Aristoteles und Athen. 2 vols. Berlin, 1891; 1910; reprinted [1 vol.] Berlin, Dublin, and Zürich, 1966; 1985.

Aischylos Orestie griechisch und deutsch. Zweites Stück: Das Opfer am Grabe. Berlin, 1896; Dublin and Zürich, 1969. Translation reprinted in *Griechische Tragödien,* vol. 2. Berlin, 1900; 1901; etc.

Griechische Tragödien übersetzt. Erster Band. Sophokles Oedipus, Euripides Hippolytos, Euripides Der Mütter Bittgang, Euripides Herakles. Berlin, 1899; 1900; 1901; 1904; etc. All translations published separately. Berlin, 1899, etc.

Die Textgeschichte der griechischen Lyriker. AGWG 4.3, 1900; Berlin, 1900; reprinted
Nendeln, 1970.

Griechische Tragödien übersetzt. Zweiter Band. Orestie. Berlin, 1900; 1901; 1904; etc.
All translations published separately. Berlin 1900, etc.

Bion von Smyrna, Adonis, deutsch und griechisch. Berlin, 1900.

Reden und Vorträge. Berlin, 1901; 2d ed., 1902; 3d ed., 1913; 4th ed. [2 vols.],
1925–1926; reprinted in 1 vol. Zürich, 1967.

Griechisches Lesebuch. 2 vols. in 4. Berlin, 1902; 1903, etc.; 13th ed. of 1.1, 1936, 6th
ed. of 1.2, 1926, reprinted in 1 vol. Zürich and Berlin, 1965; 9th ed. of 2.1,
1929, 5th ed. of 2.2, 1932, reprinted in 1 vol. Dublin and Zürich, 1966;
Dutch translation Utrecht, 1902; Italian translation Palermo, 1905; partial
English translation and adaptation in 2 vols. Oxford, 1905–1906.

Timotheos: Die Perser. Leipzig, 1903; reprinted Hildesheim and New York, ca. 1973.

Die griechische Literatur des Altertums. P. Hinneberg, *Die griechische und lateinische
Literatur und Sprache.* Die Kultur der Gegenwart Teil 1, Abt. 8. Leipzig and
Berlin, 1905: 1–236; 2d ed., 1907: 3–238; 3d ed., 1912: 3–318.

Bucolici graeci. Oxford Classical Texts. Oxford, 1905; rev. ed. 1910.

Griechische Tragödien übersetzt. Dritter Band. Euripides Der Kyklops. Euripides
Alkestis. Euripides Medea. Euripides Troerinnen. Berlin, 1906; 1910; 1916,
etc. All translations published separately. Berlin, 1906, etc.

Die Textgeschichte der griechischen Bukoliker. Philologische Untersuchungen 18.
Edited by A. Kießling and U. von Wilamowitz-Moellendorff. Berlin, 1906.

Epische und elegische Fragmente. Berliner Klassikertexte 5.1. With W. Schubart.
Berlin, 1907.

Greek Historical Writing and Apollo. Two lectures delivered before the University of
Oxford June 3 and 4, 1908. Translated by Gilbert Murray. Oxford 1908;
reprinted Chicago, 1979.

Staat und Gesellschaft der Griechen. P. Hinneberg, *Staat und Gesellschaft der Griechen
und Römer.* Die Kultur der Gegenwart, Teil 2, Abt. 4.1. Leipzig and Berlin
1910; reprinted New York 1979: 1–207; rev. ed. Leipzig and Berlin, 1923:
1–214.

Sappho und Simonides. Untersuchungen über griechische Lyriker. Berlin, 1913; 1966;
1985.

Aeschyli tragoediae. Berlin, 1914; editio minor 1915; 2d ed. revised by K. Latte.
Berlin, 1958.

Aischylos: Interpretationen. Berlin, 1914; reprinted Dublin and Zürich, 1966.

Reden aus der Kriegszeit. Hefte 1–2, Berlin, 1914; 3–5, 6–8, 9–12, 1915; 1–12, 1915.

Die Ilias und Homer. Berlin, 1916; 1920; Berlin, Zürich, and Dublin, 1966.

Vitae Homeri et Hesiodi in usum scholarum. Kleine Texte für Vorlesungen und
Übungen 137. Bonn, 1916; Berlin 1929.

Platon. 2 vols. Berlin 1919; 2d ed., 1920; 3d ed., 1929; revision of 3d ed. by B. Snell.
Berlin, 1948; 1959; revision of 3d ed. by R. Stark. Berlin, 1962.

Griechische Verskunst. Berlin, 1921; reprinted Darmstadt, 1958; 1984.

Geschichte der Philologie. A. Gercke, E. Norden, *Einleitung in die Altertumswissenschaft* 1.1. 3d ed., Leipzig, 1921; 1927; 1959; Italian translation Turin, ca. 1967; 1971; English translation Baltimore, 1982.

Pindaros. Berlin, 1922; 1966; 1985.

Griechische Tragödien übersetzt. Vierter Band. Sophokles Philoktetes. Euripides Die Bakchen. Die griechische Tragödie und ihre drei Dichter. Berlin, 1923. Both translations published separately. Berlin, 1923, etc.

Hellenistische Dichtung in der Zeit des Kallimachos. 2 vols. Berlin 1924; rev. ed. in 1 vol. 1962; Dublin and Zürich, 1973.

Menander Das Schiedsgericht (Epitrepontes) erklärt. Berlin, 1925; 1959; 1969.

Euripides Ion erklärt. Berlin, 1926; Dublin and Zürich, 1969.

Die Heimkehr des Odysseus. Neue homerische Untersuchungen. Berlin, 1927; reprinted Dublin and Zürich, 1969.

Aristophanes Lysistrate erklärt. Berlin, 1927; 1964.

Erinnerungen 1848–1914. Leipzig, 1928; rev. ed. 1929; English translation London, 1930.

Hesiodos Erga erklärt. Berlin, 1928; 1962; 1970.

Der Glaube der Hellenen. 2 vols. Berlin, 1931–1932; 2d ed. Berlin, Darmstadt, 1955; 1984; 3d ed. Basel, Darmstadt, 1959.

ΕΛΕΓΕΙΑ. Edited by W. Buchwald. Berlin, 1938.

In wieweit befriedigen die Schlüsse der erhaltenen griechischen Trauerspiele? Ein ästhetischer Versuch. Edited by W. M. Calder III. Leiden, 1974.

Cultura classica e crisi tedesca. Gli scritti politici di Wilamowitz 1914–1931. Edited and translated by L. Canfora. Bari, 1977.

Tra scienza e politica: quattro saggi. Edited with an introduction by L. Canfora, Antiqua 18. Naples, 1982.

Articles (Collected)

Kleine Schriften 1. Klassische griechische Poesie. Edited by P. Maas. Berlin, 1935; reprinted Berlin, 1971 = KS 1.

Kleine Schriften 5.1. Geschichte, Epigraphik, Archäologie. Edited by E. Schwartz, F. Frhr. Hiller von Gaertringen, G. Klaffenbach, G. Rodenwaldt. Berlin, 1937; reprinted Berlin 1971 = KS 5.1.

Kleine Schriften 5.2. Glaube und Sage. Edited by L. Malten. Berlin, 1937; Berlin, 1971 = KS 5.2.

Kleine Schriften 2. Hellenistische, spätgriechische, lateinische Dichtung. Edited by R. Pfeiffer, R. Keydell, H. Fuchs. Berlin, 1941 = KS 2.

Kleine Schriften 4. Lesefrüchte und Verwandtes. Edited by K. Latte. Berlin, 1962 = KS 4.

Kleine Schriften 3. Griechische Prosa. Edited by F. Zucker. Berlin, 1969 = KS 3.

Kleine Schriften 6. Philologiegeschichte, Pädagogik und Verschiedenes. Nachlese zu den Bänden I und II. Nachträge zur Bibliographie. Edited by W. Buchwald. Berlin, 1972 = KS 6.

Articles (Selected)

Zukunftsphilologie! eine erwidrung auf Friedrich Nietzches . . . 'Geburt der Tragödie.' Berlin, 1872. Reprinted in *Der Streit um Nietzsches "Geburt der Tragödie."* Die Schriften von E. Rohde, R. Wagner, U. von Wilamowitz-Moellendorff. Edited by K. Gründer. Hildesheim, 1969: 27–55.

Zukunftsphilologie! Zweites Stück. Berlin, 1873. Reprinted in K. Gründer, op. cit.: 113–135.

"Abrechnung eines boiotischen Hipparchen." *Hermes* 8 (1874) 435–441 = KS 5.1:245–255.

"Liber Nucis." *Commentationes philologae in honorem Theodori Mommseni scripserunt amici.* Berlin, 1877: 390–401 = KS 2:231–245.

"Die Thukydideslegende." *Hermes* 12 (1877) 326–367 = KS 3:1–40.

"Commentariolum Grammaticum I–IV." *Index scholarum . . . Gryphiswaldiae* (WS 1879; WS 1880); *Index scholarum . . . Gottingae* (SS 1889; WS 1889) = KS 4:583–696.

"Parerga 1–27." *Hermes* 14 (1879) 161–186 = KS 4:1–23.

"De Lycophronis Alexandra commentatiuncula." *Index scholarum . . . Gryphiswaldiae* (WS 1883) = KS 2:12–29.

"Curae Thucydideae." *Index scholarum . . . Gottingae* (WS 1885) = KS 3:62–84.

"Thukydideische Daten." *Hermes* 20 (1885) 477–490 = KS 3:85–98.

"Oropos und die Graer." *Hermes* 21 (1886) 91–115 = KS 5.1:1–25.

"Demotika der attischen Metoeken I–II." *Hermes* 22 (1887) 107–128, 211–259 = KS 5.1:272–342.

"Die erste Rede des Antiphon." *Hermes* 22 (1887) 194–210 = KS 3:101–116.

"Zu Plutarchs Gastmahl der Sieben Weisen." *Hermes* 25 (1890) 196–227 = KS 3:117–148.

"Die Überlieferung der Aischylos-Scholien." *Hermes* 25 (1890) 161–170.

"Die sieben Tore Thebens." *Hermes* 26 (1891) 191–242 = KS 5.1:26–77.

"De tribus carminibus latinis commentatio." [Horace *Carmina* 1.28; Statius *Achilleis*; Plautus *Persa*] *Index scholarum . . . Gottingae* (WS 1893) = KS 2:249–274.

"Über die Hekale des Kallimachos." *NAWG* (1893) 731–747 = KS 2:30–47.

"Ein Weihgeschenk des Eratosthenes." *NAWG* (1894) 15–35 = KS 2:48–70.

"Aratos von Kos." *NAWG* (1894) 182–199 = KS 2:71–89.

"Hephaistos." *NAWG* (1895) 217–245 = KS 5.2:5–35.

"Die Herkunft der Magneten am Maeander." *Hermes* 30 (1895) 177–198 = KS 5.1:78–99.

"Des Mädchens Klage." *NAWG* (1896) 209–232 = KS 2:95–120.

"Der Chor der Hagesichora." *Hermes* 32 (1897) 251–263 = KS 1:209–220.

"Lesefrüchte 1–280."*Hermes* 33 (1898) – 65 (1930) = KS 4:24–527.

"Die griechischen Technopaegnia." *JDAI* 14 (1899) 51–59 = KS 5.1:502–513.

"Der Landmann des Menandros." *Neue Jahrb.* 3 (1899) 513–531 = KS 1:224–248.

"Asianismus und Atticismus." *Hermes* 35 (1900) 1–52 = KS 3:223–273.

"Die sechste Rede des Antiphon." *SPAW* (1900) 398–416 = *KS* 3:196–217.

"Hieron und Pindaros." *SPAW* (1901) 1273–1318 = *KS* 6:234–285.

"Die hippokratische Schrift περὶ ἱρῆς νούσου." *SPAW* (1901) 2–23 = *KS* 3:278–302.

"Geschichte der griechischen Religion." *Jahrb. des freien deutschen Hochstifts* (Frankfurt 1904) 3–30. Reprinted in *Reden und Vorträge*, 3d ed.: 169–198.

"Panionion." *SPAW* (1906) 38–57 = *KS* 5.1:128–151.

"Über die ionische Wanderung." *SPAW* (1906) 59–79 = *KS* 5.1:152–176.

"Theodor Mommsen." [1907] *KS* 6:11–17.

"Der Menander von Kairo." *Neue Jahrb.* 21 (1908) 34–62 = *KS* 1:249–270.

"Pindars siebentes Nemeisches Gedicht." *SPAW* (1908) 328–352 = *KS* 6:286–313.

"Thukydides VIII." *Hermes* 43 (1908) 578–618 = *KS* 3:307–345.

"Erklärungen Pindarischer Gedichte." *SPAW* (1908) 328–352 = *KS* 6:314–343.

"Über die Wespen des Aristophanes." *SPAW* (1911) 460–491, 504–535 = *KS* 1:284–346.

"Die Spürhunde des Sophokles." *Neue Jahrb.* 29 (1912) 449–476 = *KS* 1:347–383.

"Neue lesbische Lyrik." *Neue Jahrb.* 33 (1914) 225–247 = *KS* 1:384–414.

"Die Samia des Menandros." *SPAW* (1916) 66–86 = *KS* 1:415–439.

"Oedipus auf Kolonos." Tycho von Wilamowitz-Moellendorff, *Die dramatische Technik des Sophokles*. Philologische Untersuchungen 22. Edited by A. Kießling, U. von Wilamowitz-Moellendorff (Berlin, 1917; Zürich, 1969): 313–373.

"Theodor Mommsen." [Written in 1917.] *KS* 6:18–28.

"Kerkidas." *SPAW* (1918) 1138–1164 = *KS* 2:128–159.

"Theodor Mommsen. Warum hat er den vierten Band der Römischen Geschichte nicht geschrieben?" [1918] *KS* 6:29–39.

"Athena." *SPAW* (1921) 950–965 = *KS* 5.2:36–53.

"Melanippe." *SPAW* (1921) 63–80 = *KS* 1:440–460.

"Sphakteria." *SPAW* (1921) 306–318 = *KS* 3:406–419.

"Die griechische Heldensage I–II." *SPAW* (1925) 41–62, 214–242 = *KS* 5.2:54–126.

"Pherekydes." *SPAW* (1926) 125–146 = *KS* 5.2:127–156.

"Storia italica. Conferenza tenuta in Firenze nel maggio, 1925." *RFIC* n.s. 4 (1926) 1–18 = *KS* 5.1:220–235.

"Ein Siedelungsgesetz aus West–Lokris." *SPAW* (1927) 7–17 = *KS* 5.1:467–480.

Geschichte der griechischen Sprache. Vortrag auf der Philologenversammlung in Göttingen, 27. Sept. 1927. Berlin, 1928.

"Die Καθαρμοί des Empedokles." *SPAW* (1929) 626–661 = *KS* 1:473–521.

"Kronos und die Titanen." *SPAW* (1929) 35–53 = *KS* 5.2:157–183.

Sources

Autobiographies

Erinnerungen 1848–1914. Leipzig, 1928; rev. ed., 1929; English translation as *My Recollections*, London, 1930.

Calder, W. M. III "Ulrich von Wilamowitz-Moellendorff: An Unpublished Autobiography." GRBS 12 (1971) 561–577. Reprinted in Studies in the Modern History of Classical Scholarship. Antiqua 27 (Naples, 1984): 125–145.

―――. "Ulrich von Wilamowitz-Moellendorff: An Unpublished Latin Autobiography." A&A 27 (1981) 34–51. Reprinted in Studies in the Modern History of Classical Scholarship 147–164.

Bibliographies

Hiller von Gaertringen, F. Frhr. Klaffenbach, G. Wilamowitz-Bibliographie 1868 bis 1929 (Berlin, 22 December 1929).

Buchwald, W. "Ergänzung und Fortsetzung der 1929 erschienenen Wilamowitz-Bibliographie." U. von Wilamowitz-Moellendorff, KS 6.394–400.

Biographical

Abel, W. "Studium Berolinense I. Ulrich von Wilamowitz-Moellendorff (†25.9.1931)." Gymnasium 88 (1981) 389–408.

―――. "Ulrich von Wilamowitz-Moellendorff." Berlinische Lebensbilder Geisteswissenschaftler. Berlin, 1989: 231–251.

Berner, H.-U. "Index dissertationum Udalrico de Wilamowitz-Moellendorff promotore conscriptarum." QS 15 (1982) 227–234.

Bertolini, F. "L'Omero di Wilamowitz." PP 30 (1975) 382–400.

Brandl, A. Zwischen Inn und Themse. Lebensbeobachtungen eines Anglisten. Berlin, 1936: 56, 219–223, 331–332.

vom Brocke, B. " 'Von des attischen Reiches Herrlichkeit' oder die 'Modernisierung' der Antike im Zeitalter des Nationalstaats. Mit einer Exkurs über die Zerschlagung der Wilamowitz-Schule durch den Nationalsozialismus." HZ 243 (1986) 101–136. Review of Wilamowitz nach 50 Jahren. Edited by W. M. Calder III, et al.

Calder, W. M. III. Studies in the Modern History of Classical Scholarship. Antiqua 27. Naples, 1984.

―――. "Schwester Hildegard von Wilamowitz-Moellendorff: Meine Erinnerungen beim Lesen der Erinnerungen meines Vaters." QS 24 (1986) 121–126.

―――. "Ulrich von Wilamowitz-Moellendorff: Sospitator Euripidis." GRBS 27 (1986) 409–430.

―――. "F. G. Welcker's Sapphobild and its Reception in Wilamowitz." In Friedrich Gottlieb Welcker Werk und Wirkung. Hermes Einzelschriften 49. Edited by W. M. Calder III, Adolf Köhnken, Wolfgang Kullmann, Günther Pflug. Stuttgart, 1986: 131–156.

Calder, W. M. III, H. Flashar, and Th. Lindken, eds. Wilamowitz nach 50 Jahren. Darmstadt, 1985. (Essays by many contributors.)

Calder, W. M. III and Schlesier, R. "Wilamowitz on Mommsen's 'Kaisergeschichte.' " QS 21 (1985) 161–163.

Demandt, A. "Wilamowitz 1918 an die Deutschen." QS 24 (1986) 127–132.

Dessoir, M. Buch der Erinnerung. Revised ed. Stuttgart, 1947: 15–16.

Favuzzi, A. trans. "Ricordi su Wilamowitz di Eduard Schwartz e Friedrich Frhr. Hiller von Gaertringen." *QS* 7 (1978) 211–216.

Fowler, R. L. Review of *Wilamowitz nach 50 Jahren*, ed. W. M. Calder III et al. *CJ* 82 (1986–1987) 67–72.

Fraenkel, E. "Ulrich von Wilamowitz-Moellendorff." [1921] *Kleine Beiträge zur klassischen Philologie* 2 (Rome, 1964) 555–562.

———. "The Latin Studies of Hermann and Wilamowitz." *JHS* 38 (1948) 28–34. Reprinted in *Kleine Beiträge* 2:563–576.

———. "Wilamowitz." *QS* 5 (1977) 101–118.

Friedländer, P. *Studien zur antiken Literatur und Kunst.* Berlin, 1969: 681.

Galiano, M. F. "Ulrich von Wilamowitz-Moellendorff y la filología clásica de su tiempo." *EClás* 13 (1969) 25–57.

Gigante, M. "Dal Wilamowitz al Pfeiffer. Storici della filologia classica." *PP* 29 (1974) 196–224.

Harder, R. "Ulrich von Wilamowitz-Moellendorff." *Gnomon* 7 (1931) 557–560. Reprinted in Harder's *Kleine Schriften.* Munich, 1960: 466–470.

Hiller von Gaertringen, D., née von Wilamowitz-Moellendorff. "Bericht über den Nachlass von Ulrich von Wilamowitz-Moellendorff." *A&A* 4 (1954) 14–15.

Hölscher, U. "Ulrich von Wilamowitz-Moellendorff." *Die neue Rundschau* 73 (1962) 166–185. Reprinted in *Die Chance des Unbehagens. Drei Essais zur Situation der klassischen Studien.* Göttingen, 1965: 7–30.

Hüffmeier, F. "Unvermutete Begegnung mit Wilamowitz." *Gymnasium* 83 (1976) 238–239. (On the grave at Markowitz.)

Jaeger, W. "Gedächtnisrede auf Ulrich von Wilamowitz-Moellendorff." *SPAW* (1932) 123–128 = *Die Antike* 8 (1932) 319–324 = W. Jaeger, *Humanistische Reden und Vorträge*, 2d ed. Berlin, 1960: 215–221.

———. "Rezension von Theodor Mommsen und Ulrich von Wilamowitz-Moellendorff, Briefwechsel." *DLZ* (1936) 271–281 = Jaeger's *Scripta Minora.* Rome, 1960: 2:137–147.

———. "Classical Philology at Berlin: 1870 to 1945." [1960] *Five Essays.* Translated by A. M. Fiske. Montreal, 1966: 47–74.

Kassel, R. "Wilamowitz über griechische und römische Komödie." *ZPE* 45 (1982) 271–300.

———. Review of *Wilamowitz nach 50 Jahren*, ed. W. M. Calder III et al. *GGA* 239 (1987) 188–228.

Körte, A. Review of *Hermann Usener-Ulrich von Wilamowitz-Moellendorff. Ein Briefwechsel. Die Antike* 11 (1935) 211–235.

Landfester, M. "Ulrich von Wilamowitz-Moellendorff und die hermeneutische Tradition des 19. Jahrhunderts." H. Flashar, K. Gründer, A. Horstmann, *Philologie und Hermeneutik im 19. Jahrhundert. Zur Geschichte und Methodologie der Geisteswissenschaften.* Göttingen, 1979: 156–180.

Lanza, D. "Il suddito e la scienza." *Belfagor* 29 (1974) 1–32.

Lehnus, L. "Verso Wilamowitz," *Maia* n.s. 36 (1984) 171–180. Review of W. M. Calder III, ed. *Ulrich von Wilamowitz-Moellendorff: Selected Correspondence 1869–1931*. (With excellent bibliography.)

Mejer, J. "Henrik Ibsen and the Revival of Euripides." *GRBS* 27 (1986) 399–407.

Mensching, E. "U. von Wilamowitz-Moellendorff, W. Kranz und das 'Dritte Reich.' " *Hermes* 116 (1988) 357–376.

Momigliano, A. "Premesse per una discussione su Wilamowitz." *ASNP* 3.3.1 (1973) 105–117 = *RSI* 84 (1972) 746–755 = A. Momigliano, *Sesto contributo alla storia degli studi classici e del mondo antico* 1. Rome, 1980: 337–349.

Müller, F. "Ulrich von Wilamowitz-Moellendorff 1848–1931 (extr. Port. 1862–1867, val.)." In H. Gehrig, *Schulpforte und das deutsche Geistesleben: Lebensbilder alter Pförtner Almae Matri Portae zum 21. Mai 1943 gewidmet*. Darmstadt, 1943: 120–130.

Murray, G. Review of *My Recollections* by U. von Wilamowitz-Moellendorff. *The Observer* (22 July 1930) 5.

——. "Wilamowitz." *CR* 45 (1931) 161–162.

——. "Memoirs of Wilamowitz." *A&A* 4 (1954) 9–14.

Norden. E. "Worte des Gedächtnisses an Ulrich von Wilamowitz-Moellendorff." [1931] *KS zum klassischen Altertum* (Berlin, 1966) 664–668. Excerpted in *CP* 27 (1932) 66–69.

Parente, M. I. "Rileggendo il *Platon* di Ulrich von Wilamowitz-Moellendorff." *ASNP* 3.3.1 (1973) 147–167.

Pasquali, G. "Ulrico di Wilamowitz-Moellendorff." *Pegaso* 4 (1932) 8–33 = Pasquali's *Pagine stravaganti*. Florence, 1968: 1:56–92.

Patzer, H. "Wilamowitz und die klassische Philologie." In H. Kusch, *Festschrift Franz Dornseiff zum 65. Geburtstag*. Leipzig, 1953: 244–257.

Pfeiffer, R. "Nachruf auf Ulrich von Wilamowitz-Moellendorff." *Süddeutsche Monatshefte* 25 (1931–1932) 148–152 = Pfeiffer's *Ausgewählte Schriften. Aufsätze und Vorträge zur griechischen Dichtung und zum Humanismus*. Edited by W. Bühler. Munich, 1960: 269–276.

Pohlenz, M. "Ulrich von Wilamowitz-Moellendorff." *NAWG* Geschäftliche Mitteilungen Fachgr. 1.10 (1931–1932) 74–85.

Reinhardt, K. "Ulrich von Wilamowitz-Moellendorff." *Die großen Deutschen. Deutsche Biographie. Ergänzungsband*. Edited by H. Heimpel, Th. Heuss, B. Reifenberg. Berlin, 1957: 415–421 = K. Reinhardt, *Vermächtnis der Antike. Gesammelte Essays zur Philosophie und Geschichtschreibung*. 2d ed. Göttingen, 1966: 361–368.

Rossi, L. E. "Rileggendo due opere di Wilamowitz: *Pindaros* e *Griechische Verskunst*." *ASNP* 3.3.1 (1973) 119–145.

Schadewaldt, W. "Ulrich von Wilamowitz-Moellendorff zum 100. Geburtstag am 22.12.1948." *Gymnasium* 56 (1949) 80–81 = Schadewaldt's *Hellas und Hesperien*, 2d ed. Zürich and Stuttgart, 1970: 2.698–699.

Schindel, U. "Wilamowitz in den GGA." *GGA* 234 (1982) 1–11.

Schwartz, E. "An Ulrich v. Wilamowitz-Moellendorff." [1928] *Gesammelte Schriften* 1: *Vergangene Gegenwärtigkeiten* (Berlin 1938).

———. "Ulrich von Wilamowitz-Moellendorff." *Jahrb. d. Bay. Akad. d. Wiss.* (1932) 29–41 = Schwartz's *Gesammelte Schriften* 1:368–382.

———. "Zur Einführung." *Mommsen und Wilamowitz. Briefwechsel 1872–1903,* V–XVIII.

Snell, B. "Klassische Philologie im Deutschland der zwanziger Jahre." [1932] *Der Weg zum Denken und zur Wahrheit. Studien zur frühgriechischen Sprache.* Hypomnemata 57 (1978) 105–121.

Snell, B. "Wilamowitz und Thomas Mann." *A&A* 12 (1966) 95–96.

Solmsen, F. "Wilamowitz in his Last Ten Years." *GRBS* 20 (1979) 89–122 = Solmsen's *Kleine Schriften,* 3. Hildesheim, Zürich, and New York, 1982: 3:430–463.

Vogt, E. "Ein neues Zeugnis zur Lehrtätigkeit des jungen Wilamowitz." In *Festschrift für Franz Egermann.* Edited by W. Suerbaum and F. Maier. Munich, 1985: 171–180.

Wilamowitz-Moellendorff, Fanny Gräfin von, née Baronin von Fock. *Erinnerungen und Begegnungen.* Berlin, 1936.

Wilamowitz-Moellendorff, H. "Erinnerungen an meinen Vater, U. von Wilamowitz-Moellendorff." In *wieweit befriedigen die Schlüsse der erhaltenen griechischen Trauerspiele.* Edited by W. M. Calder III. Leiden, 1974: 159–163.

Letters

Accame, S. "Premessa." G. De Sanctis, *Atthis* 3d ed. Florence, 1975: xx–xxi. Letter to De Sanctis.

Aland, K. *Glanz und Niedergang der deutschen Universität. 50 Jahre deutscher Wissenschaftsgeschichte in Briefen an und von Hans Lietzmann (1892–1942).* Berlin and New York, 1979.

Bertolini, F. "Wilamowitz a Wissowa: 'Krieg,' 'Studenten,' 'Wissenschaft' (tre inediti)." *QS* 4 (1976) 47–54.

———. "Wilamowitz a Wissowa e Praechter." *QS* 7 (1978) 185–210; reprinted and translated in L. Canfora, *Cultura classica e crisi tedesca. Gli scritti politici di Wilamowitz 1914–1931.* Bari, 1977: 181–209.

Berufungspolitik innerhalb der Altertumswissenschaft im wilhelminischen Preußen. Die Briefe Ulrich von Wilamowitz-Moellendorffs Friedrich Althoff (1883–1908). Edited by W. M. Calder III and Alexander Košenina. Frankfurt am Main, 1989.

Calder, W. M. III "Wilamowitz on Demosthenes." *CW* 72 (1978–1979) 239–240.

———. *Ulrich von Wilamowitz-Moellendorff. Selected Correspondence 1869–1931.* Antiqua 23. Naples, 1983.

———. "Wilamowitz on Adolf Erman." *QS* 18 (1983) 273–282.

———. "Ulrich von Wilamowitz-Moellendorff to Kekule von Stradonitz on Friedrich Gottlieb Welcker." *SIFC* 3.2 (1984) 116–133.

———. "Ulrich von Wilamowitz-Moellendorff to Hermann Sauppe: Two Unpublished Letters." *Philologus* 129 (1985) 286–298.

―――. "Wilamowitz' Call to Göttingen: Paul de Lagarde to Friedrich Althoff on Wilamowitz-Moellendorff." *SIFC* 3.3 (1985) 136–160.

Calder, W. M. III and Fowler, R. L. *The Preserved Letters of Ulrich von Wilamowitz–Moellendorff to Eduard Schwartz. Edited with Introduction and Commentary.* SBAW 1986, Heft 1.

Calder, W. M. III and Hoffmann, C. "Ulrich von Wilamowitz-Moellendorff on the Basel Greek Chair." *MH* 43 (1986) 258–263.

Dieterich, H. and F. Frhr. Hiller von Gaertringen, eds. *Usener und Wilamowitz. Ein Briefwechsel 1870–1905.* Leipzig and Berlin, 1934.

Dummer, J. "Ulrich von Wilamowitz-Moellendorff und die Kirchenväterkommission der Berliner Akademie." Edited by J. Irmscher and P. Nagel. *Studia Byzantina.* Folge II. Berlin, 1973: 351–387.

Gigante, M. "Premesse." A. Maiuri, *Epicedio napoletano.* Naples, 1981: 12–14. Letter to Maiuri.

Hiller von Gaertringen, F. Frhr. and D. *Mommsen und Wilamowitz. Briefwechsel 1872–1903.* Berlin, 1935.

Malitz, J. "Nachlese zum Briefwechsel Mommsen-Wilamowitz." *QS* 17 (1983) 123–150.

Mansfeld, J. "The Wilamowitz–Nietzsche Struggle: Another Document and Some Further Comments." *Nietzsche-Studien* 15 (1986) 41–58. (Letter to Ernst Howald.)

Mette, H. J. "Nekrolog einer Epoche: Hermann Usener und seine Schule." *Lustrum* 22 (1979–1980) 5–106. (Republication, occasional corrections of some of the Usener-Wilamowitz letters.)

Pintaudi, R. Römer, C. "Le Lettere di Wilamowitz a Vitelli." *ASNP* 3.11 (1981) 363–398.

Prete, S. *Tra filologi e studiosi della nostra epoca dalla corrispondenza di Günther Jachmann.* Pesaro, 1984: 119–128. (Seven letters to Jachmann.)

Skutsch, O. "Wilamowitz an Norden über dessen 'Ennius und Vergilius.' " *A&A* 29 (1983) 90–94.

Tièche, E. *Briefe von Ulrich von Wilamowitz-Moellendorff an Georg Finsler. Der Bund* 145, Literatur– und Kunstbeilage (27 March 1953); also printed separately Bern, 1953.

Papers

The Wilamowitz-Nachlaß resides in the Niedersächische Staats- und Universitätsbibliothek, Göttingen. Other papers are preserved among the archives of various correspondents; for details see the editions of his letters. Wilamowitz's working library and his collection of offprints are housed in the Akademie der Wissenschaften der Deutschen Demokratischen Republik.

F. A. Wolf

15 February 1759 – 8 August 1824

HERMANN FUNKE
Mannheim University

Friedrich August Wolf is the founder of *Altertumswissenschaft*, the scientific study of classical antiquity. The work of the Humanists had laid the foundations; in many cases only the gathering of the material had yet to be done. The seventeenth and eighteenth centuries were remarkable for industry, erudition, and the zeal for collecting information; important critics form a minority. Wolf, in his *Literarische Analekten* (1816–20), expressly chose one of the greatest of them, Richard Bentley (1662–1742), as his model. Like Bentley, Wolf realized the magnitude of the tasks that scholarship must assume, was a master of historical criticism, and knew how to discern the genuine transmission of a text. Like him, Wolf was an autodidact who possessed genius and literary gifts; like him, he was forever engaged in unedifying quarrels with his colleagues. But Wolf transcended Bentley's narrow rationalism by a combination of factual historical proof and intuitive penetration.

In his scholarly work and in his pedagogical influence alike, Wolf embodied the transition from the aesthetic estimation of antiquity (the so-called neo-Humanism) to historical science (the so-called Positivism). He was likewise a symbol of the transition from the men of universal minds (Winckelmann, Lessing, Herder, Goethe) to the pure philologists (Boeckh, Bekker, Hermann, K. O. Müller, Lachmann). He himself was both; he expanded the frontiers of *Altertumswissenschaft*. Wolf's work was respected and discussed by the leading minds of his time—Wieland, Herder, Goethe, Schiller, Humboldt, Niebuhr, Friedrich Schlegel.

Wolf superseded the encyclopedism of the Baroque polymaths by means of his historical research; he superseded the hitherto standard practice of merely passing on empirical data by employing his principle of personal critical investigation and the communication of this principle to his fellow researchers. He founded the philological seminar, with which he gave *Altertumswissenschaft* its place as an independent discipline. In contrast to the Göttingen seminar of J. M. Gesner and Heyne, his seminar completed the separation of the teacher's training from that of the preacher. With Wolf, philology ceased to be an ancillary discipline to the Bible and the Corpus Juris. The science of classical antiquity had to find an independent path; Wolf was convinced—and in his *Darstellung* (see below) gave reasons for his belief—that it was capable of doing so. Niebuhr, with justice, called him "the eponymous hero for the whole race of philologists."

His early years, up to his call to Halle, are described by Wolf himself in an *Entwurf einer Selbstbiographie*. He was born on 15 February 1759 at Hainrode (in the province of Hohenstein), not far from Nordhausen. By the end of his sixth year he already knew "much Latin and French, also some Greek." Although he profited from his teachers' attention, at the age of eleven he conceived the plan of giving himself further training by private study of books. On 8 April 1777, he matriculated at Göttingen as *studiosus philologiae*, to the astonishment of Heyne and the Prorector Baldinger; they tried to dissuade him on the grounds that this was no way to make a living. In the latter half of 1778 he read through Homer (whom he had already read) in about four months and first began to notice unevennesses in Homer's tone and language. Next came eager study of Plato, which produced an edition of the *Symposium* (Leipzig, 1782) with explanatory notes "in German and not in the old-fashioned dress" (i.e., in Latin). A few years later he was a teacher in Ilfeld and then a rector in Osterode. On 3 April 1783 Wolf received a call to Halle "as Prof. Ord. Philos. and spec(ialiter) Paedagogices." He entered on his duties in August of the same year, and in 1784, at his own request, he was released from the professorship of pedagogy and given the professorship "for Eloquence and Poesy." As Weitz put it (1805), Wolf "founded a fifth faculty: the Philological Faculty." The next twenty-three years in Halle were the happiest and most productive of his life, both for himself and for others.

In the years 1783–1784 Wolf published an edition of Hesiod's *Theogony* "with a sort of commentary"; this was the first and only time that he "combined a course of lectures with literary work." In the "Praefatio" to this edition he first sketched out the methods that he later followed in the *Prolegomena ad Homerum*. Further publications followed, among them editions of the *Odyssey* (1784) and the *Iliad* (1785), Lucian (1786 and 1791), selected Greek dramas (1787), and Demosthenes (1789). As a "guide for academic lectures" Wolf edited *Antiquitäten von Griechenland* (1787) and wrote a *Geschichte der römischen Literatur* (1787). He regarded himself entirely as a teacher; he decidedly preferred to exert his influence by the spoken word (" . . . since I prefer teaching to writing and, with Callimachus, look upon a big book as a big evil"— letter of 9 December 1807). Goethe complained that Wolf's finest publications "echo off the walls of the lecture room and die away" (letter to Wolf, 28 November 1806).

In this period of productive teaching Wolf produced *Homeri opera omnia ex recensione F. A. Wolfii, Tomus Prior*; (second title: *Prolegomena ad Homerum sive de operum Homericorum prisca et genuina forma variisque mutationibus et probabili ratione emendandi*, Vol. I [no more appeared], Halle, 1795)—the book that made him famous overnight.

What Wolf said in this work was not completely new. From the point of view of French rationalism, François Hedelin, Abbé d' Aubignac, in his *Conjectures académiques ou Dissertation sur l'Iliade* (1715), had already concluded from contradictions in the Homeric epics that these works were without merit or coherence and therefore that they had been put together out of numerous ancient poems. In 1735 Thomas Blackwell in London published his *Enquiry into the Life and Writings of Homer*, in which he viewed Homer as an improvising rhapsode whose main contribution was to fill in the gaps in the works that he recited from memory. Robert Wood, in his *Essay on the Original Genius of Homer* (London, 1767) tested the trustworthiness of the Homeric epics by comparing them with the realities of geography and ethnography. Thus Wolf's idea that the *Iliad* and *Odyssey* were not the work of one poet but had later been constructed, more or less skillfully, out of separate songs, was common in his day. Wolf's real accomplishment lay in the positive side of his criticism: his aim was, by careful consideration of all the available evidence, to throw light on the origin of the "Homer" that has been transmitted to us, to replace formal and rationalistic evidence with historical evidence. Wolf was not simply refining scholarly techniques; in philology he began the era of historical thinking. As for Homer, Wolf maintains that the Homeric age was without writing; that the *Iliad* and *Odyssey* were derived from individual songs by various authors; that they had not been assembled into the works that we possess until the days of Peisistratus; and that philology could at best only reconstruct the vulgate text of late antiquity, which had been based on the Alexandrian recensions. The *Prolegomena* contain a wealth of detailed information and observations on particular points, with which Wolf again and again sought to support his conclusions. He was aware that the attempt to reconstruct a part of the distant past was possible only through empathy, intuition, and divination, but at the same time he knew that it could be persuasively communicated only through scientific proof. Wolf's outstanding importance in Homeric criticism lies in the fact that he possessed at once scholarly perspicacity and intuitive genius. He had seen that in historical research neither a single quotation nor wishful thinking carried any weight; rather, all depended on the coherence of the whole and the mutual interconnection of all the evidence and arguments. Obliged to choose between classicism (the unity of Homer) and the principles of historical research (multiplicity of authorship), Wolf, albeit with hesitation, chose the latter and thereby set the philology of succeeding generations on its course.

When on 17 October 1806 the University of Halle was closed by Napoleon, Wolf, at Goethe's suggestion, used his leisure to commit to writing a course of lectures that he had frequently given, the "Encyclopaedia philologica." The result was his *Darstellung der Altertumswissenschaft*, which begins with a dedication to Goethe and concludes with a quotation from Jean Paul. In both passages the author expresses his devotion to an article in the creed of German neo-Humanism: that the Greeks were the supreme models for our imitation. In accordance with this is Wolf's assertion (page 5) that in this work he wished "to elevate to the dignity of a well-ordered philosophical and historical science all that pertains to the complete understanding of learned antiquity." Encyclopedism, idealism, and lofty aims here enter into the alliance that gave (German) classical philology its unique character. Wolf defines *Altertumswissenschaft* as the knowledge of all aspects of antiquity (language, literature, art, science, religion, customs, etc.) with a view to (a) understanding them and (b) comparing them with modern conditions. The sources are literature, art (monuments), and everyday technology (coins, inscriptions, etc.), which are to be regarded both as evidence of the life of the past and as aesthetically beautiful works. The beautiful confronts the useful as the Greek does the oriental. Wolf ends his work by affirming that "only the ancient Greeks possessed the qualities that go to make the foundations of a character perfected in genuine humanity" (132). For him *Altertumswissenschaft* takes the place of theology when he proclaims that all that is loftiest and most important for man is to be gained from the study of Greek antiquity. What "the epopteia or the contemplation of the most holy was for the priests at Eleusis" is for us "the knowledge of ancient humanity itself, a knowledge which proceeds from the contemplation, conditioned by the study of the ancient remains, of an organically developed, significant national education," transmitted by the "knowledge of the beautiful and classical works in the genres in which the ancients worked" (124ff.). Wolf views *Altertumswissenschaft* as a religion, of which the "most holy" is nonetheless to be attained by the route of scholarly discipline, the component parts of which he not only describes in detail, aiming at completeness, but also connects to pedagogical and methodological problems. Thus antiquity, employed as the raw material for instruction, can be used for the training of patience and dogged industry, and the distracted mind of youth will learn to pull itself together (81). "The more distant and different from us a people is in customs and manner of thought—and the more difficult, consequently, the learning of a language is—the greater is the gain in acquiring new ideas and unwonted views of things" (95). This insight into the effect of contrast and the conviction that language is the medium by which one acquires knowledge of reality, which can be acquired in no other way (and from this it follows that for Wolf the study of the ancient languages was an end in itself), not only show that Wolf was a highly modern linguistic scholar, but also show, in connection with the religious aspect of the discipline which he proclaims, that the Humanists' irrational feeling of superiority can be traced all the way back to Wolf's manifesto.

From 1807 until his death in 1824 Wolf lived in Berlin. He was involved in the founding of the University in that city (middle of October 1811), and, as a member of the Berlin Academy, he was affiliated with the University, though in a rather remote way. There was no return to a happy and productive teaching career. Wolf always felt himself to be a teacher rather than a writer; his domain was the investigative type of lecture; he challenged his listeners to think along with him; he shared not only his results but also the process by which he had arrived at them.

Wolf's influence was extraordinary; his conception of scholarship passed far beyond the boundaries of *Altertumswissenschaft*; he left a lasting impression on all humanitistic disciplines throughout the nineteenth and twentieth centuries. Wolf had the good fortune to work during a period in which the intellectual and scholarly tendencies of the next hundred years were determined. This period was conditioned through and through by its involvement with the ancient world. Wolf freed *Altertumswissenschaft* from the polyhistorism of the Baroque age; on the other hand, he placed it in the isolation of Winckelmann's paganism; for him, Christianity and the Orient do not exist. Finally, Wolf helped to exalt the idea of pure scholarship and contempt for utilitarianism. Perhaps not all of this was new, perhaps predecessors and "midwives" of these thoughts can be named; but Wolf can still serve as a shining example to show that in the humanities one's influence depends not so much on what one has said and written as on the fact that it is a personality that formulates a thought. His *Prolegomena* are the proof of this, for his contemporaries and successors felt it to be so when they credited him with the accomplishment even though they were able to enumerate his precursors.

Translated by Michael Armstrong

Books

Homeri Opera omnia ex recensione F. A. Wolfii. Tomus prior. Second title: *Prolegomena ad Homerum sive de operum Homericorum prisca et genuina forma variisque mutationibus et probabili ratione emendandi* . . . Vol. I (all published). Halle, 1795.

Prolegomena zu Homer, ins Deutsche übertragen von H. Muchau. Mit einem Vorwort über die Homerische Frage und die wissenschaftlichen Ergebnisse der Ausgrabungen in Troja und Leukas-Ithaka. Leipzig, 1908. English translation *Prolegomena to Homer 1795*. Translated with Introduction and Notes by A. Grafton, G. W. Most, and J. E. G. Zetzel. Princeton, 1985.

Vermischte Schriften und Aufsätze in lateinischer und deutscher Sprache. Halle, 1802.

Museum der Alterthums-Wissenschaft. Edited by Wolf and P. Buttmann. Two vols. Berlin, 1807–08. Vol. 1:3–145 = *Darstellung der Alterthums-Wissenschaft nach Begriff, Umfang, Zweck und Werth.* With a postscript by Johannes Irmscher. Berlin (DDR), 1985; Weinheim, 1986.

Literarische Analekten, vorzüglich für alte Literatur und Kunst, deren Geschichte und Methodik. 2 vols. Berlin, 1816–20.

Vorlesungen über die Alterthumswissenschaft. Edited by J. D. Gürtler. Six vols. Leipzig, 1831–1839.

Darstellung der Alterthumswissenschaft nebst einer Auswahl seiner Kleinen Schriften und literarischen Zugaben zu dessen Vorlesungen über die Alterthumswissenschaft. Edited by S. F. W. Hoffmann. Leipzig, 1833.

Über Erziehung, Schule, Universität ("Consilia Scholastica"). Aus Wolfs literarischem Nachlasse zusammengestellt von W. Körte. Quedlinburg and Leipzig, 1835.

Kleine Schriften in lateinischer und deutscher Sprache. Edited by G. Bernhardy. 2 vols. Halle, 1869.

Sources

Bibliography

List of Wolf's writings in *Ein Leben in Briefen* (see below) 3:258–260.

Wolf, Friedrich August. "Entwurf einer Selbstbiographie." In *Ein Leben in Briefen* (see below) 2:337–345.

Biographical

Arnolt, J. F. J. *Friedrich August Wolf in seinem Verhältnis zum Schulwesen und zur Pädagogik dargestellt.* 2 vols. Braunschweig, 1861–62.

Bursian, C. *Geschichte der Klassischen Philologie in Deutschland.* Munich and Leipzig, 1883: 517–548.

Fuhrmann, M. "Friedrich August Wolf." *Deutsche Vierteljahrsschrift für Literaturwissenschaft und Geistesgeschichte* 33 (1959) 187–236.

Horstmann, A.. "Die 'Klassische Philologie' zwischen Humanismus und Historismus. Friedrich August Wolf und die Begründung der modernen Altertumswissenschaft." *Berichte zur Wissenschaftsgeschichte* 1 (1978) 51–70.

Kern, O. *Friedrich August Wolf.* Hallische Universitätsreden 25. Halle, 1924.

Körte, W. *Leben und Studien Friedrich August Wolf's des Philologen.* Essen, 1833.

Pattison, Mark. "F. A. Wolf." *Essays.* 2 vols. Oxford, 1889. 1:337–414.

Paulsen, F. *Geschichte des gelehrten Unterrichts auf den deutschen Schulen und Universitäten vom Ausgang des Mittelalters bis zur Gegenwart.* 2d ed. Leipzig, 1897: 2:208–27.

Volkmann, R. *Geschichte und Kritik der Wolfschen Prolegomena zu Homer. Ein Beitrag zur Geschichte der Homerischen Frage.* Leipzig, 1874.

Wilamowitz-Moellendorff, U. von. *Geschichte der Philologie.* Berlin, 1921; English translation by Alan Harris as *History of Classical Scholarship*, London, 1982.

Letters

Goethes Briefe an Friedrich August Wolf. Edited by M. Bernays. Berlin, 1868.

Friedrich August Wolf: Ein Leben in Briefen. Edited by S. Reiter. 3 vols. Stuttgart, 1935. Supplement volume 1. Edited by R. Sellheim. Halle, 1956.

INDEX RERUM